A HANDBOOK
on
THE ACTS OF THE APOSTLES

The Handbooks in the **UBS Handbook Series** are detailed commentaries providing valuable exegetical, historical, cultural, and linguistic information on the books of the Bible. They are prepared primarily to assist practicing Bible translators as they carry out the important task of putting God's Word into the many languages spoken in the world today. The text is discussed verse by verse and is accompanied by running text in at least one modern English translation.

Over the years church leaders and Bible readers have found the UBS Handbooks to be useful for their own study of the Scriptures. Many of the issues Bible translators must address when trying to communicate the Bible's message to modern readers are the ones Bible students must address when approaching the Bible text as part of their own private study and devotions.

The Handbooks will continue to be prepared primarily for translators, but we are confident that they will be useful to a wider audience, helping all who use them to gain a better understanding of the Bible message.

Helps for Translators

UBS Handbook Series:

A Handbook on . . .

Leviticus

The Book of Joshua

The Book of Ruth

The Book of Job

Psalms

Lamentations

The Book of Amos

The Books of Obadiah, Jonah, and Micah

The Books of Nahum, Habakkuk, and Zephaniah

The Gospel of Matthew

The Gospel of Mark

The Gospel of Luke

The Gospel of John

The Acts of the Apostles

Paul's Letter to the Romans

Paul's First Letter to the Corinthians

Paul's Second Letter to the Corinthians

Paul's Letter to the Galatians

Paul's Letter to the Ephesians

Paul's Letter to the Philippians

Paul's Letters to the Colossians and to Philemon

Paul's Letters to the Thessalonians

The Letter to the Hebrews

The First Letter from Peter

The Letter from Jude and the Second Letter from Peter

The Letters of John

The Revelation to John

Guides:

A Translator's Guide to . . .

Selections from the First Five Books of the Old Testament

Selected Psalms

the Gospel of Mark

the Gospel of Luke

Paul's Second Letter to the Corinthians

Paul's Letters to Timothy and to Titus

the Letters to James, Peter, and Jude

Technical Helps:

Old Testament Quotations in the New Testament

Short Bible Reference System

New Testament Index

The Theory and Practice of Translation

Bible Index

Fauna and Flora of the Bible

Marginal Notes for the Old Testament

Marginal Notes for the New Testament

The Practice of Translating

A HANDBOOK ON

The Acts of the Apostles

by Barclay M. Newman
and Eugene A. Nida

UBS Handbook Series

United Bible Societies
New York

Books in the series of **UBS Helps for Translators** may be ordered from a national Bible Society or from either of the following centers:

United Bible Societies
European Production Fund
D-70520 Stuttgart 80
Postfach 81 03 40
Germany

United Bible Societies
1865 Broadway
New York, NY 10023
U. S. A.

L. C. Cataloging-in-Publication Data

Newman, Barclay Moon, 1931-
   [Translator's handbook on the Acts of the Apostles]
   A handbook on the Acts of the Apostles / by Barclay M. Newman and Eugene A. Nida.
      p.   cm. — (UBS handbook series) (Helps for translators)
   Originally published: A translator's handbook on the Acts of the Apostles, 1972.
   Includes bibliographical references and index.
   ISBN 0-8267-0159-0
   1. Bible. N.T. Acts—Translating. I. Nida, Eugene Albert, 1914-   . II. Title. III. Title: Acts of the Apostles. IV. Series. V. Series: Helps for translators.
BS2625.5.N497 1993
226.6'077—dc20   92-40063
                                                                        CIP

ABS-10/93-200-4,800-CM-6-102677

PREFACE

The form of A Translator's Handbook on The Acts of the Apostles, the third volume in the series of Handbooks published by the United Bible Societies, reflects the judgment and advice of the Translations Consultants of the United Bible Societies, whose experience in the use of A Translator's Handbook on the Gospel of Mark has resulted in several important innovations in this Handbook on Acts. In the first place, the running text is Today's English Version, since this is a more accurate and meaningful representation of the underlying Greek text than is available in more literal translations. At the same time, however, the basic underlying text for this Handbook is the UBS Greek text, published especially for the aid of translators. In the second place, transliterations of the forms of the Greek text are avoided, except where some special reference to a Greek term is required. Those who know Greek can readily determine the Greek equivalents and those who do not know Greek are not helped by the heavy use of transliteration. In the third place, every attempt has been made to avoid technical terminology. In some instances a limited number of technical terms has been indispensable, but these are explained in the Glossary of Technical Terms. And in the fourth place, exegetical problems are described without going into detail concerning the history of controversies over various viewpoints. Where scholarly judgment seems to favor one or another alternative, this is stated; but where there is no consensus, no attempt is made to legislate what particular interpretation should be followed.

As is indicated in the introductory chapter, "Translating The Acts of the Apostles," no translator should regard this Handbook as all he needs for dealing with the many exegetical and linguistic problems of Acts. He will certainly need to supplement this Handbook with two or three standard commentaries on Acts. Moreover, he will want to employ several different English or foreign language translations, if he is to benefit fully from scholarly judgment on the meaning of various passages.

To some users of this Handbook certain of the treatments of exegetical and linguistic problems may seem somewhat repetitious. It has been difficult to know just when readers should be referred back to other sections and when they should be provided with helpful suggestions at recurring points in the text. There is a good deal of cross-referencing, and in the Index special attention is paid to the various treatments of key words and phrases. If we have erred in this matter, it has been on the side of being repetitious, but this has been done for the sake of being as helpful as possible.

This Handbook is only one of a continuing series of helps that is currently being prepared. The manuscripts of Handbooks on Romans and First John are now complete and will be published in the near future. Work has begun on several other volumes. But if these Handbooks are to be of the greatest help to translators, they must benefit from the advice of the translators who use them. Accordingly, the authors will be deeply indebted to all who will be kind enough to communicate their reactions as to the strengths and weaknesses of this volume and who will suggest ways in which such helps may be improved.

The authors of this Handbook are deeply indebted to the members of the UBS Committee on Helps for Translators who have carefully reviewed various sections of the manuscript, to Mrs. Jean Newman for typing initial drafts of the exegetical sections, and to the staff of the Translations Department at American Bible Society for typing revised drafts, editing the manuscript, and preparing the typescript as a basis for offset reproduction.

Barclay M. Newman
Eugene A. Nida

April 1972

CONTENTS

TRANSLATING THE ACTS OF THE APOSTLES

In comparison with certain other books of the New Testament, The Acts of the Apostles affords the translator several distinct advantages. In the first place, it is an exceptionally well-organized account, with clearly marked transitionals to mark the connections between events. In this respect the text of The Acts of the Apostles is quite different from some portions of the Gospels, where the connections between sections are not clearly indicated, and from some of the Epistles, which treat a number of matters for which background information is characteristically not supplied and hence the relationship between sections is frequently obscure. In fact, it is precisely the explicit lack of information shared by a writer and his audience which is a mark of the genuineness of a letter. Luke, however, addresses The Acts of the Apostles to persons whom he wants to instruct carefully in the important developments of early Christianity, and hence he takes pains to show the relationship between episodes and sections.

The Acts of the Apostles presents another advantage to the translator in that it is primarily narrative in its structure, and therefore indicators of time and space are rather more precise than in most other types of writing. Of course, Acts also contains a number of discourses, but these are always carefully inserted into the narrative structure. One should not expect a book such as Acts to contain everything that happened in the early history of the church. Like any competent historian, Luke selects those particular events which are in keeping with his overall intent.

In contrast with the Synoptic Gospels (Matthew, Mark, and Luke), Acts does not confront the translator with the serious difficulty of representing accurately both the similarities and differences in the parallel passages. On the other hand, Acts does contain some parallel accounts of the same events, for example, Peter's experience with Cornelius (10. 9-33 and 11. 4-18), and Paul's conversion on the way to Damascus (9. 1-19; 22. 6-16; 26. 12-18). Quite understandably, Acts avoids slavish repetition of identical words and phrases, but because of this there are some expressions which seem to be contradictory. It is not, however, a translator's responsibility to attempt to eliminate these discrepancies of details. Rather, a conscientious translator will try to reproduce the text as Luke wrote it, leaving any seeming problems of difference to those who deal with such matters in commentaries.

Acts also affords the translator the advantage of containing sentences which are rarely ambiguous or oddly constructed. In contrast with some of the Pauline writings, in which the author was obviously so full of his subject that he scarcely seemed to know just how and when to bring a sentence to a normal grammatical end, and hence often shifted to another grammatical structure (thus producing what is generally called anacolutha), Acts contains for the most part carefully constructed sentences in which the syntactic relationships are usually quite evident. One should not, however, conclude that Acts is overly simple. Though the sentences are not especially long and though the relationships between the sentences are usually quite evident,

1

nevertheless the structure of the discourse (that is, of the paragraphs and the larger sections) is quite subtly and intricately developed. The translator must, therefore, pay special attention to these elements in the structure of the narrative, and it is for this reason that this Handbook on Acts attempts to call attention to precisely these features of the larger structure. If, however, one is to appreciate fully the significance of these larger structures, it is essential to have some understanding and appreciation of the overall purpose and structure of Acts.

The Purpose and Structure of Acts

The book of Acts is a literary work of art, and like any other work of art it must be viewed from a proper perspective in order to be fully appreciated. Although the translator must not translate word for word, he must deal with each word of the text, and in doing so he runs the risk of failing to see the book in its overall significance. That is, by concerning himself with all of the many exegetical and translational details, he may miss seeing the themes that hold the book together and that contribute toward its purpose. It is therefore essential to make a brief survey of some of the major threads that are intertwined throughout the book and that bind it together in a unity.

However, before looking into the book of Acts itself, it is important to see where Acts fits in with the total Lukan viewpoint of history, because Luke clearly shows both in his Gospel as well as in the Acts of the Apostles (the second part of Luke's two-volume work) that he is not only an artist but a theologian and an interpreter of history. For him, history may be viewed as falling into three major periods. The first was the time of "the Law and the Prophets," which was brought to an end through the ministry of John the Baptist (Luke 16.16). His second period of time comprises the earthly ministry of Jesus. Though each of the three epochs is significant in God's purpose, this second one may be said to be the most significant, since it stands at the midpoint of time. The importance of the first period is that it looks forward to, and prepares for, this moment, while the final period of time—that of the Church—proclaims the meaning of this event for all mankind. The book of Acts records the beginning of this third movement of history and interprets its theological significance.

One of the most noticeable themes in the book is the geographical spread of Christianity from Jerusalem to Rome. This is accomplished in six stages, each ending with a summary statement. The first stage focuses attention on the church in Jerusalem and the preaching of Peter; this is concluded with the observation: "And so the word of God continued to spread. The number of disciples in Jerusalem grew larger and larger, and a great number of priests accepted the faith" (6.7).

The next stage is the spread of the Christian message throughout Palestine, with the summary: "And so it was that the church throughout all of Judea, Galilee, and Samaria had a time of peace. It was built up and grew in numbers through the help of the Holy Spirit, as it lived in reverence for the Lord" (9.31).

2

A third stage of the movement is reached when the disciples carry the Good News as far as Antioch. Luke concludes that period with the observation: "The word of God continued to spread and grow" (12. 24).

Then the church reaches out beyond the boundaries of Syria and goes as far as Asia Minor. At the end of this stage, Luke notes: "So the churches were made stronger in the faith and grew in numbers every day" (16. 5).

In its fifth stage of development, the church extends itself as far as Europe, with Paul's work in Corinth and Ephesus as the focal points of attention. Of this work Acts records: "In this powerful way the word of the Lord kept spreading and growing stronger" (19. 20).

Finally, the Gospel reaches Rome; and the summary at this point reveals that all along Luke has seen more than a geographical significance in the spread of the Christian message to Rome: "He (Paul) preached ... about the Lord Jesus Christ, speaking with all boldness and freedom" (28. 31). The word translated "with ... freedom" is an adverb, the last word in the book, and it serves as a clue for understanding Luke's purpose in writing Acts. This word literally means something like "without being hindered," and would seem to reflect at least two areas of meaning in Luke's thought: the theological and the political. It has been Luke's intention to show that the Gospel is no longer hindered by the narrow, nationalistic outlook of the first apostles, and that in Rome itself, the center of the Roman government, Paul is allowed to preach without being hindered. We must now survey briefly how Luke has carried through these themes by the use of historical narrative, and how they both reach their climax in the arrival of the Gospel in Rome.

The outlook of the apostles is aptly expressed in the early part of the book, "Lord, will you at this time give the Kingdom back to Israel?" (1. 6). And even though the events of Pentecost attested to the universal nature of the message their Lord had preached, the majority of the church in Jerusalem failed to perceive its universal implications. It is an interesting observation that the spread of the message beyond Palestine is not the work of the apostles, and that even in the taking of the message to Cornelius, Peter does so with much fear and trembling. Moreover, after the list of the apostles is given in the first chapter, nine of them are not mentioned again, James and John come in only for brief mention, and Peter fades from the center of the picture after Chapter 12. All of this is to say that the apostles are not identified by Luke as sharing actively in the spread of the Gospel beyond the borders of Judaism. The first man really to see the universal implications of the Christian faith was Stephen; but he was stoned in Jerusalem, and of the subsequent events Luke says, "That very day the church in Jerusalem began to suffer cruel persecution. All the believers, except the apostles, were scattered throughout the provinces of Judea and Samaria" (8. 1).

As a result of the persecution in Jerusalem, the message was taken to Samaria by Philip, one of the seven. The Samaritans were both racially and religiously related to the Jews, though they were staunch enemies; and the proclamation of the message in Samaria caused some concern to the apostles, who sent Peter and John to investigate. However, when the Holy Spirit was received by the Samaritans, this was evidence that God had approved of this taking of the Gospel one step beyond the Jews.

In the same eighth chapter is recorded a second step in taking the Christian message outside of Judaism. Although the Ethiopian eunuch had accepted the God of Judaism, it was impossible for him to be accepted by the Jews as a full convert because of his physical condition. But Philip proclaims the message to him, and he accepts the Lordship of Jesus Christ.

A third step in the liberation of the Gospel comes when Peter is instructed by God to visit Cornelius. Cornelius was a Gentile who was strongly attached to the Jewish faith but had never become a full convert. He believed and, to the amazement of the Jewish believers, God showed his approval by sending the Holy Spirit. News of this came to the church at Jerusalem, and once again they were upset over the events. However, when Peter told them the full account of what had happened, they responded, "Then God has given to the Gentiles also the opportunity to repent and live!" (11.18). Evidently, however, the Jerusalem church either failed to see the full significance of this judgment or they were not eager to work out its full implications, since there is no indication that they began actively to proclaim the message to the Gentiles.

The final stage in the liberation of the Gospel comes as it is preached in Antioch, a predominantly Gentile city. And the impact of this event is that the opportunity to believe is not offered to isolated individuals who were in some way previously related to the Jewish faith, but to a group of Gentiles who obviously had no previous ties to Judaism.

So by the time Luke has given less than half of his account, he has told of the way in which the Holy Spirit has led the church in taking the message to the Gentiles as well as to the Jews; and he has recorded the experience of Paul, in which God chose him to be a missionary to the non-Jewish peoples of the world. From Chapter 13 on, Paul becomes the center of attention, and his primary concern is to fulfill the task to which God has called him, though he also is eager to share the message with his own people as well. Doubts and questions still arise among some of the Jewish believers (see especially Chapter 15), but the conviction is firm that God intends his message for all peoples. The apostle to the Gentiles finally reaches Rome, the center of the non-Jewish world (and, indeed, the center of the ancient world, as known to Luke and his contemporaries), but Luke is quick to point out that the Jewish people as a whole continue to reject the message (28.23-27). Nevertheless, despite the rejection, the message in unhindered: "You are to know that God's message of salvation has been sent to the Gentiles. They will listen!" (28.28).

As was stated earlier, the meaning of "without being hindered" applies not only to the theological freedom of the Gospel from the confines of Judaism, but also to the fact that the Gospel is now allowed to be proclaimed "without hindrance" in Rome itself. This theme could be elaborated in great detail, but that is not necessary for the purposes of this presentation. It is necessary only to recall how in each of Paul's trials, whether before a Jewish or a non-Jewish court, Paul is declared to be innocent of stirring up trouble, and when he is finally sent to Rome (at his own request!), there are no charges against him. This is significant. Luke intentionally includes this information to indicate that the Christian faith is not a political movement, attempting to stir up insurrection. On the contrary, the concern of the Christian faith is to bring men into a right relationship with God, into a Kingdom which is not of this world; its enemies are not the Roman Empire, or any government as such, but the Kingdom of Evil, which opposes the good of all men. Luke, then, intends for his readers, who were primarily Gentiles, to realize that the Christian faith did not rise as an insurrectionist movement, and its primary exponent, the apostle Paul, was not looked on as an enemy by the government. The truth of what he said is verified by the freedom granted Paul during his stay in Rome: "For two years Paul lived there in a place he rented for himself, and welcomed all who came to see him. He preached about the Kingdom of God and taught about the Lord Jesus Christ, speaking with all boldness and freedom" (28.30-31).

One might summarize Luke's approach to the problem of the growing Christian movement in the totalitarian Roman Empire as a message to the Christians that the government was not to be regarded as an implacable enemy of the church, but in certain respects as an ally. To non-Christians, and especially to Roman officials, Luke's intent was apparently to show that the church was not a political movement, but a spiritual one.

Organization of this Handbook on Acts

In view of the features of the text of Acts which are of special relevance to the translator, this Handbook has been designed to help the translator in dealing with the many textual, exegetical, and translational difficulties which he is likely to encounter. The underlying text for this Handbook is the Greek New Testament, published by the United Bible Societies, even though the running text (that is, the English text which is used as a basis of reference) is Today's English Version. A Translator's Handbook on the Gospel of Mark had as a running text the Revised Standard Version, which constitutes a relatively literal rendering of the Greek text. However, too much time had to be spent in explaining to translators that the literal renderings were in fact not the proper way to represent the meaning of the Greek text. Accordingly, it has seemed much more efficient and helpful to the writers to employ a running text which is a more natural and accurate reflection of the meaning of the original. There are, however, a number of references in this Handbook on Acts to the literal form of the Greek expressions. Such references are made so that the translator, who may not be familiar with the Greek text, will understand better not only the basis for certain widely divergent renderings which he encounters in various translations, but also the necessity of rather extensive semantic restructuring if the meaning of the original text is to be comprehensible to the average reader in the receptor language.

Wherever there are important variants in the Greek text (especially in passages where traditional translations based primarily on the Textus Receptus differ in important ways from modern translations following more scientifically justified texts), these facts are carefully noted and discussed. Furthermore, the translator is advised to include at such points some marginal help which will call the attention of the reader to the differences in the manuscript traditions.

In this Handbook the basic units for discussion are the paragraphs, or sets of closely related paragraphs. This is also in contrast with the practice of the Handbook on Mark, which followed the more traditional practice of discussing translation problems primarily on the basis of verse divisions. However, an approach based essentially on verse or sentence units is too circumscribed and tends to neglect the crucial features of the overall discourse. Both for analyses of exegesis and for translation the larger units are the indispensable bases for discussion. Otherwise, one fails to see the forest because of the trees.

One important aspect of this Handbook is the inclusion of essential background information which will enable the translator to see the events in terms of their wider historical settings. In this way he is much better prepared to select the right words and phrases to characterize those features of the events which the author has chosen to describe. Of course, there is much additional background data which cannot be supplied in a handbook of this nature. Hence, translators are urged to employ other commentaries which are designed to discuss in much greater detail the historical and cultural elements relevant for the understanding of particular objects and events referred to in Acts.

In addition to providing background information for the understanding of certain events, this Handbook also attempts to discuss all the basic exegetical questions. In this respect the problems treated in standard commentaries are also contained in this Handbook, but the perspective is often quite different. This Handbook is concerned only with attempting to reconstruct the original communicative event, that is, "who said what to whom, under what circumstances, and with what intent"; while many commentaries give considerable attention to the history of doctrine related to such exegetical questions, and provide extensive discussions of the theological implications of one or another interpretation. Such considerations, though important, go beyond the immediate purposes of this Handbook.

On the other hand, in dealing with a number of exegetical and translational problems, this Handbook goes considerably beyond what is to be found in standard commentaries. In the first place, it takes up the problems of linguistic categories which are unknown to persons familiar only with Indo-European or Semitic languages, for example, honorifics, inclusive and exclusive first person plural, aspects of beginning, terminating, continuing, and repeated activities. In the second place, it discusses many objects and events which have little or no correspondence in other cultures, or which may have quite different meanings in such cultures. For example, how does one describe a shipwreck for people who know only their own desert habitat? Or how can one refer to circumcision as a symbol of ethnic and religious belonging when the receptor culture understands it only as a symbol of initiation into sexual maturity? Perhaps the greatest difficulty encountered in the preparation of this Handbook has been in the selection of materials for discussion. Obviously, it would be entirely impossible to mention systematically even a majority of the problems which translators are likely to face in languages throughout the world. Even such a simple problem as shifts from active to passive or from passive to active can only be mentioned where the difficulty appears to be especially complex, because the agent of the action may be contextually obscure. In the matter of cultural diversities, the problems are even greater, since one cannot resolve the problems merely by discussing a few terms which may cause complications, for example, prophet, spirit, law, apostle, and repentance. One must also deal with entire semantic domains (that is, related sets of words), involving such areas of translation as legal systems, religious sacrifice, vows, and weights and measures. Even though it is quite impossible to deal with all of the translation problems in each of their places of occurrence, at least some attempt has been made to select those elements of the text which are most likely to produce difficulty and to suggest possible solutions at certain crucial points. In this way the translator is constantly alerted to the types of problems with which he must deal.

In discussing various ways in which certain biblical expressions may be rendered, this Handbook does not indicate the particular languages which may have employed such renderings. This was done in the Handbook on Mark, but this practice proved somewhat more misleading than helpful. Some people objected to the fact that languages in their part of the world were not sufficiently represented. Furthermore, some translators systematically neglected to consider problems which were not illustrated by languages which they regarded as related to their own. In addition, some translators were hesitant to have their own renderings mentioned, since they feared that persons lacking the necessary background information to evaluate the solutions might criticize what they had done. Furthermore, in some languages revisions have taken place since the time that data on particular renderings were recorded, and this could lead to misunderstanding. Moreover, the listing of specific languages which might have a particular rendering is of no real value to the translator. What is important is the nature of the translational problem and how it may be resolved.

Throughout this Handbook special attention has been paid to the rendering of section headings, not only because these are so valuable to the reader, but also because such headings often require rather radical adjustments in order to make them comprehensible and acceptable. For example, nouns must often be changed into verbs (with accompanying mention of participants), tenses must be changed from present to past (or past to present), and short phrases must be expanded into complete sentences. At the same time, one must not employ section headings which explain the content of the following section (headings should not be interpretive), but rather those which serve to identify the contents for the reader. These section headings are not, however, merely "tags for content." In a sense, they also serve as transitional devices.

As has been indicated, this Handbook gives special prominence to the discourse structure, that is, the structure of the communication which goes beyond the limits of the individual sentences and serves to unite into an organized whole the sentences, paragraphs, and major sections. Failure to consider sufficiently the essential features of the discourse structure often results in very inferior translations. The sentences may all be accurately translated, but the whole may not hang together, and as a result the reader gets the impression of a series of more or less unrelated statements. This means that much of the impact of any account is largely lost.

Some of the basic problems of discourse structure have been discussed in The Theory and Practice of Translation, pp. 131-162. Further analyses of these matters will be dealt with in Introduction to Semantic Structures (forthcoming). As is evident, each language has its own distinctive discourse structures, even as it has its own special syntactic patterns. Accordingly, one cannot, in a Handbook such as this, deal fully with all the types of problems which diverse discourse structures would involve; but the translator can be made aware of some of the complications and how they can be effectively treated. However, the translator must not assume that diversities in discourse structures between languages justify his reediting or rewriting the text. He is still a translator, not the original author, and he must aim at the closest natural equivalent, not merely some reworked approximation.

Concern for the larger units of the text naturally focuses attention upon the problems of differences in linguistic and historical order of events (involving, for example, so-called "flashbacks"), settings in time and space, and transitions (including not only transitional particles, such as then, next, later, therefore, and accordingly, but also transitional phrases, sentences, and even paragraphs), and identification of participants (including how they are introduced, referred to in the successive parts of the narrative, and finally removed from an account).

In the discussion of various problems of translation and their solutions, a certain number of technical terms are indispensable. To dispense entirely with such terms, it would be necessary to employ long, involved descriptive phrases, which would in themselves be not only cumbersome but even misleading. However, for any of the terms which may not be understood by the reader, there is a Glossary of Technical Terms in the Appendix, and this should be adequate to help the reader understand how such words are used. In addition, there is a Glossary of Biblical Terms, which may serve as a basis for marginal helps or glossaries to accompany the publication of the translation of Acts. The reader will want to make use of New Testament maps, a Bible dictionary, and a couple of standard commentaries as supplementary material to what he will find in this Handbook. Only in this way will he have all the necessary information to serve as background for the solution of some of the exegetical and translational difficulties mentioned in this volume. He will also want to read The Theory and Practice of Translation as well as A Translator's Handbook on the Gospel of Mark and A Translator's

<u>Handbook on the Gospel of Luke</u>, since especially in these Handbooks a number of key biblical terms are discussed somewhat more fully than in this present volume. It is assumed that by the time a translator has undertaken to work on Acts he has already made certain basic decisions with respect to many terms of biblical vocabulary.

CHAPTER 1

Originally the book of Acts had no title, and at various times in the early
church it was given different names. However, the name which finally won
out was "The Acts of the Apostles," a title which seems to go back to about
the middle of the second century A.D.

The translation of this title, The Acts of the Apostles, is not too easy
to reproduce in a number of languages. Acts must be rendered as a verb
since it refers to events, for example, "What the Apostles Did." In other
instances, one can use an expression such as "work" either in the verbal form
"How the Apostles Worked," or "The Work of the Apostles." In such instances,
"work" must include the general concept of "doing, accomplishing, performing."

> 1 Dear Theophilus:
> In my first book I wrote about all the things that Jesus did and
> taught, from the time he began his work 2 until the day he was taken up
> to heaven. Before he was taken up he gave instructions by the power of
> the Holy Spirit to the men he had chosen as his apostles. 3 For forty
> days after his death he showed himself to them many times, in ways
> that proved beyond doubt that he was alive; he was seen by them, and
> talked with them about the Kingdom of God. 4 And when they came to-
> gether, he gave them this order, "Do not leave Jerusalem, but wait for
> the gift my Father promised, that I told you about. 5 John baptized with
> water, but in a few days you will be baptized with the Holy Spirit."
> (1.1-5)

A possible section heading for this first paragraph might be "The Promise of the Holy Spirit"; however, it would be ambiguous for it could mean
"what the Holy Spirit promises" or "the fact that God promised the Holy
Spirit." It is, of course, the latter meaning which is correct. The translation of this section heading in many languages can be "The Holy Spirit Whom
God Promised."

This section, along with the following section (1.6-11), serves as a
transition between the Gospel of Luke and the book of Acts. Whereas the
Gospel indicates the mighty things that God did in and through the person of
Jesus Christ, the book of Acts represents the continuing activity of God
through the Holy Spirit. In fact, the focus of the Acts of the Apostles might
be said to be upon "the acts of the Holy Spirit," and it is not without significance that the Holy Spirit is introduced twice in this initial paragraph, both
in terms of the "commandments" given to the apostles and the "baptism"
which is to come.

The discourse structure of 1.1-5 is typically "expository," with an
initial general statement (vv. 1-2a), followed by three amplifications of this
in more specific terms: (1) verse 2b, (2) verse 3, and (3) verses 4 and 5.

There are three major problems in this discourse: (1) the introduction of Theophilus, (2) the time sequence, and (3) the shift to direct discourse toward the end of verse 4.

If we had more information about Theophilus it would be much easier to introduce this person in an appropriate manner. While nothing is known of Theophilus to whom Luke addresses his book, the name must be understood and translated as a real name and not as a symbolic one, for example, "beloved by God." In ancient times it was customary for an author to dedicate his book to a person who either had contributed toward the cost of its writing or had otherwise been related closely to its purpose. But lacking specific information about Theophilus, one can only employ a form which will be as personal and as noncommittal as possible. An expression such as "dear Theophilus" tends to suggest a letter, but this book is obviously not a letter. At the same time, an English expression such as "oh Theophilus" sounds old-fashioned. Some languages require some such explanatory introduction as "this book is written to (or for) Theophilus." What makes a direct reference to Theophilus rather awkward, however, is the fact that a direct discourse occurs toward the end of the paragraph. As noted below, this discourse must be so introduced as not to give the impression that Jesus was speaking to Theophilus. In most languages it is best to place the name "Theophilus" at the very beginning of the paragraph, rather than later in the text. Nevertheless, the fact that this book is addressed to a particular person is important for the manner in which many languages employ first person plural inclusive and exclusive forms of "we" (see 20. 5 ff.).

The time sequences are quite difficult in the passage. The first problem of relative time occurs in the transition between verse 2a and 2b. Verse 2a already mentions the ascension, but the rest of the paragraph precedes this event. This type of "flashback" must be made quite explicit; compare TEV before he was taken up. The second problem occurs in 2b, for the dependent clause which mentions the choosing of the apostles is prior to the earlier part of the verse. The third difficulty occurs at the beginning of verse 4, which describes an event that is simultaneous with what occurs in verse 3. The fourth problem occurs at the end of verse 4, where the "hearing" is considerably prior to what Jesus was then saying. It is not advisable to attempt to shift the order of the verses, for this structure is not primarily narrative, but expository. Furthermore, there is a very important climax in verse 5. However, it is most important that the shifts in time sequence be carefully indicated.

The introduction of the direct discourse in verse 4 is quite difficult, for the form of the Greek does not specify how much is to be included. The solution suggested by the TEV has a number of distinct advantages in comparison with certain other translations.

1. 1-2a

In my first book I wrote represents a Greek sentence in which the focus is on "book," and so the TEV has translated in this way. The adjective means "first," rather than "former" or "earlier," but does not imply that Luke intended another volume beyond Acts. The Greek word translated "book" may mean a variety of things (for example, "word," "treatise," "account"), but the meaning "book" (perhaps with specific reference to a writing covering more than one roll of papyrus) seems evident in the present context.

The combination "write ... book" may not exist in some languages. One may "make a book," that is, publish, but not "write a book." Therefore, in some cases one must employ some such translation as "write a statement" or "write a treatise, an account."

Jesus did and taught represents the Greek "Jesus began both to do and to teach." It is thought by a few that the word "began" is emphatic and therefore should be translated; but most translators and commentators understand the phrase "began both to do and to teach" as simply an equivalent of "to do and to teach," with no particular stress on the word "began."

The statement all the things that Jesus did may need to be recast somewhat in certain languages as "all the work that Jesus did." Usually there is very little trouble in finding some quite general equivalent of "do."

In a number of languages teach requires certain types of goals, for example, "teach the words to the people" or "what he taught the people."

The clause from the time he began his work must be related to the "did and taught" and not to the "writing of the account." The expression "time" is often translated as "day," as a more specific, but nonetheless general, reference to time.

The TEV, along with several other translations (see JB and NEB), adds to heaven to the verb "he was taken up" in order to make explicit for the reader what was evident in the mind of Luke. (So also in v. 9; in v. 11 Luke explicitly states into heaven.)

The passive he was taken up to heaven must be shifted to an active in many languages, and the appropriate agent for this is "God," that is, "until the day that God took Jesus up to heaven" or "until God caused Jesus to go up to heaven." In some languages a term "take" may suggest "grab on to" and hence must be changed to a causative.

1.2b

As noted above, the temporal sequence at this point must be made clear, either by some expression which simply signals prior time, for example, "previously" or "beforehand," or which states the relationship of the events in the form of complete clauses, as in the TEV, before he was taken up.

Although most translations connect by the power of the Holy Spirit with the verb "give instruction," some (such as JB) connect it with the verb "choose."

By the power of the Holy Spirit is literally "by the Holy Spirit," but the context clearly implies that the instrumental use of "Holy Spirit" is a reference to the power of the Holy Spirit. In this phrase Jesus is the primary or initiating agent, while the Holy Spirit is the secondary agent. The equivalent of this type of expression in a number of languages is "Jesus caused them to know (be commanded, instructed) by means of the Holy Spirit," "Jesus caused the Holy Spirit to command them," or "...to give them instructions."

Due to the complications of the causative expression, it may be necessary to provide a transition for the discourse, for example, "these were the men whom Jesus chose to be his apostles."

Apostles occurs twenty-eight times in Acts and always refers to the twelve (or eleven) in Jerusalem, with the exception of two verses (14.4, 14) where it refers to Barnabas and Paul.

An adequate term for "apostles" is not easy. Many languages have simply borrowed a term. Other languages have endeavored to reproduce something of the root meaning, namely, "the sent ones." A very useful equivalent is "his messengers" or, as in some languages, "his special messengers."

1.3

For forty days (literally "through [a period of] forty days") may be taken to mean that Jesus did not leave the presence of the apostles throughout the entire period of forty days; while, on the other hand, it may indicate that Jesus appeared to them at intervals during that time. The TEV interprets the phrase in this latter fashion and so translates for forty days...he showed himself to them many times, that is, on many different occasions.

In ways that proved beyond doubt translates one Greek word which is a very strong term meaning clear and evident proof. Proved beyond doubt may be restructured as "he showed them clearly" or "showed them so clearly that people could not doubt."

After his death translates the expression "after he had suffered," but in the context "to suffer" includes everything that Jesus experienced in connection with his trial, crucifixion, and death, with the primary focus upon his death.

The expression he was alive may give rise to serious complications, since in some languages a wrong form of the verb could suggest that Jesus had really not died but had just continued to live. Accordingly, one must sometimes translate as "came back to life and was alive."

He was seen by them is rendered "he appeared to them" in most translations and represents a Greek verb form that may be either active "appear to," or passive "be seen by." This is the only place where this particular verb occurs in the New Testament; however, the other verb stems to which it is related suggest that this form should be translated in the active. In some languages the equivalent expression is "they clearly saw him" or "he caused them to see him clearly."

Throughout this verse the pronoun them refers specifically to the apostles, though in reality other persons were involved.

The Kingdom of God refers to the sovereign authority and rule of God in the lives of his people rather than to the territory or the people over which God rules. In many languages the most appropriate equivalent is "the rule of God" or "God's ruling." The phrase is of crucial importance for the entire

New Testament, and especially for the Gospels. In some languages "rule" requires a goal and this should be "people," not "the earth," for the <u>Kingdom of God</u> refers to his rule over mankind, not his control of the physical universe.

1.4

The verb which is translated <u>when they came together</u> may have two different meanings. It may be derived from a stem meaning "eat salt together with" and thereby have reference to a meal: "while he was eating a meal with them." On the other hand, it may come from a root meaning "camp out with" or "stay with," and so be translated "while he was staying with them." The most generic manner of dealing with this verb is to translate it as "while he was with them." It may be necessary to employ some temporal modifier, for example, "still" or "yet," as in "while he was still with them."

The original manuscripts were left without any type of punctuation. For this reason, translations many times differ in details of punctuation. For example, the TEV places in direct discourse everything beginning with <u>do not leave Jerusalem</u> down to the end of verse 5. Other punctuation alternatives are possible, and one may compare, for example, the RSV and the NEB, both of which punctuate differently. However, it is very useful to introduce the direct discourse as in the TEV, so that the relationships may be quite explicit. The phrase <u>gave them this order</u> may be variously rendered, for example, "he ordered them in this way," "he commanded them with these words," "he ordered them," or "he told them strongly."

The TEV translates "to wait for the promise of the Father" by <u>wait for the gift my Father promised</u>. This has been done since the meaning is clearly that the disciples are to wait for that which the Father had already promised, namely, the Holy Spirit. They were not told to wait for the Father to promise them something.

Some translators have wanted to introduce "Father God" here, but it is not necessary---certainly not at this point in the development of the New Testament narrative. The addition of "God" would seem to remove some of the personal character of the expression.

The clause <u>that I told you about</u> may be rendered as an independent (but closely linked) sentence, for example, "I have told you about it." If it is advisable in the receptor language to keep the disciples in focus, one may translate as "which you heard me mention" or "you heard me speak about this."

1.5

In the Greek there is an evident contrast between John who baptized with water and the disciples who will be baptized with the Holy Spirit; this is brought out in the TEV by <u>John...but</u>.

The verb <u>baptize</u> may require a direct object, that is, "John baptized people with water."

The Greek negative-positive expression "not many" is often rendered as few, since this is much easier to understand.

The term water should be treated as the instrument, in the same way that Holy Spirit is an instrument. To force a distinction here between the dative with "water" and Greek en plus dative with "Spirit" is artificial.

In languages which require a shift from passive to active, the last clause can be rendered as "God will baptize you with the Holy Spirit." Some translators have objected to using the same term for "baptism of the Holy Spirit" and "baptism with water." For "baptism with water" they may have some such expression as "to enter the water" or "to receive water on the head"; while for "baptism of the Holy Spirit" they have "for the Holy Spirit to enter people." Not to employ parallelism in these two expressions is, however, unfortunate. One can usually employ some sort of related structure, for example, "to cause water to come upon" and "to cause the Holy Spirit to come upon."

Jesus Is Taken up to Heaven

6 When the apostles met together with Jesus they asked him, "Lord, will you at this time give the Kingdom back to Israel?"
7 Jesus said to them, "The times and occasions are set by my Father's own authority, and it is not for you to know when they will be. 8 But you will be filled with power when the Holy Spirit comes on you, and you will be witnesses for me in Jerusalem, in all of Judea and Samaria, and to the ends of the earth." 9 After saying this, he was taken up to heaven as they watched him; and a cloud hid him from their sight. (1.6-9)

The section heading Jesus Is Taken up to Heaven must be rendered in some languages in the active form. This will require the mention of the agent, namely, God, for example, "God Takes Jesus up to Heaven" or "God Causes Jesus to Go to Heaven." It may also be possible to speak of the ascent of Jesus without indicating an agent, for example, "Jesus Goes up to Heaven."

These paragraphs form a tightly structured narrative, with an initial expression of time, when the apostles met..., which joins the first paragraph to the preceding one. The two direct discourses, (1) a question by the disciples and (2) the answer by Jesus, form the central core of the paragraphs, terminating with a reference to the ascension, already noted in verse 2a. This reference serves to help link verse 9 with verse 2, and thus provides a unity of theme for the two paragraphs.

It is characteristic of Luke's style to suggest a theme, refer to it later more specifically, and finally to deal with it quite fully. Note, for example, Chapter 2 and the expansion of the statement concerning the baptism of the Spirit. Similarly, the rest of the book of Acts may be treated as an amplification of verse 8. Luke introduces Saul (Paul) in a similar way.

When the apostles met together with Jesus (Greek "when they met together") may be taken to include only the apostles. However, the TEV understands they to indicate not only the apostles but Jesus as well, and this is
supported by the observation that immediately following their gathering together the apostles ask Jesus a question. In most languages one must be quite explicit about the participants, as in the TEV the apostles...Jesus.

Although Lord may merely mean "sir," in the present context the meaning Lord is to be preferred (see also 1.22). By the question which the apostles
asked Jesus (Lord, will you at this time give the Kingdom back to [the nation
of] Israel?), they indicate that they are still conditioned by the Jewish expectation of a national kingdom to be set up on earth.

In many languages Lord requires some indication of those who acknowledge his lordship, for example, "our Lord" or "you who command us."

The phrase at this time is a very general statement of time contemporary with another event. In other languages one may require "in these days,"
"now," or even "very shortly," since the restoration had obviously not begun.
It is for this reason that some languages require an expression for the immediate future rather than for the present.

The English expression give the Kingdom back is quite impossible in
most languages. In fact, in most languages one cannot "give a rule" to anyone. This is essentially a causative in most instances and must usually be
translated as "cause the Israel people to rule again." Some have interpreted
this merely as "to be self-governing" or "to be free," but what is asked about
is not independence from Rome but a dominant role in governing. If a goal
for "to rule" is required, then one may use some such expression as "to
cause the Israel people to rule other nations again." In other words, the restoration of the period of David and Solomon.

1.7

The term which introduces the direct discourse must in many languages
be changed from said to "answered," since what follows is in response to a
question.

Although times refers primarily to chronological time and occasions
relates basically to special periods of time, it is quite likely that in a set
phrase such as this no basic distinction can be made between the two terms.

The meaningful relationships in the clause the times and occasions are
set by my Father's own authority are extremely complex. In many languages,
in fact, the relations must be quite completely restructured so as to make the
Father the direct agent and the times and the occasions the goal, even though
these are really temporal qualifications for certain events. As a result, one
may need to translate this clause as "my Father alone decides just when
these things will happen." The components of set (or "establish") and authority are often combined in a verb such as "decide." This is reinforced by
"alone," which indicates that it is his own decision, and therefore authority.

The shifting of "the Father" to <u>my Father</u> is almost obligatory in English and completely so in many languages. In fact, in many languages kinship terms must always occur with so-called "possessives." Since fathers are always in relationship to someone else, many languages require that such a person be specified in the immediate context.

The phrase <u>it is not for you to know</u> is equivalent in many languages to "you do not have the right to know" or "you are not permitted to know." If an agent is required, then it must be God; that is, "God has not permitted you to know."

<u>1.8</u>

It is important that the conjunction <u>but</u> not be interpreted as being in contradiction to what has just been said. This is not an adversative "but." Rather, it may be called a "diversionary" one, for example, "rather" or "on the other hand," a transitional expression which shifts the focus of attention from a previous statement to something else which has other, and perhaps even more, significance.

<u>You will be filled with power</u> translates the Greek "you will receive power," though the related expression in 2.4 is literally <u>they were all filled with the Holy Spirit</u>. The reference is to the miraculous power to be given to the disciples, by which they would be able to work miracles. The coming of the Holy Spirit upon the disciples and their being filled with the Holy Spirit are to be understood as simultaneous actions.

The passive expression <u>will be filled</u> (Greek "will receive") is difficult in many languages. Accordingly, one must often employ an agent, namely, God, for example, "God will fill you" or "God will give to you." However, <u>be filled with power</u> may require a somewhat different type of structure, such as "cause you to be powerful" or "cause you to be strong," provided, of course, that this strength is not merely physical.

Where the term "power" or "strength" must have some complement, in order to avoid a wrong interpretation, it is often appropriate to use some such expression as "the power (or strength) to witness."

<u>You will be witnesses for me</u> is not simply a statement of future fact, but it is given in the nature of a command. The Greek term usually translated as "witness" is found thirteen times in Acts, and the basic meaning is "one who testifies." Only in 22.20 can it possibly be stretched to mean "martyr," and even in that context the primary meaning is that of "one who gives testimony."

The phrase <u>witnesses for me</u> must often be shifted to a verbal expression, for example, "tell people what you know about me." The focus in "witness" is speaking from personal experience.

The locative expressions <u>in Jerusalem, in all of Judea</u> refer to places where people are, and this must be specified in some languages, for example, "tell about me to people in Jerusalem, in all Judea,..." <u>And to the ends of the earth</u> appears frequently in the Septuagint as a common phrase referring to distant lands; it is quite improbable that the expression must be understood as a specific reference to Rome. The phrase to the ends of the earth is variously expressed, for example, "to as far as there is land," "far, far away," or "to other countries."

1.9

The order of grammatical elements in the Greek must often be shifted to represent the order of events, as in the TEV. That is to say, first, Jesus finishes speaking; second, he is taken up into heaven; third, the disciples watch; and, fourth, the cloud hides him.

The phrase after saying this may be rendered in many languages as "first he said" or "he finished speaking and then." This makes the reference to the speaking relate to the previous statement.

The passive expression was taken up may require a subject, which should be God; that is, "God took him up to heaven." However, it is important that one not get the impression that God grabbed him by the head and hauled him into heaven---as in the case of one translation. Therefore, in some languages it may be better to translate "God caused him to go to heaven." (See also 1.2a.)

The verb watch so often occurs in a continuative form, thus focusing upon the duration of the process. A cloud hid him from their sight translates "a cloud took him up out of their sight." In a number of languages the phrase "a cloud hid him" causes some difficulty, since a "cloud" is essentially an instrument, not an agent. Therefore, one may prefer to employ "he was hidden by a cloud" or "he was no longer visible because of a cloud." If the verb hid suggests some intentionality on the part of the cloud, one may employ "because of the cloud he could not be seen" or "...they could not see him."

> 10 They still had their eyes fixed on the sky as he went away, when two men dressed in white suddenly stood beside them. 11 "Men of Galilee," they said, "why do you stand there looking up at the sky? This Jesus, who was taken up from you into heaven, will come back in the same way that you saw him go to heaven." (1.10-11)

The structure of this fourth paragraph of Chapter 1 is relatively simple since it consists of three basic elements: (1) the transitional clause, which ties the event of this paragraph with the previous, for example, the fact of looking up into heaven, (2) the introduction of two new participants, two men dressed in white, and (3) their statement to the apostles.

In keeping with proper Greek style, the introductory clause is dependent and serves to link the following sentence to the preceding event. However, to translate this clause in a dependent form in English tends to do violence to the meaning, for it would suggest that in some way or other the participants anticipated some such event as the appearance of the angels from heaven. (Compare a similar treatment of this type of problem in the NEB, Luke 15.14.) The TEV has rightly made the first clause independent, with the second clause dependent, thus reflecting the proper relation between the two events.

<u>1.10</u>

To have one's eyes fixed on something is a favorite Lukan expression (the verb he uses here is used fourteen times in the New Testament, twelve times by Luke himself). It means to look at something intently. Furthermore, the form of the verb, as well as the meaning of the verb itself, underscores the intensity with which the disciples were staring into the sky as Jesus was taken away.

An expression such as <u>had their eyes fixed on the sky</u> is effective in present-day English, but in most languages a verbal form of "seeing" or "looking" is required, for example, "looked continuously toward the sky," "gazed strongly at the sky," or "tried very hard to see into the sky." In a number of languages one can and should shift the order of the "going," for example, "as Jesus was going away up into the sky, the apostles looked constantly." This expression is then followed by the dependent expression introducing the <u>two men</u>.

The <u>two men dressed in white</u> are, of course, angels; "white" is the traditional dress of angels in Jewish and Christian tradition. <u>Suddenly</u> is rendered in some other translations by "behold." The word itself is a particle which generally is used to call attention to what follows; but in certain contexts it may be translated in other ways, and here the meaning "suddenly" or "all at once" (NEB) seems best suited to the context.

Even though these <u>two men</u> were angels, it is better in the translation to preserve the meaning of the original text and use simply "two men." A footnote could be used to indicate that angels are often spoken of in Scripture in this manner.

The phrase <u>dressed in white</u> may be rendered as "with white clothes" or "wearing shining garments."

The verb "stand" suggests something more than "stand up" or "be standing." In some languages one must use a compound verb phrase "came and stood" or "arrived and stood," since the men were not continuously there, at least not visibly so. In other languages, the verb "stand" may be translated as "begin to stand" or "came to stand."

<u>1.11</u>

Since the statement of the two men is a question, it must be introduced by a question term in many languages, for example, "they asked,..." For problems of word order involving verbs of speaking, see 7.27.

The phrase <u>men of Galilee</u> is equivalent to "men who come from Galilee" or "men whose home is in Galilee." All languages have a means by which people may be identified as coming from a particular locality.

<u>On the sky</u> (v. 10), <u>at the sky</u> (v. 11), and <u>into heaven</u> (v. 11) all translate the same expression, literally "into the heaven." But the Greek word

"heaven" may be used either as the abode of God, that is, heaven, or merely as the sky. Jesus is taken into heaven, whereas the disciples gaze up at the sky.

For many languages there is simply no distinction between the physical sky and the abode of God. When there is no distinction in terminology, it is quite unnecessary to try to translate "heaven" always as "the place where God lives." In a context such as this, a term for "sky" will normally serve quite well for both "heaven" and "sky."

The expression this Jesus may require certain adjustments in other languages, since proper names may not occur with a demonstrative such as "this." An equivalent could be "this person Jesus" or "this one, called Jesus"—some sort of appositional relation is found in all languages.

In the same way refers to the manner of the Lord's return, that is, on the clouds of heaven, as is depicted in other passages of the New Testament. This may be rendered in some languages as "just like he went."

Judas' Successor

12 Then the apostles went back to Jerusalem from the Mount of Olives, which is about half a mile away from the city. 13 They entered Jerusalem and went up to the room where they were staying: Peter, John, James and Andrew, Philip and Thomas, Bartholomew and Matthew, James, the son of Alphaeus, Simon the Patriot, and Judas, the son of James. 14 They gathered frequently to pray as a group, together with the women, and with Mary the mother of Jesus, and his brothers. (1.12-14)

The section heading Judas' Successor is very short and clear in English, but it involves rather complex semantic relations. In most languages it is necessary to expand this expression into something more or less equivalent to "Someone Takes the Place of Judas," "Matthias Takes the Place of Judas," or "Matthias is Designated to Do Judas' Work."

The transitional paragraph 1.12-14 is designed to set the stage for the next major section, which deals with the selection of Judas' successor. In this transitional paragraph, Luke (1) makes a connection with the preceding event, while adding information as to where it took place, (2) identifies the persons who were involved in the event and who would be involved in the following events, and (3) introduces the community of believers as a way of preparing for the events described in the rest of Chapter 1 and in Chapter 2. Luke is a very skillful narrator in the way in which he "plants details" before they are specifically required.

The particle then, at the beginning of 1.12, serves to link the following statement to the preceding event, while the clause as a whole brings the action back from the scene of the ascension to the city of Jerusalem, already mentioned in 1.4. The beginning of 1.13, they entered Jerusalem, is a typical transitional statement which sets the stage for the following statement.

21

1.12

In speaking of the Mount of Olives it is most important to avoid a name which may be misleading. For example, in some languages a literal rendering of this phrase name would imply that the mountain consisted of olives. In other languages, such a rendering suggests that the mountain consisted of olive trees. A more appropriate rendering is "mountain called 'Olive Grove'," "mountain on which there were olive groves," "mountain known for its olive trees," or "mountain with olive trees." One or another of these basic structures is almost always represented in the structure of place names in various languages.

In some languages it is useful to employ a classifier, for example, "city," with a proper name such as Jerusalem, but this should normally be done at the first occurrence of a name in a discourse, such as in verse 4, and it is not necessary to repeat the classifier at this point.

Although the Greek does not make the subject of went back explicit, it is evident that the apostles are meant.

About half a mile away from the city translates "which is near Jerusalem the distance of a Sabbath day's journey." The expression "a Sabbath day's journey" is regarded as having originated during the time Israel was wandering through the desert. The calculation was ostensibly based on the distance from the place of worship to the tent in the camp farthest from it. In later times the phrase was often used merely as an expression of distance, and that is how Luke has used it in this passage. For this reason, the TEV translates the phrase as about half a mile away from the city (of Jerusalem). In metric measurements this is "about one kilometer."

1.13

In some languages it is difficult to say entered Jerusalem, since one only enters an enclosure, such as a house or temple, and cities are not in this same class of enclosed objects. Under such circumstances one can "go to," "arrive at," or even "walk past the borders of."

The room is literally "the room upstairs," and this word is used elsewhere in the New Testament only in Acts 9.37,39 and 20.8. The type of room referred to is a tower-like construction built on the flat roof of an oriental house and reached by a stairway from the outside. Nothing further is known regarding the identity of this particular room.

Staying translates a word that is often used in the papyri to refer to a temporary residence as opposed to a place of permanent residence. One may need to translate as "where they were remaining temporarily" or even "where they were living for a short time."

The problems of transliteration of proper names are entirely too complex to be treated in this passage, and by the time one has come to Acts basic decisions on transliteration must have already been worked out. For guidance in such matters see Bible Translating, Toward a Science of Translating, and The Theory and Practice of Translation.

As can be seen clearly from the Greek text, the names in this list are grouped in a rather unusual way. The first four names form a unit, while the next four names are paired off, and the following three are listed in a series with special identification. The TEV has attempted to reproduce something of this structure, but in a form much more natural than the literal rendering employed in the RSV.

The Patriot identifies Simon as a member of the Zealot party, a group of Jewish nationals who advocated the violent overthrow of Roman rule. Judas is the son of James and not the brother of James, as some translations have it. There is nothing in the New Testament which permits one to identify this Judas with Judas the brother of James in Mark 6.3 or Jude 1.

For many languages there is a ready equivalent of "patriot," but in certain instances a descriptive phrase must be employed, for example, "one who wanted independence for his country" or "one who opposed the foreign rulers of his country."

<u>1.14</u>

Although the word translated as a group originally meant something like "with one mind" or "of one accord," it seems quite likely that by New Testament times it had become weakened to mean simply "together."

Frequently precedes the verb phrase to pray in order to bring out the meaning of the Greek verbal construction which emphasizes that the praying was done either continuously or frequently. A similar emphasis is also brought out by the JB, "these joined in continuous prayer," and by the NEB, "these were constantly at prayer together." But it seems preferable to translate "frequent" rather than "constant" or "continuous."

It is difficult to define precisely the relationship between Mary the mother of Jesus and the women spoken of, though it is very unlikely that the women should be understood as the wives of the men involved. Perhaps Mary was included within the group of the women, but because of her unique relationship to the Lord she was given specific mention; and in any case Luke elsewhere, as in the nativity narratives, lets his high regard for Mary be known.

The fact that the participants who joined together in prayer are syntactically divided between they and the postponed series the women, and with Mary ... and his brothers makes for a very awkward statement in many languages. Accordingly, the arrangement is often recast, for example, "the apostles, together with the women, and Mary the mother of Jesus, and his brothers, joined together in a group to pray frequently."

15 A few days later there was a meeting of the believers, about one hundred and twenty in all, and Peter stood up to speak. 16 "My brothers," he said, "the scripture had to come true in which the Holy Spirit, speaking through David, predicted about Judas, who was the guide of those who arrested Jesus. 17 Judas was a member of our group, because he had been chosen to have a part in our work." (1.15-17)

1. 15

The discourse structure of 1. 15-26 consists of (1) an introductory section, verse 15, which gives the setting for the direct discourse and the following narrative, (2) an introduction to the narrative concerning Judas, verse 16b, (3) a parenthesis about events associated with Judas (a kind of flashback), (4) the statement of the Scriptures, referred to by Peter (who is introduced in v. 15), (5) the conclusion as to what should be done, and (6) the result of the activity, including prayer for guidance in the casting of the lots.

The transitions between the various sections often present difficulties at the following points: (1) the parenthesis about Judas' activities (this section, vv. 18-19, usually needs to be set off by parentheses and is often introduced by temporal particles indicating that the events had already happened), (2) the transition back to what Peter has said (beginning with v. 20), which may require a new introduction of the name of Peter and a verb of speaking, for example, "Peter continued to say," and (3) the shift from the quotation of the Scriptures to the reasoning of Peter. This latter shift is aided visually by the indentation of the lines quoting Scripture, but it may be necessary to introduce another verb of speaking so as to specify that Peter is no longer quoting but addressing the audience directly.

The discourse structure of the brief paragraph 1. 15-17 is relatively simple, for the first verse sets the stage for the discourse by specifying the time, the participants, and the speaker. The difficulty with the sequence of the narrative in verses 16 and 17 is that the linguistic order is not historical. This lack of agreement between linguistic and temporal sequence often needs to be very clearly specified or the linguistic order changed.

1. 15

A few days later (literally "in those days") is merely a way of designating a vague and indefinite period of time (see 2. 18; 9. 37), and is used by Luke here and in two other places (6. 1; 11. 27) to indicate either a transition in, or the beginning of, a new story.

By the addition of there was a meeting the TEV makes explicit for its readers the situation in which Peter stood up to speak: it was a meeting of the believers (see NEB "before the assembled brotherhood"). Believers translates the word "brothers," which is used here in the specific sense of "those who belong to the Christian fellowship." "Brothers" was a term frequently used both in Jewish and in non-Jewish sources to indicate members of a particular religious community.

In place of an impersonal type of noun expression, for example, a meeting of the believers, many languages employ a verb expression, such as "the believers met together."

About one hundred and twenty in all is generally understood to be a parenthetical statement given by Luke, and so is set off by commas in the TEV. About one hundred and twenty literally translates the expression "the crowd of names was about one hundred and twenty," but "names" is used in this context as the equivalent of "persons." Although the Greek phrase translated

24

in all may also be used as a designation of place, meaning "at the same place" (see 2.1 in one place), in the present context it appears to have the meaning "in all" or "together," a usage which is supported by the papyri.

Most languages have very little difficulty in specifying "one hundred and twenty," whether the system is based on tens or twenties. Where languages do not have such high numbers (this is true of some so-called primitive languages), one can use a more general term "many" or "a crowd of."

In some languages a term for speaking requires the personal goal to be specified, in which case one can say "Peter stood up and spoke to the people there" or "...to those people."

Where, as in some languages, a double verbal expression is required for the introduction of direct discourse, one can say "he spoke to the believers; he said,..."

1. 16

My brothers translates the expression "men brothers." Since in this phrase the word "men" is used in a general sense and does not exclude women, it is best left untranslated (see also fellow Jews, literally "men Jews," 2.14; men of Israel, literally "men Israelites," 2. 22; and brothers, literally "men brothers," 2. 29).

An expression such as my brothers may cause considerable difficulty in languages in which a term for "brother" is not generalized. In these instances one can often generalize a term for "relative," "kinsman," or "companion." This must, of course, be a term which can include women.

The scripture refers to a passage or a text of Scripture rather than to the entire Old Testament.

Had to (literally "it was necessary" or "it had to be") is used here, as in many other passages of the New Testament, to denote something necessary in the purpose of God. The tense of the verb indicates that this necessity had already been accomplished at the time that Peter speaks, that is, it was brought about by the actions of Judas.

In order to specify that the scripture consisted of some passages of the Old Testament, one can often use a term such as "holy writings" or "writings of God" without, of course, implying that God himself actually wrote the documents.

Come true (see also NEB and Phillips) is rendered by most translations as "be fulfilled." The root idea of the verb is that of filling something, but it is here used in the extended sense of "give full meaning to" or "make come true." The primary meanings of the Scripture passages to which Peter has reference (see v. 20 below) are to be found in their original Old Testament setting. But because the character and actions of Judas are similar to those reflected in these passages from the Psalms, Peter can say that these Scriptures apply to Judas. This is quite typical of the manner in which the first Christians interpreted the Old Testament; they read it in light of the things which had taken place in connection with the life and ministry of Jesus.

What is really difficult about this verse is the association of ideas in an order which is not easy to communicate in other languages. At the same time, one should attempt to preserve the focus of concern, namely, the fact that Scriptures had to come true. This can often be done by introducing first a general statement, to be followed by an explanation which provides the remaining data in a more extended form. For example, the first clause can be rendered as "what is written in the holy Scriptures had to happen" or "it was necessary that the words in the Scriptures should prove to be true." Then one can refer to the contents of the rest of the verse in such a manner as to preserve as much as possible of the historical order, for example, "The Holy Spirit caused David to speak about Judas. He told ahead of time what Judas would do, this Judas who guided the men who came to arrest Jesus."

The secondary agent, that is, <u>speaking through David</u>, is often best reproduced as a causative statement, for example, "caused David to speak."

<u>Predicted</u> is merely "said in advance what was going to happen" or "what Judas would do."

A term for <u>guide</u> is normally quite easy, for example, "man who showed the way to" or "person who guided the men to Jesus."

<u>Arrested</u> refers to a rather formal procedure, relatively well-known in most societies. But if there is no definite expression for "arrest," one can always use "tied him up and led him away."

1.17

The only serious problem in this verse is likely to be the casual expression which precedes in time the content of the first clause. In many languages the order must be changed, for example, "because Judas was chosen to work with us, he was a member of our group." The Greek "he was numbered among us" simply means, as the TEV has expressed it, <u>Judas was a member of our group</u>. An idiomatic way of rendering <u>member of our group</u> may be "he was with us," "he associated with us," or "he went around with us." In some languages the most natural equivalent is "he was a friend to us," in the sense of a close associate.

Even though <u>had been chosen</u> may mean "to receive something by the casting of lots," it is doubtful if that meaning is to be found in this present context. The passive expression <u>he had been chosen</u> can be rendered as active, such as "Jesus had chosen him."

<u>Work</u> of the TEV is rendered by most translations "ministry"; the idea is that of the service or work which the apostle performs rather than the office which he holds. <u>To have a part in our work</u> is too general and abstract to be translated literally in some languages. Therefore, "to work together with us" or "to be one with us in working" may be more idiomatic and accurate.

Insofar as possible it is wise to employ for <u>work</u> a general term which can also include service to God. In some languages the connotative values of the term for "work" require that some more adequate expression be chosen. Therefore, some translators have used "in our working for God," since this is a direct reference to Judas' function as an apostle and not to his activity as a laborer.

> 18 (With the money that Judas got for his evil act he bought a field, where he fell to his death; he burst open and all his insides spilled out. 19 All the people living in Jerusalem heard about it, and so in their own language they call that field Akeldama, which means "Field of Blood.")
> 20 "For it is written in the book of Psalms,
> > 'May his house become empty;
> > let no one live in it.'
> It is also written,
> > 'May someone else take his place of service.' (1.18-20)

It is generally agreed that verses 18 and 19 are parenthetical, having been introduced into the narrative by the author for the benefit of the reader. It would have been unnecessary for Peter to have given this explanation to his hearers, and the allusion to in their own language (v. 19) is a reference to Aramaic and sounds more natural coming from Luke than from Peter.

The discourse structure of verses 18 and 19 is narrative, with only a slight shift in linguistic and temporal order. In some languages these problems can be readily resolved in the following way, "Because Judas did what was bad, he received money. By means of this he bought a field, and there he fell down, he burst open, his intestines came out, and he died." As noted from this sequence, it may be necessary to shift the order of the activity and the money, as well as the reference to the way in which Judas died.

At the beginning of verse 19 it may be necessary to introduce a connective, "as a result" or "because of this."

1.18

With the money that Judas got for his evil act translates the ambiguous phrase "reward of wickedness." It may mean money which is undeserved, or else it may mean money which is gotten for doing something evil. Most translations understand it in this latter sense. A field or a piece of land seems to be what Judas purchased with his money; that he would have been able to have purchased a farm or an estate, as some translations render it, seems quite unlikely. The word translated field is used elsewhere in 4.34; 5.3, 8; 28.7.

Although there is considerable doubt regarding the meaning of he fell to his death (this may mean "his body swelled up"; see Phillips, Moffatt, Goodspeed), the majority of translations reflect the same interpretation of the text as that given in the TEV.

There is, of course, no way in which in the translation one can harmonize this description of events with the record in Matthew 27.6-8. The reconciliation of such accounts involves quite a different level of biblical scholarship from what is involved in the translator's faithful rendering of what is said in this specific context.

27

1.19

The phrase <u>heard about it</u> may need to be somewhat more specific, for example, "heard what had happened to Judas."

<u>In their own language</u> may be rendered in some languages as a verbal expression, for example, "in the way in which those people spoke."

<u>Field of Blood</u> should not mean a field consisting of blood, or a "bloody field," but rather a field with which blood was associated. In some languages this requires a specific reference, for example, "field on which blood poured out" or "field on which blood was shed."

1.20

Peter's speech, interrupted by verses 18 and 19, is now resumed. <u>For</u>, however, refers back to verse 16, and thus gives the reason why it was necessary that Judas should have been <u>the guide of those who arrested Jesus</u> (v. 16).

Very frequently the Greek conjunction <u>gar</u> "for" presents a number of problems in translation, since it is often not related to the immediately preceding statement. In some passages it serves only to show that the argument is proceeding. In some languages it is best to omit the conjunction entirely in a construction such as here and to emphasize the use of Greek <u>oun</u> "therefore" at the beginning of verse 21. The basic meaning here is "since the Scriptures have indicated what should be done, therefore someone must be chosen to take Judas' place." The argument relates the content of verse 20 to what follows, not to what precedes.

<u>It is written</u> is a set formula used for the introduction of a quotation from the Old Testament. The first passage quoted is Psalm 69.25. The Psalm has the plural form:

> "May their houses become empty,
> Let no one live in their tents."

Peter uses it in the singular since he applies the meaning of the Psalm solely to Judas. The second passage quoted (Psalm 109.8) is an almost exact quotation from the Septuagint. Whereas the first passage expresses the wish that the house or home of Judas would be left empty, the second passage expresses the need for <u>someone else</u> to <u>take his place of service,</u> and thus serves as a transition to verses 21-26. <u>Place of service</u> (variously rendered "office," "ministry," "charge") should be translated in such a way as to show that the emphasis is upon the service that the apostle renders rather than the office which he holds. It is not at all likely that at this early date the institutional life of the church had become so developed as to have had an office of apostleship. In any case, Luke defines the primary function of an apostle as <u>a witness to the resurrection of the Lord Jesus</u> (vv. 21-22).

In many languages such an "impersonal passive" construction as "it is written" cannot be employed. In some languages one must have an active expression, for example, "The one who wrote the book of the Psalms said,"

"There are words in the book of the Psalms which say," or "In the book of the Psalms one may read."

The most satisfactory translation for Psalms is normally "songs," though in some instances one may need some type of qualifier, for example, "religious songs," or "songs of worship."

The third person imperative in Greek expressions translated as "may ...become" and "let...live" is equivalent in many languages to an emphatic obligatory mood, for example, "his house must become empty" and "no one must live in it." The use of English "may" and "let" is quite misleading, for neither potentiality nor permission is implied in the original.

The concept of a house becoming empty is not easy to render literally in many languages. One may speak of an empty container, for example, a box, sack, or bucket, but not of a house. Therefore, it may be necessary to restructure the semantic components, for example, "everyone must leave the house," with a verb for "leave" which implies permanent abandonment.

The construction may...take represents a Greek imperative. As in the case of the two preceding imperatives, it may be necessary to employ an obligatory mood, for example, "someone else must take his place," or, as suggested above, "must do his work," or "must do what he was supposed to do."

21-22 "So then, someone must join us as a witness to the resurrection of the Lord Jesus. He must be one of those who were in our group during the whole time that the Lord Jesus traveled about with us, beginning from the time John preached his baptism until the day Jesus was taken up from us to heaven."

23 So they proposed two men: Joseph, who was called Barsabbas (he was also called Justus), and Matthias. 24 Then they prayed, "Lord, you know the hearts of all men. And so, Lord, show us which one of these two you have chosen 25 to take this place of service as an apostle which Judas left to go to the place where he belongs." 26 Then they drew lots to choose between the two names. The name chosen was that of Matthias, and he was added to the group of the eleven apostles.

(1. 21-26)

Verses 21-22 serve as a conclusion to the preceding sections and as an introduction to this paragraph. Note that there is an emphatic so then at the beginning of this paragraph. In Greek these verses comprise a very complex sentence, with the verb as the first word in verse 21 and the subject as the last three words of verse 22. In order to make the meaning of this sentence immediately intelligible to English readers, the TEV has restructured the sentence and made it into two English sentences.

The following sentences are essentially narrative in structure, providing a series of succeeding events which are the practical outworking of the conclusion reached in the first two sentences. Verse 23, however, begins with a transitional particle "so," indicating that this is the result of the proposition presented in verses 21-22.

1.21-22

Peter feels as if it is necessary (must of the TEV translates here the same word as had to translates in verse 16) for someone from their larger group to join the group of the apostles and to assume the place Judas held. Must join us is often rendered as "must become one of us," "must become one with us," or "must become one of our group."

The nominal phrase a witness to the resurrection of the Lord Jesus may need to be shifted to a verbal expression, for example, "who will witness to the people that the Lord Jesus rose from the dead." In some languages this must even be put into a form of direct discourse, for example, "say to the people, We know that the Lord Jesus arose from the dead."

During the whole time that the Lord Jesus traveled about with us translates the Greek phrase "during the time that the Lord Jesus went in and out among us." "To go in and out among" is simply a Semitic idiom meaning "to live or be with someone."

The Greek expression "from the baptism of John" is translated by the TEV from the time John preached his baptism. The phrase itself can have more than one interpretation, and may have reference either to the time when John began his ministry (as TEV) or else to the time that Jesus was baptized by John. The parallel account in 10.37 tends to support the TEV interpretation.

The expression of duration of time, for example, beginning from the time...until the day is not always easy. In some languages one can only represent this as a continuous event, for example, "he must have been with us when John was preaching about his baptism and he must have remained with us until the day Jesus...."

As noted above (v. 9), the passive expression was taken up may have to be shifted to an active, for example, "God took Jesus up." (See also 1.2a and 1.9.)

In the choice of a word for Lord it is important to avoid a mere title of respect. Rather, one should have some expression which will indicate the power to command and the corresponding obligation to obey, for example, "our chief," or "the one who orders us."

1.23

Following Peter's speech two men are nominated by the group: Joseph, who was called Barsabbas..., and Matthias. After the election of Matthias neither of these men is again mentioned in the New Testament.

The pronoun they refers undoubtedly to the entire group of believers. Accordingly, it is probably necessary to introduce the nominal expression at this point, for example, "the believers spoke the names of two men" or "the believers suggested the names of two men."

The additional names of Joseph may need to be introduced in a somewhat different way in some languages, for example, "people also called him Barsabbas and they also called him Justus." In other languages one may say, "he was also known as Barsabbas and some people called him Justus" or "he had two other names, Barsabbas and Justus."

1. 24

It is difficult to know if the prayer of the group is addressed to God, the Father, or to Jesus, since Lord may refer to either. However, 1. 2 indicates that it is Jesus who has chosen the other apostles, and it is quite likely that they are asking Jesus to choose this one.

The pronoun they also refers at this point to the believers. Probably there will be no difficulty in the reference to "believers," if these are specified in the preceding verse.

In some languages "Lord," as a term of direct address, must be related to the verb of speaking, for example, "they prayed to the Lord,..." Otherwise, it might appear that the people were summoning the Lord.

The expression know the hearts may require some slight modifications, for example, "you know how men think in their hearts," "you know what all men are like in their hearts," or "you really know how men truly are."

Some type of transitional, for example, and so, is quite important at this point, for it ties together the two parts of the prayer: (1) the general recognition of the Lord's understanding of all men's motives and (2) the specific request for guidance in the choice of a successor to Judas.

Insofar as possible it is important to preserve the tense relation in have chosen. What is requested in the prayer is simply confirmation of what the Lord had already decided. In some languages, this may need to be made even more specific, for example, "which one of the two you have already decided should be the one."

1. 25

This place of service as an apostle translates "the place of this ministry and of apostleship." But in a Greek construction of this type it is quite proper to take the second noun as a qualifier of the first, and so this phrase could be understood as the ministry which an apostle performs. Evidently this expression is an expansion and further qualification of the similar phrase used in verse 17. In some languages this place of service as an apostle is equivalent to "doing the work of an apostle."

Due to the relatively complex relations of the events in this sentence, involving as they do several shifts of subjects, it may be necessary to divide the sentence into at least two parts, for example, (1) "So then, Lord, make us to know which one of these two men you have chosen so that he can do the work of an apostle," and (2) "This is the work that Judas left to go to the place where he belongs." In other languages the break may be as follows, "...whom you have chosen to be an apostle in Judas' place. Because Judas left us to go to the place where he should be."

1. 26

The place where he belongs is literally "his own place," but the meaning is that Judas went to the place which was proper for him, that is, he got what he deserved.

The translation of belongs may in some languages be expressed either in terms of "where he should be" or "to a place which he deserves" (with the connotation that it is punishment).

1. 26

They drew lots to choose between the two names translates "they gave them lots." The precise meaning of this clause is unclear, but the next clause (literally, "the lot fell on Matthias") helps to clarify it. These two clauses when taken together seem to indicate that the choice was made in a manner similar to that in which the Urim and the Thummin were used in Old Testament times. The names, written on stone, would have been placed in a vessel which was then shaken; the first stone to fall out would indicate the man chosen.

The phrase drew lots involves a number of complications in some languages. In the first place, where the custom does exist, one may have a number of different types of expressions to identify the procedure, for example, "threw down the names," "picked up the lots," or "saw the way the names fell." At the same time it is important that any expression for the casting of lots does not involve heavy connotations of magic.

Where the custom of casting lots is not known, one can employ a kind of descriptive equivalent, for example, "decided which person it would be by writing the names on pieces of stone," with a fuller explanation of the possible procedures and their cultural function in a marginal note.

In a number of languages one does not choose between the two names but "must choose between the two men."

The use of choose would imply some agent, but it would be both awkward and ill-advised to try to introduce God as the specific manipulator of the lots. Rather, one may often have an equivalent such as "the lot showed that the right man was Matthias" or "the name on the lot was that of Matthias."

He was added to the group translates the Greek word which appears only here in the New Testament. Originally the verb meant "to choose (by a vote) together with," but in this verse the meaning seems to be simply "to be added (to the eleven apostles)."

The passive expression he was added to the group may need to be put into an active form, for example, "the believers considered Matthias as one of the twelve."

Languages differ considerably in the ways in which they specify the relation of one person to others, for example, "he was one with the eleven," "he was one among the twelve," "he was added to the eleven," or "with the eleven he became the twelfth."

CHAPTER 2

For Luke the coming of the Holy Spirit into the life of the church ranks in importance with the coming of our Lord into human history, since it is only by the Spirit's presence and power that one can understand the significance of the coming of Jesus into the world. The primary purpose of Chapter 2 is to tell about the coming of the Holy Spirit. Verses 12-15 are transitional and serve to introduce the occasion for Peter's message, while the body of the message itself is contained in verses 16-36.

The Coming of the Holy Spirit

1 When the day of Pentecost arrived, all the believers were gathered together in one place. 2 Suddenly there was a noise from the sky which sounded like a strong wind blowing, and it filled the whole house where they were sitting. 3 Then they saw what looked like tongues of fire spreading out; and each person there was touched by a tongue. 4 They were all filled with the Holy Spirit and began to talk in other languages, as the Spirit enabled them to speak. (2.1-4)

The section heading The Coming of the Holy Spirit must frequently be shifted into a clause form, for example, "The Holy Spirit Comes" or even more frequently "The Holy Spirit Comes to the Believers." In some languages a more common expression is "The Holy Spirit Enters the Believers" or "The Believers Are Filled with the Holy Spirit."

The discourse structure of 2.1-4 is quite simple. The first clause provides the temporal setting for the second clause, and the entire first sentence, consisting of the two clauses, provides the setting for the following narrative.

2.1

The day of Pentecost (Greek pentecostē "the fiftieth [day]") was the fiftieth day after Passover; it was the day the Jews celebrated the Feast of the Grain Harvest (see Exodus 23.16; 34.22; Leviticus 23.15-21; and Deuteronomy 16.9-12). It is important to have a marginal note at this point to explain what Pentecost is. In the text, one can employ a phrase such as "day which was called Pentecost," or "day which was called fifty days after," but this latter type of expression is rarely acceptable.

All the believers represents the Greek word all which may refer either to all the Christians or merely to all the apostles. Most translations choose to make this ambiguous, whereas the TEV has made it explicit, that is, the total Christian community. In a number of languages one cannot employ a term such as "believers" without indicating the one in whom they believed, for example, "all those who believed in Jesus." There may be in some languages a problem with the use of "all," since this is obviously not an absolute "all." Therefore, it may be necessary to say "all the believers there," referring to the believers who were presumably associated with the group in Jerusalem.

33

2.2

In one place translates the Greek phrase which was discussed in 1.15; whereas it had one meaning in the earlier verse, it is obvious that it is used here in the sense of "at the same place." The expression in one place is further expanded in verse 2 to indicate that this refers to a particular house. It may, therefore, be necessary to be somewhat more specific and indicate "in the same house." Otherwise the reader may have the impression that it was the same town or the same land, since a general term such as "place" may not exist in the receptor language.

2.2

Noise, rather than a strong wind, is the subject of the verb filled. The house in which the believers were meeting may either have been a private house or else a part of the temple; there is no way to make a definite decision inasmuch as the word may refer to either.

An impersonal type of construction such as there was a noise is not possible in many languages. "Noises" cannot exist apart from their being heard. Therefore, in some languages one must say "the people heard a noise."

Some restructuring of relationships may be necessary in the first clause because of the comparison, for example, "the people heard a noise that was coming from the sky; the noise was just like what a wind makes when it blows strong." As may be noted, "strong" is shifted from its position as an attributive to "wind," to a position as attributive to the process of "blowing." This is frequently required, since the force is regarded not as a character of the wind, but as an aspect of the blowing.

Note that the pronoun it must be related to the noise, and not to the wind. In some cases this must be made explicit, for example, "the noise filled the house" or "everywhere in the house the people heard the noise." The latter expression may be necessary, since in many languages one cannot speak of a "noise filling" anything.

2.3

In the English text then simply serves to mark the temporal sequence. A similar device may be useful in other languages.

The verb phrase which is rendered by the TEV they saw is rendered in most translations as "appeared to them." This is a verb stem related to the one discussed in 1.3, and, as mentioned there, it is quite likely that in the New Testament this verb has an active meaning.

What appeared to them were not tongues of fire, but what looked like tongues of fire. This is Luke's way of reminding his readers that the natural object named (that is, tongue) is not intended to be an exact description, but only a likeness of that which actually appeared to the believers. The Greek expression "a tongue sat on each of them" is rendered variously in different translations, but it should be kept in mind that the text itself does not state how this was accomplished or where the tongues "sat" on each person. This is why the TEV has translated <u>each person there was touched by a tongue.</u>

There is a semantic problem in the expression <u>tongues of fire,</u> since this type of combination does not make sense in many languages. In some instances one can employ a descriptive equivalent which is somewhat more explicit, for example, "like little flames which resembled tongues." Note, however, that one does not wish to say that these were actual "flames." One may have, for example, "they saw something which looked like little flames, in the shape of tongues."

These tongues were <u>spreading out</u> (not "cloven tongues" or "divided tongues," as some earlier translators described them), which means that each tongue was going out separately and resting on some person. The total picture then is that of many tonguelike objects, each looking like fire, and darting out separately and touching (or "resting on") someone. The expression <u>spreading out</u> may be translated in some languages by a distributive expression, for example, "divided one to each person."

The relationship of each person to a tongue may be described either by focusing upon the "tongue" or upon the "person," for example, "a tongue was on (touched) each person," "each person had a tongue on him," or "each person was touched by a tongue." It may be necessary, of course, to indicate that this "tongue" was one which "looked like a flame resembling the shape of a tongue." Usually one can avoid some of this difficulty of reference by certain pronominal forms, for example, "one of these was on each person."

2.4

The major semantic difficulty in this first clause is the expression <u>filled with the Holy Spirit.</u> Since in many languages people are not regarded as "empty," they cannot be filled. One must, therefore, shift the semantic framework and employ some such equivalent as "the Holy Spirit possessed them completely" or "the Holy Spirit came into them entirely." It is also important to note that <u>with the Holy Spirit</u> specifies the object which fills and not the agent of the filling.

The Holy Spirit enabled the believers <u>to talk in other languages,</u> that is, to speak a language which was different from the one they normally spoke. <u>As the Spirit enabled them to speak</u> represents a Greek construction that suggests the ability to speak in other languages was given successively to them as individuals, and not to all of them at the same time.

That the language is a meaningful language, fully intelligible to the hearers, is suggested not only by what comes in the following verses but by the word which Luke chose for "speaking." This verb is used both in the Septuagint and in classical Greek to indicate solemn or inspired speech, but not ecstatic utterance. Elsewhere in the New Testament this verb occurs only in Acts 2.14 and 26.25.

<u>To talk in other languages</u> must be rendered in many instances as "to speak the languages of other peoples," "to speak foreigners' languages," or "to speak like the strange people speak." Some languages simply do not have

a noun for "language," but express the same concept by means of a verb "to speak."

The clause <u>as the Spirit enabled them</u> may be rendered in many languages as "it was the Spirit who caused them to speak" or "it was the Spirit who made them able to speak." It may be useful to employ a verb form meaning "speak in turn" or "speak one after the other."

> 5 There were Jews living in Jerusalem, religious men who had come from every country in the world. 6 When they heard this noise, a large crowd gathered. They were all excited, because each one of them heard the believers talking in his own language. 7 In amazement and wonder they exclaimed, "These men who are talking like this— they are all Galileans! 8 How is it, then, that all of us hear them speaking in our own native language? 9 We are from Parthia, Media, and Elam; from Mesopotamia, Judea, and Cappadocia; from Pontus and Asia, 10 from Phrygia and Pamphylia, from Egypt and the regions of Libya near Cyrene; some of us are from Rome, 11 both Jews and Gentiles converted to Judaism; and some of us are from Crete and Arabia—yet all of us hear them speaking in our own languages of the great things that God has done!" 12 Amazed and confused they all kept asking each other, "What does this mean?"
>
> 13 But others made fun of the believers, saying, "These men are drunk!" (2.5-13)

2.5

The narrative is continued in 2.5-13, but it is essential, in light of the shift of viewpoint, that new participants be introduced. Therefore, verse 5 is essentially a means of introducing the crowd which heard the believers speaking in tongues.

The English introductory expression <u>there were</u> provides a good transition, but in some languages it is important to make the link with the preceding more evident, for example, by carrying over the reference to the city of Jerusalem, as "in this city of Jerusalem Jews from everywhere were living." This reference to the city picks up a specific identification in 1.12, but the same location is implicit in all the preceding sections.

<u>Religious men</u> refers to the Jews living in Jerusalem and not to a category of Gentile believers or others separate from the Jews. An abstract such as <u>religious</u> must often be made more specific, for example, "those who regularly worshiped God" or "those who customarily prayed to God." Some languages do not have an abstract such as "religious," but they indicate essentially the same content by a set expression referring to customary worship or prayer.

The phrase <u>every country</u> is here not to be understood in an absolute sense, but in no language are terms such as "all" and "everyone" always construed as absolute.

2. 6

The pronoun they must refer back in some way to the Jews who have been introduced in the preceding verse, for example, "when these men heard."

This noise may have a reference either to the noise accompanying the arrival of the Holy Spirit (v. 2) or to the talking in other languages (v. 4). The word itself is a different word for noise from the one which is used in verse 2, though this is no argument against identifying this noise with the noise mentioned in that verse. However, the nearest antecedent is the sound of the believers talking in other languages (v. 4), for example, "when they heard the believers talking in strange languages." It is also possible to preserve a measure of ambiguity, for example, "when they heard what had happened" or "...what was happening."

A large crowd (the Greek has only plēthos "crowd," but this normally refers to a "large gathering") must, in some languages, be semantically redistributed, for example, "many people gathered together."

The Greek sentence continues through verse 6a and 6b, but the TEV has introduced a break, since the causal clause goes more appropriately with the event of being excited.

This is the excitement of amazement and bewilderment, not the excitement of good news or of some thrilling spectacle. It is important, therefore, that insofar as possible the appropriate term be selected.

The causal clause may need some greater clarification of roles and events, for example, "because then each person heard the believers speak; they were speaking in that person's own language." In some instances one must specify "own language" as "the language which he spoke in his own town."

2. 7

The nominal expression in amazement and wonder must often be shifted to a verbal form, "they were amazed and wondered." However, in some languages it is quite impossible to find two verbs which have essentially the same area of meaning. Therefore, one can employ one verb, but qualify it with an intensive, for example, "they were completely amazed," since in Greek the use of the two verbs is essentially a device to indicate intensity. In other words, the second verb does not introduce any semantic components which are not already suggested in the first verb.

These men who are talking like this—they are all Galileans! represents the translation of a Greek rhetorical sentence ("Are not all of these who are talking Galileans?"), in which the expected answer to the question is "Yes." The mention that the persons talking are Galileans is here probably intended to indicate nothing other than the fact that the languages which they are speaking are not their own native languages.

Rather than attempt to make up some adjectival form such as "Galileans," one can often retain the name of the country and produce a text which is more idiomatic, for example, "they are all from Galilee." On the other hand, many languages have regular formatives which indicate people from a particular town or region, in which case, of course, one should certainly use such forms.

2.8

In Greek the question in verse 7 is strictly rhetorical (no need for a reply is suggested), but in verse 8 there is a legitimate question, for the men do not understand how they can possibly hear, each in his own language. However, they are directing the question to themselves and to each other.

There is the problem of number in this sentence. Therefore one must often be somewhat more specific, for example, "each one of us hears in his own native language" or "all of us hear in our own native languages." This solution may not, however, be admissible in some languages, for example, "How is it that each one of us must say, I hear them speaking in my own language?"

For native language one can use an identification-associated place, age, or kinship, for example, "language of my hometown," "language which I spoke when I was a child," or "language my parents taught me."

2.9-11

Verses 9-11 are linguistically a part of the statement made by the people in the crowd to each other. In reality, however, they are an explanation of the author in order to identify the backgrounds of the crowd. In many languages it is better to preserve the strict linguistic setting, as in the case of the TEV, in which the appropriate references to the first person plural are introduced. In other languages, such an explanatory statement fits better as a kind of parenthesis, from verses 9 through 11a. The list of nations from which the Jews had come is probably intended to indicate every country in the world (v. 5).

As for the names of these regions and countries, all major languages have well-established forms, but for minor languages it is usually better to make the necessary phonological adaptations, so as to facilitate pronunciation, on the basis of the major languages of the area, rather than to attempt to go back to the Greek forms.

In general, the introduction of classifiers is warranted, for example, "from the countries of Parthia, Media,..." But in any event, no text of Acts, or of the New Testament, should be published without some maps to indicate the locations of these countries.

In the Greek text certain of these place names are grouped together, as in the TEV text, but this is not necessary in all translations. In fact, in some receptor languages such grouping might suggest a connection between some of the countries which would simply not be accurate.

The phrase the regions of Libya near Cyrene may need to be more specific, for example, "from the regions in the country of Libya which are near the town of Cyrene."

From Rome translates a Greek word which is normally used to indicate a person who is a citizen of the Roman Empire rather than a person who is from the city of Rome, but Luke seems to have used it in the latter sense in this passage. These persons from Rome were temporary residents of, or visitors to, Jerusalem rather than permanent residents.

Gentiles converted to Judaism is a phrase indicating persons of non-Jewish birth who had become full converts to Judaism. In order to become a full convert it was necessary for a person to be baptized and to offer sacrifice in the temple; if he were a man he would also have to accept circumcision.

For Gentiles many languages employ simply "non-Jews." In many ways this is a very convenient solution, for it avoids a number of wrong denotations and connotations implicit in expressions such as "the other people," "the different ones," or "the outsiders."

The phrase Gentiles converted to Judaism may be rendered in many languages as "people who have become Jews" or "people who have changed their religion and are now considered Jews."

If verses 9-11a are rendered as parenthetical (using third-person references), it is usually necessary to introduce another verb of speaking so that 11b may be properly related to the preceding direct discourse, for example, "they said, But we all hear them speaking...."

In a number of instances it is necessary to break verse 11b into two parts, for example, "yet all of us hear them speaking in our own languages; they are telling about the great things God has done." In some languages the last clause must itself be in the form of direct discourse, for example, "...speaking in our own languages. They are saying, God has done very great things."

2.12

The verbal expressions amazed and confused pick up the theme introduced at the beginning of verse 7 and can be related to the following verb of speaking as a cause, for example, "because they were thus so amazed and confused, they all asked one another repeatedly (or kept asking one another), What does this mean?"

In some languages, a verb "to mean" is not easy to find, especially one with such a wide range of meaning as the English verb mean. Rather, one must often employ other terms, which contain the same components, but with somewhat different orientations, for example, "What does all this say?" "How are we to understand all this?" "How can we explain this?" or "What does all this teach?"

There are always plenty of terms for derision, for example, "made fun of," "mocked," "laughed at," or "made jokes about." In some languages derision is expressed by reference to certain facial or body gestures, for example, "their heads moved up and down," "they moved their heads back and forth," or "they raised their noses at."

2.13

Though the Greek itself refers to "sweet wine" or "new wine" (that is, in the process of fermentation), the intent was to insist that the believers were drunk. At present drunkenness is a universal cultural feature, for even if it was not practiced in prior times in a particular indigenous society, the state of drunkenness is well-known.

Peter's Message

14 Then Peter stood up with the other eleven apostles, and in a loud voice began to speak to the crowd, "Fellow Jews, and all of you who live in Jerusalem, listen to me and let me tell you what this means. 15 These men are not drunk, as you suppose; it is only nine o'clock in the morning. 16 Rather, this is what the prophet Joel spoke about,

17 'This is what I will do in the last days, God says:
   I will pour out my Spirit upon all men.
Your sons and your daughters will prophesy;
   your young men will see visions,
   and your old men will dream dreams.
18 Yes, even on my slaves, both men and women,
   I will pour out my Spirit in those days,
   and they will prophesy.
19 I will perform miracles in the sky above,
   and marvels on the earth below.
There will be blood, fire, and thick smoke;
20   the sun will become dark,
   and the moon red as blood,
   before the great and glorious Day of the Lord
      arrives.
21 And then, whoever calls on the name of the Lord will
      be saved.' (2.14-21)

The section heading Peter's Message must often be restructured into a complete clause, for example, "What Peter Said to the Crowd," "Peter Speaks to the People," or "Peter Talks to the Jews There."

The third principal portion of Chapter 2 is this response of Peter to the statements of the crowd. The structure of this statement is important, for it contains an introduction (vv. 14-16), a series of quotations from Joel (vv. 17-21), followed by another direct statement to the people (vv. 22-24), and another quotation from the Old Testament (vv. 25-28). This is followed by still another direct appeal (vv. 29-31a), a quotation (v. 31b), another direct statement to the crowd (vv. 32-34a), a quotation (vv. 34b-35), and a final statement to the people (v. 36). This alternation between direct statements to the crowd and quotations from the Old Testament poses a number of serious difficulties. The format of indented lines helps the reader to some extent, but quite naturally this does not carry over to the one who merely hears the reading.

Therefore, special attention must be paid to the proper introduction of of the included quotations.

Except for the quotation from the prophet Joel, the rest of the quotations are given as from David, and fortunately the text contains sufficient information about David so as not to cause much difficulty in the introduction of this included speaker.

In three of the transitions (that is, from the words of the Scripture to the sentences addressed to the crowd), there is a participant identifier, for example, men of Israel (v. 22), brothers (v. 29), and all the people of Israel (v. 36), but at the beginning of verse 32 it may be necessary to introduce some expression which will make the relation of the following verses clear, such as "I tell you."

It is significant to note that the last four statements addressed to the crowd (vv. 22-24, 29-31a, 32-34a, and 36) all have as their theme the death and resurrection of Jesus.

Since all of the paragraphs involve certain internal problems of discourse structure, they will be commented upon in order.

Verse 14 is structurally only an introduction to what follows, in that it contains a statement of the circumstances of the speaking and an explicit reference to those who are addressed. A direct response to the statement of the crowd is contained in verse 15, but verse 16 begins the real answer as to why the people were so amazed and confused in hearing the proclamation of those who spoke in tongues.

2.14

It is important at the beginning of verse 14 to have some type of transitional expression, which will help to shift the attention from what the crowd has said to what Peter is now going to reply, for example, "then," "in response," or "in answer to them."

With the other eleven may be taken as the TEV has translated it, or the phrase may be understood as a title (see NEB and JB). In some languages it is necessary to state more precisely the relation of Peter to the other apostles. Did all of the twelve stand together, or was Peter, as one with the eleven, the only one to stand? He was certainly the only one to address the crowd. It would probably appear more natural to say, "Peter, who was with the eleven apostles, stood up."

To "lift up one's voice" (literally in the Greek) may merely mean "to begin to speak"; but most translators understand the phrase here to mean "to begin to speak in a loud voice." In a loud voice is more often rendered simply as "to speak loudly to" or "to shout to."

It is interesting that the Greek verb which Luke has chosen for speak is one which places emphasis upon the high quality and articulate nature of the words spoken (see 2.4). The word occurs here, following the charge of drunkenness, and in 26.25 after the charge of madness.

The rendering fellow Jews is quite appropriate for this passage, since it not only identifies the audience but indicates a degree of identification between the speaker and the audience. In some languages the equivalent is "you who are Jews with us." However, in some languages one cannot employ this type of vocative, except when one is actually calling to a person or group. Hence, such a reference must be related more specifically to the subject of the verb listen, for example, "You who are fellow Jews and all of you who live in Jerusalem, listen to me."

The two verbal expressions listen and let me tell you are really only emphatic supplements one of the other; they do not actually introduce any new information. Accordingly, in some languages only one verb is used, but it is often reinforced with some intensifier, for example, "pay very close attention to," "listen well," or idiomatically "open your ears well," "track down closely my words."

2.15

These men may be either the eleven (Peter does not seem to include himself among those who are thought to be drunk) or the larger group of the one hundred and twenty. The first part of verse 15 may be rendered in some languages as "you think these men are drunk, but they are not."

Nine o'clock in the morning is literally in the Greek "the third hour of the day." The first hour of the day was six o'clock in the morning, and the third hour of the day was nine o'clock in the morning. This was the hour of prayer for the Jews; breakfast would be eaten at ten o'clock in the morning. The point that Peter makes is that since the men had not yet eaten, they could not possibly be drunk.

The reason given for not believing that the men were drunk, namely, that it was only nine o'clock in the morning, may not be very convincing in many societies, but the reason must be given as Peter gave it. However, it may be quite useful to have a marginal note at this point, indicating that Jews normally ate only after the time of morning prayer at nine o'clock.

2.16

The quotation which is introduced in this verse, and which is given in the verses following, comes from Joel 2.28-32, and follows the Septuagint with some changes.

The total shift of viewpoint at the beginning of verse 16 should be made quite explicit. In English the word rather serves this function well, but in other languages it may be necessary to be even more explicit, for example, "you must think differently" or "the truth is very different."

The pronoun this in the first clause must refer to the speaking in tongues and not to the presumed drunkenness. In many languages one must make this reference somewhat more specific, for example, "this that has happened" or even "this that you see and hear."

Many languages require some supplementary verb of speaking to introduce direct discourse, for example, "spoke about, when he said," while other languages never employ such doublets of speaking.

Though in English we may employ two different orders, the prophet Joel or "Joel the prophet," in many languages only one order is regarded as correct for combining a proper noun (the name) and a function. More often than not, the proper name comes first and the function is treated as a qualifier, for example, "Joel, who was a prophet." Prophet should focus attention on the fact that such a person "spoke for God" rather than on his function of foretelling the future. In other words, the focus is upon his function as a revealer of God's will and word, rather than his role as a foreteller of the future.

2.17

The pronoun this at the beginning of verse 17 must be related to what follows; in fact, it stands for the following direct quotation. For many languages the first line of verse 17 must undergo considerable change of order, for example, "God says, This is what I will do in the last days," or "In the last days I will do this" (that is, the following).

In the last days is a typical Jewish expression used to describe the time of the Messianic age in which God would fully accomplish those promises that he had made to his people. It was taken over by the first·Christians and applied to the period that began when Jesus came into the world, especially from the time of his resurrection onward. It is quite significant that these words are not in the Hebrew or Greek texts of Joel but are supplied by Peter.

An expression for last days is often not easy to find. In fact, it is entirely too easy to adopt some expression which is entirely wrong, for example, "in the most recent days," or "in the days that have just passed." The real focus of meaning is "the days just before the end," or as in some instances "the days just before the new time," or "the days just before the new age."

I will pour out my Spirit is literally "I will pour out of my Spirit" (see KJV; Phillips "forth of my Spirit"; NEB "a portion of my spirit"). What Peter means by the use of this phrase is obvious: God will let all people share in his Spirit. So it seems best to translate as TEV and most other translations have done. In many languages, however, one cannot "pour out Spirit," since "Spirit" is not regarded as a mass. In such instances one may "give my Spirit to" or "cause my Spirit to come to."

Upon all men is literally "upon all flesh," a Semitic idiom meaning "all mankind." In the biblical setting to prophesy primarily means to "proclaim God's message to men," rendered in some languages as "they will say to people, This is what God says,..." However, in certain contexts this term refers to foretelling the future.

To see visions and to dream dreams are in biblical thought ways of receiving divine revelation. In many languages it is not easy to distinguish between visions and dreams. Technically, visions occur in trancelike states in which people are not regarded as asleep, while dreams are related to the state of sleep. In other cultures, however, any vision or dream which has some supernatural significance, that is, which involves a message from the spirit world, is identified by a single term. When there is only one term, it is possible to combine the subjects "your young men and your old men will...."

Since in this context visions and dreams are spoken of only as vehicles for the communication of divine truth, one must sometimes make the reference more explicit, since visions and dreams as such may convey no reference to the revelation involved. Hence, one can have, "your young men will see truth from God in visions and your old men will know about the truth from God through their dreams."

In societies where terms for age-grading are very specific, the term for young men can refer to young men before marriage and the term for old men can most appropriately refer to men who are the respected leaders— the type of men who make up the group of older counselors of the chief. Of course, insofar as possible, one should avoid expressions which are too specific.

2.18

Due to the particularly emphatic form of the Greek expression, the TEV text introduces an emphatic use of yes and the form even on...both... and. This is formally different from the Greek, but it is a very effective and close equivalent.

In some languages the term for slaves carries such unfortunate connotations that one can scarcely use it, especially in this type of context in which God speaks of his slaves. Hence, one may use the equivalent of "servant," "those who work for me," "those who do what I say," or "those who obey me."

In those days, of course, refers to in the last days of the preceding verse.

2.19

The discourse structure, both syntactic and semantic, of this quotation (vv. 17-21) is essentially poetic. This is not too obvious in verses 17 and 18, but in verses 19 and 20 the poetic nature of the lines, that is, the typical parallelism and the figurative symbolism, is evident. In such passages the rendering in the receptor language should have a similar amount of nonprose structure.

Miracles...and marvels represents a set phrase in Greek (it occurs here and also in 2.43; 4.30; 5.12; 6.8; 7.36; 14.3; 15.12). Although the word translated miracles taken by itself would most naturally refer to a happening that evokes awe, and the word translated marvel (literally "sign") is often used to point to a truth beyond itself, in a set phrase such as this it is not possible to establish any significant difference between the two words. If a receptor language has two terms for such miraculous happenings, one is likely to refer to portents—special signs in the heavens which foretell important events, or which symbolize significant changes or happenings. This is the term which would most closely parallel the first of the two Greek terms. Frequently, however, such terms occur most naturally in causative expressions, for example, "I will cause portents to occur in the sky" or "I will cause people to see portents in the sky." Where only one term exists in a receptor language, a person may employ a single statement, such as "I will cause portents to exist in the sky and on the earth."

The precise meaning of the phrase thick smoke (literally "vapor of smoke") is difficult to define, though the translation represented by the TEV (see also Goodspeed) seems most probable. The equivalent of "thick smoke" is in many languages "a cloud of dark smoke," "heavy smoke," or "big smoke." The closest normal equivalent is what comes from a volcano—both smoke and vapor.

2. 20

The sun will become dark, and the moon red as blood accurately translates the meaning of the literal expression "the sun will be turned into darkness and the moon into blood." The sun will become dark may be rendered simply as "the sun will not shine," but a more poetic form would be "the sun will become like night." In choosing a word for red it is important to select the precise term which is used in speaking of blood. In some languages, for example, the color area of red is divided into three parts: one designates orange and other yellowish forms of red; a second refers to light reds, including pinks; and still a third specifies dark red, shading toward purple. It is normally this latter area of color which is most appropriate.

In many languages a Day cannot "come" or "arrive." It may "happen" or "people may arrive on that day." Under such circumstances, one must make some adjustment in the semantic structure. Furthermore, in some languages one cannot speak of a day as "great." It can be "important," but not "great"—the latter being applicable only to persons.

The description of that day as a glorious Day comes from the Septuagint; the Hebrew has "fearful" or "awesome," which became in the Septuagint "glorious." A glorious Day is "a wonderful day" in some languages—but this quality of being "wonderful" is not in terms of the quality of the day, for example, sunshine and warmth, but in terms of the significance of the day. Hence, great and glorious really stand for the importance of the event, and in some languages the two concepts must be coalesced into one, with a compensatory expression of intensity of degree, such as "that very important day of the Lord."

The possession of a day, for example, Day of the Lord, as suggested by the genitive usage in Greek, has no direct parallel in many languages, since people simply do not possess days. One can, however, often use "the very important day for the Lord," but this use of "for" must not suggest that the importance is merely a matter of special interest for the Lord himself. What is important is that it is the day on which the Lord will act, that is, "that very important day for what the Lord will do."

It should be noted that in the use of Lord there is an evident ambiguity, but an intentional one. In the Old Testament passage Lord refers to Jehovah (Yahweh), but for the writer of Acts the application to Jesus is implied (see specifically v. 36). It is, therefore, important to employ some term which

can be doubly applicable, both to God as Lord (in the OT) and to Jesus Christ
as Lord in these typical New Testament contexts.

<u>2.21</u>

By using <u>and then</u> the TEV employs a type of transition to introduce a
summary. This fits in well with the structure of the quotation and is a good
equivalent of the special forms found in the corresponding position in the
Greek text.

In many languages one may "call the name," but one does not "call upon
the name." That is to say, the first expression is purely vocative but the second is simply not used. Accordingly, in such a language one must say "call
upon the Lord." Here <u>name</u> is only a symbolic substitute for the person, and
as such it is highly redundant. However, it is a common Semitic idiom.

Finding a fully adequate term for <u>save</u> is very difficult in many languages. In the meanings of "heal" or "rescue" there are few problems, since
there are usually quite specific terms to cover these areas of meaning. However, for the theological meaning of <u>save</u> there are a number of difficulties,
largely because of certain false concepts which tend to be clustered around
the meaning of <u>save</u>. This term does not refer primarily to "being safe."
The process is far more dynamic than this. The fundamental semantic components associated with "save" are (1) existence in a bad state (moral or
physical), (2) activity of someone to relieve that condition, and (3) beneficial
change of condition resulting from this activity. Some terms for "save" come
from the area of healing, such as "restore life to," while others depend upon
concepts related to rescue from physical danger, for example, "release" or
"help from danger." But frequently none of these is fully adequate for the concept of "save" in its theological perspective. In some languages an attempt
has been made to introduce the concept of "to renew," in order to focus upon
the positive element in <u>save</u>. This may even be made more specific in a
phrase such as "to give new life to." In other instances the focus is upon the
new quality of life, for example, "to cause to truly live."

22 "Listen to these words, men of Israel! Jesus of Nazareth was
a man whose divine mission was clearly shown to you by the miracles,
wonders, and signs which God did through him; you yourselves know
this, for it took place here among you. 23 God, in his own will and
knowledge, had already decided that Jesus would be handed over to you;
and you killed him, by letting sinful men nail him to the cross. 24 But
God raised him from the dead; he set him free from the pains of death,
because it was impossible that death should hold him prisoner. 25 For
David said about him,
'I saw the Lord before me at all times;
he is by my right side, so that I will not be
troubled.

26 Because of this my heart is glad
        and my words are full of joy;
    and I, mortal though I am,
        will rest assured in hope,
27 because you will not abandon my soul in the world of
        the dead;
        you will not allow your devoted servant to suffer
        decay.
28 You have shown me the paths that lead to life,
        and by your presence you will fill me with joy.'

(2. 22-28)

The basic structure of 2. 22-24 is narrative, with one parenthetical statement, the last two clauses of verse 22. What is important about the three principal statements is that in each instance God is the primary agent.

The first sentence is essentially transitional, to mark the shift from quoted material back to a statement addressed to the crowd. (The discourse structure of vv. 25-28 will be discussed just before the treatment of v. 25.)

2. 22a

The phrase these words refers to what is going to be said, not to what has been said. This distinction is very important in many languages.

The expression men of Israel may need to be made somewhat more general in many languages, for example, "people of Israel." This phrase should not, however, be constructed in such a way as to suggest that the people referred to here were "followers of Israel" or people loyal to a certain chief called "Israel." Where there is a widely used pattern of family names to mark descent this is naturally the best type of construction to employ; but where this is lacking (many languages do not possess such constructions) one can use "people called Israel" or "people who are Israel." The use of this term in the New Testament is not a reference to descent from Israel but to the nation as a religious and ethnic entity.

2. 22b

A man whose divine mission was clearly shown to you is literally "a man designated/appointed/authenticated by God to you." "Appointed" is used in the papyri, on inscriptions, and by historians to describe a person who has been appointed to a given office. Understood in that sense, the meaning of the phrase "a man appointed by God" means a man with a divine mission or task. However, the idea is not merely that he was appointed, but that he was clearly shown to have been appointed by God; and this by the miracles, wonders, and signs which God did through him. In the miracles, wonders, and signs the first word is the same one which occurs in 1. 8; the other two terms are those which appear in 2. 19.

In Greek, verses 22b through 24 are one well-organized sentence. However, it is almost impossible to reproduce this as one sentence in most other languages, not primarily because such languages cannot construct long sentences, but because the long sentences which are appropriate in such languages are simply not the types which occur in Greek.

Since the attestation of Jesus' ministry was basically the work of God, it may be useful in some languages to shift this expression into an active form, for example, "God has shown clearly to you by the miracles, wonders, and signs, that he was working through Jesus; that is how Jesus did these" ("these" being a reference to the miracles, wonders, and signs).

The expression "in your midst" (compare the Greek) is associated in the TEV text with the following statement about the evident knowledge of such events: for it took place here among you. Though the syntactic structure does link this expression with the fact that God worked these miracles through Jesus, nevertheless the semantic link of "in your midst" is certainly with the evident knowledge of the people. It is for this reason that such a shift, as in the TEV, can be made.

You yourselves know this may need to be somewhat altered, for example, "you yourselves know about these happenings." This will permit the various miracles, wonders, and signs to be included. The final clause may then be rendered as "since these miracles happened right here among you" or "right here where you live."

2. 23

Verse 23 begins with a dependent clause that the TEV has made into a sentence. God, in his own will and knowledge, had already decided that Jesus ... represents "this one by the predetermined will and foreknowledge of God." "This one" refers back to Jesus, while the phrase "predetermined will and foreknowledge of God" means God had already decided and had already known what was going to take place.

The translation of will and knowledge is not easy, and in many languages these terms must be rendered as verbs, for example, "God himself planned it that way and he knew all about it beforehand." However, these expressions may need to be placed after the description of the event, such as "God had already decided that Jesus would be handed over to you; that is the way he planned it and he knew all about it beforehand" (or "before you did it").

The verbal phrase handed over in the original actually has no indication of the persons to whom Jesus was handed over. In the historical situation it was the Jews to whom Jesus was handed over, and therefore the TEV has added to you (see also Barclay, and JB "who was put into your power").

The expression you killed him must in many languages be changed to a causative, since these men did not physically kill him, but caused others to do it, even as the text itself stipulates.

The use of letting in English is misleading. This should not have the sense of "permitting" but of "causing," for example, "you caused sinful men to nail."

2. 24

In Greek this verse is a relative clause, without an adversative conjunction or particle. However, the rendering but God raised him is fully
justified since there is a very definite contrast between the men who killed
Jesus (v. 23) and God who raised him from the dead (v. 24).

The implied causative in raised him from the dead may need to be semantically recast as "caused him to rise from the dead" or "caused him to
live again."

He set him free from the pains of death in the Greek is a subordinate
clause dependent upon the main verb raised, and prior in time to the action
of the main verb. Pains of death is a phrase which comes from the Greek
text of the Old Testament and which literally means "birth pangs of death";
so the meaning of the phrase is that of "bringing the pangs to an end" or
"doing away with the pain." The Hebrew text has "bonds of death," but Luke
quotes the Greek, and it is this text which must be translated.

The phrase "birth pangs of death" (compare the Greek) is an extremely
difficult expression to translate. Some scholars have insisted that the interpretation of "birth pains" implies that death is suffering these birth pains.
"God released him from death, which as it were was suffering birth pains"
(that is, in the sense of restoring such a person to life again). It may be
necessary to introduce some such expression as "as it were" or "like" in
order to indicate that this is a strictly figurative expression and that birth
pains are not normally attributable to such an event as death. One should,
however, be cautioned against reading too much into the meaning of "birth
pains." Some scholars interpret "birth pains" as being the subject or agent
of the act of dying or death, and they translate as "from the pain that death
was causing" or possibly "from the anguish that he was suffering in dying."

A special difficulty exists in languages in which there is no noun for
"death," and therefore no way in which death can be regarded as doing anything, either "having pain" or holding him prisoner (as in the last clause of
this verse). When there is no such noun for "death" the closest equivalent is
"the place where the dead are," since in some languages this may be regarded as being capable of such "pain." It is interesting to note that just such
a change did take place in the textual tradition, for "Hades" as the place of
the dead was substituted in some manuscripts for "death."

The expression it was impossible that... can be restructured simply
as "death could not keep him a prisoner" or "death could not cause him to
remain a prisoner." This figurative sense of prisoner may, however, need
to be made more specific, for example, "he could not be kept a prisoner of
death" or even "a prisoner in the place of the dead," for those languages in
which "death" has to be related more specifically to some location.

2. 25

The structure of verses 25-28 is relatively simple, since it consists
of an introductory statement of speaking and the following direct address

(Psalm 16. 8-11), which in its original setting referred to David, but which is applied by Peter in this total discourse to Jesus. The explanation of this application is made quite explicit in the following paragraph, verses 29-31.

After the introductory statement as to the relationship of David (in the first person singular reference) to the Lord, there is a reference to happiness (v. 26a), followed by a statement as to why this is true, namely, the rescue from death (vv. 26b-28a), and finally a return to the earlier theme of joy (v. 28b). This is typical of such expository discourse.

The statement which introduces the direct discourse should indicate clearly that David is speaking about Jesus. In some languages the proper name must be introduced. I saw is translated by some translations "I foresaw"; but it is best to take the form of the verb in the sense of "to see (in front of oneself)" rather than "to see beforehand."

The term for Lord must, of course, be the regular expression used in speaking of Jesus as Lord, for this is the contextual setting of this New Testament usage.

There is a problem in some languages in the shift of figurative usage in before me and by my right side, for people argue that he cannot be in two places at the same time. However, since by my right side refers primarily to a position taken by one who wishes to help and sustain another, it is entirely appropriate that this be rendered as "with me." This makes it possible to preserve the sense of location without introducing seemingly contradictory expressions.

The clause so that I will not be troubled may be shifted into the active form as "so that people will not trouble me" or "so that people will not be able to trouble me" (some languages require the indication of potentiality in such a result clause projected into the future).

In most languages one can speak of an organ such as the heart (though the equivalent may be "liver," "kidneys," or "stomach") as being "glad." In fact, there may be a regular idiom for such an emotion, for example, "my heart is warm," "my heart dances," or "my heart is cool"; but in some languages only a "person can be glad in his heart." Under such circumstances, the translation needs to be appropriately adapted.

2. 26

My words are full of joy translates "my tongue rejoiced," but in many languages it is difficult to say "my words are full of joy," for obviously the words do not experience the joy, but the person has this experience, as manifested in his speaking. Hence, one may be required to shift the semantic structure so as to translate "I am very joyful as I speak."

One may argue that such shifts inevitably impair the poetic character of such a passage. From our standpoint this is certainly true, for the semantic shifts seem to be much less poetic. However, the poetic character of such a passage may be enhanced in many languages by appropriate shifts in word order, fixed length of lines, alliterative devices, and parallelism of structure, so that not all the poetic values are lost. When certain semantic shifts are required, it is important for the translator to attempt to compensate for these by such formal modifications as may be appropriate so as to reflect as much as possible of the poetic structure.

The Greek use of sarks, literally "flesh," is a similar type of poetic figure which must be changed in English if the passage is to make sense. The TEV has compensated somewhat for the loss of the figure of speech by introducing a rather elaborate syntactic device, and I, mortal though I am. This is entirely in keeping with the somewhat elaborate introductory particles in Greek eti de kai "yet but also."

The phrase mortal though I am is equivalent in many languages to "just a man like all others" or "a person destined to die." When David spoke of "his flesh" he would have been characterizing himself as a mortal being, weak and frail, in contrast to God who is eternal and powerful.

The phrase rest assured in hope involves two different events, which in most languages must be specified as related events, often as coordinate, for example, "rest and hope." However, an expression for "confidence" may require a specification of the goal of the confidence, such as "rest, having confidence in God." Other languages may employ such phrases as "hope in what God will do for me" or "hope for God's promises."

2.27

The pronoun you of verse 27 refers to God, and in many languages this must be made explicit, "you, God."

As used in this context, the term for soul should identify that part of the individual which is regarded as going on to the next world---the immaterial portion of man, in contrast to his body, referred to in verse 27b.

For David the meaning of this verse was that God would save him from death, that is, God would not let him die and go down into the world of the dead. Peter has applied the verse to Jesus, and has given the meaning that God will not abandon the soul of Jesus in the world of the dead, that is, God will not let Jesus stay there.

Your devoted servant translates "your holy one," which is used in the sense of one who belongs to and serves God. The translation of Greek hosion "holy one" is difficult, since it involves in this possessed form two principal components: (1) dependency and (2) dedication to. The TEV has attempted to indicate these two components in the phrase devoted servant. In other languages, one may have "your loyal servant" or "the one who is dedicated to worship you."

In many languages one cannot speak of a servant suffering decay. Rather, it is the body of such a person which decays; it is the person who dies and the body which rots. This means that in some languages this final clause would be rendered as "you will not permit the corpse of your devoted servant to decay."

51

"Decay" is variously expressed in different languages. In some it is specifically associated with worms and maggots, for example, "you will not permit maggots to eat the corpse."

2.28

The first line of verse 28 presents only one serious difficulty in the use of the abstract form of "life," paths that lead to life. In many languages there is simply no general noun for "life," only verbs for "living." This does not, however, seriously hamper the translation of this passage, for one may render this as "you have shown me the paths which I must take in order to live" (or "to truly live," for there is a qualitative element involved in this use of "life").

In a number of languages a noun such as presence (literally "face") cannot be the instrument by which an agent can do anything. However, one can semantically restructure this to read, "because you are with me, I have complete joy." This indicates that the real agent of the state is "you." This can be made even more specific by rendering "because you are with me, you cause me to be completely happy."

The phrase fill me with joy is impossible to render literally in some languages. "To be full" only specifies the completeness of the event of joy, and this in turn is only an expression of a state, that is, "being happy." The final clause may, therefore, be rendered as "because you are with me I am completely happy" (or "very very happy," with an expression of intensive degree).

29 "Brothers: I must speak to you quite plainly about our patriarch David. He died and was buried, and his grave is here with us to this very day. 30 He was a prophet, and he knew God's promise to him: God made a vow that he would make one of David's descendants a king, just as David was. 31 David saw what God was going to do, and so he spoke about the resurrection of the Messiah when he said,
'He was not abandoned in the world of the dead;
his flesh did not decay.'
32 God has raised this very Jesus from the dead, and we are all witnesses to this fact. 33 He has been raised to the right side of God and received from him the Holy Spirit, as his Father had promised; and what you now see and hear is his gift that he has poured out on us.
34 For David himself did not go up into heaven; rather he said,
'The Lord said to my Lord:
Sit here at my right side,
35 until I put your enemies as a footstool under your feet.'
36 "All the people of Israel, then, are to know for sure that it is this Jesus, whom you nailed to the cross, that God has made Lord and Messiah!" (2.29-36)

Beginning in verse 29 Peter reinterprets the psalm as referring to Jesus. He points out that evidently the psalm did not have an ultimate application to David, since David died and was buried and his grave is still there. Rather, the ultimate meaning of the psalm is to be found in Jesus Christ, whom God did not abandon in the world of the dead and whose body did not decay.

This final section, verses 29-36, constitutes a single discourse unit, even though it contains two included quotations. This section is introduced by another direct reference to the audience—an important device to show that the following words are not a part of the quotation. The first sentence also acts as an introduction to the contents.

The subsection, verses 29b-31, deals primarily with David, and the following subsection, verses 32-35, deals primarily with Jesus, while verse 36 stands as a final conclusion, set off in the TEV as a separate paragraph, but structurally simply a conclusion to the preceding argument.

Each subsection concludes with a Scripture quotation which gives the biblical support for the position taken, namely, that in respect to both the resurrection and the exaltation, the true reference is to Jesus and not to David.

Note, however, that at the beginning of the conclusion there is another reference to the audience being addressed, an important device to show that the following words are not to be taken as part of the direct quotation.

The semantic connections within the first subsection are rather difficult, for after the first sentence, which defines the topic to be discussed in the following sentences, the second sentence summarizes David's life, while the third and fourth sentences give information about what David did prior to his death. This backward movement in temporal sequence may need to be made quite clear.

2.29

If a term for brothers does not lend itself to generalization in identifying fellow countrymen, one can often use another kinship term which will have this essential function, for example, "relatives," "kinsmen," or "cousins."

Quite plainly translates "with boldness" or "with confidence." The same phrase is used in 4.31 and is translated there with boldness; the expanded phrase occurs in 4.29 and 28.31 where it is translated with all boldness. A literal rendering of the phrase speak to you ... plainly may turn out in some languages to be only a reference to the quality of utterance or pronunciation. Hence, one may need to shift the focus to something like "I must make you to understand clearly."

Patriarch (a word which occurs in the New Testament only here and in 7.8, 9 and Hebrews 7.4) implies progenitor and "founder of the nation," but in the present passage it is an honorary title applied to David, the king of Israel. The term patriarch is equivalent in many languages to "forefather," "grandfather in ancient times," "our big grandfather," or "elder many years ago."

2.30

If it is necessary to specify the agent of the expression <u>was buried</u>, one can simply say "he was buried by the people" or "the people buried him." Nothing more explicit is required.

In order to avoid speaking as though Peter was addressing the crowd in a cemetery, one may wish to shift the expression <u>here</u> to "near here." In some languages, however, one cannot speak of a grave as "near" someone or something, since graves are not regarded as "movable." Therefore, it may be necessary to shift the focus, for example, "and we here are near to (or, not far from) his grave."

2.30

In this context the word <u>prophet</u> has the specific meaning of "one who sees and foretells the future." As noted in the section on the discourse structure, there is a shift in temporal sequence from verses 29b to 30. Verse 29b contains a reference to David's death, while verse 30 describes what David did while still alive. In some languages verse 30 must begin with an explicit reference to this shift in time, for example, "While David was still living, he was a prophet" or "David had been a prophet."

In the Greek text the reference to the oath comes directly after the verbal form <u>knew</u>, but in the TEV the rather full expression "to swear by means of an <u>oath</u>" is reproduced as <u>promise ... made a vow</u>. Note, however, that in the TEV the promise is the fact that God would make one of David's descendants a king; it is not that God would make a vow.

In most languages an expression for "swearing" or "promising by means of an oath" is not difficult to find or to employ in this type of context, but where such formal oath-taking is not normally practiced one may need to employ some substitute type of expression which will communicate the essential components of the Greek terms, for example, "he made a strong promise to him" or "he promised David with powerful words." In many other contexts one can translate "to make an oath" as "to promise, calling God to witness," but since in this context it is God who makes the oath, such a phrase, designed to indicate the religious nature of the promise, cannot be employed.

The expression <u>make ... a king</u> may be rendered as "would cause ... to become a king." Two Semitic idioms are translated in the TEV expression <u>one of David's descendants</u> (literally "from the fruit of his loins") and <u>a king, just as David was</u> (literally "to sit upon his throne"). The second of these idioms is easily understood; and so is the first when it is realized that "loins" was often used by the Hebrews to specify the reproductive organs. The passage referred to is Psalm 132.11.

It is obviously necessary in most languages to modify the idiom "fruit of his loins," but even a general term for <u>descendant</u> is not easy to find in some languages. So many kinship terms are entirely too specific. However, one can often use such phrases as "distant grandchild" or "grandchild much later." Other acceptable solutions may be "a man in David's lineage" or "a later man in David's family," in which "lineage" and "family" must be terms to indicate a relatively long succession.

Beginning in verse 29 Peter reinterprets the psalm as referring to Jesus. He points out that evidently the psalm did not have an ultimate application to David, since David died and was buried and his grave is still there. Rather, the ultimate meaning of the psalm is to be found in Jesus Christ, whom God did not abandon in the world of the dead and whose body did not decay.

This final section, verses 29-36, constitutes a single discourse unit, even though it contains two included quotations. This section is introduced by another direct reference to the audience—an important device to show that the following words are not a part of the quotation. The first sentence also acts as an introduction to the contents.

The subsection, verses 29b-31, deals primarily with David, and the following subsection, verses 32-35, deals primarily with Jesus, while verse 36 stands as a final conclusion, set off in the TEV as a separate paragraph, but structurally simply a conclusion to the preceding argument.

Each subsection concludes with a Scripture quotation which gives the biblical support for the position taken, namely, that in respect to both the resurrection and the exaltation, the true reference is to Jesus and not to David.

Note, however, that at the beginning of the conclusion there is another reference to the audience being addressed, an important device to show that the following words are not to be taken as part of the direct quotation.

The semantic connections within the first subsection are rather difficult, for after the first sentence, which defines the topic to be discussed in the following sentences, the second sentence summarizes David's life, while the third and fourth sentences give information about what David did prior to his death. This backward movement in temporal sequence may need to be made quite clear.

2. 29

If a term for brothers does not lend itself to generalization in identifying fellow countrymen, one can often use another kinship term which will have this essential function, for example, "relatives," "kinsmen," or "cousins."

Quite plainly translates "with boldness" or "with confidence." The same phrase is used in 4. 31 and is translated there with boldness; the expanded phrase occurs in 4. 29 and 28. 31 where it is translated with all boldness. A literal rendering of the phrase speak to you ... plainly may turn out in some languages to be only a reference to the quality of utterance or pronunciation. Hence, one may need to shift the focus to something like "I must make you to understand clearly."

Patriarch (a word which occurs in the New Testament only here and in 7. 8, 9 and Hebrews 7. 4) implies progenitor and "founder of the nation," but in the present passage it is an honorary title applied to David, the king of Israel. The term patriarch is equivalent in many languages to "forefather," "grandfather in ancient times," "our big grandfather," or "elder many years ago."

If it is necessary to specify the agent of the expression <u>was buried</u>, one can simply say "he was buried by the people" or "the people buried him." Nothing more explicit is required.

In order to avoid speaking as though Peter was addressing the crowd in a cemetery, one may wish to shift the expression <u>here</u> to "near here." In some languages, however, one cannot speak of a grave as "near" someone or something, since graves are not regarded as "movable." Therefore, it may be necessary to shift the focus, for example, "and we here are near to (or, not far from) his grave."

2.30

In this context the word <u>prophet</u> has the specific meaning of "one who sees and foretells the future." As noted in the section on the discourse structure, there is a shift in temporal sequence from verses 29b to 30. Verse 29b contains a reference to David's death, while verse 30 describes what David did while still alive. In some languages verse 30 must begin with an explicit reference to this shift in time, for example, "While David was still living, he was a prophet" or "David had been a prophet."

In the Greek text the reference to the oath comes directly after the verbal form <u>knew</u>, but in the TEV the rather full expression "to swear by means of an <u>oath</u>" is reproduced as <u>promise...made a vow</u>. Note, however, that in the TEV the promise is the fact that God would make one of David's descendants a king; it is not that God would make a vow.

In most languages an expression for "swearing" or "promising by means of an oath" is not difficult to find or to employ in this type of context, but where such formal oath-taking is not normally practiced one may need to employ some substitute type of expression which will communicate the essential components of the Greek terms, for example, "he made a strong promise to him" or "he promised David with powerful words." In many other contexts one can translate "to make an oath" as "to promise, calling God to witness," but since in this context it is God who makes the oath, such a phrase, designed to indicate the religious nature of the promise, cannot be employed.

The expression <u>make...a king</u> may be rendered as "would cause...to become a king." Two Semitic idioms are translated in the TEV expression <u>one of David's descendants</u> (literally "from the fruit of his loins") and <u>a king, just as David was</u> (literally "to sit upon his throne"). The second of these idioms is easily understood; and so is the first when it is realized that "loins" was often used by the Hebrews to specify the reproductive organs. The passage referred to is Psalm 132.11.

It is obviously necessary in most languages to modify the idiom "fruit of his loins," but even a general term for <u>descendant</u> is not easy to find in some languages. So many kinship terms are entirely too specific. However, one can often use such phrases as "distant grandchild" or "grandchild much later." Other acceptable solutions may be "a man in David's lineage" or "a later man in David's family," in which "lineage" and "family" must be terms to indicate a relatively long succession.

The term king differs from other words for "ruler" simply by virtue of the fact that there is a succession of leadership from father to son. In some societies, however, this type of succession is quite unknown, and therefore it may be necessary to translate king merely as "a great chief" or "a big chief." A note in the margin or glossary may indicate that in ancient Israel it was the practice for a son to succeed his father as the ruler of the people.

The idiom "to sit on the throne" must usually be altered, for it may only mean the occupation of a big chair. However, if one wishes to retain the term "throne," then it may be useful to employ an attributive, "the seat for ruling"), for example, "occupy a seat for ruling just as David did." However, in many languages the most appropriate equivalent is "rule as David ruled."

2.31

By the addition what God was going to do the TEV links the promise that God made (v. 30) to its fulfillment in the resurrection of the Messiah. The Greek expression of "foreseeing" is very elliptical, and particularly in this type of context it requires some degree of redundancy, even as in the TEV.

The nominal phrase he spoke about the resurrection of the Messiah may be rendered as "he said that the Messiah would rise from the dead." The difficulty with this expression is that it requires some verb of speaking, but this produces a conflict with the following verb of speaking, which introduces direct discourse. Hence, to relate the two expressions it may be necessary to say, "David was really talking about the fact that the Messiah would rise from the dead when he said, He was not abandoned...." In other languages it may be necessary to reverse the order, for example, "When David said, He was not abandoned in the world..., he was really talking about the fact that the Messiah would rise from the dead."

Messiah is the same word which is translated elsewhere "Christ"; but where the term occurs as a title the TEV renders it Messiah. The Messiah (meaning "the anointed one") was a technical name for one whom God had promised to send to save his people. In popular Jewish thought of the first century A.D., the title had political overtones and implied a descendant of David who would come and overthrow the Roman rule. Here, of course, Messiah is used apart from its political connotations; it is used rather to link Jesus to a spiritual fulfillment of the Jewish hope.

In many languages a term for Messiah is simply borrowed, but this does not make much sense, unless the meaning is taught or the reader is referred to a note in the glossary. In a number of languages Messiah is translated as "God's specially chosen one." Literally, of course, Messiah refers to anointing, but since the process of anointing to symbolize the selection of a person for some divinely appointed task is very rare, a literal rendering can rarely be employed. In any event, the meaning and significance of the term Messiah should be explained in the glossary.

2.32

Though in the quotation from the Old Testament the pronoun he must be so used as to refer to the Messiah, it is not warranted to introduce the noun "Messiah" into the quotation. One can, of course, always change the passive to the active, for example, "God did not leave him in the world of the dead."

2.32

In order to signal a shift from a quotation to direct address to the crowd, it may be useful to invert the order of the two clauses of verse 32, for example, "Now we are all witnesses to the fact that God has raised...." Some translators would like to employ the inclusive "we" at this point, to indicate that all the people were witnesses to the fact of the resurrection of Jesus. However, Jesus appeared only to his disciples and followers, and hence it is essential to use the exclusive first person plural, which included Peter and the believers, but not the crowd.

This very Jesus is the emphatic element in this sentence. Although very has no verbal equivalent in the Greek text, its use in the English translation helps to carry out the stress intended in the Greek sentence structure. A term for witnesses may simply be "we have seen him with our own eyes." To this fact corresponds to a relative pronoun in the Greek, and it may refer either to Jesus (for example, "to whom we are witnesses") or to the reality of the resurrection, as most translators understand it.

2.33

The passive expression he has been raised can be placed in the active, with God as the agent, for example, "God has raised Jesus to his right side." To the right side of God, indicating the place of authority and power, may possibly be rendered "by means of the right hand (that is, power) of God." But inasmuch as the reference in verse 30 is to "sitting upon the throne" and the reference in verse 34 is to "sitting at the right side of God," it seems most likely that the phrase has a local reference in this verse, that is, "at God's right side." However, one may also translate as "at the place of honor at God's side."

In some languages he ... received from him the Holy Spirit is more naturally rendered as "God gave him the Holy Spirit." This restructuring is particularly useful if the first clause is shifted to an active form, with God as the agent.

The clause as his Father had promised is one way of rendering the elliptical Greek expression "promise of the Holy Spirit." When the text says literally that Jesus "received the promise of the Holy Spirit from the Father," it really means that he "received the Holy Spirit, who had been promised by the Father."

Though the Greek text does not employ a possessive pronoun with "Father," it is essential in many languages to add some pronominal relation, even as in the TEV his Father.

It is important in translating this verse not to suggest that God and his Father are two different persons. Hence, one may need to employ an appositional expression, for example, "God, his Father, had promised."

"He poured out this which you see and hear" is translated by the TEV what you now see and hear is his gift that he has poured out on us. "This" of the Greek may refer back to the Holy Spirit (as many translations have it), but the TEV understands "this" as referring back to the total experience that the believers have shared in connection with the coming of the Holy Spirit; and since this experience comes from God, it is spoken of as his gift (see also NEB "all that you now see and hear flows from him").

This last part of verse 33 is difficult to translate. One usually cannot speak of "pouring out" an event. One can "cause" an event, but not "pour it out." Moreover, if one says "pour out this gift," then it would appear that Jesus is pouring out the gift of the Spirit, which has just been given to him by God, but the Scriptures consistently speak of God as pouring out his Spirit. In many languages the most satisfactory way of treating this last portion of the verse is to translate "and Jesus is the one who has caused what you now see and hear."

2.34-35

A still further argument against the assumption that in the previous quotations David was speaking about himself is now introduced. This recapitulates what was said in verse 29b, but in a different way, since now the focus is shifted to the exaltation (vv. 32-33).

It is probably necessary to have some marginal note for verse 34 to indicate that this reference to going to heaven applies to the special exaltation of Jesus to the right hand of God. In some instances one can simply indicate this contrast between David and Jesus by adding to the first clause "as Jesus did," for example, "For David himself did not go up into heaven as Jesus did." The quotation from Psalm 110.1, given in verses 34-35, is almost an exact reproduction of the Septuagint. In the original context of the Psalm it was God[1] telling his[1] chosen king[2] to sit at his[1] right side until he[1] had made the king's enemies a place for him[2] to put his[2] feet. As used in the present context the Lord is God the Father and my Lord refers to Jesus; by raising Jesus from the dead God made him Lord and Messiah. Although the word translated until may in other contexts indicate that the action of the main verb will be terminated at the point indicated by until, it is impossible to suppose that the same holds true in the present context. This is simply another way of saying that God has given the Lord Jesus his power and authority, and all of Jesus' enemies will be made subject to him.

If the literal form of the phrase The Lord said to my Lord is retained, it is almost certain that some marginal note is required to indicate that this is God who is speaking to my Lord.

As suggested above, there is a real problem involved in rendering until, since in many languages such a conjunction specifies the end of a period, after which some other arrangement is presumed. Therefore, it may be more in keeping with the proper exegesis of this passage to translate until as "in the meantime" or "during that time," for example, "Sit here at my right side and during that time I will put your enemies . . . ."

In many languages the figure of the footstool is meaningful, especially if one can supplement this with some marginal note to indicate that this is a figure of speech, indicating victory over one's enemies. However, in languages in which the figure is inadmissible, one can always employ a non-metaphorical equivalent, for example, "until I cause you to have victory over your enemies" or "I cause your enemies to be subjected to your authority." The concept of being "subjected to your authority" may be rendered in some languages as "must obey your words."

2.36

In verse 36 the emphatic element in the sentence is for sure (literally "surely" or "certainly" which occurs in 16.23, and is there translated tight). This final verse in the discourse unit, which begins at verse 14, summarizes the point which has been made about Jesus, whom the people crucified, but whom God has exalted. Note that this verse also assists in shifting the discourse from the quotation to the direct address to the crowd. In some languages, however, it is important to make this direct reference explicit by introducing "you," for example, "all you people of Israel" (literally "house of Israel").

The relatively heavy clause structure of this verse may require some breaking up of the syntactic units, but this must not be done at the price of sacrificing the relations between the parts. One can introduce Jesus as the emphatic element in the discourse and then make the two contrastive statements about him, for example, "know for sure that I am talking about this Jesus. You nailed him to the cross. But God has made him Lord and Messiah."

In employing a causative at this point, such as "made him Lord," it may be useful to employ a specifically applicable verb, for example, "named him" or "designated him."

The term for Lord must be the same one as is normally used in speaking of Jesus. It must not be a mere title of respect, but something which indicates his authority to command. The term Messiah is probably best treated here as "his chosen one" or "his specially designated one."

> 37 When the people heard this, they were deeply troubled, and said to Peter and the other apostles, "What shall we do, brothers?"
> 38 Peter said to them, "Turn away from your sins, each one of you, and be baptized in the name of Jesus Christ, so that your sins will be forgiven; and you will receive God's gift, the Holy Spirit. 39 For God's promise was made to you and your children, and to all who are far away—all whom the Lord our God calls to himself." (2.37-39)

Verses 37-39 reintroduce a dialogue between Peter and the crowd. The first clause in verse 37 shows the shift in the participants, and at the beginning of verse 38 there is another indicator of change in speakers.

2.37

The first clause when the people heard this helps to identify a shift in the viewpoint of the characters. The pronoun this refers to all that Peter had said, such as "when the people heard what Peter had said."

Deeply troubled is literally "stabbed to the heart" (the corresponding Greek verb occurs only here in the New Testament). To be deeply troubled may be expressed in a number of ways, often idiomatically, for example, "their hearts were cut," "they did not know what to do," or "they were split" (referring to their divided thoughts).

The term brothers in this verse should be the same as the expression used by Peter in verse 29.

2.38

When any statement is a direct reply to a question, it may be necessary in the receptor language to specify this fact, for example, "Peter replied to them."

Though in the Greek there is a formal difference of subject for the verbs "repent" ("turn away from your sins") and "be baptized," there is no semantic difference.

Turn away from your sins is "repent" in most translations; however, "repent" is not used with the same meaning in contemporary English that the Greek word had in its distinctive biblical setting. The literal meaning of the Greek word itself is "to change one's mind," but even this is not adequate for the meaning of the word. The meaning of this term must be sought in its Jewish, rather than in its Greek, background. Although the word is Greek, the meaning behind it came from the Old Testament context and signified either "to turn from one's sins" or "to turn to God," which from the biblical standpoint are essentially the same.

The context at this point indicates that the focus is upon the sin of the people in rejecting Jesus as Lord. Therefore, turn away from your sins is appropriate. For a fuller treatment of "repent," see the componential analysis of this term in The Theory and Practice of Translation, pp. 51-55 and 66-68.

Insofar as possible it is important to avoid introducing the agent with be baptized, but if the receptor language in question has no passive construction nor any substitute passive, for example, "receive baptism," one can introduce "we" (exclusive) as the subject, such as "we will baptize you."

In the name of Jesus is literally in Greek "on the name of Jesus." This is the only place in the New Testament where this particular expression occurs with the word "baptize" (though it does occur with speak in 4.17 and 5.40, and with teach in 4.18 and 5.28). The phrase more commonly used with baptism is literally "into the name." Most English translations simply employ "in the name of," and it is not likely that one can justify any meaningful distinction between these New Testament expressions.

The expression in the name of Jesus Christ is extremely difficult to translate meaningfully. It is more or less a formula which people accept but which they normally do not understand. In languages in which one cannot use "name" in any sense as a functional symbol for the personality, translators have used "be baptized as a believer in Jesus Christ" or "be baptized as a follower of Jesus Christ."

So that your sins will be forgiven (literally "into a forgiveness of your sins") in the Greek may express either purpose or result; but the large majority of translators understand it as indicating purpose. The phrase modifies both main verbs: turn away from your sins and be baptized.

The clause your sins will be forgiven may be restructured in an active form as "God will forgive your sins."

The Greek phrase "the gift of the Holy Spirit" is translated in the TEV by God's gift, the Holy Spirit in order to make the meaning explicit.

Though the expression you will receive God's gift seems formally quite simple, it is semantically very complex. The pronoun you, though it is in the subject position, is actually the goal of the activity suggested by receive. Receive is only a substitute for a formal passive. Therefore, in many languages this clause must be semantically restructured as "and God will give you the Holy Spirit."

2.39

Verse 39 is an expansion on the theme of verse 38—implying that these benefits are the right not merely of the Jews, but of all those whom God calls. In the present context God's promise refers to his promise regarding the Holy Spirit; and your children indicates not merely the children of the people who are listening, but all of their descendants as well. In place of the passive promise was made, one may have an active form, such as "God has promised you and your children." The difficulty with such a verb form is that it may require a specification of what is specifically promised. This may be done by referring to the contents of verse 38, for example, "God has promised this (or, these same things) to you and your children."

To all who are far away is interpreted by some in a temporal sense, referring to persons not yet born; but more naturally it is taken to mean "persons in far-off distant lands" or "all people whose villages are many days' walk away." This may be a reference to the Jews of the dispersion or to the Gentiles.

The verb rendered calls to himself is elsewhere used in the sense of "invite" or "summons" (see 5.40; 6.2; 13.2,7; 16.10; 23.17,18,23), for example, "this includes all the people whom the Lord our God invites to come to him."

40 Peter made his appeal to them and with many other words he urged them, saying, "Save yourselves from the punishment coming to this wicked people!" 41 Many of them believed his message and were baptized; about three thousand people were added to the group that day. 42 They spent their time in learning from the apostles, taking part in the fellowship, and sharing in the fellowship meals and the prayers.

(2. 40-42)

This final paragraph of Peter's message serves as a summary to what has been introduced in the preceding discourse (that is, from v. 1), and also provides a transition to the next section (vv. 43-47). Verse 40 summarizes the discourse (from v. 14). Verse 41 indicates the immediate response of the people, and verse 42 indicates what they did as a result, while introducing the subject of the following discourse, namely, the activities of the believing community.

The three verses clearly mark the shift of participants. First, it is Peter who makes the appeal; second, it is the persons who respond; and third, it is the group which shares in the life of the Christian community.

2. 40

Made his appeal to them is a strengthened form of the verb "testify" and may also have the meaning "testify by argument." It is not always easy to find two words for verbal appeals, for example, "made an appeal...urged," which are strong and at the same time not completely redundant. However, to introduce the phrase many other words, and at the same time to provide the appropriate measure of emphasis, one may sometimes employ a negative expression followed by a positive, such as "this was not all that he said to them; he urged them strongly with many other words." Though this is not a close formal correspondence, it may be an excellent dynamic equivalence, for by means of a negative-positive expression some languages succeed in reproducing the heavily loaded expression contained in the Greek text. In some languages, however, one "cannot urge with words" (in which "words" is used as instruments). One can, on the other hand, "urge by speaking more."

Save yourselves from the punishment coming to this wicked people represents what in the Greek text is literally "save yourselves from this wicked people." But what Peter means is that those who hear are to try to save themselves from the fate which God will bring upon the wicked people who have crucified Jesus. In languages in which "punishment" must be treated as a verb, one can restructure the sentence to read, "save yourselves, so that you will not be punished as this wicked people are going to be punished." Some languages require a shift from "punishment," as an outwardly imposed event, to "suffering," with its focus upon the person directly involved (this is particularly true if the agent of the punishment is not specified). Accordingly, one may translate as "save yourselves; then you will not suffer the way these wicked people will suffer." The expression wicked people (literally "crooked generation") comes from Deuteronomy 32. 5 and Psalm 78. 8. The reference

2.41

to this wicked people must be made more explicit in some languages, for example, "the wicked people here in this country" or "the bad people who killed Jesus." In the first instance, the identification is geographical (the people of that country) and in the second instance, the identification is behavioral (those who specifically rejected and crucified Jesus). In either event, the dynamic equivalence is essentially the same. It is, of course, also possible to employ a temporal identification, such as "all the people living now," but this is in some respects somewhat too wide, for Luke's focus at this point is upon the Jewish nation.

2.41

It could well be that Luke intends verse 41 to begin a new paragraph or a new section, since he uses the same transitional formula here that he used in 1.6.

If there is any problem involved in a nominal form of message, the phrase believed his message may be restructured as "believed what Peter had said."

People is literally "souls"; the use of the word "soul," meaning "person" or "individual," goes back to the Septuagint, and is also used in Acts 3.23; 7.14; and 27.37.

The expression added to the group is very difficult to render in many languages, quite apart, of course, from the difficult passive without an agent. An equivalent in some languages is simply "there were about 3,000 more believers that day" or "about 3,000 more believers joined their group." On the other hand, one can make the agent explicit, by saying "that day the Lord increased the group of believers (made the group bigger) by about 3,000 persons."

In languages which may not have elaborate number systems, one can borrow a term from the dominant language of the area and then make a detailed explanation of the significance of such a number, based on the indigenous counting system.

2.42

The Greek text of this verse (literally "they were devoting themselves to the teachings of the apostles and to the fellowship, to the breaking of bread and to prayers") lends itself to two possible arrangements. It is possible to take the four items listed as being in two pairs, with the two items in each pair joined by the connective and, or it is possible to understand these as four separate items. The TEV has followed this latter arrangement.

Though the subject of the four events mentioned in this verse is, strictly speaking, the group of new believers, nevertheless this listing of the four aspects of the life of the believers serves primarily to introduce what is to come in the following paragraphs. At the same time, the immediately following paragraph serves as an introductory statement to much of what is in the succeeding chapters (3.1---5.16).

62

The translation of the Greek term proskarterountes (TEV they spent their time in) is by no means easy, especially when it is necessary to relate this to the events which follow. In some languages one may use "they gave themselves to," "they were eager for," or "they were very desirous of."

The learning from the apostles may be rendered as "to have the apostles teach them."

Fellowship (a word which occurs only here in Acts) may refer either to the common spirit which the believers shared with the apostles, or, more likely, to the communal spirit which they shared with the total group, and which is described in verses 44-46. In many languages this fellowship may be described as "they shared what they had with the others" (or "the other believers") or "they were one with the others."

Sharing in the fellowship meals (in Greek literally "in the breaking of bread") represents a Greek phrase which occurs only here and in Luke 24.35. It is generally agreed that these fellowship meals were common meals shared in by the early Christian community, and followed by the celebration of the Lord's Supper.

A literal translation of "breaking bread" is rarely satisfactory, especially in areas where bread is not broken, but cut or divided. The implication of this expression is that "they ate together as believers." Obviously, there is more than merely having one's meals with one another. This eating together was an aspect of their common loyalty to Jesus Christ. In view of the fact that the agapē (the fellowship meal) did involve the celebration of the Lord's Supper, it would be entirely appropriate to have a marginal note to explain the precise nature of these meals, which were so characteristic of the believing community.

The prayers which the disciples shared in were probably not limited to the prayers of the Christian community only, but likely included as well the Jewish prayers at their stated hours (see 3.1). The prayers may be translated as "they prayed to God together."

Life among the Believers

43 Many miracles and wonders were done through the apostles, and this caused everyone to be filled with awe. 44 All the believers continued together in close fellowship and shared their belongings with one another. 45 They would sell their property and possessions and distribute the money among all, according to what each one needed. 46 Every day they continued to meet as a group in the temple, and they had their meals together in their homes, eating the food with glad and humble hearts, 47 praising God, and enjoying the good will of all the people. And every day the Lord added to their group those who were being saved. (2.43-47)

The section heading Life among the Believers is difficult to translate in a language in which there is no noun such as life to designate the manner in which people relate to one another. In such instances one can often employ

63

a verb expression, for example, "How the Believers Lived with Respect to One Another" or "How the Believers Treated One Another."

As noted above, this paragraph is structurally transitional, for it links what has gone before with what is to follow. At the same time it contains more or less an outline of the immediately following chapters. Verse 43 introduces miracles (3.1-10 and 5.12-16). Verses 44-45 indicate the sharing of possessions (4.32-37 and 5.1-11). Verses 46-47a describe the humble life of the believers (with general acceptance by the people, in contrast with official opposition, 4.1-22 and 5.17-42). Verse 47b emphasizes the constant growth of the community (4.4, 31 and 5.42). It is important to note that the participants in each of these events are the same, namely, the believers.

2.43

Miracles and wonders is the same expression which was discussed in 2.19. The force of the Greek verb is such as to indicate that the apostles were continuously causing miracles and wonders and that the people were constantly filled with awe.

One should note that the apostles are not spoken of as the primary agents of the miracles, but only as the secondary ones. God himself is the initiator, and he works through the apostles. In some instances this type of secondary agency can be expressed as "many miracles and wonders happened because of (or, through) the apostles," but obviously not in the sense of "for their sake." However, one can also translate as "the apostles did many miracles and wonders," especially in those receptor languages which have no convenient devices for indicating secondary agency.

And this caused everyone to be filled with awe, the second clause in the English sentence structure, is the first clause in the Greek sentence, which has been inverted by the TEV. This inversion of the order of the Greek text is made so as to follow the temporal sequence (first the miracles and then the awe), and in order to employ a cause-and-effect sequence (the events and the reactions to them). The phrase to be filled with awe is equivalent in some languages to "had great respect for" or "were deeply impressed by"; idiomatically, "their heads were bowed" or "they saw them (that is, the miracles) with open mouths."

Everyone (literally "every soul") may refer either to the believers (as the TEV understands it) or to the nonbelievers. If everyone is taken to refer to the believers, then awe perhaps describes best their response; if everyone refers to nonbelievers, then the best description of their reaction may be that of "fear."

2.44

The term believers may require some grammatical goal, for example, "all those who believed in Jesus."

Continued together in close fellowship includes the same Greek expression which was rendered "in all" (1.15) and "in one place" (2.1). The meaning of the phrase here seems to be that they were drawn together in Christian fellowship (see NEB "all whose faith had drawn them together") rather than that they were all living in one place (see JB "the faithful all lived together"). The expression continued together in close fellowship is an excellent rendering in English of a rather abstract expression in Greek. In other languages, however, quite different forms may be required, for example, "they remained near one another," "they continued to be one group," "they continued as a loyal group," or "they were very much together."

Shared their belongings with one another correctly translates the meaning of "they were having all things in common." As is indicated in the following verse, the believers did not immediately give up everything they possessed or give their goods to a common community storehouse. Verse 45 indicates that they only gave up something when there was a specific need within the Christian community; and the fact that Barnabas received so much attention from the selling of his piece of property would further indicate that this was not something everyone in the Christian community was doing. Shared their belongings may be rendered in some languages as "they brought together what they owned and used them together," "each one's things belonged to all of them," or "they gave to one another what was needed."

2.45

The last clause of 2.44 is a general statement, of which verse 45 is a more specific description. It may even be useful to introduce this verse by a transitional phrase, "that means" or "that is to say," in which one indicates clearly that the preceding statement is explained by what follows. Otherwise, one might get the impression that the two clauses refer to different events. If there is to be a distinction made between the two words property and possessions, the first should be taken to refer to real estate and the second to personal property. These terms are collectively translated as "what they owned" or "what belonged to them." They would sell...and distribute correctly carries out the force of the Greek verb tense, which indicates that this was an action that was carried on whenever the need arose, for example, "from time to time." The fact that they could sell their goods is still further indication that the believers did not turn everything over to a community fund as may be suggested by some translations of verse 44.

Among all has reference to all believers who were in need.

2.46

As a group is the same word which is translated together in 1.14. The expression continued to meet as a group may simply be "came together."

The temple is in many languages the "house of God," "holy place," or "sacred house," a phrase used in the Old Testament to describe the temple in Jerusalem (see also 3.1).

They had their meals together in their homes (literally "they were breaking bread from house to house") should be taken to mean that the believers met at different homes from time to time and there shared in their fellowship meals together.

The concept of simultaneous experience of eating and having gladness in one's heart must be expressed in some languages in a more explicit manner than is employed in the TEV or in the Greek, for example, "they ate and at the same time they were happy."

Humble hearts (literally "singleness of heart") may signify either humility or generosity, such as "they gave to one another gladly."

2.47

The specific content of "praise" may need to be introduced in some languages, for example, "they said, God is very good."

Enjoying the good will of all the people means that the believers were liked by all the people in Jerusalem; but the expression "enjoying the good will of all the people" must often be semantically restructured so that the persons who experience the attitudes toward the believers are put into focus, for example, "all the people regarded the believers favorably," "all the people thought of the believers as being good," or "all the people felt warm in their hearts about the believers."

It may be necessary to introduce "Jesus" with Lord in order to make the reference clear at this point.

To their group translates the expression which first appeared in 1.15 (and was discussed also in 2.1, 44). Although some scholars have raised questions regarding the meaning of the phrase in this context, it seems best to translate it with a meaning similar to that of the TEV (see NEB, RSV, JB). Added to their group may be expressed in a number of different ways, for example, "caused the group to be bigger by these," "put them into the group," "made them a part of the group," or "counted them also as part of the group."

Those who were being saved must be understood in light of every day. The meaning of the verb phrase were being saved is temporal and not theological, that is, Luke is not concerned in this passage to present a theory of salvation as a progressive experience; rather he is saying that day after day the Lord kept adding to their group those people who became believers. Those who were being saved may be shifted into the active, for example, "those whom God was saving."

CHAPTER 3

This next episode in Acts is the story of the healing of the lame man. It includes not only all of Chapter 3 but also the first 22 verses of Chapter 4. Moreover, this story provides the basis for the emphasis upon prayer and the life of the Christian community beginning in 4.23. It serves as an illustration of the miraculous power that came upon the disciples by means of the Holy Spirit (see 1.8) and indicates how important the name of Jesus was for the first believers.

This discourse (3.1—4.22) consists of three major parts: (1) 3.1-10 is the story of the healing of the lame man; (2) 3.11-26 is the message of Peter to the people in the temple; and (3) 4.1-22 is the account of Peter and John before the Council, including not only the arrest and the accusations but also the defense of Peter and the final outcome of the decision of the Council. This last section has a more complex internal structure than the first two sections.

The Lame Man Healed

1 One day Peter and John went to the temple at three o'clock in the afternoon, the hour for prayers. 2 There, at the "Beautiful Gate," as it was called, was a man who had been lame all his life. Every day he was carried to this gate to beg for money from the people who were going into the temple. 3 When he saw Peter and John going in, he begged them to give him something. 4 They looked straight at him and Peter said, "Look at us!" 5 So he looked at them, expecting to get something from them. 6 Peter said to him, "I have no money at all, but I will give you what I have: in the name of Jesus Christ of Nazareth I order you to walk!" 7 Then he took him by his right hand and helped him up. At once the man's feet and ankles became strong; 8 he jumped up, stood on his feet, and started walking around. Then he went into the temple with them, walking and jumping and praising God. 9 The whole crowd saw him walking and praising God; 10 and when they recognized him as the beggar who sat at the temple's "Beautiful Gate," they were all filled with surprise and amazement at what had happened to him. (3.1-10)

A section heading such as The Lame Man Healed can be rather difficult to translate, especially in a language in which such a participial form as healed is not easily combined in this type of passive construction. Therefore, in a number of languages it is preferable to introduce the subject "Peter and John Heal a Lame Man." The tense of the verb to be used in this type of title will depend upon the way in which the particular receptor language treats such identificational statements. The term healed itself may require some type of causative formation such as "cause him to become well."

The section 3.1-10 has a relatively simple narrative structure. A temporal transitional item occurs in 3.1, namely, one day, and the setting is given in the first two verses. Verse 1 includes the participants, Peter and John; the place, the temple; and the time, the hour for prayers. Verse 2 specifies more precisely the location; introduces the third participant, namely, the lame man, and explains his activity and how he got there. Luke is masterful in his handling of such transitions and settings.

The following verses have some interesting shifts in agents and goals. Note that in verse 3 the focus is upon the lame man introduced in verse 2. In verse 4 the focus shifts to Peter and John. In verse 5 the focus shifts back to the lame man, and in verse 6 there is another shift of focus so that Peter becomes the subject.

In verse 7b there is a further shift to the condition of the lame man, and in verses 8 and 9 the lame man is in focus. Notice that in verse 9 the shift is to the crowd which sees the lame man and expresses amazement as to what has happened.

This alternation in focus is one of the difficult aspects of this type of narrative. Since each language tends to have its own particular way of handling such shifts, it is important that care be exercised in the treatment of such rapid changes in subjects.

3.1

In the Greek text there is a problem of transition at the beginning of the first verse. In Greek the conjunction de, usually rendered "but," may be sufficient to suggest a major change in content. However, the problem of transition was recognized by early scribes who tended to make a difference in the division of verse content, taking the last three words of verse 47 and associating them with the first verse of Chapter 3 so as to provide more satisfactorily for the transition.

In the King James Version this transition is indicated by the conjunctive adverb "now" but this tends to be rather misleading. Accordingly, the TEV has employed simply one day, since this would be normal in English, and probably the closest natural equivalent. Other languages, however, have expressions such as "and then," "later," or "at another time."

It is possible that John is John Mark, but most commentators understand him to be John the son of Zebedee.

Throughout the New Testament there are two words used for temple: one indicates the central sanctuary itself; the other (used here) is a more comprehensive term and includes the whole temple area. As noted elsewhere, a term for temple may be very well rendered as "the house of God." However, in some languages this becomes confusing since it may already be used for "the church building." Some have amplified the phrase, for example, "a house of God of the Jews," but this can become rather ambiguous in indicating that it is only "the God of the Jews." An expression such as "the house of prayer" can likewise be somewhat confusing since it might also be applicable to a "synagogue." Therefore, some translators have used a more general expression such as "the house of worship," and to distinguish this from a synagogue they have called it "the great house of worship" and have called the synagogue "a small house of worship of the Jews."

Three o'clock in the afternoon is literally "the ninth hour" (see 2.15). Josephus, the Jewish historian, tells that temple sacrifices were offered twice a day: at sunrise and about the ninth hour, that is, about three o'clock in the afternoon.

There are very few languages in which one can use an expression such as "at the ninth hour." In some languages it has been possible to preserve a rough equivalent such as "nine hours after sunrise," but this is usually awkward. An adjustment to a modern reckoning of time is no doubt more satisfactory, namely at three o'clock in the afternoon. In some languages, however, this is still a rather artificial way of speaking and therefore a more indigenous expression may be regarded as more satisfactory; for example, "when the sun is halfway down in the sky," "at the time of the afternoon rest," or "when the sun is leaning on its side." If such terms are consistently and habitually used for expressing a time such as three o'clock in the afternoon, they are quite satisfactory in the translation.

An expression such as the hour for prayers can be rendered as "the time when the people habitually pray" or "the time when people normally pray." Some languages may require a goal for a term such as "prayer," and therefore it is perfectly acceptable to have "a time when people normally pray (or, talk) to God."

In the selection of a term for prayer it is important to emphasize the fact of communication rather than primarily "begging for" or "asking for."

In languages which make a clear distinction between prayer as simply speaking to God and more elaborate religious functions involving prayer, it is preferable to use the latter term in this instance. Therefore it could legitimately be translated essentially as "the time when people normally worshiped."

3.2

The Greek sentence of 3.2 is usually best divided into two parts: the first identifies the place and the man, and the second tells about his activity of begging from the people who came to the temple.

No positive identification can be made of the Beautiful Gate referred to. Generally it is understood to have been one of the gates on the eastern side of the temple (near the Shushan Gate or the Nicanor Gate); but Jewish tradition knows nothing of a gate called the Beautiful Gate, and any attempt to be specific in identification is hazardous.

A translation of the term gate turns out to be, in many languages, a term for "door." A word for gate is associated far more with an opening in a fence or some other type of enclosure rather than as a more or less elaborate solid structure which could close off such an important area as the temple. A term for "door" should, however, refer to "a doorway" rather than to the object which closes the opening.

In the TEV the transition between the first and second sentences, that is, between verse 1 and verse 2a, consists of a reference to the place there. In some languages it is necessary to be more specific, "the beautiful doorway of the temple."

69

Sometimes the expression the "Beautiful Gate," as it was called must be restructured in a somewhat more explicit fashion, for example, "the doorway that was called the Beautiful Doorway," "the doorway that people commonly called the Beautiful Doorway," or "the doorway, it had a name, the Beautiful Doorway."

After the transitional elements which add further information as to the location, the lame man is introduced and described in terms of the length of time that he had been lame. In some languages lameness is expressed as "he could not walk." In other languages some more specific reference to his feet may be included, for example, "his feet were weak," "his legs could not hold him up," or even "his legs were twisted."

Lame all his life translates "lame from his mother's womb," another Semitic idiom. An expression such as all his life may be shifted into a verbal form such as "for as long as he had lived." On the other hand, it may include a specific reference to his birth, for example, "he was even lame in his mother's stomach" or "even when he was born he was lame."

The TEV has given initial position to every day, which in the Greek comes after the verb. This is one of the most satisfactory transitions in English for a narrative discourse, and highlights the use of the Greek imperfect tense which indicates habitual action.

He was carried to translates two verbal phrases: "he was being carried" and "whom they were placing." The second of these verbs is an impersonal third person plural with an object. In Semitic speech this kind of construction is often the equivalent of a passive verb with the object of the impersonal verb being equivalent to the subject of the passive verb. That is, "whom they were placing" is the equivalent of "he was being placed." Rather than combine these two verbs, as the TEV has done, one may prefer to render them separately, for example, "they carried him there and put him down." The main argument for translating these verbs separately is so that the reader can clearly see that at the very moment the disciples were standing there the lame man was being carried past them.

If the passive expression he was carried to this gate can be employed, it is desirable to retain it since in this way one does not introduce additional participants. If an active form is required then one must usually say something like "some people carried him each day to this gate." However, it is important to distinguish carefully between the people who carried him to the gate and the people from whom he begged money.

An expression such as beg for money from the people represents such a common experience that one can usually translate it without special difficulty. In some languages, however, an expression for begging can only be given in direct discourse, for example, "he said to the people, Please give me money."

In view of the particular setting of this discourse the use of the expression going into the temple is most appropriate, although it is not designed to exclude his begging from people as they came out of the temple. The real meaning here is simply "those who went in and out of the temple" or "those who visited the temple."

3.3

Since the lame man is the subject of the preceding sentence, he can probably be referred to by some pronominal substitute such as "he"; but some languages may require a specific mention of the lame man by some nominal form. It is probably necessary to specify Peter and John, since a pronominal substitute might be confused with people in general.

As noted in the preceding verse, it may be necessary to translate an expression for begging in the form of direct discourse, for example, "he asked them strongly, Give me something."

3.4

The Greek form of 3.4 focuses upon Peter and therefore introduces John in a subordinate prepositional phrase. In most languages it is essential to indicate clearly that both Peter and John looked upon the lame man. One must, however, also indicate that it is Peter who does the speaking.

They looked straight at him translates the same verb as was used in 1.10; there it is translated they...had their eyes fixed on.

In a number of translations, problems have been encountered in the expression Look at us!---not because this cannot be readily said, but simply because it seems rather strange. One would assume that Peter and John would ask permission to look at the lame man rather than tell the lame man to look directly at them. Due to the unexpectedness of such an expression, and also the shift in subject which occurs in the next verse, it is essential that the meaning of Peter's statement be perfectly clear.

3.5

The TEV marks the transition in activity by the particle so. This is a legitimate as well as a useful transitional device.

In English the lame man as well as Peter and John can be identified by pronouns, but in some languages one or another of the participants may need to be specified by nouns.

He looked at them is not the same verb as is used in the preceding verse (Look at us!), although in the context the meanings of both verbs are essentially the same. The Greek verb in this verse is actually one which normally occurs with a direct object ("fix [object] on someone"), but in this Greek sentence there is no object expressed. The object may either be one's mind or one's eyes; the TEV takes it to mean he fixed his eyes on them, that is he looked at them.

It may not be easy to translate a term such as expecting. This may need to be shifted to a form such as "thought in himself (or even, said to himself), I will get something from them."

3.6

As this is the second statement which Peter has made to the lame man, it may be necessary to highlight this fact by a transition, for example, "and then" or "and further he said."

The meaning of the phrase "silver and gold I do not have" is accurately rendered by I have no money at all, since in this passage "silver and gold" simply means money. The emphatic expression no money at all is completely justified by the emphatic form of the Greek original.

In the name of is a frequently occurring biblical phrase meaning "by the authority or power of the person whose name is mentioned." Some translators have employed simply "mentioning the name of" or "pronouncing the name of." This, however, is quite unlikely to communicate the real meaning. Some translators have used expressions such as "by the power of," "by the authority of," or even "because Jesus Christ of Nazareth has given me the power," or perhaps more satisfactorily "because Jesus Christ of Nazareth has the power."

In some languages an expression such as "has the power to" must be more specifically qualified so that it may read "because Jesus Christ of Nazareth has the power to heal you, I order you to walk."

All expressions such as order or "command" must in some languages be shifted into direct discourse, for example, "I order you, Walk" or "I say to you, You must walk."

The expression Jesus Christ of Nazareth can usually be translated in a straightforward manner, since most languages have relatively simple ways of identifying the hometown of a person with his name. However, in some languages it is necessary to say "Jesus Christ, who came from Nazareth town."

Some persons may wish to employ a translation of Christ as "the anointed one." But in this type of context the expression Jesus Christ is simply a fuller name. Therefore, some transliteration of the name is the most warranted equivalent.

3.7

The use of the transitional particle then is useful to highlight the next development in the narrative.

Since Peter is the subject of the preceding verse, it may not be necessary to specify the subject of verse 7. However, there can be ambiguity in the series of pronouns he ... him ... his ... him, and these references must be clearly sorted out in the receptor-language text.

The act of taking the man by the hand must be understood as a friendly gesture and not some type of "grabbing." In some languages the more appropriate equivalent is "touched his right hand" or even "felt his right hand."

The phrase helped him up involves two semantic problems. First, it is likely to be a causative in the sense of "caused him to get up," but this is accomplished not merely by verbal command but by physical assistance. The second problem involves the nature of "getting up." Was this from a lying position to a standing position, or from a sitting position to a standing position? It is likely that it is the latter, namely, he stood up from a sitting position.

At once describes the immediacy with which the healing takes place. Luke has made evident the immediate healing of the man by combining the use of an adverb with a verb tense, which means something done at that particular time, for example, "immediately" or "just then."

In some languages one would not speak of feet and ankles, since a term for "feet" may include "ankles." Therefore, a more natural expression might be "feet and legs," though even this expression may have complications in view of the fact that in some languages the common word for "legs" also includes the feet.

3. 8

The very abruptness of the transition between verses 7b and 8a may require no transitional particle, but in some languages it may be necessary to add "therefore," "hence," or "as a result." Started walking around ... walking and jumping and praising God translate Greek verb tenses which emphasize the continuousness of the action. Luke evidently intends a contrast between the instantaneousness with which the healing took place and the ongoing of the action expressed by these particular verbs. A phrase such as walking around does not, of course, refer to any circular motion. It is simply that he began "walking here and there."

In order to indicate the transition between the activity of the man in the direct presence of Peter and John and what he did in the temple, one can conveniently use an expression such as "then," "and next," or "after that."

In this particular sentence an expression such as jumping refers to "leaping into the air."

In a number of languages an expression such as praising God must be put into direct discourse, for example, "he said, God is wonderful" or "he declared, How great God is!"

3. 9

From the standpoint of the discourse there is a problem beginning with verse 9 in that a new set of participants is introduced who were only indirectly mentioned before, that is, at the end of verse 2. These are the persons who were going into the temple. One can translate simply as "all the people there in the temple."

In a number of languages a construction such as saw him walking must be broken up into two closely combined expressions, for example, "saw him; he was walking."

A translation of praising God may need to be turned into an expression of direct quotation, as suggested in the previous verse.

3. 10

When they recognized him involves a Greek verb tense which describes a process of gradual recognition on the part of the people in the temple.

Recognized, particularly in this type of context, may be rendered in some languages as "came to know," "saw who he was," or "saw and knew he was the beggar."

The phrase temple's "Beautiful Gate" may be rendered in some languages as the "Beautiful Doorway to the house of God."

No real distinction between the two Greek words translated surprise and amazement can be made. In many languages surprise and amazement are expressed by idiomatic phrases, for example, "they no longer sat with intelligence in their hearts," "they no longer could think," "their minds had been grabbed," or "their mouths were shut."

The relation between the amazement and what had caused it may need to be expressed as a relation of cause and effect, for example, "they were amazed because of what had happened to the lame man," or, as in some languages, "what had happened to the lame man caused them to be amazed."

Peter's Message in the Temple

11 As the man held on to Peter and John, all the people were amazed and ran to them in "Solomon's Porch," as it was called. 12 When Peter saw the people, he said to them, "Men of Israel, why are you surprised at this, and why do you stare at us? Do you think that it was by means of our own power or godliness that we made this man walk? 13 The God of Abraham, Isaac, and Jacob, the God of our ancestors, has given divine glory to his Servant Jesus. You handed him over to the authorities, and you rejected him in Pilate's presence, even after Pilate had decided to set him free. 14 He was holy and good, but you rejected him and instead you asked Pilate to do you the favor of turning loose a murderer. 15 And so you killed the one who leads men to life. But God raised him from the dead—and we are witnesses to this. 16 It was the power of his name that gave strength to this lame man. What you see and know was done by faith in his name; it was faith in Jesus that made him well like this before you all. (3.11-16)

The section heading Peter's Message in the Temple is effective in English and in any language which uses primarily nominal forms. However, when verbal forms are required, it may be necessary to modify this somewhat, for example, "Peter Speaks to the People in the Temple" or "Peter Explains to the People in the Temple." A term such as "explains" is an attempt to link what follows with the significance of the event which has just been described.

The section 3.11-26 consists of a setting (v. 11), an introduction to direct discourse (v. 12a), and two major sections of the discourse (vv. 12-16 and 17-26). It is interesting to note that both of these sections of the discourse have somewhat the same type of structure. Both begin with a mention of Jesus, after appropriate introduction, and then return to the theme of Jesus at the end.

The statement of the setting picks up the fact that these individuals have already been surprised by what has happened (v. 10); this serves as a transitional link to the preceding paragraph. In verse 13 Peter idenfifies God as the source of this miracle through his Servant Jesus, but God is here closely related to the Jewish tradition as the God of Abraham, Isaac, and Jacob.

What follows is an historical flashback (vv. 13b-15). Verse 14 is essentially a restatement of verse 13b with a slightly different emphasis; and verse 15a is a conclusion to verses 13b and 14. Verse 15b, however, gives the divine aspect of the event, and verse 16 returns to the event which has caused the surprise in the first place.

In summary, the discourse structure of this portion may be analyzed in terms of the following segments:

1. The setting (v. 11).
2. The introduction to direct discourse (v. 12a).
3. The link with the preceding event (v. 12b).
4. The introduction of God and his Servant Jesus (v. 13a).
5. An historical background, flashback (vv. 13b-15).

6. A conclusion consisting of the restatement of what is implied in verse 13a (v. 16).

3.11

The introductory clause as the man held on to Peter and John forms an excellent transition from the preceding paragraph, since it introduces all the principal participants and shows the continuing relation between the lame man, Peter, and John.

Though the Greek text introduces the concept of amazement by an adjective at the end of verse 11, it may be more satisfactory to change the order, as has been done in the TEV, to indicate clearly the temporal sequence and the implied cause and effect.

The phrase ran to them may in some languages be better rendered as "ran to where they were."

Solomon's Porch was a type of roofed colonnade or portico. It is usually conjectured that it was the colonnade that ran the length of the east side of the outer court, but identification cannot be made with certainty. It is mentioned again in 5.12 and also in John 10.23.

The expression Solomon's Porch may require a certain degree of elaboration if it is to be fully comprehended, for example, "a porch which was known as Solomon's" or "a porch called by the people Solomon's Porch."

In some relatively primitive areas there is no construction which immediately parallels this type of colonnade. One can sometimes use a more general term such as "a long shelter" or "a roofed-over shelter." In many areas such a shelter is constructed for special festivities and therefore the name of this type of even temporary construction can probably be employed as the closest natural equivalent. If the differences are too great then some type of marginal note is necessary.

3.12

In Greek there is no expressed object of the verb saw; many translations, as the TEV, prefer to understand the people as the object of the verb,
though it is possible to understand the object as being the total experience of
the people rushing toward Peter (see Barclay, Phillips "when Peter saw this").

The expression men of Israel is a means of identifying Peter with those
to whom he speaks and would include both men and women. In some languages
this is simply equivalent to "fellow tribesmen" or even "my relatives" (if this
involves the extended ethnic unit). (See also 2.14.)

The term Israel may be used in most languages as a rough equivalent
to the identification of the tribal or national unit. Sometimes this is specifically indicated in terms of descent, for example, "my kinsmen descended
from Israel." In other instances it implies an ethnic unit, such as "people
of my tribe called Israel."

A translation of surprised can be precisely the same as has occurred
in the previous verses (vv. 10 and 11).

An expression for stare at us may be "look at us so strong" or even
"see us and see nothing else."

Do you think that it was by means of our own power or godliness that
we made this man walk? is much more natural in English than would be a
literal translation of the Greek, "Do you think that our own power or godliness has made this man walk?"

The expression by means of our own power or godliness is more often
than not expressed as a cause since both power and godliness must frequently
be introduced by verbal expressions, for example, "because we are so strong
personally and because we worship God so well" or "because we have special
power or because we are so good before God."

In a number of languages there is an expression for "spiritual power."
This is the type of power that the medicine man has in working miracles or
in the control of natural phenomena. It is often a useful equivalent at this
point.

The term godliness refers to one's own personal piety and religiosity,
and therefore an expression which speaks of a person's "goodness before God"
or "manner of worshiping well" may be an adequate functional equivalent.

3.13

The God of Abraham, Isaac, and Jacob is a phrase which goes back to
Exodus 3.6,15. It is a familiar Old Testament way of addressing God as the
God of those men who were the founders of the Jewish nation. In many languages, however, it is difficult to speak of the God of Abraham, Isaac, and
Jacob since it might imply that these three men owned God. Moreover, in
some languages a term for God is very close to "ancestor spirit" and therefore there is real confusion at this point since God would be nothing more
than the ancestor spirit of Abraham, Isaac, and Jacob. Accordingly, it may be

important to make the relation much more specific by translating "the God whom Abraham, Isaac, and Jacob worshiped."

The phrase the God of our ancestors has, of course, the same basic problems as the phrase the God of Abraham, Isaac, and Jacob. It is quite naturally in apposition to the preceding phrase and therefore this must be made perfectly clear in some languages by some kind of marker, for example, "that is to say," "that is," or "he is."

The phrase our ancestors is rendered in a number of different ways— "our fathers," "our grandfathers," "our forefathers of many years ago," "those who began our clan," or "those from whom we have all come."

God...has given divine glory (literally "God glorified") may be taken as referring to the resurrection of Jesus that is explicitly mentioned in verse 15 (so TEV); while others believe it refers to the act of healing that had just been performed on the lame man.

A translation of given divine glory to, or "glorified," is extremely difficult to translate effectively in this kind of context, for there is not enough of the specific involvement of Jesus Christ to help the reader understand just how Jesus is "glorified." In some languages, however, the concept of "giving glory to" can be expressed as "caused him to count for something," "caused him to be very important," or "caused people to look at (or remember) Jesus as being very great." In other languages it is possible to say "God showed how really wonderful his Servant was" or "God demonstrated how great his Servant was."

The Greek word translated Servant may either mean "child" or "servant"; the meaning here, however, is determined by the sense of the word as used in the Septuagint translation of Isaiah 52.13 and other related passages where "the servant of the Lord" was a Jewish Messianic title (see Isaiah 41.8; 42.1; 44.1,2,21).

Terms for "servant" are normally related to two aspects of serving: (1) the obeying of orders and (2) performing specific tasks on behalf of someone. In the first instance, a term for servant may be "one who obeys" (and this may require some direct goal such as "Jesus who obeyed God"). In other instances one can simply have "one who did what God said." When the focus is upon performing some service, an idiom may be "one who worked for" or "one who helped." It is rare that one can employ a term which will combine not only the concept of serving but also the prestige which comes from serving an eminent person. This is certainly part of the implication of the term Servant in this Semitic expression.

With the process of "handing over" (which contrasts with what precedes) the implied goal, the authorities, is supplied, while the act of "rejection" is related to what took place before Pilate. In a number of languages it is important to make clear that the authorities are "those who rule the Jews" or "the leaders of the Jews." Some may object that the people (referred to as you) did not themselves participate directly in the handing over of Jesus, but one cannot alter this involvement of the people, as clearly stated by Luke in his report of Peter's message.

3.14

A translation of <u>rejected</u> or "denied" is not always easy. In some languages one may render this as "spoke bad about him before Pilate," "would have nothing to do with him when he was in front of Pilate," or "you accused him of being bad when he was before Pilate." In one translation this is rendered as a direct discourse: "you said, He is a liar." This is the local equivalent of denial.

The problem of sequence of tenses in the last clause of 3.13b may cause some difficulties since the decision by Pilate was prior to the rejection of the people. This time relation may need to be made quite specific, for example, "you did this even when Pilate had decided beforehand to set Jesus free" or "you did this even after Pilate had decided...."

3.14

<u>Holy and good</u> would also have been understood both by Peter and by his Jewish listeners as a Jewish Messianic title. <u>Good</u> (or "righteous") as a Messianic title probably had its origin in Isaiah 53.11, and in the present context it has specific reference to Jesus' perfect obedience to the will of God and to his innocence in contrast to those who put him to death.

Rather than attempt to reproduce the Messianic title, "the holy and righteous one," as a goal of the verb "reject," this semantically heavy substantive phrase has been restructured in two clauses in the TEV, where the first clause indicates that Jesus was <u>holy and good</u> and in the second clause the rejection is specified.

In many languages one of the most difficult terms is a word for <u>holy</u>. This is especially true in a context such as this, where <u>holy</u> is not in any sense related to "taboo." Here the emphasis is certainly upon the dedication of Christ to the will of God, and therefore in many languages one must translate "he was dedicated to God," "he gave himself to God," or "he served God only." This is much more likely to convey the meaning of the biblical concept of "holy" than any term which means "separation" or "isolation." In fact, the translation of <u>holy</u> by a term for "separated" is almost always erroneous since it is the dedication to the service of God which then requires separation, rather than separation which results in dedication to God. This is particularly true in a religious system in which positive taboo is a significant factor in the concept of "holy."

In many languages a translation of <u>good</u> or "righteous" may be rendered as "straight," in the sense of "conforming to a standard." This standard is naturally that which God expects. Sometimes this must be expressed as "did right before God," "did that which was good in God's eyes," or "did what God said was good."

<u>You asked Pilate to do you the favor of turning loose a murderer</u> properly gives the meaning of the Greek, "you asked for a man who was a murderer to be given to you" (see also NEB "you begged as a favor the release of a murderer").

A clause such as <u>asked Pilate to do you the favor</u> must in many languages be expressed as direct discourse, for example, "you pleaded with Pilate, Instead of Jesus let a murderer loose" (with possibly a specific reference to Barabbas).

The idea of <u>favor</u> may be indirectly expressed in some languages by a form of direct discourse, including an expression such as "please," "do us a kindness," or "be good to us."

3.15

The expression <u>and so</u> provides a useful transition by preparing the reader for a type of conclusion.

The direct form <u>you killed</u> may need to be shifted into a causative in some languages since these people themselves did not crucify Jesus but by their behavior caused him to be crucified by the Romans. Therefore, a causative form such as "you caused him to be killed" or "you caused him to die" may be more appropriate and accurate.

<u>One who leads men to life</u> may be understood as "one who causes people to really live," "one who causes true life," or "one who shows true life"; there is no way of knowing precisely what meaning Peter had in mind. The meaning "prince" does not fit the context and is usually quite inadequate.

<u>But God raised him from the dead</u> correctly translates the Greek relative clause "whom God raised from the dead." The contrast between the activity of the people in causing Jesus' death and what God did in raising him from the dead is so great that it usually needs to be specifically highlighted by a conjunction such as "but."

As noted in previous sections, <u>raised him from the dead</u> is essentially a causative, for example, "caused him to rise from the dead."

The substantive expression <u>witnesses to this</u> may be changed into a verbal expression "we ourselves saw this." <u>To this</u> translates a relative pronoun that may refer either to the fact of the resurrection (so the TEV), or else "to him," that is, to Jesus who was raised from the dead.

3.16

In many languages the expression <u>of his name</u> is extremely difficult to render since there is no use of "name" as a substitute symbol for the personality. Therefore, the closest equivalent of <u>the power of his name</u> is "his power." Some persons may insist that in this instance the meaning is "the power which results from speaking the name of Jesus." This, however, would tend toward an interpretation involving "word magic." This first sentence of verse 16 may be translated as "It was Jesus' power which caused this lame man to be strong." The cause-and-effect relation may need to be more specific in some languages and can be rendered as "because Jesus was powerful this lame man was given strength."

There is an ambiguity in the expression <u>by faith in his name</u>, since the faith may be that of the lame man or that of the apostles. In many languages one cannot be so ambiguous but must specify whether this faith was experienced by the lame man or by Peter and John. If one assumes that it is the faith of the lame man, one can translate "What you have seen and know happened because this man believed in Jesus." If, however, one interprets the faith as being that of Peter and John, an appropriate rendering may be, "What you see and know happened because we two believed in Jesus." The phrase in his name may also have the meaning "through his name," and so refer to the faith awakened in the man by the name of Jesus (see NEB "And the name of Jesus, by awakening faith, has strengthened this man").

Any term for faith or "belief" must imply more than mere intellectual assent to the existence of some one or some thing. There must be some measure of "trust" or "confidence." In many languages this is translated as "to lean on," "to depend on," or "to hang on to with the heart." Mere intellectual acknowledgment of the truth of a proposition is certainly not what is meant in this type of context.

The second sentence of verse 16 consists of two clauses which are to some extent "mirror images" of each other. Essentially the same fact is stated twice in order to make it more emphatic. In both instances it is the faith in Jesus which is the cause (or instrument), the process is the healing, and in one instance the result is described in terms of what you see and know, and in the second instance as well like this before you all.

In some languages an expression such as before you all must simply be rendered as "and you can see it for yourselves." It is not essentially a matter of the place where the event occurred, but the fact that it was visible to all concerned.

17 "And now, my brothers, I know that what you and your leaders did to Jesus was done because of your ignorance. 18 God long ago announced by means of all the prophets that his Messiah had to suffer; and he made it come true in this way. 19 Repent, then, and turn to God, so that he will wipe away your sins, 20 so that times of spiritual strength may come from the Lord's presence, and that he may send Jesus, who is the Messiah he has already chosen for you. 21 He must remain in heaven until the time comes for all things to be made new, as God announced by means of his holy prophets of long ago. 22 For Moses said, 'The Lord your God will send you a prophet, just as he sent me, who will be of your own people. You must listen to everything that he tells you. 23 Anyone who does not listen to what that prophet says will be separated from God's people and destroyed.' 24 And the prophets, including Samuel and those who came after him, all of them who had a message, also announced these present days. 25 The promises of God through his prophets are for you, and you share in the covenant which God made with your ancestors. As he said to Abraham, 'Through your descendants I will bless all the people on earth.' 26 And so God chose and sent his Servant to you first, to bless you by making all of you turn away from your wicked ways." (3.17-26)

The discourse structure of 3.17-26 is somewhat complex. It begins with a direct address, which repeats a similar expression occurring at the beginning of the discourse in verse 12. The first sentence of this section (v. 17) echoes what has already been said in the previous section, namely, that the people and their leaders caused the death of Jesus.

Verse 18, however, is a flashback which states that this very event had already been announced by God earlier through the prophets. Verse 19 brings the discourse back to the present time and indicates what the people should do in view of what has happened. Verse 20 projects this into the future, while verse 21 introduces still further future implications.

Verse 22 is another flashback which takes up the words of Moses and expands on what has already been introduced in verse 18. The second half of verse 22 repeats the same theme as verse 19, and this is continued in verse 23. Verse 24 enlarges upon the theme of verse 22 (and v. 18) and makes it more general. Verse 25, however, brings the implications of these promises of God back to the present circumstances. Finally, verse 26 repeats the theme of repentance suggested in verses 19 and 22 and serves as a conclusion to the message.

This section (3.17-26) has three essential elements: (1) what happened to Jesus, (2) the message of the prophets, and (3) the response of the people in repentance. These three elements are repeated in slightly varying ways three different times, thus illustrating a typical expository type of discourse.

3.17

The transitional expression and now indicates that the speaker, though treating the same general theme, is approaching it from a somewhat different perspective, namely, the implication of what has happened for the people in question. This aspect is reinforced by the introduction of the expression my brothers. In a number of languages this is simply equivalent to "fellow tribesmen," "relatives," or even "friends." The use of a specific term such as "brothers" in this more general meaning is relatively restricted.

The leaders are the chief priests and the scribes who took the leading part in accusing Jesus before Pilate.

The translation of the expression because of your ignorance is not easy since it can be interpreted in so many different ways. This is certainly no reference to the general ignorance of the people. It is simply "because you didn't understand really what you were doing" or, as in some languages, "you didn't understand the meaning of what you were doing." These people obviously knew what they were doing in betraying and rejecting Jesus, but they did not understand the significance of what they were doing. It is this aspect of ignorance which must be made quite clear.

3.18

Long ago announced is rendered by most translations as "foretold." Elsewhere in the New Testament this verb appears only in Acts 7.52.

3.19

Some such expression as <u>long ago</u> is essential in order to indicate clearly the flashback in this discourse structure. In some languages this is specifically "many generations ago" or even "many, many moons ago" (if "moon" is used as a general reference for time).

The concept of a secondary agent implied in <u>God ... announced by means of all the prophets</u> is not easy to translate in some languages. In some instances one can more satisfactorily render this as "God caused the prophets to announce" or in other instances "God put into the mouths of all the prophets." In still other cases the whole structure may be shifted, for example, "All the prophets announced because God told them to."

<u>He made it come true</u> (see Phillips "this was how his words came true") translates the literal statement, "he fulfilled it in this way" (see the comments at 1.16 where the same verb occurs). In other languages, however, this is normally a causative of occurrence, for example, "he made it to happen" or "he caused it to occur."

The phrase <u>in this way</u> may be rendered as "just as it did," such as "he caused it to happen just as it did."

In some languages, however, the causative must be related to some concept of "order" or "command," for example, "it happened just the way he had commanded it." This does not mean, in the language in question, that God specifically ordered people to behave as they did. It is simply that in such languages some expression for "commanding" is the way in which secondary agency is expressed.

3.19

The syntactic structure of verses 19 and 20 is somewhat complex. The clause <u>so that he will wipe away your sins</u> (v. 19b) is the direct purpose of "repenting and turning to God." There is, however, an additional purpose, namely, the content of verse 20 which is divided into two parts: (1) the coming of the times of spiritual strength and (2) the coming of Jesus as the Messiah. In a number of languages it is necessary to divide verses 19 and 20. Otherwise, the purpose expressed in verse 20 is dependent upon "the wiping away of sins." In reality, the two parts expressed in verse 20 are dependent upon the total experience represented by verse 19. In order to show the appropriate relation between these, the first part of verse 20 may repeat the repentance and turning to God expressed in verse 19, for example, "do that so that the times of spiritual strength may come ...."

The term <u>repent</u> should focus upon the significant change in one's attitude. This is here reinforced by the verb <u>turn to</u>. Under these circumstances <u>repent</u> can be related to the experience of <u>sin</u>, while the <u>turning</u> can be the positive response to God. Such a phrase can therefore be translated as "then repent from your sins and turn to God."

Due to the psychological factors involved in "repentance" a number of different idioms may be employed, for example, "turn your back on your sins," "give up your sins," or "change your heart about sin."

In a number of languages turn to God is rendered as "return to God." This does not presuppose that these people were formerly reconciled to God, but simply that being "with God" is regarded as the natural or appropriate relation which man should have with his creator, and therefore "return" seems to be a widespread usage.

So that he will wipe away your sins represents the Greek expression "so that your sins may be wiped away," but the Greek reflects a Semitic construction in which the subject of the passive voice is recognized as being God.

As noted also in other contexts, expressions for "forgiveness" are quite varied. Here wipe away is paralleled by a number of different expressions, for example, "erase your sins," "blot out your sins," or "cause your sins not to appear." On the other hand, some languages shift the focus to a state of "innocence," such as "cause you to be innocent" or "cause you to have no guilt."

3. 20

Both the background and the exact meaning of the expression times of spiritual strength are difficult to define. The word translated spiritual strength occurs only here in the New Testament and in the Septuagint (Exodus 8. 15). Its meaning is given as "breathing space, relaxation, relief." This expression does not appear in rabbinic literature, and as it stands is evidently not a Semitic idiom. However, most commentaries believe the phrase to mean those periods of refreshment during which God strengthens the human spirit.

In a number of languages times do not come. Rather, one can have "it will happen that" or as in this context, "so that you will have a time of rest" or "so that you will rest in your spirits."

A literal translation of "rest" can be badly misunderstood. Obviously this passage does not refer to physical rest but to "rest for your spirits." It is for that reason that an expression such as spiritual strength may be translated as "rest for your spirits" or "recuperation for your spirits."

Not only is it difficult to speak of "times coming" in some languages, but they certainly would not come from the Lord's presence. This is semantically almost impossible in most languages. Obviously the agent of this "coming" is the Lord himself. Therefore in some languages the structure must be altered so as to read "so that the Lord will send to you a time of renewing for your spirits."

Where it is necessary to make a distinction in the use of Lord when it refers to God or Jesus, it is certainly possible in verse 20a to employ "Lord God."

The second purpose to be accomplished through the repentance and turning to God is God's sending of Jesus. This may be made very clear in some languages by saying "Do this so that the Lord will send a time of renewal for your spirits and so that he will also send Jesus." The introduction of "also" is simply a way of indicating that there is a dual purpose.

It is possible to understand Messiah either as a title in apposition with the proper name Jesus (Jesus, who is the Messiah) or as a part of a proper name, Jesus Christ. Most translations have the former.

He has already chosen for you in the Greek is also a passive construction; but again it is obvious that God is the intended subject of the passive voice. Although the verb translated has already chosen may in itself simply mean "to choose" or "to appoint" without the idea of "beforehand" or "ahead of time" connected with it (see 22.14; 26.16, the only other places where this verb occurs in the New Testament), both the context and the tense of the verb suggest that here the idea is that of "choosing beforehand."

3.21

This verse concludes a sentence which began in the Greek with verse 19. The Greek clause "whom it is necessary for heaven to keep" is meaningfully rendered by the TEV he must remain in heaven.

The phrase until the time comes causes certain difficulties. An equivalent may be "until it happened that ..." or "until the time when all things are made new."

For all things to be made new is an expression which occurs only here in the New Testament (it translates a noun phrase, the verb form of which is rendered give ... back in 1.6), and offers the possibility of two different interpretations: (1) it may mean that God will bring about all the things that he had spoken through the prophets concerning the person of Jesus Christ or (2) it may be a reference to God's promise that he will make a restoration of the entire created order, as he had promised through his prophets (see "universal restoration" of the JB, NEB, Phillips). The fact that this word is used in the papyri for the renewal or repair of temples and public places tends to support the latter interpretation.

Rather than the passive expression be made new, it is often necessary to use a phrase denoting "becoming," for example, "until all things become new." In some languages the semantic structure is so shifted as to employ a phrase such as "there is a new becoming-time for all things" or "the time God makes all things new."

It may be useful to break the last clause of verse 21 into a separate sentence, for example, "This is just the way God announced it by means of his holy prophets of long ago." As noted in several other instances, announced by means of may be variously expressed as "caused his holy prophets to speak," "put the words into the prophets' mouths," or "caused the voices of the prophets to speak."

The term holy in this type of context indicates "those dedicated to him" or even "those who served him." The emphasis here is upon the prophets' relation to God, not upon any quality of taboo which they might have.

In the translation of the phrase of long ago it is important to avoid the suggestion of "mythological time." Some languages make a very clear distinction between "long ago" as referring to presumed historical events, and "long ago" when they mean mythological or even legendary events. It is important in this instance to maintain the historical perspective.

3.22

Verse 22 is an amplification of verse 21b, namely, the statement by ... his holy prophets. In this instance there is no causal relation as might be suggested by the word for. Rather, it may be necessary to indicate that the contents of verse 22 simply represent a specific instance of what has already been said. This can be effectively indicated by English "for," but a conjunction of cause would not do this in certain other languages. A closer equivalent in such languages would be "for example, it was Moses who said."

In some languages the so-called possessive your related to the phrase the Lord your God must be shifted from God to Lord, that is to say, "God your Lord." This is because people are regarded as related to Lord but they certainly are not thought of as in any possessive relationship to God. Even with Lord the possessive pronoun represents a semantic goal, for the Lord is "the one who commands the people."

"Like me" (TEV just as he sent me) may in this present passage be taken to refer either to the fact that God will send a prophet in the same way that he sent Moses, or to the fact that the one whom he sends will be a prophet just like Moses was a prophet. The TEV follows the first of these possibilities and gives the second as an alternative rendering.

The last clause of verse 22a who will be of your own people must in some languages be a separate sentence, since it should be attributive to prophet and not to the intervening phrase just as he sent me.

The phrase of your own people should refer to the "nation" and not merely to some family or clan. This means that the final clause of verse 22a might read "he will be one of your nation" or "he will be one of you," though in this instance the pronoun "you" must refer to the totality of the people and not to the specific group gathered to hear Peter.

You must listen to involves more than merely hearing. The implication is "you must obey" or "pay attention to all that he tells you," implying conformance in behavior.

3.23

In Greek this verse is a free rendering of what is said in Deuteronomy 18.19 and Leviticus 23.29. Anyone here is literally "every soul."

As noted in the previous verse, the implications of listen to here are essentially obedience or heeding, for example, "anyone who does not heed what the prophet says." In a number of languages referring to an individual in terms of a particular potential activity may be rendered as a condition, such as "if a person does not heed ...." Will be separated from God's people and destroyed renders the Greek "will be destroyed out from the people." The people referred to are God's people; and the preposition "out from" indicates

3. 24

that those persons who are to be put to death will be separated from God's people and then put to death.

In some languages this statement of excommunication in terms of separated from God's people is quite difficult in the passive voice since it might imply that God himself had excommunicated the individual. This problem is dealt with in some languages by saying "he must leave God's people" or "he will no longer be a part of God's people." This prevents the passage from being overly specific.

<u>3. 24</u>

Verse 24 has essentially the same position in the discourse structure as verse 22, which is itself an amplification of the general statement occurring in verse 21b.

The Greek phrase "from Samuel" means "from (the time of) Samuel"; and since it is obvious that Samuel is intended as one of the members of this group the TEV has translated including Samuel.

Since the expression the prophets is not designed to exclude Moses (mentioned in v. 22), it may be necessary to say "and the other prophets." The syntactic and semantic structure of the first part of verse 24 is awkward for there are two types of apposition following the prophets. First, there is the phrase including Samuel and those who came after him and, second, all of them who had a message. In some languages it is better to take the phrase including Samuel and those who came after him and place it at the end of verse 24, for example, "And the other prophets, that is, all of them who had a message, also announced these present days. These included Samuel and those who came after him."

The phrase those who came after him may be slightly restructured as "those who lived later than Samuel" or even "those who followed Samuel."

The clause all of them who had a message may seem rather obscure. The implication is that the message came from God, and it may be necessary to specify this in some instances, for example, "all the prophets who had a message from God" or, in a more direct form, "all the prophets whom God caused to speak."

The relation between announced and these present days in not easily represented in some languages. One may announce what is going to happen, or announce what has happened, but one does not "announce a day." Therefore it may be necessary to modify slightly the structure so as to read "also announced what would happen in these present days." This is a perfectly legitimate specification of components of the term "days," for here it represents not merely a temporal element but the feature of time at which certain important events took place.

<u>3. 25</u>

The first part of this verse may be literally rendered as "you are the sons of the prophets and of the covenant which God made with your ancestors."

But "sons of the prophets" and "sons of the covenant" reflect idiomatic Semitic usage and must be understood to mean those persons who will receive the promises that the prophets have made and will share in the covenant that has been agreed upon.

Though the TEV has attempted to render in modern English the meaning of the Semitic phrase "the sons of the prophets," the form the promises of God through his prophets are for you may involve certain difficulties in transfer, since the phrase for you goes directly with the event of promises. Therefore, if this can be shifted into a verbal form it may be more satisfactorily rendered as "through his prophets God made promises for your sakes" or "God caused his prophets to promise for your sakes." The phrase for you is obviously a benefactive, and the phrase through his prophets is a normal expression of secondary agency in Greek and English.

It may also be useful to say that "the covenant is for your sakes." This would then make it parallel with the promises. However, in order to relate the second part of verse 25a, one may require some minor shifts of relations, for example, "God made a covenant with your ancestors and it is for you," "the covenant God made with your ancestors is for your sakes," or "...applies to you."

An adequate term for covenant is extremely difficult in many languages since a receptor-language term so frequently implies a compromise agreement arising out of the procedures of bargaining. The covenant of the Old Testament, of course, was one which was initiated by God and accepted by the people. Moreover, it was the faithfulness of God which made the covenant valid. In some languages a term such as "pact" or "alliance" is perhaps the best equivalent which can be found. However, it may be important that some marginal note be employed or that an explanation be made in a glossary to indicate clearly certain unique features of the covenant as represented in the Old and New Testaments.

In some languages it may be necessary to specify "God" as the subject of the speaking in verse 25b.

Through your descendants translates "in your seed," a Jewish way of referring to one's descendants. In some languages a term for "descendants" is not as easy to render as one might think. In a number of instances it is equivalent to "lineage," in other cases it implies "clan," but always the focus is upon those who come from a particular ancestor. Sometimes a phrase is employed "those who will follow you" or "those whom you will cause to be born." In some instances one employs an idiom such as "from the children of your children." One may even have such an expression as "from your family vine" or "from the twigs of your family."

I will bless all the people on earth is a rendering of a passive construction in Greek (literally "all the people on the earth will be blessed"), in which God is the implied subject. The quotation in this verse is from Genesis 22.18 and agrees very closely both with the Hebrew and the Septuagint.

In translating bless some prefer an expression which implies simply verbal activity. Others contend that this "blessing" really refers to "causing good for." In this case there is a double causative, for example, "I will cause your descendants to cause good for all people on earth."

3.26

And so God chose and sent his Servant to you first literally translates "to you first of all God having raised up his Servant sent him." "Having raised up" is ambiguous; it may refer either to the resurrection of Jesus or to the sending of Jesus to earth. In verse 22 the same verb is used (there translated sent) of the sending of a prophet into the world; and inasmuch as this verse takes up the thought of verse 22 and uses the same word as is found in the quotation there, it seems most likely that the reference is to God's sending Jesus into the world rather than to his raising him from the dead. The TEV employs the verb chose, indicating it has something to do with the expression of God's purpose in sending his Servant.

In some languages it is difficult to employ single goals such as his Servant as the object of the verbs "choose and send." The action of "choosing" implies one person from among a number, and the "sending" can have only a single goal. Therefore in some languages it may be preferable to have "and so God chose Jesus as his Servant and sent him."

In a number of languages it is necessary to indicate clearly the meaning of first. Does it mean, for example, that the people were the first ones to whom he sent his Servant, or was this the first thing which God did, namely, to send his Servant? It is the first meaning which should be clearly indicated here, for the emphasis in Acts is upon the message going first to the Jews and then to the Gentiles.

In this particular context "blessing" is described as making all of you turn away from your wicked ways. This is therefore more than some mere verbal formula and can be translated in a number of languages as "caused good to you" or "caused you to be richly benefited." The final clause then specifies how this took place.

By making all of you turn away involves a causative expression which may be indicated clearly in some languages as "God caused good to you; he did this by causing you to turn away from your wicked ways."

The metaphorical usage of turn away from your wicked ways is paralleled in a number of languages, for example, "to turn from your wicked road," "to turn from the wicked road on which you are walking," or "to turn from the road on which you are walking so wickedly." In the same way that "righteousness" may be expressed as "to walk on God's road," so evil may often be described as "to walk on a wicked road," or simply "to do wicked deeds" or "to act evilly."

CHAPTER 4

This chapter introduces the basis for the first external difficulty faced by the church: persecution because of the teaching about Jesus, especially as it pertained to the resurrection. On the other hand, the following chapter describes the first internal problem faced by the early Christian community: the disruption of the Christian community by the selfishness of Ananias and Sapphira.

As noted in the analysis of discourse structure beginning in Chapter 3, the episode of Chapter 3 continues into Chapter 4 up to verse 22. The portion which occurs in Chapter 4 is divided essentially into four parts: (1) the events immediately following Peter's speech (vv. 1-4), (2) the events of the next day, including the introductory statement by Peter (vv. 5-12), (3) the argumentation back and forth within the Council (vv. 13-18), and (4) the answer of Peter and John, including the conclusion to the episode (vv. 19-22).

Peter and John before the Council

1 Peter and John were still speaking to the people when the priests, the officer in charge of the temple guards, and the Sadducees came to them. 2 They were annoyed because the two apostles were teaching the people that Jesus had risen from death, which proved that the dead will rise to life. 3 So they arrested them and put them in jail until the next day, since it was already late. 4 But many who heard the message believed; and the number of men came to about five thousand. (4.1-4)

The English section heading Peter and John before the Council is often unsatisfactory as a basis for transfer or adaptation into another language, since some type of event needs to be indicated. Merely to introduce a verb such as "to stand" or "to be in position" is likewise usually not successful. Therefore, one must frequently introduce some such expression as "Peter and John Defend Themselves before the Council," "Peter and John Are Brought before the Council," or "Peter and John Are Arrested and Accused before the Council."

The first section of Chapter 4 (vv. 1-4) has a narrative structure consisting of (1) the arrival of the officer of the temple guard and Sadducees, (2) their annoyance at the teaching of Peter and John, (3) the arrest, and (4) the response of the people. In addition there is a transitional element in the first verse and a conclusion in the fourth verse. The conclusion is stylistically important since it indicates the response of the crowd, which is not referred to subsequently in the episode.

4.1

Verse 1 of Chapter 4 consists of a transitional statement (the fact that Peter and John were still speaking to the people) and the arrival of those who were concerned about what was happening in the temple.

There is a problem with regard to the statement Peter and John were still speaking to the people, since this might imply in some languages that

89

Peter and John were both saying exactly the same thing, or that they were both speaking at the same time but saying something different. Since the preceding discourse has been attributed directly to Peter, some languages require some such statement as "Peter was still speaking to the people with John at his side" or "Peter, with John helping him, was still speaking to the people."

Though in the Greek text this transitional material is in a participial construction and the following clause is the independent clause, it is quite necessary in a number of instances to shift the structure of the Greek sentence and make the initial portion the independent sentence, while the second clause becomes the dependent portion. There are important stylistic reasons for this type of shift, for if the first clause began with "when," it would seem to imply that something was anticipated.

Some manuscripts read "chief priests" (see NEB) rather than priests. However, the word for "chief priest" occurs 122 times in the New Testament, while the word for "priest" is used only 31 times. Accordingly, it is more likely that a scribe would substitute the more frequently used word for the less frequent word. Moreover, the reading "chief priests" seems to be an attempt by a scribe to heighten the seriousness of the persecution.

A number of different expressions for priest are used in various languages. The important thing is that this be a term to designate a professional religious functionary. All so-called "world religions" have their priestly castes or groups. In so-called animistic societies there may, however, be difficulty in obtaining a satisfactory word for priest. In some instances the closest equivalent is the shaman or the medicine man. In other instances it may be important to have some type of descriptive phrase as "the one who sacrifices" or "the one who functions in the house of God."

The officer in charge of the temple guards was himself a priest and the highest officer in the temple, ranking second only to the High Priest. In many languages the equivalent of temple guards is simply the "policemen of the temple."

The Sadducees (mentioned also in 5.17 and 23.6,7,8) were a religious party among the Jews composed largely of priests. They were in some respects a very conservative group, and, as the text indicates, did not believe in the resurrection of the dead. For the term Sadducees it is essential that some type of transliteration be employed. However, a brief explanation of the sect of the Sadducees should be contained in a glossary.

In some languages great care is exercised in indicating the composition of a group. For example, if one says "the priests" and "the Sadducees" this would mean all the priests and all the Sadducees. One must, therefore, employ a type of partitive construction in some languages and say "some of the priests" and "some of the Sadducees."

4.2

The closest equivalent of they were annoyed is in many languages simply "they were angry" or "they did not like it."

Teaching the people that Jesus had risen from death, which proved that the dead will rise to life translates "teaching the people and proclaiming in Jesus the resurrection from the dead." The TEV, along with many commentaries and translations, treats the phrase "proclaiming in Jesus the resurrection from the dead" as meaning that they were using the case of Jesus' resurrection to prove that others would be raised from the dead (see JB "teaching the people the doctrine of the resurrection from the dead by proclaiming the resurrection of Jesus"; Zürich "they taught the people and proclaimed on the basis of the example of Jesus the resurrection from the dead").

The short expression in the Greek text "announcing in Jesus the resurrection from the dead" is justifiably expanded into two clauses in the TEV, for there are evidently two relations of Jesus to the resurrection. First, the fact that he himself rose from the dead, and second, the fact that this proved that people generally would rise from the dead. Since this was directly contradictory to the doctrine of the Sadducees, it is understandable that they would be "annoyed."

The passive expression had risen can be shifted into an active, for example, "God had raised Jesus from the dead," but one can also use a form which may omit an agent, such as "Jesus rose from among the dead."

Some languages may prefer to make a complete sentence of the last clause, for example, "This proved the dead would be raised to life" or "What happened to Jesus showed that the people who are dead would live again." At the same time one must be sure to avoid in an expression such as "live again" the notion of resuscitation.

As is so often the case with verbs of teaching or explaining, it may be necessary to put some of the content into the form of direct discourse, for example, "talked to the people and said, Jesus has risen from the dead." The relation between the two events of rising may be expressed as "saying, Jesus rose from the dead. Therefore people will rise from the dead."

4.3

A transitional item to show the conclusion or result of a previous situation is effectively expressed by so.

Since the process of arresting is so common all over the world, there are usually no problems involved. However, in some languages it is literally "they grabbed hold of them," "they tied them up," or "they surrounded them."

The institution of jails is likewise widespread in the world, but in some so-called primitive areas a number of interesting idioms are employed, for example, "the house of darkness," "the house of iron," or "the house with chains."

The clause since it was already late must, of course, refer to the time of day. This is expressed in a number of languages as "since the sun was already going down."

4.4

The contrast between the response of the priests and Sadducees, and the reaction of the people in the crowd, is such that a contrastive conjunction such as but is important.

It may be essential to elaborate somewhat on many, since this may need to be linked directly to the crowd, for example, "many of the people in the crowd."

Message is literally "word," but it is used here in the specialized sense of the Christian message, a meaning which it has in a number of places throughout Acts. However, in this context one may need to translate as "what Peter and John had preached."

Many languages require some goal to the term believed. The closest goal is the message, for example, "they believed it." On the other hand, it is also possible to employ a frequently recurring formula "they believed in Jesus."

The number of men came to about five thousand indicates that the total number of believers was now five thousand (see 2.41), not that an additional five thousand persons were added to the group, for example, "all the believers totaled five thousand" or "the number of believers became five thousand." It is impossible to say whether the term men includes women as well.

> 5 The next day the Jewish leaders, the elders, and the teachers of the Law gathered in Jerusalem. 6 They met with the High Priest Annas, and Caiaphas, and John, and Alexander, and the others who belonged to the High Priest's family. 7 They made the apostles stand before them and asked them, "How did you do this? What power do you have, or whose name did you use?"
> 8 Peter, full of the Holy Spirit, answered them, "Leaders of the people and elders: 9 if we are being questioned today about the good deed done to the lame man and how he was made well, 10 then you should all know, and all the people of Israel should know, that this man stands here before you completely well by the power of the name of Jesus Christ of Nazareth---whom you crucified and God raised from death. 11 Jesus is the one of whom the scripture says,
> 'The stone that you the builders despised
> turned out to be the most important stone.'
> 12 Salvation is to be found through him alone; for there is no one else in all the world, whose name God has given to men, by whom we can be saved." (4.5-12)

The discourse structure of this second section of Chapter 4 is relatively simple. The first two verses (5 and 6) provide the setting. Verse 7 consists of the challenge of the Jewish leaders to the apostles, and verses 8-12 represent the response of Peter. The response is essentially the same type of statement as occurred in Chapter 3: (1) the fact of the miracle, (2) the power of Jesus Christ in performing the miracle, (3) the witness of the Scriptures to Jesus Christ, and (4) the necessity of people to respond to this offered salvation.

4.5

In the Greek text the transition which marks this next episode is indicated by egeneto de (literally, "and it happened"). This is one of Luke's favorite devices for marking a transition in an episode. However, this is quite unnecessary to represent literally in English and the Greek temporal transition the next day is the most satisfactory way of indicating the sequence of events.

The Jewish leaders probably refers to the chief priests as the leading members of the Jewish Council. The elders were respected laymen, of advanced age, who exercised various political and religious functions, particularly as judges. The teachers of the Law were the official teachers and interpreters of the Jewish Scriptures, and not merely secretaries, as the usual translation "scribes" might suggest.

In most languages there is no difficulty involved in selecting three terms for leaders, elders, and teachers. In some so-called primitive societies, however, this may represent some difficulty. The "leaders" are those that have the political power. These consist of the chief and his immediate assistants. The "elders" are the older men who serve as his counselors. The teachers of the Law is rendered in some languages as "the specialists in the Law," implying a sort of professional status.

Since the reference to the Law is obviously to the Pentateuch, it is possible in some languages to add here "the Laws as given by Moses," or at least to use the plural form "the Laws," since in many languages a singular cannot be used as a general term to include a body of regulations.

In some languages it is not sufficient to say that these people gathered in Jerusalem. It is true that they had to come to Jerusalem, for some of them did not live within the city itself; but one must be somewhat more specific in certain instances, such as "came together in one place in Jerusalem."

4.6

Annas actually functioned as High Priest from A.D. 6-14, though he can be called the High Priest since it was customary for a man who had once held that position to maintain that title throughout life. Actually at this time Caiaphas, the son-in-law of Annas, was the High Priest, and held this office from A.D. 18-36. Nothing is known of John and Alexander, but it is possible that John was one of the sons of Annas who later became High Priest. Some manuscripts read "Jonathan" in place of John, and this text is followed by the NEB and the JB. The manuscript evidence is in favor of the reading John, and since the Jewish historian Josephus states that Jonathan, son of Annas, was appointed high priest in A.D. 36 in succession to Caiaphas, it appears likely that the reading "Jonathan" is an attempt by some scribe to make Luke conform.

4.7

One may render this passage as "they met with Annas, the High Priest" or "with Annas who was the High Priest," and show the relationship of the other persons to this event by repeating the verb "they also met with Caiaphas, and John, and Alexander, and others who belonged to the clan of the High Priest."

In very few languages can one use an attributive such as "high" to indicate superior rank. One must more often be spoken of as "the big priest" or "the great priest." In other instances he is "the boss of the priests" or "the one who controls the priests." In still other languages one can simply employ "the chief of the priests."

4.7

It seems to have been customary for the Jewish Council to have sat in a semicircle with the accused persons standing before them. Whatever the reason for the arrest, it becomes immediately evident that the concern of the Council is to learn by what authority the apostles performed the miracle on the lame man. Within the composition of Acts itself the question put to the disciples serves primarily as a literary technique for introducing another message by Peter. As given in the Greek, the emphatic element in the question is you; and in order to make this evident to the reader, the TEV has prefaced the questions regarding the power and the name with the question, How did you do this?

The expression they made the apostles stand before them is a causative of commanding and therefore in many languages it must be rendered as "they commanded the apostles, Stand before us." In some instances it may be necessary to identify the particular apostles concerned as "Peter and John."

In most languages there is no difficulty involved in having a multiple subject for a verb such as "asked." However, this is not possible in other languages and therefore one must say "one of them asked," since presumably only one person would be speaking on behalf of the others.

The question How did you do this? may need to be made somewhat more specific since the reference to the healing of the lame man is somewhat removed from this verse, for example, "How did you make the lame man well?" or "How did you make the lame man walk?"

In most instances a term such as power must either be qualified as belonging to some person or being of a particular character. Therefore, "By whose power did you do this?" or "By what kind of power did you do this?" In some languages, however, a term such as power as used in this more or less abstract sense, is not available. Therefore, one must translate "How is it you were able to do this?" "How were you strong enough to do this?" "Who made you able to do this?" or "Who made you strong enough to do this?" This type of reference to "strength" must, of course, be understood as being more than physical prowess.

The expression whose name did you use? must be made slightly more specific in some languages as "whose name did you pronounce when you did this?" or "whose name did you say when you healed the man?"

In many languages, however, the use of <u>name</u> has very little meaning, and therefore a more satisfactory equivalent is "by whose authority" or "who gave you the right."

4.8

<u>Full</u> translates a Greek verb tense that indicates it was at that very moment that Peter became filled with the Holy Spirit. This passage and others (see 2.14-21 and Luke 12.12) intimate that in Luke's thought the gift of the Holy Spirit was in a certain sense granted on specific occasions to carry out a particular task.

The filling of the Holy Spirit and the response of Peter may be regarded in many languages as two parallel but closely related events more or less equivalent to cause and effect, for example, "The Holy Spirit filled Peter's heart and therefore he answered them...."

In some languages it is extremely difficult to speak of being <u>full of the Holy Spirit</u>. The Holy Spirit "may possess completely," the Holy Spirit "may come into and command," but merely to be <u>full of the Holy Spirit</u> is not too meaningful. Moreover, even terms for filling sometimes distinguish between fullness as of a bucket, and fullness as of a sponge which is completely saturated with something. It is the latter term which is sometimes used for the filling of the Holy Spirit.

A vocative expression such as <u>leaders of the people and elders</u> presents certain problems in some languages, since one cannot use this type of direct address. Rather than seeming polite (as it is in the Greek text) it would be offensive, since one would seem to be calling to, or summoning, individuals. Therefore, such an expression must be made the goal of the preceding verb, for example, "answered the leaders of the people and elders." In other instances these individuals must be identified by a second person plural pronoun, "you who are the leaders of the people and elders."

4.9-10

In Greek the use of the conditional sentence introduced by <u>if</u> is very effective. However, in some languages this would be nonsense since there is absolutely no doubt as to the fact that Peter has just been asked how the lame man was made to walk. Therefore, this type of expression must be changed into a declarative, for example, "we are evidently being questioned today about...." Though in Greek the form is conditional, there is obviously no real condition implied---it is only a rhetorical device.

In the Greek text the use of the passive makes possible the elimination of a direct reference to the agent. In other languages, however, an active form may require the agent, for example, "you are evidently questioning us today about...."

<u>Questioned</u> translates a Greek word (see 12.19; 17.11; 24.8; 28.18) which suggests a judicial hearing.

In the phrase the good deed done to the lame man there is no reference to the agent. This may need to be supplied because of the passive form and the semantically redundant expression deed done. One may use "the good which we did for the lame man" or even "how we helped the lame man."

The passive expression in how he was made well may be shifted to an expression indicating change of state, for example, "how he became well."

Some type of transitional element at the beginning of verse 10 (see then in TEV) is very important. In some languages one may employ an expression such as "evidently" at the beginning of verse 9 and a corresponding "therefore" at the beginning of verse 10.

It should be noted that no reference has been made in the introduction to this section (vv. 5-7) of the presence of the man who has been healed. However, his presence is indicated in verse 10 and he is further mentioned in verse 14.

The instrumental relationship expressed by the power of the name of Jesus Christ of Nazareth may need to be expressed as a causative subject in some languages, for example, "the power of the name of Jesus Christ has caused this man to stand here before you completely well." In certain instances a distinction must be made between the healing and the standing, such as "the power of the name of Jesus Christ has healed this man and therefore he stands before you."

As has been noted in other contexts, the use of name as a substitute for the personality, or as a symbol of the personality, is not understood in some languages, and therefore the more satisfactory equivalent may be simply "the power of Jesus Christ."

The last clause whom you crucified and God raised from death must in many languages be expressed as a separate sentence with an emphatic identification of the subject, for example, "This is the one you crucified but whom God raised from death." In these two expressions the contrastive features may require some such conjunction as "but."

When there is no specific term for crucify, it may be important to employ some type of descriptive equivalent which will indicate both the execution and the means by which it was done, for example, "killed him by nailing him to a cross" or "put him on a cross and in this way killed him."

4.11

Jesus is the one (literally in Greek "this one is") represents the meaning "this (man) is." This interpretation is followed by a number of translations and commentaries. Others, however, understand the Greek to mean "this (stone) is." Of whom the scripture says is added by the TEV in order to clarify for its readers that Peter is referring to a passage of Scripture in what follows. The passage referred to comes from Psalm 118.22, and is also quoted in Matthew 21.42, Mark 12.10, and Luke 20.17, where it follows the Septuagint. Here the verse is not taken from the Septuagint and may represent an original translation from the Hebrew by Luke.

Without some type of identification of the direct quotation as coming from the Scriptures and as being applied specifically to Jesus, a good deal of confusion could arise in this verse. One could also use some such expression as "Jesus is the one about whom the Scripture is talking when it says." This makes it clear that the stone refers to "Jesus"—a relation which is quite clear in the original text.

An expression such as the stone that you the builders despised can be expressed in a number of ways, for example, "the stone you the builders put to one side" (in the sense of neglecting), "the stone you the builders neglected," or "the stone you the builders thought was no good."

An expression such as turned out to be may be rendered as "was found to be," "the builders discovered it was," or "it became."

The most important stone is literally "the head of the corner," a literal translation of which has no meaning at all. Some translators understand this to be a reference to the stone which held together the walls, that is, "the cornerstone," while others take it to be the final stone in the building which was placed over the entrance, a kind of "keystone." Whichever of these stones it may have been, the concern of Peter is to point out that it is "the most important stone" in the building.

In some instances translators have wanted to employ a different figure, for example, "the most important stake in the house," referring to the upright poles placed in the ground and forming the main "columns" for the construction of huts in tropical regions. However, in the Scriptures as a whole there are so many references to construction employing stone, for example, the many references to the temple, that it is generally wise to retain the figure of stone. Where necessary, of course, a marginal note may be employed to indicate something about the type of stone construction employed in the Middle East.

<u>4. 12</u>

Salvation, a word which can also mean "healing," represents a play on words that is difficult to reproduce in English: (Christian) salvation and/or the healing (of the lame man) are possible only through the name of Jesus. The strong double negative expression in the Greek text (not...in no one) is represented in the TEV by a positive (a completely legitimate equivalent), and one which forms a much more frequent basis for transfer into other languages. However, the use of a nominal construction such as salvation is to be found is difficult since normally salvation must be expressed by a verb, for example, "you can only be saved through him alone" or "he alone is able to save you." (See also 2. 21.)

As can be clearly seen, verse 12b is simply an elaboration of the statement in verse 12a, stated in a slightly different form.

In all the world literally translates "under the heaven." For some languages there is a problem involved in two relative clauses being attributive to such an expression as no one else in all the world. Moreover, these two relative clauses are not coordinate. The first is restrictive before the second. In some languages it means that the first restriction must be stated as a pre-posed clause, with the second restriction coming in the next clause, for example, "God has given his name to men and there is no one else in all the world by whom we can be saved."

Whose name God has given to men represents another one of the passive constructions in Greek in which God is the implicit subject, "name...which God has given to men."

By whom we can be saved is the meaning of the Greek expression "by whom (i.e. by which name) it is necessary for us to be saved" (see JB "by which we can be saved" and NEB "by which we may receive salvation"). The passive expression by whom we can be saved can be shifted to an active "who can save us."

> 13 The members of the Council were amazed to see how bold Peter and John were, and to learn that they were ordinary men of no education. They realized then that they had been companions of Jesus. 14 But there was nothing that they could say, because they saw the man who had been made well standing there with Peter and John. 15 So they told them to leave the Council room, and started discussing among themselves. 16 "What shall we do with these men?" they asked. "Everyone living in Jerusalem knows that this extraordinary miracle has been performed by them, and we cannot deny it. 17 But to keep this matter from spreading any further among the people, let us warn these men never again to speak to anyone in the name of Jesus." (4.13-17)

The discourse structure of this third section, verses 13-17, is relatively simple, since the subject throughout, except for certain portions of direct discourse, refers to the members of the Council. The sequence of events in verses 13-15 is without special difficulty since the linguistic and temporal orders are parallel. Beginning with verse 16 the direct discourse is likewise without particular complications.

4.13

The Council was the supreme religious court of the Jews; it was composed of seventy leading Jewish men and was presided over by the High Priest. Though the Greek text itself (which simply has "they") makes no specific reference to the Council, this is an important device in identifying the group of individuals who were meeting together to consult on this matter. A phrase such as "those who were consulting together" may be an appropriate way of identifying the various individuals brought together for this consultation.

Bold comes from a word which literally means "freedom of speech," and may indicate that the members of the Council were amazed at the boldness with which Peter and John had spoken in the name of Jesus. How bold Peter and John were can be expressed as "how Peter and John spoke without fear." In some languages this may be expressed idiomatically as "how they said every-thing" or "how they did not cover up anything."

The expression for <u>learn</u> must not imply either formal instruction or any outside information. This is something which the members of the Council deduced from the way in which Peter and John had spoken.

<u>Ordinary men of no education</u> translates two words, the first of which, "ordinary men," means a person who is not a specialist in a particular field; while the second, "of no education," means a person who is unschooled, and in the papyri even refers to one who cannot write. This latter term is taken by some translators to refer to a person who is untrained in the Jewish Law, though it is doubtful if that is the meaning in the present context. For the two words JB has "uneducated laymen," NEB "untrained laymen," and Goodspeed "uneducated, ordinary men."

Expressions for <u>ordinary men</u> vary widely in different languages, for example, "the little people," "those who do not count for much," "those who live at the edge of the village," and "those who did not command others."

Lack of formal education (in the rabbinical sense) is not so easily ex-pressed. In some situations this is expressed in rather unique ways, for ex-ample, "they did not know paper," "they could not instruct from books," or "they had not gone off to school."

The meaning of the Greek clause "they had been with Jesus" is <u>they had been companions</u>, that is, close friends, <u>of Jesus</u>. It is important to indicate that Peter and John had been with Jesus over a period of time. It is for that reason that the TEV has employed <u>companions of Jesus</u>. In other languages one may have "experienced living with Jesus," "associated with Jesus," or "followed along with Jesus for some time."

4. 14

The shift of viewpoint at the beginning of verse 14 is well indicated by a conjunction such as <u>but</u>. While one can always say something such as <u>there was nothing that they could say</u>, it is often possible to render the same type of expression in an idiomatic way, for example, "their mouths were shut," "there were no words for their voices," or "their thoughts gave them no words." The implication is that "they had nothing to say in response" or "... in return."

In the translation of this verse the Greek sentence order has been re-versed; in the Greek the emphatic element is "the man whom they saw stand-ing there with them," that is, with Peter and John. The last clause of verse 14 may be broken up into two parts, for example, "they saw the man who had been made well; he was standing there with Peter and John."

4. 15

Since verse 15 introduces a result of the Council's inability to make any formal accusations, some such transitional particle as <u>so</u> is helpful.

It may be necessary to identify <u>them</u> as referring directly to Peter and John and probably also to the man who had been healed.

99

4.16

Nothing is known regarding the location of the Council room where the Jewish Council met at that time.

A term for discussing must not suggest "arguing" but rather "conferring." Evidently all the persons involved were joined in trying to find a practical solution to the problem.

4.16

The reference to these men must identify Peter and John. There is, of course, no implication that an accusation is brought against the man who was healed. It may, therefore, be necessary to say "What shall we do with these men Peter and John?"

Since, however, these individuals were actually not asking anyone else for advice, it may be necessary to translate "They were asking one another."

Inasmuch as the following direct discourse is not a question, or even an answer to the question, it may be necessary to introduce a further statement of speaking, for example, "They were saying to one another." The Greek text has an introductory participle of "speaking."

Extraordinary miracle (see also NEB "notable miracle") is literally "a well-known (or notable) sign"; but it is clear that the Greek word traditionally translated "sign" (see 2.19) in the present context indicates a "miracle." The phrase this extraordinary miracle may be rendered as "this great miracle" or "this marvelous thing."

The passive construction in has been performed by them can, of course, be shifted into the active, for example, "Peter and John have done this great miracle."

An expression for we cannot deny it can be "we cannot say it did not happen" or "we cannot say, They did not do it."

4.17

Since the contents of verse 17 contrast abruptly with the contents of verse 16, a conjunction such as but, "on the other hand," or "on the contrary" may be useful.

In a number of languages the purpose of an activity always follows that event. In such cases, it would mean that the first clause in verse 17 (in the TEV) must be placed at the end of the verse.

In many languages one cannot speak of a matter spreading. Rather, one must say "in order that more people will not hear about it."

The equivalent of a hortatory such as let us warn is in many languages an obligatory mode, for example, "we must warn" or "it is necessary that we warn." There is, of course, nothing permissive in the use of the form let in English.

The last part of verse 17 must frequently be expressed as direct discourse, "we must warn them, You must never again speak to anyone using the name of Jesus." (See also 4.21.)

In the name of Jesus is literally "upon (the basis of) this name." The name referred to is that of Jesus, and the Greek preposition "upon (the basis of)" is equivalent in meaning to "in."

> 18 So they called them back in and told them that under no condition were they to speak or to teach in the name of Jesus. 19 But Peter and John answered them, "You yourselves judge which is right in God's sight, to obey you or to obey God. 20 For we cannot stop speaking of what we ourselves have seen and heard." 21 The Council warned them even more strongly, and then set them free. They could find no reason for punishing them, because the people were all praising God for what had happened. 22 The man on whom this miracle of healing had been performed was over forty years old. (4.18-22)

This final section to the episode of the healing of the lame man consists essentially of four conclusions: (1) the conclusion of what was recommended in verse 17, (2) the statement of Peter and John (vv. 19 and 20), (3) the conclusion of the Council (v. 21), and (4) a summary statement on the man who was healed (v. 22), which links the story to its beginning (see 3.2). It should be noted that though Luke did not specifically say what happened to the lame man at the time of the Council's deliberation, he has not forgotten to make final mention of the lame man at the end of the episode. This is an important characteristic of well-structured discourse.

4.18

The importance of the command for the disciples no longer to speak or to teach in the name of Jesus is that it now gives the legal basis for the further persecution recorded in the next chapter.

The contents of verse 18 are a conclusion to what has been recommended in verse 17 (hence the transitional particle so) and a transition to the following paragraph.

Inasmuch as the pronoun them in this context refers specifically to Peter and John, it is perhaps necessary to specify these individuals. Otherwise some may understand this to include the man who was healed. From the standpoint of the discourse structure, this is a somewhat awkward situation in that the lame man has been dropped from the episode without specific mention of what happened to him.

Many languages require the substance of what was told to Peter and John to be expressed in direct discourse, for example, "told them, In no way are you to speak or teach using the name of Jesus."

Though the term name certainly figures prominently in this type of context, it may be necessary in some instances to translate as "you must under no circumstances speak or teach about Jesus."

4.19

The contents of verse 19 are in contrast with verse 18; therefore it is appropriately introduced by a conjunction such as but.

Since a coordinated subject such as Peter and John might imply that both were talking at the same time, some languages require "Peter together with John" or "Peter spoke; John was with him."

The imperative expression in you yourselves judge must often be rendered as an obligatory "you yourselves must judge," or "it is necessary that you yourselves judge."

The expression which is right in God's sight is equivalent in some languages to "which God says is right" or "which God thinks is right."

The final expression to obey you or to obey God is an implied question and must be rendered as a question in some languages, for example, "Shall we obey you or shall we obey God?"

4.20

A phrase such as cannot stop speaking is equivalent in some languages to "we must continue speaking." In other instances it is equivalent to "there can be no end to our speaking" or "our speaking will not finish."

What we ourselves have seen and heard refers to the deeds and words of Jesus, especially to his resurrection.

4.21

This verse gives the two reasons why the Council decided to release the apostles: (1) there were no legal grounds for arrest, and (2) the Council was afraid of the people who had witnessed this miracle.

Warned them even more strongly is an intensive form of the verb used also in verse 17; in both instances the verbs may mean something even stronger than warn; they may mean "threaten." A term such as "warn" is rather general and must be expressed in somewhat more concrete ways in some languages, for example, "threatened them with punishment," "said, We will punish you," or "said strongly, You will suffer."

An expression such as set them free is rendered quite literally in some languages as "untied them" or "let them go out the door."

The expression find no reason is sometimes rather radically restructured, for example, "they could not say, This is why we will punish them." In other instances this expression may be restructured as "they could not justify punishing them" or "they could not give an answer to people who said, Why are you punishing them?" In some languages a term for punish is literally "to cause to suffer."

An expression for praising God may need to be expressed as direct discourse since it implies speaking, for example, "they said, What has happened shows that God is wonderful."

Though the Greek text has <u>gar</u> (literally "because" but often signifying only a general connection in thought), there is no direct causal relationship between verse 22 and the preceding statement. The fact that the man was over forty years of age simply enhances the significance of the miracle. Accordingly, in many languages one cannot translate by a causal conjunction meaning "for."

The expression <u>the man on whom this miracle of healing had been performed</u> presents a number of difficulties for transfer into other languages. Accordingly, one sometimes finds "the man who was healed in this miraculous way," "the man who experienced healing by a miracle," or "the man whom a miracle made well."

The phrase <u>over forty years old</u> is variously expressed in different languages, for example, "he had lived more than forty years" or "his years were more than forty." In languages in which there is a poorly developed numerical system (as, for example, in the languages of the primitive tribes in South America), one can express relative age in terms of the time of life, for example, "he was no longer the age of a warrior" or even "he was so old that his children would be men." (This does not, of course, imply that the man had children, but simply that if he had had children, they would already be adults.)

The Believers Pray for Boldness

23 As soon as they were set free, Peter and John returned to their group and told them what the chief priests and the elders had said. 24 When they heard it, they all joined together in prayer to God: "Master and Creator of heaven, earth, and sea, and all that is in them! 25 By means of the Holy Spirit you spoke through our ancestor David, your servant, when he said,

'Why were the Gentiles furious;
    why did the peoples plot in vain?
26 The kings of the earth prepared themselves,
    and the rulers met together
    against the Lord and his Messiah.'

27 For indeed Herod and Pontius Pilate met together in this city with the Gentiles and the people of Israel against Jesus, your holy Servant, whom you made Messiah. 28 They gathered to do everything that you, by your power and will, had already decided would take place. 29 And now, Lord, take notice of the threats they made and allow us, your servants, to speak your message with all boldness. 30 Stretch out your hand to heal, and grant that wonders and miracles may be performed through the name of your holy Servant Jesus."

31 When they finished praying, the place where they were meeting was shaken. They were all filled with the Holy Spirit and began to speak God's message with boldness. (4.23-31)

103

The discourse unit, verses 23-31, focuses upon prayer in the Christian community. It is introduced by a transitional sentence (v. 23) which provides the setting for the following section. The first part of verse 24 introduces the theme of prayer, and from verse 24b through verse 30 there is a presumed summary of the prayer of the community of believers.

The structure of this prayer is of interest, consisting as it does of the following parts: (1) an invocation to God, with certain of his attributes indicated, (2) a reference to Old Testament Scriptures (vv. 25 and 26), (3) a recounting of historical events (vv. 27 and 28), and (4) a request for boldness and the power to perform miracles (vv. 29 and 30). Verse 31, which consists of a separate paragraph, indicates a transition from the state of prayer to the filling of the Holy Spirit and the proclamation of the message as an answer to the prayer that has just been uttered.

Within this context the section heading The Believers Pray for Boldness is fully intelligible in English. However, it may require certain modifications when transferred into another language, such as "The Believers Pray to God to Help Them to Speak without Fear." In some instances it may be somewhat better to express primarily the thanksgiving of these prayers, for example, "The Believers Give Thanks to God" or even "The Believers Pray to God."

4.23

The clause as soon as they were set free is purely transitional, in order to link what follows to what precedes.

To their group translates the phrase "to their own (people)," that is, to those who were believers. "To their friends," used in several translations, is not explicit enough to define the meaning of the group to which the disciples returned.

What the chief priests and the elders had said refers to the threats in verses 17 and 21. The chief priests are simply "the leaders of the priests" or "those who command the priests."

4.24

The expression joined together in prayer is rendered in some languages as "prayed to God with one heart" or "joined their words as they prayed to God."

The direct address to God must in some languages be represented as "You who are Master and Creator of heaven...."

Master translates a word which may also mean "Lord" or "Sovereign." The word appears only here in Acts, and Luke uses it elsewhere only in 2.29 of his Gospel. In the New Testament it occurs also in 2 Peter 2.1; Jude 4; and Revelation 6.10. It means essentially the same thing as the word customarily translated "Lord." An equivalent of Master is simply "Lord" in the sense of "one who controls or rules over." The phrase Creator of heaven, earth, and sea, and all that is in them reflects the wording of Exodus 20.11. A term for Creator may be simply "you who made."

The reference here to heaven is not the abode of God so much as the celestial universe, which in many languages is simply "the sky."

The phrase all that is in them may be taken as a reference to "all that live in them," that is, to the plants, animals, and men who dwell in these three areas.

A term for sea should, if at all possible, include any body of water. From the standpoint of the Hebrew usage this would be either salt water or fresh water. This means that in so..ne instances where specifically different words are used it may be necessary to employ "oceans and lakes." Otherwise, by omitting one term, one might imply that God had created only certain bodies of water.

4.25a

The Greek text underlying the translation of by means of the Holy Spirit you spoke through our ancestor David, your servant is not strictly grammatical nor entirely clear. In the textual commentary prepared by the UBS committee on the Greek text there is a detailed discussion of the grammatical and theological problems involved. But since most translations interpret the Greek text in essentially the same manner that the TEV has done, no further discussion of the problem will be given here, except to mention that the textual committee considered this reading closer to what the author wrote than any of the other possibilities represented by the various manuscripts. For a different interpretation of the text, and for one which follows a slight emendation, see Moffatt: "who (that is, God) said to our fathers by the holy Spirit through the lips of thy servant David."

In verse 25a the semantic problems are acute because of the statement of instrument by means of the Holy Spirit and of secondary agency through our ancestor David. These problems become compounded with the appositional expression your servant and by the two verbs of speaking, one relating to God and the other to David. The TEV has very effectively brought all of these together, but in many languages one cannot reproduce this type of coalesced utterance. A restructured form which may be useful for transfer into other languages may be "You caused our ancestor David to speak. He was your servant and the Holy Spirit inspired him when he said ...." In some instances, to speak through another individual is represented as "you gave him the words to speak" and therefore one might say "By means of the Holy Spirit you gave our ancestor David, your servant, the words to speak when he said ...."

The expression ancestor may be rendered as "our father of long ago," "our father many generations ago," or even "our great father."

Since the immediately following expressions are questions rather than statements, it may be necessary to change the verb of speaking to one of "asking."

4. 25

<u>4. 25b-26</u>

    The biblical quotation in these verses comes from Psalm 2.1-2 and follows the Septuagint. In the original context of Psalm 2 "his Messiah" was the king whom God had chosen for the people of Israel; in the present context <u>his Messiah</u>, of course, is Jesus.

    A term for <u>Gentiles</u> may be expressed as "those who are not Jews" or simply "non-Jews." In some languages one must employ "the other nations" or "the other tribes." Sometimes "otherness" is more effectively rendered as "different," therefore "the different people."

    A term for <u>furious</u> is often "exceedingly angry," or idiomatically "their faces got very hot" or "their hearts were burning." An expression for <u>plot in vain</u> is difficult to express without some type of goal. Therefore, in some languages it is necessary to add the goal from the end of verse 26, "plot against the Lord, but their plans will not succeed," or "they make plans against the Lord, but they will not be able to carry them out."

    The expression <u>the peoples</u> must be equivalent to <u>the Gentiles</u>. As such it may sometimes be rendered as "the different peoples." If, however, there is no way in which <u>Gentiles</u> can be referred to with two different phrases, a pronoun can be used in this last clause of verse 25, thus indicating that there is no real difference between <u>the Gentiles</u> and <u>the peoples</u>.

    The phrase <u>the kings of the earth</u> must in many languages be "the rulers of the earth," since the earth is substantially the location in which they rule— not the fact that they rule over the earth. On the other hand, if this is to be taken as "the kings of the lands," then lands can be a semantic goal of the ruling.

    The phrase <u>prepared themselves</u> is equivalent to "got themselves ready to fight."

    The first two lines of verse 26 are complete parallels in which <u>kings</u> and <u>rulers</u> are the subjects, while <u>prepared themselves</u> and <u>met together</u> constitute the parallel activities. The goal in each instance is <u>the Lord and his Messiah</u>. Therefore, this goal must be meaningfully attached to <u>prepared themselves</u> "against" and <u>met together against</u>, that is, "met together to fight."

    In this particular context the expression <u>the Lord</u> may need to be specified as "the Lord God," so that the relationship of this to <u>Messiah</u> may be meaningful.

    The phrase <u>his Messiah</u> may be translated in some languages as "the one whom he has specially chosen" or "the one whom he has designated." Rarely can the concept of "anointing" be carried across.

<u>4. 27</u>

    Since verse 27 is presumed to be an explanation of the meaning of verses 25b and 26, it can rightly begin with the transitional phrase <u>for indeed</u>. The conjunction <u>for</u> indicates the causal relationship, and <u>indeed</u> emphasizes the reality of what has just been announced in the previous verse. In some languages this is equivalent to "because in just this way" or "because that is just how it happened."

As may be readily noted, the order of elements in the Greek sentence is rather radically altered in the TEV structure. However, this modified order of semantic units makes possible a much more readily transferable set of relationships.

Peter interprets every aspect of Psalm 2.1-2 to apply explicitly to Jesus: Herod (see Luke 23.6-12) represents the kings of the earth, Pontius Pilate stands for the rulers, the Gentiles are most likely the Roman soldiers, and the people are the people of Israel.

In a number of languages all participants in such a meeting together must be related in a so-called "subject position," for example, "Herod and Pontius Pilate, together with the Gentiles and the people of Israel, met together."

Note that the expression in this city is merely locative and its position may be altered depending upon the treatment of the receptor language.

The multiple concepts expressed in met together...against may require two different verbs, for example, "met together and plotted against." In English the preposition "against" implies more than mere positional relationship, and therefore in such a context some event word of "plotting," "planning," or "antagonism" needs to be introduced.

For your holy Servant see 3.13. Whom you made Messiah properly translates the expression "whom you anointed" (see NEB "whom thou didst anoint as Messiah"; and Barclay "whom you anointed as Messiah").

The appositional expression your holy Servant is parallel to the clause whom you made Messiah. In some languages these may be treated as parallel relative clauses "who is your holy Servant" and "whom you made Messiah."

It is not always easy to qualify Servant by the attributive holy, particularly if the latter is expressed as some kind of event, with an implied relationship, for example, "one who is dedicated to." Therefore, one may be obliged to have "who is dedicated to you and who serves you." Under these circumstances the final clause may need to be expressed as a closely associated but separate clause, such as "this is the one you caused to be the Messiah" or "you designated as Messiah."

4.28

Your power translates "your hand"; "the hand of God" is a biblical phrase which signifies "the power or might of God," especially as seen in his mighty acts of salvation.

The statement of the principal event "gathering together" and its purpose to do everything that...had already decided is not difficult to combine in most languages. What complicates the picture is the addition of the phrase by your power and will. This explanation of the means, or as some might interpret it the attendant circumstances, may need to be expressed as a separate clause.

4.29

The first clause can be rendered as "they came together to do exactly what already had been decided would happen." The parenthetical expression can then be rendered as "you could decide it this way because of your power and will." An even fuller statement of this might be "you could decide exactly what would happen because you had the strength and because this is the way you wanted it." It is difficult to know in all instances whether Greek boulē should be rendered "wanted it," as a close translation of "will," or whether the concept is closer to "design" or "plan," in which case one could translate "because you had planned it this way."

<u>4.29</u>

The transitional phrase <u>and now</u> shifts the attention from the historical event to the circumstances faced by the believers, for example, "but as for now" or "but as for our circumstances." The expression <u>take notice of</u> may be rendered as "listen to." The phrase <u>the threats they made</u> may be rendered in some languages as "how they have threatened us" or "how they have said, You will suffer."

The expression <u>allow us</u> is not really a request for permission. It is far more a prayer for the strength to be able to do something, for example, "make it possible for us to speak" or "give us the strength to speak." The words <u>us, your servants</u> are equivalent in many languages to "we who serve you."

<u>To speak your message</u> translates an expression that has become a technical term for the early Christian missionary preaching. It is literally "to speak the word," and may be accompanied by a variety of modifiers, such as "of God" (see v. 31), "of the Lord," or "of the Good News," that is, the good news about Jesus.

As in other contexts, an expression such as <u>with all boldness</u> can be rendered as either "without fear" or as "speaking everything plainly."

<u>4.30</u>

<u>Stretch out your hand</u> is in the Greek a subordinate clause dependent upon the main verb phrases <u>take notice of the threats</u> and <u>allow us ... to speak</u> (v. 29). It may be related to the main verbs as temporal "while you are stretching out your hand," or as instrumental "by means of stretching out your hand." However, it is also possible to do as the TEV has done and to understand this verb and the following verb, <u>grant</u>, as an extension of the imperative content of the main verb. If the passage is understood in this fashion, then there are four requests made on the part of the disciples: <u>take notice of the threats</u>, <u>allow us ... to speak your message</u>, <u>stretch out your hand</u>, and <u>grant that wonders and miracles may be performed</u>.

The phrase <u>stretch out your hand</u> is in many languages quite meaningless. A nonfigurative equivalent in some languages is "show your power," "make people see your strength," or "cause people to see that you are strong."

The verb to heal must frequently have some goal, for example, "to heal people" or "to cause people to become well." The causative implied in grant...may be performed may be restructured as a straightforward causative in a number of languages, such as "caused wonders and miracles to happen" or "...to be performed."

Whenever two terms such as wonders and miracles or "signs and wonders" can be employed, this is, of course, preferable. However, in some languages there is simply no way of designating two different types of miracles, and in this context there is no special emphasis upon the distinctive varieties. Therefore, in some languages it is simply "great miracles," since the two terms tend merely to reinforce one another rather than to provide distinctions between types of events.

The passive construction may be performed may be equivalent in some languages to "happen." In other languages an agent, such as "we," may be introduced, for example, "so that we may perform wonders and miracles."

If one retains the use of the word name, it is possible in this type of context to use the phrase "using the name of your holy Servant Jesus." Where the use of name is misleading, this expression may be equivalent to "by the power of your holy Servant Jesus."

4.31

When they finished praying (see NEB "when they had ended their prayer") correctly translates the meaning of the Greek verb tense. The meeting place was shaken after they had finished praying, not while they were praying. The shaking of the meeting place (an indication that God had answered their prayers) and the filling with the Holy Spirit are most probably intended to be interpreted as simultaneous actions.

Rather than employ a passive was shaken with an ambiguous agent, it may be more satisfactory to use an intransitive such as "shook" or even "moved as in an earthquake."

The passive expression they were all filled with the Holy Spirit can be rendered as "the Holy Spirit filled them all" or "the Holy Spirit came into all of them." In some languages, however, the relationship of the Holy Spirit to the people must be one of "possession" or "commanding." (See 1.8.)

Again Luke indicates that in his thinking the filling with the Holy Spirit is something which takes place on specific occasions in order to empower people to do a particular task. In this case, as in the earlier instances, the Holy Spirit enables them to speak God's message with boldness.

The TEV has tried to capture the flavor of the Greek verb tense by stating they began to speak, which apparently is the meaning in the context. Although some few understand the speaking in this present passage to be that of ecstatic speech, this is quite unlikely, inasmuch as the phrase used here, speak God's message, along with several related phrases (see speak your message, v. 29), appear in the New Testament as technical terms for preaching the Christian message.

The phrase <u>God's message</u> would certainly seem to be, especially in this type of context, "the message that comes from God," or in a more analytical form "they began to speak what God had told them to say."

An expression for <u>boldness</u> should reflect the usage in verse 29 in which the people had prayed for <u>boldness</u>.

All Things Together

32 The group of believers was one in mind and heart. No one said that any of his belongings was his own, but they all shared with one another everything they had. 33 With great power the apostles gave witness of the resurrection of the Lord Jesus, and God poured rich blessings on them all. 34 There was no one in the group who was in need. Those who owned fields or houses would sell them, bring the money received from the sale 35 and turn it over to the apostles; and the money was distributed to each one according to his need.

36 And so it was that Joseph, a Levite born in Cyprus, whom the apostles called Barnabas (which means "One who Encourages"), 37 sold a field he owned, brought the money, and turned it over to the apostles. (4.32-37)

The English section heading <u>All Things Together</u> is effective, but in many languages this would be quite obscure, for it could be understood to mean "all things piled together." The meaning of this is better conveyed in some languages as "The Believers Own Everything Together," "The Believers Share Their Possessions," or "The Believers Give to One Another as Needed."

At this point the narrative is interrupted and the stories about Barnabas and Ananias are introduced. The narrative continues again, beginning in 5.12.

This final section of Chapter 4 consists of two parts. The first (vv. 32-35) gives a description of the way in which the believers shared their possessions. The second (vv. 36-37) not only serves to indicate a specific example of this sharing, but also introduces Barnabas whose role becomes important at a later point. The mention of what Barnabas did also sets the stage for the following episode involving Ananias and Sapphira.

Within the first paragraph of this section is a general statement (v. 32a) followed by specific characterizations of how the believers were <u>one in mind and heart</u>. This is a typical so-called "expository text," with imbedded narrative to be found in verses 34b and 35.

4.32

The word translated <u>group</u> is used in the book of Acts in two senses: (1) a crowd or a large group of persons, (2) a religious community, whether Jewish or Christian. Here it is used in the specific sense of the entire Christian community. The phrase <u>the group of believers</u> is equivalent in many languages to "all the believers." This does not specifically introduce the idea of "the community," but by the use of "all" and their joint activity, the component of community is implied.

One in mind and heart is literally "one in heart and soul." In Jewish thought "heart" was the center of intellectual activity, and "soul" the seat of the will. Taken together they are inclusive of the total inner being of the person. The expression one in mind and heart may be expressed verbally as "they thought the same things and they wanted the same things." When, however, the idiomatic formula can be preserved it is preferable, for example, "they were just like one person in their mind and heart" or "they had only one mind and heart."

They all shared with one another everything they had seems to be the meaning of the literal statement "they had all things in common." The context suggests that the believers continued to possess their own personal belongings (see v. 32b), and that even when someone sold a piece of property the money remained his own (see 5.4). See also the earlier discussion at 2.44.

The first clause of verse 32b must frequently be expressed as direct discourse, for example, "No one said, What I own belongs just to me" or "No one said, All I have is just for me."

The adversative element between the two clauses of verse 32b is strong and therefore the introduction of a conjunction such as but is important.

In some languages it is not possible to use the plural they. Rather, one must use a singular to identify the fact that each individual on his own initiative shared, for example, "each person shared with each other person anything which he had."

4.33

The first phrase with great power probably typifies not only the activity of the apostles but also the effect of their witness upon the people. This may be rendered in some languages as "in a powerful way" or "by showing great power." In other languages this may be equivalent to "very strongly."

A nominalized expression such as gave witness of the resurrection of the Lord Jesus may need to be shifted into a verbal form in a number of languages, for example, "witnessed that the Lord Jesus had risen from the dead," or in the form of direct discourse "announced to the people, The Lord Jesus has risen from the dead."

In the expression "great grace was upon them all" the grace referred to is probably God's grace; for this reason the TEV has translated God poured rich blessings on them all. On the other hand, if the reference is to the attitude of the people toward the believers, the translation of the NEB may be followed: "they were all held in high esteem" (see also JB "they were all given great respect").

The expression poured rich blessings is quite figurative, though it may not seem to be so in English. In many languages it must be rather radically altered, for example, "God showed great favor to them all," "God was exceedingly good to them all," or "God blessed them all very much."

4.34-35

The verb tenses in these two verses are such as to suggest continued or repeated action on the part of the Christian community: whenever the believers would sell a field or a house they would bring the money they received and "place it at the feet of the apostles," that is, they turned the money over to (the authority of) the apostles (see 4.37 and 5.2). Then the money would be distributed by the apostles to each one according to his need.

It is generally impossible to employ the idiom "placed it at the feet of the apostles," since it might not imply entrusting it to their care. It is also important to be careful in the choice of a word for "give," since this might indicate that it was merely a gift to the apostles rather than something entrusted to them to be used for the believers. In some instances this must be made specific, for example, "gave it to the apostles for the believers."

The agents of was distributed were the apostles. Therefore, in the active form one can have "the apostles distributed the money to each one as that person had need."

4.36-37

Verses 36 and 37 constitute a particular instance of the immediately preceding generalized statement of the behavior of people in the believing community. At the same time these verses serve as an introduction to Barnabas and as a transition to the following story. It is, therefore, essential that this brief section be carefully structured so as to fulfill these important requirements in the discourse.

And so it was that translates a particle which Luke uses to indicate a transition in a narrative. It is rendered variously in different translations: "for instance" (NEB), "it was at this time" (Phillips), "there was a" (JB), and it is not translated at all by Goodspeed.

A transition in a number of languages is "and so it happened that" or "and so it was with Joseph."

One who Encourages is literally "a son of encouragement"; but the Semitic phrase "son of" is used to indicate the qualities or characteristics which distinguish a person. Evidently Barnabas had the gift for encouraging his fellow Christians (see 11.23 where a verb is used which comes from the same stem as this noun: he [Barnabas] was glad and urged [that is, "encouraged"] them all to be faithful...).

The heavy set of attributives to Joseph requires in many languages a series of closely related, complete sentences. He was not only a Levite, but he was born in Cyprus; the apostles called him Barnabas and, in addition, there is an explanation of what this name meant. In some languages such a series could be translated as "And so it happened with Joseph. This man was a Levite born in Cyprus. The apostles gave him the name Barnabas. (In their language the name meant 'he is the One who Encourages'.)" It is understood, of course, that the term <u>Levite</u> will be explained in a glossary and that a map will be published with a translation of any book such as Acts so that people can identify where Cyprus is. In some languages a classifier such as "island" can be added to the term <u>Cyprus,</u> so as to give people some idea as to what this geographical proper name refers.

CHAPTER 5

The first part of Chapter 5 consists of the story of Ananias and Sapphira (vv. 1-11). In a sense this portion belongs to the last of Acts 4 in which the church is described as having all things together. The story of Ananias and Sapphira adds emphasis and contrast to this joint holding of property and the sharing of resources.

The second section of this chapter, concerning Miracles and Wonders (vv. 12-16), is a somewhat natural transition, since already in the story of Ananias and Sapphira there has been a miracle which attracted a great deal of attention. Having discussed the miracles and wonders and the very favorable reaction of the people, it is not strange, therefore, that the next section introduces persecution (vv. 17-42). But despite this persecution, the church continues its ministry and keeps on growing, thus giving rise to the need expressed in Chapter 6 for The Seven Helpers.

For the most part the transition between the principal sections of Acts 5 is not difficult since the content itself helps to show the relationships. The translator, however, must make certain that the connections are not obscured by faulty handling of the initial sentences in each section. These will be noted below.

Ananias and Sapphira

1 But there was a man named Ananias, whose wife was named Sapphira. He sold some property that belonged to them, 2 but kept part of the money for himself, as his wife knew, and turned the rest over to the apostles. 3 Peter said to him, "Ananias, why did you let Satan take control of your heart and make you lie to the Holy Spirit by keeping part of the money you received for the property? 4 Before you sold the property it belonged to you, and after you sold it the money was yours. Why, then, did you decide in your heart that you would do such a thing? You have not lied to men---you have lied to God!" 5 As soon as Ananias heard this he fell down dead; and all who heard about it were filled with fear. 6 The young men came in, wrapped up his body, took him out, and buried him. (5.1-6)

The section heading Ananias and Sapphira is probably all that is required in most languages. However, in some instances it may be advisable to employ "The Story about Ananias and Sapphira."

This first paragraph of Chapter 5 is a narrative text, with included direct discourse. The important discourse feature of this paragraph is the contrast between this story and what has preceded. In English this contrast is effectively shown by the introductory but. In some languages, however, it may be necessary to employ a more amplified contrastive expression, somewhat equivalent to "in contrast with this" or "but it was not always this way."

5.1

The Greek text introduces Ananias as the subject of the verb sold, but the introductory particle tis ("a certain") indicates clearly that this is someone previously unidentified in the discourse. In English the most satisfactory way of handling this type of reference is to place the name in the predicate position with a kind of "dummy subject" using there. It is for this reason that the TEV has there was a man named Ananias. The manner in which unidentified participants are introduced into a story differs from language to language. It is therefore very important that one make the necessary adaptations.

The phrase named Ananias must frequently be translated as "people called him Ananias" or "his name was Ananias." As in the case of all such proper names, terms such as Ananias and Sapphira should be adjusted in form so as to make them most easily pronounceable in terms of the system of the receptor languages. These two names, however, normally represent relatively minor difficulties.

The term for property in verse 1 is different from the term translated property in verse 3. The term in verse 1 is a very general term for any kind of possession, while in verse 3 the reference is directly to a "field."

It is important to indicate clearly in this verse that Sapphira participated in this deal, not only as one who knew about it (as specified in v. 2), but as one who shared in the possession. Though Ananias is the one who sold the property, Sapphira obviously participated in the sale as one who shared in the possession (note the TEV rendering).

5.2

The phrase kept part . . . for himself translates a verb which appears in two other places in the New Testament, Acts 5.3 and Titus 2.10. This verb is also used in the Septuagint in the story of Achan (Joshua 7.1), and it is tempting to see a parallel between this account and the story of Achan. In Hellenistic Greek this verb is commonly used of money taken secretly from a quantity belonging to a group of people.

Though the Greek text literally says "laid it at the apostles' feet," it is frequently more satisfactory to translate simply "turned it over to the apostles" or "gave it to the apostles." A literal translation of the Greek idiom could be, and often is, badly misunderstood.

The phrase as his wife knew can sometimes be translated by a separate clause "his wife knew all about it."

5.3

Peter, who acts as the spokesman for the Christian community (a position clearly described in previous chapters) now speaks to Ananias. Since, however, what he says is in the form of a question, it is necessary in some languages to translate "asked him."

The phrase take control of is literally "fill," but such a figurative meaning of "fill" is extremely difficult to render in many languages. It is particularly difficult to use with the expression heart. Therefore in some languages this phrase is translated as "brought your mind to." In other languages "Satan entered your heart so that you."

The term heart must be rendered by some expression which indicates thought with strongly emotional content. In some languages this is the liver, in other languages the stomach. It is, however, more than just thinking. There must be the implication of desire as well.

In verse 3 the object of the Greek verb translated lie is in the accusative case, while the objects of the same verb in verse 4 are in the dative case. However, it is very unlikely that Luke wishes to make any distinction at this point. These are only alternative grammatical usages.

The phrase the money you received for the property can be translated "the money you received when you sold the property."

5.4

The first sentence of this verse in Greek is in the form of a question which suggests the answer "yes." However, it is not easy to have two questions in a row, the first implying an affirmative answer and the second being neutral. This is why in the TEV the first question has been shifted to a statement. However, if in a particular receptor language the question expecting an affirmative answer is more effective, this first sentence should certainly be employed in the form corresponding most closely to the Greek expression.

The phrase the money was yours translates a Greek expression "was in your power." In some languages this is rendered as "you could say what you wanted to do with it" or "you could do anything you wanted."

Decide in your heart (see also Luke 21.14) is literally "place on your heart," an expression which occurs in the Septuagint (1 Samuel 21.13; 29.10; Jeremiah 12.11).

5.5

In some languages the expression fell down dead is rendered as "died and fell down," since it is the dying which causes the falling.

All who heard about it refers to people other than those who were present and saw what happened. Most probably the reference is to Christians and non-Christians alike.

5.6

Young men seems merely to be a statement regarding the age of the men rather than a description of their precise status or function in the Jerusalem church. In a number of languages young men may be translated by a term designating unmarried men. This is probably the closest functional equivalent. Came in translates the Semitic expression "getting up" and is merely a way of speaking of the initiation of an action; it does not imply that the young men were either sitting or lying down, though most translations render the expression something like "got up." Wrapped up (with a shroud for burial) is employed by most translations, though no one is at all certain as to the exact meaning of this word.

A receptor-language term for bury may have certain local denotations which need to be avoided. For example, in some languages the closest equivalent is "burn the body." In other cultures it may specify placing the body on a special platform for putrefaction. It is preferable, therefore, to try to represent the biblical pattern of burial which means "place the body in the ground" or "place the body in a tomb." Since there are so many references to burial in the Bible, it is important to represent carefully the ancient customs in a consistent manner.

> 7 About three hours later his wife came in, but she did not know what had happened. 8 Peter said to her, "Tell me, was this the full amount you and your husband received for your property?"
>
> "Yes," she answered, "the full amount."
>
> 9 So Peter said to her, "Why did you and your husband decide to put the Lord's Spirit to the test? The men who buried your husband are at the door right now, and they will carry you out too!" 10 At once she fell down at his feet and died. The young men came in and saw that she was dead, so they carried her out and buried her beside her husband. 11 The whole church and all the others who heard of this were filled with great fear. (5.7-11)

This second section of Chapter 5 begins with a temporal transition about three hours later and ends with a conclusion (v. 11) to the account as a whole. The internal structure of the section is quite simple, since all the events are in historical order and the participants clearly marked.

5.7

There is a subtle difficulty in the rendering of came in since the previous paragraph does not specify where the apostles were at the time that Ananias presented the money and died. In some languages it is necessary to make the indication of place quite specific and therefore must sometimes be rendered as "came into the room where Peter was" or "came to the place where Peter was."

Such a general phrase as what had happened must often be made more specific, for example, "what had happened to her husband" or "that Ananias had died."

5.8

The Greek plural verb form "you received" is made explicit in the TEV translation by you and your husband received.

5.9

The Greek expression translated in the KJV as "for so much" is extremely difficult to render satisfactorily in a literal manner. It is for this reason that the TEV has employed was this the full amount. In some languages the term this must be amplified as "this much money" or even "this money here."

5.9

Put the Lord's Spirit to the test means, as the commentators point out, that Ananias and Sapphira had put the Spirit to the test by seeing if they could get away with their scheme. In the phrase Lord's Spirit, Lord presumably stands for God (see v. 3 Holy Spirit; v. 4 God; and here Lord's Spirit). It is important in rendering the word decide to specify that both Ananias and Sapphira had joined together in the decision.

It is obviously necessary to avoid the traditional rendering "tempt the Spirit of the Lord," for there is no implication of "tempting to sin" but of "testing." Even the term test is not easily employed, for in a sense Ananias and Sapphira were not trying to determine the qualities of the Lord's Spirit but were attempting to see what they could get by with. In some languages this particular process must be described rather specifically, for example, "decided if you could lie to the Lord's Spirit and not suffer punishment" or "decided to see whether you thought you could deceive the Lord's Spirit and not suffer."

Right now translates a frequently used particle of emphasis, literally "behold."

5.10

The phrase she fell down at his feet can mean in some languages "to implore" or to "ask a great favor of." In this context, however, she collapsed in death, or, as in some languages, "died and fell down in front of him."

In this verse the Greek term translated young men is not the same word as occurs in verse 6; and came in represents a different Greek expression from the corresponding term in verse 6. This may or may not suggest that the same persons were referred to in both instances; but in either case it supports the earlier judgment that the phrase young men is not a technical term for a church office or function.

5.11

This is the first time in the book of Acts where the word church appears. Although the word is used in a variety of ways throughout the book of Acts, it is used in the present passage as a technical term for the description of the Christian community in Jerusalem.

In many languages there are serious problems in finding an adequate term for church. Too often the term simply identifies a building, and certainly in the New Testament its primary reference should be to the group of believers. It is for this reason that in a number of languages church in this context is translated as "gathering of believers" or "the group of believers," or even as in some instances "all those believing in Christ."

It is not known who all the others are. It is possible that they are all the others in the Christian community as contrasted with the apostles. It is also possible that all the others could refer to anyone who heard this account. In any event, a translation should be so constructed as to include others but not necessarily exclude any particular group.

The expression were filled with great fear poses certain problems in many languages since one cannot be filled with...fear. One can, however, "fear very much," "have great fear," or "great fear can possess one."

Miracles and Wonders

12 Many miracles and wonders were being performed among the people by the apostles. All the believers met together in a group in Solomon's Porch. 13 Nobody outside the group dared join them, even though the people spoke highly of them. 14 But more and more people were added to the group—a crowd of men and women who believed in the Lord. 15 As a result of what the apostles were doing, the sick people were carried out in the streets and placed on beds and mats so that, when Peter walked by, at least his shadow might fall on some of them. 16 And crowds of people came in from the towns around Jerusalem, bringing their sick and those who had evil spirits in them; and they were all healed. (5.12-16)

In some languages it may be necessary to employ a complete clause for the title, for example, "The Apostles Perform Miracles and Wonders" or "Miracles and Wonders Happen."

As noted in the introduction to this chapter, verses 12-16 form a type of summary to the preceding chapters in that the activity of the church is described in considerable detail and the results of the ministry of the apostles are pointed out. This paragraph also serves to introduce the persecution which follows.

There is an important unity to this paragraph, even though the connections between the individual sentences are not always clearly indicated. The paragraph begins with a mention of miracles and wonders, then calls attention to Peter's special role, and concludes with a more general statement about healing. For the translator the principal discourse problem is the proper identification of the participants, for these shift frequently, for example, people, apostles, believers (v. 12); group (vv. 12 and 13); people, group, crowd (v. 14); apostles, people, Peter, some of them (v. 15); and crowds, people, evil spirits (v. 16). Whether in each instance these participants should be identified by nouns or pronouns will depend upon the structure of the receptor language.

5.12

Miracles and wonders reflects the same Greek expression which appears
in 2.19. A number of languages require a somewhat different expression for
"performing miracles," and in many instances it is useful to employ an active
rather than a passive construction, for example, "the apostles caused many
miracles and wonders to happen." In other languages one must "show miracles
and wonders" or even "cause them to be seen."

Some languages require a goal to the term believers, for example, "believers in Jesus."

Together in a group is the same word which is translated by NEB,
Phillips, JB as "by common consent"; for the meaning of this word see 1.14.
The emphasis upon unity in the expression together in a group is rendered in
some languages as "united just as though one person." In other languages,
"together like a single family."

5.13

It is not known exactly who nobody outside the group (literally "none of
the others") may be, though the TEV (see also NEB) understands them to be
the non-Christian group. This conclusion receives support both from the context and from the observation that earlier (Luke 8.10) Luke changed the
Markan Greek phrase "to those outside" (Mark 4.11) to "to the others." There
are certain complications in the phrase nobody...dared join them. This
might imply that no one other than the believers could become a believer.
This is obviously not true since in verse 14 Luke indicates clearly that more
and more people were becoming Christians. Accordingly, in some languages
this first clause in verse 13 may be translated as "nobody who was not a believer dared to pretend to be a believer when he was not." On the other hand,
this clause may refer to the fact that the believers met separately from other
people and therefore could be rendered as "nobody who was not a believer sat
with them."

The connective even though may be rendered in some languages by an
expression equivalent to "nevertheless." The logical connection between the
two clauses is not easy to represent accurately.

The people spoke highly of them is rendered in many languages as "the
people spoke well of them" or "the people said the believers were good."

In some instances, however, the expression the people must be more
definitely identified, either by using "the nonbelievers" or "the people in
Jerusalem" (as a designation of people in general in the area rather than the
believers specifically).

5.14

The Greek phrase "to/in the Lord" makes possible two different interpretations of this verse: (1) it may mean "believers in the Lord joined their
group" (so TEV, Moffatt, Goodspeed, NEB) or else (2) it may mean "believers were added to the Lord" (so RSV, JB).

The use of a dash in verse 14 makes the second part a kind of parenthetical explanation of the term group. This is, however, very difficult to
render literally in some languages. The closest equivalent is often "there
were so many men and women...." Though the Greek expression rendered
as were added is passive, thus suggesting that the agent may be God himself,
most translations omit the specific addition of the agent and therefore employ
a phrase such as "joined themselves to" or "became a part of." This latter
expression has the advantage of not indicating specifically whose initiative
was involved.

5.15

As a result of what the apostles were doing translates one Greek word
meaning "so that." However, it is most likely that verses 12b-14 are to be
understood as a parenthetical statement, and that "so that" in this verse refers back to the first part of verse 12. A number of commentators understand
the connection in this fashion, and some translators have made this relationship explicit (see JB, Goodspeed, Moffatt). On the other hand, there are some
who think that the result clause should be connected with the description of the
high regard in which the Christians were held (as mentioned in v. 13).

In some languages the transitional clause (the first clause in the TEV
rendering) can be rendered as "because of all that was happening" or "because
of the miracles which the apostles were doing" (making the reference specifically to v. 12a).

If there is any distinction made between the words beds and mats, it
is that the second of these terms refers to a poor man's bed or mattress.
Luke does not state explicitly that the people over whom Peter's shadow passed
were healed, but he writes in such a fashion as to make this clearly implicit
in the text. Nor does he make clear who carried out the sick persons, though
it is thought by a number of commentators that the non-Christian community
is intended.

If the agent of carried out must be specified, then one can employ a
phrase such as "the people there" or even "many people," with the resulting
active rendering "the people there carried members of their family who were
sick out in the streets...." It is to be assumed that those who carried people
out in the streets would be at least members of the same household.

The expression his shadow might fall on some of them can be rendered
in some languages as "his shadow might touch some of them" or "his shadow
might pass over them."

5.16

The phrase crowds of people is a reference primarily to the great number of people. Therefore in many languages "many people" or "very, very
many people" might be used.

A term for towns must distinguish smaller communities from the large
city of Jerusalem. In some contexts, therefore, a word for town will be more

or less equivalent to "village." It is the relative size, not the specific number of people, which is significant in this type of context.

The phrase bringing their sick will probably need to be translated in many languages as "carrying their sick." The manner of bringing those with evil spirits may need to be contrasted as "and leading those who had evil spirits in them."

In many languages evil spirits do not live in people but "control them" or "command them." Those who had evil spirits in them literally translates "those who were being troubled by unclean spirits." But in biblical terminology "evil spirits" and "unclean spirits" are essentially synonymous. There are, however, serious difficulties encountered in employing an adjective such as "unclean," for this can turn out to be simply "dirty." Quite naturally the emphasis in the Bible is on the fact that these spirits caused people to become unclean in a religious sense, that is, they defiled them, so that they could not worship God.

The passive expression they were all healed may be transformed into an active as "they all got well" or "none was any longer sick."

The Apostles Persecuted

17 Then the High Priest and all his companions, members of the local party of the Sadducees, became extremely jealous of the apostles; so they decided to take action. 18 They arrested the apostles and placed them in the public jail. 19 But that night an angel of the Lord opened the prison gates, led the apostles out, and said to them, 20 "Go and stand in the temple, and tell the people all about this new life." 21 The apostles obeyed, and at dawn they entered the temple and started teaching.

(5.17-21a)

The section heading The Apostles Persecuted must in some languages be changed into an active expression, for example, "The Jewish Leaders Persecuted the Apostles" or "The Apostles Suffer."

This account regarding the persecution of the apostles reminds one of the earlier account given in Chapter 4. The present narrative falls into four principal sections: (1) the arrest, imprisonment, and miraculous release of the apostles (vv. 17-21a); (2) the discovery of the escape and the rearrest (vv. 22-26); (3) the apostles before the Council and Peter's statement to the Council (vv. 27-32); and (4) the advice of Gamaliel and the subsequent release of the apostles (vv. 33-42).

It is interesting to note that in each of the principal paragraphs of this final section, verses 17-42, the High Priest and his associates in the Council are the first participants indicated, and they are the ones who constantly take the initiative for what happens.

5.17

In Greek, verses 17 and 18 comprise one sentence that begins with the word translated in the KJV as "rose up." This is the same word that is used in verse 6 and does not indicate whether the High Priest was sitting or lying down before he got up. It is used simply to indicate the initiation of an action, and is translated by the TEV so they decided to take action (see NEB "...were goaded into action"). In many languages High Priest is rendered as "the big priest," "the chief of the priests," or "the priest who commands the other priests."

His companions are "his henchmen" or, as in some languages, "his helpers" or "his followers." (See also 5.21b.)

The appositional phrase members of the local party of the Sadducees must be clearly marked as apposition in some languages, for example, "his followers, that is to say, the members of the local party of the Sadducees" or "his followers who were part of the local group of the Sadducees."

In translating party it is useful to employ a term which designates primarily a political group, not a religious group, for in this context the emphasis is upon the political role of the Sadducees.

In the phrase the local party of the Sadducees, local translates a Greek participial construction which is taken by commentators to mean "what is current in time or local in place." Similar constructions are also found in 11.22 and 13.1.

It is interesting that throughout the book of Acts the Pharisees, who were representative of the heart of Judaism, are presented as generally favorable toward the Christian movement, whereas the Sadducees are strongly opposed to the Christian community.

In many languages jealous is expressed by an idiomatic phrase, for example, "their hearts burned" or "their livers were yellow." In some instances, however, one must employ a rather full description of precisely what was involved, such as "they were not happy because everybody liked the apostles" or "they were unhappy because the apostles were doing so much."

The verb take action must sometimes specify the goal, particularly when some kind of opposition is involved, for example, "to take action against the apostles" or "to make the apostles suffer."

5.18

Arrested represents the same phrase (literally "lay hands on") as appears in 4.3. Public jail (or "common jail") is the translation accepted by most, though it is possible that the phrase may be taken to mean "they publicly put them in custody." Three other times this phrase occurs in the New Testament (without being joined with the word "jail") and each time it has an adverbial force and is translated something like "in public" (see 16.37; 18.28; 20.20).

In a number of languages the equivalent of "common" is "jail where bad people are kept." This contrasts with jails for political prisoners.

5.19

Angel of the Lord is a phrase which appears frequently in the Septuagint, and many times refers to a manifestation of the Lord himself. In the book of Acts, however, it refers to an angel whom the Lord has sent (see 8.26; 12.7, 11; and "angel of God" 10.3; 27.23). The rendering of opened is frequently "caused the prison gates to open." In many languages, however, one must speak of "doors" rather than "gates."

The term led can be rendered "led by the hand" or "caused to go out."

5.20

The term stand is not primarily a reference to a particular body position, but where the apostles are to be. In some languages this is equivalent to "go into the temple."

Tell the people all about this new life (see also JB, Goodspeed, Phillips) literally translates "tell the people all the words (or things) of this life."

The reference to the people must be made somewhat more specific in some languages as "the people there."

In the context the meaning of this ... life is the Christian life, therefore the basis for translating the phrase new life. The phrase this new life is difficult to translate in many languages since life is not a noun but a verb. Therefore, the phrase may be rendered as "this new way" or "this new way of living." In some languages new is equivalent to "different," for example, "this different kind of way to live."

5.21

The apostles obeyed is literally "when they heard," but "to hear" in this context obviously means "to obey." In translating they entered ... started teaching the TEV brings out the contrast between the Greek tenses; the second of these verbs is a Greek imperfect, and here probably indicates the beginning of an action. A goal of the verb obey is an angel, hence "obeyed the angel."

> 21b The High Priest and his companions called together all the Jewish elders for a full meeting of the Council; then they sent orders to the prison to have the apostles brought before them. 22 But when the officials arrived, they did not find the apostles in prison; so they returned to the Council and reported, 23 "When we arrived at the jail we found it locked up tight and all the guards on watch at the gates; but when we opened the gates we did not find anyone inside!" 24 When the officer in charge of the temple guards and the chief priests heard this, they wondered what had happened to the apostles. 25 Then a man came in who said to them, "Listen! The men you put in prison are standing in the temple teaching the people!" 26 So the officer went off with his men and brought the apostles back. They did not use force, however, because they were afraid that the people might stone them. (5.21b-26)

5.21b

The last part of verse 21 actually begins with a participle that has been rendered as a finite verb in a number of translations (see, for example, RSV "came"; NEB "arrived"). It is possible, also, to take this participle as a Lukan stylistic device indicating a transition in the discourse, and so a redundant feature in English. The TEV understands it as conveying no new information, and has taken it merely as a transition, which has been indicated by the introduction of a new paragraph.

"Those with him" is translated his companions (TEV), "his colleagues" (NEB), "his supporters" (JB), and "his allies" (Phillips). The expression itself is a rather loose term, and may mean any group sharing together in a common undertaking.

"The Council and all the council of elders of the sons of Israel" represents a literal translation of the Greek which has been rendered by the TEV all the Jewish elders for a full meeting of the Council. It is generally assumed that the two terms used here by Luke (that is, "Council" and "council of the elders") are synonyms, the latter term simply explaining the former. It is best either to translate as the TEV has done, or else to translate something like "a meeting of the Council, that is, of the full Jewish senate" (see NEB, Barclay, JB).

The Jewish elders simply identifies those persons who constituted the Council. In some societies these are the "advisers." In other instances elders may be translated as "the old men" or "the wise men."

The final clause of verse 21 is somewhat complex from the standpoint of participants and causal relationships. In some languages these must be made more explicit, for example, "they sent men (or officials) to the prison to tell the guards to bring the apostles to the Council."

5.22

The officials (see 13.5) are either officers of the Jewish Council or Levites of the temple guard under the officer in charge of the temple guards (see v. 24). In some languages the term officials is equivalent to "policemen." In other instances the closest equivalent is "soldiers."

To the Council has been added to the verb they returned in order to indicate to what place they returned.

The verb reported may be rendered as "said to the men in the Council."

5.23

When we arrived at the jail is implicit in the Greek text and the TEV has made this information explicit. Most translators prefer to render without a transitional (NEB "we found the jail securely locked").

The phrase found it locked up tight may require some slight modification since in some languages one does not "lock a jail," but rather one "locks the doors of the jail"; therefore, "found the doors securely locked."

5.24

The clause <u>all the guards on watch at the gates</u> is equivalent in many languages to "all the soldiers carefully guarding the doors."

There is a potential problem in the phrase <u>did not find anyone inside</u>. This could be interpreted to mean that the angel of the Lord led out not only the apostles but all of the criminals in the jail. Some translators have therefore preferred to render this as "did not find either of the apostles inside." Note that in verse 24 the concern is only for the apostles who had apparently escaped.

5.24

The <u>officer in charge of the temple guards</u> is the same term used in 4.1. <u>They wondered what had happened to the apostles</u> is one possible meaning of the difficult Greek expression in this verse. Goodspeed ("they were very much at a loss as to what would come of it") and JB ("they wondered what this could mean") are two other possible translations of this somewhat puzzling expression.

5.25

The location indicated by <u>in</u> must be made more specific in some languages, for example, "into the Council" or "where the leaders were gathered together."

The particle translated <u>listen</u> may have the force of "at this very moment" (see JB). It is the same particle that the TEV translates <u>right now</u> in 5.9 and <u>suddenly</u> in 1.10.

The reference to <u>standing</u> is again not so much a designation of posture as one of location.

In some languages the relationship between <u>standing</u> and <u>teaching</u> is expressed by two closely combined clauses: "they are in the temple; they are teaching the people."

5.26

The <u>officer</u> is the same word used in verse 24, <u>the officer in charge of the temple guards</u>.

Many languages are quite specific in the use of terms such as <u>brought ...back</u>. In this context a rendering may be "caused them to return with them" or "commanded them to return with them." The text clearly states that no physical force was used.

In order to indicate clearly that <u>they did not use force</u>, one may say in some languages "they did not grab them" or "they did not tie them up." In other languages a common expression is "they did not beat them."

It is important that in the final clause the goal of the stoning is the officer and the soldiers, not the apostles.

27 They brought the apostles in and made them stand before the Council, and the High Priest questioned them. 28 "We gave you strict orders not to teach in the name of this man," he said; "but see what you have done! You have spread your teaching all over Jerusalem, and you want to make us responsible for his death!"

29 Peter and the other apostles answered back, "We must obey God, not men. 30 The God of our fathers raised Jesus from death, after you had killed him by nailing him to a cross. 31 God raised him to his right side as Leader and Savior, to give to the people of Israel the opportunity to repent and have their sins forgiven. 32 We are witnesses to these things—we and the Holy Spirit, who is God's gift to those who obey him." (5.27-32)

This section consists of an introduction, followed by an accusation and a defense. It is particularly important that the defense of Peter be clearly marked as a response to the accusation. This is done in English by answered back, but in some languages it is important to begin verse 29 with some contrastive statement, for example, "but in response" or "as a rebuttal to what the High Priest had said, Peter...."

5.27

In view of the paragraph break beginning with verse 27 it may be necessary to specify who they are, that is, "the officer and the guards."

Brought...in may be rendered as "caused them to go in where the Council was meeting." It is frequently necessary to specify the place when an adverbial form such as in is used.

The term questioned must be altered in a number of languages since what follows is not a question but an accusation.

5.28

A Semitic idiom ("with an order we ordered you") lies behind the translation we gave you strict orders; and the verb "order" is used in a technical sense in the papyri of a summons to court or a court injunction.

The phrase teach in the name of this man is difficult to render in some languages. One equivalent is "teach the people on the authority of this man" or "teach the people on the authority of Jesus" (since "this man" may be misleading). In other languages the closest equivalent is "teach what this man taught," since this may be the only way in which the authority of the original teacher can be indicated clearly. In still other instances one may use "teach what this man said should be taught."

But see what you have done translates the same particle as used in verse 25 above.

In some languages spread your teaching is an impossible combination, therefore an equivalent such as "cause people all over Jerusalem to hear your teaching" may be employed.

5.29

You want to make us responsible for his death is literally "you want to bring on us the blood of this man," which is simply a Semitic way of saying exactly what the TEV has said in English. This clause may be expressed in other languages as "you want to blame us because he died" or "you want to say, You caused him to die."

5.29

Peter and the other apostles is in Greek "Peter and the apostles," but a literal translation might imply that Peter was not an apostle.

A term for answered must indicate that this is not answering a question but replying to an accusation.

In many languages obey is rendered as "do what we are told (by God) to do."

The ellipsis implied in not men may need to be filled out, for example, "we are not obligated to do what men tell us to do."

5.30

The account of Peter's message as given in these verses has much in common with that in 3.13 ff.; not all the ideas are the same, but much of the wording is similar.

The so-called possessive relationship in the God of our fathers must be rather radically restructured in many languages, for example, "the God whom our fathers worshiped" or "the God whom our ancestors worshiped." The equivalent of fathers may be "grandfathers," "those of long ago," or "our grandfathers who died long ago."

From death has been added to the verb raised in order to make explicit that the resurrection is referred to, though it is possible that the reference is to the bringing of Jesus into the world (see 3.26). The context, however, seems to favor the interpretation given by the TEV, since there follows immediately the affirmation that these people had been the ones responsible for killing Jesus.

The expression raised ... from death cannot be literally translated in many languages. The equivalent may be "cause to get up from death," "cause to come back from having died," or "caused to live again."

Nailing him to a cross is in Greek "by hanging him on a tree" and recalls the language of Deuteronomy 21.22. It should be noted, however, that the passage in Deuteronomy refers to the custom of hanging the dead body of an executed criminal on a tree, not to the Roman method of execution by crucifixion.

Some languages may require some specific mention of the place of the nailing, therefore "nailed his hands and feet to a cross."

5.31

For a translation of to his right side see 2.33. The important element in this idiom is, of course, the place of honor.

128

The closest equivalent of <u>Leader</u> is in many languages "chief" or "one who commands."

The subject of the verb <u>to give</u> is the same one who is <u>Leader and Savior</u>. In some languages it is necessary to employ a purpose clause and this may be conveniently done with a passive construction since the reference to forgiveness is likewise in passive form, for example, "in order that the people of Israel might be given an opportunity to repent and have their sins forgiven." In some languages the expression of <u>opportunity</u> is most closely paralleled by a phrase such as "be able to."

If the forgiveness of sins must be expressed in an active form, then obviously it is "God who forgives."

5.32

The phrase <u>witnesses to these things</u> may be expressed as "those who tell what has happened" or even "those who tell what God has done."

To emphasize the joint witness of both the apostles and the Holy Spirit, it may be necessary to employ an expression such as "the Holy Spirit also tells" or "the Holy Spirit also shows."

The pronoun <u>him</u> in the phrase <u>obey him</u> refers, of course, to God.

33 When the members of the Council heard this they were so furious that they decided to have the apostles put to death. 34 But one of them, a Pharisee named Gamaliel, a teacher of the Law who was highly respected by all the people, stood up in the Council. He ordered the apostles to be taken out, 35 and then said to the Council, "Men of Israel, be careful what you are about to do to these men. 36 Some time ago Theudas appeared, claiming that he was somebody great; and about four hundred men joined him. But he was killed, all his followers were scattered, and his movement died out. 37 After this, Judas the Galilean appeared during the time of the census; he also drew a crowd after him, but he also was killed and all his followers were scattered. 38 And so in this case now, I tell you, do not take any action against these men. Leave them alone, because if this plan and work of theirs is a man-made thing, it will disappear; 39 but if it comes from God you cannot possibly defeat them. You could find yourselves fighting against God!"

The Council followed Gamaliel's advice. 40 They called the apostles in, had them whipped, and ordered them never again to speak in the name of Jesus; and then they set them free. 41 The apostles left the Council, full of joy that God had considered them worthy to suffer disgrace for the name of Jesus. 42 And every day in the temple and in people's homes they continued to teach and preach the Good News about Jesus the Messiah. (5.33-42)

These two paragraphs are very well organized, and there should be no difficulty except for possible confusion in the speech of Gamaliel, which is included within this passage from verse 35 through the first part of verse 39.

5.33

If a format is used which requires special paragraphing for such included direct discourse, this may be a distinct advantage. Note, however, that within Gamaliel's speech there are three clearly marked temporal transitions: some time ago (v. 36), after this (v. 37), and and so in this case now (v. 38). These temporal markers must be made perfectly clear.

Verse 42 serves not only as a summary of this account of the imprisonment, but serves to reemphasize the function of the church in teaching and preaching both in the temple as well as in people's homes.

5.33

Members of the Council and the apostles have been substituted in place of the pronouns "they"..."them" in order to make the pronominal referents explicit (see, for example, JB "this so infuriated them that they wanted to put them to death"). They were so furious translates a verb which appears only here and in 7.54 in the New Testament; it literally means "to saw through," and is used in both passages in Acts in a figurative sense.

5.34

The Pharisees were the largest, most important, and most influential religious group of the Jews; they were very faithful in their observation of the Law of Moses. Gamaliel, mentioned here and in 22.3, is Gamaliel I, a noted and respected Jewish teacher. The expression highly respected by all the people may be rendered in some languages as "all the people thought he was very great" or "all the people honored him very much."

Ordered the apostles to be taken out may be shifted into an active form "ordered the guards to lead the apostles out."

The Greek includes an adverb with the verb phrase to be taken out. Although the adverb may mean either "a little distance" or "a little while," most translations follow the latter interpretation. In 27.28 the TEV renders this same adverb by a little later.

5.35

The Council replaces the pronoun "them," and serves to make clear to the reader that Gamaliel is addressing the Council and not the apostles.

Since Gamaliel is also a member of the Council, it may be necessary to employ an expression such as "fellow-men of Israel."

A translation of be careful may be rendered in a number of ways—for example, "think again," "be concerned about," or "have fear about."

5.36

Theudas is mentioned only here in the New Testament. Although there are certain questions of chronology raised by the mention of Theudas in this verse and by the mention of Judas the Galilean in the following verse, the details of these questions are not important for the translator, and so they will not be dealt with here. The temporal expression some time ago is perhaps best translated as "a few years ago." One should avoid giving the impression of a long period of time.

Claiming that he was somebody great may be of necessity shifted into direct discourse, for example, "said, I am a great leader."

The expression joined him may be translated variously, for example, "became his helpers," "followed him," "became his henchmen."

The passive construction was killed may be shifted into an active in two forms, either "died violently" or "died by violence" (implying some agent who killed him), or one may say "some people killed him" not specifying precisely the agent. The passive were scattered may simply be shifted to "went in all directions."

In many languages movements cannot die out. They can, however, "stop," "cease," or "become nothing."

5.37

Galilean is simply "a man from the province of Galilee."

During the time of the census may require some descriptive equivalent in some languages, for example, "while all the people were being counted," or "while officers were writing down the names of all the people." However, since census taking is increasingly more frequent in most parts of the world, there is usually a convenient expression for this process of registration.

Drew a crowd after him may be equivalent to "caused many people to follow him" or "caused many people to become his helpers."

5.38

In this case now translates a Greek expression which means "now" or "as far as the present situation is concerned." It is the same phrase which is translated "now" in 4.29; and it appears in 17.30; 20.32; 27.22. A related expression appears in 24.25.

Do not take any action against is equivalent to "do nothing against" or "do nothing to harm."

The clause if this plan and work of theirs is a man-made thing is often not easy to translate, since man-made can only be expressed by making people the subject of the clause, for example, "if only people have made these plans and do the work" or "if it is only a man who is commanding this plan and their work."

5.39

If it comes from God should be rendered in a form somewhat parallel to the corresponding expression in verse 38, for example, "if it is God who has commanded this," "if it is God who has helped them," or "if God is the one who gives them power." Only rarely can one employ a pronoun such as it to refer to this plan and work of theirs. Furthermore, it is difficult in most languages to speak of an event as "coming."

5.40

The equivalent of you could find yourselves fighting against God is in some languages "you would see that you are fighting God" or "you would come to know that you are trying to defeat God."

Followed Gamaliel's advice may be rendered as simply "did what Gamaliel said" or "decided that what Gamaliel said was right."

5.40

The passive causative had them whipped may be restructured as "ordered the guards to whip them" or "caused the guards to whip them."

After the verb ordered one frequently must employ direct discourse, for example, "ordered, Do not ever again speak in the name of Jesus."

The phrase speak in the name of Jesus is not easy to render. In some languages it is simply "authority of Jesus" but in other languages the closest equivalent is "speak to the people, using Jesus' name."

5.41

Left the Council is literally "left from the face of the Council," another Semitic idiom.

Full of joy is variously expressed in different languages, "they had great joy," "they rejoiced very much," "they were very, very happy," or idiomatically as "their hearts were very sweet" or "their livers were cool."

The concept of worthy is difficult to render satisfactorily in a number of languages. In some contexts it is equivalent to "to be able to be" or "to be important enough." In this context the equivalent may be "considered them good enough to suffer."

The expression suffer disgrace is rendered as "to suffer punishment," "to suffer being whipped," or "to be punished."

For the name of Jesus in this context may be rendered "for Jesus' sake."

5.42

In people's homes is the same expression which appeared in 2.46; whether they taught only in the houses of believers or in the houses of believers and unbelievers alike the text does not state.

Preach the Good News translates one Greek word, which appears fifteen times in the book of Acts and is somewhat of a technical term for the preaching of the Good News. In the Greek sentence structure (about) Jesus the Messiah is actually the object of the verb preach the Good News.

Messiah may be understood as in the TEV, that is, as a title; or it may be taken as a part of a proper name, Christ Jesus. If it is understood as a title the meaning may be that they were preaching the Good News that Jesus is the Messiah.

CHAPTER 6

Chapters 6 and 7 constitute an important unit, with the principal character being Stephen, the first martyr. The beginning of Chapter 6 contains two transitional devices, the first a reference to time, and the second a reference to the rapidly growing church referred to at several points in the preceding narrative. This same theme of growth is reiterated in verse 7.

It is Stephen's important contribution to the growing church as one of the specially designated helpers that leads to his arrest (vv. 8-15). Chapter 7 consists primarily of the speech of Stephen, followed by his being stoned. Note, however, that this particular episode contains a reference to Saul (v. 58), who is then introduced at the beginning of Chapter 8.

The Seven Helpers

1 Some time later, as the number of disciples kept growing, there was a quarrel between the Greek-speaking Jews and the native Jews. The Greek-speaking Jews said that their widows were being neglected in the daily distribution of funds. 2 So the twelve apostles called the whole group of disciples together and said, "It is not right for us to neglect the preaching of God's word in order to handle finances. 3 So then, brothers, choose seven men among you who are known to be full of the Holy Spirit and wisdom, and we will put them in charge of this matter. 4 We ourselves, then, will give our full time to prayers and the work of preaching."

5 The whole group was pleased with the apostles' proposal; so they chose Stephen, a man full of faith and the Holy Spirit, and Philip, Prochorus, Nicanor, Timon, Parmenas, and Nicolaus, a Gentile from Antioch who had been converted to Judaism. 6 The group presented them to the apostles, who prayed and placed their hands on them.

7 And so the word of God continued to spread. The number of disciples in Jerusalem grew larger and larger, and a great number of priests accepted the faith. (6.1-7)

The section heading The Seven Helpers may be syntactically impossible in some languages, since one may need to specify who is helped. Furthermore, in certain languages one may find it necessary to make an entire clause of this section heading. Accordingly, one may adapt the section heading to read "Seven Men Help the Apostles," "Seven Men Are Chosen to Help the Apostles," "The Church Chooses Seven Helpers," or "Seven Men to Help the Apostles Are Chosen."

These three initial paragraphs are closely linked, since the second paragraph describes the action proposed in the first, and the third specifies the result of the continuing ministry and outreach of the church. The three important transitional features of these three paragraphs are (1) the initial transition of time some time later and of circumstance as the number of disciples kept growing of verse 1, the latter linking this paragraph with the im-

133

mediately preceding statements in Chapter 5; (2) the words the whole group and proposal of verse 5, linking the second paragraph semantically with the preceding paragraph, and the conjunction so, marking the conclusion; and (3) the introductory phrase and so of verse 7, indicating that this verse marks the conclusion to what has preceded.

6.1

This is the first time in the book of Acts where disciples is used as a designation of the Christians. Altogether the corresponding Greek term is used more than twenty-five times in Acts: once with the addition "of the Lord" (9.1); and in 9.25 the reference may be limited to the followers of Paul, Saul's followers.

It may be necessary to employ a term for disciples which is different from the expression used in the translation of the Gospels. If in the Gospels one has used a phrase such as "those whom Jesus taught" or "those who learned from Jesus," in Acts it is necessary to employ an expression which will indicate indirect association with Jesus, for example, "those who were followers of Jesus" (if the word "followers" means adherents to rather than immediate companions) or "believers in Jesus." In fact, many translations use simply "believers" for disciples in Acts.

The number of disciples kept growing is rendered in many languages as "there were more people who became believers" or "more and more people believed in Jesus."

Kept growing accurately translates the continuous aspect of the Greek present tense.

Quarrel is translated by some as "complaint" or "disagreement," while others understand the word to mean a secret murmuring that was not done openly.

Greek-speaking Jews is rendered by most translations as "Hellenists"; and native Jews is usually translated as "Hebrews." Although there is fairly unanimous agreement regarding the meaning of this latter term (it refers to Aramaic-speaking Jews of Palestine), there is some disagreement regarding the meaning of the former of these words. However, most commentators understand "Hellenists" to mean Greek-speaking Jews (see NEB "those of them who spoke Greek"); compare 9.29 and 11.20.

The phrase native Jews is not complicated in some languages. Some would like to render this simply as "those who lived in Jerusalem," thus implying that Greek-speaking Jews were visitors from other areas. Others prefer to render this phrase as "Jews who spoke only the Jewish language" or "Jews who spoke only Aramaic."

In Jerusalem there were many widows of men who had lived most of their lives outside of the Holy City, but had come to Jerusalem to die and to be buried. In order to care for these widows the Jews had set up means whereby they would be given money for food. Evidently the Christian community had adopted a similar custom. The daily distribution of funds is literally "in the daily distribution," and may be taken to refer either to funds (as in the TEV) or else to food. In light of the manner in which the Jews themselves handled the care for the widows, it is quite likely that the distribution is that of money rather than food.

The passive expression were being neglected may be rendered in some languages by a kind of substitute passive "they did not receive."

The daily distribution of funds may be rendered as "money that was given to the widows each day" or "money that was given for the widows' needs of each day."

6.2

The twelve apostles (a term which occurs only here in the book of Acts) should probably be taken as a title rather than simply as a number; and the whole group of disciples means the whole church body.

It is doubtful that the apostles' statement it is not right for us to neglect the preaching of God's word in order to handle finances is intended to convey the idea that this ministry was distasteful to the apostles. Rather, it is to suggest that their particular ministry was that of preaching God's word. To neglect the preaching of God's word is literally "to neglect the word of God," but in this context the evident meaning is that of preaching the word of God (see Phillips and Goodspeed).

To handle finances (see Phillips "to look after the accounts"; Goodspeed "to keep accounts") may be taken either as the TEV has it or else in the sense of "to serve tables." However, one finds it difficult to believe that the responsible task referred to was that of waiting on tables, so that even if the latter alternative is followed, it should be broadened to mean something like "to see that the widows' needs are properly cared for."

The phrase God's word is obviously "the message that comes from God."

6.3

So then is an important transitional device to indicate the logical conclusion to the immediately preceding sentence. For the word brothers, see 1.16.

Men...who are known to be appears in some other translations as "men of good reputation" (NEB, Phillips; see RSV); and so are described as having three qualifications (a good reputation, full of the Holy Spirit, and full of wisdom) rather than two (known to be full of the Holy Spirit and wisdom). Most translations assume that the reference is to the Holy Spirit, even though the word "holy" is not in the Greek text; however, Phillips thinks "full of the Spirit" means they were "spiritually minded."

In a number of languages one cannot speak of full of the Holy Spirit. Rather, one must use a term such as "whom the Holy Spirit commands," "whom the Holy Spirit directs," or even "whom the Holy Spirit possesses."

Similarly, it may be impossible to use a phrase such as full of...wisdom. One, however, can "be very wise" or "know things very well."

6.4

Put them in charge of this matter may be rendered as "give them this work to do" or "cause them to do this work."

6.4

We ourselves brings out the emphasis intended in the Greek sentence structure. Give our full time (a verb which appears in 1.14) is rendered in most translations as "devote ourselves" (see RSV, NEB, Phillips, JB); but the "devotion" referred to is that of giving one's entire time to this particular aspect of the Christian work. The work of preaching is literally "the ministry of the word," but the context makes it obvious that the meaning is "preaching the word of God."

The phrase give ... full time to should not be understood as meaning that prayer and preaching were the only activities of the apostles; rather, it was their main work. In some languages, therefore, the equivalent is "we ourselves will have the work of praying and preaching the good news."

6.5

As in verse 2, the whole group refers to the entire church community. Another reflection of Luke's Semitic style lies behind the translation of the whole group was pleased with the apostles' proposal, which is literally "the word was pleasing before all the group." The phrase the apostles' proposal may be simply "what the apostles said."

They chose refers to the whole congregation (see v. 3). Of the seven men chosen, only two are mentioned further in Acts: Stephen (other than Chapter 7 see 8.2; 11.19; 22.20) and Philip (Chapter 8; 21.8). The Philip mentioned here should not be confused with Philip the apostle. The Antioch from which Nicolaus came was probably Antioch in Syria. On the phrase a Gentile ... who had been converted to Judaism see 2.11.

It is important in introducing the phrase a man full of faith and the Holy Spirit that this not be related to Stephen in such a way as to suggest that the other men were not in this same category. It is only that for Stephen this expression is an emphatic qualifier. In some languages this portion of verse 5 is translated as "they chose Stephen. He was a man who believed firmly, and the Holy Spirit possessed him; they also chose Philip, Prochorus,..."

As indicated, the phrase full of faith must frequently be restructured as "believe strongly," "believe very much," or even "believe without any doubting." The expression had been converted to in this type of context may be rendered as "had become" or, as in some languages, "had made himself into a Jew" or "had come to be just like a Jew."

6.6

In Greek the subject of the verb presented is not explicit, as the TEV has made it, but obviously the entire congregation is referred to. Neither is the subject of prayed and placed their hands on them explicit in the Greek; the apostles may be the subject (as TEV, NEB, Moffatt, Phillips), or the entire

136

congregation may be taken as the subject. Some translations (see RSV, JB, Goodspeed) have left the text ambiguous. Although the JB has left the text ambiguous, the translators have given a footnote: "possibly a gesture of the community, cf. 13.1-3; more probably (v. 3) of the apostles."

The laying on of hands was a gesture taken over by the Christian community from the Jewish community. It symbolized not only the giving of a responsibility but, what is more important, the imparting of strength and of the community's blessing.

It may be necessary to specify where the hands were placed, in which case one may say "placed on their heads." Notice, however, that in many instances this type of distributive meaning must be rendered with care. A plural "heads" might imply that each person had more than one head. Therefore, in some languages one must say "placed their hands upon each person's head."

6.7

The statement the word of God continued to spread (literally "the word of God increased") means that the preaching of the Good News was successful in winning more and more people to the Christian faith. The expression the word ... spread must be semantically restructured in many languages since one cannot speak of "a word" or "message" spreading, particularly when referring to the acceptance of such a message. The equivalent of this clause in some languages is "more and more people believed the word of God" or even "more and more people heard and believed the word from God."

Disciples again is used in the sense of "believers."

Apart from other considerations, the text would indicate that the great number of priests who accepted the faith must have come from Jerusalem; but it is possible that some may have come from Qumran and other Jewish communities. From all indications there were about 18,000 priests and Levites in Palestine during this time, 8,000 of whom were priests. Accepted the faith is literally "were obedient to the faith"; and in this context the word faith may be taken as practically synonymous with "the Good News." For a similar use of the faith in Acts see 13.8; 14.22; 16.5.

The Arrest of Stephen

8 Stephen, a man richly blessed by God and full of power, performed great miracles and wonders among the people. 9 But some men opposed him; they were members of the synagogue of the Free Men (as it was called), which had Jews from Cyrenia and Alexandria. They and other Jews from Cilicia and Asia started arguing with Stephen. 10 But the Spirit gave Stephen such wisdom that when he spoke they could not resist him. 11 So they bribed some men to say, "We heard him speaking against Moses and against God!" 12 In this way they stirred up the people, the elders, and the teachers of the Law. They came to Stephen,

seized him, and took him before the Council. 13 Then they brought in
some men to tell lies about him. "This man," they said, "is always
talking against our sacred temple and the Law of Moses. 14 We heard
him say that this Jesus of Nazareth will tear down the temple and
change all the customs which have come down to us from Moses!"
15 All those sitting in the Council fixed their eyes on Stephen and saw
that his face looked like the face of an angel. (6. 8-15)

The section heading The Arrest of Stephen may be made into a complete
clause by the indication of the agent, for example, "The Jewish Leaders
Arrest Stephen" or "The Jewish Leaders Cause Stephen to be Arrested."

The transitions in this paragraph are very important: but (v. 9), but
(v. 10), so (v. 11), in this way (v. 12), and then (v. 13). Note that Stephen is
the focal person in the entire paragraph, but in most instances other participants are the subjects of the sentences. In some languages (for example, in
the Malayo-Polynesian languages of the Philippines) this discrepancy between
the semantic subject of the paragraph and the grammatical subjects of the
various verbs requires some restructuring.

6. 8

A man richly blessed by God translates the Greek expression "full of
grace." In the biblical sense to be "full of grace" means that God's grace and
blessing are uniquely present and perceptible in the life of a person; whereas
in contemporary English "full of grace" might suggest that a person is full of
charm and persuasiveness. Power must be taken to mean "the power to perform miracles."

6. 9

Opposed is not actually a part of the Greek text, but that these men
did oppose Stephen is immediately evident from the context and beginning the
verse in this fashion enables the translator to render into intelligible English
a very difficult Greek construction. The sentence itself begins with a Greek
verb meaning "they got up" (used here, as in 5. 6 and 17, merely to indicate
the initiation of an action), which must be taken together with the participle
"arguing." The TEV combines these two verbs ("they got up" and "arguing"),
and translates started arguing (see also Moffatt "started a dispute" and Goodspeed "undertook to debate").

The synagogue was used by the Jews as a place of worship on the Sabbath day and on other set days; it was also the place where Jews met for
social activities, and throughout the week the building was used as a school
for Jewish children. There is no unanimous opinion as to how many synagogues are referred to in this verse, but it seems most likely that the choice
must be between (1) two synagogues: (a) the synagogue of the Free Men,
whose members were Jews from Cyrenia and Alexandria, and (b) a synagogue
whose members were Jews from Cilicia and Asia; or (2) one synagogue, the

synagogue of the Free Men, whose members were Jews from Cyrenia and Alexandria; while the other Jews from Cilicia and Asia are mentioned as another group of persons, but without reference to any synagogue. If this conclusion is valid, then there is one synagogue and two groups of persons mentioned.

Free Men is to be understood in the sense of "freed men," meaning that previously they had been slaves but later obtained their freedom.

The parenthetical expression as it was called implies that this is an explanation of an otherwise foreign name. (The phrase Free Men actually comes from a Latin term.) Such an explanation may be rendered idiomatically as "that is the way people called it" or "this was the name of the synagogue."

6.10

The Greek of this verse is literally "and they were not able to resist the wisdom and the spirit with which he was speaking." Most commentators and translators agree that the spirit referred to is the Holy Spirit, and the sentence construction lends itself to the interpretation of the text that the TEV has given: But the Spirit gave Stephen such wisdom that when he spoke they could not resist him (see also JB, "They found they could not get the better of him because of his wisdom, and because it was the Spirit that prompted what he said").

Gave ... such wisdom is equivalent in some languages to "caused him to be so wise" or "caused him to speak such wise words."

The expression could not resist him may be rendered as "were not able to answer him" or "were not able to argue against him."

6.11

The first verb in this verse may mean either bribe (see also Phillips) or "to instigate secretly." In the phrase speaking against Moses and against God, the meaning of the accusation apparently is that Stephen's interpretation of the Law of Moses and his understanding of God's purpose for the Jewish people conflicted with the nationalistic outlook of these people.

In some languages speaking against is equivalent to "saying bad things about" or "speak evil words against."

6.12

It is difficult to determine exactly the subjects of the verbs in this and the following verse. The subject of they stirred up may be either the men who argued with Stephen (v. 9) or the men who testified against him (v. 11); while the subject of they came to Stephen, seized him, and took him before the Council may be either of the above or else the people, the elders, and the teachers of the Law. The same three possibilities exist for the subject of they brought in some men to tell lies about him (v. 13). One logical solution to these complex problems is to suggest that the subjects of they bribed some men and of they stirred up the people are the same: that is, the men who argued with Stephen (v. 11); and that the subjects of the next series of verbs are the people, the elders, and the teachers of the Law. If this conclusion is accepted, then it was the men who disputed with Stephen who stirred up the people, the elders, and the teachers of the Law; and it was these, in turn, who seized him, and took him before the Council.

Stirred up may be rendered as "caused to be angry," "caused to become excited," or "caused to be fearful." All of these emotions may occur in expressions denoting the process of stirring up a group of people.

In this context took him implies "leading by force."

6.13

They brought in some men to tell lies about him is literally "they set up false witnesses," but the meaning of the noun phrase "false witnesses" is better understood when restructured into a verb phrase, as the TEV has done.

Against our sacred temple and the Law of Moses translates "against this sacred place and the Law," but the meaning of "this sacred place" is the Jerusalem temple, and "the Law" is obviously the Law of Moses. The translator should, of course, keep in mind that the term "Law," although an accurate translation of the Greek word, does not convey fully the meaning of the word law in the Jewish setting. In Jewish life "law" referred essentially to the Law of Moses, the first five books of the Scriptures.

Sacred temple may be translated in some languages as "temple dedicated to God." The Greek term which means "sacred" and "holy" must often be translated by quite different terms in receptor languages when it refers to different types of objects, for example, people, the Spirit of God, and objects such as the temple, ark, or priestly clothing. For objects, a rendering such as "dedicated to the worship of God" is often the most satisfactory.

The Law of Moses is quite naturally the law which comes from Moses, or the law which Moses gave, not the law which belonged to Moses. The meaning here is a secondary agent, because the law is described as coming primarily from God, but through Moses. In some instances, therefore, the appropriate rendering is "the Law through Moses."

6.14

This Jesus of Nazareth is obviously intended as a derogatory term. The two accusations made against Jesus are designed to appeal both to the Sadducees (whose main religious interests were centered about the temple service) and to the Pharisees (whose basic concern was with the interpretation of the Law of Moses and with the perpetuation of the customs they believed had their basis in the Law of Moses).

The connotative value in the phrase this Jesus of Nazareth may almost be equivalent to "this fellow Jesus from Nazareth" or "this guy Jesus from Nazareth." Note that the relationship in the phrase Jesus of Nazareth is source, that is, "Jesus who comes from Nazareth."

Tear down is to be understood in the sense of "destroy" or "ruin."

Change all the customs is equivalent in some languages to "cause us to live differently from what Moses taught our ancestors" or "make us follow ways which are not the ones Moses gave to our ancestors."

As implied in the previous paragraph, there are difficulties in the expression come down to us from Moses. Normally, traditions do not "come down," and the source of traditions is usually not expressed in a phrase such as "from Moses"; rather, "Moses" must be made the agent. These are, therefore, "the traditions which Moses taught" or "the traditions which Moses ordered."

6.15

Fixed their eyes on translates the same verb as was used in 1.10. Fixed their eyes on is equivalent to "looked directly at" or "watched Stephen carefully."

The indication that Stephen's face looked like the face of an angel doubtless means that his face shone like that of Moses (see Exodus 34.29-30) and of Jesus (Luke 9.29; Matthew 17.2). In some languages resemblance may be expressed negatively as not being able to make a distinction, for example, "they could not see that his face was different from the face of an angel." In other languages the equivalent is "Stephen's face and an angel's face were alike."

CHAPTER 7

Chapter 7 consists of two main parts: first, the speech by Stephen, and second, the account of the stoning of Stephen, beginning with verse 54. The first sentence of Chapter 8 structurally belongs to Chapter 7, for this mention of Saul's approval of the murder of Stephen is an important conclusion to the preceding paragraph.

Stephen's speech is not a direct answer to the charges which have been made against him. Rather, it is a frontal attack on the way in which Jewish leaders had traditionally rejected the persons whom God had sent to them, and it ends with strong arguments against traditional Jewish attitudes toward the temple (vv. 44-50). Indirectly, of course, Stephen's speech can be regarded as a reply to the accusations contained in verse 13 of Chapter 6, for the two principal issues were "the sacred temple" and "the Law of Moses."

Stephen reminds his hearers that God appeared to Abraham outside the Holy Land before the giving of the Law or the building of the temple. He points out that throughout their history the Jewish people constantly rejected the persons whom God had sent to them, for example, Joseph and Moses; and he tells the persons to whom he is speaking that they themselves had rejected the One whom God had sent to them (that is, Jesus), and that by their devotion to the temple they had failed to recognize God when he spoke to them in the person of Jesus Christ.

Stephen's defense (vv. 2-53) is an exceptionally well-organized discourse. Note that the second paragraph concentrates on the experience of Abraham and ends with an introduction of the twelve patriarchs. This immediately provides the transition for the third paragraph (vv. 9-16) in which the patriarchs are described as having rejected Joseph, who was God's provision.

The third paragraph ends with a reference to Abraham, and in so doing provides an excellent transition for the fourth paragraph (vv. 17-22), since it is the promise made to Abraham which constitutes the basis for God's calling Moses.

The fifth, sixth, and seventh paragraphs all deal with Moses. The fifth (vv. 23-29) recounts the killing of the Egyptian and Moses' flight to Midian, the sixth (vv. 30-34) describes the episode of the burning bush, the seventh (vv. 35-38) begins with the theme of rejection, thus tying the story closely to the fifth paragraph, and the eighth again introduces the theme of rejection with the long quotation from Amos (Amos 5.25-27).

Having repeatedly emphasized the theme of rejection, Stephen's speech continues to deal with the problem of the temple in two paragraphs (vv. 44-50), and finally (vv. 51-53) Stephen summarizes the theme of rejection and resistance. In the light of such strong accusations, it is no wonder that the reaction of the members of the Council was so strong. Hence the transition in verse 54 is quite natural.

Because of the well-structured nature of this discourse, it is most important that a translator pay particular attention to the transitions and to the manner in which the participants in these various historical events are clearly identified.

Stephen's Speech

1 The High Priest asked Stephen, "Is this really so?"

2 Stephen answered, "Brothers and fathers! Listen to me! The God of glory appeared to our ancestor Abraham while he was living in Mesopotamia, before he had gone to live in Haran, 3 and said to him, 'Leave your family and country and go to the land that I will show you.' 4 And so he left the land of Chaldea and went to live in Haran. After Abraham's father died, God made him move to this country, where you now live. 5 God did not then give Abraham any part of it as his own, not even a square foot of ground; but God promised that he would give it to him, and that it would belong to him and his descendants after him. At the time God made this promise Abraham had no children. 6 This is what God said to him, 'Your descendants will live in a foreign country, where they will be slaves and will be badly treated for four hundred years. 7 But I will pass judgment on the people that they will serve,' God said, 'and afterward they will come out of that country and will worship me in this place.' 8 Then God gave to Abraham the ceremony of circumcision as a sign of the covenant. So Abraham circumcised Isaac a week after he was born; Isaac circumcised Jacob, and Jacob circumcised the twelve patriarchs. (7.1-8)

The section heading Stephen's Speech may be transformed into a clause, "Stephen Speaks," but more often than not some goal of the speaking is required, for example, "Stephen Speaks to the Council" or "Stephen Defends Himself before the Council."

7.1

Although Stephen is not explicitly mentioned either in verse 1 or verse 2 of the Greek text, the TEV has included his name in the translation in order to make it immediately evident to the reader whom the High Priest addressed and whose speech is given in the following verses.

The question Is this really so? may require some expansion so that the reference of the pronoun this may be clear, for example, "Is what these men have accused you of true?" or "Are these accusations against you true?" or "Did you say what these men claim you said?" What is, of course, important in the High Priest's question is not the validity or truth of what Stephen had said, but whether Stephen himself was guilty of having made the statements.

7.2

On the term brothers (literally "men brothers") see 1.16. This is exactly the same formula of address that Paul uses in speaking to the Jews in 22.1.

The God of glory is an expression which occurs elsewhere only in Psalm 29.3 (LXX 28.3), but it is doubtful that either Stephen or Luke had this in mind. Some take the phrase to mean simply "the glorious God," while others see another meaning in the word glory, on the basis of 1 Corinthians 2.8 and James 2.1; that is, "the God who reveals himself in glory." Not only is the exegesis of the God of glory difficult, but the rendering of such a phrase in other languages is equally complicated. In many languages glory is related to the concept of "shining" or "brightness." Thus the God of glory may be rendered as "the God who shines" or, as in one language, "God the light-owner," indicating that he possesses special light. In other languages glory is associated with "majesty" or "regal appearance" and therefore is rendered as "the majestic God" or "the God with great majesty." A term for "majesty" in some languages is very closely related to words for "conspicuousness," with the accompanying denotation of "attractiveness."

According to Genesis 12.1 the command for Abraham to leave his family and country and go to a land that God would show him was given in Haran after he and his father Terah had moved there from Ur of the Chaldees.

In a number of languages it may be useful to terminate verse 2 with a complete sentence, beginning verse 3 then as a new sentence and reintroducing God as the subject of speaking.

7.3

The command leave your family and country has reversed the order of the words "country and family," as they appear in the passage quoted from Genesis; but the TEV has done this inasmuch as the command go to the land that I will show you more naturally follows after "country" than after "family."

It is sometimes difficult to translate the verb show by a term which may be used for revealing or showing objects, since a country does not fall into the same class of demonstrable things. One may be required, therefore, to translate as "the country I tell you to go to" or "the country I say is the right country for you to go to."

7.4

Whoever reads the accounts in Genesis 11.27---12.4 is left with the impression that it was after Abraham's father died that God made him move; but if one takes into consideration the ages of Terah and Abraham as given in Genesis 11.26,32 and 12.4, then Terah must still have been alive when the move was made from Haran. Neither this discrepancy nor the one mentioned in the previous verse is important to Luke or to Stephen; the purpose of both men is merely to indicate that God appeared to Abraham outside the Holy Land.

The TEV has made explicit the subject of made him move, that is, God. Stephen now points out that even though it was God who made Abraham move to the country in which they now live, God did not then give Abraham any part of it as his own. As his own translates one Greek word which is usually rendered "inheritance," but the meaning is not something which one inherits but rather something which one possesses.

If it is necessary to identify the place name <u>Haran,</u> one can always add
"city," preferably, of course, in the place of first occurrence of this term,
namely, in verse 2.

7.5

A <u>square foot of ground</u> in Greek is technically a linear measurement
(see RSV "a foot's length"), but for English speakers it is more common to
measure ground in square feet than in linear feet (see JB "a single square foot
of this land"). This phrase occurs in Deuteronomy 2.5 of the Septuagint. The
measurement of <u>a square foot of ground</u> must, of course, be adjusted. It may
be rendered by a rather general expression such as "not even a very small
piece of ground." But in some languages there is a corresponding idiomatic
expression, "not even a piece of ground where a cooking pot could be placed."

The promise referred to in the last half of this verse is based on Genesis
17.8. <u>That it would belong to him</u> translates the Greek expression "for a possession"; the meaning is that God would give the land to Abraham and to his
descendants as a permanent possession.

In some societies personal possession of land is rather unusual, since
land is not normally possessed by individuals but belongs to a tribal group.
It may, therefore, be necessary to make such possession rather explicit,
often by means of direct discourse, for example, "God did not give Abraham
any part of the land so that Abraham could say, This land belongs just to me."

7.6

The Scripture passage referred to in verses 6-7a comes from Genesis
15.13-14, and the passage referred to in verse 7b comes from Exodus 3.12.
In these verses the promise made to Abraham is one of deliverance from
Egypt and the opportunity to worship God.

In many languages the expression <u>foreign country</u> is "another country"
or "a country ruled by other people." The latter expression, of course, fits
well in the context in which the Jews are spoken of as "slaves."

Since most societies at least know about the custom of slavery, there is
very little difficulty in obtaining a satisfactory term. Where slavery is unknown there may be equivalents such as "forced labor" or "those who are made
to work and do not receive pay."

In must circumstances there is little difficulty in obtaining an expression
for <u>badly treated</u>, but where it is necessary to make this expression somewhat
more specific, one can use "they will be whipped in order to make them work."

7.7

The expression <u>pass judgment</u> implies, of course, condemnation and
punishment. It is, therefore, most effectively rendered in some languages as
"I will punish the people that they will work for as slaves."

Though a term for <u>worship</u> is usually available, it frequently represents
an extension of meaning of the term "to pray." In this particular context, of

course, the expression "will pray to me in this place" is a close natural equivalent.

"On this mountain" (that is, Mount Horeb or Sinai) of Exodus 3.12 has been adapted by Luke to in this place (that is, Palestine or Jerusalem).

7. 8

This verse serves as a transition between the story of Abraham and that of Joseph (vv. 9-16). The literal phrase "covenant of circumcision" means the covenant which was agreed upon between God and Abraham and which had circumcision as its external sign. Therefore, the TEV has translated the phrase as ceremony of circumcision as a sign of the covenant.

The Greek text of verse 8 is not clear; it could mean either "Isaac was the father of Jacob, and Jacob was the father of the twelve patriarchs" or "Isaac circumcised Jacob, and Jacob circumcised the twelve patriarchs." Most translations follow the former alternative, while the TEV takes the latter one. This seems also to be the understanding of the JB, "So when his son Isaac was born he circumcised him on the eighth day. Isaac did the same for Jacob, and Jacob for the twelve patriarchs."

Though in many languages one can speak of "giving a covenant" or "making a covenant," it is much more difficult to speak of "giving a ceremony." It may, therefore, be necessary to modify somewhat the structure of this first sentence of verse 8, for example, "God made an agreement with Abraham, and he told Abraham that if the people were circumcised this would show that they accepted the agreement." Such a rendering is, of course, rather extended, but it tries to indicate the relationship between the covenant and circumcision and to state precisely that the agreement was one proposed by God and accepted by the people.

The term for covenant is not easy in a number of languages. So often a term suggested for covenant implies a kind of bargaining session. This, of course, is not the biblical concept. Rather, it is an agreement reached on the basis of a proposal by God and acceptance by the people. It is thus closely equivalent to the relationship which exists between a chief and his people in many face-to-face societies. An equivalent in some languages may be "an alliance"; in still others, "a bond of friendship." (See 3.25.)

Where the practice of circumcision is either carried out or known about, there is normally a quite adequate term. In some societies, however, circumcision is entirely unknown and a descriptive phrase would be regarded as very vulgar. Under such circumstances many translators have employed a more general expression such as "a mark by cutting" or "a sign by cutting the skin." It is essential, however, that such a phrase be carefully identified by a glossary note so that people will comprehend the precise nature of the practice.

There are certain problems involved in the introduction of the twelve patriarchs. If one adopts the interpretation "was the father of the twelve patriarchs," there is very little difficulty. In some languages, however, this has been rendered literally as "gave birth to the twelve old men"—something which is obviously ludicrous. The term patriarch must usually be translated as "important ancestor" or "famous grandfather" (if the term "grandfather" can be used in a general sense for male ancestor). In many societies, however, there is a special term to identify the person who has been regarded as the founder of a tribe or important clan. Such a technical term may here be employed for patriarch.

If, however, one follows the TEV in translating circumcised the twelve patriarchs, there may still be problems involved since this might imply that the circumcision took place when the patriarchs were adults. Such an implication must be carefully avoided.

> 9 "The patriarchs were jealous of Joseph, and sold him to be a slave in Egypt. But God was with him, 10 and brought him safely through all his troubles. When Joseph appeared before Pharaoh, the king of Egypt, God gave him a pleasing manner and wisdom. Pharaoh made Joseph governor over the country and the royal household. 11 Then there was a famine in all of Egypt and Canaan, which caused much suffering. Our ancestors could not find any food. 12 So when Jacob heard that there was grain in Egypt, he sent his sons, our ancestors, on their first visit there. 13 On the second visit Joseph made himself known to his brothers, and Pharaoh came to know about Joseph's family. 14 So Joseph sent a message to his father Jacob, telling him and the whole family to come to Egypt; there were seventy-five people in all. 15 Then Jacob went down to Egypt, where he and our ancestors died. 16 Their bodies were moved to Shechem, where they were buried in the grave which Abraham had bought from the tribe of Hamor for a sum of money. (7. 9-16)

This third paragraph of Chapter 7 is narrative in structure, with very explicit and important connectives: but (v. 9), then (v. 11), so (v. 12), on the second visit (v. 13), so (v. 14), and then (v. 15). Since there is also a rapid shifting between participants: patriarchs, Joseph, Pharaoh, our ancestors, brothers, Jacob, and Abraham, one must make certain that these are properly introduced and identified.

7. 9

It may be necessary to identify the relationship of the patriarchs to Joseph. This may be done by some marginal help which would refer to the passage in Genesis and indicate that Joseph was himself one of the patriarchs, being a brother of the other eleven. Or it may also be possible to provide an identifier for the name Joseph by saying "the patriarchs were jealous of their brother Joseph." The term jealous is often expressed in an idiomatic manner, for example, "their hearts were not on him," "they were sour toward him," or "they could not listen to his name."

A literal translation of sold him to be a slave in Egypt may require some expansion in certain languages, for example, "sold him to men who took him as a slave to Egypt" or "sold him to men who then sold him as a slave in Egypt."

The expression <u>God was with him</u> is rendered in many languages as "God continued to help him" or even "God caused him to succeed."

The clause <u>brought him safely through all his troubles</u> may be rendered in some languages as "helped him whenever he was in trouble," "caused him to be safe even when he was in difficulties," or "caused him to be safe even when people tried to harm him."

<u>When Joseph appeared before Pharaoh, the king of Egypt, God gave him a pleasing manner and wisdom</u> does not necessarily refer to one formal appearance that Joseph made before Pharaoh. The Greek simply says, "He [God] gave to him [Joseph] grace and wisdom before Pharaoh king of Egypt." This statement may mean that Joseph's <u>pleasing manner and wisdom</u> (perhaps a specific reference to his ability to interpret dreams) was such as to attract the attention of Pharaoh (see JB "by making him wise enough to attract the attention of Pharaoh king of Egypt"). <u>Pleasing manner</u> translates the word "grace," which here refers not to the grace of God but rather to the impression that Joseph made before Pharaoh. <u>The royal household</u> is taken by most to be the meaning of the words, "his [Pharaoh's] house," though in light of Genesis 41.43 some understand this to refer to Pharaoh's property. The subject of the verb <u>made</u> is not explicitly stated; some understand it to be God, but most understand it to be Pharaoh, which seems to go better with <u>over... the royal household.</u>

The equivalent of <u>royal household</u> is in many languages "all the houses that the king had."

"A famine and much suffering" would be a Jewish way of saying <u>a famine ...(which) caused much suffering,</u> and so the TEV has translated it in this way (see JB, NEB, Phillips; and also Goodspeed and Moffatt). The word translated <u>food</u> appears only here in the New Testament; in the Septuagint and the papyri it refers specifically to food for domesticated animals, but the meaning in this context seems to be food in general.

An expression for <u>famine</u> is usually readily available, but in some areas it is translated as "the people had no food."

A rendering of <u>could not find any food</u> should not be translated to imply that they were hunters and gatherers; rather, they "could not obtain any food" in the sense that there was no food even to be bought.

The word translated <u>grain</u> is in Greek a plural, generally taken to mean "food" rather than <u>grain</u>; but a number of translators understand it to mean <u>grain</u> (see JB, RSV).

7.13

Made himself known translates a verb form which may have a middle
force as in the TEV (see also Moffatt, Goodspeed, JB, RSV), though it is possible to translate it passively (see Phillips and NEB "Joseph was recognized
by his brothers"). The Greek may either mean that Pharaoh came to know
about Joseph's family (see RSV, NEB, JB) or that "Pharaoh learned of Joseph's
parentage" (Goodspeed; see also Moffatt and Phillips). However, in light of
the fact that Pharaoh already knew of Joseph's lineage, it seems most likely
that the meaning here is that Pharaoh came to know (about) Joseph's family.

7.14

The first clause of verse 14 must frequently be translated as direct discourse, for example, Joseph told his brothers, "Say to my father Jacob, You
and all of your family must come to Egypt."

Seventy-five people is literally "seventy-five souls," but once again
"souls" means people. Seventy-five comes from the Septuagint (Genesis 46.27)
and differs from the Hebrew text, which has seventy. The figure in the Septuagint is arrived at by adding the sixty-six who came from Canaan (Genesis
46.26) to the nine descendants of Joseph who were born in Egypt (Genesis
46.27) and omitting both Joseph and Jacob. The figure in the Hebrew text is
arrived at by adding the sixty-six who came from Canaan (Genesis 46.26) to
the two sons of Joseph (Genesis 46.27) and Joseph and Jacob also.

7.15

Though the text mentions only Jacob as having gone down to Egypt, quite
naturally the implication is that Jacob and the whole family went to Egypt. In
some languages it is necessary to specify this fact, for example, "Jacob and
the rest went down to Egypt" or "they all went down to Egypt."

Since, in certain languages, he and our ancestors might be understood
to exclude Jacob from among the ancestors, one must translate as "he and our
other ancestors."

7.16

Their bodies translates "they," but the reference is of course to the
bodies of Jacob and Joseph. In a number of languages were moved must be
translated by an active phrase, indicating more specifically the action involved, e.g. "they carried the bodies back." From the tribe of Hamor is a
Semitic expression which reads literally "from the sons of Hamor."

17 "When the time drew near for God to keep the promise he had
made to Abraham, the number of our people in Egypt had grown much
larger. 18 At last a different king, who had not known Joseph, began to
rule in Egypt. 19 He tricked our people and was cruel to our ancestors,
forcing them to put their babies out of their homes, so that they would

die. 20 It was at this time that Moses was born, a very beautiful child. He was brought up at home for three months, 21 and when he was put out of his home the daughter of Pharaoh adopted him and brought him up as her own son. 22 He was taught all the wisdom of the Egyptians, and became a great man in words and deeds. (7.17-22)

The third paragraph in Stephen's speech (vv. 17-22) serves not only to advance the story, but also functions as a transition between the account of Joseph, who was rejected by his brothers, and Moses, who was rejected by his fellow Israelites. Note how skillfully verse 17 draws together the promise made to Abraham with the increase of the people in Egypt.

7.17

In many languages one cannot say time drew near. One may say that "people approach a time," but time does not itself "move." In such languages one can sometimes say "when it was about that day," "when the day was not far away," or "when they would soon see the day."

To keep is not expressed in the Greek ("when the time of the promise which God made to Abraham was drawing near"), but the meaning is clearly implicit in the text (see JB "as the time drew near for God to fulfill the promise"; and also NEB, Phillips, Goodspeed). Had grown much larger translates two verbs which are almost synonyms: "grow" and "multiply." The JB translates: "grew larger and larger."

7.18

This verse actually continues the sentence begun in verse 17 and is a subordinate temporal clause beginning with "until the time in which." In order to make the sentence less difficult for the English reader, the TEV has divided it into two parts (see also JB, NEB, Phillips). Who had not known Joseph is true in a temporal sense, but the primary reference is to the unwillingness of the new king to be guided by what Joseph had done for Egypt.

7.19

Tricked is a word which appears only here in the New Testament; it means "to take advantage by trickery." In most languages this is equivalent to "deceive."

The equivalent of cruel is in many languages more specific, for example, "beat," "tortured," or "caused to suffer."

To put ... out of their homes is rendered by most translations as "to expose." In either case the meaning is clear: the Egyptians made the Hebrews put their newborn children outside and leave them there to die. So that they would die is a positive way of expressing the Greek negative statement, "so they would not go on living."

In a number of languages an expression such as put their babies out of their homes would not necessarily imply immediately the concept of exposure.

Of course, the final clause makes this perfectly clear. A more normal expression in some languages, however, is "to abandon their children" or "to leave their children outside."

7.20

A very beautiful child translates the Greek expression "he was beautiful to God." However, the addition of the phrase "to God" or "before God" was evidently a way of forming a strong superlative. For example, in Jonah 3.3 Nineveh is said to have been "a city great before God," that is, a very great city; while the statement in Genesis 10.9, "Nimrod was a mighty hunter before the Lord," simply means that Nimrod was "the greatest hunter in the world."

At home is the meaning of the expression "in the house of his father." The phrase at home may be equivalent to "was taken care of at home" or even "nursed at home."

7.21

Adopted literally means "to lift up" (in 2.23 it means "to kill"), and may be translated either as the TEV (see NEB, RSV, JB, Phillips) or literally, that is, "to take up (from the river)," which is the meaning it has in the narrative of Exodus 2.5 (see Zürich "the daughter of Pharaoh lifted him out of the water").

The term adopted may be rendered as "made him her son" or "treated him just like her own." Under such circumstances it may be necessary to coalesce, adopted...brought...up, for example, "took care of him just as her own son and called him her child."

7.22

In Exodus 4.10 Moses indicates that he was not a capable speaker (in fact, he stuttered!), but later Jewish tradition made him out to be a powerful speaker; and the phrase a great man in words is most naturally taken to mean "one who has a great ability to speak." Some, however, interpret this phrase as being a reference to the importance of what he said, that is, "a great man in what he said and in what he did."

23 "When Moses was forty years old he decided to visit his fellow Israelites. 24 He saw one of them being mistreated by an Egyptian; so he went to his help and took revenge on the Egyptian by killing him. 25 (He thought that his own people would understand that God was going to use him to set them free; but they did not understand.) 26 The next day he saw two Israelites fighting, and he tried to make peace between them. 'Listen, men,' he said, 'you are brothers; why do you mistreat each other?' 27 But the one who was mistreating the other pushed Moses aside. 'Who made you ruler and judge over us?' he asked. 28 'Do you

151

want to kill me, just as you killed that Egyptian yesterday?' 29 When
Moses heard this he fled from Egypt and started living in the land of
Midian. There he had two sons. (7.23-29)

7.23

When Moses was forty years old translates "but as a time of forty years
was being filled for him." The TEV is representative of what most translators have done, though the NEB has "he was approaching the age of forty";
and Moffatt has "when he had completed his fortieth year" (see KJV). The
Greek phrase itself apparently means "when he was about forty years old."

"It came upon his heart" is merely a Semitic way of saying he decided
(see JB, NAB) or "it occurred to him" (Moffatt, Goodspeed, NEB).

Although most translations have to visit, the Greek verb may mean "to
look into the conditions of" (NEB).

His fellow Israelites is literally "his brothers, the sons of Israel."

7.24

By an Egyptian has been added to the first clause of this sentence so as
to let the reader know immediately who it was that was mistreating the Israelite. The verb which the TEV has translated killing literally means "to hit,"
but here the meaning is extended to "strike down," that is, "to kill."

The translation of verse 24 is complicated by problems of pronominal
reference to three different persons: Moses, the man who was being mistreated, and the Egyptian. In some translations the closest natural equivalent
is "saw an Egyptian beating one of the Israelites, therefore Moses went to
help the Israelite and took revenge on the Egyptian; he killed him."

7.25

God was going to use him to set them free translates "God through his
(Moses') hand is giving them freedom"; "through one's hands" is merely a
Semitic way of saying "through one's power."

The rendering of set ... free in some languages is "caused to escape"
or "caused them not to be slaves any longer."

7.26

He saw two Israelites fighting translates a clause that literally reads
"he appeared to them as they were quarreling." From the context it is obvious
that Moses came across two men (most translations add "two"), and that these
men were fellow Israelites.

Tried to is implied in the meaning of the verb tense, which is literally
translated as "he was making peace between them." Expressions for make
peace differ radically from language to language, for example, "caused them
to cease fighting," "caused them to receive one another again," or "caused

them to snap fingers together again," the local equivalent in some languages of "shaking hands."

7.27

The other is literally "his neighbor," but the meaning in this context is obviously "fellow countryman" (JB). It is interesting that in Exodus it is not said that the one Israelite pushed Moses aside. This expression does, however, emphasize the similarity between the way that the Israelite treated Moses and the way that the Jews treated Jesus.

The terms ruler and judge may be more conveniently rendered as verbs, for example, "to rule over us and to judge us."

Note that in the TEV the positions of speaking, for example, he said (v. 26) and he asked (v. 27), occur at different positions in the direct discourse largely for stylistic reasons. The position of such verbs of speaking should be ordered in such a way as to make them seem completely natural. In most languages they tend to go at the beginning of direct discourse, in some languages they occur at the end, and in certain languages there is both an introductory expression for speaking as well as another term identifying the end of direct discourse.

7.28

In the Greek the question Do you want to kill me ... ? expects a negative answer, though many translations imply that the expected answer is "yes."

7.29

Started living is literally "he became an alien," an idea which is brought out by the RSV, NAB, Phillips, and Moffatt, but is not emphasized in the TEV, JB, NEB, or Goodspeed, unless one assumes that it is implied by the additional phrase in the land of Midian.

The expression started living is rendered in some languages as "became a resident of" or "built a house in," this being the idiomatic way of indicating taking up residence.

A translation of he had two sons must be indicated in a somewhat more expanded fashion in some languages, for example, "his wife gave him two sons" or "he and his wife had two sons." Many languages, however, have a special term for "begetting" (that is, the function of the male in reproduction), for example, "he begot two sons" or "he became the father of two sons."

30 "After forty years had passed, an angel appeared to Moses in the flames of a burning bush in the desert near Mount Sinai. 31 Moses was amazed by what he saw, and went near the bush to look at it closely. But he heard the Lord's voice: 32 'I am the God of your ancestors, the God of Abraham, Isaac, and Jacob.' Moses trembled with fear and dared not look. 33 The Lord said to him, 'Take your sandals off, for the place

where you are standing is holy ground. 34 I have looked and seen the
cruel suffering of my people in Egypt. I have heard their groans, and
I have come down to save them. Come now, I will send you to Egypt.'

(7.30-34)

This paragraph (vv. 30-34) begins with an expression of temporal setting,
after forty years, and ends with a statement concerning Egypt, thus preparing
the way for the next paragraph (vv. 35-38).

It should be noted that the expressions an angel (v. 30), the Lord's voice
(v. 31), and the Lord (v. 33) are here used interchangeably (compare Exodus
3.2 and 4).

7.30

In many languages one cannot say forty years had passed. One can, however, "live in a place for forty years," and it is this latter expression which
is often employed as a transitional device in this verse.

The literal expression "in a flame of fire of a bush" probably means, as
the TEV has it, in the flames of a burning bush (see also NEB, JB, Phillips,
Goodspeed). The place where the angel appeared to Moses was in the desert
as most translations have it, not "in the wilderness." The Old Testament
narrative says this revelation took place at "a Mount called Horeb," but in
the biblical accounts Horeb and Sinai are identified as the same mountain.

It is difficult in some languages to translate the term desert since in
some parts of the world a barren area is almost inconceivable. It is, therefore, better under such circumstances to translate this term as "an uninhabited area." In many situations this is the closest natural equivalent.

7.31

What he saw translates a word that is most often used in the sense of a
"vision," that is, something subjective and unreal (see 12.9); here, of course,
the meaning "sight" or "something seen" best suits the context.

In many languages the equivalent of heard the Lord's voice is "heard the
Lord speak." In fact, in some languages there is no noun for "voice," only a
verb for "speaking."

7.32

In verse 32 the words of God are quoted exactly from Exodus, whereas
the response of Moses is described with more freedom by Luke.

Many languages possess no such convenient device as the preposition of
employed in an expression such as the God of your ancestors. Such a construction is often spoken of as a "possessive genitive," but obviously the ancestors
do not possess God. Accordingly, in a number of languages one must translate this expression as "I am the God whom your ancestors worshiped" or "I
am the one whom your ancestors acknowledged as God."

With fear is added by the TEV to the verb tremble in order to make clear for the reader why it was that Moses trembled (see Phillips "trembled and was afraid"). In a number of languages it is necessary to employ two verbs "trembled and feared" since this is the most natural way of indicating the nature of the trembling.

In a number of languages a rendering of dared not look involves a statement of lack of capacity, for example, "did not have the strength to look" or "was not able to look." In other languages the failure to look is related to the fear, "was so afraid he did not wish to look." In the choice of a term for dare it is important to avoid the meaning often associated with "daring someone to do something."

7.33

Moses would have been wearing sandals rather than "shoes," as most translators render the word. In the command take your sandals off the words "from your feet" have been omitted by TEV as redundant for the English reader (see JB, NEB, Goodspeed). According to ancient oriental custom one was not permitted to wear shoes in or at a holy place.

The rendering of holy ground is not easy in some languages. One can readily speak of a person being holy, but holy ground is rather unusual. However, it can be rendered in many languages as "ground dedicated to God," and in this context it would be "ground specially dedicated to me," since God is speaking. In other languages the rendering may be "ground which is specially mine," since anything possessed by God takes on this quality of "holiness." In still other languages, of course, there is a term for positive taboo and one can readily speak of a location as being "taboo," in the sense that it is so filled with spirit power that it requires special behavior on the part of those who are in it or nearby.

7.34

Some languages do not possess two such distinct terms as "look" and "see." Both forms of perception may be included in a single verb. I have looked and seen translates a Semitic idiom "seeing I have seen," which may be taken as a means of expressing emphasis (see RSV "I have surely seen"; NEB "I have indeed seen").

The construction seen the cruel suffering of my people in Egypt must often be changed to read "seen how my people in Egypt suffer so much" or as in some languages "seen how the people in Egypt beat my people so severely."

The sequence involved in I have heard their groans may be restructured in some languages as "they groan and I hear them."

In the statement come now, I will send you to Egypt, the first phrase come now translates an imperative, and I will send represents a subjunctive with a hortatory meaning, "let me send" (see JB, NEB). A literal rendering of come now may be quite vague. Therefore, one may wish to use, as in some languages, "come here" or "come listen."

155

A number of languages are quite specific with regard to whether a person has been in a place before. Accordingly, the last clause of verse 34 must then be rendered as "I will send you back to Egypt."

> 35 "Moses is the one who was rejected by the people of Israel. 'Who made you ruler and judge over us?' they asked. He is the one whom God sent as ruler and savior, with the help of the angel who appeared to him in the burning bush. 36 He led the people out of Egypt, performing miracles and wonders in Egypt and the Red Sea, and in the desert for forty years. 37 Moses is the one who said to the people of Israel, 'God will send you a prophet, just as he sent me, who will be of your own people.' 38 He is the one who was with the people of Israel assembled in the desert; he was there with our ancestors and with the angel who spoke to him on Mount Sinai; he received God's living messages to pass on to us. (7.35-38)

There is an important transition beginning with verse 35. Not only is there a shift from the historical narrative to an application of the story, but there is an important shift in speakers. The Lord is the one who speaks in verses 33 and 34, but it is again Stephen who speaks beginning with verse 35. In order to make clear this transition it is necessary in some languages to introduce Stephen again by some such expression as "Stephen continued, as he said" or "Stephen continued to speak."

This shift of focus from the largely historical narrative to the emphasis upon Moses as the individual rejected by the people of Israel, is indicated clearly by the very structure of the Greek sentences themselves. Moses is the one (vv. 35 and 37), he (v. 36), and he is the one (v. 38), are the emphatic elements in the Greek sentences. The Greek clause "this is the Moses whom they rejected" has been restructured into a passive sentence by the TEV with the subject made explicit, Moses is the one who was rejected by the people of Israel.

7.35

The concept of rejected may be expressed in some languages as "refused to listen to," "put aside," or "refused to accept."

The word translated savior by the TEV appears only here in the New Testament; in other translations it is rendered "deliverer" (RSV, NAB, Phillips; Goodspeed "to deliver them"), "redeemer" (JB; Moffatt "to redeem them"), and "liberator" (NEB) (see 5.31).

The tense of the verb sent, though almost impossible to reproduce in English, seems purposely intended to emphasize the idea of permanence, not expressed by the other verb tenses in this sentence.

"With a hand of an angel" may mean with the help of the angel (Goodspeed, Phillips; see Moffatt "by aid of the angel"); or it may mean "by means of" (see JB and NAB "through the angel"). The NEB understands the phrase to mean that it was through an angel that God spoke to Moses and gave him the commission ("speaking through the angel").

7.36

As mentioned above he (that is, Moses) is the emphatic element in this sentence.

If the strictly temporal aspect of the participle performing (miracles and wonders) is stressed, then it technically means action which was done before Moses led the people out of Egypt. For this reason it is best to take the participle purely in its instrumental aspect, that is, "by performing miracles and wonders." The KJV translation ("after that he had showed wonders and signs in the land of Egypt, and in the Red sea, and in the wilderness forty years") is a correct translation if the temporal aspect of the participle is emphasized; but this makes poor sense, inasmuch as all these actions must be looked upon as happening prior to the main verb led the people out. The JB attempts to bring out the temporal notion of the participle, but the translators seem to have gone too far in rearranging it, "It was Moses who, after performing miracles and signs in Egypt, led them out across the Red Sea and through the wilderness for forty years."

If one interprets performing miracles and wonders as being primarily instrumental, that is, "the means by which Moses was able to lead the people out of Egypt," then one can combine much more effectively Egypt, the Red Sea, and the desert. However, it is necessary in many languages to translate "in the country of Egypt," "along the Red Sea," and "in the desert," with desert often rendered as "uninhabited lands."

Note, however, that the temporal expression for forty years must be associated only with what was done in the desert. In some languages it is necessary, therefore, to introduce a verbal expression which would refer to the performing of miracles and wonders, for example, "he continued to perform miracles in the desert for forty years."

7.37

The people of Israel correctly translates the Semitic idiom "the sons of Israel."

For the two possible interpretations of just as he sent me see 3.22.

The clause who will be of your own people may be rendered in some languages as "who belonged to your clan" or "who belonged to your lineage." In some instances, of course, it is also "who belonged to your nation." The choice of terms such as "clan," "lineage," or "nation" depends upon the most normal way of speaking about one's belonging to an ethnic group related by blood descent.

7.38

In order to make it obvious what "assembly" is referred to by the expression "in the assembly in the desert" the TEV has translated the people of

Israel assembled in the desert. Phillips is confusing in employing "in that church in the desert..."; and most other translations have not done much by way of improvement.

According to the Hebrew text it was the Lord himself who gave Moses the Law, but later Jewish tradition introduced an angel as a mediator, thus maintaining God's distinctiveness and separateness from the world. Even though Phillips has evidently tried to capture the flavor of the tense of the participle "the angel who used to talk with him," it is doubtful if Luke intends for his readers to look upon the conversation between Moses and the angel as an habitual action in past time.

It is important to indicate that the pronoun he of verse 38 refers to Moses. Unless one is careful, the reference may be to the prophet who was to come.

The term assembled is in some languages translated as "came together," but in other languages it is more equivalent to "who formed a large group."

God's living messages is literally "living oracles." An "oracle" means "a message from God." This phrase is translated variously: "words of life" (JB), "living oracles" (RSV), "oracles of life" (NAB), "living utterances of God" (NEB), "living words" (Phillips and Moffatt), and "utterances that still live" (Goodspeed). In this context living seems to mean that these words are enduring or lasting. If one assumes that living refers to the contents of the message, then one may translate as "message concerning how one is to live." This interpretation is, however, much less satisfactory than living as an expression of an enduring quality, for example, "a message which continues" or "a message which lasts always."

> 39 "But our ancestors refused to obey him; they pushed him aside and wished that they could go back to Egypt. 40 So they said to Aaron, 'Make us some gods who will go in front of us. We do not know what has happened to that Moses who brought us out of Egypt.' 41 It was then that they made an idol in the shape of a calf, offered sacrifice to it, and had a feast to celebrate what they themselves had made. 42 But God turned away from them, and gave them over to worship the stars of heaven, as it is written in the book of the prophets,
> 'People of Israel! It was not to me
> that you slaughtered and sacrificed animals
> for forty years in the desert.
> 43 It was the tent of the god Moloch that you carried,
> and the image of the star of your god Rephan;
> they were idols that you had made to worship.
> And so I will send you away beyond Babylon.' (7.39-43)

This paragraph (vv. 39-43) emphasizes again the concept of rejection, but adds another dimension. Not only do the people reject Moses and his leadership, but God turns away from his people (v. 42). The conjunction but at the beginning of verse 39 is particularly important in order to show the contrast between the passing on of God's living messages and the response of the people. In some languages it is necessary to indicate this shift by a rather emphatic introductory statement, for example, "but rather than accept the message, our ancestors refused...."

7.39

Since this is a new paragraph it may be necessary to reintroduce Moses as the object of refusing to obey, for example, "they would not listen to (or obey) Moses."

Wished that they could go back to Egypt (see NEB "they wished themselves back in Egypt") translates the Greek "they turned in their hearts towards Egypt."

7.40

It may be useful to introduce a marginal note to explain who Aaron is, since Aaron has not been previously introduced in this particular book.

In many languages one cannot "make a god." Rather, it is necessary to say "make us idols of gods" or "make us images to be our gods."

The expression who will go in front of us must be related in many languages to the role of idols, for example, "who will be carried in front of us."

The Scripture reference is to Exodus 32.1 and 23. In the second sentence of this verse the emphatic element is that Moses: "for that Moses, who brought us out of Egypt, we do not know what happened to him." The force of this construction is to speak contemptuously of Moses.

7.41

In the shape of a calf may be rendered as "it looked just like a calf."

Offered sacrifice is equivalent in many languages to "killed animals in honor of" or "killed animals in order to worship."

As the context of the story in Exodus 32.4-6 makes clear, the idea is not merely that the people "rejoiced" (KJV), "had a festive celebration" (NAB), or "were perfectly happy" (JB), with what they had done, but rather that they held a religious feast in honor of what they had made (see Goodspeed "held a celebration over" and NEB "had a feast in honor of"). What they themselves had made translates the Hebraic expression "the work of their hands," and here refers, as it often does in the Old Testament, to idols.

In some languages there is a problem caused by the different agents implied in verse 40 make us some gods and the phrase what they themselves had made (v. 41). In the first instance it is obviously Aaron who undertakes to make the gods or is commissioned to see that they are made, and in verse 41 the people as a whole are regarded as the ones who make the gods. In some languages a seeming discrepancy of agents constitutes a problem which may be resolved by an expression such as "they asked to have made for themselves" or "they asked Aaron to make for them."

The idea that God gives men over (TEV gave them over) to the consequence of their sin appears three times in Romans 1 (vv. 24, 26, 28), and implies that God not merely passively deserts such people, but that he actively hands them over to the result of their sins.

The "hosts of heaven" is a Jewish way of speaking of the stars of heaven (see Moffatt, Goodspeed "the starry host").

The book of the prophets is not a comprehensive term referring to the section of the Hebrew Bible known as "the prophets"; it is rather a reference to the single scroll which contained all of the so-called minor prophets. The quotation which follows is from Amos 5. 25-27; and as given here it follows the Septuagint text, which departs significantly from the Hebrew text. Not only is there a textual difference between the Septuagint and the Hebrew, but there is a basic difference of application of these verses by Amos and Stephen. Amos is arguing against the priestly emphasis upon sacrifice, and points out that the absence of sacrifice in the desert was an indication that God did not command his people to offer sacrifice to him; whereas Stephen uses these verses to prove that the Israelites were idolatrous all during the time of their desert wanderings. In Greek the quotation from Amos is a rhetorical question expecting the answer "no," with the people addressed coming last in the sentence: "you did not sacrifice to me ... did you ... house of Israel?" In order to make this a more natural and readable English construction, the TEV has transformed the rhetorical question into a statement and has put the people addressed first in the verse. Also, the Greek uses two nouns which are virtual synonyms ("slaughtered animals" and "sacrificed animals") as objects of the verb "you offered (as sacrifices in worship)." But these have been restructured by the TEV to read it was not to me that you slaughtered and sacrificed animals.

7.43

It is often not difficult to find an equivalent for the word tent, for example, "sanctuary" or even "canopy," since in so many societies it is common practice to provide some type of covering for the image of a god when it is carried in a public procession.

The TEV has added the god before Moloch and the image of before the star in order to indicate that Moloch was a god, and what the people of Israel actually carried was a likeness, or an image, of the star of the god Rephan (unless the reference to the star of your god Rephan is taken in some general way to suggest that they worshiped this particular star). Moloch was the Canaanite god of sun and sky, and Rephan may have been the Egyptian god of the planet Saturn. The statement I will send you away beyond Babylon agrees neither with the Hebrew nor with the Septuagint, both of which have "beyond Damascus."

In most languages there is no distinction made between image and idol. Technically, an image is only a representation of a god and has no inherent power within itself, while an idol not only represents the god but has certain inherent characteristics of special spirit power.

The expression <u>I will send you away</u> is not to be understood in the normal sense of "sending on a commission" but rather "cause you to be taken away" or "cause you to be led away."

> 44 "Our ancestors had the tent of God's presence with them in the desert. It had been made as God had told Moses to make it, according to the pattern that Moses had been shown. 45 Later on, our ancestors who received the tent from their fathers carried it with them when they went with Joshua and took over the land from the nations that God drove out before them. And it stayed there until the time of David. 46 He won God's favor, and asked God to allow him to provide a house for the God of Jacob. 47 But it was Solomon who built him a house.
>
> 48 "But the Most High God does not live in houses built by men; as the prophet says,
>> 49 'Heaven is my throne, says the Lord,
>> and earth is my footstool.
>> What kind of house would you build for me?
>> Where is the place for me to rest?
>> 50 Did not I myself make all these things?' (7.44-50)

These paragraphs are complexly structured and consist of essentially two contrasting viewpoints. The first relates to the tabernacle, which finally became a temple in the historical development of the Jewish people. Verse 48, however, introduces the contrast which declares that God himself does not live in such constructions built by men. Without special care in the translation one may very readily fail to bring out this important distinction.

The first half of the paragraph (vv. 44-47) consists of a tightly organized historical sequence which is essentially a description of the development and role of the tabernacle/temple. The temporal transition between the sentences is exceptionally important.

7.44

The <u>tent of God's presence</u> is rendered in most translations as "the tent of witness" (RSV; see Phillips "the Tabernacle of witness") or "the Tent of the Testimony" (JB, NEB). This <u>tent</u> was called "the tent of witness" because either in a general sense it was a witness to the presence of God among his people, or else, in a more specialized sense, it contained the covenant box (Exodus 25.22) in which were deposited the stones on which the Law had been written and which were a witness to God's covenant with his people.

The phrase <u>tent of God's presence</u> may be rendered in a number of different ways, for example, "tent which showed that God was present," "tent which contained that which showed that God was present," or "tent which said to the people, God is here."

7.45

The literal expression "the one speaking to Moses" (see RSV, Zürich, Goodspeed) is made explicit in the TEV, God had told Moses (see JB, NEB, Phillips). The TEV translation according to the pattern that Moses had been shown accomplishes at least two things: (1) it clears up the ambiguity in the Greek phrase "according to the pattern that he had seen" (which the reader could possibly understand to mean the pattern that God had seen), and (2) it indicates that what Moses saw was something that had been shown him by God.

A term for pattern is essentially the word "model." In certain languages, however, the closest equivalent is "picture," as any kind of representation.

7.45

In order to indicate the time lapse between the making of the tent of God's presence and the carrying of the tent into Palestine, the TEV has connected verse 45 with verse 44 by the adverbial statement later on.

Who received ... from their fathers translates the same Greek word that has been rendered "in turn" by the RSV. The word itself means "to receive from a former owner"; and though the participial construction is rather awkward in the present sentence, the meaning is clear enough: it refers to something that was handed down from one generation to another (see JB "it was handed down from one ancestor of ours to another").

The difficult noun phrase "in the possessing (that is, taking possession) of the nations" is transformed into a more readily understood verbal expression by the TEV, they ... took over the land from the nations (see JB "the country we had conquered from the nations" and NEB "they dispossessed the nations").

The first sentence of verse 45 is rather complex since it involves a number of diverse activities of our ancestors and includes two dependent clauses. In a number of languages such a complex sentence will need to be broken up, for example, "Later on, our ancestors received the tent from their fathers. They carried it with them when they went with Joshua. They carried it when they took over the land from the nations that God drove out before them."

Because of the problem of temporal sequence in the last two verb expressions in the first sentence, it may be necessary to change the order, for example, "as God drove nations out ahead of the Israelites, they took over the land from these nations."

The expression the time of David is often rendered as "the time when David lived" or "until the days (or years) of David."

7.46

He won God's favor (see JB, NEB, Phillips, Moffatt, Goodspeed) is literally "he found grace before God," but the meaning of "grace" in this passage is the same as in verse 10. The phrase won God's favor is not easy to translate in a number of languages. Frequently it must be expressed as a type of causative; for example, "he caused God to be favorable to him" or "he acted in such a way that God was good with him."

Although the text literally reads "he (that is, David) asked to find," it seems most probable that Stephen intended the word "to find" in the sense of to provide (see NEB, Goodspeed) or "to build" (JB; see Moffatt "devise"). Whatever may be the precise meaning of this verse in its Old Testament context (Psalm 132.5), in Acts it seems quite clear that David is not requesting that he be permitted to look around and find something already built, but rather that he be allowed "to build" or "to provide" a place for God.

The word which the TEV has translated house may also mean "tent" (most translations are vague, for example, "dwelling," "dwelling place," or "habitation"), but the point seems to be that David was asking to build God a permanent place, that is, the temple (see JB "to have a temple built"), as opposed to the tent which was formerly used as the place of God's presence.

As is indicated in the TEV list of alternative readings, there is a textual problem which may be resolved in one of two ways: (1) David's request may have been to build a temple for the "house of Jacob," that is, for the nation of Israel (see JB "to have a temple built for the House of Jacob"); or (2) David's request may have been to build a temple for the God of Jacob (as the TEV and most other translations have done). The UBS committee on the Greek text prefers the alternative reading suggested by the TEV, both on the basis of the diverse manuscript evidence in support of this reading and for the reason that it is easy to see why a scribe would change the reading "house" to "God," but not vice versa.

If the TEV is followed, it is most important to avoid a rendering of the God of Jacob which will seem to imply that this God is different from the God which is mentioned twice previously in the same verse. In some languages it may even be necessary to introduce a marginal note at this point to indicate that God is spoken of as the God of Jacob, or as expressed in some languages "the God whom Jacob worshiped."

7.47

As mentioned in the preceding verse, the word translated house may also mean "tent," and for that reason some commentators understand a contrast between what David asked and what Solomon built. These commentators would say that David asked to build God a temporary dwelling place, whereas Solomon built him a permanent dwelling place, that is, a temple. If this conclusion is valid, then these two verses are a rebuttal on the part of Stephen against the very existence of the Jerusalem temple.

7.48

The Most High God is a term taken from the Septuagint, and translates a Hebrew word that was often used by non-Israelites who confessed the true God. In many languages the concept of "highness" also means "greatness," but this is not necessarily true. A literal translation of Most High might imply merely a position on top of other gods but without necessarily suggesting greater importance. In such instances the closest equivalent of <u>the Most High God</u> is "the Greatest God."

The word translated <u>houses built by men</u> is a term frequently used to describe temples devoted to idols; and it may be that the term is used here in a derogatory sense by Stephen, with the meaning that the actual building of the temple was wrong in itself.

7.49

The Scripture quote in verses 49-50 comes from Isaiah 66.1-2, and follows the Septuagint closely. <u>Footstool</u> is used in this passage as an illustration of the greatness of God, for whom the whole world is merely a small footstool; the significance of a footstool is different in the earlier passage (2.35), where it is a figure of subjection.

<u>What kind of house</u> correctly translates the force of the qualitative interrogative in Greek.

In many cultures there is no equivalent to a <u>throne</u> as a seat of authority. One may, however, render this first clause of verse 49 as "heaven is the place from which I rule."

7.50

If the form of the question is to be retained in verse 50, it must be so structured as to imply a strong affirmation that God had himself made all such things. If this cannot be brought out clearly in the question, then one may shift to an emphatic statement. After all, the question is merely rhetorical even as the preceding two questions are, and in some languages such expressions must be restructured as emphatic statements. God is obviously not asking for information, but by means of the question form is emphasizing his lack of dependence upon what man has built.

> 51 "How stubborn you are! How heathen your hearts, how deaf you are to God's message! You are just like your ancestors: you too have always resisted the Holy Spirit! 52 Was there any prophet that your ancestors did not persecute? They killed God's messengers, who long ago announced the coming of his righteous Servant. And now you have betrayed and murdered him. 53 You are the ones who received God's law, that was handed down by angels---yet you have not obeyed it!" (7.51-53)

Stephen has completed his survey of Jewish history; he has shown how the Jews have consistently rebelled against God and rejected those whom he had sent to them. Now he points out that the present generation of Jews have behaved in the same fashion by their rejection of the one whom God sent to them.

This paragraph (vv. 51-53) begins with a general statement how stubborn you are and then illustrates or amplifies the statement by several examples. One could, of course, take the entire first half of verse 51 as the general statement and the rest of the paragraph as being illustrative of this initial declaration.

7.51

How stubborn you are translates a single Greek word (literally "stiffnecked"), which is used in Exodus 33.3 and other places in the Septuagint to describe the rebellious attitude of Israel. In the phrase "uncircumcised in heart and in ears" the word "circumcised" must be understood as the equivalent of "pagan" or "heathenish." Therefore, the TEV has translated the first part of this expression as how heathen your hearts, and the second part has been rendered how deaf you are to God's message! To be "heathen in heart" means either that one has not heard, or refuses to hear, God's message.

In translating how heathen your hearts one may make specific reference to the heathen, for example, "your hearts are just like the hearts of heathen people" or "your hearts are just like the hearts of those who do not believe in God." However, this portion of verse 51 may be somewhat restructured, for example, "just like those who reject God, you will not let your hearts listen to God's message" or "...you are deaf to what God has said."

The phrase resisted the Holy Spirit may be rendered as "refused to listen to the Holy Spirit" or "would not obey the Holy Spirit."

7.52

The initial question of verse 52 is obviously rhetorical, for Stephen is not asking for any information. It is, therefore, necessary in a number of languages to render this as an emphatic statement, for example, "your ancestors persecuted every prophet" or "there was not one prophet that your ancestors did not cause to suffer."

Who long ago announced has been expanded by the addition of God's messengers, since the context makes it clear that those who announced the coming of his righteous Servant were the messengers whom God had sent. His righteous Servant (literally "the righteous one") is without doubt used here as a technical term referring to the Savior whom God had promised he would send. The same expression is used of Jesus in 3.14 and 22.14. In the former of these passages it is translated holy and good, while in the latter passage it is rendered righteous Servant, as in the present passage. Inasmuch as the name appears to identify Jesus with the servant of God in the Old Testament (see 3.13), the TEV has sought to maintain that identity by translating righteous Servant both in the present passage and in 22.14.

In this context, righteous refers to one who does what God requires. This is somewhat more, therefore, than mere "good behavior" and can be rendered by the same expression used for righteous in a number of contexts, for example, "God's servant who does what he requires."

7.53

As is frequently done in the TEV, nouns that contain verbal ideas have here been translated as verbs: "you became betrayers and murderers" appears as <u>you have betrayed and murdered him</u>.

<u>7.53</u>

The word <u>law</u> has been made specific by rendering <u>God's law,</u> so that the English reader would understand the correct meaning of the word in this type of context. <u>God's law</u> is, of course, "the law that comes from God" or "the law that God gives." It is rarely translated by a "possessive construction," for it is not "the law that God possesses." In some instances the source of the law can be combined with a rendering of <u>received</u>, for example, "the ones to whom God gave the law."

Although the words translated <u>that was handed down by angels</u> comes from a very difficult Greek expression, most exegetes agree that this is the meaning. As used by Stephen the words are intended to underline the greatness of the significance of the law which the Israelites received, though Paul uses a similar expression in exactly the opposite fashion (see Galatians 3.19). It should be noticed that the Hebrew Old Testament does not mention that God used angels as mediators to give his law to his people, but the Septuagint of Deuteronomy 33.2 adds "angels with him (that is, with the Lord), at his right hand."

The difference in the role between God who gives the law and the angels who act as mediators may be expressed in some languages as "God gave the law...the angels spoke it to Moses." On the other hand, one may also say "the law came from God by means of the angels." This latter translation leaves the specific relationship to the event more ambiguous.

The Stoning of Stephen

54 As the members of the Council listened to Stephen they became furious and ground their teeth at him in anger. 55 But Stephen, full of the Holy Spirit, looked up to heaven and saw God's glory, and Jesus standing at the right side of God. 56 "Look!" he said. "I see heaven opened and the Son of Man standing at the right side of God!"
57 With a loud cry they covered their ears with their hands. Then they all rushed together at him at once, 58 threw him out of the city and stoned him. The witnesses left their cloaks in charge of a young man named Saul. 59 They kept on stoning Stephen as he called on the Lord, "Lord Jesus, receive my spirit!" 60 He knelt down and cried out in a loud voice, "Lord! Do not remember this sin against them!" He said this and died.
1a And Saul approved of his murder. (7.54---8.1a)

The reaction of the Jewish Council to the speech of Stephen serves as the final verification of his words. As the Jewish people had rejected and put to death God's messengers in times past, so now they reject and put to death Stephen.

Note that the first clause of Chapter 8 is included as a portion of this account of the stoning of Stephen. First, Saul is introduced in verse 58, and second, his approval is stated in the first clause of Chapter 8. This provides the transition for a brief account of Saul's activities and sets the stage for a fuller description of Saul's experiences, beginning with Chapter 9.

7.54

The subject of the verbs became furious and ground their teeth is not explicit in the Greek; but the TEV has made the subject explicit, the members of the Council, inasmuch as the last previous reference to the Jewish Council appeared in 6.15. As...listened...they became furious attempts to represent the significance of the Greek verb tenses. "As they heard these things" has been expanded to read as the members of the Council listened to Stephen, while in anger has been added to the expression ground their teeth at him in order to indicate for the English reader the significance of this Jewish expression. The idiom ground their teeth at him is quite meaningless in many languages. In fact, the impression may simply be of some ludicrous activity. In some languages, therefore, another idiom with equivalent meaning is employed, for example, "their hearts were very hot against him," "their faces burned against him," or "their hearts were very angry."

7.55

The subject of the Greek verb is not explicit; the Greek simply has "he," the TEV Stephen. The statement that Stephen was full of the Holy Spirit may imply that the Holy Spirit is, in some contexts, to be regarded as a gift for special occasions, this time enabling Stephen to look into heaven itself.

It is important in translating saw God's glory not to imply that Stephen sees God himself; rather, what he sees is the "glory" or "majesty" of God. This is rendered in some languages as "the bright shining of God." This expression is, of course, a reference to the Shekinah of God, often referred to in the Old Testament in relationship to the presence of God in the temple.

For the phrase at the right side of God see 2.33.

7.56

The rendering of heaven opened must not be such as to suggest that "heaven is split open." It is necessary, therefore, in some languages, to translate as "the entrance to heaven is open." Otherwise the term "opened" would suggest some damage having occurred to heaven.

This is the only passage outside the Gospels where the phrase the Son of Man appears. It is obvious that by the use of this term Stephen was referring to Jesus, and it is just as obvious that the Jewish Council understood him in this fashion. This explains the reaction of the Jewish Council toward Stephen; in their minds he has committed blasphemy by identifying Jesus with God. However one translates the title Son of Man, it should be translated in such a fashion as to indicate that it is a term of dignity and power and not

merely that the person to whom he referred was a man. For new readers and
other persons who may have a limited background for understanding the meaning of this term, the name Jesus could be substituted in the text for the Son of
Man with a footnote explaining what has been done. Commentators offer different explanations of the reason that he was standing at the right side of God,
but most generally it is assumed that Jesus stands in order to welcome his
faithful witness.

7.57

In order to avoid defilement by even hearing the blasphemous things that
Stephen was saying, the members of the Jewish Council do two things, they
shout and cover their ears. All...together...at once translates the same
Greek word as appeared in 1.14; it is translated "as one man" by NAB and
"like one man" by Moffatt.

7.58

It is difficult to determine whether Luke intends for his readers to
understand the stoning of Stephen to be the result of legal action on the part
of the Jewish Council or whether it is to be taken as mob violence. The method
of stoning is altogether different from the description of execution by stoning
as described in the Mishnah, the Jewish source which tells how the Jews carried out this action. For this reason many understand the stoning here to be
that of mob action rather than as a carrying out of the legal decision of the
court. In cases demanding the capital offense, the Jewish court required the
testimony of two witnesses. If a man were convicted, it was the duty of one
of these witnesses to push him headfirst off a precipice and then roll a stone
over him. If this did not kill him, then the second witness rolled another
stone on him which was supposed to crush his chest. In the Mishnah there is
nothing said of the witnesses taking off their outer garments, though the Mishnah does state if the criminal is a man then he must be unclothed before he is
put to death. From reading Luke's account one is of the opinion that Stephen
was put to death by people throwing stones at him, and that the persons who
threw the stones removed their outer garments so they would have better
freedom in throwing the stones.
Though the Greek term literally means "threw out," the action of the
mob would suggest more "drive out forcibly." There seems to be no suggestion that Stephen was literally thrown down from a wall or over any cliff.
Stoned him is simply equivalent to "threw stones at him" or "killed him
by means of throwing stones at him." In this particular verse, however, the
rendering may need to be "were killing him" since they continued the process
for some time, as noted in verse 59.

7.59

They kept on stoning underlines the force of the Greek verb tense. The verb translated called on means "to call on (in prayer)." One might compare this prayer with the prayer of Jesus in Luke 23.46.

7.60

Do not remember this sin against them is in some languages equivalent to "forgive this sin of theirs." With this prayer one might compare the prayer of Jesus in Luke 23.34.

Died translates a euphemistic expression (literally "he fell asleep") which means "to die." See Phillips who tries to bring out this aspect, "he fell into the sleep of death."

8.1a

Even though "death" is a legitimate translation of the word used here, it seems too colorless and meaningless to suit the present context, which demands the meaning of murder (so also NEB).

Approved may be rendered as "agreed that the murder was right" or "agreed that Stephen should have been killed." In some languages the approval is expressed by "said yes to the murder" or "his heart was good because they had killed Stephen." (In such a context "good" would refer only to the feeling in the person's heart, not to his behavior.)

CHAPTER 8

Chapter 8 consists of three principal sections. The first (vv. 1b-3) serves as a transition, since it relates what happened in Chapter 7 to a more general persecution, and highlights the role of Saul. The statement on persecution also forms an appropriate reason for the preaching of the gospel in Samaria (note how the account of the scattering of the believers is picked up in v. 4).

The second section, which deals with the preaching in Samaria, concentrates on the work of Philip, but then shifts to Peter and John. Philip is again the center of attention in the third section of Chapter 8 (vv. 26-40), which tells the story of Philip meeting the Ethiopian official.

Saul Persecutes the Church

1b That very day the church in Jerusalem began to suffer cruel persecution. All the believers, except the apostles, were scattered throughout the provinces of Judea and Samaria. 2 Some devout men buried Stephen, mourning for him with loud cries.

3 But Saul tried to destroy the church; going from house to house, he dragged out the believers, both men and women, and threw them into jail. (8.1b-3)

The term Persecutes in the section heading to these paragraphs can be translated as "Causes to Suffer." It may also be necessary to render Church as "Believers," since in some languages one can only cause people, not institutions, to suffer. Therefore, one may need to employ as a section heading "Saul Causes the Believers to Suffer."

These verses look both forward and backward: verse 1b looks back to the persecution which resulted from the death of Stephen, and at the same time points forward to the preaching of the gospel in Samaria. Verse 2 points back to the death of Stephen and constitutes the climax of that story; while verse 3 takes up once again the theme of persecution against the church, and points forward to Chapter 9, where the story of Saul is given in more detail.

8.1b

That very day renders a corresponding emphatic expression in the Greek sentence structure.

The phrase suffer cruel persecution may simply be rendered as "suffered very much," but it is important to emphasize the intensity of the "persecution," for example, "suffered because people were treating them very badly."

In order to make the subject of the verb scattered explicit, the TEV has expanded all to all the believers (see Phillips "all Church members"). Throughout the provinces is a difficult expression, but the basic idea seems to be the country regions as opposed to the city regions (see JB and NEB "country districts").

170

A term for scattered must of course be applicable to people, not merely to things. Therefore, a rendering which is often employed is "were caused to flee."

The phrase except the apostles must apply to the activity of fleeing, not to believing. In some languages this can only be done by a positive and negative expression, for example, "all the believers were caused to flee...; only the apostles didn't flee."

8.2

The devout men who buried Stephen may either be Christians, pious Jews, or both Christians and pious Jews. Elsewhere in the New Testament this phrase is used of Jews, and when used of Ananias, who was a Christian, it was used of him as a Jew (22.12). In general the term devout can be appropriately rendered as "worshipers of God."

Mourning for him with loud cries is literally "they made a great mourning for him." It has been pointed out by some commentators that Stephen's death must not have been an official execution by the Jewish Council, otherwise there would have been no public mourning for him and no burial, since according to the Mishnah neither of these was allowed for a man who had been executed by stoning. However, it is quite likely that the Mishnah describes what was felt should have been right in the second century A.D. rather than what was necessarily the practice in the first century.

8.3

The conjunction but should contrast the activity of those who wept for Stephen with the behavior of Saul, who was determined to destroy the church.

Tried to destroy translates a Greek imperfect tense, which seems to have this force in the context. (See JB "Saul then worked for the total destruction of the Church.") Some exegetes have, however, taken it simply in the sense of continuous action "was destroying." On the other hand, it is possible to translate this verb, which appears only here in the New Testament, with the meaning of "harass" or "bring great trouble to." If this is done, then it is unnecessary to indicate the fact that this is something that Saul tried, and it may be stated as something which in fact he did do (see NAB "Saul began to harass the church"; Goodspeed "but Saul harassed the church").

The term destroy must be relatable to a group of people, not simply to a building, which might be suggested by a term such as is often employed for church. Sometimes destroy may be rendered as "cause to disappear" or "cause them not to be."

The Greek literally states that Saul dragged out "both men and women," but these "men and women" were believers, as the TEV has indicated.

Saul's role in the persecution of the church was that of a prosecutor, and therefore the phrase threw them into jail may need to be expressed by a causative "caused them to be put into jail." In some languages this is referred to variously as "caused them to be tied up," "caused them to be locked up," or "caused them to be put away."

The Gospel Preached in Samaria

4 The believers who were scattered went everywhere, preaching the message. 5 Philip went to the city of Samaria and preached the Messiah to the people there. 6 The crowds paid close attention to what Philip said. They all listened to him and saw the miracles that he performed. 7 Evil spirits came out with a loud cry from many people; many paralyzed and lame people were also healed. 8 So there was great joy in Samaria. (8.4-8)

In a number of languages one cannot employ a participial construction such as occurs in the section heading The Gospel Preached in Samaria. Rather, a complete sentence may be required, for example, "The Gospel (or Good News) Is Preached in Samaria," but more often than not a verb such as "preach" requires some agent, "Philip Preaches the Good News in Samaria."

The account of the revival in Samaria (contained in vv. 4-25) is a skillfully written account with clearly marked transitions and excellent development of events.

Verse 4 introduces the reason for the movement into Samaria as the result of the persecution described briefly in the preceding verses. Philip's success immediately brings him into competition with Simon, who had dominated the religious life of Samaria (vv. 9-13). This revival in Samaria also attracts the attention of the apostles in Jerusalem, who send Peter and John, presumably to investigate developments. Simon, who has been introduced in the second paragraph of this major section, now becomes the focus of attention as he seeks from Peter the gift of laying on of hands so that people may receive the Holy Spirit (vv. 18-24). Finally, verse 25 summarizes the events and takes Peter and John back to Jerusalem so that Philip's experience with the Ethiopian official can be introduced, beginning with verse 26.

Note closely the transitional devices beginning the various paragraphs: scattered (v. 4), referring back to verse 1; in that city (v. 9), referring back to Samaria in verse 8; the people of Samaria had received the word of God (v. 14), referring to the contents of the two preceding paragraphs; Simon saw that the Spirit had been given to them when the apostles placed their hands on them (v. 18), an immediate reference to verse 17; and after they had given their testimony (v. 25), a reference to the preceding events. The proper treatment of these transitional devices is essential if the story is to hang together.

8. 4

Luke begins this section with a favorite formula (see 1.6) that is not rendered in most translations, though it appears in the RSV as "now" and in the KJV as "therefore."

"Those who were scattered" has been expanded in the TEV to the believers who were scattered, while went everywhere translates a verb which means "to go from place to place" (see JB). For the use of "word" in the sense of message see 4.4.

8.5

Philip is one of the seven (see 6.5).

Translations are divided as to whether Luke said the city of Samaria or "a city of Samaria" (NEB, RSV). In New Testament times the Old Testament city of Samaria was known as Sebaste, and the word Samaria referred to the province; so by the expression the city of Samaria is meant the (main) city of Samaria, that is, Sebaste. The Samaritans, as the Jews, lived in the expectation of a coming Messiah; among the Samaritans he was known as Taheb, "one who restores."

In this context the TEV employs Messiah rather than "Christ," since the former term applies specifically to Christ's having been sent by God on a special mission. To introduce this distinction in some languages it is necessary to render Messiah as "the one specially sent by God."

Though in English one may say preached the Messiah, this is rendered in many languages as "told the people about the Messiah."

8.6

The phrase paid close attention may be rendered in a number of different ways, for example, "listened to him well," "opened their ears to him," or "received his word with care."

They all translates the same word as gathered frequently...as a group in 1.14.

8.7

The Greek text of verse 7 contains a very unusual grammatical reference. Many people (rather than evil spirits) is technically the grammatical subject of came out; however, it is perfectly clear from the context that evil spirits are to be understood as having come out of the people.

Came out with a loud cry is often rendered by two verbal expressions, for example, "they screamed and came out."

Paralyzed...people is usually rendered as "persons who could not move their legs" or "those who could not move their bodies." Lame people are simply "those who walk haltingly" or "those who could not walk properly."

8.8

The phrase "in that city" is taken to mean the city of Samaria by the TEV, so there was great joy in Samaria. In many languages, however, one cannot simply speak of "there being joy." Rather, it is people who must experience joy. Therefore, one must translate as "the people in Samaria were very joy-ful" or "the people in Samaria were glad in their hearts."

> 9 In that city lived a man named Simon, who for some time had astounded the Samaritans with his magic. He claimed that he was someone great, 10 and everyone in the city, from all classes of society, paid close attention to him. "He is that power of God known as 'The Great Power,'" they said. 11 He had astounded them with his magic for such a long time that they paid close attention to him. 12 But when they believed Philip's message about the Good News of the King-dom of God and the name of Jesus Christ, they were baptized, both men and women. 13 Simon himself also believed; and after being baptized he stayed close to Philip, and was astounded when he saw the great wonders and miracles that were being performed. (8.9-13)

In Greek, a new participant in a discourse is frequently introduced by a pronominal element tis, often translated as "a certain." In English, it is much more common to have a new participant in a discourse introduced after a verb, even in a situation such as the first sentence of verse 9, in which a man, although the subject, occurs after the verb lived. The phrase in that city serves as the appropriate transition from the preceding sentence.

8.9

The main verb in this sentence (literally, "to be for some while") has two participles dependent upon it, "practicing magic" and "astounding." The meaning is that Simon had been in the city for some time and all the while had been practicing magic and astounding the people. The rendering "who had previously practiced magic" (RSV) might suggest that at the time that Philip came to Samaria Simon was no longer practicing magic, but the force of the Greek indicates that Simon had been doing this for a long time and was still doing it at the time of Philip's arrival in the city. The Greek literally says "the nation of the Samaritans" (see RSV), but the meaning of the expres-sion is simply "the Samaritan people," that is, the Samaritans (see NEB, Phillips, JB). He claimed that he was someone great is very similar to what was said of Theudas in 5.36.

The Greek term translated "practicing magic" is a technical expres-sion relating to the use of sorcery. It is not a term for "performing mira-cles." Since magic in one form or another, whether "white" (beneficial) or "black" (harmful), is of common occurrence in most cultures, there is usu-ally no difficulty in finding some closely corresponding terms.

8.10

Everyone in the city, from all classes of society is literally "all from little unto great," an idiom used to include all members of a given group. The JB renders this phrase "eminent citizens and ordinary people alike." In some languages the equivalent of this expression is "all the people, little people and big people."

Paid close attention to him is the same verb as used in verse 6 above; Barclay translates "listened eagerly to." The commentators agree that The Great Power is a name referring to the Highest God and not merely to one who possesses a great power from God. What the people believed was that Simon himself was a manifestation of God.

If one is to render correctly the meaning of he is that power of God known as The Great Power, it is often necessary to restructure the expression rather radically in order for the reader to understand that the people regarded Simon as a kind of god. The closest equivalent to this may be "The god called The Great Power has come down in the form of Simon" or "Simon is the one who the god, known as The Great Power, has become."

8.11

Note that verse 11 does not add any new information which is not already contained in the two preceding verses. It is simply an emphatic repetition of the essential information. In some languages one must add a term such as "really," for example, "he had really astounded them." By such emphatic forms one can justify the repetition of the information.

8.12

When they believed translates a verb tense expressing so-called "point action," as opposed to the linear or continuous action of the verb tenses in verses 6 and 10, paid close attention to.

Philip's message may have the meaning "as Philip was preaching" (see RSV, Phillips) or "what Philip was preaching" (see JB "they believed Philip's preaching, Barclay "believe the Good News which Philip was bringing").

On the Kingdom of God see 1.3; and on the name of Jesus see 3.6.

To preach the Good News about the name of Jesus Christ would mean "to preach the Good News about Jesus Christ," and in the present context specifically the Good News that Jesus was the Messiah.

8.13

In most languages it is necessary to have some goal for the verb believed. Therefore, "believed Philip's message" or "believed in Jesus Christ."

By translating great wonders and miracles the TEV has reversed the order of the Greek phrase "signs (that is, miracles) and great wonders."

Though the phrase were being performed is passive, it can be changed to an active by making Philip the subject, for example, "the great wonders and miracles that Philip was doing."

14 The apostles in Jerusalem heard that the people of Samaria
had received the word of God; so they sent Peter and John to them.
15 When they arrived, they prayed for the believers that they might
receive the Holy Spirit. 16 For the Holy Spirit had not yet come down
on any of them; they had only been baptized in the name of the Lord Jesus.
17 Then Peter and John placed their hands on them, and they received
the Holy Spirit. (8.14-17)

This paragraph is deceptively easy. In reality, the system of pronominal
reference is quite complex. There are three sets of plural participants: the
apostles in Jerusalem, the people of Samaria (or the believers), and Peter and
John. In referring to these participants this paragraph in English has ten occurrences of they, them, or their, and without special care in the translation
of such pronouns one can very readily make a wrong reference.

8.14

In the Greek text Samaria is the subject of receiving the word of God,
but this obviously is a reference to the people of Samaria. In many languages,
one cannot speak of "receiving the word of God." One can only "believe the
word of God." Many languages, moreover, make a clear distinction between
the word that comes from God (that is, the message which comes from God)
and God's own spoken words. In this context, of course, it is a message which
comes from God and is about Jesus Christ.

Some persons have thought that John might here refer to John Mark (who
in 13.5 and 13 is called simply John in the Greek text, though identified as
John Mark in the TEV), but this is quite doubtful.

8.15

For the believers takes the place of "for them" in order to clear the
possible ambiguity in the Greek statement "when they arrived, they prayed
for them (that is, for the believers) that they might receive the Holy Spirit."

In some languages there is a problem in the phrase receive the Holy
Spirit, for it could imply that they were refusing to receive the Holy Spirit
and that the prayer of Peter and John was that they might be willing to receive
the Holy Spirit. This, of course, is not the meaning of the original text.
Therefore, one must sometimes translate as "they prayed for the believers
that the Holy Spirit would come to them." This interpretation is reinforced
by verse 16.

8.16

It is frequently possible to speak of the Holy Spirit coming down on, but
in many languages it is necessary to say "the Holy Spirit comes into," "the
Holy Spirit comes to possess," or "the Holy Spirit comes to live in them."

For the expression in the name of the Lord Jesus see 2.38.

The subject of "they placed their hands" has been made explicit by the addition of Peter and John. As in other contexts, it may be necessary to indicate where the hands were placed and this would presumably be on the heads.

A term for received the Holy Spirit must of course be the same as is employed in verse 15.

> 18 Simon saw that the Spirit had been given to them when the apostles placed their hands on them. So he offered money to Peter and John, 19 and said, "Give this power to me too, so that anyone I place my hands on will receive the Holy Spirit."
>
> 20 But Peter answered him, "May you and your money go to hell, for thinking that you can buy God's gift with money! 21 You have no part or share in our work, because your heart is not right in God's sight. 22 Repent, then, from this evil plan of yours, and pray to the Lord that he will forgive you for thinking such a thing as this. 23 For I see that you are full of bitter envy, and are a prisoner of sin."
>
> 24 Simon said to Peter and John, "Please pray to the Lord for me, so that none of these things you said will happen to me."
>
> 25 After they had given their testimony and spoken the Lord's message, Peter and John went back to Jerusalem. On their way they preached the Good News in many villages of Samaria. (8.18-25)

The first three paragraphs in this section contain the conversation between the apostle Peter and Simon, who practiced magic in Samaria. The last paragraph is a conclusion to the entire episode. It is important that the reference to their testimony not be merely an allusion to what Peter had said to Simon. The testimony and the message were to all the people.

8.18

The passive expression rendered as had been given suggests that God is the agent of the giving. If this phrase must be shifted into an active form, one can therefore translate that "God had given the Spirit to them when the apostles placed their hands on them."

When the apostles placed their hands on them is not merely a statement of time, but indicates "by means of placing their hands on them" (see NEB and RSV "through the laying on of the apostles' hands"). To Peter and John translates "to them" of the Greek text.

8.19

Give this power to me is equivalent in many languages to "make me able to" or "cause me to be strong enough to." The final clause of verse 19 may need to be radically restructured if the expression receive the Holy Spirit requires some modification, as suggested in the discussion of verse 15.

<u>8.20</u>

The full force of Peter's wish is accurately translated by the TEV: <u>may you and your money go to hell</u> (see Phillips "to hell with you and your money," who adds the note, "these words are exactly what the Greek means. It is a pity that their real meaning is obscured by modern slang usage"; JB "may your silver be lost forever, and you with it"). In some languages this forceful expression may be rendered as "may your money die and you too" or "you and your money will certainly die."

In the present context <u>God's gift</u> is the power to communicate the Holy Spirit through the laying on of hands. The phrase <u>God's gift</u> may be difficult to render in this context since <u>gift</u> does not refer to an object but to an ability to perform a particular function. The entire clause may be rendered, therefore, as "thinking that you can pay money and have God cause you to have this ability to give the Holy Spirit" or "...cause the Holy Spirit to come upon people."

<u>8.21</u>

The expression <u>you have no part or share</u> is equivalent to "you are not really one with us" or "this is certainly not your work."

<u>In our work</u> literally translates the phrase "in this word," but in Greek as in Hebrew, "word" may also mean "matter" or "business."

In the expression <u>your heart is not right</u> the word <u>right</u> translates a term which means "straight"; but inasmuch as "straight" in a moral sense is indicated, the meaning is "right" or "upright." Moffatt "your heart is all wrong in the sight of God" renders accurately the meaning. NEB "for you are dishonest with God" and Phillips "your heart is not honest before God" seem to have somewhat missed the full impact of the word. In some languages, however, one cannot say <u>your heart is not right</u>. Rather, one must employ a rendering such as "you are not right (straight) in your heart."

<u>In God's sight</u> is equivalent to "as God sees you," "from God's point of view," or "as God judges you."

<u>8.22</u>

The TEV understands the evil within Simon in the sense of an <u>evil plan</u>, though most translators simply render the word by "wickedness." The expression "the intent of your heart" is rendered by the TEV as <u>for thinking such a thing as this</u>, since in Jewish thought the heart was the seat of one's thoughts.

<u>Forgive you for thinking</u> may be rendered as "forgive you because you have thought."

<u>8.23</u>

The language of this verse is drawn from Old Testament passages such as Deuteronomy 29.17b and Isaiah 58.6. The TEV understands "gall of bitterness" in the sense of bitter envy; but others, in light of the fact that in Deuteronomy the phrase is connected with idolatry, refer this specifically to heathen worship: "bitterness like gall which godless worship brings" (Barclay). The interpretation of this particular phrase is also related to the overall understanding of the verse, since the Greek preposition with which the verse begins may mean either "in" or "into." Most translations accept the same conclusions of the TEV: you are full of (that is, "in") bitter envy, and are a prisoner of sin (see RSV, NAB, JB, Phillips, Zürich, Moffatt). Others understand the phrase to mean "I see you are a prisoner of sin and headed for" (that is, "into") "a bitter fate" (see NEB and Barclay).

The phrase full of bitter envy is especially difficult to translate in a number of languages. In the first place, full of must usually be rendered as "being very envious." The term bitter is not so much a description of envy itself as the effect which envy has upon the individual who is envious. On the other hand, it may refer to the intensity of envy or its evil nature.

The phrase prisoner of sin is equivalent to "being made a prisoner by sin" or "sin makes you its prisoner." However, in many languages one cannot employ a term such as sin, which refers to an event, as the agent of causing someone to be a prisoner. There is a causal relationship and therefore one can say in some languages "because of your sin you are a prisoner" or "because of your sin you are tied like a prisoner."

8. 24

In Greek the subject of the verb pray is masculine plural, and for this reason the TEV has made explicit the persons to whom Simon addressed his request: to Peter and John.

8. 25

This verse is transitional as is indicated by the particles that Luke uses to begin it. Although it is thought by some that the subject of the verb went back should include Philip, most commentators understand the subject to be only Peter and John.

The phrase had given their testimony may require a goal in certain languages, for example, "said what they knew concerning Jesus Christ" or "had shared with people what they knew about Jesus." The term of "knowing" should imply personal experience. The Lord's message may be understood as "the message which the Lord had spoken" or "the message about the Lord."

Philip and the Ethiopian Official

26 An angel of the Lord spoke to Philip, "Get yourself ready and go south to the road that goes from Jerusalem to Gaza." (This road is no longer used.) 27-28 So Philip got ready and went. Now an Ethiopian eunuch was on his way home. This man was an important official in charge of the treasury of the Queen, or Candace, of Ethiopia. He had

been to Jerusalem to worship God, and was going back in his carriage.
As he rode along he was reading from the book of the prophet Isaiah.
29 The Holy Spirit said to Philip, "Go over and stay close to that carriage." 30 Philip ran over and heard him reading from the book of the
prophet Isaiah; so he asked him, "Do you understand what you are
reading?"

31 "How can I understand," the official replied, "unless someone
explains it to me?" And he invited Philip to climb up and sit in the carriage with him. 32 The passage of scripture which he was reading was
this,

> "He was like a sheep that is taken to be slaughtered;
> he was like a lamb that makes no sound when its
>   wool is cut off;
> he did not say a word.
> 33 He was humiliated, and justice was denied him.
> No one will be able to tell about his descendants,
>   because his life on earth has come to an end." (8. 26-33)

These paragraphs, verses 26-33, are a typical narrative sequence with
completely embedded conversation and a quotation. It is for this reason necessary that careful attention be paid to the transitional devices, for example,
so, now, this man, as, so that there may be no confusion concerning prior
information about the Ethiopian eunuch and what he was actually doing when
Philip met him.

8. 26

Luke now directs his attention back to Philip. Get yourself ready (see
JB "be ready") is the same verb which appears in 5. 6 and indicates the initiation of action (NEB translates "start out").

Though most translators and commentators understand that Philip was
directed to go south, it is possible that this expression is intended to be taken
in the sense of "at midday" (see JB, Zürich). This road is no longer used is
generally understood to have been a parenthetical statement added by Luke
for the benefit of his readers. The TEV gives an alternative rendering of this
passage (this is the desert road); and there is also the possibility that the adjective translated no longer used and desert may refer back to Gaza. If so,
then the old Philistine city of Gaza, having been destroyed, is now distinguished from the new city of Gaza, built on the coast some two miles west
of the old city. Although a number of commentators accept this viewpoint,
only a few translators follow this interpretation (see Goodspeed "... from
Jerusalem to Gaza. [The town is now deserted]"; and Knox).

8. 27-28

Some equivalent of the transitional particle so is especially useful to
point up the response of Philip to the immediately preceding command from
the Lord.

The following sentence about the Ethiopian eunuch introduces another participant in the story. It is very important, therefore, to have some kind of transitional device to highlight the fact that another person is being introduced. In the TEV this is done by the use of the conjunction now.

Although the word eunuch basically means "a man who has been emasculated," the word is often used in the Old Testament as a synonym for a high political or military official; and the word translated important official (see NEB "high official") indicates the importance of the position that he held in the court of Ethiopia. In some languages a literal equivalent of eunuch has such unfortunate connotations that in certain translations this type of reference has been omitted completely and simply an equivalent of "official" has been employed. This is perfectly acceptable within such a context, since there is no special reference to the physical condition of the official, only his position and prominence.

Jewish law forbade a eunuch to become a full convert to Judaism (see Deuteronomy 23.1); but hope was given to those eunuchs who obeyed the Law of the Sabbath day (Isaiah 56.3-8), and they were permitted to worship the God of the Jewish people. This eunuch had been to Jerusalem to worship God (perhaps it is too much to describe him as having been there "on a pilgrimage," so NEB, though the identical expression in 24.11 may support this translation).

Candace (transliterated as Kandake in the NEB) is not the name of the queen but rather the title of the queens of Ethiopia, as Pharaoh was the title of the kings of Egypt. An equivalent of treasury may be "valuable possessions," "the money of the kingdom," or "the gold and silver which belonged to the queen." An equivalent of Queen is in many languages simply "a woman ruler" or "a woman who ruled over the whole land."

Carriage or "wagon" suits the context better than "chariot," which suggests a two-wheeled cart used in war. As the eunuch rode along he was reading aloud, as was the custom in antiquity.

The expression the book of the prophet Isaiah must clearly indicate that this was "the book containing the words of the prophet Isaiah" or "the book written by the prophet Isaiah." It is not "the book which belonged to Isaiah."

8.29

An angel of the Lord had supernaturally instructed Philip to go down towards Gaza, and now the Holy Spirit points out to Philip the reason for the previous instructions. In the Greek text "Holy" is not used as a modifier of Spirit in this passage, but it is evident that Luke means the Holy Spirit.

The expression stay close to that carriage is translated in a number of languages as "walk along close beside the carriage." Obviously the eunuch was continuing his journey as he read.

8.30

It may be necessary to specify where Philip ran to, for example, "ran over to where the Ethiopian was riding along."

8.31

The question Do you understand what you are reading? must not be so translated as to suggest that the Ethiopian did not know the language nor that he was unable to read correctly. The question really involves the interpretation of what he had read. Therefore, in some languages, the question is framed as "Do you understand the meaning of what you are reading?"

8.31

The invitation of the Ethiopian official to Philip must frequently be expressed as direct discourse, for example, "he said to Philip, Please come up and sit in the carriage with me."

In some languages it is important to specify that the carriage continues to go forward, and therefore a term for "sitting" must also imply "riding," for example, "ride along in the carriage with me."

8.32

Even though the words translated passage of scripture here and in verse 35 are different words, there is no essential difference of meaning. The passage quoted in these verses comes from the Septuagint of Isaiah 53.7-8, and it is the first time in the book of Acts that the "Suffering Servant" passage is applied to our Lord. (Note, however, 3.13.)

The verb taken must not suggest "seized" or "grabbed," but rather "being led away."

Though sheep are not particularly well-known in certain parts of the world (for example, the tropics or arctic regions), there is usually some knowledge concerning these animals and normally some term for them. Even the Eskimos speak of sheep as "woolly goats," since they know wild goats and are acquainted with wool. Furthermore, sheep and lambs are so important in the biblical account and figure so prominently as symbols that one cannot substitute any other type of animal. If necessary, it is entirely possible to employ some kind of descriptive note in a glossary, and pictures of sheep and lambs may be introduced so as to make clear to the reader what type of animal is being spoken of.

8.33

He was humiliated, and justice was denied him is literally "in his humiliation his judgment was taken away." The first part of this expression is easily taken to mean he was humiliated, but the second half causes difficulty. Most translations tend either in the direction of the TEV or in the direction of JB, "he has been humiliated and has no one to defend him" (see also NEB "he has been humiliated and has no redress"). The second line of verse 33 (in Greek a rhetorical question) is rendered by the TEV no one will be able to tell about his descendants, since he was put to death without leaving any posterity. This view is followed by NEB, JB, and Goodspeed, among others. There is also the possibility that the word translated descendants may mean "contemporary generation." If this is the case, the question can mean "who can relate the evil of his contemporaries?" Phillips has "His generation who shall declare?" Like the KJV rendering, "who shall declare his generation?," this makes little sense. Because his life on earth has come to an end (literally "his life was lifted from the earth") is best understood as referring, in this context, to Christ's death, though some commentators understand this verse to refer to his exaltation from the earth to heaven.

> 34 The official said to Philip, "Tell me, of whom is the prophet saying this? Of himself or of someone else?" 35 Philip began to speak; starting from this very passage of scripture, he told him the Good News about Jesus. 36 As they traveled down the road they came to a place where there was some water, and the official said, "Here is some water. What is to keep me from being baptized?"
> [37 Philip said to him, "You may be baptized if you believe with all your heart."
> "I do," he answered; "I believe that Jesus Christ is the Son of God."]
> 38 The official ordered the carriage to stop; and both of them, Philip and the official, went down into the water, and Philip baptized him. 39 When they came up out of the water the Spirit of the Lord took Philip away. The official did not see him again, but continued on his way, full of joy. 40 Philip found himself in Ashdod; and he went through all the towns preaching the Good News, until he arrived at Caesarea.
> (8.34-40)

These final paragraphs (vv. 34-40) conclude the story of Philip and the Ethiopian official, and in so doing provide an excellent opportunity for an exposition of this passage of Scripture from Isaiah. Note that in the conclusion of the story Luke has very effectively disposed of the participants by indicating where they went and what they did, thus preparing the discourse for the introduction of a new participant, Saul, beginning with Chapter 9 verse 1.

8.34

The supplementary question, Of himself or of someone else?, must frequently be filled out, for the ellipsis which is perfectly appropriate in English may not be satisfactory in other languages. Therefore, one may translate: "Was he talking about himself or was he talking about someone else?"

8.35

In some languages the expression began to speak is regarded not only as redundant but meaninglessly repetitious. Therefore, the passage is sometimes rendered as "Philip began with this very passage of Scripture and told the Ethiopian official the Good News about Jesus."

8.36

The expression this very passage of scripture may be rendered as "at that very place in the book of the Holy Writings." Sometimes the term passage may be referred to as "those very words."

8.36

In many languages it is quite impossible to speak of water without specifying the particular nature of such water. Was it, for example, simply water in the road; was it water in a container, a spring, a well, a pond, a lake? In view of the action described in verse 38, one would presume the most appropriate term would be something equivalent to a pond or a pool of water in an otherwise dry riverbed.

The question What is to keep me from being baptized? may be rendered as "Is there any reason why I should not be baptized?" or, as in some languages, "If I want to be baptized, is there anyone who says I cannot be baptized?"

8.37

This verse is placed in brackets by the TEV and is omitted by most modern translations of the New Testament as not being an original part of the book of Acts. Its content is in keeping with the thought of the book of Acts, but it is not to be found in the earliest and best Greek manuscripts available. If it had been an original part of Acts, it is difficult to see why a scribe would have omitted it.

In so many languages a term for believe must have some grammatical object; for example, "believe in Jesus Christ."

8.38

The order given by the Ethiopian official would imply that someone was driving the carriage. Obviously, in many languages one cannot order a carriage to stop. It is only possible to "order someone to cause the carriage to stop." Accordingly, in some languages, this first clause is translated as "the official ordered the driver to have the carriage stop," "to cause the horses to stop," or "to cause the oxen to stop."

In order to avoid possible ambiguity, the TEV has made the subject of baptized explicit: Philip baptized him (see JB, Moffatt).

8.39

Out of the water implies "walking out of the water."

Took (Philip) away translates a verb which appears here and in 23.10 (get away), and literally means "snatch away" or "take away by force." In the present context the idea of force is not involved, but possibly Luke chose this particular verb in order to emphasize the suddenness with which the action took place. In any case the tense of the verb stresses suddenness of action, whether or not this is to be found in the verb stem. Luke does not

184

state how this was accomplished, but the intimation seems to be that in some miraculous fashion Philip was taken bodily away and transported to Ashdod.

As in his Gospel, so in Acts, Luke takes every opportunity to express the joy which one has in discovering the Christian experience, and so he states the official... continued on his way, full of joy. However, the idiom full of joy can rarely be translated literally. Rather, one must have some such expression as "his heart was joyful," "his heart was very sweet," or "he was cool in his liver."

8. 40

Philip found himself in Ashdod (see NEB, JB, Moffatt, Phillips) correctly translates the force of the Greek verb; "Philip was found at Azotus" (KJV) sounds rather odd and seems to suggest a passive force for the Greek verb form. The phrase found himself in Ashdod is equivalent in some languages to "saw that he was in Ashdod." One must, of course, avoid a term for found which would suggest "looking for something."

Ashdod (Azotus, the Greek form of the name as used in many translations) was an ancient Philistine city, twenty miles north of Gaza. Caesarea (meaning "the city of Caesar") was the chief city of Palestine and the residence of the Roman governor. It was on the coast, fifty-five miles northwest of Jerusalem. Philip seems to have made Caesarea his home, and he was there when he next appears in the Acts narrative (21. 8). The clause until he arrived at Caesarea would imply that all the towns would be those towns lying between Ashdod and Caesarea.

CHAPTER 9

The chapter division is rather artificial, since it contains first the account concerning Saul and then shifts to the story of Peter in Lydda and Joppa. This particular section, beginning with verse 32, is closely linked with the following account contained in Chapter 10. Note, however, the way in which Saul (or Paul) has been introduced: first, only mentioned in verse 58 of Chapter 7, and then next in the first part of Chapter 8. This is followed by the experience of Philip and the ministry of Peter and John. Luke again returns to Saul in the first part of Chapter 9, but then shifts back to the ministry of Peter from 9.32 through 11.18. Saul is again mentioned in the latter part of Chapter 11 (vv. 25-30). After this Luke again returns to the ministry of Peter in Chapter 12, and only beginning with Chapter 13 is Paul the center of attention for the rest of the book of The Acts of the Apostles. This skillful interweaving of important historical episodes is carefully designed. In the Greek text there are always important indicators of time and place, so the reader is carefully orientated as to who is being spoken of. These must be skillfully reproduced, if the reader is to understand clearly the nature of the story and the important implications of such an interweaving of the accounts of Peter and Saul.

The Conversion of Saul

1 In the meantime Saul kept up his violent threats of murder against the disciples of the Lord. He went to the High Priest 2 and asked for letters of introduction to the Jewish synagogues in Damascus, so that if he should find any followers of the Way of the Lord there, he would be able to arrest them, both men and women, and take them back to Jerusalem. (9.1-2)

The section heading The Conversion of Saul involves two problems: (1) the noun form (it is only a topic and not a complete statement) and (2) the term Conversion, which is very difficult to render satisfactorily in a number of languages. One can change the noun expression The Conversion of Saul into a verbal phrase or clause (for example, "Saul Is Converted"), but this presupposes a close link between a noun and a corresponding verb with a highly specialized meaning. In most languages one must restructure the meaning of Conversion and use a phrase—for example, "Saul Becomes a Believer," "Saul Begins to Believe in Jesus," or "Saul Acknowledges Jesus as Lord." The emphasis of conversion in this type of context is not upon a change of behavior but upon a change in loyalties.

9.1-2

In the Greek text verses 1 and 2 are actually one sentence, which the TEV has broken up into two sentences for ease of understanding. In the meantime (see JB, NEB "meanwhile") translates a Greek particle (rendered in most translations as "and" or "but") that merely indicates the resumption of an old

186

narrative or the beginning of a new narrative. Since this story is a continuation of the one in 8.3, the TEV has indicated that the events of the preceding chapter were not prior in time to the events of the present narrative, but happened simultaneously with this story.

The idiomatic phrase "breathing threats and murder" has been rendered in the TEV as violent threats of murder (see Knox "threatened the disciples of the Lord with massacre"). The TEV has incorporated the meaning of the adverb "yet" or "still" into the verb kept up (his violent threats of murder).

The Roman government had given the Jewish Council authority over the Jews living in foreign cities, and for this reason Saul went to the High Priest (the head of the Jewish Council) to ask for authority over the persons whom he wanted to arrest. The letters that Saul asked for were evidently letters of introduction and for this reason the TEV has made letters explicit. Saul would have found the persons he was looking for at worship in the Jewish synagogues, since the Jewish Christians considered belief in Christ the fulfillment of their Jewish hopes.

The expression letters of introduction may require some marginal explanation or perhaps a descriptive equivalent in the text itself. In some languages one may employ "letters telling who Saul was." However, there were also letters indicating the authority vested in Saul, for example, "letters saying who Saul was and the power that had been given to him." If the term synagogues indicates primarily buildings, then it may be impossible to speak of letters being addressed to buildings. Therefore one can have "letters addressed to the leaders of the synagogues saying who Saul was."

There was a large colony of Jews in Damascus (after the war of A.D. 70 some 18,000 of them were massacred), and Saul had probably gone to Damascus in order to arrest Jewish Christians who had fled from Jerusalem and had taken refuge in the city of Damascus. Followers of the Way (literally "those of the Way") is one of the many terms that Luke uses to describe Christians in this chapter, for example, disciples, people of God, those calling on the name of the Lord, and brothers.

The phrase the Way of the Lord must be translated with care so as not to imply that this is simply "the road that belongs to the Lord" or "the road that the Lord followed" (as though it were some reference to a road on which Jesus walked). Rather, one must have some such expression as "the Way shown by the Lord" or "the Way that the Lord said people should walk" (or "live"). (See also 18.25,26; 19.9,23; 22.4; 24.14,22.)

"Bring them bound to Jerusalem" means simply arrest them...and take them back to Jerusalem (see JB "to arrest and take to Jerusalem," and NEB "to arrest...and bring them to Jerusalem"). In this context the word "bound" merely means "in custody" or "under arrest," and does not indicate necessarily that the people were in chains or ropes.

3 On his way to Damascus, as he came near the city, suddenly a light from the sky flashed around him. 4 He fell to the ground and heard a voice saying to him, "Saul, Saul! Why do you persecute me?"

5 "Who are you, Lord?" he asked.

"I am Jesus, whom you persecute," the voice said. 6 "But get up and go into the city, where you will be told what you must do."

7 The men who were traveling with Saul had stopped, not saying a word; they heard the voice but could not see anyone. 8 Saul got up from the ground and opened his eyes, but could not see a thing. So they took him by the hand and led him into Damascus. 9 For three days he was not able to see, and during that time he did not eat or drink anything. (9.3-9)

9.3

In Greek the first clause of this verse is rather complex and any literal translation of it is awkward in English. It is for that reason that the TEV has somewhat restructured the form of this clause to read on his way to Damascus, as he came near the city. The Greek text contains a transitional verb that literally means "it happened," but this is simply a Semitic expression often used by Luke to mark the introduction to a story or the beginning of a particular episode within an account.

A description of the bright light which flashed in the sky is not always easy to render effectively. In some languages the closest parallel is that of lightning. In other languages, terms suggesting the blazing up of fire have been employed. In all instances, the source of this light as from the sky must be clearly indicated. In some languages the equivalent is "light suddenly shown bright from the sky. It was bright every place around Saul."

9.4

In rendering fell to the ground it is important to imply that this is not from merely a standing position, but from a position mounted on a horse or mule.

In some languages one does not hear a voice. Rather, it is necessary to say "he heard someone say to him."

In this context persecute may be rendered as "cause harm to me" or "cause me to suffer." (See also 8.1.)

9.5

Saul's reply was either who are you, Lord? (TEV and most translations) or "who are you, sir?" The problem is that the word may mean either Lord or "sir." Moffatt deliberately left this word untranslated (as in 10.4; 22.8; and 26.15), since, according to him, "any English rendering would imply too much or too little." Though it may be risking the possibility of implying too much, it seems best in the context to translate by the technical Christian term Lord.

Get up indicates rising to a standing position. The clause where you will be told what you must do must, in some languages, be shifted into an active expression, for example, "there someone will tell you what you must do."

9. 7

They heard the voice contradicts 22. 9 where it says that the men who were traveling with Saul did not hear the voice. In Greek it is possible for the verb "to hear" to take either the genitive case or the accusative case as its object. And so some have sought to resolve the difficulty by stating that when used with the genitive case (as here) the meaning is that the men heard the sound of the voice, but did not understand the specific words that were spoken; whereas when it is used with the accusative case (as in 22. 9), the meaning is that the men both heard and understood the specific words themselves. By this reasoning the present passage would not contradict what is said in 22. 9, since there it would be taken to mean that Saul's companions did not hear (so as to understand) the words/voice. However, this conclusion is judged by most scholars as invalid; for upon examination of Luke's usage of the verb "to hear" in Acts, it is clear that he makes no consistent distinction between "to hear" with the genitive case and "to hear" with the accusative case (see 22. 1). The contradiction must remain, as must the statement in this chapter that Saul's companions remained standing, whereas in 26. 14 it is said that they all fell to the ground. Luke has simply told the same story three times (a narrative which he doubtless considers to be of great importance in the spread of the Christian message throughout the world), and we must not deny him the freedom of using differences of detail in narrating the event. It is not the responsibility of the translator to try to resolve such difficulties which he thinks may exist, but to translate faithfully what the writer has given him to translate.

9. 8

Saul ... opened his eyes (see JB "with his eyes wide open" and NEB "when he opened his eyes") correctly translates the force of the Greek participial expression; the KJV ("when his eyes were opened") may wrongly imply that someone else opened Saul's eyes for him.

An expression for opened his eyes must indicate clearly that this simply meant opening his eyelids, for he obviously was not able to see. A number of languages make a clear distinction between the opening of the eyelids and the capacity to see.

> 10 There was a disciple in Damascus named Ananias. He had a vision, in which the Lord said to him, "Ananias!"
> "Here I am, Lord," he answered.
> 11 The Lord said to him, "Get ready and go to Straight Street,

189

and at the house of Judas ask for a man from Tarsus named Saul. He is praying, 12 and in a vision he saw a man named Ananias come in and place his hands on him so that he might see again."

13 Ananias answered, "Lord, many people have told me about this man, about all the terrible things he has done to your people in Jerusalem. 14 And he has come to Damascus with authority from the chief priests to arrest all who call on your name."

15 The Lord said to him, "Go, because I have chosen him to serve me, to make my name known to Gentiles and kings, and to the people of Israel. 16 And I myself will show him all that he must suffer for my sake." (9.10-16)

These paragraphs (vv. 10-16) are a combination of narrative discourse with included conversation. It is particularly important that in each instance the speaker be clearly identified. Note also that in the first verse (v. 10) a new person, Ananias, is introduced into the account.

9.10

This verse opens a new scene in which the central figures are Ananias and the Lord. This particular Ananias appears only in this chapter (vv. 10, 12, 13, 17) and in 22.12.

A vision (see 7.31) indicates a supernatural experience in which a divine revelation is given to a person. The commentators compare this scene to the call of Samuel in 1 Samuel 3.1 ff.; the same words here I am appear in this narrative as in the Septuagint translation of 1 Samuel.

9.11

On get ready see 8.26. Straight Street is a much more natural English idiom than the literal phrase "the Street called Straight" (see JB, NEB, Goodspeed). Most likely Straight Street was the important street which ran east and west through Damascus. During Roman times it had long colonnades and ended with large porches at either end.

It may be useful to identify Tarsus as "the city of Tarsus."

As in so many contexts, it is best to leave untranslated the Greek word idou, usually translated "behold" in traditional translations.

9.12

The words in a vision appear in different positions in various manuscripts and are omitted by some manuscripts, though all translations apparently include them. Regardless of whether this phrase is an original part of the Greek text, it may be included on translational grounds, since verse 10 makes it clear that what Ananias saw was in a vision.

9.13

"I heard from many people concerning this man" appears in the TEV as many people have told me about this man. The NEB transforms the idea of "many" into "often": "I have often heard about this man," but the Greek would seem to lend itself more naturally to the interpretation given in the TEV. To your people (Goodspeed; see NEB "to thy people") appears in NAB and Phillips as "to your holy people," and in JB " to your saints" (see Moffatt "to thy saints"), with an extensive note in JB explaining the meaning of the term. The phrase is literally "the holy ones," and is the common Pauline term for Christians. In Acts it appears only in this chapter (vv. 13, 32, 41) and in 26.10. The use of this term goes back to the Old Testament concept of the people of Israel as belonging to God in a unique sense. Since, for a number of reasons, "saints" or "holy ones" is misleading in contemporary English, the TEV, as well as most modern translations, has adopted throughout either your people or God's people.

All the terrible things he has done to your people may be rendered as "how much he has caused your people to suffer."

9.14

"Here," as employed in most translations, appears in the TEV as to Damascus and in Moffatt as "in this city too."

With authority from the chief priests is often equivalent to "the chief priests have given him the power" or "the chief priests have said that he is able to." The phrase call on your name is equivalent to "worship you." It must not be understood merely in the sense "speaking a person's name." It can, however, be understood as "using your name as they pray."

9.15

I have chosen him to serve me translates "he is to me a vessel/instrument of choice." The phrase "vessel/instrument of choice" is merely a Jewish way of saying "(someone) chose a vessel/instrument"; while "vessel/instrument," when applied to a person, is equivalent in meaning to "someone who serves (someone else)." Finally "he is to me" defines both who chooses ("to me") and who is chosen ("he"): that is, I have chosen him (to serve me).

To Gentiles and kings is taken by several translators to mean "to Gentiles and their kings" (see NEB, Moffatt, Goodspeed).

As in many instances, the term name must be translated as a more direct reference to the person himself, since name in this type of context is simply a substitute for a reference to a person. Therefore in many languages one may translate "to make me known to the Gentiles...."

9.16

In Greek the pronoun subjects of verbs are expressed by a suffix on the verb form itself; but when a separate form of the pronoun is used as a subject, this usually indicates that the subject is to be stressed. Since I does appear as a separate form in this sentence, the TEV has brought out the intended emphasis by translating I myself.

The final phrase of verse 16 for my sake must not be understood as an expression of cause but as an expression of purpose. Such purpose must in some languages be made relatively explicit by a purpose clause, for example, "in order to make me known" (an expansion based upon the immediately preceding statement in v. 15).

> 17 So Ananias went, entered the house, and placed his hands on Saul. "Brother Saul," he said, "the Lord has sent me—Jesus himself, who appeared to you on the road as you were coming here. He sent me so that you might see again and be filled with the Holy Spirit." 18 At once something like fish scales fell from Saul's eyes and he was able to see again. He stood up and was baptized; 19 and after he had eaten, his strength came back. (9.17-19a)

9.17

The transitional particle so is particularly important, since it marks the conclusion of the preceding paragraph and introduces the result stated in this paragraph.

Who appeared to you may be also taken in the sense of "whom you saw" (see 1.3). Has sent me—Jesus himself captures the intended emphasis of the Greek sentence structure which is missed by a translation such as "the Lord Jesus...has sent me" (RSV).

The expression filled with the Holy Spirit must conform to the normal usage of such an expression in the receptor language, for example, "whom the Spirit will control," "into whom the Holy Spirit comes," etc. (See also 2.4; 4.8,31; 6.3,5,8; 7.55; 9.17; 11.24; 13.9.)

9.18

Something like fish scales appears in most translations as "something like scales." The TEV has added the qualifier fish in order to indicate to the reader the kind of scales that are meant, that is, fish scales as opposed to weight scales.

Saul Preaches in Damascus

> 19b Saul stayed for a few days with the disciples in Damascus.
> 20 He went straight to the synagogues and began to preach about Jesus. "He is the Son of God," he said.
> 21 All who heard him were amazed, and asked, "Isn't this the man who in Jerusalem was killing those who call on this name? And didn't he come here for the very purpose of arresting them and taking them back to the chief priests?" (9.19b-21).

The section heading Saul Preaches in Damascus may require certain modifications since it may be necessary to render Preach by a phrase, and since a personal goal may be required in some languages, for example, "Saul Tells the Good News in Damascus" or "Saul Announces the Good News in Damascus."

9.19b

Since this section introduces a new narrative, the TEV, along with others (KJV, Phillips, Goodspeed), has made the Greek pronoun subject ("he") into Saul. For a few days is merely a way of indicating an indefinite, but brief, period of time.

9.20

The full impact of the adverb "immediately" ("and immediately in the synagogues he was preaching") is retained by the TEV he went straight to... and began. Goodspeed accomplishes this by "(Saul) began at once"; while it is expressed "without delay" by Phillips, and "soon" in the NEB; but the meaning is missed by JB ("he began preaching").

This is the only place in Acts where the title Son of God is applied to Jesus (see, however, the quotation of Psalm 2.7 in 13.33).

9.21

As the TEV makes clear, the Greek is in the form of a question which expects a "yes" answer; but the TEV has divided this question into two parts for ease of understanding. In many languages one must specify to whom the question was addressed. Therefore, one can say "asked one another."

In some instances one must make somewhat more specific the reference intended in the phrase on this name, for example, "Jesus."

On the phrase arresting them and taking them back see verse 2. Killing (corresponding to a Greek word which appears only here and in Galatians 1.13 and 23) literally means "pillage," "ravage," or "destroy" (see NEB "trying to destroy"). Other translations see in this word an expression of the fact of the persecution rather than its outcome: "organized the attack" (JB), "so bitterly persecuted" (Phillips), and "carried on a merciless campaign against" (Barclay).

Though these two questions are framed in such a way as to appear to be asking for information, they are in reality rhetorical questions indicating clearly a positive answer. In many languages the closest equivalent is a strong affirmative statement; for example, "This is certainly the man who in Jerusalem was killing those who worshiped Jesus. He surely came here for the very purpose of arresting such people and taking them back to the chief priests."

22 But Saul's preaching became even more powerful, and his proofs that Jesus was the Messiah were so convincing that the Jews who lived in Damascus could not answer him.

23 After many days had gone by, the Jews gathered and made plans to kill Saul; 24 but he was told of what they planned to do. Day and night they watched the city gates in order to kill him. 25 But one night Saul's followers took him and let him down through an opening in the wall, lowering him in a basket. (9.22-25)

9.22

Saul's preaching became even more powerful (see Barclay "but Saul preached with increasing power") translates "but Saul was becoming stronger and stronger." However, in the context the reference is not to Saul's physical condition; it is rather to his increased activity in preaching the gospel, and this is what is meant by JB "Saul's power increased steadily." The RSV "Saul increased all the more in strength" and Moffatt "Saul became more and more vigorous" tend to suggest that Saul's health is referred to.

In many languages it is extremely difficult to speak of "preaching becoming powerful." A literal rendering of this would suggest simply the increase of volume of his voice or even of the length of his preaching. The implication, of course, is the increased manner in which Saul was convincing the people of what he was saying. Therefore, in some languages, the closest equivalent is "Saul, by his preaching, was convincing more and more people."

The remainder of this sentence has been made to read in reverse order from the way that it appears in Greek: literally "he was confusing the Jews who lived in Damascus by proving that this one (that is, Jesus) is the Messiah." His proofs...were so convincing (see NEB "with his cogent proofs," JB "by the way he demonstrated that," and Phillips "by proving beyond doubt") translates the Greek participle "by proving that"; while the Jews...could not answer him (see NEB "silenced," JB "able to throw...into complete confusion," and Moffatt "put...to confusion") translates "he was confusing the Jews."

It is not possible in some languages to speak of "proofs being convincing." Persons or objects can be convincing, but not a "proof." In fact, the word proof must correspond in many languages to a verb "to prove." Therefore the equivalent is "he proved so surely that Jesus was the Messiah."

An expression for answer must imply "a rebuttal of arguments." This is not merely answering a question, but responding to an argument with some kind of convincing, contrary evidence.

9.23

After many days had gone by is another expression of indefinite time. Some try to stress the linear or progressive action in the verb by translating "as the days mounted up" (NEB) or "as time went on" (Lake's commentary). However, the Greek verb tense represented by gathered and made plans (the verb has both of these ideas rather than merely "make plans" or "plot") indicates that the Jewish gathering did not take place until after many days had gone by.

194

In many languages one cannot speak of "days going by." One can, however, say "many days later," "after the sun had gone down many times," or even as in some languages "after many moons" (often not a reference to months but to nights).

9.24

In order to bring out the intended focus of the Greek sentence order ("but was made known to Saul their plan"), he was told of has been placed first, followed by what they planned to do. Goodspeed has accomplished this goal by "Saul found out about the plot."

The equivalent of watched the city gates is in many languages "waited for him at the city gates." The men obviously were not simply watching the gates, but "waiting for him at the city gates."

9.25

One night (so NEB, Phillips, Goodspeed, Moffatt) translates a genitive construction which may be intended to emphasize the qualitative aspect of "nighttime" as opposed to "daytime" (see JB "when it was dark"). This genitive may, however, simply specify the time during which an event took place.

Through an opening in the wall (see Phillips, Zürich) translates a rather ambiguous phrase. The rendering of the TEV seems to express the meaning of the Greek preposition, though a number of translations have "over the wall" (Goodspeed, Moffatt, Barclay; see JB "from the top of the wall"), NAB "along the wall," and NEB "by the wall." The words used for basket in this passage and in 2 Corinthians 11.33 are two different words. The word used in 2 Corinthians refers to a large woven bag or basket which may be used for straw or for bales of wool; the basket here is made of similar material, but was probably smaller, though it was evidently large enough for a man to stand in.

Saul in Jerusalem

26 Saul went to Jerusalem and tried to join the disciples. They would not believe, however, that he was a disciple, and they were all afraid of him. 27 Then Barnabas came to his help and took him to the apostles. He explained to them how Saul had seen the Lord on the road, and that the Lord had spoken to him. He also told them how boldly Saul had preached in the name of Jesus in Damascus. 28 And so Saul stayed with them and went all over Jerusalem, preaching boldly in the name of the Lord. 29 He also talked and disputed with the Greek-speaking Jews, but they tried to kill him. 30 When the brothers found out about this, they took Saul down to Caesarea and sent him away to Tarsus. (9.26-30)

A section heading such as Saul in Jerusalem may seem quite awkward in some languages. One may need to introduce a verb such as "visits" or "goes back to," for example, "Saul Visits Jerusalem," "Saul Visits the Believers in Jerusalem," or "Saul Goes Back to Jerusalem."

9.26

The Greek participle translated <u>went</u> in the TEV is rendered as a temporal clause by most translators, for example, "when he reached Jerusalem" (NEB). Both this sentence and the following sentence serve as good illustrations of one of the techniques followed in the TEV translation. Very frequently the TEV translates such participial constructions as simple statements, since these are more easily understood by the English reader. This same technique is frequently followed by other English translations; however, they generally translate participles as subordinate clauses rather than as coordinate clauses. For example, the participle "not believing" (see Phillips "finding it impossible to believe") is rendered by the NEB as "because they did not believe" and by the RSV as "for they did not believe." Of course, in many instances it is necessary to translate participles as subordinate clauses, and the TEV has done this when the meaning requires such a usage. By reversing the order of the Greek clauses the TEV has introduced the causative meaning of the Greek sentence into the corresponding English expression without using a subordinate clause. That is, the causative force of the participle has been brought out by putting <u>they would not believe</u> first in the sentence, followed by <u>and they were all afraid of him.</u> The average reader will then understand that their not believing him caused them to be afraid.

<u>Join the disciples</u> may be rendered as "to become one with the disciples" or "to be considered one of the disciples."

9.27

The expression <u>Barnabas came to his help</u> is equivalent in many languages to "Barnabas helped him."

<u>Took him to the apostles</u> must imply "took him in order to talk with the apostles." It is not simply that Paul was led to the apostles but was brought by Barnabas so they might talk with the apostles.

So as to avoid a possible misunderstanding of the Greek sentence (literally "and that he had spoken to him") the TEV has translated <u>and that the Lord had spoken to him</u> (see Phillips "and how the Lord had spoken to him"). <u>Boldly ...had preached</u> translates one verb which appears six other times in Acts (9.28; 13.46; 14.3; 18.26; 19.8; 26.26), and is related to the noun discussed in 2.29.

It may be necessary in some languages to specify where the road was, for example, "on the road to Damascus."

It is often not easy to translate the term <u>boldly</u> since so much depends upon the particular context and situation. The meaning of <u>boldly</u> can be effectively reproduced in a number of ways, for example, "he did not care to whom he was speaking," "he would speak to everyone just the same," "he had no fear when he was talking," or "he would say everything regardless of who was listening." All of these expressions define in one way or another the concept of boldness in a communication.

If one wishes to retain a specific reference to <u>name</u> it may be necessary to employ an expression such as "preached, using the name of Jesus."

9.28

And so Saul stayed with them and went all over Jerusalem translates a Semitic idiom (literally "and he was with them going in and out in Jerusalem") that is used to describe the freedom of relationship that one shares with others. NEB renders this "Saul...stayed with them, moving about freely in Jerusalem"; Goodspeed "he associated with them freely in Jerusalem"; and Phillips "Saul joined with them in all their activities in Jerusalem."

9.29

He also talked and disputed translates verb tenses in Greek which indicate that this is something which Paul habitually or frequently did.

Greek-speaking Jews translates the same word as was used in 6.1.

In the statement they tried to kill him the verb translated <u>tried</u> does not necessarily indicate failure; the idea of failure comes, not from the verb itself, but from the context. The NEB is correct in understanding the meaning of this as "they planned to murder him." Although Phillips tries to express the meaning of the Greek verb tense, which may signify continuous action in past time, he certainly reads too much into the meaning of the verb by his translation "but they made several attempts on his life." Had Luke intended to say that "they made several attempts" he could certainly have said this clearly and easily. The meaning of the verb and the force of its tense much more naturally mean something like "they were continuously looking for a way to kill him."

> 31 And so it was that the church throughout all of Judea, Galilee, and Samaria had a time of peace. It was built up and grew in numbers through the help of the Holy Spirit, as it lived in reverence for the Lord. (9.31)

This short paragraph, consisting of verse 31, serves as an important transitional device, summarizing what has immediately preceded, and also preparing the way for the introduction of Peter's experiences in Lydda, Joppa, Caesarea, and then in Jerusalem. Furthermore, this verse serves to highlight the geographical extension of the church---something which is suggested in Chapter 1 verse 8 as being a significant theme of this book.

9.31

This is clearly the beginning of a new section as is indicated by the words which Luke has used to begin it (TEV <u>and so it was</u>). On the formula that Luke has used here see 1.6. With the conversion of Saul the persecution of the church is for a while brought to an end and there are Christian communities not only in Jerusalem but in Judea, Galilee, and Samaria. <u>Throughout</u>

all of Judea, Galilee, and Samaria in the Greek modifies church rather than had a time of peace (KJV seems to intimate that this phrase modified the verb rather than the noun).

The phrase had a time of peace is often expressed negatively, for example, "were no longer suffering," "there was no longer persecution," or "the people no longer had fear."

This verse offers two possibilities for punctuation: it was built up may be taken with what precedes, had a time of peace, or with what follows, grew in numbers. Most translations take this, as does the TEV, with what follows; however, JB and Zürich take it with what precedes. For most of the important alternatives of punctuation, the translator will find valuable evidence in the punctuation apparatus occurring in the Greek text published by the United Bible Societies.

Most translators understand it was built up in a passive sense with the Holy Spirit as the agent; whereas the JB takes it with a middle force, "building themselves up" ("themselves" referring to "churches" rather than "church" of most translations).

In some languages one cannot speak of a church (referring to individuals) as "being built up." This could only refer to a building, not to an institution. Therefore, it may be necessary to change the figure of speech to something equivalent to "became strong." Grew in numbers is rendered in many languages simply as "more and more people believed."

Through the help of the Holy Spirit is rendered by most translators as "in the consolation/comfort of the Holy Spirit." But "consolation" or "comfort" carry too much the notion of relief from sorrow; the full meaning of the word is better expressed by "encouragement," "assistance," or "help." Through the help of the Holy Spirit may be restructured in some languages as "this happened because the Holy Spirit was helping" or "the Holy Spirit caused this to happen" (in which case "this" refers to the building up and the growth of the church).

In the expression "walking in the fear of the Lord," "walking" (in Greek) refers to conduct or way of life, and "fear" means "respect" or reverence (see Moffatt, Goodspeed).

Peter in Lydda and Joppa

32 Peter traveled everywhere, and one time he went to visit God's people who lived in Lydda. 33 There he met a man named Aeneas, who was paralyzed and had not been able to get out of bed for eight years. 34 "Aeneas," Peter said to him, "Jesus Christ makes you well. Get up and make your bed." At once Aeneas got up. 35 All the people living in Lydda and Sharon saw him, and they turned to the Lord. (9.32-35)

As in the case of the previous section heading, this one may also seem unduly short and abrupt. One can restructure it into a complete sentence by saying "Peter Goes to Lydda and Joppa" but probably better "Peter Performs Miracles in Lydda and Joppa."

The two miracles performed by Peter in Lydda and Joppa seem to prepare the way for the even greater miracle of the giving of the Holy Spirit to Cornelius in Caesarea. The shift back to Peter does seem rather abrupt in the English text, but in Greek the use of "it happened" at the very beginning of verse 32 clearly marks another type of episode. It may, therefore, be necessary to reproduce something of this same kind of transitional device.

9.32

Everywhere, of course, does not mean all over the world, and the idea may be limited to the many villages of Samaria (see 8.25). However, this may be imposing too great a limitation upon the meaning of the word as used by Luke.

On the translation of "the saints" as God's people see 9.13.

Lydda was a small village lying northwest of Jerusalem, some ten miles from Joppa.

9.33

For eight years may mean "since he was eight years old," but most translations and commentaries render this phrase in the sense of the TEV.

9.34

The expression Jesus Christ makes you well is a kind of third person command. In some languages the equivalent is "Jesus Christ will make you well right now" or "Jesus Christ causes you to become well."

Make your bed (so the large majority of the commentaries and translations) may mean "get yourself something to eat," since the Greek is literally "spread for yourself." However, the natural meaning in this particular context would seem to be make your bed. The phrase make your bed must of course not be translated in a form which would imply building or constructing the bed. It is only arranging or rolling up the bed or mat.

9.35

Sharon is the coastal plain extending thirty miles along the sea from Joppa to Caesarea. A translation should make clear that Sharon is not a town, but the coastal plain (see Twentieth Century "all the inhabitants of Lydda and of the Plain of Sharon"; see also Zürich).

Turned to the Lord must be understood in the sense of "became believers in the Lord." In many languages the mere process of "turning" implies no figurative extension of believing in or becoming a disciple of.

36 In Joppa there was a woman named Tabitha, who was a believer. (Her name in Greek is Dorcas, meaning a deer.) She spent all her time doing good and helping the poor. 37 At that time she got sick and died. Her body was washed and laid in a room upstairs. 38 Joppa was not very

far from Lydda, and when the disciples in Joppa heard that Peter was in Lydda, they sent two men to him with the message, "Please hurry and come to us." 39 So Peter got ready and went with them. When he arrived he was taken to the room upstairs. All the widows crowded around him, crying and showing him the shirts and coats that Dorcas had made while she was alive. 40 Peter put them all out of the room, and knelt down and prayed; then he turned to the body and said, "Tabitha, get up!" She opened her eyes, and when she saw Peter she sat up. 41 Peter reached over and helped her get up. Then he called the believers and the widows, and presented her alive to them. 42 The news about this spread all over Joppa, and many people believed in the Lord. 43 Peter stayed on in Joppa for many days with a leatherworker named Simon.

(9.36-43)

This particular episode is introduced in the Greek text by a specific reference to place, namely, Joppa, and by the pronoun tis often rendered "a certain." This is a device frequently used by Luke to show the beginning of another story. In fact, in some translations it is an advantage to separate these two accounts by two different section headings. For example, "The Healing of Aeneas" could be a heading to the paragraph verses 32-35, while another heading "The Raising of Dorcas" could be used for the paragraph verses 36-43.

9.36

Joppa is the modern city of Jaffa, the most important port in southern Palestine, about ten miles northwest of Lydda. Who was a believer translates a word which appears only here in the New Testament, meaning literally "a woman disciple." Luke explains that her Aramaic name Tabitha means gazelle when translated into Greek; and the TEV has sought to do for the English readers what Luke did for his Greek readers, that is, to explain the meaning of the name both in Aramaic and in Greek: named Tabitha...(her name in Greek is Dorcas, meaning a deer).

Technically, of course, this animal is a gazelle, not a deer, but such a technical distinction did not seem to be warranted in a translation such as Today's English Version.

"She was full of good works and of the almsgiving which she was doing" is simply a Jewish way of saying she spent all her time doing good and helping the poor. Spent all her time is in many languages equivalent to "continually did good."

9.37

In all languages there are ways of speaking about "getting sick" but there are a number of different idioms employed: "fever grabbed her," "sickness entered her," and even in some languages "God took her" (a reference to mysterious divine power overcoming an individual).

The passive expressions was washed and laid may readily be made active; for example, "people washed her body and laid it."

"Urging, 'Do not delay to come to us'" becomes in TEV with the message, "Please hurry and come to us." (See JB "with an urgent message for him, 'Come and visit us as soon as possible'" and NEB "with the urgent request, 'Please come over to us without delay.'") In Greek "do not delay" is simply a polite way of making a request, equivalent to please; the urgency of the situation is brought out in the TEV by the addition of the word hurry.

9. 39

In the expression shirts and coats, the first word describes the garment which was worn next to the body, while the second term refers to the outer garment (the same word as was used in 7. 58). Shirt and coat (see NEB and Goodspeed) seem to be the nearest natural equivalents in modern English. On the other hand, it is important not to employ terms which only designate clothing worn by men. After all, the clothing was most certainly for the widows.

Was alive is the meaning of "while she was with them."

9. 40

The word translated all is masculine; however, it is used in a generic sense and refers both to men and women.

When praying, it was quite common for Jews and for other people of the ancient world to kneel. After the verb prayed, it may be necessary to indicate the grammatical goal—for example, "prayed to God."

The command addressed to Tabitha, get up, means "stand up."

The verb sat up appears only here and in Luke 7.15, where it is also used of a dead person coming back to life.

9. 41

Helped her get up is "helped her stand up."

The believers translates the same word as was translated God's people in verse 32 (see also v. 13). The phrase the believers and the widows does not imply that the widows were not Christians (see 1. 14 the women... and Mary; also Mark 16. 7). In a number of languages one must indicate clearly the inclusion of "the widows" in the group of "believers," therefore "the believers, including the widows."

9. 42

In a number of languages one cannot speak of "news spreading." One can, however, say "people all over Joppa were hearing about what happened."

9. 43

Verse 43 serves as a transitional section. In the first place, it begins with a Greek verb often translated "it came to pass" or "it happened that," and this marks the beginning of another episode (Chapter 10.1-48). At the same time, this verse serves as a kind of conclusion to the preceding account of what happened to Dorcas in Joppa. The information, however, that Peter was staying with a leatherworker named Simon is important for understanding information given in 10.6.

The term leatherworker is essentially a "tanner." In other words, one who tans the hides of animals. This does not imply that he is the one who makes articles out of leather, as a sandal maker or shoe cobbler would be. A tanner's trade was considered unclean by the Jews, since it involved handling the skins of animals they considered ceremonially unclean.

CHAPTER 10

In this chapter Luke deals with two issues which were basic to the life of the Christian community: (1) the admission of Gentiles to the Christian faith and (2) fellowship between Jews and Gentiles. The chapter may be divided into six parts: (1) Cornelius' vision (vv. 1-8), (2) Peter's vision (vv. 9-16), (3) Cornelius' request (vv. 17-23a), (4) Peter comes to Cornelius (vv. 23b-33), (5) Peter's preaching (vv. 34-43), and (6) the coming of the Holy Spirit (vv. 44-48). These six divisions are closely paralleled by the first eighteen verses of Chapter 11, that is, Peter's report of his experience to the church in Jerusalem.

The divisions of Chapter 10 are integrally related to one another. The transition between the first and second sections is indicated by a temporal marker the next day. The third section begins with a shift of subjects, for this is Peter's response to the vision which he has just seen. The fourth section again introduces a temporal connection, the next day; while the following paragraph, beginning with verse 30, introduces a new speaker, Cornelius. The shift back to Peter marks the beginning of the paragraph starting with verse 34, and the final section begins with another temporal marker while Peter was still speaking.

Peter and Cornelius

1 There was a man in Caesarea named Cornelius, a captain in the Roman army regiment called "The Italian Regiment." 2 He was a religious man; he and his whole family worshiped God. He did much to help the Jewish poor people, and was constantly praying to God. 3 It was about three o'clock one afternoon when he had a vision, in which he clearly saw an angel of God come in and say to him, "Cornelius!"

4 He stared at the angel in fear and said, "What is it, sir?"

The angel answered, "God has accepted your prayers and works of charity, and has remembered you. 5 And now send some men to Joppa to call for a certain man whose full name is Simon Peter. 6 He is a guest in the home of a leatherworker named Simon, who lives by the sea." 7 Then the angel who was speaking to him went away, and Cornelius called two of his house servants and a soldier, a religious man who was one of his personal attendants. 8 He told them what had happened and sent them off to Joppa. (10.1-8)

In a number of languages a section heading such as Peter and Cornelius may seem quite inadequate, since it does not suggest the relation between these two men. Accordingly, one may employ a title such as "Cornelius Sends for Peter," "Peter Visits Cornelius," or "Peter Preaches the Good News to Cornelius."

The first part of this section (vv. 1-2) consists of an expository type of discourse, in which first Cornelius is mentioned and then various facts about him are presented. This is followed by a narrative text (v. 3), with a temporal setting about three o'clock one afternoon (the first part of which is relatively specific and the second part quite indefinite).

10.1

As so frequently in Luke's writings, a new person is introduced into the story by the Greek particle tis attributive to the word man and, in traditional translations, often translated as "a certain man."

Caesarea, the city which was rebuilt by Herod the Great in honor of Caesar Augustus, was the headquarters of the Roman governor and of the Roman garrison. Cornelius was an especially frequently used name. Captain appears in most other translations as "centurion." The word itself refers to an officer in the Roman army who was in command of one hundred men. In most languages there is an equivalent for the word captain since the use of soldiers, under the leadership of this type of officer, is common in all areas of the world. However, if a term for captain is not available, one can always use a general expression such as "one who commands soldiers" or even a more specific phrase "one who commands a hundred soldiers."

A regiment (or "cohort") was one of the basic divisions in the Roman army, consisting of six hundred men (one-tenth of a legion), and was commanded by an officer of higher rank than the centurion. Where there is no equivalent term for regiment, one may use simply a term for "group of soldiers" or even "many soldiers." It is also possible to borrow a term such as regiment and then explain its meaning in a marginal help.

The title The Italian Regiment can be translated as "the regiment from Italy."

10.2

Religious translates a word which comes from the same root as the word rendered godliness in 3.12; it appears also in verse 7, and refers to a person who was "pious," "devout," or "godly." He...worshiped God translates a technical expression denoting Gentiles who had accepted certain aspects of the Jewish religion without becoming full converts; that is, they had not undergone circumcision. This term occurs also in verse 22 and 13.16, 26. Cornelius was evidently a devout Gentile, who worshiped the God of the Jews and devoted himself to certain pious Jewish activities, such as prayer and the giving of money to the poor.

In many languages a translation of the word religious is equivalent to "worship God." The full expression, therefore, may be "he faithfully worshiped God" or "he constantly worshiped God." This must, of course, also be expanded to include both Cornelius and his whole family, a phrase which would normally include not only members of his immediate family, but also members of the household including permanent servants and slaves.

He did much to help the Jewish poor people (see NEB "he gave generously to help the Jewish people" and JB "he gave generously to Jewish causes") accurately translates the meaning of the expression "he gave many alms to the people." "Alms" are, of course, gifts given to poor people; and "the people" is a term used in the Septuagint and throughout the New Testament to refer specifically to the Jewish people.

The term constantly is not to be taken in the sense of "continuously without interruption" for obviously Cornelius had to carry out his responsibilities and duties as a Roman soldier. In attempting to do justice to this term in Greek, some translators have used "regularly" or "consistently." In some languages a form of the verb expressing habitual action is an effective equivalent. Barclay has employed the translation "constant in private prayer to God" but this is perhaps reading somewhat too much into the meaning of the verb.

10.3

For the phrase about three o'clock one afternoon (literally "about the ninth hour of the day"), see 3.1. The fact that this was the regular hour of prayer stresses the piety of Cornelius.

For the term vision see 9.10, and for angel of God see 5.19.

In a number of languages the use of only the proper name as in the case of Cornelius would require a special verb of speaking, for example, "addressed him by name," "called him by name," or "spoke his name."

10.4

Stared is the same verb translated had their eyes fixed on in 1.10. In the question What is it, sir? the word translated sir may also mean "Lord." The problem is that the word sir may mean too little, whereas "Lord" may be taken to mean too much. Cornelius clearly recognizes that this is a heavenly messenger, though it is doubtful if he would address him in the same way that one addresses God, that is, "Lord." A number of translations have "Lord," but the NEB has followed essentially the same conclusion as that of the TEV, "What is it, my lord?" Moffatt again believes that any English translation would imply either too much or too little (9.5), so he simply translates "What is it?" In many languages there is simply no equivalent for the term sir as merely a polite means of addressing a person. Under such circumstances one is justified in omitting such an expression of polite, direct address.

The Hebraic expression "your prayers and your works of charity went up for a memorial before God" simply means God has accepted your prayers and works of charity, and has remembered you.

In translating the word accepted it is important to avoid the implication of literally "receiving" or "taking." In a number of languages the appropriate equivalent is "has heard your prayers and has seen your works of charity." In other languages it may be necessary to make the degree of acceptance more specific by saying "God is happy with your prayers and works of charity."

10.5

   Works of charity must often be translated simply as "what you have
given to the poor." This, of course, is another way of speaking of "alms."
   The verb remembered in this type of context must not be rendered as
though God had forgotten about Cornelius and that now at last he was remembering him. Rather, it is important to choose a term which will imply "is
responding to you" or "is answering you."

10.5

   The phrase to call for a certain man is equivalent in some languages to
"to find out where a certain man lives" or "to find a certain man."
   "A certain Simon who is also called Peter" appears in the TEV as a certain man whose full name is Simon Peter. The English idiom is best rendered
either as the TEV has done or else by translating something like "a certain
man known as Simon Peter."

10.6

   He is a guest in the home may be rendered in some instances as "he is
staying with" or "he is living (temporarily) with."

10.7

   The house servants were in a rather special category of servants or
slaves in that they were closely related to the affairs of the household and
were obviously trusted individuals. It would be important, therefore, to avoid
using some general term for slaves or servants, for Cornelius was obviously
very particular in the choice of persons to whom he would commit this important task. It might even be possible to employ an expression such as "personal
servants."
   One of his personal attendants (Goodspeed, Phillips; NAB "from among
those whom he could trust") describes a man who must have been "a military
orderly" (NEB).
   The term religious is the same as is used to describe Cornelius in
verse 2. The equivalent of this in a number of languages is simply "one who
worships God."

10.8

   In some languages it is important to be somewhat more specific than
the phrase what had happened would suggest. Therefore one may use "he told
them what the angel had said."
   Joppa was about thirty miles from Caesarea.

   9 The next day, as they were on their way and coming near Joppa,
Peter went up on the roof of the house about noon in order to pray.
10 He became hungry, and wanted to eat; while the food was being prepared he had a vision. 11 He saw heaven opened and something coming

down that looked like a large sheet being lowered by its four corners to the earth. 12 In it were all kinds of animals, reptiles, and wild birds. 13 A voice said to him, "Get up, Peter; kill and eat!"

14 But Peter said, "Certainly not, Lord! I have never eaten anything considered defiled or unclean."

15 The voice spoke to him again, "Do not consider anything unclean that God has declared clean." 16 This happened three times; and then the thing was taken back up into heaven. (10. 9-16)

10. 9

The next day implies that on the very day that Cornelius had the vision he sent the men to Joppa, and they arrived there the next day. About noon (literally "about the sixth hour") was no special time of prayer for Jews; and it is unnecessary to speculate, as some have done, whether this was a late morning prayer or an early afternoon prayer.

The Jewish house had a flat roof, which was reached by a stairway from outside. In areas of the world in which houses do not ordinarily have flat roofs, it may be necessary to add some marginal note or to place in the text itself the phrase "flat roof." Without some supplementary information the implication of Peter going on to the roof might appear rather ludicrous or meaningless.

10. 10

It is impossible to conclude exactly what meal was being prepared: the Romans ate a meal around noon, but the main meal of the Jewish people was eaten in the late afternoon. In any case, the fact that Peter became hungry was what prepared him for the vision. Whereas the Jews would say "a trance came upon someone," the nearest English equivalent would be to say "he fell into a trance" (see NEB, RSV, Phillips). The TEV renders "a trance fell on him" by he had a vision. This is done inasmuch as in the context the emphasis is not so much on the state of Peter (as in a trance or in ecstasy) as it is upon what he saw (that is, a vision).

10. 11

He saw is in Greek a form of the present tense for the sake of vividness (see v. 27).

The word translated something is the same word that was used in 9. 15 (literally "vessel" or "instrument"), and is used here in the most general sense possible, meaning simply a "thing." A similar use of this word is found in Mark 11. 16.

The passive expression being lowered by its four corners may cause certain difficulties in languages which cannot employ such a passive construction. Obviously, in this context there is no indication of the agents, but one can render such a passive expression as "it came down as though someone were holding it by its four corners" or "it came down as though people were holding it by the four corners." (In such an expression, however, it is necessary to make certain that one does not specifically imply that people were actually doing this. It was only "as though they were doing it.")

10.12

All kinds of must be taken in the sense of "some of every kind or species." The threefold division of the animal world is based on Genesis 6.20 (see also Genesis 1.24). Animals includes all animals, both domesticated and wild; and wild birds (see Goodspeed and Moffatt) translates "birds of the air," in which "of the air" is taken as the equivalent of wild, as opposed to domesticated. These classifications of animals, reptiles, and wild birds should not be understood in any special technical sense. The most general terms which correspond roughly to these three categories are fully satisfactory, and in most languages there are terms which more or less correspond.

10.13

The voice which said to him is obviously God. In languages in which one cannot speak of "a voice saying anything" one can introduce the obvious agent of the speaking, "God said to him."

The verb translated kill originally meant "to kill as a sacrifice," but commentators and translators agree that in the present context it has lost its specialized meaning and simply means kill, not "offer as a sacrifice." In a number of languages some grammatical goal of kill and eat must be introduced, for example, "kill and eat these animals" or "kill and eat these living things."

10.14

Certainly not is a very strong expression in Greek and is used in the Septuagint in Ezekiel 4.14 where RSV has "never."

The TEV has added to the adjectives defiled and unclean the qualifier considered (see also the verb consider anything unclean in v. 15) because Peter is referring to the Jewish religion which considered certain animals clean and others unclean. The introduction of the term considered is particularly important, for defiled or unclean do not characterize the animals in a literal sense, but obviously in the religious context. The equivalent of defiled is often "impure" or "bad," but not in the sense of behavior. A term such as "contaminated" may also be employed. A term for unclean must not be understood merely in the sense of "dirty"; rather, the meaning is "not fit to be eaten" or "not such that one should eat."

10.15

Again it may be necessary to introduce the subject, for example, "God spoke to him again." The meaning of unclean...clean in the sense of "that which should not be eaten" and "that which is suitable to be eaten" may need to be quite specific, for example, "do not think that anything is unsuitable to eat if God has said it is suitable to eat."

10.16

This happened three times may refer specifically to the command of God, for example, "God spoke to him three times" or "God commanded him three times to kill and eat." Or one may interpret the three times as a reference to the entire event, including God's statement and Peter's reply, "all this happened three times."

Was taken back up into heaven may be rendered "was drawn up into heaven." It is not that the object was carried, but that it was evidently pulled up.

17 Peter was wondering about the meaning of this vision that he had seen. In the meantime the men sent by Cornelius had learned where Simon's house was, and were now standing in front of the gate. 18 They called out and asked, "Is there a guest here by the name of Simon Peter?"

19 Peter was still trying to understand what the vision meant, when the Spirit said, "Listen! Three men are here looking for you. 20 So get yourself ready and go down, and do not hesitate to go with them, because I have sent them." 21 So Peter went down and said to the men, "I am the man you are looking for. Why have you come?"

22 "Captain Cornelius sent us," they answered. "He is a good man who worships God and is highly respected by all the Jewish people. He was told by one of God's angels to invite you to his house, so that he could hear what you have to say." 23 Peter invited the men in and had them spend the night there. (10.17-23a)

10.17

The transition between paragraphs is made possible by the reference to the vision which has just been seen.

The meaning of this vision may be rendered as "what this vision was trying to say," "what God was trying to say by means of this vision," or "what God was trying to teach by means of this vision."

The phrase in the meantime also serves as a transitional device and represents the particle translated suddenly in 1.10. The literal translation of this portion of verse 17 is "but as Peter wondered to himself...behold the man sent by Cornelius." "Behold" must be taken in connection with "as" to indicate that both actions were taking place simultaneously: that is, Peter was wondering at the same moment that the men sent by Cornelius were standing in front of the gate.

The verb translated learned means "to learn by inquiry." Compare "had been asking the way to Simon's house, and now arrived at the entrance" (NEB).

10. 18

The word gate when applied to a house indicates the gateway leading to the inner court. (In 12.13-14 the same Greek word is translated door.)

10. 18

Most translators employ indirect discourse in introducing the question asked by those who had come seeking Simon Peter. The fact, however, that the full name Simon Peter is used (rather than merely Peter) would suggest that it is more appropriate to employ direct discourse. In Greek the form of direct and indirect discourse in such a context would be identical. It is for that reason the TEV has used direct discourse.

10. 19

The simultaneous character of certain events is clearly marked by the clause Peter was still trying to understand.

It may be necessary in this context to use the full expression "Holy Spirit" rather than merely Spirit since the relationship of Spirit to visions might imply in some languages not the Holy Spirit but some other kind of spirit.

The introductory particle often translated "behold" is far more accurately rendered in this context as Listen!

Three men, that is, the two household servants and the soldier, appears in some manuscripts as "two men" (meaning the two servants without reference to the soldier escorting them), and in others by "some" as NEB and JB. The manuscript evidence favors three and, if it were original, the change to "two" may be explained as the work of a scribe who sought to make the text conform with what he read in verse 7, where the two servants are understood as messengers and the soldier as a guard to accompany them. The rendering "some" appears to be an attempt not to face the problem occasioned by the inclusion of a numeral.

10. 20

It is interesting to note that the Spirit (see v. 19) is used here in direct parallel with voice in verses 13 and 15 which Peter addresses as Lord in verse 14. Note also that the Spirit speaks of something done by an angel (see v. 3). Notice the same interchange between an angel and the Spirit in the narrative about Philip (8.26,29). Both here in verse 20 and in the following verse the pronoun I is emphatic in the sentence structure.

In rendering the expression I have sent them it may be necessary to shift the viewpoint and employ "I have caused them to come." Obviously the verb send would imply the viewpoint of Cornelius, while "come" would represent the viewpoint of Peter in Joppa. In some languages it is necessary to retain the viewpoint of the immediate discourse rather than shift to an earlier episode in a story.

210

The contents of verse 22 represent a summary of what has been said in the first paragraph of Chapter 10. The phrase highly respected by all the Jewish people may be translated as "all the Jewish people respect him very much" or "all the Jewish people think he is very good."

The verb translated was told is a word which is always used of a divine revelation or saying. By one of God's angels is literally "by a holy angel," but "holy" is used in the sense of "belonging to God." In the same way that "the holy people," that is, "the saints," is elsewhere translated as "God's people," it is permissible here to translate "a holy angel" as "God's angel."

The last sentence of verse 22 may cause a number of complications in languages which require direct discourse, particularly for the sequence he was told by one of God's angels to invite you to his house. This becomes, in some instances, "one of God's angels said to him, Send a message to Peter saying, Come to my house." In such a rendering there are three levels of discourse, but this is often necessary when languages require direct discourse.

10. 23

Had them spend the night is literally "treated them as guests," but the meaning in the present context is "to treat them as overnight guests" (see JB "gave them lodging" and NEB "gave them a night's lodging"). As in a number of languages, the verb "invite" requires some direct discourse, for example, "Peter said to the men, Come in and spend the night here."

> 23b The next day he got ready and went with them; and some of the brothers from Joppa went along with him. 24 The following day he arrived in Caesarea, where Cornelius was waiting for him, together with relatives and close friends that he had invited. 25 As Peter was about to go in, Cornelius met him, fell at his feet, and bowed down before him. 26 But Peter made him rise. "Stand up," he said, "because I myself am only a man." 27 Peter kept on talking to Cornelius as he went into the house, where he found many people gathered. 28 He said to them, "You yourselves know very well that a Jew is not allowed by his religion to visit or associate with a Gentile. But God has shown me that I must not consider any man unclean or defiled. 29 And so when you sent for me I came without any objection. I ask you, then, why did you send for me?" (10. 23b-29)

The temporal connectives are most important in this paragraph: the next day (v. 23), the following day (v. 24), as Peter was about to go in (v. 25), kept on and as he went (v. 27). Note that markers of temporal sequence are not always direct expressions of time, but may include aspect indicators, implied in the phrase kept on.

10.23

10.23b-24

The next day of verse 23 indicates the third day since the beginning of the narrative, and the following day of verse 24 indicates the fourth day. Both of these temporal expressions serve as linking devices.

Some of the brothers is rendered in certain languages as "some of the believers." This is obviously a reference to "fellow believers." A phrase such as together with relatives and close friends that he had invited may be expressed in many languages as a supplementary clause, for example, "relatives and close friends whom Cornelius had invited were also waiting for Peter."

10.25

As Peter was about to go in involves the Semitic expression "came to pass," which is essentially transitional (see 9.32). The expression met him must not be understood in the sense of "be introduced to" but rather "greeted him" or "welcomed him."

Fell at his feet must of course not imply any accident but simply "bowing low before him." In fact, in the Greek text "fell at his feet and bowed down before him" represents essentially one activity, namely, bowing low before a person in the act of worship.

10.26

Made him rise is an expression for "caused him to stand up." In saying that he was only a man Peter is obviously emphasizing that he is not an angel and therefore does not merit any kind of special regard or worship as suggested by Cornelius' actions described in verse 25.

10.27

Peter kept on talking translates a Greek present participle (as does he saw in v. 11); the present tense of the Greek verb translated found is used for the sake of making the action more vivid to the reader. The actors in the narrative are mentioned explicitly, Peter...to Cornelius as he went into the house, where he found, to avoid the possible ambiguity of the Greek text "and as he was talking with him he went in and he found."

10.28

Not allowed by his religion (see NEB "forbidden by his religion") translates the expression "it is unlawful," but in the context the reference is to the Jewish Law. Gentile is literally "one of another race"; but from the Jewish point of view these terms carry the same meaning.

Is not allowed by his religion to visit may be rendered as "must not visit." One can also employ an expression such as "the laws of the Jews say that they cannot visit or associate with a Gentile." To visit or associate with may be difficult to render effectively in some languages. Visit, however, may be translated in some languages as "go into the house of" or "stay in the house of," and associate may be rendered as "have anything to do with" or "go around with."

It is not difficult to speak of food as being unclean, for it can be described as "not fit to eat" (in the sense of negative taboo), but it is not so easy to employ unclean or defiled with reference to people. Some translators, however, have employed exactly the same terms for unclean or defiled when applied to food and to persons and then used a marginal note to explain the particular application to people. On the other hand, one can also use in speaking of people "unfit to be associated with" as the equivalent of unclean or defiled. However, this type of rendering does not do full justice to the original terms, and therefore one should probably employ some such expression as "impure (or "too bad") to be associated with." In this type of context one is concerned with negative taboo, avoidance required because of contamination. This is not positive taboo, which is based on the possession of potentially harmful supernatural potency.

10.29

Without any objection may be rendered as "I did not object in any way" or "I did not ask any questions."

> 30 Cornelius said, "It was about this time three days ago that I was praying in my house at three o'clock in the afternoon. Suddenly a man dressed in shining clothes stood in front of me 31 and said: 'Cornelius! God has heard your prayer, and has remembered your works of charity. 32 Send someone to Joppa to call for a man whose full name is Simon Peter. He is a guest in the home of Simon the leatherworker, who lives by the sea.' 33 And so I sent for you at once, and you have been good enough to come. Now we are all here in the presence of God, waiting to hear anything that the Lord has ordered you to say."
>
> (10.30-33)

This paragraph illustrates one of the techniques by which Luke emphasizes certain features of an event. For example, this is the third time in this chapter that Cornelius' piety is mentioned: first when the angel comes to Cornelius (v. 4), later when the servant of Cornelius affirms this to Peter (v. 22), and finally in Cornelius' repetition of the angel's words (v. 31). Luke no doubt regarded this fact as very important, in view of later developments.

10.30

Three days ago (JB, NAB, Phillips, Moffatt, Goodspeed, Zürich, Knox) is "four days ago" in many translations (RSV, NEB, Barclay, Luther). There is no textual difference but only a difference of interpretation of the Greek phrase "from the fourth day." Cornelius means that this was the fourth day

213

from the day on which the angel had appeared to him (see vv. 7, 9, 23, 24).
There is a difference, however, between the meaning of the Greek expression
"from four days ago" and the English expression "four days ago." If, for example, on a Friday we were to say "four days ago" we would mean Monday;
but in New Testament times this phrase would mean Tuesday, for it would include in its calculation Friday itself. The correct English equivalent therefore
is three days ago. In a number of languages, however, the New Testament
system of reckoning is employed and therefore a translation "four days ago"
would be appropriate. The particular form of this reference to time depends
upon the usage in the receptor language. It is assumed by most commentators
and translators that about this time is a correct rendering of the Greek phrase
"until this hour" (though some exegetes assume that it is a precise temporal
reference, "exactly"), and that it modifies the adverbial expression three days
ago. At three o'clock in the afternoon is literally "the ninth hour" (see 3.1).
Three o'clock in the afternoon was the time for the afternoon prayers;
hence the NEB has "I was in the house here saying the afternoon prayers."
Some manuscripts have "praying and fasting" (TEV praying), and some scholars believe that the verb "fasting" was deleted from the present verse because
some scribe recognized that nothing had been said in the previous account
about Cornelius' fasting. However, it is more likely that the words were added
by a scribe who believed that fasting should come before baptism (see 9.9).
A man dressed in shining clothes is, of course, an angel (see 1.10).

10.31-32

These verses repeat essentially the information contained in verses 1-6.

10.33

At once is in the emphatic position in the Greek sentence.
In the presence of God may be rendered as "where God is" or "and God
is with us."
The term ordered suggests "instructed you to say to us" or "has arranged
for you to say to us."
In the second sentence of this verse anything is in the Greek literally
"everything."

Peter's Speech

34 Peter began to speak: "I now realize that it is true that God
treats all men on the same basis. 35 Whoever fears him and does what
is right is acceptable to him, no matter what race he belongs to.
36 You know the message he sent to the people of Israel, proclaiming
the Good News of peace through Jesus Christ, who is Lord of all men.
37 You know of the great event that took place throughout all the land of
Israel, beginning in Galilee, after the baptism that John preached.
38 You know about Jesus of Nazareth, how God poured out on him the

Holy Spirit and power. He went everywhere, doing good and healing all who were under the power of the Devil, because God was with him. 39 We are witnesses of all that he did in the country of the Jews and in Jerusalem. They put him to death by nailing him to the cross. 40 But God raised him from death on the third day, and caused him to appear, 41 not to all the people, but only to us who are the witnesses that God had already chosen. We ate and drank with him after he rose from death. 42 And he commanded us to preach the gospel to the people, and to testify that he is the one whom God has appointed judge of the living and the dead. 43 All the prophets spoke about him, saying that everyone who believes in him will have his sins forgiven through the power of his name." (10.34-43)

Some languages have no noun form such as speech. In this section heading one can, however, adapt a verb form, for example, "Peter Speaks to Cornelius and the Household" or "Peter Tells the Good News to Cornelius and His Household."

Peter's speech follows basically the same outline as that given in Chapter 2: first, he addresses the specific situation (vv. 34-35); second, he gives the outline of Jesus' ministry, including particular reference to his death and resurrection (vv. 36-41); third, he appeals to the Scripture as proof (v. 43a); and finally he calls for repentance (vv. 42 and 43b).

10.34

Peter began to speak is literally "but opening his mouth Peter said." However, "to open one's mouth" is a Semitic way of saying "begin (to speak)." It is important to avoid the use of an expression for began to speak which will suggest that what follows is only an introduction and that the main part of the speech is to come later.

God treats all men on the same basis translates the Semitic idiom "God is not one who receives men's faces." "To receive (someone's) face" means "to show partiality to someone" on the basis of external factors such as race, religion, or nationality. Peter's statement means that God's judgment of a person is not based on any external factors (see NEB "God has no favorites," and Goodspeed "God shows no partiality"). The rendering of God treats all men on the same basis varies significantly from language to language, for example, "God goes along with everyone the same," "God doesn't look upon anyone as though he were anyone," "God does not love people just because of the way they look," "God does not distinguish faces" (implying that he looks upon the heart), or "God does not take the side of anyone."

10.36-38

In the UBS Greek text these verses comprise one sentence, although in some manuscripts they consist of two. This long, involved structure has been divided by the TEV into several sentences, three of them beginning with the

main verb you know which appears in the Greek sentence only in verse 37.
In Greek the structure is complicated and may, as suggested above, be two
sentences rather than one. If it is two sentences, then the first one in verse
36 should be rendered something like "he sent his message to the people of
Israel, proclaiming the Good News of peace through Jesus Christ, who is
Lord of all men." On the other hand, if these verses are to be understood
as only one sentence, then you know is the main verb in the sentence. The
TEV assumes that the Greek structure best supports the thesis of one sentence; and in order to carry through the force of the main verb, this verb has
been repeated in each of three shorter sentences (vv. 36,37,38).

The phrase through Jesus Christ is best understood with peace, though
it is possible to understand this as a reference to Jesus Christ being the
agent for proclaiming the Good News. In such a context peace is a reference
to peace with God or the reconciliation which has been made possible through
Jesus Christ. In some translations this second clause in verse 36 is rendered as "announcing the Good News that we may have peace with God through
Jesus Christ."

Lord of all men must be translated with a certain amount of caution, for
normally one cannot imply a possessive construction. The men do not possess
the Lord; rather, he is "the Lord over all men." This is made explicit in
some languages as "the Lord who commands all men."

The great event translates "the thing that happened" (NEB "what happened"), but from Luke's point of view this is not just "something that
happened," it is "an event," that is, a great event. To translate as does
Goodspeed, "you know the story that has gone all over Judea," could leave
the intimation that these things did not really happen, since in many languages a word such as "story" often suggests something unreal.

In some languages the great event that took place is simply equivalent
to "what happened" or perhaps "what happened that was so important." In
many languages there is simply no noun corresponding to event. The only
equivalent is a verb meaning "to happen."

After the baptism that John preached may be a reference to the specific
baptism of Jesus Christ by John, since it is then that the Gospels emphasize
how the Holy Spirit came upon Jesus with power.

God poured out on him the Holy Spirit and power is rendered in most
other translations as "God anointed him with the Holy Spirit and with power,"
which represents a more literal translation of the Greek text. However, the
problem is that most English readers do not understand "anoint" in the biblical sense of "to choose (someone) for a special task." In a number of languages, however, one cannot speak of poured out...the Holy Spirit for the
Holy Spirit is not regarded as a kind of liquid. One can, however, introduce
the meaning of "anoint" by a double verb "chose him and caused the Holy
Spirit to come into him."

It is equally impossible in many languages to speak about "pouring out
power upon." One can "cause someone to be powerful" or in some languages
"give a person power," or even "cause a person to have power." In other

216

instances the expression must be somewhat more specifically related to strength (though in a general sense) "he caused him to have strength to do ...," in which case the complement of "having strength" may be the actions specified in the final sentence of verse 38, namely, doing good and healing all.

Doing good may be rendered as "doing good to people" or "causing good to come to people."

Under the power of the Devil may be equivalent to "whom the Devil controlled" or "whom the Devil had in his power."

10.39

It is important in rendering in the country of the Jews and in Jerusalem to avoid the impression that Jerusalem was not in the country of the Jews. Of course the first phrase refers to all of the country outside of the city of Jerusalem, while in Jerusalem specifically identifies the ministry of Jesus within the city itself. However, in some languages the order needs to be changed, for example, "all that he did in the city of Jerusalem and in the rest of the country of the Jews."

For the expression nailing him to the cross see 5.30.

10.40

In this sentence him is an emphatic initial position. This emphasis is difficult, if not impossible, to indicate in an English sentence, and the TEV has sought to make this emphasis by translating the clause but God raised him from death... as a contrast to the preceding statement about his being put to death.

Caused (literally "gave") is translated allow in 2.27, but in the present passage "to give" has the extended meaning of "to cause." "To allow" (see NEB and JB) is not strong enough in the present context, since God brought Jesus back to life and thereby caused him (not merely "allowed" him) to appear.

The rendering of to appear may be in some languages "to show himself to us."

10.41

It is generally agreed that all the people is a reference to the Jewish people.

The witnesses that God had already chosen may be rendered as "we are the ones that God had already chosen to be witnesses of him" (or "of these events").

We ate and drank with him is doubtless a reference to Luke 24.13 ff., 36 ff. "Eating and drinking" is, of course, a reference simply to "having a meal with." In some languages both activities are specified, while in other languages a general term groups both activities together.

10.42

Although it is possible to understand he in the clause he commanded as a reference to God, it is more probable that the reference is to Jesus.

The verb which most translators render "preach" or "proclaim" is expanded by the TEV to preach the gospel, since this is a technical term in the book of Acts for the proclamation of the gospel.

The living and the dead is a comprehensive term for all persons, past and present. It is, of course, part of the teaching of the New Testament that at the end of time some people will still be alive on the earth.

10.43

About him translates a phrase which may be either neuter "to this fact," or masculine "to this one," that is, about him; most commentaries and translations follow the second alternative.

The expression everyone who believes in him will have his sins forgiven is somewhat difficult to render, especially in languages in which the agent of forgiving must be specified as the subject of such a verb. The equivalent may therefore be "if anyone believes in Jesus, God will forgive that person's sins."

The Greek expression "through his name" is in such a context a reference to Jesus himself. In other words, the individual believes in Jesus and it is through Jesus that God forgives sins. In some languages the equivalent is "God will forgive the man's sins by means of him," that is, Jesus.

The Gentiles Receive the Holy Spirit

44 While Peter was still speaking, the Holy Spirit came down on all those who were listening to the message. 45 The Jewish believers who had come from Joppa with Peter were amazed that God had poured out his gift of the Holy Spirit on the Gentiles also. 46 For they heard them speaking in strange tongues and praising God's greatness. Peter spoke up, 47 "These people have received the Holy Spirit, just as we also did. Can anyone, then, stop them from being baptized with water?" 48 So he ordered them to be baptized in the name of Jesus Christ. Then they asked him to stay with them for a few days. (10.44-48)

The section heading The Gentiles Receive the Holy Spirit may require certain restructuring in some languages. In the first place, Cornelius and his household are only a few Gentiles and, though they are representative, in some languages one must say "Some Gentiles...." It is also possible, however, to employ "Cornelius and His Household Receive the Holy Spirit."

The transition between the preceding speech by Peter and what immediately follows is introduced by the clause while Peter was still speaking. This paragraph ends also with a reference to time in order to explain Peter's activity and to prepare the way for the next episode, Peter's report to the church at Jerusalem.

10.44

Came down on is literally "fell down on," and is so rendered in some translations (see RSV and Phillips). However, "to fall on" might seem to imply either that the Holy Spirit tripped and fell, or else that he attacked the believers. As in so many instances, some adjustment must be made in speaking of the Holy Spirit coming upon people, for example, "the Holy Spirit came into," "the Holy Spirit came to control," or "the Holy Spirit came into their hearts."

To the message (literally "to the word") refers here specifically to the Christian message (see 4.4) rather than merely to Peter's speech as such (see NEB "to the message"). By rendering who were listening to the message as "all the listeners" the JB has left out an important element.

10.45

"The of-circumcision believers" is correctly interpreted by the TEV to mean the Jewish believers.

God had poured out his gift of the Holy Spirit is literally "the gift of the Holy Spirit had been poured out." But this is one of those passive constructions in which a passive voice is used to describe the action of God without mentioning the name of God; that is to say, "the gift has been poured out" means "God has poured out his gift." However, as noted in other instances, it is not possible in a number of languages to speak of "pouring out a gift." One simply "gives to."

10.46

In the same way that the Holy Spirit manifested himself in a unique way at Pentecost, so he does for Cornelius and the other Gentile believers. It is difficult to comprehend fully the significance of this experience for the church, for it is an indication that God offers himself, his salvation, and his Spirit, not only to Jews, but to Gentiles as well. And the fact that the Gentiles speak in strange tongues is the external indication of God's Spirit in their lives. Whereas at Pentecost the Spirit seems to have given the believers the ability to speak in other languages (2.4), the experience here seems rather to be an ecstatic experience in which they did not speak other intelligible languages but rather strange tongues (see 19.6; and compare NEB "speaking in tongues of ecstasy"). However, there are some commentators and translators that do understand this speaking as referring to foreign languages (for example, Goodspeed and Phillips).

Since phenomena at least closely paralleling speaking in tongues are to be found in the religious systems of many societies, one can usually employ some local expression which will identify this kind of ecstatic utterance. Failing, however, to find such a well-known term or phrase in the receptor language, one can describe the experience by some such phrase as "speaking strange sounds," "speaking with different sounds," or even "unrecognizable sounds."

10.47

Praising God's greatness is the translation of a Semitic idiom (literally "magnifying God"), and has the same meaning as the similar phrase translated speaking...of the great things that God has done in 2.11. A phrase such as praising God's greatness must frequently be expressed as direct discourse, for example, "saying, God is very great."

10.47

Peter's statement that these people have received the Holy Spirit, just as we also did does not imply that he is identifying the speaking in foreign languages at Pentecost with the speaking of strange tongues here. What he is saying is that in both instances God was obviously present.

The question which Peter raises, Can anyone, then, stop them from being baptized with water? is a rhetorical question expecting the answer "No."

Being baptized with water may be restructured in some languages as "using water to baptize them."

10.48

It is possible to take in the name of Jesus Christ with the verb ordered. However, most commentators and translators take it with to be baptized.

The expression baptized in the name of Jesus Christ is often rendered as "baptized using the name of Jesus Christ."

By staying with the Gentile believers for a few days Peter proved both that they were now accepted as full members of the Christian community and that it was possible for Jews and Gentiles to have fellowship with one another.

CHAPTER 11

Chapter 11 is divided into two principal sections. The first (vv. 1-18) summarizes what has been related in the preceding chapter. By including Peter's account of what happened, Luke is able to emphasize again the importance of this event for the history of the church. In a sense, however, this first section also acts as a transition to what follows, namely, the spread of the church among the Gentiles. The second section (vv. 19-30) echoes the theme of earlier persecutions (5.17-41; 6.8-15; 8.1-3), and Luke can again emphasize the spread of the church as the result of persecution. This section also reintroduces Saul and gives further background information, as well as relating the visit of Barnabas and Saul to Jerusalem as a means of providing help for the believers in Judea, something which Saul did on several occasions, as related later in Acts.

Peter's Report to the Church at Jerusalem

1 The apostles and the brothers throughout all of Judea heard that the Gentiles also had received the word of God. 2 When Peter went up to Jerusalem, those who were in favor of circumcising Gentiles criticized him, 3 "You were a guest in the home of uncircumcised Gentiles, and you even ate with them!" 4 So Peter gave them a full account of what had happened, from the very beginning: (11.1-4)

This first portion (vv. 1-4) is essentially introductory to the second (vv. 5-18), which should be regarded as included structurally within this first unit since it is simply an expansion of the statement in verse 4 about the full account of what had happened.

11.1

As in so many other contexts, brothers may need to be translated as "believers."

The Gentiles must not be understood as inclusive or definitive. This is only "some Gentiles."

In this type of context received the word of God is to be understood as "believed the word of God"; and, as in other contexts of this type, word of God refers to the "word that is from God."

11.2

The use of the expression went up in referring to going to Jerusalem (and, conversely, "going down" when going away from Jerusalem) reflects, of course, the geographical position of Jerusalem which was higher than most of the surrounding area. In translating such expressions as "going up" and "going down" it is not wise to use terms which suggest that Jerusalem is on top of some very high mountain, only that it is at the top of a ridge of hills.

In many languages, however, the most natural and accurate equivalent is simply "went to."

Those who were in favor of circumcising Gentiles translates "those of circumcision," a phrase which is taken by many as a reference to Jewish Christians (see Barclay "Jewish Christians"), while other translations understand it to refer solely to "the Jews" (so JB). Most translations are ambiguous and do not indicate specifically whether Jewish Christians or Jews are meant (see Moffatt, RSV, Phillips "the circumcision party," and Goodspeed "the advocates of circumcision"). The total context, however, and the evident concern of Peter to justify what he had done, would seem to point to the fact that those who were criticizing Peter constituted a group of Christians who still held to a belief in the necessity of circumcision.

Criticized, reflecting in Greek a verb which is sometimes used as a legal technical term meaning "to enter into legal controversy (with someone)" (see Septuagint of Ezekiel 20.35), is represented by Barclay as "questioned his action" and by NEB as "raised the question with him." It is obvious that in the present context it does not have the force of a technical legal term.

11.3

This verse, rendered as a statement in the TEV, appears as a question in some translations (see JB and RSV). The basic issue is that of fellowship between the Jewish and Gentile Christians. From the strictly Jewish point of view it was bad enough for Peter to go and preach the message to the Gentiles, but even worse for him to be willing to eat with them. Peter, however, uses this incident as an argument against requiring Gentiles to be circumcised (see 15.7 ff.).

11.4

Peter gave them a full account means that Peter told them "point by point" what had happened (see JB "gave them the details point by point"). A full account of what had happened may be equivalent to "everything that had happened."

From the very beginning may need to be somewhat more specific in some languages, for example, "he began talking about what had happened first" or "he started with the very first thing that happened."

5 "I was praying in the city of Joppa, and I had a vision. I saw something coming down that looked like a large sheet being lowered by its four corners from heaven, and it stopped next to me. 6 I looked closely inside and saw animals, beasts, reptiles, and wild birds. 7 Then I heard a voice saying to me, 'Get up, Peter; kill and eat!' 8 But I said, 'Certainly not, Lord! No defiled or unclean food has ever entered my mouth.' 9 The voice spoke again from heaven, 'Do not consider anything unclean that God has declared clean.' 10 This happened three times, and finally the whole thing was drawn back up into heaven.

11 At that very moment three men who had been sent to me from Caesarea arrived at the house where I was staying. 12 The Spirit told me to go with them without hesitation. These six brothers from Joppa also went with me to Caesarea, and we all went into the house of Cornelius. 13 He told us how he had seen an angel standing in his house who said to him, 'Send someone to Joppa to call for a man whose full name is Simon Peter. 14 He will speak words to you by which you and all your family will be saved.' 15 And when I began to speak, the Holy Spirit came down on them just as on us at the beginning. 16 Then I remembered what the Lord had said, 'John baptized with water, but you will be baptized with the Holy Spirit.' 17 It is clear that God gave those Gentiles the same gift that he gave us when we believed in the Lord Jesus Christ; who was I, then, to try to stop God!"

18 When they heard this, they stopped their criticism and praised God, saying, "Then God has given to the Gentiles also the opportunity to repent and live!" 11.5-18)

This speech by Peter, which constitutes his defense for what he did in Caesarea, is essentially a repetition of the earlier account, designed, moreover, to emphasize the importance of the event. It contains some details which are not included in the previous account, and of course omits certain items since it obviously is a shortened form of the total discourse. Most of the exegetical and translational problems have already been dealt with in the previous chapter.

11.5

On this verse see 10.9-11. From heaven is not explicitly mentioned in the earlier account, though it is implied by the statement that heaven opened (10.11). In many languages a distinction must be made between "sky" and the spiritual world or abode of God. In this context both seem to be involved, though in view of the details of the vision most translators employ "sky" if a choice must be made.

The equivalent of the verb stopped must not suggest something which would normally move horizontally and possibly under its own power, but only that the large sheet which was being lowered from heaven "stopped being lowered," "was no longer lowered," or "ceased being lowered." The Greek text reads "came near to me."

11.6

On the basis of Genesis 1.24-25, which distinguishes between domesticated animals and wild animals, it seems best to understand animals as domesticated animals and beasts as wild animals. On this verse see 10.12.

11.7-8

On these verses see 10.13-14.

11.9

On these verses see 10.15-16. It should be noticed that in verse 9 <u>from heaven</u> is added to the details of the account as given in 10.15.

11.11

On this verse see 10.17-18.

In place of <u>I was</u> some manuscripts have "we were," which may have been the original reading, since it is easy to see why a scribe would change "we were" to <u>I was</u> (to conform to v. 5), but not vice versa.

11.12

On this verse see 10.20. There the Greek text has a participle (rendered <u>do not hesitate</u>), while here there is a difference in the Greek manuscripts. Some have a participial form (rendered <u>without hesitation</u>; so NAB), while others have a different form of the participle of the same verb (translated "without making any distinction"; see RSV and Zürich). The UBS committee on the Greek text favors this latter form, since it has the earliest manuscript evidence in its favor.

<u>Into the house of Cornelius</u> is literally "into the house of the man," but the context makes it clear that Cornelius is meant, and for English readers the proper name reads more naturally in this context than the general term "man."

11.13-14

It is to be noticed that this is the fourth time in Acts that this particular story has been narrated (see 10.3,5,22,32). <u>Your family</u> (literally "your household") included not only the immediate family, but all the servants and others who were under the authority of the master of the house (see 10.7).

11.15

<u>At the beginning</u> is a reference to Pentecost, a phrase which is sometimes difficult to render since it does not specify what began. In some languages this is best expressed as "just as it happened to us at the first," "just as the Holy Spirit came to us at first," or "as the Holy Spirit came first to us." As has been noted in a number of other contexts, the particular expression used with regard to the coming of the Holy Spirit depends upon the receptor language in question, for example, "comes down on," "comes into," "comes on," "comes to control," or "possesses."

11.16

On this verse see 1.5. The passive <u>you will be baptized</u> may constitute problems in certain languages in which there is no regular passive construction for the verb "baptize." In such instances one may often employ a kind of indirect passive, for example, "you will receive baptism," but in still other languages there is no noun for "baptism," and therefore it is necessary to employ some agent. Under these circumstances probably the best expression is "God will baptize you with the Holy Spirit," thus making the clause completely parallel with the statement concerning John having baptized with water.

11.17

On this verse see 10.45,47. The same gift is, of course, a reference to the Holy Spirit. An expression such as gave...the same gift is difficult to render literally in many languages. One simply cannot "give a gift." Under such circumstances one may translate, however, as "God gave to the Gentiles in the same way that he gave to us" or, even more specifically, "God gave the Holy Spirit to the Gentiles in the same way that he gave the Holy Spirit to us."

As in practically all contexts, an expression such as believed in is to be understood not in terms of "believing what a person has said" but "trusting in" or "committing one's self to." This implies "loyalty to" or "adherence to."

Who was I, then, to try to stop God! translates a Greek construction that is very difficult to explain, but it is agreed that it contains two elements: (1) "who was I to try to stop God?" and (2) "could I stop God?" This final question in a number of languages may require some characterization of the speaker, such as "was I big enough to try to stop God?" or "did I have enough power to try to prevent God?" It may even be necessary to specify what was involved in "preventing God," for example, "prevent God from doing what he wanted to do."

11.18

The verb rendered they stopped their criticism (see NEB "their doubts were silenced") is probably to be taken in this sense rather than as "they were silenced" (RSV). The verse affirms that (1) negatively, they stopped their criticism of Peter and (2) positively, they started praising God.

God has given to the Gentiles also the opportunity to repent and live is rendered rather literally in most translations (as an example, see the RSV "to the Gentiles also God has granted repentance unto life"). The expression "repentance unto life" means "repentance which leads to life," thereby providing the basis for translating the opportunity to repent and live.

This last verse of the first section would seem to indicate quite clearly that those who criticized Peter (spoken of in v. 2) were Christians and not Jews.

The Church at Antioch

19 The believers were scattered by the persecution which took place when Stephen was killed. Some of them went as far as Phoenicia and Cyprus and Antioch, telling the message to Jews only. 20 But some of the believers, men from Cyprus and Cyrene, went to Antioch and proclaimed the message to Gentiles also, telling them the Good News about

the Lord Jesus. 21 The Lord's power was with them, and a great number of people believed and turned to the Lord.

22 The news about this reached the church in Jerusalem, so they sent Barnabas to Antioch. 23 When he arrived and saw how God had blessed the people, he was glad and urged them all to be faithful and true to the Lord with all their hearts. 24 Barnabas was a good man, full of the Holy Spirit and faith. Many people were brought to the Lord.

25 Then Barnabas went to Tarsus to look for Saul. 26 When he found him, he brought him to Antioch. For a whole year the two met with the people of the church and taught a large group. It was at Antioch that the disciples were first called Christians. (11.19-26)

These three paragraphs all relate to developments in Antioch. The first paragraph tells of the growing number of believers, the second describes briefly the visit of Barnabas from Jerusalem, and the third describes Saul's coming to Antioch. A final paragraph (vv. 27-30), closely related to this series, treats the practical expression of brotherly love on the part of the people in Antioch by sending help to the believers in Jerusalem.

11.19

This section begins with the same words as 8.4, and indicates that the story which is about to be told took place simultaneously with the events recorded in 8.5---11.18 and not subsequent to them. In many languages it may be necessary to invert the order of clauses in the first part of verse 19 so as to highlight the connection with the persecution taking place when Stephen was killed, for example, "because of the persecution which took place when Stephen was killed, the believers were scattered," "...the believers had to flee to other cities," or "...to other countries." In a number of languages it is not possible to say simply that people had to "flee." One must specify in as general a manner as possible either where they fled from or to what types of places they fled.

Phoenicia was the coastal plain along northern Palestine which included the cities of Tyre and Sidon. Cyprus (see Barnabas in 4.36) was a large island lying off the coast of Asia Minor and Syria. Antioch (see Nicolaus in 6.5) was the capital of the imperial province of Syria; it was located about fifteen miles from the coast, and was the third city in the Empire, next only to Rome and Alexandria.

Telling the message may require some more specific identification, for example, "telling the message about Jesus" or "telling the message about the Lord Jesus."

11.20

There is some question regarding the meaning of the word translated Gentiles (most translations have "Greeks"; Zürich "those who spoke Greek"; NEB "Gentiles"), but in the context these persons are apparently contrasted with the Jews in verse 19 (see Spanish Versión Popular "those who were not Jews"). For this reason Gentiles seems to be the most adequate term for the context. It is perhaps worthy of note that the message preached to the Gentiles is about the Lord Jesus (rather than "about Jesus the Messiah"). This would have had much more meaning and much more effect in the Gentile environment than the message for Jews that Jesus was the Messiah.

11.21

The Lord's power translates an Old Testament phrase, "the hand of the Lord," and probably refers to God the Father rather than to Jesus. On the other hand, in the phrase turned to the Lord, the Lord Jesus is meant. In a number of languages one cannot readily speak of power as a noun of capacity or ability. This first clause must, therefore, be restructured in a number of languages as "the Lord helped them very much," "the Lord was with them strongly," or "the Lord showed how strong he was by being with them to help."

The expression turned to must convey the concept of "committal to." In some languages this may be equivalent to "trusted," "followed as their leader," or "made him their chief."

11.22

The news about this reached the church in Jerusalem is literally "the word about these things was heard in the ears of the church in Jerusalem." (It is also possible to interpret the Greek pronoun autōn as "these people," but this interpretation is less widely held.) This is another example where "word" is used with an extended meaning (see 1.1), and the entire sentence construction reflects Semitic thought patterns. In many languages, however, one cannot speak about news...reaching. Rather, one must say "the people in the church in Jerusalem heard about what had happened in Antioch."

Barnabas now shares the same role in Antioch as Peter and John shared in Samaria (8.14).

11.23

For the translation how God had blessed the people (literally "the grace of God") see 4.33 and 6.8. The translation of blessed poses a number of problems in some languages. In general, however, it is equivalent to "God had been good to the people," "God had shown favor to the people," or "God had caused good to the people."

On the relationship between the meaning of the name Barnabas and the verb urged see 4.36.

To be faithful and true to translates a verb which literally means "to remain" or "to stay with." Here, of course, it is used in the sense "to remain faithful and/or true to." It is difficult to find two such terms as faithful and true. These are essentially synonymous expressions in English and simply

11.24

reinforce the idea of the original text. It is equivalent in many languages to
"remain loyal to," "follow steadfastly with," or even "not give up obeying."

With all their hearts translates an expression which may be taken to
mean either determination ("with resolute hearts" NEB) or devotion ("with
heartfelt devotion" JB). An expression such as with all their hearts may simply be attributive to the previous expression, for example, "being completely
loyal to" or "never once ceasing to follow."

11.24

Although the Greek has "he," it is helpful to the English reader to translate "he" as Barnabas, since the last previous mention of his name was in
verse 22. Barnabas is here described in the same way that Stephen was in
6.5.

The Greek verb, "were added to," must be understood in the sense were
brought to or "were won over to" (JB and NEB). There is, however, a difficulty with the passive construction were brought to since in many languages
this is not only awkward but grammatically impossible. The closest equivalent
may be in some instances "came to believe in."

11.25

To look for represents a Greek verb which in the papyri is used of
searching for persons and usually implies difficulty. Saul is last mentioned
in 9.30, representing a lapsed period of time of some ten years.

11.26

The verb met with may also mean "be guests of" (see RSV note and NEB,
"lived in fellowship with").

"The church" is qualified here as meaning the people of the church. It
is agreed by the commentators that Christians was a title given to the believers by the non-Christian community, perhaps because the believers said
"Christ is Lord," in contrast with the confession of the Roman world "Caesar
is Lord." Thus, the word Christian basically means "one who is a follower of
Christ." The word is used only here, 26.28, and 1 Peter 4.16. In many languages it is difficult to form an adjective on the root Christ, and therefore
one cannot so conveniently employ a term such as Christian. This means that
the closest equivalent may be a phrase such as "followers of Christ" or "adherents to Christ." One should, however, avoid expressions which will only
imply some intellectual interest in the Christian faith, for example, "learners
from Christ" or "learners of the Christ way." Some greater emphasis upon
commitment is required.

The importance of the stay in Antioch is underlined by the observation
that the two men met there for a whole year. According to Acts most of Paul's
visits were very short; Ephesus and Corinth were exceptions.

27 About that time some prophets went down from Jerusalem to Antioch. 28 One of them, named Agabus, stood up and by the power of the Spirit predicted that a great famine was about to come over all the earth. (It came when Claudius was Emperor.) 29 The disciples decided that each of them would send as much as he could to help their brothers who lived in Judea. 30 They did this, then, and sent the money to the church elders by Barnabas and Saul. (11.27-30)

11.27

About that time is another one of Luke's vague descriptions of time, and is almost verbally identical in Greek with the indication of time in 1.15.

Prophets, of course, refers to Christian prophets, and the term is used here and in 13.1; 15.32; 21.10 (see 2.16 where the reference is to Joel, the OT prophet). It should be noticed that both here and in 21.10 the only specific thing mentioned in relation to the prophets (Agabus, in both cases) is their ability to predict a future event. In many other contexts in the New Testament, and especially in the Epistles, the term prophet refers not primarily to a person who can predict future events but to one who engages in inspired preaching. In a number of languages one may require two different terms since one expression will be applicable only to foretelling future events and may even be roughly equivalent to "diviner" or "clairvoyant." In some instances both aspects of the prophetic function may be included in a phrase such as "one who speaks on behalf of God." With this type of expression the context alone will indicate whether the reference is to the prediction of future events or to inspired preaching.

11.28

"Through the Spirit" is taken by the TEV to mean by the power of the Spirit (see 1.2). This reference to "through the Spirit" may be expressed in many languages as a type of causative "it was the Spirit (or the Holy Spirit) which caused him to predict." In still other languages one may say "he predicted, the Holy Spirit told him to." This would indicate the causative force as well as the source of such divine revelation.

Predicted is literally "to indicate" or "to signify" (the word in Greek is related to the root meaning "sign"; see 2.19), but commentators and translators agree that the meaning here is "predict" (see NEB; and "foretold" in RSV and Phillips).

The Greek term translated here as earth (the same Greek term also occurs in 17.6, 31; 19.27; 24.5) means "the inhabited earth," or "the civilized world" and is equivalent to "the Roman Empire."

Claudius was emperor from A.D. 41 to 54, and evidently his reign was characterized by famines in various parts of the known world. In Palestine the famine was particularly severe around A.D. 46. The statement (It came when Claudius was Emperor.) is parenthetical, and so placed in parenthesis by the TEV (also Zürich).

11.29

The Greek of this verse involves a relatively complex sentence structure, but the meaning is made clear by the TEV and most other translations. The gift sent to Jerusalem by the disciples in Antioch (most of whom were probably Gentiles) indicates at least two things: (1) their gratitude to the Jerusalem church from which the Christian message had come and (2) their sense of unity with the Jewish believers in Jerusalem.

It is important, however, in translating this verse to indicate that the action of sending help was a collective action and not an individual one. A literal rendering of each of them would send as much as he could might suggest that each individual was sending his own particular gift. Obviously, however, this was a joint undertaking since the money was sent to the church elders in Jerusalem by means of two persons designated for the task, Barnabas and Saul.

11.30

Though the Greek text has no specific reference to money, it is clearly implied in the context (see Spanish Versión Popular "offering"; Barclay "their contributions"). "The elders" are obviously the church elders. This is the first time that Christian elders are spoken of (see further 14.23; 15.2,4,6, 22,23; 16.4; 20.17; 21.18). In none of these passages, however, is there any indication regarding either the origin or the function of these elders. In speaking of the elders there is a tendency in some translations to imply only a designation of "old men." This may not, however, be fully adequate for it suggests the leaders in the church rather than necessarily the older men, though of course there was a tendency for leadership to rest with the older adult men in the congregation, even as in most societies. In most face-to-face societies there exists a relatively well-identified group of elder counselors who often act as a kind of consultative body for the chief. Such a term may be readily employed for this group of individuals in the church.

By Barnabas and Saul is literally "by the hand of Barnabas and Saul," which simply means "by means of" (see Barclay "through"). By Barnabas and Saul may be rendered as "Barnabas and Saul carried the gift" or "Barnabas and Saul took the money to Jerusalem."

CHAPTER 12

Chapter 12 introduces a repeated theme, the persecution of the church. In this instance, however, there is a rather special development, namely, the divine justice which ends in the death of Herod, who was himself responsible not only for the death of James, but also for the imprisonment of Peter. The chapter consists of three major portions. First, the introductory paragraph (vv. 1-5); second, the release of Peter from prison (vv. 6-19); and third, the death of Herod (vv. 20-23). Verse 24 is a typical summary paragraph and re-emphasis of what was happening to the church, namely, its continued growth. Verse 25, which is also a paragraph, is transitional in character since it takes Barnabas and Saul from Jerusalem, where they had been left in 11.30, and returns them, together with John Mark, to Antioch. This is an important feature in the discourse since Chapter 13 centers on the work of Barnabas and Saul.

More Persecution

1 About this time King Herod began to persecute some members of the church. 2 He had James, the brother of John, put to death by the sword. 3 When he saw that this pleased the Jews, he went ahead and had Peter arrested. (This happened during the time of the Feast of Unleavened Bread.) 4 After his arrest Peter was put in jail, where he was handed over to be guarded by four groups of four soldiers each. Herod planned to put him on trial in public after Passover. 5 So Peter was kept in jail, but the people of the church were praying earnestly to God for him. (12.1-5)

The section heading More Persecution must often be radically restructured in translation, since the event of persecution would be more normally expressed by a verb phrase, and the greater extent of persecution will need to be indicated by some adverbial modifier, for example, "The Believers Suffer More," "The Authorities Cause the Church to Suffer More," or "The Rulers Persecute the Members of the Church More."

The temporal setting of this section is given in two different forms: (1) by the introductory phrase about this time, which relates the following to what has just preceded and (2) by the parenthetical expression (This happened during the time of the Feast of Unleavened Bread.). Note, however, that this more specific reference applies primarily to the arrest of Peter, while the persecution of the church as a whole had continued for some time. In addition to these two references to time, there are several other indications of relative time: when he saw (v. 3), after his arrest (v. 4), after Passover (v. 4), and was kept (v. 5).

12.1

About this time (see JB, NEB, Luther Revised; "about that time" RSV, Zürich, Segond) is a vague designation of time, and serves as much as a paragraph marker as it does an indication of time. Such a reference to time is equivalent in some languages to "in those days" or even "then." In other languages a verbal expression is employed "while all this was happening."

King Herod is Herod Agrippa the first, grandson of Herod the Great (Luke 1.5), who from A.D. 41 to 44 ruled over all the country of Palestine, with the title of "King."

The literal expression "he laid hands on to mistreat" is translated began to persecute (see JB "started persecuting"). In this type of context, "to lay hands on" indicates hostile action, and taken together with the verb "mistreat" (here with the specialized meaning of "persecute") means "begin to persecute" (see also NEB "attacked" and Barclay "launched a violent attack"). To attempt a literal translation (as in RSV, Phillips, Goodspeed, Moffatt, Segond, Zürich) might suggest that this is something Herod did personally with his own hands, whereas this is actually something that he ordered done and it was carried out by his subordinates. The phrase "certain ones of those from the church" is translated some members of the church (so Segond).

He had . . . put to death by the sword is literally "he killed . . . with a sword." But again to say "he killed" might suggest that this was something that Herod did personally, whereas it was something ordered by him and done by his subordinates. Put to death by the sword in this type of context may be rendered in some languages as "ordered a soldier to kill James by means of a sword" or "ordered a soldier to take his sword to kill James." In many parts of the world a sword is not employed in fighting or in warfare. The closest equivalent may be "a very large knife." In other instances a sword is "a large knife for fighting."

Pleased the Jews may be rendered as "caused the Jews to be happy about this."

He went ahead and had Peter arrested (literally, "he added to arrest Peter also") reflects a Semitic idiom ("he added [to do something]") which appears quite frequently in the Old Testament (see also Luke 19.11; 20.11-12), and most translators have employed various types of restructuring, as in the TEV. The concept of adding one crime to another may be expressed in some languages as "he did something else bad; he had Peter arrested" or "he did further evil; he ordered soldiers to arrest Peter."

From the mention of the Feast of Unleavened Bread in this verse and of Passover in the following verse one might conclude that the Feast of Unleavened Bread preceded Passover. However, this is not the case, for the Passover was celebrated on the 14th day of the month Nisan (March-April) and the Feast of Unleavened Bread was celebrated from the 15th to 21st day of the same month. Luke, a Gentile, seems to have identified these two terms as synonymous, for in Luke 22.1 he writes the Feast of Unleavened Bread, which is called the Passover.

An appropriate rendering of the expression Feast of Unleavened Bread is difficult in a number of languages. One can scarcely say "time when the people feasted on bread that did not rise," although this is possible in some languages. In general the relationship of the Feast to Unleavened Bread is expressed as the name of the feast, for example, "during the time when people had a feast called the Feast with bread that did not rise." Even the expression "unleavened" must be carefully selected for it might mean simply that someone had forgotten to put in the yeast. This is "bread in which no yeast has been placed" or, as in some languages, "bread without yeast." In some areas of the world the equivalent of yeast is "beer foam" or "sourdough," but in other areas it is "medicine that makes bread get large." (Under such circumstances "medicine" is simply a general designation for any type of potent substance, whatever its origin or purpose.)

12.4

After his arrest Peter was put in jail represents "whom also having arrested he put in prison." The reader has no difficulty in understanding that Herod is the one who made the arrest; but inasmuch as a parenthetical statement has intervened since the last mention of Peter by name, it seems best to make "whom" explicit, that is, Peter.

Four groups of four soldiers each is the meaning of the Greek phrase (see NEB, JB, Spanish Versión Popular, Segond, Zürich), but it is not made clear by the RSV and NAB ("four squads of soldiers"). One group of four men would be on guard duty for three hours, followed by the other groups who also would be on duty for periods of three hours each. Peter was chained to two of these guards, and evidently the two others stood on duty at the gate.

In rendering four groups of four soldiers each one may say "four groups of soldiers guarded him successively. Each group contained four soldiers." Or "...one group after another. Each...."

Herod planned translates the participle "planning," which a Greek reader could immediately recognize as referring back to Herod, but this is not immediately clear to the English reader, so the TEV has made it explicit. Moreover, in order to avoid a long and complicated sentence structure, the TEV has begun a new sentence here. Luke's literal expression "to bring him out to the people" should probably be taken in the sense of "to put him on public trial" (so Barclay; also JB "to try Peter in public"). In some languages this public trial of Peter can be rendered as "bring him out of jail so the people could condemn him to death" or "cause him to be tried where everybody could listen to his being condemned to death."

12.5

Was kept in jail may simply be rendered as "the soldiers continued to guard Peter in jail."

Two things emphasize the intensity of the prayer offered by the people of the church in behalf of Peter: (1) the verb itself, were praying, which indicates continuous action and (2) the adverbial expression earnestly. The expression of earnestly may be rendered as "strongly," for example, "they were praying strongly to God" or "they were praying with words they felt in their hearts."

Peter Set Free from Prison

6 The night before Herod was going to bring him out to the people, Peter was sleeping between two guards. He was tied with two chains, and there were guards on duty at the prison gate. 7 Suddenly an angel of the Lord stood there, and a light shone in the cell. The angel shook Peter by the shoulder, woke him up, and said, "Hurry! Get up!" At once the chains fell off Peter's hands. 8 Then the angel said, "Tighten your belt and tie on your sandals." Peter did so, and the angel said, "Put your cloak around you and come with me." 9 Peter followed him out of the prison. He did not know, however, if what the angel was doing was real; he thought he was seeing a vision. 10 They passed by the first guard station, and then the second, and came at last to the iron gate that opens into the city. The gate opened for them by itself, and they went out. They walked down a street, and suddenly the angel left Peter. (12.6-10)

The section heading Peter Set Free from Prison may need to be expressed in an active form in some languages, for example, "An Angel Causes Peter to Go Out of the Prison." In other instances one may employ an intransitive verb, for example, "Peter Escapes from Prison," but this should not give the impression that Peter had contrived some special means of escape.

The narrative sequences in this paragraph are fully marked by temporal transitionals, for example, the night before Herod was going (v. 6), suddenly (v. 7), at once (v. 7), then (v. 8), then (v. 10), and suddenly (v. 10).

12.6

The intimation of this verse is that Peter was chained to each of the two guards who slept beside him. It may be useful to indicate specifically how Peter was bound by the two chains, namely, "one chain bound him to a guard on one side and another chain bound him to a guard on the other side."

The reference to guards on duty at the prison gate may be translated as "soldiers were guarding the door to the prison."

12.7

For the particle that Luke has translated suddenly see 1.10.
On the expression angel of the Lord see 5.19.

The verb translated <u>stood there</u> is often used by writers to refer to persons who suddenly come on the scene, and it is used especially of the sudden appearance of divine or demonic beings.

The word translated <u>cell</u> (some translations "prison") is a very general expression, and literally means "a dwelling"; but it is obvious that Peter was in a <u>cell</u>.

For the sake of carrying out the intended force of the Greek (literally "get up quickly") the TEV has translated <u>Hurry! Get up!</u> Although the Greek has "he hit him on the side" the meaning is more naturally conveyed in English by <u>shook Peter by the shoulder</u>. Though in English <u>shook...by the shoulder</u> is a natural expression, in other languages something closer to the Greek text may be far more appropriate, for example, "slapped him on the side."

12.8

<u>Tighten your belt</u> is of course a reference to the girdle which was worn around relatively loose clothing.

<u>Cloak</u> is the outer garment (sometimes translated "coat"); <u>and come with me</u> is literally "follow me," but the verb "to follow" is often used in the sense of "go with" or "accompany."

12.9

The KJV, "and he went out, and followed him," represents a fairly literal translation of the Greek, but it suggests that first Peter went out of the prison and then followed the angel. The meaning is "he followed him out" (Phillips, NEB) or, more explicitly, <u>Peter followed him out of the prison</u>.

It is not always easy to translate the expression <u>real</u>. In some languages one must employ some such form as "he did not know whether he was really going out of the prison, or whether he was simply imagining this," "he did not know whether he was dreaming or whether this was actually happening," or "he was not sure that he was going out of the prison; he thought he was seeing a vision."

12.10

The <u>first guard station</u> can be rendered as "the first group of soldiers who were guarding." <u>The second</u> can, of course, be "the second group of soldiers who were guarding."

The mention of <u>the iron gate that opens into the city</u> has caused most commentators to assume that Peter was being held prisoner in the tower of Antonia, located at the northwest corner of the temple area, with gates leading into the temple area and into the city itself.

<u>The iron gate that opens into the city</u> may cause certain difficulties since people will not understand the nature of the prison (or palace) in which Peter had been imprisoned. In some languages the only reasonable equivalent is "door," but in other instances one can speak of "the iron gate in the wall."

One cannot, however, employ the word opens in a number of languages since this would imply opening into a room but not into the city. One must, therefore, use an expression such as "leads out into the city" or "opens and one may go into the city."

The gate opened for them by itself may be rendered as "the gate became open but no one had moved it."

It is held by some that a street (Greek "one street") may possibly have the meaning of "a certain street."

> 11 Then Peter realized what had happened to him, and said, "Now I know that it is really true! The Lord sent his angel, and he rescued me from Herod's power and from all the things the Jewish people expected to do."
>
> 12 Aware of his situation, he went to the home of Mary, the mother of John Mark. Many people had gathered there and were praying. 13 Peter knocked at the outside door, and a servant girl named Rhoda came to answer it. 14 She recognized Peter's voice and was so happy that she ran back in without opening the door, and announced that Peter was standing outside. 15 "You are crazy!" they told her. But she insisted that it was true. So they answered, "It is his angel."
>
> 16 Meanwhile, Peter kept on knocking. They opened the door at last and when they saw him they were amazed. 17 He motioned with his hand for them to be quiet, and explained to them how the Lord had brought him out of prison. "Tell this to James and the rest of the brothers," he said; then he left and went somewhere else.
>
> 18 When morning came, there was a tremendous confusion among the guards; what had happened to Peter? 19 Herod gave orders to search for him, but they could not find him. So he had the guards questioned and ordered them to be put to death.
>
> After this Herod went down from Judea and spent some time in Caesarea. (12.11-19)

The five preceding paragraphs deal with four principal features of this episode: (1) the realization by Peter that he has now escaped from Herod's power (v. 11); (2) the response of the church to Peter's presence (vv. 12-17); (3) the reaction of Herod and his punishment of the guards (vv. 18-19a); and (4) Herod's departing from Judea (v. 19b). This last brief mention of Herod's going to Ceasarea is, of course, in anticipation of the next episode which relates the death of Herod.

12.11

Realized what had happened to him is taken by most to mean "came to himself," as though he had been in a trance, and by others to signify "came to his senses," as though he had been unconscious. This rather difficult expression may be rendered in some languages as "knew that what had happened to him was true" or "knew that it was really true that he had come out of the prison."

The Lord in this verse probably refers to God rather than to the Lord Jesus.

From Herod's power translates the Semitic expression "from the hand of (Herod)," in which "hand" symbolizes the power (of someone). The noun phrase "from all the expectation of the people of the Jews" has been transformed into a verb clause by the TEV from all the things the Jewish people expected to do, which makes a much more intelligible English sentence structure (see also Spanish Versión Popular, de Beaumont, Segond). In translating rescued me from Herod's power it may, however, be necessary to restructure the semantic relationships: "rescued me so that Herod cannot harm me" or "rescued me so that I will not be under Herod's authority." Similarly, the last phrase from all the things the Jewish people expected to do may be related to the "rescuing" as "rescued me from having to suffer what the Jewish people were going to cause me to suffer."

12.12

Aware of his situation translates a single verb in the Greek (literally, "when he realized") that has no object, and so the object must be supplied from the context such as the NEB "when he realized how things stood" and the JB "as soon as he realized this." One may render aware of his situation by such expressions as "now knowing what had happened" or "seeing what had really happened."

It is interesting that Mary is identified by the addition of her son's name John Mark, though it was more natural to identify a person by the father than by his son. This is the first mention in Acts of John Mark. It is typical of Luke's writing to introduce a person such as John Mark by this kind of brief reference, particularly when he is going to be mentioned in the text later (12.25; 13.5, 13; 15.37-39).

Were praying may require in many languages some grammatical object, for example, "were praying to God for Peter."

12.13

The outside door (so JB; "the outer door" NEB) was either the door leading from the street into the inner court or else a smaller door built into the main door, and which could be used for entrance without opening the larger one. Rhoda, the name of the servant girl, means "a rose."

In many languages one cannot speak of "answering the door" as answer it would imply. Rather, one must say "a servant girl named Rhoda came to find out who was knocking" or "...came in response to Peter's knocking."

12.14

Recognized Peter's voice may be rendered as "knew that it was Peter who was speaking" or "recognized that Peter was speaking."

12.15

Though the expression was so happy that she ran back in without open-ing the door seems relatively simple in its structure in English, this may re-quire certain adjustments in other languages because of the problems of temporal sequence, for example, "she was very happy; she did not open the door but she ran back into the house."

Announced may simply be "told everyone."

Outside accurately translates the meaning of the Greek phrase, "in front of the door," for Peter would have been standing outside of the inner court of the house.

12.15

Since Rhoda's announcement in verse 14 may very well be in direct dis-course, "Peter is standing outside," it may be necessary to modify the verb of speaking referring to the response of the people, "they answered her," "they responded to her," or "they replied."

You are crazy! captures both the spirit and the meaning of the people's response to Rhoda's statement. She insisted that it was true may be rendered as "she kept saying that Peter was really there."

Among certain of the Jews it was believed that each individual had a spiritual counterpart, who could appear if the person were alive or dead, and this was known as his angel.

12.16

Meanwhile may be rendered in some languages as an entire clause, "while this was happening" or "while they were talking."

Kept on knocking (JB "was still knocking") carries through the force of the Greek verb tenses, and they opened the door at last expresses quite accu-rately the force of the Greek aorist participle "when they had opened."

The subject of the verb opened may need to be identified as "the people inside" or "some of the people inside."

The term for amazed should be one expressing a very strong reaction, for example, "utterly astounded" or "completely amazed."

12.17

The force of the present infinitive to be quiet means in Greek "to keep quiet" (see NEB, Moffatt), rather than "to get quiet" (see Phillips "to stop talking").

James and the rest of the brothers is literally "James and the brothers," which to an English reader might sound as if James was not included among the brothers. In reality this is a means of marking him out for special atten-tion as with the earlier mention of the women, and ... Mary (1.14). This James is thought to be the brother of the Lord, who became a noted leader in the Jerusalem church (see 15.13 ff.; 21.18).

Somewhere else (most translations "to another place") is extremely indefinite; it may refer either to another house in Jerusalem or to another town or city. If the translator must make a choice, the latter of these alternatives is probably to be preferred.

12.18

Tremendous (JB "great") translates one of Luke's favorite emphatic expressions (literally, "not a little bit"; see 14.28; 15.2; 17.4,12; 19.23,24; 27.20). This expression of tremendous confusion may be expressed as "the soldiers who had guarded Peter were terribly disturbed," or as in some languages "fearfully confused" or "afraid and confused." The question what had happened to Peter? must be introduced by some verb of speaking in some languages, for example, "they kept saying to one another, What has happened to Peter?"

12.19

To be put to death is literally "to be led off." Although the expression could mean "to be led off to prison," most translators and commentators understand it in the more specific sense of to be put to death, since it was customary for Roman soldiers to receive the punishment designated for the prisoners whom they allowed to escape. It is interesting that Caesarea is distinguished from Judea, although it was the Roman capital of the province. This was because Caesarea was a Gentile city, and was not considered by the Jews as actually part of their territory.

The Death of Herod

20 Herod was very angry with the people of Tyre and Sidon; so they went in a group to see Herod. First they won Blastus over to their side; he was in charge of the palace. Then they went to Herod and asked him for peace, because their country got its food supplies from the king's country.
21 On a chosen day Herod put on his royal robes, sat on his throne, and made a speech to the people. 22 "It isn't a man speaking, but a god!" they shouted. 23 At once the angel of the Lord struck Herod down, because he did not give honor to God. He was eaten by worms and died.
24 The word of God continued to spread and grow.
25 Barnabas and Saul finished their mission and returned from Jerusalem, taking John Mark with them. (12.20-25)

The section heading The Death of Herod may be altered to "Herod Dies" or "The Account about How Herod Died."
The first paragraph of this section is readily combined with the preceding since Herod has just been mentioned. The second paragraph is also quite logically related to the first, with a convenient temporal transition on a chosen day. The third paragraph (v. 24) may seem somewhat strange or

out of place, but this is a constantly recurring theme in the book of Acts and is several times mentioned as the normal consequence of persecution. Accordingly, in terms of the overall structure and theme of the book, this paragraph is quite fitting. The last paragraph (v. 25) is an important transitional paragraph, designed to reintroduce Saul, who from the beginning of Chapter 13 is the focal character in the book.

12. 20

Very angry translates a verb that literally means "to be at war with," and is here used in the figurative sense of "to be very angry with" (see NEB "furiously angry with").

They must be understood as a delegation of citizens from these two cities who came to plead their case with Herod. On the meaning of the word translated in a group see 1. 14.

Blastus, mentioned only here in the New Testament, was a very common name and nothing more is known of him than is mentioned in this verse. He was in charge of the palace translates "the one over the king's bedchamber," that is, "the king's chamberlain." "Chamberlain," the usual rendering of this term, conveys very little, if anything, to the average English reader. Primarily, the word designated the man in charge of the harem, but the duties of his office could have been much wider, and so a translation such as the TEV is much more meaningful to English readers (see also Spanish Versión Popular "a high official of King Herod").

The cities of Tyre and Sidon were free cities under the Roman administration, but they depended on the grain fields of Galilee for their food. From the king's country is literally "from that belonging to the king," but the reference is obviously to the territory or country over which Herod ruled.

12. 21

According to the account of Josephus, the Jewish historian, the chosen day was a celebration in honor of the Emperor. Luke does not state what the occasion was, or who chose the day, though the context suggests that this was a special day appointed by Herod to hear the grievances of the people from Tyre and Sidon. The chosen day can be "on a special day" or "on a day that Herod had especially selected."

Put on his royal robes may be equivalent to "put on special clothes fit for a king" or "put on clothes which he wore for special days."

Sat on his throne, and made a speech to the people does not indicate the nature of the gathering. Some scholars, however, contend that this was a court scene (Barclay "took his seat on the bench in his court"; NAB "sat on the rostrum"). The throne may be "his special seat" or "his special chair." On the other hand, it may refer to "the chair on which he sat when he pronounced judgment" or "the chair on which he sat when he ruled."

To the people may be limited to the delegations from Tyre and Sidon, or else it may be enlarged to include the people of Caesarea as well; no definite decision can be made.

12. 22

It isn't a man speaking, but a god may cause certain difficulties in some languages, for it is not possible to deny Herod being a man. Therefore one must say "he speaks like a god; he doesn't speak like a man" or "he is a god speaking, not just a man speaking."

They shouted in the Greek is a tense that suggests continuous action, "they shouted and kept on shouting."

12. 23

Struck Herod down is equivalent to "caused him to become sick."

He did not give honor to God indicates that he claimed for himself the honor that belonged only to God, and thus was guilty of pride and sacrilege. The expression give honor to God is rather too general in some languages for this kind of context. Therefore one must say "because he did not insist that he was just a man and not God." In other instances one may employ "because he did not have the people praise God rather than himself."

To be eaten by worms was a death frequently ascribed by ancient writers to extremely evil persons, especially of persons with great power and authority. The worms spoken of in this context should refer to some kind of intestinal worms rather than to maggots for, according to the text, it was the worms which caused his death and not maggots, which would eat his flesh after he had died.

12. 24

This is the third summary account given in Acts (see 6. 7; 9. 31). The word of God refers to the Christian missionary preaching and to the Christian community which grew on the basis of this preaching. However, in many languages one cannot speak of "the word of God spreading and growing." Rather, one must say "more and more people heard the word of God and believed."

12. 25

Finished their mission is equivalent to "did what they came to Jerusalem to do" or, as may be necessary in some instances, "gave the money to the elders" (a specific reference to 11. 30).

This verse presents a very severe textual problem, and the translations differ as to whether or not (they) returned from Jerusalem or "returned to Jerusalem." Although it is possible to conclude that this verse means that Barnabas and Saul finished their mission (in Antioch) and returned to Jerusalem, it is more natural to assume that 11. 30 records their arrival in Jerusalem and 12. 25 their departure from Jerusalem. NAB and Goodspeed have

12.25

"to"; while TEV, Moffatt, Barclay, Spanish Versión Popular, Segond, Luther Revised, and Zürich have "from"; Synodale "from Jerusalem to Antioch"; RSV, NEB, JB have "from," with a note indicating the possibility of "to." The UBS Greek text has "to," but gives this a D rating, as quite uncertain. From the standpoint of the discourse structure, it would seem much more natural for the reading to be from Jerusalem, so as to prepare the reader for the account of the happenings in Antioch, which immediately follows (13.1 ff.).

The beginning of Chapter 13 marks a major shift of focus in The Acts of the Apostles since from 13.1 through 28.31 the ministry of Paul is the center of attention and, for the most part, the progress in the story is related to different centers where Paul ministers. The events are essentially in historical order but the transitional devices are primarily geographical as Paul moves from one place to another.

There are three dominant themes in most of the accounts beginning with Chapter 13: (1) increased interest on the part of Gentiles for the message of the Good News, (2) opposition by the Jews, and (3) the mounting success of Paul's ministry as more and more people believe.

Chapter 13 is divided essentially into three sections. The first (vv. 1-3) deals with the commissioning of Barnabas and Saul, the second (vv. 4-12) relates the experiences in Cyprus, and the third (vv. 13-52) treats their experiences in Antioch of Pisidia.

Barnabas and Saul Chosen and Sent

1 In the church at Antioch there were some prophets and teachers: Barnabas, Simeon (called the Black), Lucius (from Cyrene), Manaen (who had been brought up with Governor Herod), and Saul. 2 While they were serving the Lord and fasting, the Holy Spirit said to them, "Set apart for me Barnabas and Saul, to do the work to which I have called them."

3 They fasted and prayed, placed their hands on them, and sent them off. (13.1-3)

The section heading Barnabas and Saul Chosen and Sent is particularly useful in English, but quite impossible in languages which cannot employ passive participles such as chosen and sent. Furthermore, in a high percentage of languages some agent of the action is called for. Some translators may prefer to focus attention upon the role of the Holy Spirit, for example, "The Holy Spirit Directs the Church in Antioch to Send Out Barnabas and Saul" or "The Holy Spirit Selects Barnabas and Saul for a Special Work." Others may prefer to focus attention upon the activity of the church in Antioch, for example, "The Church in Antioch Sends Out Barnabas and Saul" or "The Believers in Antioch Commission Barnabas and Saul."

These initial paragraphs constitute the introduction to the entire second half of the book of Acts. From this point on, Saul is the focal character, and though for a brief period he is linked with Barnabas (at first as the second name in the team), he soon takes over the leadership. What is important about this commissioning is that it was done by the church in response to directions from the Holy Spirit.

13. 1

13. 1

In the church, as in most translations, is rendered "in the local church" by Moffatt, because the same type of construction appears here as was discussed in 5. 17. It is important, however, in translating church not to give the impression that this is a building. In some languages it is even necessary to employ "among the believers who worshiped Jesus at Antioch."

In the present context **prophets** seems to be used of persons whose duty it was to proclaim the Christian message, while **teachers**, a word which occurs only here in Acts, were persons who apparently had the responsibility of instructing the Christian converts in the beliefs and duties of the Christian faith. In this type of context **prophets** may be spoken of as "those who preached the Good News" and **teachers** may be "those who taught the believers."

Black translates a Greek word brought over from Latin and means "dark complexioned" or "black" ("Niger" as used in many translations holds no meaning for the reader). **Lucius (from Cyrene)** should not be confused with Lucius mentioned in Romans 16. 21; and there is no evidence to connect him with Luke, the author of Acts.

Who had been brought up with translates one word in Greek which is often used as a title for a boy who had been brought up as the companion of a prince (this is the basis for "foster brother" of Moffatt and Phillips); but it may have the general meaning of "intimate friend," as is shown by its use in the papyri, and that seems to be its significance here.

A term for **governor** (Greek "tetrarch," literally "ruler of a fourth part") may simply be the same as "ruler," unless it is necessary to specify the area over which such a person rules, in which case one may use "ruler over a province."

13. 2

The subject of **were serving** is unclear; it refers either to the entire church community or to the five prophets and teachers mentioned in the previous verse. If the reference is to the entire church community, the verb translated **were serving** should perhaps be rendered "were worshiping," as in most translations. If, however, the reference is to the five men, the meaning may be limited to "rendering Christian service," in a way similar to the priests of the Old Testament, since the word is used in the Septuagint in this sense.

In most languages there is a more or less technical term for **fasting** which specifies going without food for religious purposes. Where there is no such term, it is sometimes possible to employ a phrase such as "going without food in order to worship God" or "not eating as a part of worshiping."

To them does not appear in the Greek text as such, but it is clearly implied. Once again, it is not clear whether the Holy Spirit is speaking to the entire church community or merely to the five men.

In the Greek text immediately following the command **set apart** is an emphatic particle, not reproduced in most translations, but rendered by

244

Moffatt "come"; the meaning of the particle is probably to be understood in the sense of "now" or "immediately" (cf. Luke 2.15; Acts 6.3). The tense of the verb I have called suggests that God had already made the decision, and it was the church's responsibility to carry out his will. In rendering set apart one must make certain that the connotations of the expression are satisfactory, for in many languages the process of "setting apart" may be carefully divided between (1) setting apart something which is good or for good purposes and (2) setting apart something because it is inferior or inadequate. The meaning here is, of course, "designate" or "commission." In some languages this is equivalent to "give a special work to" or "appoint for special tasks." This aspect of set apart is made more specific by the last clause of verse 2, but in rendering this clause it is sometimes quite difficult to employ a literal translation of called. The concept of "God calling people" is so familiar to us in English that we assume this is always possible in other languages, but frequently "call" only implies "shouting to." In this context it is "the work to which I have appointed them."

13.3

It is not clear to whom they and their refer. Once again the pronoun may refer to the remaining three men in the group of five, Simeon, Lucius, and Manaen, or to the entire congregation at Antioch; most likely the reference is to the entire church community.

For placed their hands on them see 6.6.

In Cyprus

4 Barnabas and Saul, then, having been sent by the Holy Spirit, went down to Seleucia and sailed from there to the island of Cyprus. 5 When they arrived at Salamis, they preached the word of God in the Jewish synagogues. They had John Mark with them to help in the work.

6 They went all the way across the island to Paphos, where they met a certain magician named Bar-Jesus, a Jew who claimed to be a prophet. 7 He was a friend of the Governor of the island, Sergius Paulus, who was an intelligent man. The Governor called Barnabas and Saul before him because he wanted to hear the word of God. 8 But they were opposed by the magician Elymas (this is his name in Greek); he tried to turn the Governor away from the faith. 9 Then Saul—also known as Paul—was filled with the Holy Spirit; he looked straight at the magician 10 and said, "You son of the Devil! You are the enemy of everything that is good; you are full of all kinds of evil tricks, and you always keep trying to turn the Lord's truths into lies! 11 The Lord's hand will come down on you now; you will be blind, and will not see the light of day for a time."

At once Elymas felt a black mist cover his eyes, and he walked around trying to find someone to lead him by the hand. 12 The Governor believed when he saw what had happened; he was greatly amazed at the teaching about the Lord. (13.4-12)

The section heading In Cyprus may be judged quite inadequate for some languages. A more satisfactory section heading may be "Barnabas and Saul Visit Cyprus," "Barnabas and Saul Tell the Good News in Cyprus," or "The Apostles Preach in Cyprus."

This section (vv. 4-12) refers to two different episodes: the first takes place in Salamis and the second in Paphos. In fact, verses 4 and 5 are primarily transitional in order to provide the necessary geographical details leading up to the principal account of Paul's dealings with Bar-Jesus.

13.4

The same pair of particles is used here as occurs in 1.6, and indicates the beginning of a new section in the narrative. In the Greek text Barnabas and Saul is merely "they," but there is no doubt that these two men are meant, and it is best to make this information clear for the reader, especially since a new section has been introduced.

Seleucia, on the coast sixteen miles west of Antioch, was the port city of Antioch. Cyprus, the home of Barnabas, was an island noted for its copper mines. In 57 B.C. the island was taken over by the Romans, and in 22 B.C. it was made a senatorial province governed by a proconsul (the word translated Governor).

The dependent phrase having been sent by the Holy Spirit may need to be expressed as a separate clause in an active form, "the Holy Spirit had sent them."

In translating went down to Seleucia it may be useful to specify precisely what is meant by "going down." In this case "going down to the seacoast at Seleucia."

Though in many languages it is possible to distinguish carefully between different types of boats by the use of distinctive verbs designating such travel, one should not attempt to be overly precise. Sailed in this context simply means "went by boat."

13.5

Salamis, on the eastern coast of Cyprus, was the chief city of the island. It was the seat of the government for the eastern half of the island, although the capital was Paphos on the southwestern part of the island. The city had a rather large Jewish population, as is indicated by the mention of several Jewish synagogues.

The Jewish synagogues may be rendered as "worship houses of the Jews" or "buildings where the Jews worshiped God." It is important to try to distinguish clearly between such synagogues and churches.

All commentators agree that John who was with them was John Mark, and for this reason the TEV has identified "John" by John Mark. Exactly what

John Mark's responsibilities were is not made clear in the text. The Greek word translated to help in the work is also used of the function of subordinate officers in the Jewish synagogue (see Luke 4.20), while in the papyri it describes a ministry most usually associated with written documents. On the basis of this latter observation some have concluded that Mark's responsibility was that of instructing converts in the life and teaching of Jesus. Most translators prefer to speak of John Mark as "their assistant," though the verb form of the TEV has certain advantages over the noun form. To help in the work may simply be the equivalent of "to help them." The Greek term is so general in its implications that one should not be too specific.

13.6

Paphos, on the western end of the island, was about ninety miles from Salamis. Paphos, known as "New Paphos" in New Testament times, was the official capital of the island. Though in English one may speak of all the way across, in some languages it is necessary to employ a term which would indicate clearly that this was from one end of the island to the other, for example, "went the length of the island" or "went from one end of the island to the other end of the island."

Met translates a verb which is literally "found," here used in the sense of "to find by chance."

Magician, a Persian loan word, which originally referred to one who was a member of a particular kind of priesthood, had come in New Testament times to mean "sorcerer," "magician," or even "swindler" or "charlatan."

Bar-Jesus in Aramaic would mean "son of Joshua," the Greek equivalent of Joshua being Jesus (see Hebrews 4.8). "False prophets" (the literal form of the Greek) is taken by the TEV in the sense of one who claimed to be a prophet. For Luke any person who spoke (a message) contrary to the Christian preaching would be classified as a "false prophet." Since Bar-Jesus was a prophet, even though a false one, perhaps it may be necessary in some languages to say "who claimed to be a prophet of God but was not." In this way the falseness of his activity can be made perfectly clear.

13.7

The literal Greek expression "he was with the governor" (see RSV) is understood by the TEV to mean he was a friend of the Governor. Certain other translations take this phrase to indicate that "he was a member of the court of the governor." Despite considerable uncertainty as to the evidence, scholars believe on the basis of nonbiblical sources that Sergius Paulus became a well-known leader in Christian circles, and that both his daughter and her son were distinguished by their devotion to the Christian faith. Governor (most translations employ "proconsul") was the title given one who was in charge of a Roman senatorial province. In the book of Acts two such officials are mentioned by name: Sergius Paulus of Cyprus (13.7) and Gallio of Achaia (18.12). See also 19.38.

The term <u>intelligent</u> refers to the mental capacities of the <u>Governor...</u>
<u>Sergius Paulus</u>. In a number of instances the closest equivalent is "he was a
wise man" or as in some languages "he understood things well."

The expression <u>called...before him</u> must be understood in a sense of
"invited" rather than "commanded."

<u>13. 8</u>

The Greek sentence order has been rearranged in the TEV to put the
parenthetical explanation <u>(this is his name in Greek)</u> immediately following
the name <u>Elymas</u>. <u>This is his name in Greek</u> translates "for this is the way
his name is translated." However, it is not known what <u>Elymas</u> means in
Greek. There is no connection between it and <u>Bar-Jesus</u>, neither is there
any evident play on words. For these reasons it is best to do something similar to what the TEV has done (see also JB "as he was called in Greek"). In
order to make perfectly explicit the relationship of <u>Elymas</u> to <u>Bar-Jesus</u> one
can say "when speaking Greek one used the name <u>Elymas</u> in talking about
Bar-Jesus."

The passive construction can, of course, be easily shifted to active
"the magician Elymas opposed Barnabas and Saul."

Most commentators and translators understand <u>the faith</u> to be used here
as a summary description of the Christian message, similar to 6.7, but some
understand this to refer to the governor's faith, that is, "he tried to keep the
governor from believing." It is relatively simple to translate <u>the faith</u> if this
refers to the governor's own faith, "he tried to keep the governor from believing in Jesus." However, if <u>the faith</u> is to be understood as the content of
what was believed by Christians in general, the problems are somewhat more
complex. One can say "he tried to keep the governor from believing the way
the Christians believed" or "he tried to keep the governor from trusting the
word of God as the believers in Jesus had come to trust it." In this way one
may define <u>the faith</u> as the manner or content of believing.

<u>13. 9</u>

It was common for Jews, especially those who lived outside of Palestine
proper, to have both a Hebrew and a Roman name. <u>Saul</u> was the Hebrew name
and <u>Paul</u> the Roman name. Why did Luke mention at this point that his name
was <u>Paul</u>? Was it because <u>Paul</u> now begins to assume the more prominent position and Luke desired to identify him with the name that he himself used in
his own writing? Or was it because Luke feels his Roman name is more suitable in light of the fact that he now begins the account of taking the message
to the Gentile world? <u>Also known as Paul</u> may be rendered as "people also
called him Paul" or "he had another name which was Paul."

The statement <u>Paul---was filled with the Holy Spirit</u> intimates once again
that though the <u>Holy Spirit</u> was the permanent possession of all believers,
there was also a sense in which his power was uniquely present on particular

occasions. As in so many other contexts, <u>filled with the Holy Spirit</u> may need to be semantically restructured: "the Holy Spirit came upon him," "the Holy Spirit controlled him," or "the Holy Spirit completely possessed him."

<u>He looked straight at</u> is the same verb which occurs in 1. 10.

13. 10

For the sake of emphasis the TEV has rearranged this sentence and has placed first <u>You son of the Devil!</u>

<u>Everything that is good</u> or "all that is right" (Goodspeed) correctly translates the meaning of the literal expression "of all righteousness" since "righteousness" is used in the present context in the general sense of "what is good or right." "You enemy of all true religion" (JB) perhaps limits the reference too much.

Though in most languages an expression such as <u>son of the Devil</u> is quite meaningful, there are some instances in which this could be wrongly interpreted, that is, as a declaration that he was literally the offspring of the Devil. The emphasis, of course, in this Semitic idiom is to emphasize the extent to which a person is like the individual, or quality, which follows the phrase <u>son of</u>. Accordingly, in this situation, one can employ an expression such as "you are like the Devil himself" or "you are just like the Devil."

In all languages one may be an enemy of a person but not necessarily "an enemy of what is good." One can always find some way to express this relationship, for example, "you are opposed to everything that is good" or "you are contrary to all that is good."

<u>Full of all kinds of evil tricks</u> translates two adjectives, the first of which means "deceit" or "cunning." The second, usually rendered something like "villainy" or "wickedness," originally meant "ease in doing (something)," but it later developed the bad sense of "laziness" and "wickedness." In the papyri it is used especially in connection with theft. Needless to say, the translators differ widely in the way in which they express these terms.

<u>You always keep trying to turn the Lord's truths into lies</u> in the Greek is a question which demands the answer "Yes." <u>To turn...into lies</u> is literally "to make crooked." But since it is impossible to turn <u>the Lord's truths</u> (literally "these straight ways of the Lord") <u>into lies</u>, the TEV has taken the verb in the sense of <u>trying to turn...into lies</u>. There are several ways in which the expression <u>turn the Lord's truths into lies</u> can be understood and translated. It may, for example, be equivalent to "you are saying that the truth about the Lord is a lie," "you are lying about the truth concerning the Lord," or "you are changing the truth about the Lord so that it becomes a lie."

13. 11

<u>The Lord's hand</u>, an expression used to indicate the power of the Lord (see 11. 21) is here used of the Lord's power to judge and to punish. Such an expression as <u>the Lord's hand will come down on you</u> is, however, not very meaningful in some languages. It might even imply some kind of blessing,

but of course this would not fit in the context. Some translators have employed expressions such as "the Lord will strike you down" or "the Lord will hit you" thus implying indirectly a reference to "hand." In other instances one may use an expression for judgment or condemnation, such as "the Lord will condemn you right now."

And will not see the light of day is a participial construction indicating the extent of the blindness that will come upon Elymas. For a time may be taken in an indefinite temporal sense, though it is possible also to understand the phrase in the sense of "until a given time." If this latter interpretation is followed, then the phrase would mean "until the time appointed by God."

<u>13. 12</u>

Believed is the main verb in the sentence and connected to it are two participles. Most translators apparently understand the first participle in a temporal sense, when he saw what had happened (but see JB, which takes it as a descriptive participle, "who had watched everything"). It seems better to take the second participle in a purely descriptive sense, he was greatly amazed at the teaching about the Lord, rather than to take it in a causal sense as though this was the basis for the governor's faith (see JB "became a believer, being astonished by what he had learnt about the Lord").

In Antioch of Pisidia

13 Paul and his companions sailed from Paphos and came to Perga, in Pamphylia; but John Mark left them there and went back to Jerusalem. 14 They went on from Perga and came to Antioch of Pisidia; and on the Sabbath day they went into the synagogue and sat down. 15 After the reading from the Law of Moses and the writings of the prophets, the officials of the synagogue sent them a message: "Brothers, we want you to speak to the people if you have a message of encouragement for them." 16 Paul stood up, motioned with his hand, and began to speak: (13. 13-16a)

The same objections raised about the section heading In Cyprus at the beginning of verse 4, are also relevant for a section heading such as In Antioch of Pisidia, with the additional difficulty that the reader is very unlikely to know that Antioch is a city and Pisidia a province. One can make certain types of adaptations, for example, "Barnabas and Paul Go to Antioch in Pisidia" or "Barnabas and Paul Preach the Good News in the Town of Antioch in Pisidia."

The third section of Chapter 13 is divided into two principal parts. The first part (vv. 13-41) consists of an introduction to Paul's message (vv. 13-16a) and the message which follows (vv. 16b-41). The second part (vv. 42-52) takes up the double theme of acceptance and rejection and moves back and forth between those who accept the message and those who repudiate it, the result being further persecution against Paul and Barnabas.

13. 13

Perga was a city about eight miles inland from the coast; it is presumed that the missionaries landed at Attalia and made their way by land to Perga. However it is possible that they may have sailed up the Cestrus River for eight miles, disembarking at the river port of Perga about five miles from the city itself. Pamphylia was a very poor district lying between the Taurus mountains and the sea.

In a number of languages it is important to be quite specific about geographical relationships, and therefore in such languages one may be required to use a rather technical term for sailing from an island to the mainland, equivalent in some languages to "crossed the straits." If a term such as came would represent movement over land then it may be necessary to say "reached the coast and then went to Perga."

Note also the problem of geographical viewpoint in words such as came and went. Most languages take the viewpoint of the individual who is traveling and therefore are more likely to say "went to Perga." Similarly John Mark would "go back to Jerusalem," or since he had been there before and this was his home it would be "returned to Jerusalem."

No reason is given as to why John Mark left them there and went back to Jerusalem and speculations lead nowhere.

13. 14

Antioch of Pisidia was not actually in the district of Pisidia, but near it. It was actually in Phrygia, a region lying in the Roman province of Galatia. There are also problems of geographical viewpoint in went on...came to. In many languages this is equivalent to "went on...and arrived at." A shift from "went" to "came" in the same journey would be awkward in a number of languages.

Luke does not state where they sat down. It is possible that they sat down with the Jewish teachers (rabbis) in the row of seats facing the congregation, but it is most likely that they took their place in the congregation.

13. 15

The synagogue service usually consisted first of the Jewish confession of faith called the "Shema" (see Deuteronomy 6.4: "Hear, O Israel: The Lord our God is one Lord"). After this, the leader of the worship service led in prayer and this was followed by reading from the Law of Moses, which on the Sabbath day and certain feast days was followed by a selection from the writings of the prophets. After the Scripture had been read a sermon was given by any suitable member of the congregation, and the service was then concluded with a benediction. The section of the Jewish Bible known as "(the writings of) the prophets" included the prophetic books of the Christian canon, with the exception of Daniel, and also some of those books known by Christians as "the historical books."

13. 16

> After the reading from the Law of Moses and the writings of the prophets
may be rendered as "after someone had read from the Law of Moses and the
writings of the prophets." The Law of Moses is "the law given through Moses"
or "the law given by Moses." The writings of the prophets are simply "what
the prophets wrote" or "the books which the prophets wrote." The phrase the
officials of the synagogue refers to "the leaders of the synagogue." These are
not "officials" in the sense of "government officials."

The expression sent them a message implies that the officials of the
synagogue delegated someone to speak to Paul and Barnabas, "had someone
say to them" or "caused someone to speak to them saying."

In this context brothers does not refer to fellow believers but to "fellow
Jews." We want you to speak is literally an imperative plural (see RSV "say
it"), but a literal translation in English sounds much more abrupt than the
meaning in the context (see NEB "let us hear it"; Barclay "please give it").
Although the imperative is plural, this is not intended to imply that both were
invited to speak; the plural is used because it is not known which one of the
visitors might speak.

Message of encouragement for them may be rendered as "words to encourage them" or "words to make them stronger."

13. 16a

It was customary for one who spoke in the synagogue to remain seated
(see Luke 4. 20). It may have been for the sake of his Gentile readers that
Luke said Paul stood up, since in Gentile circles it was customary for a man
to stand up when addressing a group. The fact that he motioned with his hand
indicates that he was calling for silence and attempting to get the attention of
the people.

> 16b "Fellow Israelites and all Gentiles here who worship God:
> hear me! 17 The God of this people of Israel chose our ancestors,
> and made the people a great nation during the time they lived as for-
> eigners in the land of Egypt. God brought them out of Egypt by his
> great power, 18 and for forty years he endured them in the desert.
> 19 He destroyed seven nations in the land of Canaan and made his
> people the owners of the land 20 for about four hundred and fifty
> years. (13. 16b-20a)

This message by Paul, beginning with verse 16b and going through verse
41, is roughly similar in theme to the message of Peter (2. 14-39) and of Stephen (7. 2-53). Special emphasis is placed upon the historical background of
Jesus' ministry, prophetic utterances concerning his role, and the tendency
of people to reject him.

13. 16b

Gentiles...who worship God is a term used to distinguish these persons
from natural-born Israelites. They may have been either full converts to

Judaism or Gentiles who sympathized with the Jewish faith and desired to worship the God of the Jews.

13.17

As in other instances, the expression the God of this people of Israel may need to be semantically restructured as "the God whom this people of Israel worships."

There is a particularly difficult problem of inclusive and exclusive first person plural in the expression our ancestors. The difficulty is that Paul has addressed both the Israelites and the Gentiles. If he were addressing only Israelites, our would be translated as inclusive in a language which makes a distinction between inclusive and exclusive first person plural. If he were addressing Gentiles, then our would be exclusive. But since he is addressing both groups, there are serious difficulties. This may be dealt with, however, in some instances as "chose the ancestors of the Jews of whom I am one." That is to say, one specifies who the ancestors are, but then it is necessary for Paul to identify himself as a Jew if one is to represent properly the significance of our.

Made . . . a great nation may refer either to the numerical increase of the Israelites or to their increase in power, but the former of these seems more probable inasmuch as the Israelites remained slaves while in Egypt. During the time they lived as foreigners in the land of Egypt (see NEB "when they were still living as aliens in Egypt") is the correct meaning of the Greek phrase used by Luke; a literal rendering such as "during their stay" fails to carry the full implications of the phrase.

By his great power is literally "with a high arm," a Semitic idiom indicating great strength or power. In many languages it is difficult to speak of "power" as an instrument, that is, by his great power. Generally the equivalent is represented as a causal clause "because he was so strong" or "by means of his being so strong."

13.18

As the TEV, 3rd edition, points out in its "Other Readings and Renderings," some manuscripts have "took care of" (see JB) in place of endured. Luke is apparently alluding to Deuteronomy 1.31 where the Septuagint has the same two alternative forms. Though the form meaning "took care of" is supported by a slightly stronger diversity of manuscript evidence and seems more suited to the context, the textual evidence is not at all conclusive. In fact the best, and the majority of the Septuagint manuscripts, have "took care of"; hence if the form meaning "endured" were the original reading of Acts, one can readily see why scribes would have tended to make the change to the form meaning "took care of," so that this reference in Acts would conform to the Septuagint reading. Conversely, it is difficult to see why the change would have been made in the other direction. On the whole, therefore, the form meaning "endured" seems to be the preferred reading in this verse.

13.19

The concept of endured is not easy to communicate in some languages. Sometimes there is an idiomatic expression somewhat equivalent to "put up with" or "got along with despite difficulties." In other instances endured must be expressed by some type of descriptive phrase: "he helped them despite the way they treated him" or "he stayed with them even though they did not show they wanted him."

Desert is not wholly satisfactory as a translation of the underlying Greek term, since it suggests to many people sandy wastes such as the Sahara. The term "wilderness" is also misleading. The basic meaning is "uninhabited area" and in many languages this is "the bush" or "out where no one was living."

<u>13.19</u>

He destroyed seven nations must be expressed as a causative since God himself did not actually kill the people. Therefore one may translate as "he caused seven nations to be destroyed." In many languages, however, the term "nation" is more or less equivalent to "tribe" or, more technically, "an ethnic group."

The relation between land and Canaan is one of identity. In other words, the land was called Canaan; it did not belong to Canaan.

Made ... owners of translates a verb which originally meant "to give or leave (something) as an inheritance." In New Testament times the word had developed the meaning given by the TEV. Moreover, the idea in the Old Testament of "inheritance," when used of the divine-human relationship, always has the meaning of "(something) which God gives his people"; never does it imply that God died and left something—the primary meaning of "inheritance" in present-day English usage. It may be difficult to translate made his people the owners and one may therefore readily employ "gave the land to his people."

<u>13.20a</u>

The UBS Greek text and most translations include for about four hundred and fifty years as the first part of verse 20, but the RSV includes these words as the last part of verse 19. The period of four hundred and fifty years is evidently intended to include the whole period from God's choice of Israel in Egypt to the possession of the land in Canaan, and it is arrived at by adding the four hundred years' stay in Egypt (Genesis 15.13) to the forty years in the wilderness, and another ten years from the entry into Canaan to the dividing of the land among the tribes (see Joshua 14).

20b "After this he gave them judges, until the time of the prophet Samuel. 21 And when they asked for a king, God gave them Saul, the son of Kish, from the tribe of Benjamin, to be their king for forty years. 22 After removing him, God made David their king. This is what God said about him, 'I have found that David, the son of Jesse, is the kind of man I like, a man who will do all I want him to do.' 23 It was Jesus,

254

a descendant of David, that God made the Savior of the people of Israel, as he had promised. 24 Before Jesus began his work, John preached to all the people of Israel that they should turn from their sins and be baptized. 25 And as John was about to finish his mission, he said to the people, 'Who do you think I am? I am not the one you are waiting for. But look! He is coming after me, and I am not good enough to take his sandals off his feet.' (13. 20b-25)

For the most part the events mentioned in this paragraph are in historical sequence, but with several large temporal gaps. There are a number of very important temporal transitionals, for example, after this (v. 20), when they asked (v. 21), after removing him (v. 22), before Jesus began his work (v. 24), and as John was about to finish (v. 25).

13. 20b

The judges referred to were far from being judges in the contemporary sense of the word; they were spiritually endowed leaders who arose at particular times in Israel's history and enabled Israel to overcome their enemies. It is not easy to translate properly the word judges since the systems of present-day courts and judicial procedures are so utterly different from what existed in biblical times. In reality these judges were simply leaders or "strong chiefs." In fact, the closest equivalent to the judges in many face-to-face societies is the term "chief," since it is the chief who not only gives direction to the activities of the tribe but also judges the internal disputes. It is, therefore, recommended that in many instances the term rendered judge in English be translated simply "chief."

The expression he gave them judges cannot be readily rendered in a number of languages. Rather, one must say "he caused them to have chiefs" or even "he caused chiefs to lead them."

The time of the prophet Samuel is distinguished from the period of the judges; Samuel is regarded as the beginning point of a new period in the history of God's dealings with Israel. Until the time of the prophet Samuel may cause certain complications in some languages since a conjunction such as until always suggests some type of activity, not merely a designation of time. Therefore one may have "until the day the prophet Samuel was leader" or "until the time the prophet Samuel came." In general, it is important to avoid any such possessive construction as might be suggested by the English preposition of. Most frequently this relationship is expressed in languages as being "time when."

13. 21

For the historical events referred to in this verse see 1 Samuel 10. 21-24. They asked for a king must be made more specific in a number of languages, "they asked Samuel to name a king for them" or "they asked Samuel to appoint a king to rule them." This must not, however, imply that Saul was already a king and he was simply taking over the territory of the Israelites. Rather, the implication must be that Saul is made to be a king over the Israelites.

The term gave in an expression such as God gave them Saul is frequently misleading. Rather, one must have "God caused them to have Saul as king" or "God appointed for them Saul as king."

To be their king is clearly implied in the Greek text and is stated explicitly by the TEV in order to aid the English reader in understanding an otherwise ambiguous construction (see RSV "... and God gave them Saul the son of Kish, a man of the tribe of Benjamin, for forty years").

13.22

After removing him may be rendered as "after God caused him no longer to be king."

Made David their king may be rendered as "caused David to be their king" or "appointed David as their king."

The quotation from Scripture that Paul gives is a somewhat "mixed" quotation, combining materials from 1 Samuel 13.14, Psalm 89.20, and Isaiah 44.28.

Found must be understood in the sense of "learned by experience." In some languages, however, this is implicit in the direct discourse. Therefore one may simply say "David the son of Jesse is the kind of man I like."

The kind of man I like translates the Hebraic idiom "a man after my heart." Such an expression of "liking a person" is often highly idiomatic, for example, "on whom my heart rests," "who causes my stomach to be cool," or "who causes me joy."

13.23

A descendant of David (literally "from the seed of this one") is in the stressed position in the Greek sentence structure. Most languages have a rather traditional term for "descendant." In general this reflects two different principal areas of meaning: (1) "of the same family" or "of the same clan," and (2) a more specific term which acquires a general meaning, for example, "grandson of" or "great-grandson of."

In the Greek text of Acts the title Savior appears only here and in 5.31. Note that the people of Israel are the goal of the implied event in the word Savior. In other words, "he is the one who saves the people of Israel."

The expression people of Israel represents what might be called an appositional construction, "the people are Israel" or "the people are Israelites."

The last clause of verse 23 as he had promised may require some specific indication as to the persons to whom the promise had been made, for example, "as he had promised the ancestors of the Israelites."

To all the people of Israel must not be taken to mean that John preached to each and every Israelite, but it indicates that his message was directed to all of them. "All people" is frequently used in the Old Testament with the meaning "many people." Moreover, in most languages a term for "all" is also used in the relative sense to mean "very many."

That they should turn from their sins and be baptized translates the Greek construction "a baptism of repentance." The Greek expression "a baptism of repentance" is essentially a noun phrase which has been constructed by what grammarians call transformations from a verb expression "repent and be baptized." In the noun form of this relatively complex expression in Greek there is no specified way in which the two events are related. However, from occurrences of these two expressions in other contexts, we can determine that the phrase consisting of two nouns is basically an adaptation of the verb expression. Therefore the translation turn from their sins and be baptized is fully justified.

In a number of languages the closest equivalent of "repentance" is "to turn from one's sins." "Repentance" actually involves three important meaningful components: (1) a person has done something wrong, (2) he feels deeply sorrowful for what he has done, and (3) he changes, with the intent not to commit the sin again. In both Hebrew and Greek the focus of attention in "repentance" is this last component, namely, the change. Accordingly, one should employ some term in a receptor language which will likewise focus on this aspect and not merely upon a person's feeling of contrition or sorrow for having sinned.

13. 25

John was about to finish his mission (literally, "race to run" or "course to follow") may be rendered as "John would soon finish his task" or "soon John would not have more to do."

Rather than reading the first part of John's words as a question, Who do you think I am?, some translations connect it with the following words and render it as a statement (JB, "I am not the one you imagine me to be"). As has been previously indicated, the Greek manuscripts were not punctuated and there is nothing in the sentence itself or even in the context to indicate which alternative ought to be followed. If John's words are phrased as a question, as in the TEV, then the answer which John literally gave was "I am not he." The TEV has taken this to mean I am not the one you are waiting for while others understand it in the sense "I am not the one you think I am." (See The Punctuation Apparatus in the UBS Greek New Testament for the decisions of various editions and translations.)

He is coming after me must be understood in a temporal sense, "he comes later than me" or "he comes as I am finishing."

To take his sandals off his feet must be understood as being a service to Jesus and not as robbing him of his sandals. (Taking off someone else's sandals was regarded as the menial task of a slave.) This may be introduced in some languages by saying "help him by taking sandals off his feet."

26 "My brothers, descendants of Abraham, and all Gentiles here who worship God: it is to us that this message of salvation has been sent! 27 For the people who live in Jerusalem, and their leaders, did not know that he is the Savior, nor did they understand the words of the prophets that are read every Sabbath day. Yet they made the prophets' words come true by condemning Jesus. 28 And even though they could find no reason to pass the death sentence on him, they asked Pilate to have him put to death. 29 And after they had done everything that the Scriptures say about him, they took him down from the cross and placed him in a grave. 30 But God raised him from the dead, 31 and for many days he appeared to those who had traveled with him from Galilee to Jerusalem. They are now witnesses for him to the people of Israel. 32-33 And we are here to bring the Good News to you: what God promised our ancestors he would do, he has now done for us, who are their descendants, by raising Jesus to life. As it is written in the second Psalm,

> 'You are my Son;
>   today I have become your Father.'

34 And this is what God said about raising him from the dead, never again to return to decay,

> 'I will give you the sacred and sure blessings
>   that I promised to David.'

35 As indeed he says in another passage,

> 'You will not allow your devoted servant to suffer
>   decay.'

36 For David served God's purposes in his own time; and then he died, was buried beside his ancestors, and suffered decay. 37 But the one whom God raised from the dead did not suffer decay. 38-39 All of you, my brothers, are to know for sure that it is through Jesus that the message about forgiveness of sins is preached to you; you are to know that everyone who believes in him is set free from all the sins from which the Law of Moses could not set you free. 40 Take care, then, so that what the prophets said may not happen to you,

> 41 'Look, you scoffers! Wonder and die!
> For the work that I am doing in your own day
>   is something that you will not believe,
>   even when someone explains it to you!' " (13. 26-41)

This second major portion of Paul's address to the people of Antioch in Pisidia is quite complex. It not only contains a good many historical references, but it introduces several quotations from the Old Testament. Moreover, references to historical events are not in strict historical sequence since Paul must interweave historical developments with his arguments to the people concerning their specific responsibilities and responses. The translator of this passage must therefore pay special attention to tense forms and indicators of time, many of which are specifically mentioned below.

13. 26

On the expression my brothers see 1. 16. All Gentiles here who worship God is the same expression which appeared in verse 16.

Whereas the pronoun our in verse 17 represented special problems in connection with inclusive and exclusive first person plural, in verse 26 us must be understood as inclusive for this message of salvation is obviously sent not only to the descendants of Abraham but to all the Gentiles to whom Paul was speaking.

This message of salvation is rendered in a number of languages as "this message concerning how God saves us." Salvation obviously refers to an event and must be translated as a verb in many languages with both a subject and a grammatical object.

In a number of languages one cannot speak of "sending a message." Rather, one can "send a messenger" or "cause a messenger to take a message." Therefore the introduction of someone to take the message may be necessary in verse 26, "it is to us that God has caused someone to bring this message concerning how he saves us."

13. 27

Most translators understand the Greek verb, which is rendered in the TEV by two verb expressions did not know . . . nor did they understand, as having two different grammatical objects: (1) that he is the Savior and (2) the words of the prophets. On the other hand, some take did not know to have only a single object, "For the people of Jerusalem and their leaders refused to recognize him, and condemned him, thus fulfilling the very utterances of the prophets which are read every Sabbath" (Goodspeed); while the JB elects to follow an entirely different textual tradition, known as the Western text, "What the people of Jerusalem and their rulers did, though they did not realize it, was in fact to fulfill the prophecies read on every sabbath."

Did not know that he is the Savior must often be rendered as "did not recognize that he was the Savior." The sequence of tenses between "recognizing" and "being the Savior" must be adjusted to the grammatical requirements of the receptor language. One must not, however, suggest by such tense arrangements that he was the Savior but is no longer.

Moreover, that he is the Savior translates a pronoun which may be taken either as masculine "this one," that is, the Savior, or as neuter "this thing" or "this fact," that is, that the message of salvation had been sent to the Gentiles. Most translators understand this as a masculine form of the pronoun, because the participle by condemning evidently refers back to this same pronoun as its object, or else it has no object. The TEV has rendered "this one" as that he is the Savior in the first part of the verse because of its close tie to the last part of verse 26, but in the last part of this verse "this one" becomes Jesus because of the historical reference to his condemnation and death as Jesus of Nazareth.

The expression that are read every Sabbath day must be understood in the sense of the reading of the words of the prophets in the synagogue. In some languages this passive expression are read must also be shifted into an active expression. Therefore one may render the clause as "that someone reads every Sabbath day to the people" or as in some languages, "that someone reads every Sabbath day in the synagogue."

On the expression made ... come true see 1. 16.

Condemning Jesus must be understood not merely in the sense of "denouncing" but "causing the death of Jesus."

13. 28

They, as the subject of verses 28 and 29, continues to be "the people who live in Jerusalem and their leaders."

Could find no reason to pass the death sentence may be equivalent to "could find no evidence to condemn him to death" or "were not justified in condemning him to death."

The clause they asked Pilate to have him put to death must frequently be rendered as direct discourse, for example, "they begged Pilate, Cause Jesus to be put to death."

13. 29

That the Scriptures say translates a technical formula (literally "the things which had been written") used by the early Christians of a passage from the Old Testament which was taken to refer to Jesus. Cross translates the same word as appeared in 5. 30.

In a number of languages one must make a distinction between the two pronouns they in this verse. The first they obviously refers to the Jewish people and their leaders who condemned Jesus to death. The second they would seem to refer to the friends of Jesus, specifically Joseph and Nicodemus, who took him down from the cross and placed him in a grave. In some instances one must make this clear by translating the second they as "his followers." There are some scholars, however, who believe this latter they must refer to the Sanhedrin, which arranged the removal from the cross through Joseph and Nicodemus.

13. 30

God raised him from the dead is often translated as "God caused him to live again" or "God caused him to come back alive."

13. 31

For many days must be understood to identify the total period during

260

which Jesus appeared at various times, since appeared is rendered in a number of languages in a particular repetitive form of the verb meaning "to appear
on various occasions."

He appeared to translates a verb which is rendered by some as "he was
seen" (see 1.3). Once again we see that in Luke's thought the only valid witnesses to the resurrection are those persons who had been with the Lord
during his earthly ministry, because this is precisely what is meant by the
reference to those who had traveled with him from Galilee to Jerusalem. It
may be necessary in some languages to emphasize the time element reflected
in the English verb had traveled by rendering this as "had earlier traveled."

To the people of Israel is literally "to the people," an expression used
many times in the Old Testament with the limited notion of the people of
Israel.

13.32-33

On the basis of the apostolic witness, testimony to the resurrection of
Jesus is given in the following verses. The TEV has slightly rearranged the
Greek sentence structure of these two verses in order to make clear the re-
lationship between the giving and the fulfillment of the promise.

To bring the Good News may be equivalent to "speak the Good News to
you" or "announce the Good News to you." What follows may be understood
as direct discourse, since this is the substance, in a sense, of the Good News.

What God promised our ancestors translates "the promises which came
to the ancestors," but this merely represents a Jewish way of describing the
divine activity without mention of God's name.

In place of for us, who are their descendants, some manuscripts have
"for our descendants" while still others have "for their descendants." The
manuscript evidence strongly favors the reading "for our descendants," but
this makes little sense in the context. If the promise was made to our ancestors, then one would expect the promise to be fulfilled to their descendants.
The other two possibilities are, however, so appropriate to the context that
one wonders why any change was made if either of these was the original reading. As the UBS committee on the Greek text has concluded, there is a serious
degree of doubt regarding the original reading of the text at this point.

In these verses the pronouns our and us provide serious difficulties for
languages which make a clear-cut distinction between inclusive and exclusive
first person pronouns. The pronoun our in the phrase our ancestors must refer only to the ancestors of the Jews who were present, including part of the
audience and the speaker. But it is also obvious that what God has...done for
us must include the Gentile hearers as well as those who were Jews participating in this meeting. However, the reference to us becomes complex because
of the clause who are their descendants. Some persons, of course, will interpret the clause who are their descendants as being both physical and spiritual.
But in languages where very rigid distinctions are made between inclusive and
exclusive first person plural, this type of expression can be particularly difficult and misleading. In some languages these difficult and complexly related

clauses are rendered as "what God promised the ancestors of the Jews he would do, he has now done for us who are their descendants and for all others" or "... and for the Gentiles." Only in this way can the message delivered by Paul be at all relevant to the Gentiles who were worshiping God (v. 26).

By raising Jesus to life translates the same verb as was used in 3. 26; but whereas in the earlier passage the reference was to God's sending Jesus into the world, the reference in the present context is taken by the TEV to be to the resurrection. Many translations remain ambiguous (RSV "by raising Jesus"; see also Phillips), while some, as the TEV, make the reference explicit (NEB "by raising Jesus from the dead"; see also JB).

In a number of languages, however, it is not possible simply to tack on the clause by raising Jesus to life. It must frequently be expressed as a separate clause "God has done this by raising Jesus to life" or "God has done this by causing Jesus to live again."

As a testimony to the reality of the resurrection, an appeal is made not only to the authority of the eyewitnesses but also to the testimony of Scripture. The quotation from Psalm 2. 7 occurs also in Hebrews 1. 5, where it has reference to the exaltation of Jesus. Here it refers to his resurrection, while the first part of the quote, you are my Son, appears also in the accounts of Jesus' baptism. I have become your Father (so also JB, Moffatt, Goodspeed) is much more natural for English speakers than "I have begotten you."

In a number of languages one cannot so neatly speak of "becoming a father." One can, however, say "today I make you my son" and this is often regarded as the closest natural equivalent; in fact, it is the only way in which this can be said without some reference which would be understood as being primarily sexual.

* Never again to return to decay must be translated with great care. What it really means is "never to die again." A literal rendering of return to decay may imply that Jesus' body had already decayed once and would not decay again. But obviously the reference here is to dying again, in contrast with Lazarus who was raised from the dead, then later died a normal death, and whose body decayed. However, Jesus was raised from the dead and then ascended.

I will give you the sacred and sure blessings that I promised to David is an extremely difficult expression to translate, as can be seen by the variety of ways that it has been rendered. While the TEV, Spanish Versión Popular, and NEB have essentially the same rendering, the RSV has "I will give you the holy and sure blessings of David," Phillips "I shall (KJV "will") give you the sure mercies of David," JB "I shall give the sure and holy things promised to David," and Moffatt "I will give you the holiness of David that fails not." It is assumed that the quotation comes from the Septuagint of Isaiah 55. 3, and in Greek it reads "I will give to you (plural) the holy things of David, the faithful things." But what "the holy things" and "the faithful things" are is not made clear in the Septuagint passage, and this accounts for the different translations. As is indicated by the translations quoted above, some understand these to be "promises," "decrees," or "blessings"; and Moffatt takes the plural nouns in the sense of "the holiness" that David possessed. All in all, it seems best to understand the words as referring to something that God had promised, perhaps to his blessings.

Not only is the exegesis of the clause I will give you the sacred and sure blessings difficult, but the rendering of this clause, following the TEV and other translations, is almost equally complex. In the first place, one cannot "give blessings" in a number of languages. One may use a verb expression "to bless," and one may thus render give...sure blessings as "most certainly bless you." But how is one to introduce the concept of sacred...blessings? In a number of languages this is rendered as "bless you in a sacred way" or "bless you with sacred benefits."

One must note that you in this verse is plural and emphatic. One might expect it to refer only to Jesus, but the obvious reference here is to the blessings which come to those who put their trust in Jesus.

The clause that I promised to David may be translated as "just as I also promised David."

13.35

Luke has previously quoted Psalm 16.10 (see 2.27). It is quite likely that in the early Christian tradition this verse had become closely attached to the verse taken from Isaiah and that together they formed a type of "testimony" to Jesus. There is a complication in the identification of the pronoun he in verse 35, for in both of the preceding expressions of direct discourse it is God who is speaking. However, the he of verse 35 cannot be God for then you would refer to someone else other than God. One must therefore introduce some identification for he by saying "as the Scripture says," "as it is said in the Scripture," or "as the writer of the Psalm says." In fact, in some instances it is necessary to indicate that this particular expression is directed to God, "as the writer of the Psalm says, speaking to God."

Your devoted servant is often rendered as "your servant who is devoted to you" or "your servant who is loyal to you." The Greek word for devoted here and for sacred in verse 34 is the same. This is apparently the only meaningful link between the quotations.

To suffer decay is "to die and to rot." In a sense "to die" implies the decomposition of the body, but the special emphasis upon "rotting" or "decay" (already mentioned in v. 34) may need to be made explicit, for note also the emphasis upon this same theme in verses 36 and 37.

13.36

The argument in this verse is very much the same as in 2.29 ff. David did indeed die and his body remained in the grave; therefore the prophecy does not refer to him but to Jesus Christ whom God raised from the dead. Most commentators understand the Greek of verse 36 in the same way as the TEV, that is, for David served God's purposes in his own time; and then he died. However, it is possible to connect the last clause and then he died with God's purposes, and so translate "for David served in his own time; and then he died, as was God's purpose." In fact, the Greek text may even be understood in a third way, though it makes little sense: "for David served God's purposes; and then he died in his own time/generation."

The equivalent of served God's purposes may in some languages be "did as God had planned for him."

Suffered decay is equivalent to "his body rotted."

13.37

The body of Jesus, in contrast to that of David, did not stay in the grave and suffer decay, for Jesus was raised from the dead. Note the renewed emphasis that the body of Jesus did not decay (cf. v. 34). However, here it may be necessary to reintroduce the concept of dying again and having the body decay, "God raised him from the dead but he did not die again and his body never decomposed."

13.38-39

My brothers must here refer to more persons than just Jews since Paul includes not only fellow Israelites, but also the Gentiles to whom he is speaking. Most languages permit this type of extension of a word such as "brothers" or "relatives" in view of the distinctive usage which applies such a term of lineage to those who become spiritually related through their faith in Jesus Christ.

The phrase through Jesus may be related either to the forgiveness of sins or to the verb expression is preached to you. However, the position of this phrase in the Greek text would suggest that it is related to the preaching and may be expressed in some languages as "by what Jesus himself did" or "by what Jesus experienced."

In verse 30 Paul mentions the fact of the resurrection, which he confirmed in verse 31 by the evidence of those who had seen the risen Lord. In verses 32-37 he appeals to the Scripture as further evidence of the resurrection of Jesus, and now he shows the significance that Jesus' resurrection holds for the life of the believers. Paul mentions two important results of the resurrection, and the TEV has restructured the Greek sentence order so as to show to the reader that these are basically parallel thoughts, forgiveness of sins and set free from...sins. For an English speaker it is more natural to say the message about forgiveness of sins is preached than it would be to repeat the literal Greek expression "the forgiveness of sins is preached." The verb translated set free appears only in this verse in Acts; it is the term, often translated "justified," that Paul uses so often in his letters. The Greek word itself is a term from the law courts, describing the condition of a person who has been declared innocent of the charges brought against him (see

Goodspeed "is cleared of every charge") and so it may be rendered "be set free from" (RSV), "be acquitted of" (NAB; see NEB, Barclay), or "absolve you from" (Moffatt). In the epistles, however, the emphasis is on the believer's new relationship with God, and hence the TEV usually translates the verb as "to be put right with God."

Everyone who believes in him is set free from all the sins from which the Law of Moses could not set you free may be taken to mean one of two things: (1) the Law of Moses could set a man free from some sins though not from others, but the believer is now set free from these other sins as well; or (2) the Law of Moses cannot set a person free from any sin, but belief in Christ sets (one) free from all... sins. In light of the total New Testament message, and especially in light of what Paul says elsewhere, the second of these possibilities is much more probable.

Set free from... sins may be rendered as "caused you to be guiltless of sins," but it is difficult to combine such an expression readily in the clause from which the Law of Moses could not set you free. In some languages this last clause is combined with the previous one in the following way: "is declared innocent from all his sins, but the Law of Moses could not declare him innocent of his sins." There is, however, an additional difficulty in shifting from the third person to the second person—everyone who believes...you. In many languages one cannot shift in this manner and therefore one must translate as "you are to know that if you believe in Jesus you are set free (or, he sets you free) from all your sins from which the Law of Moses could not set you free."

13.40

Take care... so that it will not happen to you may be difficult to render. One may employ an expression such as "be careful or it will happen to you" or "be on your guard, then it will not happen to you."

13.41

What the prophets said (v. 40) refers to a passage from the "book of the prophets," in particular to Habakkuk 1.5, which is quoted in verse 41. This passage quotes the Septuagint, which follows the Hebrew very closely except for the addition of one verb which is translated die by the TEV. Most translators understand this verb to mean "to die" or "to perish," but Goodspeed gives it a weakened sense, to get out of one's sight, "Then wonder and be-gone!" In their original setting these words referred to the Chaldean invasion which Habakkuk felt to be imminent; Paul applies the word to the final judgment.

Look is simply an expression to attract the attention. In some instances it must be rendered as "listen."

An expression for scoffers must sometimes have some type of goal or grammatical object, for example, "you who scoff at what God has said" or "you who speak bad about what God has said."

In your own day is equivalent to "while you are still alive."

42 As Paul and Barnabas were leaving the synagogue, the people invited them to come back the next Sabbath and tell them more about these things. 43 After the people had left the meeting, Paul and Barnabas were followed by many Jews and many Gentiles converted to Judaism. The apostles spoke to them and encouraged them to keep on living in the grace of God.

44 The next Sabbath day nearly everyone in the town came to hear the word of the Lord. 45 When the Jews saw the crowds, they were filled with jealousy; they spoke against what Paul was saying and insulted him. 46 But Paul and Barnabas spoke out even more boldly, "It was necessary that the word of God should be spoken first to you. But since you reject it, and do not consider yourselves worthy of eternal life, we will leave you and go to the Gentiles. 47 For this is the commandment that the Lord has given us,

'I have set you to be a light for the Gentiles,
to be the way of salvation for the whole world.' "

48 When the Gentiles heard this they were glad and praised the Lord's message; and those who had been chosen for eternal life became believers.

49 The word of the Lord spread everywhere in that region. 50 But the Jews stirred up the leading men of the city and the Gentile women of high social standing who worshiped God. They started a persecution against Paul and Barnabas, and threw them out of their region. 51 The apostles shook the dust off their feet against them and went on to Iconium. 52 The disciples in Antioch were full of joy and the Holy Spirit.

(13.42-52)

These last four paragraphs of Chapter 13 are treated as a unit because of the fact that they are so closely interrelated. The first paragraph (vv. 42-43) states the positive response to Paul's message. The second (vv. 44-47) describes the opposition of the Jews and then the special relevance of the message to the Gentiles. The third (v. 48) describes the positive response of the Gentiles. The fourth (vv. 49-52) repeats the opposition of the Jews and the response of the apostles, while emphasizing the positive results among the believers in Antioch of Pisidia (v. 52).

13.42

As is learned from the following verse, the subject of the verb were leaving is Paul and Barnabas, and since a new paragraph is introduced the TEV has made the subject explicit. Things, a word which may also mean "words," refers back to the content of what Paul had preached to the congregation (see JB "to preach on the same theme"; NEB "speak on these subjects"). In some languages one may say "to tell them more about what they had already said."

13.43

After the people had left the meeting translates the literal expression "after the synagogue (meeting) had broken up" (see Goodspeed "after the congregation had broken up"). It is most important that this particular expression after the people had left the meeting be related to the earlier temporal expression beginning in verse 42 as Paul and Barnabas were leaving the synagogue. In verse 42 one must indicate clearly that all the participants are still in the synagogue or at least on the way out of it. In verse 43 all the participants have left the synagogue and are now going to their homes.

Were followed by must be rendered in a number of languages as "accompanied by," since all the participants in this event were able to talk with one another.

The phrase Gentiles converted to Judaism (Greek, "proselytes") is slightly different from the one appearing in verses 16 and 26, Gentiles here who worship God. This phrase, though appearing only here in Acts, is to be differentiated from the other in that this one describes Gentiles who had become full converts to Judaism. The former term describes Gentiles who had not become full converts, that is, they had not accepted circumcision, but who felt a close attachment to the God of the Jews and to the Jewish form of worship. In rendering Gentiles converted to Judaism one can simply say "Gentiles who had become Jews" or as in some languages, "Gentiles who had made themselves Jews."

Apostles translates a pronoun (literally "they"), and refers back to Paul and Barnabas.

The expression rendered keep on living in the grace of God may be variously interpreted. Keep on living, for example, may also represent in Greek the meaning of "rely upon," "to continue reliance upon," or "to hold fast to." The emphasis is upon their continuing their relationship to the goodness of God, "urged them to continue to rely on the goodness of God." One might even say "to continue to trust in the goodness of God." If one is to preserve the concept of living one may translate "keep on living in dependence on the goodness of God." In this verse the term grace is not to be understood in any special technical sense in contrast with the Law, but is simply a reference to the nature of the Good News which comes to man as an expression of God's grace or goodness. However, the term "goodness" must be understood not as a particular inherent quality of God but as the way in which he manifests himself toward men, that is, in showing favor and goodness to them even though they do not deserve it.

13.44

The implication is that this meeting took place in the synagogue.

13.45

Most translators understand Luke to be saying that the people insulted Paul; but others take this to mean that they spoke evil things against Christ,

13.46

that is, "blasphemy" (JB, Zürich; and "abuse" of NAB). The Greek verb may have either sense.

They spoke against what Paul was saying is, in many languages, equivalent to "they said, What Paul was saying is a lie." To render insulted him one may simply say "they spoke bad things about Paul." The emphasis of this clause seems to be simply that they not only spoke about what Paul said but they also spoke about him personally.

13.46

The concept of boldly is variously expressed in different languages, "they spoke everything," "they spoke without thinking about who they were speaking to," or "they spoke without caring who heard."

The passive expression should be spoken first to you may be rendered as an active, "that someone should first speak to you"; but it also may be shifted from speaking to hearing, "that you should be the first to hear the word from God."

The concept of reject may be expressed as "insist it is not true" or "refuse to believe it." In a sense both processes are involved since those who rejected the word denied its truth and also refused to believe that it was relevant to them.

It is difficult to translate adequately the word worthy. If this is understood in a sense of "good enough to receive eternal life," then there is a very serious theological problem involved since the receiving of eternal life is by the grace of God and is in no way related to man's own personal worthiness. The emphasis of the Greek term at this point would seem to be equivalent to "appropriateness" or "the right one," for example, "do not consider yourselves the appropriate ones to receive eternal life." On the other hand, one may shift the negative aspect of this expression and render the phrase as "condemn yourselves as being unworthy to have eternal life." That is to say, the rejection of the Good News serves as the basis for the people condemning themselves. In some languages this is expressed as "you have condemned yourselves and are thus not good enough to receive eternal life."

The phrase eternal life is used only here and in verse 48 in Acts. Literally the term means "life in the age," that is, the age in which God would rule as opposed to the present evil age. Basically then the term has a qualitative rather than a quantitative significance, and so places the emphasis on the kind of life that one has when God rules in his life.

This phrase eternal life is probably one of the most difficult expressions of the Bible to render satisfactorily. Literally the meaning of "eternal" or "everlasting" refers to length of time, for example, "life that never ends." But this can be very seriously misunderstood if people are to conclude that by becoming Christians they will never die. On the other hand, to use an expression such as "life which comes from God" or "true life" is to miss some of the significance of this quality of life which does continue not only throughout one's earthly lifetime, but even after death. In some languages an attempt has been made to represent both the qualitative and the quantitative factors involved by translating "real life which never ends." This may ultimately be the best solution.

Luke evidently intends this rejection of the Christian message by the Jews to be the factor which initiated the actual mission to the Gentiles. Up to this point Paul's preaching has been directed to only one other Gentile, Sergius Paulus. The apostles now not only go to the Gentiles, but in so doing they leave the Jews; for this reason the TEV has translated leave you and go to the Gentiles (Greek "we will go to the Gentiles"). This statement does not mean that Paul and Barnabas would refuse to preach the Good News to the Jews, for Paul's policy continued to be that of preaching the Good News first in the Jewish synagogues wherever he went. However, in this city the Jews had refused the Christian message, and Paul and Barnabas would henceforth turn to the Gentiles.

13.47

In many languages one cannot speak of "giving a commandment." One must simply "command" or "speak a commandment," for example, "this is the way the Lord commanded us" or "with these words the Lord commanded us." (In this context "us" is exclusive.)

This quotation comes from the Septuagint of Isaiah 49.6, though one brief phrase of the Septuagint text is omitted by Paul. It comes from one of the "servant poems" in the Old Testament in which God sends his "servant" as a messenger to all the nations. Simeon (in Luke 2.32) applied these words solely to Jesus, while in the present passage Paul seems to be applying them first of all to Jesus and then in an extended sense to the Christian messengers, though it is possible that Paul has in mind only the Christian messengers with no reference to Jesus. However, the pronoun you in this quotation is singular.

The way of salvation may be variously rendered, for way in this context refers to the means or instrument, "it is through you that the whole world will be saved" or in the active form, "it is through you that God will save the whole world." Quite naturally world in this type of context must refer to the people of the world, not to the physical earth.

13.48

Only here in the New Testament does the verb praised (literally "glorified") have as its object the Lord's message; the usual object is God. It is relatively easy to speak of "praising a person," but in many languages one does not "praise a message." On the other hand, one may always translate the Greek term "glorified" by direct discourse, for example, "they said, The Lord's message is wonderful."

Those who had been chosen for eternal life is a phrase which occurs frequently in rabbinic literature. The meaning is clearly that those whom God had chosen became believers, and the translator must not attempt to weaken this meaning.

Chosen for eternal life may thus be rendered as "whom God had selected in order that they would have eternal life."

In certain languages the phrase became believers is difficult to render succinctly. The same concept, however, may be expressed by phrases such as "arrived at being believers" or "came to believing."

13.49

As in so many instances, one cannot speak of "the word spreading." One can, however, always say "more and more people throughout that region were hearing the word about the Lord." Region refers to the surrounding territory in general, and does not refer to any particular political unit of the country.

13.50

There is usually no difficulty in finding an appropriate term for stirred up since this is such a normal kind of activity in so many societies. One can always employ some descriptive equivalent such as "caused them to oppose."

Leading men indicates the chief citizens of the community and does not necessarily have any reference to the city officials. Such leading men may simply be "the important men" or "the big men of the city."

Of high social standing (see JB "of the upper classes") translates a term which means "prominent" or "noble." The word may also mean "rich," as is suggested by comparing the use of this word in Mark 15.43 with its parallel in Matthew 27.57 where "rich" appears. The Greek text does not state whether the women...who worshiped God ("women sympathizers" NAB, "religious and respectable women" Phillips, and "devout women" RSV, JB) were Gentiles or Jews. From the context one would assume that these were Gentile women. In most languages the functional equivalent of high social standing would be represented by a phrase such as "rich women" or "women of rich families."

Started a persecution may be equivalent to "caused the people to persecute" or "caused the people to attack Paul and Barnabas."

Threw them out may be rendered as "caused them to flee" or "caused them to leave." The phrase must not be translated in such a way as to imply literal throwing.

13.51

Perhaps the gesture of shaking the dust off one's feet originally arose as travelers returning to Palestine shook the dust off their feet before entering the Holy Land so as not to defile it. As practiced by the Jews in New Testament times, the gesture evidently indicated that those persons against whom they shook the dust off their feet were considered to be pagans (see Luke 9.5; 10.11; Matthew 10.14). In the present setting the gesture may indicate that the missionaries feel as if they have cleared themselves of all further responsibility for the city that refuses to repent. It is not easy to introduce the concept of against them in speaking of shaking the dust off one's feet. Usually one must be somewhat more specific than is suggested by merely the preposition against, for example, "they shook the dust off their feet as a sign against the people of that city." By introducing a word such as "sign" or "symbol" one can suggest the symbolic significance of this act of shaking the dust off their feet. It may also be useful to have at this point a brief marginal note indicating the historical background for this symbolic action.

Iconium was a city about 80 miles southeast of Antioch in the Roman province of Galatia, and it would probably have required four or five days' travel to arrive there.

13.52

Although the Greek text merely says "the disciples," the reference is obviously to the disciples, that is, Christian believers, in Antioch.

As in so many other instances, full of must be expressed by other types of constructions, "they were very joyful" or "joy possessed their hearts." Similarly, full of...the Holy Spirit may be rendered as "the Holy Spirit completely possessed them."

CHAPTER 14

This chapter brings to a conclusion Luke's narrative of the "first missionary journey." From Luke's point of view this journey is a necessary preparation for the official recognition of the Gentile mission in Chapter 15. The Holy Spirit sends forth the missionaries, and filled with the Holy Spirit they take the message to the Gentiles, pointing out to the Jews (see 13.47) that this is in itself the fulfillment of God's promise to them.

Chapter 14 may be regarded as being typical of Paul's ministry. At first he is accepted by the Gentiles, and then opposed by Jews who together with some Gentiles succeed in persecuting him and Barnabas. The third section of this chapter (vv. 21-28) touches on a second important theme, namely, the strengthening of the believers. Finally there is the report back to the church from which the apostles were sent.

The connections between major sections of Chapter 14 are primarily references to places, and therefore it is very important that these be adequately highlighted in the translation.

In Iconium

1 The same thing happened in Iconium: Paul and Barnabas went to the Jewish synagogue and spoke in such a way that a great number of Jews and Gentiles became believers. 2 But the Jews who would not believe stirred up the Gentiles and turned their feelings against the brothers. 3 The apostles stayed there for a long time. They spoke boldly about the Lord, who proved that their message about his grace was true by giving them the power to perform miracles and wonders. 4 The crowd in the city was divided: some were for the Jews, others for the apostles.

5 Then the Gentiles and the Jews, together with their leaders, decided to mistreat the apostles and stone them. 6 When the apostles learned about it they fled to Lystra and Derbe, cities in Lycaonia, and to the surrounding territory. 7 There they preached the Good News.

(14.1-7)

The title In Iconium serves quite well in this series in English since it indirectly refers back to the beginning of Chapter 13 and continues the listing of those places in which Barnabas and Paul ministered. However, in a number of languages one simply cannot say merely In Iconium. It may be necessary to make an entire sentence of this, for example, "Paul and Barnabas Preached in Iconium," "Paul and Barnabas Tell the Good News to People in Iconium," or "The Good News Is Told to People in Iconium."

This first section can be most conveniently divided into two paragraphs, verses 1 through 4 and then verses 5 through 7. The first paragraph deals with the initial success but anticipates the problems by virtue of the city being divided, some for the Jews and others for the apostles. The second paragraph

272

describes the persecution and the subsequent fleeing of the apostles to Lystra and Derbe where they carry on their work.

14. 1

The same thing happened translates a phrase (literally "it happened according to the same") that some take in the sense of "together" (see RSV); but though the exact meaning is not clear, it is difficult to see why Luke was concerned to point out that Paul and Barnabas entered the synagogue together. On the contrary, one can easily see why he was concerned to indicate that the same thing happened in Iconium as had taken place in Antioch.

The translation of the clause the same thing happened in Iconium is not easy in some languages, since one may not have a convenient substitute such as thing to refer to an event. In some languages the closest equivalent is "in Iconium Paul and Barnabas had the same kind of experience as they had in Antioch of Pisidia."

The subject of went is not explicit in the Greek, but since a new section is introduced, it is possible that the English reader may have difficulty in identifying "they" as a reference to Paul and Barnabas; for this reason the TEV has made the subject explicit. Something similar has been done in verse 3 where "they" is rendered apostles.

The word which the TEV has translated Gentiles literally means "Greeks." Either Luke intended this word to be taken as a synonym for Gentiles, or else he intended to differentiate the Greeks from the other Gentiles. The first of these possibilities seems more likely, in light of the observation that he mentions only two groups and one of them is Jews.

The phrase Jewish synagogue may be rendered as "synagogue where Jews met" or as in many languages, "meeting house of Jews" or even "worship house of Jews."

In most languages there is a general equivalent of a great number. This is often a term such as "many" and it differs in actual number depending upon the content. In some languages, however, there are several words for "many" and therefore one must indicate whether it is a matter of a few dozen, a few hundred, or several thousand people. It is probable that in this type of circumstance several hundred would be an appropriate equivalent, although it may very well be that even fewer believers would cause a considerable reaction.

The phrase became believers may need to be made more specific in some languages, "came to believe in Jesus" or "came to believe in the Lord."

14. 2

Would not believe is literally "disobeyed," but this word is used throughout Acts and elsewhere in the New Testament as the opposite of "to believe." The phrase would not believe may be rendered as "refused to believe in Jesus."

14.3

In the Greek sentence structure their feelings (literally "the souls of the Gentiles") is actually the object of both verbs stirred up and turned... against. The verb translated turned... against literally means "mistreat" or "treat badly" (see 7.6), and when used with "soul" as its object means "stir up feelings (in a negative way)." Some translators render the Greek expression as "poisoned their minds against." Some commentators believe that the verbs in this verse should be taken in the sense of "began to" inasmuch as the apostles stayed for a long while and did not really have any difficulty until the Jewish and Gentile leaders managed to get together (see v. 5).

The equivalent of turned their feelings against may be in some languages "caused them to be angry with." In some instances the equivalent is highly idiomatic, for example, "caused their hearts to be hot against" or "caused them to burn against."

The expression the brothers may be difficult to render in this particular context, since it might suggest that Paul and Barnabas were brothers in a physical sense. The meaning of course is "fellow believers," and this is the way in which it must sometimes be translated in order to avoid an incorrect implication.

14.3

The TEV has not translated the Greek particle oun "therefore" with which this verse begins since in combination with the particle men it is resumptive, that is, transitional.

The identification of Paul and Barnabas as apostles should not cause any difficulty since a similar reference is made in 13.51. However in some languages it may be preferable to use the names Paul and Barnabas since this would make the reference somewhat more specific.

The phrase for a long time may need to be made more specific in some languages, since in a number of instances one must distinguish between time in terms of days, weeks, or months. It is probable in this context that one is dealing with weeks, and therefore one may translate "for several weeks." However, insofar as possible one should attempt to use a term of indefinite time so as not to go beyond what the text itself suggests.

The equivalent of boldly generally comes from one of two different perspectives in communication: either from the standpoint of the speaker himself who "speaks fully," "speaks strongly," "speaks openly"; or from the standpoint of the receptors, for example, "speaks without concern for who is listening" or "speaks without fear of those who may listen."

In some languages it may be necessary to specify "Lord Jesus" since a term for Lord in this particular context might refer to God. However, in view of the total context of Acts there is no special difficulty in most languages with the use of the term Lord at this point to indicate the "Lord Jesus."

It seems highly likely in the present context that the verb "to testify to" (RSV "bore witness to") must be taken in the sense of proved or "showed to be true."

The subject of this sentence (the Greek simply has "they") is either Paul and Barnabas (from v. 1) or the apostles (from v. 3). In any event the same persons are involved.

The phrase message about his grace comes from the expression "word of his grace." Commentators are generally agreed that "word" must be taken here in the sense of message, and that the genitive construction "of his grace" means about his grace or "concerning his grace."

The expression proved that their message about his grace was true is semantically quite complex. First of all, it is the Lord who is the subject of proved. They (Paul and Barnabas) are the subjects of the implied event of proclaiming the message, and the Lord is the subject of the event indicated by the word grace. In some languages this rather complex structure must be put together in a somewhat different form, for example, "the Lord proved that what they were saying was true when they spoke about his grace" or "the Lord proved their message was true, that message was about the Lord's grace." In so many languages an expression such as their message must be rendered as "what they said"; and the phrase his grace is equivalent to "his looking on them for good," "his being kind to them," or as in some languages, "his showing them that he loved them."

By giving them the power to perform miracles and wonders is based on "granting signs and wonders to be done by their hands" (RSV, which is a rather literal representation of the Greek), but "through their hands" obviously means "by (means of) them." Thus when the phrase "by their hands" is combined with the verb "to grant" or "to give" the meaning is "give (someone) the power (to do something)." On miracles and wonders see 2.19.

The phrase giving them the power to perform may be rendered in many languages as "caused them to be able to perform" or even "gave them the strength to perform." In this latter instance, however, a term for "strength" must not refer merely to physical ability.

In many languages one "performs miracles" or "does miracles," but in some other languages a causative is required "to cause miracles to happen" or "to cause people to see miracles."

14.4

It is not certain precisely how the phrase the crowd in the city is to be translated. The Greek expression is a reference to the population of the city and does not mean merely some crowd which happened to gather in the city square. Rather, it is a reference to the many people in the city who were divided into two groups, one for the Jews and the other for the apostles. An equivalent of the crowd in the city may be translated in some languages as "the many people in the city" or "all the people of the city."

The verb was divided does not refer to "divided thoughts" but to "divided loyalties." In some languages this can be indicated as "the many people in the city separated into two groups."

14.5

The expression were for the Jews may be rendered as "approved of what the Jews were saying" or "joined sides with the Jews." Similarly, the expression for the apostles must be parallel with the phrase chosen to express for the Jews.

14.5

This verse is rendered quite differently by various translators, primarily because of different interpretations given to one word. The only other place in the New Testament where this particular word occurs is in James 3.4, and it is agreed there that it means something like "intention," "purpose," or "desire." The TEV has translated this noun, together with the verb "happened," as meaning decided, while most translators employ something like "a movement arose." Phillips qualifies the movement as a "hostile movement," basing his translation either on the original meaning of this word or else on the following events. As the context makes clear, the word indicates the formulation of a plan to kill the apostles and not the actual realization of this plan.

With their leaders may refer either to the Jews, or to the Gentiles and Jews. In the former case the leaders would be the leaders of the synagogue, and in the latter case the city officials (see NEB "city authorities"). "Insult" (Phillips) is a possible translation of what the authorities decided to do to the apostles; however, mistreat (RSV "molest") seems much better in the present context, because the implication is that they wanted to bring physical injury to the apostles.

The phrase together with their leaders may be translated either as "their leaders also approved" or "their leaders also joined with them." As noted above, their may refer either to the Jews or to both the Jews and the Gentiles.

To mistreat is in most languages "to harm physically," "to damage them," or "to wound them." This is in keeping with the last expression stone them, which in many languages is literally "kill them by throwing stones at them."

14.6

Once again the subject "they" must be made explicit for the sake of clarity, the apostles.

Learned about translates a verb which means "to become aware of or to realize (certain obscure information)." Fled translates a verb meaning "to flee for safety." The verse suggests that the sudden trip to Lystra and Derbe was not within the original plans of the apostles but that they had to hasten there in order to escape with their lives.

Lystra was about 18 miles southwest of Iconium and held the rank of a Roman colony. Derbe was a frontier city of the province of Galatia, though its exact location has not been established. According to some it was about

30 miles southeast of Lystra. <u>Lycaonia</u> was a district in the Roman province of Galatia.

In some languages there is a problem involved in translating <u>fled to Lystra and Derbe...and to the surrounding territory</u>. It is all right for people to flee to a particular town, but to flee to towns possibly 30 miles apart, and also to the surrounding territory, may seem strange indeed. In some languages the appropriate equivalent is "fled to a territory which included Lystra and Derbe which were cities in Lycaonia." This would suggest, therefore, that the apostles were relatively free to move about within this territory rather than fleeing first to Lystra, then to Derbe, and on to the surrounding territory. The difficulty with this type of rendering is that in verse 8 the narrative continues in Lystra.

<u>14. 7</u>

The reference implied by <u>there</u> must be to the entire territory, including both Lystra and Derbe. Therefore in some languages it may be rendered as "in that region they preached."

As in so many instances, it may be necessary to specify the goal or content of <u>the Good News</u>, for example, "the Good News about the Lord Jesus."

In Lystra and Derbe

8 There was a man living in Lystra whose feet were crippled; he had been lame from birth and had never been able to walk. 9 Sitting there, he listened to Paul's words. Paul saw that he believed and could be healed, so he looked straight at him 10 and said in a loud voice, "Stand up straight on your feet!" The man jumped up and started walking around. 11 When the crowds saw what Paul had done, they started to shout in their own Lycaonian language, "The gods have become like men and have come down to us!" 12 They gave Barnabas the name Zeus, and Paul the name Hermes, because he was the one who did the speaking. 13 The priest of the god Zeus, whose temple stood just outside the town, brought bulls and flowers to the gate. He and the crowds wanted to offer sacrifice to the apostles.

14 When Barnabas and Paul heard what they were about to do, they tore their clothes and ran into the middle of the crowd, shouting, 15 "Why are you doing this, men? We are just men, human beings like you! We are here to announce the Good News, to turn you away from these worthless things to the living God, who made heaven, earth, sea, and all that is in them. 16 In the past he allowed all peoples to go their own way. 17 But he has always given proof of himself by the good things he does: he gives you rain from heaven and crops at the right times; he gives you food and fills your hearts with happiness." 18 Even with these words the apostles could hardly keep the crowds from offering a sacrifice to them.

19 Some Jews came from Antioch of Pisidia and from Iconium; they won the crowds to their side, stoned Paul and dragged him out of town, thinking that he was dead. 20 But when the believers gathered around him, he got up and went back into the town. The next day he and Barnabas went to Derbe. (14. 8-20)

As in the case of the title In Iconium (at v. 1) it may be necessary to indicate what happened in Lystra and Derbe, for example, "Paul and Barnabas Preach in Lystra and Derbe" or "Paul and Barnabas Are Persecuted in Lystra and Flee to Derbe." One may, however, wish to highlight the experience of Paul in Lystra and simply have as a title "Paul Is Stoned in Lystra."

14. 8

He had been lame from birth translates the same expression as was used in 3.2 who had been lame all his life. The full details of the man's situation are given, whose feet were crippled... lame from birth... never been able to walk, in order to emphasize the greatness and reality of the cure.

By means of the device there was it is possible to introduce the lame man in Lystra as "new information" in this story. In Greek the same kind of information is indicated by the indefinite pronoun tis sometimes translated "a certain" or "one."

Terms for crippled vary widely, for example, "twisted," "weak," or "shriveled"; but in all languages there are satisfactory equivalents since this is a universal experience.

14. 9

Sitting there comes from verse 8 of the Greek, where its literal translation in combination with the phrase in Lystra would be awkward.

He listened to Paul's words may also be rendered "he listened to Paul as he was speaking."

Paul saw that he believed and could be healed is literally "(Paul saw) that he had faith to be healed"; this indicates that Luke evidently looked on the man's ability to be healed as a result of his faith in Paul's power to heal him. "To be healed" is the same verb used throughout the New Testament in the sense of "to be saved," but in the present context the meaning is obviously related to the man's physical condition.

Looked straight at him may be rendered in some languages as "looked directly at him" or even "looked at him and no one else" (see also 1. 10).

14. 10

The phrase stand up straight is not a reference to his posture but to the fact that he should stand up fully on his feet rather than lean against something or perhaps crouch over. In some languages this may be equivalent to "stand up fully" or "stand up to your full height."

On jumped up and started walking around see 3. 8.

14. 11

They started to shout translates the Hebraic expression "they lifted up their voice," which means simply "to speak (or to shout) loudly." Started to shout is an attempt to express the force of the aorist tense of the Greek verb, here indicating the beginning of the action. Of course neither Paul nor Barnabas could understand the regional language, that is, the Lycaonian language. The gods have become like men and have come down to us (NEB "the gods have come down to us in human form") is precisely the meaning of the Greek; the JB seems to have gone too far by stating that the gods came down "disguised as men."

Have come down to us may need to be more specific, for example, "have come down from heaven to us."

14. 12

Zeus was the chief god of the Greeks and Hermes was the messenger of the gods. A writer of the fourth century A.D. refers to Hermes as "the leader of the words," almost exactly the same expression which appears in the TEV as one who did the speaking. There was a local legend to the effect that an elderly and pious couple by the name of Philemon and Baucis had entertained Jupiter (= Zeus) and Mercury (= Hermes) without knowing that they were gods.

In many languages it is important to add some kind of note at this point to indicate that Zeus was regarded as the chief god of the Greeks and that Hermes was the messenger of the gods. In some instances, however, a kind of classifier may be used for both Zeus and Hermes and one may have in the text a rendering such as "they called Barnabas by the name of the god Zeus and Paul by the name of the god Hermes." However, the use of such a classifier to identify who Zeus and Hermes were is not really adequate to provide all of the necessary cultural background which may be required if people are to understand adequately this kind of context.

The names Zeus and Hermes should be transliterated on the basis of pronunciation and adjusted to the pronunciation of the dominant language in the area, unless the receptor language has its own tradition for dealing with such terms.

14. 13

The god Zeus, whose temple stood just outside the town is the way that most translators understand the meaning of the Greek; however, some think the reference is to the name of a local deity (see JB "Zeus-outside-the-gate"). The flowers (literally "wreaths of flowers") were draped around animals to be sacrificed. Commentators differ as to whether the gate referred to was the gate of the city, the gate of the temple, or the gate of the house where the apostles were staying; but it seems more in keeping with the story to suppose that the gate referred to was the gate of the temple. The purpose of the sacrifice that the priest wanted to offer is clearly evident in the context; it was to

14.14

be offered to the apostles, and for this reason the TEV has made the purpose of his intended sacrifice explicit (see vv. 14 ff.).

The phrase the priest of the god Zeus may need to be somewhat more explicit in some languages—for example, "the priest who served the god Zeus" or even "the priest in the temple of the god Zeus."

The phrase whose temple may be translated as "the building in which people worshiped Zeus."

The verb brought must frequently be translated by two quite different verbs, one which would apply to "bulls" and another to "flowers." In the first instance it may be "caused to be led" or "caused to be driven," while in the second it would be either "carried" or perhaps "caused to be carried."

In this instance the term gate may often be rendered as merely "entrance" or "place where people went in."

For languages which have no sacrificial system, to offer sacrifice to may be translated as "to kill an animal in honor of" or "to kill an animal as a gift to show respect for." However, there must be direct implication of "worship"—for example, "to kill an animal in order to show worship to."

14.14

This verse begins with the phrase "the apostles Barnabas and Paul" (TEV Barnabas and Paul), but since "the apostles" was stated explicitly as the object of the intended sacrifice in the preceding verse, it is unnecessary to repeat this qualifier. In the Greek text the verb heard has no expressed object, but the reference is to all that was described in verse 13; therefore the TEV has given what they were about to do as the object of heard.

Barnabas and Paul tore their clothes as a protest against the intended action of the crowd. In Jewish rabbinic literature, the tearing of one's clothes is given as the proper reaction towards blasphemy (see Mark 14.63); but perhaps also the apostles realized that if they behaved in this fashion, they might more easily convince the crowds that they were merely men, and not gods.

The tearing of clothes obviously has quite different cultural meanings in different societies. It may be necessary to have some kind of marginal note at this point to explain to the reader precisely what is involved in this action of tearing the clothes. Such an action might, in fact, suggest to many people that Paul and Barnabas had simply become insane. In some languages one can suggest something of the purpose of tearing the clothes by translating as "they tore their clothes in protest" or "they tore their clothes to show they did not approve of what was happening." However, this supplement to the text is not sufficient in most instances, and some marginal note is necessary.

14.15

This verse begins with the participle "and saying" (see KJV "crying out, and saying"). This represents Hebraic usage, but it is redundant for the English reader, and therefore practically all modern translations omit it.

Human beings like you translates an adjective which means "of similar feelings" or "of the same nature." In the context the word is employed to show that the apostles are merely human in the same way that other men are. It is thus parallel to the previous statement we are just men.

In some languages it may be useful to reverse the order suggested in the TEV just men, human beings like you. One may have, for example, "we are just like you; we also are men." This, however, may seem relatively strange in some languages, and therefore a more vivid contrast may be necessary—for example, "we are men like you; we are not gods." Only in this way can the contrast between their previously given names and their actual humanity be specifically indicated.

As in other contexts, it may be necessary to specify the content of the Good News—for example, "the Good News about Jesus."

These worthless things is a term used in the Septuagint to refer to idols, and it may have that specific meaning in the present context (see JB "empty idols"). Although the definite article "the" does not appear in the Greek text, the translation should be to the living God rather than "to a living God" (RSV), which might imply that there were several living gods, something which could never be true in Jewish or Christian thinking.

The expression to turn you away from...to... implies considerable ellipsis, and it may be necessary to fill out the implied events and relationships—for example, "to turn you away from worshiping these worthless objects and to cause you to worship the living God" or "to cause you no longer to worship in this way which has no value, but to cause you to worship the living God."

The attributive living may be rendered as a qualifying clause, "God who lives" or "God who is alive."

The terms heaven, earth, sea represent the three divisions of the universe as recognized by ancient peoples. In many languages it is necessary to distinguish between "heaven" as "the abode of God" and "the sky." It is this latter meaning which is implied in this context.

Some languages are not able to employ a general expression such as all that is in them. Rather, they must specify whether these objects are persons, animals, or plants. If in a particular language it is necessary to be more specific, one can then say "persons, animals, and plants," since this would include the totality of creation. From the biblical viewpoint celestial beings were also included, but it is not necessary to be that specific, particularly in view of the very general way in which the creation is referred to.

14.16

To go their own way means that God permitted them "to go as they pleased," without a specific revelation of his will for them in Jesus Christ. Paul's point here, as in 17.30, is that men had been ignorant of the truth about the living God in times past, and God had overlooked their idolatry because of this ignorance, but now that the truth had been proclaimed, they were obliged to turn from their idols to the living God.

The idiom to go their own way is useful in English but may be quite misleading in another language, since it may refer only to actual movement from one place to another. A more equivalent expression in some languages is "to do as they themselves thought best," "to determine themselves what was right," or "to worship as they thought it was best to worship."

<u>14.17</u>

The Greek particle translated but appears only here and in Hebrews 4.3. In the present context it is used to qualify the statement that God allowed all peoples to go their own way in the past, and perhaps denotes concession, "but even though he did this." The equivalent in some languages is "nevertheless."

The clause rendered he has always given proof of himself states positively what the Greek affirms in a negative fashion, "he did not leave himself without proof." The word translated proof is related to the verb translated proved...true in verse 3. As in the former passage, so in the present, the meaning is that God gives evidence that something is true by the way in which he acts. Here the good things that he does are understood to be the proof that is given of himself.

In some languages the equivalent of he has always given proof of himself is to state "he has shown very clearly just who he is" or "he has shown people clearly just what kind of God he is." The final phrase by the good things he does may be related to the previous clause by translating "he has shown this by the good he has done for people." It is frequently necessary to specify "for people," since otherwise "good" is too vague and even misleading. However, in some instances the following clauses may be sufficient to provide the proper conditioning for the expression good.

Crops at the right times translates a phrase which means "harvest seasons," the seasons in which the fields yield their harvest. The last clause in verse 17 literally reads "filling your hearts with food and happiness," which the TEV has restructured to read he gives you food and fills your hearts with happiness (see JB "he gives you food and makes you happy"). Goodspeed understands the clause to mean "giving you food and happiness to your heart's content."

Gives you rain may be rendered in some languages as "causes the rain to come" or "causes the rain to fall." In this clause the term heaven specifies the sky, not "the abode of God."

In many languages one cannot speak about "giving" crops at the right times, but one can say "he causes plants to produce grain when it is the right time for them" or "he causes trees to produce fruit when they should."

As in so many instances, it is not possible to speak of "filling one's heart." This is more generally translated as a causative, "causes your hearts to be happy."

14.18

Even with these words may be understood either as indicating means, "by saying these things," or concession, "even though they said these things." Most translators prefer the latter alternative. The relationship of the phrase with these words to the rest of the clause is not easy to express in some languages. It may even be necessary to say "the apostles spoke these words but they found it difficult to prevent the crowds...."

The semantic structure of hardly keep the crowds from offering is rather complex. In some languages the equivalent is "only by trying very hard did the apostles prevent the crowds from offering" or "the apostles caused the crowds not to offer a sacrifice to them, but it was not easy for the apostles to prevent them from doing so."

14.19

Throughout Acts, Luke is careful to point out that Paul's troubles are almost always caused by the Jews and that sometimes the Jews come from great distances to cause him trouble. Even though Antioch of Pisidia was about 100 miles from Iconium, the cities did share a close connection, as is indicated by the fact that the people of Lystra once built a statue in Antioch. Some Jews should probably be taken as the subject of all the verbs in this sentence, won, stoned, dragged, thinking; but it is possible also to consider the crowds as taking part in the stoning and dragging and thinking that Paul was dead.

The expression won the crowds to their side may be rendered as "caused the crowds to believe what they said," "...to follow them," "...to be on their side," or "...to go along with them."

In some languages it may be more appropriate to translate: "dragged his body out of town." This would reflect more accurately what the people thought they were doing, since they regarded Paul as being dead.

14.20

Luke's phrase "the disciples" has been rendered as the believers; the reference is to the Christians in Antioch. The fact that Paul was able to get up and go back into the town, and the next day go to Derbe, suggests that Luke intended this to be read as a miraculous event.

The Return to Antioch in Syria

21 Paul and Barnabas preached the Good News in Derbe, and won many disciples. Then they went back to Lystra, then to Iconium, and then to Antioch of Pisidia. 22 They strengthened the believers and encouraged them to remain true to the faith. "We must pass through many troubles to enter the Kingdom of God," they taught. 23 In each church they appointed elders for them; and with prayers and fasting they commended them to the Lord, in whom they had put their trust.

283

24 After going through the territory of Pisidia, they came to Pamphylia. 25 They preached the message in Perga and then went down to Attalia, 26 and from there they sailed back to Antioch, the place where they had been commended to the care of God's grace for the work they had now completed.

27 When they arrived in Antioch they gathered the people of the church together and told them of all that God had done with them, and how he had opened the way for the Gentiles to believe. 28 They stayed a long time there with the believers. (14. 21-28)

The section heading The Return to Antioch in Syria may need to be made into a complete sentence in some languages, "Paul and Barnabas Return to Antioch in Syria."

14. 21

Derbe is the final city reached in the course of the first missionary journey. After winning many disciples there, the two apostles returned to Antioch by way of Lystra and Iconium. The expression won many disciples frequently cannot be translated literally. The Greek itself simply means "cause to become disciples," and it is this form which can most generally be employed. The equivalent in many languages is simply "caused many people to believe in Jesus" or "caused many people to become followers of Jesus." It is particularly important to avoid a term for disciples which may in any way imply that these people became followers of Paul or Barnabas.

14. 22

The return visit to these cities was to strengthen the believers (literally "strengthening the souls of the disciples") and to encourage them to remain true to the faith. The faith is used in a way similar to its use in 6. 7 and 13. 8. Strengthened the believers must, of course, not be understood in a literal sense. Rather, it means "caused the believers to believe more firmly" or "caused those who believed in Jesus to be strong in their faith." To remain true to the faith may need to be somewhat recast in certain languages as "to remain faithful to what they had believed" or "to continue true in their trust in Jesus." Here faith is to be understood in this active sense of personal trust in the Lord.

We must pass through many troubles to enter the Kingdom of God is direct discourse in the Greek sentence structure (see JB), though a number of translations reproduce this as indirect discourse (see RSV, NEB). We includes both the apostles and their hearers and hence is inclusive. In a more general sense, of course, the pronoun could be applied to all the believers. Paul meant, "All who believe must pass through many troubles in this life in order to enter the Kingdom of God in the age to come."

The phrase Kingdom of God is to be understood in terms of the rule of God, not some particular place (see also 1. 3). It is related to time, and not essentially to space. In some languages the closest equivalent to the latter part of this admonition to the believers may be rendered as "in order that we may enjoy at last God's ruling over us."

14. 23

Although the verb rendered appointed originally meant "to elect by a show of the hands," it is apparent that in the present context it means "to appoint." Most translations have "appointed," while Moffatt has "they (the apostles) chose ... for them (the church)," which amounts to the same thing. In the New Testament this verb occurs only here and in 2 Corinthians 8.19. The same verb stem with the prefix "before" appears in Acts 10.41, where it refers to the witnesses whom "God had already chosen." The sense of appointed may be indicated in some languages as simply "chose," but in other languages it may be necessary to specify the kind of activity which is implied—for example, "gave a task to," "assigned for work," or "gave responsibility to."

Elders, a term which comes from the Jewish background, is frequently used as an official Christian title in Acts (see 11.30).

The phrase with prayers and fasting may be taken either with the verb appointed or with commended. Most translations connect it with commended, as does the TEV, though a few connect it with appointed. In translating with prayers and fasting one may need to employ verb expressions—for example, "after praying to God and fasting." The term fasting may itself require some more specific type of identification—for example, "going without food in order to worship" or "going without food as a part of one's worship of God."

In the clause they commended them to the Lord, it is not certain to whom them refers. Reference may be limited to the elders, but in light of the qualifying statement, in whom they had put their trust, it is most likely to be enlarged to include the entire Christian community. Commended may be rendered literally as "turned them over to." In some languages it may be rendered more idiomatically as "put them in the hands of" or "placed them under the eyes of." Basically, this is an expression of "entrusting to the care of."

14. 24-26

In translating preached the message in Perga, it may be necessary to indicate the persons who received the message—for example, "preached the Good News to people in Perga."

Attalia was the chief seaport of Pamphylia. One went down to it when coming from inland.

Commended to the care of God's grace (literally "commended to the grace of God") is to be taken in the sense of "to be commended to God's providence and care" (see NEB and Moffatt "commended to the grace of God," which is to be preferred to Goodspeed "commended to God's favor"). It is not easy to render satisfactorily the expression commended to the care of

14. 27

God's grace. It is quite easy to talk about "turning people over to God" or "entrusting them to God," but to "entrust a person to God's grace" may produce certain complications. Therefore, in many languages it is necessary to break this expression into two phrases: "they entrusted them to God for him to care for" or "they entrusted them to God in order that God would show his goodness to them."

It is essential that God's grace be closely related to the work they had now completed, since it is "God's care for them so that they could do the work which they had finished."

14. 27

With them is capable of two principal interpretations: it may refer to all that God had done "for them" (Knox "all God had done to aid them"), but more likely it is to be taken in the sense of what God had done "in union with them" (NEB "all that God had done through them"; Zürich "all the great things God, who had been with them, had done"; Goodspeed "how God had worked with them"; Barclay "all that God had done along with them").

The rendering he had opened the way for the Gentiles to believe implies that the expression "to open a door of faith" should be interpreted to mean "to give (someone) the opportunity to believe." The phrase opened the way for may be equivalent in some languages to "showed how it was possible for" or "showed that the Gentiles could believe."

14. 28

As in the case of so many other translations, the TEV has transformed Luke's negative phrase, "no little time," into a positive one, a long time. It is impossible for us to know how long a time is implied, but in many languages the closest equivalent is probably "for a number of months" or "... moons." The unit of time is certainly more than would be reckoned by days or weeks, but it would probably be wrong to imply "a number of years," since this would distort the chronology of Paul's activities.

CHAPTER 15

Chapter 15 is both the midpoint and the turning point in the book of Acts. By counting the number of pages in the UBS Greek text, one can see that this chapter begins almost exactly at the midpoint of the text. But more important, it is the turning point in the book of Acts, and this can be seen in several ways: (1) Jerusalem is no longer central. Until the time of the Jerusalem Council (Chapter 15) all roads led either to or from Jerusalem, but after Chapter 15 Jerusalem is mentioned only once (Chapter 21), and there it is in connection with the story of Paul. (2) Peter is mentioned for the last time in Chapter 15; and Barnabas, who may be regarded as representative of Jerusalem Christianity, is no longer active in the narrative after this chapter. In fact, Barnabas has a dramatic break with Paul, around whom the rest of the narrative of Acts is centered. (3) The apostles no longer hold their high positions in sending forth the Christian message (they are last mentioned in 16.4), and "the elders" of the various churches now become the recognized leaders of the Christian movement. (4) The Gentile mission, which had its beginning in Antioch (11.19 ff.) and which was again forced upon Paul and Barnabas after their experiences in Antioch of Pisidia (13.46 ff.), now receives primary focus throughout the remainder of the book.

The question the Jerusalem Council had to answer was of central importance to the Christian movement: Were Gentiles to be admitted into the Christian fellowship upon the basis of faith alone, or must they be circumcised and follow the demands of the Law of Moses in order to become legitimate Christian disciples? In answer to this question the Council made several observations: (1) God, who knows the hearts of men, showed his approval of the Gentiles by giving the Holy Spirit to them just as he had done to the Jews. (2) God made no distinction between the Jews and the Gentiles; he had forgiven the Gentiles in the same way that he had forgiven the Jews. (3) Both Jews and Gentiles are saved by the grace of the Lord Jesus, and to place any further burdens on the Gentile believers would be putting God to the test. (4) God had worked the same wonders and miracles among the Gentiles that he had among the Jews, thereby giving divine approval to the bringing of the Christian message to them and to the reception of the Gentiles into the Christian fellowship.

The discourse structure of this chapter is rather complex. The first part (vv. 1-35) deals essentially with the issue of the admission of Gentiles to the Christian community without undergoing the requirements of the Mosaic law. The second major section (vv. 36-41) deals with the conflict between Paul and Barnabas. Within the first section, however, there are a number of important features in the narrative. The first paragraph (vv. 1-2) introduces the issue in Antioch. The second paragraph (vv. 3-5) shifts the scene of the conflict to Jerusalem, where essentially the same problem exists among those who belong to the party of the Pharisees. Verses 6-21 introduce essentially two speeches: one by Peter (vv. 7b-11), and the second the statement by James (vv. 13b-21). The report by Barnabas and Paul is mentioned briefly in verse 12.

15.1

As a result of the consultation, the church prepares a letter (vv. 23b-29), and Paul and Barnabas are sent off to Antioch with this letter. Verse 35 serves to summarize the activities of Paul and Barnabas and to provide a transition for the next section (vv. 36-41), which describes the conflict between Paul and Barnabas.

The Meeting at Jerusalem

1 Some men came from Judea to Antioch and started teaching the brothers, "You cannot be saved unless you are circumcised as the Law of Moses requires." 2 Paul and Barnabas had a fierce argument and dispute with them about this; so it was decided that Paul and Barnabas and some of the others in Antioch should go to Jerusalem and see the apostles and elders about this matter. (15.1-2)

The section heading The Meeting at Jerusalem may be adequate in many languages, but in a number of instances one must specify who is meeting. Thus one can say, "The Apostles and Elders Meet Together in Jerusalem." This statement, however, is not particularly significant and therefore it may be useful to employ a section heading which deals with the issue of conformance to the Law of Moses; for example, "The Question of Whether Gentile Christians Should Be Circumcised," "Should Christians Obey the Law of Moses?," "The Law of Moses and the Gentile Believers," or "Questions about the Law of Moses."

15.1

Some men is intentionally given by Luke as a vague and indefinite reference. The Greek text has "came down from Judea," but the place to which they came is Antioch, and the TEV has made this information explicit, some men came from Judea to Antioch. This mention of Antioch also serves as a transitional device to link the first part of Chapter 15 to the immediately preceding paragraph.

In this context it is not easy to translate satisfactorily the term brothers. These are, of course, the "fellow believers." In most languages the Christian community does develop a term for relatives which is applicable to the community of believers, but this may be a highly specialized usage and can create a number of problems. In some situations one must employ an expression which is practically equivalent to "believers who formed a family" or "the family of believers," since the term brothers implies two essential components of meaning: (1) the close relationship which the members of the Christian community felt for one another and (2) their common faith in Jesus Christ.

Started teaching is a verb tense which indicates action in progress, with emphasis upon the initiation of the action (see also NAB, NEB, Phillips "began to teach").

In a language which cannot employ a passive expression one must make some adaptation of the phrase cannot be saved. In general this is rendered as "God will not save you unless..." or even "God cannot save you unless...." (See also 16.30.)

As the Law of Moses requires translates "according to the custom of Moses," but "the custom of Moses" refers to the requirements of the Mosaic Law (cf. NEB "in accordance with Mosaic practice"). As noted previously, the expression the Law of Moses must indicate that this is the law that comes through Moses. It is not the law that he possessed. The equivalent of requires may be rendered as "you must be circumcised just like the Law of Moses says you must."

15.2

Fierce is literally "not a little" (see 14.28), and is used by Luke as the means of making a strong emphasis. The NEB also has "fierce," and the JB "long"; while Phillips translates the entire expression as "a serious upset... and much earnest discussion." In the present context the words translated argument and dispute are practically synonyms. It is important in rendering the expression had a fierce argument to indicate by the total context that this was not an argument between Paul and Barnabas, but with Paul and Barnabas on one side and the men who came from Judea on the other side. In some languages it may be necessary to say "Paul and Barnabas had a fierce argument with them and disputed with them about this matter."

It was decided (see JB and NEB "it was arranged") is literally "they appointed." The subject of the verb "appointed" is not at all clear from the context, and most translations prefer to render the verb phrase either by a passive construction or by an impersonal construction, since in Greek the active third person plural frequently has this meaning. If a passive or impersonal construction is impossible in the receptor language, it is perhaps best to take the subject as "the men who came from Judea," though some commentators believe the subject was the brothers, that is, the Christians at Antioch.

In many languages it is quite impossible to use the verb "see" in the meaning of "to talk with people about." Therefore one must render the last clause as "and talked with the apostles and elders about this matter."

In the Greek only one definite article connects apostles and elders, thus intimating that they are to be regarded as a single group, rather than as two separate groups. Thus the apostles and elders appears to be a better rendering than "the apostles and the elders," which might imply two separate groups. The final phrase about this matter must refer to the insistence of those from Judea that Gentiles were to be circumcised according to the Law of Moses. It may be necessary to specify this by translating "to talk with the apostles and elders about the Gentile believers being circumcised according to the Law of Moses." On the other hand, it is often possible to suggest the same content by saying "to talk with the apostles and elders about this disputed matter" or "...about the dispute."

3 They were sent on their way by the church, and as they went through Phoenicia and Samaria they reported how the Gentiles had turned to God; this news brought great joy to all the brothers. 4 When they arrived in Jerusalem, they were welcomed by the church, the apostles, and the elders, to whom they told all that God had done with them. 5 But some of the believers who belonged to the party of the Pharisees stood up and said, "They have to be circumcised and told to obey the Law of Moses." (15.3-5)

15.3

The particle that Luke uses to begin this verse (see 1.6) suggests that this is the beginning of the story and that the previous two verses are merely introductory. The TEV does not express this particle by the translation of any given word, but it is indicated stylistically by the introduction of a new paragraph. In a number of languages the appropriate transitional equivalent to introduce this paragraph would be "so" or "therefore," since this second paragraph is a logical result of what had been described in the first paragraph.

In the expression "the conversion of the Gentiles" (see RSV, NEB, Phillips) the word "conversion" obviously means "the turning (of the Gentiles) to God," and is made explicit in the TEV. Evidently there were Christian communities in Phoenicia as well as in Samaria, though Luke has told us nothing of a mission to Phoenicia. This is a reminder that Luke has been selective in what he has recorded and does not intend to give an exhaustive history of the Christian movement. Luke writes with definite purposes in mind, and one of his obvious goals is to point to the universal nature of the Christian faith.

It may be necessary in some languages to specify Christians as constituting the church, since it may not be possible to say "the church sent them on their way"; therefore an expression such as "the members of the church sent them on their way" or "the people of the church...."

It may be necessary to specify to whom Paul, Barnabas, and others reported the turning of the Gentiles to God; for example, "they reported to the believers there how the Gentiles had turned to God." The expression turned to God may be rendered in some languages as "came to believe in God," "became followers of God," or "became worshipers of God."

The phrase brought great joy to may need to be recast as a causative; for example, "this news caused all the fellow believers to be very joyful" or, in a more idiomatic manner, "this news caused all the fellow believers to have warm hearts."

15.4

The term welcomed may be rendered in many languages as "received as guests." In contrast with verse 2, the Greek text of verse 4 employs an article with both apostles and elders. The fact that the construction may occur either with or without the article (see v. 2) indicates that at this time in the development of the church there was no hard and fast distinction.

To whom appears in the TEV for the sake of clarity, and refers back to the church, the apostles, and the elders. Told translates a verb which literally means "declare" or "announce," but the meaning in the context is either "give an account" (JB) or simply "tell."

15.5

The Pharisees comprised one of the major groups within Judaism, and not a "sect" (KJV). Luke does not state that these believers "formerly" belonged to the party of the Pharisees. His account suggests that for the earliest Christians there was no distinction between being a Jew and a Christian believer; to be a Christian meant that one had accepted the fulfillment of one's Jewish faith and could thus still maintain his ties with his religious party within Judaism. With them (v. 4) is the same phrase that appears in 14.27. It is important to avoid in a term for party an expression which would imply a political entity. In some languages the appropriate expression would be "belonged to a group called the Pharisees" or "were members of a group called Pharisees." The term Pharisee is best rendered as a transliterated proper name, but with supplementary information being supplied in a glossary.

The passive expression indicating obligation have to be circumcised may be rendered in some languages as "must undergo circumcision" (the term "undergo" followed by a noun is a kind of substitute passive). One can, however, make an active expression out of this, as "someone must circumcise them." Similarly, the passive expression told to obey may be made active by saying "you must tell them that they must obey the Law of Moses."

Though in many languages there is a perfectly satisfactory collective singular which can be used in an expression such as the Law of Moses, in some languages this must be plural since it involves a number of ordinances; therefore "the laws of Moses" or "the laws that came to the people through Moses."

6 The apostles and the elders met together to consider this question. 7 After a long debate Peter stood up and said, "My brothers, you know that a long time ago God chose me from among you to preach the message of Good News to the Gentiles, so that they could hear and believe. 8 And God, who knows the hearts of men, showed his approval of the Gentiles by giving the Holy Spirit to them, just as he had to us. 9 He made no difference between us and them; he purified their hearts because they believed. 10 So then, why do you want to put God to the test now by laying a load on the backs of the believers which neither our ancestors nor we ourselves were able to carry? 11 No! We believe and are saved by the grace of the Lord Jesus, just as they are." (15.6-11)

15. 6

15. 6

Met together may be taken either in the reflexive sense as the TEV has done (see JB and Phillips "met") or in a passive sense ("were gathered" RSV). The Greek idiom (literally "to look concerning this word") has been rendered by the TEV to consider this question and by most other translations "to look into this matter."

15. 7

The term for debate should not imply a serious dispute. It simply indicates a long discussion where differences of opinion were expressed.

On my brothers see 1.16. A long time ago is taken by some translators to mean "in the early days (of the Christian faith)." Peter is here referring to the events narrated in Chapter 10, which had taken place some ten years before. God chose me...to preach is obviously the meaning of the Greek expression "God chose through my mouth...for the Gentiles to hear" (see RSV "God made choice...that by my mouth the Gentiles should hear"). As in so many instances, it may be necessary to supply some goal to the verb believe, for example, "believe in the Lord."

15. 8

Luke uses the verb "to testify" with the extended meaning of "to show one's approval of": God... showed his approval of the Gentiles (so also NEB and JB). This verb stem is from the same root as the adjective in 14.17 and is used with a very similar meaning.

The idiom knows the hearts of men is in many languages equivalent to "knows exactly what men think," "knows men's thoughts," or even "knows just what men are." The phrase his approval of the Gentiles may require certain semantic modifications in some languages; for example, "showed that the Gentiles could also believe" or "showed that it was all right for Gentiles also to become believers."

The phrase by giving the Holy Spirit to them may be rendered as "by causing them to have the Holy Spirit" or "by causing the Holy Spirit to come upon them."

15. 9

The first clause of verse 9 he made no difference between us and them may be translated as "he showed that there was no difference between us and them" or, as in some languages more specifically, "he showed that both we and they were to become believers in the same way." The distinction between us and them must be made clear in some languages; for example, "we who are Jews and they who are Gentiles."

The participial phrase in Greek (literally "having cleansed their heart") is taken by some in a causal sense (see NEB and JB), while the TEV takes it as an expression of manner or means. "To cleanse one's heart" is equivalent in meaning to "to remove the sin from one's heart" which is what the New Testament means by forgiveness, that is, the removal of sin which separates one from God. The noun phrase "by faith" is possibly ambiguous if rendered literally, and so has been transformed into a verbal clause <u>because they believed</u>.

15.10

<u>To put God to the test</u> is an Old Testament expression (see Exodus 17.2; Deuteronomy 6.16). A similar expression is used in 5.9, and in both cases the meaning is the same, that is, to go against the revealed will of God to see if he would bring the deserved punishment. The JB has adopted a translation of this verse which mentions the end result, "it would only provoke God's anger." The closest equivalent to the expression <u>to put God to the test</u> is in some languages "to do what God has shown us we should not do in order to see how God will react" or "...to see if God will be angry."

<u>By laying a load on the backs of the believers</u> translates an infinitive clause intended to explain what is meant by putting God to the test. The commentators are agreed that in the present context "yoke" (RSV "a yoke upon the neck") is equivalent to "burden." For this reason the TEV has rendered the expression <u>a load on the backs</u> (JB "you imposed on the disciples the very burden," Phillips "by trying to put on the shoulders of these disciples a burden"). An expression for "burden" fits very well in a number of languages, but in some instances such an expression as <u>laying a load on the backs of the believers</u> would only be understood in a literal sense. A closer equivalent may be "to cause them unnecessary difficulty," "to cause them to have problems which they should not have," or "to add unnecessarily to their difficulties."

15.11

In order to carry through the full impact of the particle with which this verse begins, the TEV has translated <u>No!</u> (so also NEB), though one could employ "but," "on the contrary," or "surely...not." In some languages one cannot use a negative such as "no." Rather, it is necessary to employ an entire negative expression; for example, "that is not the way it should be." However, the contrast between verses 11 and 10 may be indicated by a connective such as "but on the other hand" or "but in contrast with this."

The remainder of this verse may be understood in one of three ways: (1) <u>We believe and are saved by the grace of the Lord Jesus, just as they are</u> (saved), a present experience. This viewpoint is also followed by Moffatt, JB, and NEB. (2) "We believe that we shall be saved through the grace of the Lord Jesus, just as they will" (RSV), a reference to the future. (3) "We believe we have been saved through the grace of the Lord Jesus Christ, just as they have," a past fact. The reason for these three different interpretations is the use of the aorist infinitive in the Greek phrase "we believe to be saved." The infinitive "to be saved" may refer to a past fact, a future possibility, or a present reality that expresses a timeless truth; and many modern exegetes believe that this context points more naturally to the last of these possibilities.

Regardless of the tense of the verb selected to render the word believe, this must be satisfactorily combined with the following expression for saved. In languages where an active form is required, one may say "we believe that God saves us." However, this salvation must also be meaningfully connected to the expression of grace; for example, "God saves us through the kindness (grace or favor) which the Lord Jesus showed us."

The last clause just as they are may be rendered in some languages as "and God saved them in the same way."

12 The whole group was silent as they heard Barnabas and Paul report all the wonders and miracles that God had done through them among the Gentiles. 13 When they finished speaking, James spoke up, "Listen to me, brothers! 14 Simon has just explained how God first showed his care for the Gentiles by taking from among them a people to be all his own. 15 The words of the prophets agree completely with this. As the scripture says,

16 'After this I will return, says the Lord,
    and I will raise David's fallen house.
 I will restore its ruins,
    and build it up again.
17 And so all other people will seek the Lord,
    all the Gentiles whom I have called to be my own.
18 So says the Lord, who made this known long ago.'

(15.12-18)

15.12

Was silent may also be taken in the sense of "became silent," while the expression they heard translates a tense signifying continuous action. Also as represents a word normally meaning "and"; so the entire sentence may be rendered: "The whole group became silent, and listened to Barnabas and Paul...."

On wonders and miracles see 2.19.

The phrase rendered through them is a different one in Greek from the phrase translated with them in 14.27 and 15.4. Whereas in the former two passages the precise meaning of the phrase is unclear, here it definitely refers to a secondary agency, that is, "by means of them." As has been noted in other passages, secondary agency is often expressed by a causative. In this context it is God who takes the initiative, but he performs the wonders and miracles through the apostles; therefore one may translate: "which God had caused Barnabas and Paul to do among the Gentiles." The phrase among the Gentiles may be rendered in some languages as "where the Gentiles were."

15.13

The James referred to here is presumably the brother of the Lord (Galatians 1.19; Mark 6.3; see also 12.17), but this is general background information and should not be made explicit in the text. Spoke up is literally "answered," but the verb is quite often used in this more general sense.

On the expression brothers see 1.16.

15.14

The root meaning of the verb translated showed his care for is "to visit." But this verb is used here (as also in Luke 1.68,78 and 7.16) of God's redemptive care for his people. Goodspeed has translated this "showed an interest in" and Barclay "demonstrated his care for." The KJV, which makes an attempt at a literal rendering of the Greek text, makes little sense, "God at first did visit the Gentiles, to take out of them a people for his name." The Greek infinitive "to take" is used here to denote means, by taking. "For his name" must be understood either in the sense of "to bear (that is, have) his name" (NEB), or to be all his own. This first meaning of "for his name" may be rendered as "to be called by his name." The second meaning is equivalent to "to belong to him" or "to be his possession."

15.15

On the expression the words of the prophets see 13.40; the quotation comes from Amos 9.11-12. The expression the words of the prophets must sometimes be expressed as a verbal construction; for example, "what the prophets said agreed..." or "when the prophets spoke, their words agreed...." In many languages one can readily speak of "people agreeing" but it is often difficult to talk about "words...agreeing." Therefore, in some languages one must say "when the prophets spoke, this is exactly what they talked about" or "what the prophets said was precisely about this very matter."

The clause as the scripture says is perfectly acceptable in many languages, but in certain languages one cannot speak of "the scripture saying." Rather, it is necessary to have "these are the words of the scriptures," "in the scriptures one reads," or "in the scriptures the prophet said."

15.16-18

The passage quoted from Amos differs significantly from the Hebrew text and has several minor differences from the Septuagint. The argument that James introduces in this passage is based upon the Septuagint and cannot be made upon the basis of the Hebrew text. It is unnecessary to make a comparison of the relationship between the Hebrew text, the Septuagint, and the text as Luke has given it here. The task of the translator is to translate the passage as Luke has given it and to bring out the emphases which he intended.

In translating this passage the TEV has included the words says the Lord in verse 16. This has been done in order to indicate to the reader that the words which are being quoted are the words of the Lord and not merely a promise made by the prophet, as verse 15 might suggest.

The expression <u>after this</u> may be equivalent to "later" or "in the future."

In many languages it is possible to refer in poetic form to a <u>house</u> as representing a family or lineage, and therefore the figurative expressions in verse 16 may be fully comprehensible. However, in other languages there is simply no metaphorical value in this reference to <u>David's fallen house</u> and therefore the translator is faced with two alternatives. Either he may preserve the figurative expression and indicate in a marginal note the significance of the figure of speech, or he may endeavor to change the figure and speak of David's lineage rather than his <u>house</u>. In general, however, it is preferable to follow the first alternative when this is possible. In the first place, people expect in poetic discourse to encounter such figurative expressions, and often they are able to understand them far more readily than some translators might imagine. Furthermore, if one is going to change the figure of speech, then there must be radical semantic restructuring which will result in a form of expression quite different from what one is likely to encounter in a corresponding Old Testament text, where the figures of speech will usually need to be preserved more carefully because of the total context.

However, in the translation of the figurative expressions in this verse, there are several complications. If one renders literally <u>raise David's fallen house</u>, it may simply mean to raise up in the air a house which is in a collapsed condition. It may be necessary, therefore, to translate: "David's house has collapsed, but I will build it again." Similarly, in the third line, <u>I will restore its ruins</u>, a literal translation might imply that the person would fix up the ruins while still leaving them in the form of ruins. A more acceptable equivalent may be "I will rebuild the ruins," "I will take what has been ruined and make it good again," or "though it is ruined, I will build it up again."

Because of the highly repetitious nature of the three lines referring to the reconstruction of the <u>fallen house</u>, it may be necessary to coalesce these into two principal expressions.

In verse 17 the two expressions <u>all other people</u> and <u>all the Gentiles</u> are probably equivalent phrases referring to the Gentiles in contrast to the Jewish people. On the other hand, the Greek expression underlying the phrase <u>all other people</u> may refer to "the rest of the people," and therefore some scholars make a distinction between the two expressions <u>all other people</u> and <u>all the Gentiles</u>.

The literal expression "and all the nations upon whom my name has been called upon them" has been rendered <u>all the Gentiles whom I have called to be my own</u>, since in biblical language to have God's name called upon someone is to indicate that that person belongs to God.

In verse 18 <u>so says the Lord</u> may be rendered as "this is what the Lord has said." The expression <u>made this known</u> may be equivalent to "caused people to hear" or "caused people to know."

19 "It is my opinion," James went on, "that we should not trouble the Gentiles who are turning to God. 20 Instead, we should write a letter telling them not to eat any food that is unclean because it has been offered to idols; to keep themselves from immorality; not to eat any animal that has been strangled, or any blood. 21 For the Law of Moses has been read for a very long time in the synagogues every Sabbath, and his words are preached in every town." (15.19-21)

15.19

It is possible that James' words express a decree issued by him (so Lake "I decree"), but the words more naturally mean it is my opinion ("in my opinion" Goodspeed, Moffatt). It is important at this point to introduce James as the speaker, and hence a phrase such as James went on is necessary. In some languages this is literally "James continued to speak" or "this is then what James said." At this point one may need to indicate that the following are James' own words rather than being his quotation from the prophet Amos speaking on behalf of the Lord.

Trouble the Gentiles may be equivalent to "cause difficulty for the Gentiles" or "bother the Gentiles."

15. 20

There are textual problems regarding certain aspects of this verse and two related verses (15. 29; 21. 25), and the difficulties relate primarily to the nature of the prohibitions contained in the apostolic decree, whether ethical, ceremonial, or a combination of both. For a detailed discussion of the problems see Bruce M. Metzger, A Textual Commentary on the Greek New Testament (London: United Bible Societies, 1971).

The demands which James suggested should be placed upon the Gentiles were of four kinds. The first two demands related to sins for which the Gentiles were notorious, that is, idolatry and sexual immorality; while the other two related to matters which would endanger (table) fellowship between the Gentiles and Jewish Christians, that is, eating animals that had been strangled and eating blood. Most commentators agree that the expression "pollutions of idols" has a specific reference to food that is unclean because it has been offered to idols. This would be a quite difficult command for the Gentiles to obey, inasmuch as it demanded that they no longer participate in any of the feasts given in the names of pagan gods, and it would possibly mean that they could no longer purchase meat from the public markets, since much of the meat sold in the public market had come from idol temples.

The term unclean in this context must not be rendered as "dirty." The meaning is "religiously defiled," that is, from the standpoint of the standards of the Christian community. In a number of languages this passage may be most conveniently and effectively translated as "not to eat any food that should not be eaten because it has been offered to idols."

The expression <u>offered to idols</u> may be translated as "brought as a gift to idols" or "sacrificed in honor to idols."

The command to <u>keep themselves from immorality</u> may refer (1) to the marriage relationships such as were forbidden in Leviticus 18. 6-18 or (2) to sexual immorality, since this was often connected with idolatrous worship.

The Jews believed that the life essence of an animal was contained in its blood, and therefore people were forbidden to eat it. This is why they could neither eat strangled animals, since these still had the blood in them, nor could they eat blood by itself. In order to avoid a possible breach in the (table) fellowship between the Jews and the Gentiles, James thought it wise to forbid the Gentiles to continue to eat blood.

The expression <u>not to eat any animal that has been strangled</u> may require some marginal explanation, or it may be more appropriate in some languages to speak of "not eating any animal whose blood has not been drained out." It is the "draining out of the blood" which is obviously the essential element, and <u>strangled</u> is only a type of indirect reference to the existence of the blood in the meat. One can, however, retain <u>strangled</u> and the functional equivalent, as in "not eating any animal whose <u>blood</u> has not been drained out, since it was strangled."

<u>15. 21</u>

There are no textual problems connected with this verse, though it is quite difficult to see its real relationship with what has preceded. Perhaps the meaning is that the Jews, who heard the Law of Moses read every Sabbath day in the synagogue, would be offended if the Gentiles did not keep these restrictions. Furthermore, certain of the important regulations observed by Jews were well known to Gentiles, and this may be the basis for the statement by James.

The expression <u>for a very long time</u> must refer not to the actual process of reading the Scriptures in a particular synagogue, but to the many years during which it was the practice of the Jews to read the Law of Moses in the synagogues every Sabbath.

In many languages one cannot say <u>his words are preached</u>. It is possible, however, to say "they preached about what he said" or "they talked to the people about Moses' words."

The Letter to the Gentile Believers

22 Then the apostles and the elders, together with the whole church, decided to choose some men from the group and send them to Antioch with Paul and Barnabas. They chose Judas, called Barsabbas, and Silas, two men who were highly respected by the brothers. 23 They sent the following letter by them:

"We, the apostles and the elders, your brothers, send greetings to all brothers of Gentile birth who live in Antioch, Syria, and Cilicia. 24 We have heard that some men of our group went out and troubled and upset you by what they said; they had not, however, received any instructions from us to do this. 25 And so we have met together and have all agreed to choose some messengers and send them to you. They will go with our dear friends Barnabas and Paul, 26 who have risked their lives in the service of our Lord Jesus Christ. 27 We send you, then, Judas and Silas, who will tell you in person the same things we are writing. 28 The Holy Spirit and we have agreed not to put any other burden on you besides these necessary rules: 29 eat no food that has been offered to idols; eat no blood; eat no animal that has been strangled; and keep yourselves from immorality. You will do well if you keep yourselves from doing these things. Good-bye." (15.22-29)

The section heading The Letter to the Gentile Believers may need to be rendered as a complete sentence; for example, "The Apostles and Elders Send a Letter to the Gentile Believers" or "The Gentile Believers Are Sent a Letter."

Although in Greek verses 22 and 23 comprise one sentence, the TEV, along with most other translations, has broken this sentence up into smaller units for the sake of clarity.

15.22

It is important to have some kind of transitional device represented in the TEV text by then. In other languages the equivalent may be more appropriately "as a result" or "so" since what follows refers to the preceding discussion.

It may be somewhat awkward to introduce the expression together with the whole church, but it is important to indicate that this action was not merely the decision of the apostles and the elders. In some instances one may translate as "the apostles and the elders decided, and all the believers together also decided" or "the apostles and the elders as well as all the church decided."

Although the word translated decided (so also Moffatt, Barclay, JB) may have the technical sense of "voted" (see Lake "it was voted by the apostles and elders with the whole church"), most translations are not so specific and prefer to have a more general term (Goodspeed, NEB "resolved"; Phillips "agreed"). To choose is in reality a participle rather than an infinitive, and so the expression may be rendered "decided to send chosen men"; but most translators prefer to take the participle as active rather than passive and therefore refer it back to the apostles and elders, the apostles and the elders...decided to choose some men. Some men from the group may be limited to the apostles and the elders, though it seems more natural to assume that the whole church is indicated.

Some persons have conjectured that Judas, called Barsabbas is the brother of Joseph Barsabbas mentioned in 1.23, and many New Testament scholars are of the opinion that Silas is to be equated with the Silvanus mentioned in the Pauline Epistles. In some languages there are complications in an expression such as Judas, called Barsabbas, and Silas. This might imply that Judas had two different names, Barsabbas and Silas. Therefore, in some instances it is necessary to reverse the order of names and say "Silas and Judas, who was also called Barsabbas."

Highly respected translates a participle which has been rendered "leading men" by most other translations. Although "leading men" or simply "leaders" appears to be a more natural translation of the participle, highly respected is possible if one assumes that the participle is passive rather than middle. The passive sense, reflected in the use of respected, may be made active by "the fellow believers regarded these two men very highly" or "the fellow believers thought these two men were very good."

15. 23

They sent the following letter by them translates the Greek expression "having written through their hands," which might appear to mean that "they (the apostles and the elders) wrote letters by them (the messengers)" (KJV). However, most commentators agree that what is meant is that the apostles and elders wrote the letter and sent it by the messengers. In some languages it may be necessary to translate this introductory clause as "They sent the following letter to the believers in Antioch. They caused Judas and Silas to carry the letter."

"Brothers," which appears in the Greek without the possessive "your," is taken by almost all scholars to refer back to the apostles and the elders, and so is translated your brothers (so also JB). It is interesting to note that the introductory formula "so-and-so send their greetings to so-and-so," and the concluding expression Good-bye (v. 29), are precisely the forms that were used by letter writers of the first century A.D. In many languages it is necessary to introduce the first person plural pronoun in this introductory sentence; therefore, "we the apostles and elders, your brothers, send our greetings." The expression brothers of Gentile birth would be "fellow believers who are Gentiles" or, as in some languages, "fellow believers who are not Jews."

It may be useful and even necessary to distinguish between Antioch as a town and Syria and Cilicia as regions; therefore, "in the city of Antioch and in the provinces of Syria and Cilicia."

15. 24

Some men of our group is a deliberately vague phrase (cf. v. 1). Upset you is literally "upsetting your souls," with "souls" used as equivalent to "persons." The word rendered upset is a very strong term, and it refers to reversing what has been done or to tearing down what has been built.

The final clause they had not, however, received any instructions from us to do this may be equivalent to "we did not, however, tell them that they should do this."

15.25

Together translates the same word rendered "as a group" in 1.14. However, some translators have interpreted this expression in this context to mean "of one accord," for example, "we are unanimously agreed" (see Phillips). Agreed translates the same word as was rendered decided in verse 22; and to choose some messengers translates a construction similar to the one in verse 22 (that is, to choose some men).

The phrase our dear friends may be translated as a verbal expression: "Barnabas and Paul, whom we love very much" or "Barnabas and Paul, whom we like very much."

15.26

Who have risked their lives in the service of our Lord Jesus Christ translates "who have given their souls in behalf of the name of our Lord Jesus Christ." Most translations take "given their souls" as the equivalent in meaning to "risked their lives," whereas the NEB understands it in the sense of "have devoted themselves to." Risked their lives may be equivalent to "were in danger of being killed" or "people threatened to kill them."

In biblical thought the "name" of a person represents what he is or what he stands for. Thus in the present passage it is perfectly legitimate to understand "in the name of" as equivalent to in the service of. In combining risked their lives with the phrase in the service of, one may say "risked their lives because they were serving our Lord Jesus Christ." A term for service is often equivalent to "working for" or "helping."

15.27

We send is literally "we have sent," a verb tense which reflects the point of view of the readers of the letter and not of the writer. Who will tell you in person the same things we are writing is literally "and they through a word will tell the same things." "Through a word" means "by word of mouth," which the TEV takes as equivalent to in person. And "the same things" is a specific reference to what was written (see JB "what we have written in this letter"). The meaning of this entire verse is that the written message from the Council and the oral message by the messengers would be identical. This last clause may be rendered in some languages as "they themselves will tell you the same thing as we have written" or "their words, which they will tell you themselves, will be the same as the words which we have written."

15.28-29

Though the Greek text has the conjunction gar "for," in many languages it is necessary to omit this conjunction, since it obviously does not express a causal relationship. It merely signifies that what follows is a logical outgrowth of what has preceded. In many languages it is best to represent this logical development simply by starting another sentence without a connective, as in the case of the TEV.

The verb has agreed may be rendered as "are of the same mind," "think the same thoughts," or even "say the same thing."

Besides these necessary rules is a very difficult grammatical construction in Greek and, though there are no textual variations present, some scholars have made suggestions as to how the text may have been damaged and therefore should be changed. The word rendered necessary rules (NEB, JB "the essentials") is used elsewhere in Greek as an adverb, but never with the article before it, as it appears here. If we accept the text as it stands, then Luke has evidently made this word the equivalent of a noun by the addition of the definite article. As an adverb the word means "necessarily," and so as a noun it would mean "that which is necessary"; here, in the plural, it means "those necessary (things/rules/regulations)." Besides these necessary rules may be rendered "it is only that you should follow certain rules" or "you should, however, do the following things." In reality, however, since the regulations specified in verse 29 are all negations, it may be necessary to use a negative expression in verse 28, "but you must not do the following."

Keep yourselves from immorality is simply "do not commit immorality" or "do not have illicit sex relations."

You will do well may be understood either in the sense of "you will prosper" (see Phillips "you will make good progress") or with the meaning "you will be doing right."

Keep yourselves from doing these things may be equivalent to "if you do not do these things." In some languages, however, it may be necessary to shift the focus somewhat by saying "if you do just as we have said."

Good-bye ("farewell" of many translations) translates a fixed expression used at the end of letters and frequently found in the papyri. A translator may employ, as an equivalent of good-bye, whatever expression is normally used in the salutation of a letter. If in the receptor language there is no such custom employed in writing letters, such an expression may be omitted; or one may introduce, as a final phrase, the type of expression generally used when people part from one another.

> 30 The messengers were sent off and went to Antioch, where they gathered the whole group of believers and gave them the letter. 31 When the people read the letter, they were filled with joy by the message of encouragement. 32 Judas and Silas, who were themselves prophets, spoke a long time with the brothers, giving them courage and strength. 33 After spending some time there, they were sent off in peace by the brothers, and went back to those who had sent them. [34 But Silas decided to stay there.]
> 35 Paul and Barnabas spent some time in Antioch. Together with many others, they taught and preached the word of the Lord. (15.30-35)

15. 30

Luke begins this verse with a particle that he often uses to introduce a new scene; the TEV has indicated this, not by a literal reproduction of the words, but by a paragraph division (on this word see 1. 6). The TEV has made the subject of were sent off explicit, that is, the messengers (so also Moffatt; see Goodspeed "the delegates," JB "the party"); and "the group" (RSV, Phillips, NEB "the congregation") has been qualified as the whole group of believers.

15. 31

This is a very brief sentence in Greek, consisting of only six words. For the English reader, however, there are certain ambiguities if it is rendered literally (see RSV "And when they read it, they rejoiced at the exhortation"); and so this necessitates a longer sentence than appears in Greek. If the first "they" is qualified as the people, there is no problem of understanding the referent of the next "they." In Greek there is no object expressed, but what they read was the letter. "At the encouragement" is an evident reference to the message of encouragement (contained in the letter). It may be necessary to shift the passive expression were filled to an active one and to make somewhat more explicit the relationship between message and encouragement. Moreover, the people are the ones who have joy and are being encouraged; therefore one may restructure this second clause as "the message encouraged the people and filled them with joy" or "... caused them to have great joy."

15. 32

Prophets in this particular context is primarily not a reference to "foretelling the future" but to "speaking on behalf of God." It is this latter meaning which should be introduced at this point in the selection of a term for prophets.

Most translators take who were themselves prophets as a simple qualifying statement, while a few see in it the grounds for their actions, "for they themselves were prophets" (Barclay).

The phrase a long time may refer to the particular occasion when the letter was read and the subsequent explanation or confirmation by Judas and Silas. It may, however, refer to the fact that they stayed in Antioch for some time and exhorted their fellow believers on various occasions.

In many languages one cannot speak of "giving someone courage and strength." One may, however, often use a causative, "caused them to be courageous" and "caused them to be strong."

15. 33

The temporal expression some time should probably be interpreted in terms of several weeks. It is surely not a matter of hours or days and certainly should not be interpreted as years. If it is necessary to specify, one can introduce the concept of weeks.

In peace represents a salutation common to the Jews (see Luke 7.50; 8.48); the JB translates "(the brothers) wished them peace." In peace may be in some languages merely the equivalent of "wished them a good journey" or "sent them off with their blessings."

15.34

This verse was evidently not a part of the original text (it is omitted or placed in the margin by NEB, JB, Moffatt, Goodspeed, Phillips, Barclay), and it has been placed in brackets by the TEV. Apparently verse 34 was added by some scribe on the assumption that verse 40 makes it impossible to conclude that Paul went to Jerusalem to get Silas or sent a message for him to come to Antioch. However, this assumption is without foundation, and the addition of verse 34 contradicts the plain meaning of verse 33.

15.35

Once again Luke uses an indefinite expression of time, some time, and it is impossible to define precisely what is meant. If it is necessary to specify some temporal unit, the most appropriate equivalent is probably "some months."

The word of the Lord is "the message about the Lord."

Paul and Barnabas Separate

36 Some time later Paul said to Barnabas, "Let us go back and visit our brothers in every city where we preached the word of the Lord, and find out how they are getting along." 37 Barnabas wanted to take John Mark with them, 38 but Paul did not think it was right to take him, because he had not stayed with them to the end of their mission, but had turned back and left them in Pamphylia. 39 They had a sharp argument between them, and separated from each other. Barnabas took Mark and sailed off for Cyprus, 40 while Paul chose Silas and left, commended by the brothers to the care of the Lord's grace. 41 He went through Syria and Cilicia, strengthening the churches.

(15.36-41)

The section heading Paul and Barnabas Separate can usually be rendered quite readily into other languages. One may, however, have to specify "... Separate from Each Other." In other instances it may be preferable to indicate the basis for the separation, "Paul and Barnabas Argue and Therefore Separate."

15.36

Some time later (literally "after certain days") is another vague expression of time. The word "after" is used with indications of time throughout the last half of Acts in a similar way that the particle referred to in
verse 35 (see 1.6) is used in the earlier part of the book. Where a receptor
language does not permit a completely vague expression of time, one can employ some such transitional device as "after some months," since this is
likely to be the most satisfactory equivalent.

Some translators render the emphatic Greek particle in this sentence
by "come" (RSV, Goodspeed, Moffatt), while others believe that a translation of the verb in itself is sufficient, let us go back. From the statement of
Paul's purpose as given by this verse, he obviously intended this merely as a
journey to visit the previously established Christian communities and not as
another "missionary journey." In keeping with what most other translators
have done, the TEV has translated the idiomatic Greek expression "how they
have it" by how they are getting along. The final expression how they are
getting along should not be understood merely as a reference to their physical
condition or prosperity, since it is obviously a reference to their spiritual
welfare. It may be necessary, therefore, in some receptor languages to say
"how they are getting along in their faith" or "how they are continuing in
their believing."

15.37

According to 13.13, John Mark had returned to Jerusalem. He has not
been mentioned since that time, but now he shows up in Antioch.

15.38

This entire verse requires a good deal of restructuring from the Greek
because the verb phrase is divided, the first part coming at the beginning of
the sentence and the last part at the very end, with the clause describing
John Mark coming in between.

Either did not think it was right or "was not in favor of" (JB) correctly
translates the meaning of the verb that Luke has chosen to describe Paul's
attitude. The choice of a word for right should not imply moral rightness,
in contrast with something which was morally wrong. It is simply a matter
of whether it was a good thing to have John Mark go along with them.

The literal expression "to the work" is translated to the end of their
mission inasmuch as "work" is used in several places in Acts as a specific
term of reference for the Christian missionary effort (see 13.2; 14.26).
Moreover, it is obvious that Paul meant that John Mark had left them and had
not completed the mission that they had intended to undertake. In some languages the expression not stayed with them to the end of their mission may
be rendered as "did not stay with them until they had completed their work"
or "did not stay with them until they finished what they had started to do."

15.39

15.39

The word which Luke has chosen to describe the disagreement between Paul and Barnabas originally meant "an irritation," but in this context something much stronger is indicated, that is, a sharp argument (see JB "violent quarrel"). After the separation, Barnabas, who was originally from Cyprus (4.36), took Mark and sailed off for Cyprus.

15.40

On the expression commended ... to the care of the Lord's grace see 14.26.

15.41

There is a problem in the subject of this verse since the use of he might imply that Paul went alone, in which case it may be necessary to say "he went with Silas through Syria...."

The phrase strengthening the churches must refer, of course, to the members of the churches and not to the buildings, as might be understood if the term for church refers primarily to the buildings rather than to the congregations. In some languages one may translate this as "causing the believers of the churches to be strong in their faith" or "causing the congregations to be firm in their faith." (See also 16.5.)

CHAPTER 16

The main interest of Chapter 16 centers about the taking of the Christian message to Philippi, a city populated mainly by Roman citizens. Luke is careful to remind his readers that it was the Holy Spirit who had led them in this direction (see vv. 6-7) and that it was a direct revelation from God himself that brought them to the city of Philippi (vv. 9-10).

The first paragraph (vv. 1-5) serves essentially as transitional material and as a means of introducing Timothy, who was to accompany Paul and Silas. In verses 6-40 the focus is essentially upon the ministry in Macedonia: first the call (vv. 6-10), then the favorable response in Philippi (vv. 11-15), and finally the persecution (vv. 16-40), a typical conclusion to so many of the experiences which Paul had. Note, however, that in verse 10 there is an introduction of we. From this point on, until the end of the chapter, the first person plural includes the writer Luke, who seems to have joined Paul, Silas, and Timothy at this time. He appears again in 20.5. In languages which distinguish between inclusive and exclusive first person plural it is necessary to use the exclusive form, since this entire book is addressed to Theophilus who obviously was not present at these happenings.

Timothy Goes with Paul and Silas

1 Paul traveled on to Derbe and Lystra. A believer named Timothy lived there; his mother, also a believer, was Jewish, but his father was Greek. 2 All the brothers in Lystra and Iconium spoke well of Timothy. 3 Paul wanted to take Timothy along with him, so he circumcised him. He did so because all the Jews who lived in those places knew that Timothy's father was Greek. 4 As they went through the towns they delivered to the believers the rules decided upon by the apostles and elders in Jerusalem, and told them to obey these rules. 5 So the churches were made stronger in the faith and grew in numbers every day. (16.1-5)

The section heading Timothy Goes with Paul and Silas is easily rendered in this form in almost any language, although it may be that a term such as "Accompanies" or "Travels with" may be selected instead of the more general term "Goes with."

16.1

The Greek has "he traveled on," which the TEV has rendered Paul traveled on, since the last mention of Paul occurs in the preceding chapter (v. 40).

Notice that in the TEV text the introductory verb in Greek has been rendered as traveled on. This is not only a completely legitimate translation of this verb, but the adverbial particle on serves as an important transitional device to combine this first paragraph of Chapter 16 with the last sentence of Chapter 15.

The second sentence of this verse begins with a particle which often denotes emphasis (see 1.10) but which in many contexts is left untranslated. Most translators have not rendered this particle, but in the KJV it appears as "behold." This Greek particle, however, serves not only for emphasis but may also help to introduce a new participant, in this instance Timothy.

Believer is literally "a disciple," but commentators are agreed that the meaning of "disciple" in the present context is "one who is a Christian." Most commentators agree that there is a reference to the city of Lystra.

The second time the word believer is translated in this verse it means exactly that and is not the same word as is used above.

16.2

The verb translated spoke well of may also be understood in the sense of "thought highly of" (see Goodspeed and Moffatt). The passive verb form in the Greek text (literally "Timothy was spoken well of by all the brothers") has been changed to an active form: all the brothers...spoke well of Timothy.

As in so many passages in Acts, there are problems involved in the translation of brothers. In languages in which this type of kinship term is obligatorily possessed (that is to say, in which the term brothers must occur with some kind of pronoun indicating whose brothers are involved), it is sometimes possible to use a standard form such as "our brothers" or, as in some languages, "our relatives"---provided, of course, that this type of expression can be used of people who associate together rather than those who are strictly biological brothers. After the introduction of we, which includes Luke in verse 10, the possessive usage "our brothers" may be quite appropriate. It can, however, be used even before this point in the text of Acts. On the other hand, in languages where there is no such kinship term which can be employed in this sense of persons who are closely united within a particular group, it may be necessary to employ some such phrase as "fellow believers" or "those who believed together with us."

16.3

The Greek text says that he (Paul) circumcised him (Timothy). This is taken by some to mean that Paul himself actually circumcised Timothy, but most scholars understand it to mean that Paul had him circumcised (that is, by someone else). The reason for Paul's action is given in this verse: since the Jews knew that Timothy's father was a Gentile, and Timothy had therefore not been circumcised, it would presumably have been difficult for Paul to use him to take the Christian message to the Jewish people. It may be necessary in some instances to add a marginal note at this point to indicate that, since Timothy's father was a Gentile, Timothy had not been circumcised in his infancy.

Some understand the clause Timothy's father was Greek to indicate that Timothy's father was dead, and so translate "Timothy's father had been a Greek" (see Moffatt and Barclay).

16.4

By translating literally, the KJV (see also Phillips) misrepresents the meaning of the Greek text: "as they went on their way through the cities, they delivered them the decrees." The meaning of this in English would be that they delivered to the cities the decisions which had been reached by the apostles and elders. However, in Greek the word "cities" is feminine gender while "to them" is masculine. For this reason the TEV has made the meaning explicit: as they went through the towns they delivered to the believers. In many languages one cannot deliver...rules. One can, however, say "they told the believers what the apostles and elders in Jerusalem had decided should be done." It may even be necessary to characterize the rules as "how believers should behave."

They delivered...the rules...and told them to obey these rules translates "they delivered to them to obey the rules." The meaning of this Greek clause is precisely as the TEV has rendered it, and the same type of translation has been followed by several others (see NEB, JB, Barclay).

16.5

This is the third statement of the progress of the Christian churches that Luke has so far given (see 6.7; 9.31). By use of his favorite particle (translated so in TEV), Luke brings down the curtain on this act of the Christian drama. This is the same particle referred to in 1.6 and used frequently throughout the book.

As has been pointed out in several other passages, it may be necessary to translate churches as "members of the churches" or "people who belong to the churches." This is necessary in some languages since only people can be made stronger. Even the term stronger must, in some instances, be recast as "to become more firm," "to be made to stand steady," or even in a negative expression, "not to change in their faith."

The churches...grew in numbers every day must be rendered in some languages as "there were more and more believers each day," "more and more persons believed each day," or "the number of persons who believed was larger each day."

In Troas: Paul's Vision

6 They traveled through the region of Phrygia and Galatia, because the Holy Spirit did not let them preach the message in the province of Asia. 7 When they reached the border of Mysia, they tried to go into the province of Bithynia, but the Spirit of Jesus did not allow them. 8 So they traveled right on through Mysia and went down to

Troas. 9 Paul had a vision that night in which he saw a man of Macedonia standing and begging him, "Come over to Macedonia and help us!" 10 As soon as Paul had this vision, we got ready to leave for Macedonia, because we decided that God had called us to preach the Good News to the people there. (16. 6- 10)

Though the section heading In Troas: Paul's Vision is effective in English, this is not a form of expression which can be readily adapted in another language. Rather, one is likely to have some such form as "Paul Sees a Vision in Troas," "Paul Receives a Vision in Troas," or "A Vision Comes to Paul when He Is in Troas."

16. 6

Commentators are sharply divided on their interpretation of the phrase rendered the region of Phrygia and Galatia. Is Luke referring to the Roman political division of the land, according to which a part of Phrygia belonged to the Roman province of Galatia, or does he refer in a popular way to the border district which separated the ethnic regions of Phrygia and Galatia? The Greek defines the region as being both Phrygian and Galatian (literally "the Phrygian and Galatian region"), and therefore the second alternative appears more natural. In order to render the expression the region of Phrygia and Galatia properly in other languages, it is very important in most instances to be precise about the geographical relationships. Obviously this is not a reference to traveling through the two regions, Phrygia and Galatia, but traveling through a border area in some way related to both. If one adopts the second alternative, as suggested here, it may be possible to translate "traveled through the area shared by Phrygia and Galatia" or "traveled through the area between Phrygia and Galatia," though this latter expression is not fully accurate.

Some translators have wanted to introduce at this point a marginal note with regard to the geographical problem involved, but this detail is hardly vital for the average reader.

Did not let them preach translates a Greek participle which seems to have a causal force: "because the Holy Spirit did not let them preach." The Greek text implies that Paul and his group planned to go to the Roman province of Asia (probably to its capital city Ephesus). However, since the Holy Spirit would not let them preach in Asia, they passed through the Phrygian-Galatic region, on to the border of Mysia (v. 7). The Greek text simply has "Asia," but the TEV has expanded this to read the province of Asia. In an even narrower sense "Asia" could be used of the coastal region of the province along the Aegean Sea where the seven cities referred to in Revelation 2-3 were located.

The rendering of did not let them preach involves some serious difficulties in certain languages, since one needs to specify the basis for not having let Paul and his group proceed with their preaching mission. Was this a direct revelation?—that is, did the Holy Spirit tell them "you shall not preach in Asia"? or were Paul and his group led by circumstances not to go into the province of Asia? It is quite impossible to tell on the basis of the Greek text itself. It is preferable under such circumstances to use some rather general expression such as "the Holy Spirit prevented them from speaking"; but if one cannot be as general as this, it may be possible to say "the Holy Spirit showed them that they should not speak."

16.7

When they reached the border of Mysia (so NEB, Barclay, Twentieth Century) is apparently the meaning of the expression used by Luke. It seems to be the meaning given by certain other translators who do not use the word border—for example, "came to Mysia" (NAB, Phillips), "reached Mysia" (Goodspeed), "got as far as Mysia" (Moffatt), "reached the frontier of Mysia" (JB). Mysia was a region in the northwest part of the province of Asia. The province of Bithynia (literally "Bithynia," but with the meaning province of Bithynia) was located northeast of Mysia. Only here in the New Testament does the phrase the Spirit of Jesus appear. Luke obviously intends it as a reference to the Holy Spirit (v. 6).

The translation of the last clause of this verse, namely, the Spirit of Jesus did not allow them, involves the same problems as in verse 6 with the phrase the Holy Spirit did not let them. The Greek verbs in question are different (one is positive and the other negative), but the meaning is essentially the same and should be handled in the same general manner.

16.8

The TEV transitional particle so is an important element in connecting verse 8 with verse 7. Since this introduces the result of Paul and his group not having been able to go where they had expected to go, it is useful to indicate the resulting alternative, namely, going on through Mysia.

For the average reader, a number of these details of geographical relationships are obviously obscure and therefore need to be supplemented by maps. It is for that reason that the Bible Societies urge that in any publication of a book such as The Acts of the Apostles there be an accompanying map which will show the relationships of these various areas. Of course, for some people who are just emerging from a nonliterate state (that is, in translations for peoples who have not previously had a written language), maps present obvious difficulties, since people need to learn how to "read maps." Nevertheless, people do learn readily, and it is important that publications for such persons, as well as for any public, have adequate maps. Otherwise the text is unduly obscure and may be misleading.

The verb which the TEV has translated traveled right on through has as its primary meaning "passed by" (see alternative rendering in TEV). However, the problem is that it would have been impossible for them to have gone from the border of Mysia straight to Troas without passing through Mysia, since they had been forbidden to go to Bithynia. Moreover, there are places where this verb definitely means "to travel through," and most scholars understand it to mean such in the present passage. Went down is the normal expression that one would use to describe a trip from the interior down to the coastal region. Troas was a port city of Mysia on the Aegean Sea, near the spot where the city of Troy had once been.

16.9

It is more natural for the English speaker to say Paul had a vision than to say, as does the Greek, "a vision appeared to Paul." Luke probably intends to say that the vision came to Paul that night (NEB "during the night"), rather than to say, in a general sense, "one night." The meaning that night (the first night after his arrival) is supported both by the context and by the article which appears in Greek before night (literally "the night"). Macedonia was a Roman province, across the Aegean Sea from the province of Asia, and its capital was Thessalonica.

In translating begging him, one must obviously avoid the connotation of "begging for money." In many languages the appropriate equivalent is "asking him strongly" or "pleading with him."

16.10

We got ready to leave for Macedonia begins a series of "we" sections in which the author explicitly includes himself in the narrative. This particular section goes through verse 17, and it is assumed that the author was also present in Philippi for the remainder of Paul's stay there. When Paul leaves Philippi, however, the author does not appear to be in the group (see v. 40, they...left).

In some languages it is necessary to stipulate the kind of transportation which is implied in a word such as to leave—in this case, "to go by boat."

As in so many passages, one must be careful in translating called. In this instance there is no physical "calling," but rather guidance and instruction. It is for this reason that in some languages one must translate "God had instructed us to preach" or "God had shown us that we should preach."

In Philippi: the Conversion of Lydia

11 We left by ship from Troas and sailed straight across to Samothrace, and the next day to Neapolis. 12 From there we went inland to Philippi, a city of the first district of Macedonia; it is also a Roman colony. We spent several days in that city. 13 On the Sabbath day we went out of the city to the riverside, where we thought there would be a Jewish place for prayer. We sat down and talked to the women who gathered there. 14 One of those who heard us was Lydia,

from Thyatira, who was a dealer in purple goods. She was a woman who worshiped God, and the Lord opened her mind to pay attention to what Paul was saying. 15 She and the people of her house were baptized. Then she invited us, "Come and stay in my house, if you have decided that I am a true believer in the Lord." And she persuaded us to go.

(16.11-15)

The section heading In Philippi: the Conversion of Lydia is not a very useful model for adaptation into other languages. In some instances one may use "In Philippi Lydia Is Converted," or one may simply employ "The Conversion of Lydia" or "Lydia Becomes a Believer."

16.11

We left by ship translates a technical term which means "to put out to sea." Evidently they had a favorable wind behind them because they sailed straight across to Samothrace. Samothrace was an island about 38 miles from Troas; it was half way between Troas and Neapolis, the port city of Philippi, which was about 10 miles south of Philippi.

In some languages very careful distinctions are made in terms for sailing or going by ship. One verb may stipulate going from a mainland to an island, while another is used to describe travel from an island to the mainland. It is important in a passage such as this to employ a proper set of terms so as to coincide with the geographical relationships.

16.12

The phrase a city of the first district of Macedonia represents an attempt to make sense out of a very difficult Greek text, and there are other possibilities, as the TEV alternative renderings indicate: "the main city of the district of Macedonia" or "the main city of that district in Macedonia." The problem is that Philippi was not the chief city in the province of Macedonia; Thessalonica was both the leading city and the capital. Moreover, Macedonia had been divided into four districts, and Philippi was not the leading city of the district in which it was located; that honor had gone to the capital city of the district, Amphipolis. The rendering in the TEV actually translates a conjecture as to what may have been the original reading of the Greek, and it seems to make the best sense in the context.

In rendering the expression a city of the first district of Macedonia, it may be necessary to be somewhat more specific than the TEV phrase is—for example, "a city which was located in the first region of the province of Macedonia." In order to supplement the meaning of first district, it may be useful to have a marginal note indicating that there were four districts and that Philippi was simply located in what was regarded as the first of these districts. Where already existing translations have established a tradition of regarding Philippi as a "leading city" or "very important city," it may be necessary to provide some supplementary note which will indicate the basis for this different translation.

313

16.13

Apart from a geographical location, there was no difference between living in a city located in Italy and in a Roman colony abroad. The rights of a colony were essentially threefold: self-government, freedom from taxes and tributes, and the same privileges as the citizens of any Italian city. It is not easy in some languages to find an adequate expression for Roman colony. In some instances the closest equivalent is "a city which had been built by the Romans" or "a city which had been populated by people who came from Rome." It may even be useful at this point to have a marginal note describing precisely what a Roman colony was. This would be useful to the average reader in understanding something of the implications of the latter part of this chapter.

16.13

The Sabbath day referred to is evidently the first Sabbath day after their arrival in the city. Out of the city is literally "out of the gate" but the gate referred to is the "city gate" (NEB, JB). The river mentioned is the Gangites (or Angites).

Place for prayer (see JB, Moffatt, Barclay) translates a word which generally means merely "prayer," but here and in verse 16 it means "place for prayer," a meaning which is also attested outside the New Testament. It is better to translate this term in the generalized sense of "a place for prayer" rather than with a specific meaning of "synagogue," since Luke did use the word synagogue elsewhere and could have used it here had he so desired.

16.14

Lydia was not only a personal name, but it was also the name of a region in the western part of the Roman province of Asia where the city of Thyatira was located. Since purple goods were luxury materials worn by the rich, it is thought by many that Lydia herself must have been well off. In order to indicate that purple goods were a luxury item, some translators have employed "expensive purple cloth." The goods in this particular instance refers obviously to cloth.

By the statement that she was a woman who worshiped God, Luke indicates that she was a Gentile participating in Jewish worship. In Jewish thought the heart is looked upon as the center of one's intellectual activities; therefore, the TEV has translated the literal expression "opened her heart" by opened her mind. In translating opened her mind, one may employ some such phrase as "caused her to be receptive," "caused her to accept," or even "caused her to understand."

The verb translated pay attention to (used also in 8.6) is taken by some in the sense of "to believe" or "to accept" (see JB). In some languages it is important to combine opened her mind with the phrase pay attention to as being two subsequent actions---for example, "caused her to be receptive to what Paul was saying and to believe it."

The word translated the people of her house (most translations "house-hold") has as its basic meaning "house" (see latter part of this verse), but it may also mean "family" (see 10.2). Since Lydia was the head of the house, it is assumed that she was either unmarried or a widow; and because her marital status is unknown, the people of her house perhaps suits the present context better than "family." In rendering the expression the people of her house, it may be necessary to stipulate "the people who lived with her in the house." In general this would include not only relatives but also servants and slaves.

If you have decided that I am a true believer in the Lord translates a conditional sentence in Greek that presupposes that the "if" clause is true to fact. That is, Lydia was saying, "Since you have decided...." True believer is literally "faithful," which in the context describes one whose faith is genuine, and so is "a true believer." In rendering true believer into another language there may, however, be a number of complications. In the first place one may need to place this into a verb expression "that I genuinely believe" or "that I really believe." A term for true must refer to the quality of faith, not simply to some person who is "true" in character or who "tells the truth." In combining the final phrase in the Lord with an expression for belief, one may have in some languages "that I truly trust the Lord" or "that I am one who truly trusts the Lord."

In Prison at Philippi

16 One day as we were going to the place of prayer, we were met by a slave girl who had an evil spirit in her that made her predict the future. She earned much money for her owners by telling fortunes. 17 She followed Paul and us, shouting, "These men are servants of the Most High God! They announce to you how you can be saved!" 18 She did this for many days, until Paul became so upset that he turned around and said to the spirit, "In the name of Jesus Christ I order you to come out of her!" The spirit went out of her that very moment. 19 When her owners realized that their chance of making money was gone, they grabbed Paul and Silas and dragged them to the authorities in the public square. 20 They brought them before the Roman officials and said, "These men are Jews, and they are causing trouble in our city. 21 They are teaching customs that are against our law; we are Romans and cannot accept or practice them." 22 The crowd joined the attack against them; the officials tore the clothes off Paul and Silas, and ordered them to be whipped. 23 After a severe beating they were thrown into jail, and the jailer was ordered to lock them up tight. 24 Upon receiving this order, the jailer threw them into the inner cell and fastened their feet between heavy blocks of wood. (16.16-24)

The section heading In Prison at Philippi may need to be made somewhat more specific: "Paul and Silas Are Put in Prison at Philippi." On the other hand, it may be quite sufficient to say "Paul and Silas Are Thrown into Prison" or "Paul and Silas Are Arrested." Being placed in prison may be regarded as an obvious result of being arrested.

The temporal relationship between this incident and the one described in verses 13-15 is not quite clear. In verse 13 it is said that Paul and his group went out of the city to find the Jewish place of prayer. Does Luke intend for his readers to understand that on the way to the place of prayer Paul met these women and sat down and talked with them and now (v. 16) proceeds with them to the Jewish place of prayer? Or does Luke mean that Paul actually met the women at the Jewish place of prayer and that the incident related in 16 ff. happened at another time when they were going to the place of prayer? The latter alternative seems more probable, and for that reason most translators have either added "one day" or "once" to the first part of verse 16 in order to suggest this interpretation. On the other hand, the RSV and a few others (NAB, Barclay, Zürich) tend to leave the impression that these events took place on the same day spoken of in verse 13, as Paul was going to the place of prayer.

In view of the contents of verse 15, in which Lydia had persuaded Paul and his group to stay in her house, it would seem that the events of the following paragraph took place at another time. Certainly it would have been difficult for this event to have occurred at the same time as the events of verse 13. It is for that reason that some satisfactory transition as marked by the sequence of events (as in the TEV one day) is so necessary. In some languages, in fact, it is obligatory to indicate "we were going to the place of prayer again," otherwise there will be serious misunderstanding and confusion with the contents of verse 13.

One should note, however, that this paragraph (vv. 16-24) is only the first of eight paragraphs describing the imprisonment and difficulties in Philippi. The transitions between the major divisions are carefully marked by temporal particles—for example, in verse 25 about midnight, and at the beginning of verse 35 the next morning. These markers of transition are extremely important if the proper sequence of events is to be clearly indicated.

16.16

The phrase the place of prayer is the same as the one referred to in verse 13. In the earlier verse one can render this as "a place where Jewish people habitually gathered together to pray to God." In verse 16 a similar expression can be employed "a place where people habitually gathered to pray to God." It may be necessary to specify habitual action and also the goal of prayer, namely, God. Otherwise the reader might assume that this was only a place where someone on some particular occasion happened to be praying.

We were met by a slave girl may, of course, be rendered in the active form as "a slave girl met us." However, "met" must not be understood in the technical sense of becoming acquainted with, but simply "coming across" or "chance meeting up with."

A slave girl may be rendered in some languages as "a girl who had been sold into slavery" or "a girl who had been bought as a slave."

Who had an evil spirit in her that made her predict the future is literally "who had a python-spirit." "Python" was originally the name given to the snake that guarded the sacred place at Delphi where divine oracles were given. Later, the word "python" was used of anyone who possessed the power to foretell the future. Looked at from the Christian point of view, this "python-spirit" would have been an evil spirit, and therefore the TEV has rendered the phrase an evil spirit (in her) that made her predict the future. Predict the future may be rendered as "tell people what would happen in the future" or "tell people what was going to happen."

Some persons have assumed that the owners were a man and his wife, but the incidents which took place later would seem to indicate that several men were involved as the owners of this slave girl.

Much money may also be taken in the sense of "much profit." Telling fortunes (see NEB, JB) better qualifies what she was doing than "foretelling the future" (Phillips). The word translated by telling fortunes appears only here in the New Testament, but when used in the Septuagint it never refers to true prophecy but is always used of lying prophets and of forbidden ways of seeking God's will. In practically all languages there are expressions for telling fortunes---this is simply the practice of divination. But if there is no generally recognized term or expression for this practice, one can always translate "telling people what would happen to them in the future."

16.17

The forms of the Greek verbs translated followed and shouting indicate that this was a continuous action. Note also the fact that this is made explicit in the beginning of verse 18. One can, therefore, translate "she kept following Paul and us and kept shouting" or "she continually followed Paul and us and kept shouting."

The Most High God was a term current among both Jews and Gentiles. The expression the Most High God is usually translated in one of two different ways. Either Most High refers to position, that is, "the highest God" (indirectly a reference to "the God in heaven") or "the God who is higher than all other gods," that is to say, "the most important God." Here the reference would certainly seem to be to "God who is greater than all others."

How you can be saved (JB "to tell you how to be saved") translates the noun phrase "a way of salvation" (so NAB, NEB, Goodspeed), but which has been rendered by a number of translators as "the way of salvation" (RSV, Moffatt, Barclay, Phillips). There is no problem in transforming a noun phrase into a verbal expression as the TEV and JB have done, since this often provides a much better basis for understanding the meaning. The real problem that faces the translator is the meaning of the expression "way of salvation."

Is it legitimate to understand this in the sense of "the way of salvation," which can then be transformed into a verbal expression such as how you can be saved? In this regard there are several observations that are important. (1) When the definite article "the" is used in Greek, it is usually safe to assume that the definite article can be used in English translation; however, it does not follow that when no article is used in Greek, the equivalent expression in English is the indefinite article "a." For example, in 17.23 the literal expression "to unknown God" may be legitimately taken either as to "an" unknown God or to "the" unknown God; and it is definitely to be concluded that the expression "Son of God" in Mark 15.39 means "the Son of God." (2) Luke certainly intends for his readers to understand that there is but one way of salvation; and for this reason "way of salvation" must be understood in the sense that Luke himself would have taken it, "the way of salvation."

As long as the passive expression can be preserved, for example, how you can be saved, there are usually no problems involved. However, it may be necessary to place this in the active, in which case God must be made the subject: "how God can save you."

16.18

Became so upset may also mean "became annoyed," a verb which appears only here and in 4.2. This is the first instance of exorcism in the name of Jesus Christ in the book of Acts, but there is no basic difference between this and the healing in the name of Jesus in the earlier chapters.

Note that in this verse Paul addresses the spirit, not the girl. However, in some languages one must say "said to the spirit that was in the girl." Otherwise the connection between the spirit and the girl may not be evident.

The use of the phrase in the name of Jesus Christ may be extremely difficult to render in a comprehensible manner. In many instances one can employ "by speaking the name of Jesus Christ." However, this may be relatively meaningless in some languages and therefore one may use "by the power of Jesus Christ" or "by the authority of Jesus Christ." In still other instances one may combine both of these concepts—for example, "by the power which is in the name of Jesus Christ."

The literal expression "that very hour" (RSV) is much more naturally expressed in English by that very moment (Phillips "immediately"; JB "then and there").

16.19

In Greek verses 19-21 are one sentence, but it is obviously useful to break up this rather long sentence into a number of shorter sentences in order to show relationships more effectively and to deal more meaningfully with the sequence of events.

The expression their chance of making money was gone may be rendered as "that they would no longer be able to make money out of the girl" or "that the slave girl would no longer be able to make money for them."

The authorities translates a general term which is used of the magistrates of a city. Although "market place" is what the Greek literally says, public square (so also Goodspeed), "main square" (NEB), or "city square" (Barclay) is more naturally the meaning, because the reference is to a place where public court was conducted. (See JB "to the law courts in the market place.")

16.20

The Roman officials (most translations "magistrates") were the chief magistrates of a Roman colony, and they were two in number. The text does not make it clear whether these were the same authorities referred to in the previous verse, though it is quite likely that they were. It is to be noticed that Paul and Silas were brought before the Roman officials on the charge that they were Jews, not that they were Christians.

The expression causing trouble should be understood in the most general sense. In some languages it would be "causing trouble for the people in our city." In terms of this particular context, however, it is sometimes rendered as "causing a disturbance."

16.21

It is not known what customs are referred to. Perhaps the reference is to the fact that although the Romans recognized the Jewish religion, they did not permit them to go about actively seeking converts. In the eyes of the Roman officials Paul and Silas were at best Jews seeking converts for their religion.

Teaching customs that are against our law may be rendered as "teaching us to do things which our law says we should not do."

We are Romans is rendered in some languages as "we belong to the city of Rome" or "we are the same as people who live in the city of Rome." (See also 16.37.) And cannot accept or practice them may be rendered as "therefore we must not do as these men are telling us."

16.22

Joined the attack against refers not to verbal charges made against the two men, but to an attempt on the part of the crowd to do them physical harm. Joined the attack may be translated as "also started hitting."

The officials tore the clothes off Paul and Silas translates an ambiguous expression in Greek. It is possible to understand this to mean that the officials tore their own clothes (as Jews did when someone committed blasphemy), but most translators and commentators understand it in the sense that the TEV renders it. It was not the custom for Romans to tear their clothes under such circumstances, and the context suggests that the officials themselves tore the clothes off Paul and Silas so that they could have them whipped. On the other hand, it is more likely that the Roman officials ordered the clothes of Paul and Silas to be torn off by soldiers who no doubt would be standing nearby.

The word translated whipped literally means "to be beaten (with a stick)," but it is possible that some other instrument, such as a whip, was used. It may be necessary to stipulate precisely who received the orders and who did the whipping—for example, "ordered soldiers to whip Paul and Silas." One may, of course, employ a general term for "beating," implying that they were beaten with sticks or some type of instrument.

16.23

A severe beating is literally "with many blows," the meaning of which is accurately rendered by the TEV (see also Phillips, NEB). It may be necessary to indicate who did the beating and who put Paul and Silas in prison. One may therefore translate: "after the soldiers had beaten Paul and Silas very severely they threw them into jail," or, as in some languages, "...they tied them up in jail," or "...they locked them into the jail." One should avoid a term such as "throw" if this means literally throwing through the air.

The subject of ordered is obviously the officials, and therefore one may render this second clause of verse 23 as "the officials ordered the jailer to lock them up securely." It may even be necessary to place this in the form of direct discourse: "the officials said to the jailer, You must lock these men up securely." Even the term "securely" may need to be specified as "so that they cannot possibly escape."

16.24

It is not necessary to assume, as some commentators have done, that the inner cell was an underground cell. The inner cell was simply "the farthest cell in the prison." This may be translated in some instances as "the most guarded cell of the prison," since one would need to pass through several other cells in order to arrive at this inner cell.

Between heavy blocks of wood is rendered by most translators as "stocks." The term "stocks" was avoided by the TEV for two reasons: (1) it was felt that its meaning would not be readily understood by the readers for whom the TEV was designed and (2) the stocks utilized by the Romans were of a different sort from those otherwise known. The Romans used this as an instrument of torture. It had more than one pair of holes for the legs, so that a prisoner's legs could be spread wide apart, causing him great pain.

25 About midnight Paul and Silas were praying and singing hymns to God, and the other prisoners were listening to them. 26 Suddenly there was a violent earthquake, which shook the prison to its foundations. At once all the doors opened, and the chains fell off all the prisoners. 27 The jailer woke up, and when he saw the prison doors open he thought that all the prisoners had escaped; so he pulled out his sword and was about to kill himself. 28 But Paul shouted at the top of his voice, "Don't harm yourself! We are all here!"

29 The jailer called for a light, rushed in, and fell trembling at the feet of Paul and Silas. 30 Then he led them out and asked, "What must I do, sirs, to be saved?"

31 "Believe in the Lord Jesus," they said, "and you will be saved —you and your family." 32 Then they preached the word of the Lord to him and to all the others in his house. 33 At that very hour of the night the jailer took them and washed off their wounds; and he and all his family were baptized at once. 34 He took Paul and Silas up into his house and gave them some food to eat. He and his family were filled with joy, because he now believed in God. (16. 25-34)

The number of temporal transitions in these relatively brief paragraphs are most important. Note the following: about midnight (v. 25), suddenly (v. 26), at once (v. 26), then (v. 30), at that very hour (v. 33). Since the actions in these paragraphs clearly alternate between Paul and Silas on the one hand and the jailer on the other, it is most important that the participants in the action be clearly identified.

16. 25

Praying and singing hymns may be rendered as "they were singing psalms as prayers to God." Singing hymns to God is equivalent in some languages to "singing hymns in honor of God."

Listening to them is potentially ambiguous in English. It may refer to listening to the hymns which were sung or listening to Paul and Silas. In some languages, entirely different verbs are used, depending upon the goal. Essentially, there is no real difference in meaning.

16. 26

There was a violent earthquake may be rendered in some languages as "the earth shook very much." In practically all areas there are earthquakes, and some equivalent expression is normally well known. In some instances, however, it is highly idiomatic—for example, "the volcano snored," "mother earth had a fit," or "the giant rolled over."

Shook the prison to its foundations may be rendered as "even shook the foundations of the prison" or "even shook the ground on which the prison was built."

16. 27

The jailer was about to kill himself either for a point of military honor or, more likely, because of the reason given in 12.19: that a jailer who allowed prisoners to escape would receive the same punishment due the prisoners. It may be useful to have at this point some marginal note to explain that the jailer's intention to kill himself was based upon the fact that in ancient times a jailer who allowed prisoners to escape would receive their punishment, and, in view of the fact that evidently some of the prisoners

16.28

were slated for capital punishment, the jailer assumed that he himself would be killed. Otherwise, such an action would be regarded as quite incomprehensible in some societies.

16.28

Luke does not explain how Paul knew that the jailer was about to kill himself or that the prisoners had not escaped. Speculation at this point is of no value to the translator.

16.29

The word translated light is actually plural ("lights"), but the TEV takes it in a collective sense, meaning simply "light" and not "lamps." In a number of languages, however, it would be very appropriate to have a translation such as "called for someone to bring a lamp."

The expression fell trembling must not be rendered so literally that it implies the jailer stumbled at the feet of Paul and Silas. Rather, "he threw himself down..." or "he bowed down at the feet of Paul and Silas." It may also be necessary to explain the significance of trembling, that is, "trembling with fear."

16.30

Saved should be taken with full theological meaning, since this is evidently the meaning intended by Luke, and not simply as a reference to what the jailer hopes to do in order to save himself from this bad situation. However, in many languages a term for saved implies both physical escape as well as moral and spiritual change. If both can be combined in this context, the meaning becomes even more relevant.

16.31

Family is the same word translated the people of her house in verse 15 and family in 10.2. The relationship between the jailer's belief in the Lord Jesus and the salvation of his family is not clear. Did Paul say that the jailer's belief was sufficient both for him and for his family, or did Paul tell the jailer that if he believed he would be saved, and if his family believed they also would be saved? The first of these alternatives more naturally suits the meaning of the Greek.

16.32

The expression the word of the Lord is here to be understood, as in other contexts, as "the message about the Lord."

16.33

The expression took them may be difficult to translate for he did not actually carry them away. What is perhaps better understood is "led them into another room." In certain instances where the TEV has used washed off their wounds, one may simply want "washed their wounds" in the sense of to cleanse and to take care of.

"All of his" (so literally in Greek) may be taken either as the equivalent of the jailer's family or, in the expanded sense, of his entire "household" (JB), as was the case with Lydia (v. 15).

16.34

The Greek idiomatic expression "he set a table" is properly understood as he...gave them some food to eat.

The word which Luke has chosen to use for family appears only here in the New Testament. It is in the dative case, and how one understands it in relationship to the two verbs filled with joy and believed makes a great deal of difference in a translation. In Greek the verb translated filled with joy is actually a third person singular verb and would literally be translated: "he was filled with joy along with his family." Believed is actually a participle in agreement with "he": "because he had believed (in God)." If one understands "with his family" to go with the first verb, one may follow the RSV: "and he rejoiced with all his household that he had believed in God." On the other hand, if "with his family" is to be taken both with the verb and with the participle, the meaning is: "he along with his family were filled with joy because he along with his family now believed in God." The TEV has followed the first alternative and so has translated: he and his family were filled with joy, because he now believed in God (but see JB "the whole family celebrated their conversion to belief in God").

Filled with joy may be equivalent in many languages to "were very happy" or possibly with a causative "were caused to be very happy." As has been pointed out in other instances, renderings of the concept of joy or happiness may frequently involve highly idiomatic or figurative phrases—for example, "their hearts were singing."

35 The next morning the Roman authorities sent police officers with the order, "Let those men go."

36 So the jailer told it to Paul, "The officials have sent an order for you and Silas to be released. You may leave, then, and go in peace."

37 But Paul said to the police officers, "We were not found guilty of any crime, yet they whipped us in public—and we are Roman citizens! Then they threw us in prison. And now they want to send us away secretly? Not at all! The Roman officials themselves must come here and let us out."

38 The police officers reported these words to the Roman officials; and when they heard that Paul and Silas were Roman citizens, they were

afraid. 39 So they went and apologized to them; then they led them out of the prison and asked them to leave the city. 40 Paul and Silas left the prison and went to Lydia's house. There they met the brothers, spoke words of encouragement to them, and left. (16.35-40)

This final episode in the imprisonment in Philippi shifts back to the Roman authorities mentioned in verses 20 ff. Since, however, one must deal not only with the authorities but also the police officers and Paul and Silas as well as the jailer, it is essential that the proper participants in the events be carefully designated.

Note especially the introductory temporal transition the next morning and also the final sentence, which is so typical of Luke's description of what happened after persecution, namely, encouragement to the fellow believers.

16.35

The next morning (Phillips "when morning came") is literally "when day came." It is doubtful if the Roman officials would have acted as early as the NEB ("when daylight came") and the JB ("when it was daylight") intimate. Roman authorities is the same word translated Roman officials in verse 20.

The word translated police officers appears in the New Testament only here and in verse 38. Each of the two Roman officials in a colony (see v. 20) had a special attendant. In Latin these attendants were called lictors, and this is the rendering in the translation by Moffatt. The average reader will, however, not understand this technical Latin term, and it is best to do either as the TEV has done or to follow the NEB ("their officers") or Barclay ("their attendants").

The sequence of orders in verse 35 is not easy to express in some languages. Note first the Roman authorities give an order to the police officers, and the police officers are in turn directed to order the jailer to let the men go. In languages in which orders must be expressed in direct discourse, one may translate: "The next morning the Roman authorities said to the police officers, Go and tell the jailer, Let those men go." In some languages let those men go may be rendered as "release those men from prison" or "untie those men."

16.36

For some languages there is an additional problem of discourse in relaying the orders of the Roman authorities. One may therefore translate: "So the jailer said to Paul, The officials have ordered me, Let those men go." However, it is better to employ some indirect discourse, if at all possible, so as not to produce two levels of direct discourse. This may be done either as in the TEV or as "So the jailer told Paul that the officials had sent an order saying, Let those men go."

A literal translation into English of the words spoken by the jailer to Paul may be misleading---for example, "the officials have sent an order for you to be released." In Greek this was no problem, since the plural form of "you" was used. To represent this meaning for the English reader, the TEV has translated for you and Silas. Most translators seem to understand the expression go in peace in one of three ways: (1) "go quietly away," that is, leave without making any further disturbance; (2) "go unmolested" (Goodspeed), that is, you may leave without any further punishment; (3) "blessings on your journey" (NEB), or "and all good things go with you" (Barclay), that is, the Roman officials wish the Jewish prisoners a safe and happy journey, which in the context seems rather strange. The appropriate interpretation of the Greek expression in peace is to be found in the manner in which Paul speaks of being sent away "secretly" (v. 37).

16.37

Note that in the first clause of verse 37 Paul is not responding to what the jailer has told him but is speaking directly to the police officers. Evidently he had demanded from the jailer the opportunity of speaking to the police officers.

The adjective which the TEV has rendered not found guilty of any crime (NEB "not been found guilty") may be understood in this sense, or it may mean "without a trial" (Phillips, Goodspeed, Barclay). Were not found guilty may need to be restructured in some languages as "the authorities could not prove that we were guilty of a crime" or "the authorities did not prove that we were guilty."

They whipped us must be understood as a causative "the authorities caused us to be whipped in public" or "they ordered the police authorities to whip us in public."

In public may be rendered as "with all the people looking on" or "with everyone there present."

It is essential to set off in some contrastive manner the clause and we are Roman citizens. This is done in the TEV by a dash and followed by an exclamation mark. In many languages, however, one must introduce this expression by some kind of contrastive particle---for example, "but we are Roman citizens."

Translating Roman citizens is not easy in some languages. In fact, an entire clause may be required, and it may also be necessary to have some marginal note. One may render Roman citizens as "we are just like those who live in Rome," "we have the same privileges as those who live in Rome," or "we are to be treated just like those who come from Rome."

On the basis that the context expresses purpose or intent, the TEV has rendered the verb expression "they are sending us away" as they want to send us away (so also Phillips; see JB "and then think they can push us out"). Not at all represents a very strong rejection of their proposal by Paul.

16.38

Reported these words may be rendered as "the police officers told the Roman officials what Paul and Silas had told them." It is also important to make perfectly clear that the final they of verse 38 refers to the Roman officials and not simply to the police officers. These Roman officials were justifiably afraid, since severe penalties were often placed upon persons who violated the rights of Roman citizens.

16.39

Apologized may be rendered as "asked them to forgive them" or (perhaps better) "asked them to overlook." In some languages the equivalent is "they said to them, We are sorry for what we did."

The final verb expression asked them to leave the city may need to be expressed as direct discourse in some languages––for example, "said to them, Please leave the city."

16.40

Note that though Paul and Silas left the prison, they did not immediately leave the city but went to Lydia's house. There they met with the brothers, that is, "the fellow believers."

Words of encouragement are "words which encouraged the people" or, as in some languages, "they encouraged the fellow believers by what they said to them." The final verb left must refer to "leaving the city."

CHAPTER 17

The material on Chapter 17 can readily be divided into three major sections relating to the three locations where the various events took place: Thessalonica, Berea, and Athens. Verse 1 forms a geographical transition from Chapter 16. The first sentence of verse 10 is a transition from the preceding paragraph in order to introduce what happened in Berea. The last verse of the second section (v. 15) forms, in a sense, a transition to the third part of the chapter, and this final section (vv. 16-34) is further introduced by the initial clause of verse 16. These transitional devices are extremely important if one is to follow the account satisfactorily.

In Thessalonica

1 They traveled on through Amphipolis and Apollonia, and came to Thessalonica, where there was a Jewish synagogue. 2 According to his usual habit, Paul went to the synagogue. There during three Sabbath days he argued with the people from the Scriptures, 3 explaining them and proving from them that the Messiah had to suffer, and rise from death. "This Jesus whom I announce to you," Paul said, "is the Messiah." 4 Some of them were convinced and joined Paul and Silas; so did a large group of Greeks who worshiped God, and many of the leading women. (17.1-4)

The section heading In Thessalonica may be quite satisfactory in a number of languages, but frequently it is not sufficient since a mere geographical location does not tell the reader what is presumably involved. It may be useful, therefore, to employ a section heading such as "Paul and His Colleagues (or Companions) Are Persecuted in Thessalonica," "People Riot in Thessalonica Because of What Paul Has Said," or "...Because of Paul's Preaching."

17.1

The means of travel is not indicated, whether by animal or by foot, though if Amphipolis and Apollonia were the only two cities in which Paul stopped on his way to Thessalonica, it would imply that at least part of the journey was made on horseback. The road on which Paul was traveling would have been the Via Egnatia, which extended all the way across Macedonia from Neapolis to the city of Dyrrhachium. Amphipolis, located about three miles from the sea, was the capital of the first district of Macedonia and was about 30 miles southwest of Philippi. Apollonia was 30 miles southwest of Amphipolis and 35 miles east of Thessalonica. Thessalonica was a free city and was the capital of the province of Macedonia.

It may be useful to use a classifier with the cities Amphipolis, Apollonia, and Thessalonica, since it is possible that these might be interpreted as provinces or territories. However, in the ancient world the name of a city

normally applied not only to the immediate built-up area, but also to the surrounding farmlands, which were regarded as being a part of the city.

In a number of languages Jewish synagogue must be rendered as "a
synagogue for Jews" or, as in some instances, "a worship house for Jews"
or "a building where Jews worshiped God."

According to his usual habit is rendered in some languages as a verb
expression, usually with a form of the verb indicating habitual action—for
example, "Paul habitually went to the synagogue and therefore on this occasion he went to the synagogue (in Thessalonica)."

Three Sabbath days translates an unusual expression which most scholars understand in the sense represented by the TEV. The RSV and Zürich,
however, take the expression to mean "for three weeks." The verb translated
argued (so most translations) may also mean "discussed" (see Goodspeed).
It is doubtful if from the Scriptures can be understood in the sense of "quoting texts of Scripture" (NEB; see Moffatt, Phillips). What Paul evidently did
was to read passages of Scripture and to explain these in light of their fulfillment in Jesus Christ. The relationship of argued to from the Scriptures
may be indicated by "he argued with the people by referring to the Scriptures"
or "he discussed with the people by reading from the Scriptures."

17. 3

The literal expression "opening (the Scriptures)" should be taken to
mean "explaining," "interpreting," or "expounding" them. However, in some
languages one cannot use the phrase "explain the Scriptures." One can only
"explain what the Scriptures say," in other words, the content of the writings,
not the writings themselves. An expression for explaining may be simply
"say what it means" or "make it clear."

Proving from them (that is, the Scriptures) is taken by some in the
sense of "quoting passages to prove" (see Barclay, Moffatt). In rendering
the phrase proving from them it may be necessary to employ rather extensive restructuring—for example, "reading the words of the Scriptures and
showing to the people that it was necessary therefore that..." or "showing
to the people that the words of the Scriptures meant that...."

The concept of obligation or necessity suggested by the clause that the
Messiah had to suffer, and rise from death is difficult to express in some
languages since the usual expression for necessity would indicate that Jesus
was compelled by Roman authorities to suffer death. This is true, but it is
not what is meant by this first portion of verse 3. What Paul is saying is that
the Scriptures showed that the Messiah would suffer and then rise from death,
and it was the fulfillment of that prophecy which was important. Therefore
in many languages one must simply translate "he showed from the Scriptures
that the Messiah would suffer and be raised from death."

Announce may be rendered as "tell you about for the first time" or "whom I am just now telling you about."

Since the second half of verse 3 is in direct discourse, it is often important to introduce Paul as the speaker. It is evident that in the present context "the Christ" is to be taken in the sense of a title rather than with the meaning of a proper name. Accordingly, the TEV has translated the Messiah (so NEB, Moffatt, Barclay), rendered in some languages as "God's specially commissioned one" or "the one whom God chose to send."

17.4

Convinced may be rendered as "believed that what Paul had said was true" or "believed Paul's words." The term joined must not be understood in the technical sense of joining an association but in the more informal meaning of "counted themselves one with Paul and Silas," "took the part of Paul and Silas," or "identified themselves as being companions of Paul and Silas."

The Greeks who worshiped God were persons who had not been fully converted to Judaism, but who believed in and who worshiped the God of Judaism. The phrase translated leading women (so most translations) may be translated as "important women in the town." However, it may be understood to mean "the wives of the leading men" (Barclay).

> 5 But the Jews were jealous and gathered some of the worthless loafers from the streets and formed a mob. They set the whole city in an uproar, and attacked the home of Jason, trying to find Paul and Silas and bring them out to the people. 6 But when they did not find them, they dragged Jason and some other brothers to the city authorities and shouted, "These men have caused trouble everywhere! Now they have come to our city, 7 and Jason has kept them in his house. They are all breaking the laws of the Emperor, saying that there is another king, by the name of Jesus." 8 With these words they threw the crowd and the city authorities in an uproar. 9 The authorities made Jason and the others pay the required amount of money to be released, and then let them go. (17.5-9)

It is most important that this paragraph begin with some kind of particle which will show the contrast with the preceding paragraph. This is indicated in the TEV by but. In some languages it is necessary to have an even stronger expression of contrast.

17.5

In some languages there is no term for jealous which covers this particular area of meaning. Therefore one may have to describe the basis for their feelings --- for example, "the Jews were angry that so many people believed Paul" or "the Jews were very unhappy that so many people joined with Paul and Silas."

Loafers from the streets is literally "men of the market place." Commentators agree that this expression is used in a bad sense, referring either to persons who were "lazy" or to "trouble makers." The TEV has taken this term in combination with the word worthless (literally "evil"), and renders the whole phrase worthless loafers from the streets. Formed a mob (see Goodspeed, Moffatt, Barclay) appears much more in keeping with the context than the more generic statement "gathered a crowd" (Phillips). In some languages a mob is rendered as "noisy crowd" or "angry crowd."

The subject they of the second part of verse 5 must include not only the worthless loafers but also the Jews who had formed them into a mob. In some languages this must be specified as "the Jews and the rest of the mob." Otherwise it may imply that only the worthless loafers...attacked the home of Jason.

Set the whole city in an uproar is equivalent to "caused a riot." In some languages this is simply "made a lot of noise" or "caused much angry noise."

It is necessary in some languages to specify the particular way in which the home of Jason was attacked. Most languages have a number of words for attacking a person, but not so many for attacking a house. One can say "they threw rocks on the house," but under the circumstances it is probably better to say "they broke down the doors of the house," since this was apparently what happened in their attempt to find Paul and Silas and to bring them out to the people.

Jason was a common name in Greek and was often used by Jews in place of the more Jewish sounding "Joshua." Nothing further is known about Jason; he may have been a believer, or he may have been the person for whom Paul was working in the city. The phrase to the people may refer either to the mob that had been gathered or to "the town assembly" (NEB; see JB "People's Assembly"), by which is meant the citizens assembled for judicial purposes. This same phrase is translated to the people in 12. 21.

17. 6

The phrase which the TEV has rendered Jason and some other brothers is literally "Jason and some of the brothers" (see JB). The question is whether Jason was or was not a Christian. Considered solely upon the basis of the Greek text of this verse, one would conclude that Jason was not one of the "brothers." However, when other passages are taken into consideration, there is sufficient evidence to indicate that Luke may have intended Jason to have been included among the "brothers." For example, 1.14 mentions the women, and...Mary the mother of Jesus, with the evident indication that Mary is not to be excluded from among the women. Again, the expression the believers and the widows in 9. 41 does not imply that the widows were not believers. One may also argue, from the casual way in which Luke has introduced Jason, that he probably should be considered as one of the believers. Otherwise, one would have expected that Luke would have indicated clearly Jason's relationship to the believing community.

The city authorities (in Greek, the word appears only here and in 17. 8) is a technical term used to describe the five or six members of the city council in a Macedonian city. These men have caused trouble everywhere is more literally translated by the NEB as "men who have made trouble all over the world." The word translated "world" by the NEB is a word which refers to the civilized world (more specifically the Roman Empire) and is here used in an exaggerated sense. In the idiom of today everywhere seems much more natural.

The our in our city is, of course, inclusive since the Jews were addressing the city authorities.

17. 7

Kept them in his house translates a verb indicating that the brothers were guests in Jason's home. This phrase kept them in his house is equivalent to "has welcomed them to his house," "has had them in his house as guests," or even "has given them food and a bed in his house."

The (Roman) Emperor referred to in this verse is Claudius, who ruled from A.D. 41 to 54. The accusation against the Christians is not merely that they were saying that there is another king, by the name of Jesus, but that someone else other than Claudius was king, and his name was Jesus. The JB renders this entire statement: "they have broken every one of Caesar's edicts by claiming that there is another emperor, Jesus." The laws of the Emperor are simply "the rules which the Emperor has given us" or even "what the Emperor has told us we must do." In many societies there are no terms such as king and emperor, nor are there any parallel cultural features. In the ancient Roman world kings were traditional rulers (normally with hereditary descent) in various regions, while the emperor was the highest authority over the entire Roman Empire. In some situations one can only speak of a king as "a ruler" and the emperor as "the biggest ruler." In societies which only know chieftainship, one can employ for a king "a big chief" and for the emperor "the biggest chief," "the chief who is controlling all the other chiefs," or "the chief who is giving orders to all the other chiefs."

The final phrase by the name of Jesus may be expressed as "and his name is Jesus" or "and this other king has the name Jesus."

17. 8

The expression threw ... in an uproar may be equivalent to "caused a terrible disturbance among" or "caused complete confusion for." In this instance the crowd is not primarily the mob that had been formed previously, but the crowd that had gathered as a result of the violence done to Jason and the other brothers in their being dragged before the city authorities.

17. 9

The required amount of money to be released translates a technical

term which refers to the security or money which was given to the city officials and which would have been forfeited by Jason had the offense been repeated. Although the subject of the verb made . . . pay is not explicit in Greek,
the context makes it clear that the authorities are the subject.

In Berea

10 As soon as night came, the brothers sent Paul and Silas to
Berea. When they arrived, they went to the Jewish synagogue. 11 The
people there were more open-minded than the people in Thessalonica.
They listened to the message with great eagerness, and every day they
studied the Scriptures to see if what Paul said was really true. 12 Many
of them believed; and many Greek women of high social standing and
many Greek men also believed. 13 But when the Jews in Thessalonica
heard that Paul had preached the word of God in Berea also, they came
there and started exciting and stirring up the mobs. 14 At once the
brothers sent Paul away to the coast; but both Silas and Timothy stayed
in Berea. 15 The men who were taking Paul went with him as far as
Athens. Then they went back to Berea with instructions from Paul that
Silas and Timothy join him as soon as possible. (17.10-15)

The section heading In Berea may need to be modified in the same manner as the first section heading In Thessalonica—for example, "Paul and His
Companions Have Trouble in Berea." On the other hand, one may express the
positive response of many of the people in Berea, "Many of the People in Berea Believe Paul."

The first sentence of this third paragraph of Chapter 17 is very important from the standpoint of transition. The first clause indicates time, and
the second clause relates to space and brings Paul and Silas to Berea, thus
setting the stage for the second major episode in this chapter.

17.10

The literal Greek expression "through night" obviously refers to that
very night, so that the entire expression "immediately through night" is rendered as soon as night came. The brothers most likely refers to the entire
Christian community of Thessalonica and not merely to the ones who had been
released (v. 9). Berea was about 60 miles west of Thessalonica and south of
the Ignatian Way.

The second part of verse 10 simply indicates that, as was his custom,
Paul visited the Jewish synagogue as one of the first things which he did upon
arrival in any new town or community.

17.11

Open-minded translates a word which originally referred to persons of
noble birth (see RSV "noble"), but which later came to be used of those qualities which were expected in a person of such birth. In the present context

the reference is to the attitude of the Bereans toward the Christian message and is best understood in the sense of "receptive." In a context such as this, open-minded may be rendered in some languages in a negative fashion—for example, "their minds were not closed" or "their ears were not stopped up." On the other hand, expressions for open-minded may be positive: "their minds received what he said," "their ears were opened to hear," or "they were willing to listen."

Listened to the message with great eagerness is rendered in some languages as "wanted very much to listen to the message" or "desired very much to hear what Paul said." The term eagerness is essentially the quality with which the people desired to listen and it is therefore possible to transfer this element of the meaning to a verb such as "to desire" or "to want to."

To see if what Paul said was really true literally translates "to see if these things were so." But the meaning, of course, is that the people of Berea studied the Scriptures to see if what Paul taught them was true. The NEB at this point is ambiguous, since the final "they" in the expression "whether it was as they said" could be understood in two different ways.

In some languages a translation of true, in referring to some statement or declaration, must be rendered by a verb "to agree with." Therefore, one may need to restructure this final sentence of verse 11 to read "every day they studied the Scriptures in order to see if what Paul had said agreed with what the Scriptures said" or "...to see if what was written in the Scriptures agreed with what Paul had said."

17.12

There are two possible interpretations of verse 12. One may assume that many of them refers to those who were in the synagogue and so were thus either Jews or the so-called "devout people" who accepted Jewish beliefs about God but who had not become proselytes. In this case, the additional expressions many Greek women and many Greek men would refer to other persons who had become interested in the message that Paul preached. On the other hand, it is possible to understand many of them believed as a general expression made more specific by the additional phrases many Greek women and many Greek men. If the latter is the interpretation adopted, one may translate: "Many of the people there believed. This included many Greek women of high social standing and many Greek men." Otherwise one may translate: "Many of the people there believed, and in addition there were many Greek women of high social standing and many Greek men who also believed."

Of high social standing translates the same word as was used in 13.50. This expression of high social standing may be rendered as "important" or, as in some contexts, "rich" (a designation for "rich" is equivalent in some societies to "important").

If some goal to the verbs believed is required, it is probably better to put in "Jesus" or even "Lord Jesus" rather than "what Paul had said." On the other hand, one can also introduce the phrase the word of God from verse 13.

17.13

The participles translated exciting and stirring up in the TEV have been interpreted by some scholars as expressing purpose---for example, "came there in order to excite and stir up the mobs." However, the present form of these participles would seem to suggest more the continuous nature of their activity rather than primarily the purpose for their coming, though obviously purpose is also suggested in the nature of the context itself. One should avoid the implication that the mobs were there all the time and that they were just stirred up by the Jews from Thessalonica. Therefore it may be necessary to say: "excited the people so that they formed mobs."

17.14

To the coast (literally "to the sea") in this instance refers to the Aegean Sea, where Paul could catch a ship for Athens. It is important, however, in translating the verb sent to indicate that Paul was not sent off alone; in verse 15 there were men who accompanied Paul and went with him as far as Athens. Therefore it may be necessary in verse 14 to translate: "sent Paul away with some other men to the coast."

17.15

In choosing a verb for taking, one should not suggest that Paul was being in any way escorted against his will. These men were simply "accompanying him."

In languages which clearly specify different means of travel, it may be necessary to employ here "sailed as far as Athens." Otherwise there would have been no point in Luke having commented about Paul going to the coast.

The word here translated instructions is often translated "command," a rendering which is too strong for the present context. The final clause of verse 15 must be rendered as direct discourse in a number of languages--- for example, "went back to Berea with words from Paul, Silas and Timothy must join me as soon as possible."

In Athens

16 While Paul was waiting in Athens for Silas and Timothy, he was greatly upset when he noticed how full of idols the city was. 17 So he argued in the synagogue with the Jews and the Gentiles who worshiped God, and in the public square every day with the people who happened to come by. 18 Certain Epicurean and Stoic teachers also debated with him. Some said, "What is this ignorant show-off trying to say?"

Others said, "He seems to be talking about foreign gods." They said this because Paul was preaching about Jesus and the resurrection.

19 So they took Paul, brought him before the meeting of the Areopagus, and said, "We would like to know this new teaching that you are talking about. 20 Some of the things we hear you say sound strange to us, and we would like to know what they mean." 21 (For all the citizens of Athens and the foreigners who lived there liked to spend all their time telling and hearing the latest new thing.) (17.16-21)

As in the case of the two preceding section headings, the expression In Athens may need to be somewhat augmented in order for it to make sense in this context—for example, "Paul Visits Athens" or "Paul Speaks to the People of Athens."

Paul's experiences in Athens are centered about two incidents: the preaching in the public square (vv. 16-21) and the speech before the council of the Areopagus (vv. 22-31). It is interesting to note that Athens is the only city where Paul preached without bringing persecution against himself.

17.16

In Paul's day Athens was a relatively small city and lived in the glory of its past. In light of the contribution that Athens had made to the world, the Roman government permitted the city to be free and an allied city with Rome.

The introductory clause, while Paul was waiting in Athens for Silas and Timothy, forms an excellent transition from the preceding verse 15 and also provides a setting for what follows.

Greatly upset is rendered as "exasperated" in several translations (NEB, Phillips, Goodspeed). The Greek literally says "his spirit was stirred up within him," and the reference may be either to Paul's anger, to his grief, or to his desire to win the Athenians over to the Christian message. In the present context it would seem that "angered" (Barclay) is too strong a term, and that Paul's reactions may best be described by saying either "he was upset" or "he was disturbed." An expression such as greatly upset is often rendered in a highly idiomatic form: "his heart was eating him" or "his stomach was hot." What is important about this expression is that it should indicate severe emotional concern without loss of temper, for Paul's whole approach to the people of Athens is reasoned as well as full of positive concern.

In many languages one cannot speak of a city being full of idols. One may, of course, have a "box full of idols" or even "a room full of idols," but a city simply is not capable of being "full of something." Therefore one must translate as "there were many, many idols in the city."

17.17

The transitional particle so introduces what Paul did as the result of his great concern about the city being full of idols.

Paul obviously divided his ministry in Athens between (1) the synagogue, where he argued with Jews and devout Gentiles concerning Jesus, and (2) the public square, where he discussed with people the theme of the Good News. The public square is literally "the market place," and it is felt by some that this was the market northwest of the Acropolis, where pottery was sold and which was the center of Athenian life and trade.

In rendering the expression with the people who happened to come by, it is important not to suggest that Paul grabbed such people and forced them to listen to him. In fact, it may be necessary to translate as "talked with the people who happened to come by and would listen to him."

17.18

The Epicureans and the Stoics were groups representing different schools of philosophy in Athens. For a description of these see the glossary. It is quite probable that some should be taken as a group other than the Epicurean and Stoic teachers. In translating the phrase Epicurean and Stoic teachers, one may wish to use some such expression as "teachers who were known as Epicureans or as Stoics." It will be important at this point to introduce some kind of marginal help to explain to the reader the major tenets of the Epicurean and Stoic philosophies.

Many languages do not have a term such as debate to express formalized arguing. Therefore one may simply employ "also argued with him."

It may be necessary to translate some said, in the second sentence of verse 18, as "some others said." This would mean that the following expression others said would need to be translated as "still others said."

Ignorant show-off translates a term which is rendered differently in almost every translation: "fellow with his scraps of learning" (Moffatt; see Barclay "fellow with his ill-digested scraps of knowledge"), "rag-picker" (Goodspeed), "parrot" (JB), "charlatan" (NEB), and "cock sparrow" (Phillips). The word was originally used of a small bird that went around picking up grain, and later was applied to persons who picked up food scraps and other odds and ends in the market place. Still later it came to be used figuratively of any person who picked up odd bits of information, and especially of one who was unable to put them together properly. In some languages the equivalent of this expression ignorant show-off may be "uneducated teacher," "self-declared wise man," or "word beggar."

Foreign gods may also be taken in the sense of "strange gods" (see JB "outlandish gods," Phillips "some more gods"), but most translators follow the former alternative, in the sense of "gods of foreign peoples."

They said this because Paul was preaching about Jesus and the resurrection is a parenthetical statement given by Luke and is not the comment of the persons with whom Paul was disputing.

The phrase Jesus and the resurrection is understood in one of two ways: (1) Paul was preaching about Jesus and the resurrection (probably not only about the resurrection of Jesus, but the doctrine of the resurrection in general), or (2) Paul's hearers thought he was speaking about two deities, Jesus (the male deity) and Resurrection (the female deity). In light of the fact that there were a number of religions in which the male deity was brought back to life by the female deity, it is possible that Paul's hearers understood him to be speaking of two gods, Jesus and Resurrection. However, inasmuch as Luke gives this as an explanation of what Paul was in fact preaching, it is extremely doubtful if the translation should be other than the TEV and most other translations have rendered: Jesus and the resurrection. In many languages, however, it is necessary to translate the resurrection as a verb expression---for example, "and that people rise from the dead." Note that the resurrection of the dead was a central issue. It is also introduced in verse 31 and was the element which provoked the protest described in verse 32.

17.19

The transitional particle so is important, since it marks the beginning of the next episode, resulting from what Paul had been saying to various persons.

In the choice of words for took and brought, one should not suggest that Paul was under arrest. In some languages it is necessary to render this as "invited him to come to" or "asked him to come to."

The Areopagus was "the hill of Ares." Ares was the Greek god of war, equivalent to the Roman god Mars. It was on this hill that the Athenian council met, and for this reason most commentators understand the reference to the Areopagus to be to the meeting of the council rather than to the hill itself. This is why the TEV has expanded Areopagus to the meeting of the Areopagus. See also "the Council of the Areopagus" (JB) and "the Court of Areopagus" (NEB), but in some languages the nearest equivalent may be "the council that met on the Areopagus." In Athens there were several places where speakers might lecture to the public, and it was the responsibility of this council to hear and pass judgment on those lecturers.

17. 20

Sound strange to us may be rendered as "we have never heard this before," "these are completely new to us," or "these are very different from what we have heard before."

17. 21

This sentence constitutes a parenthetical explanation by Luke concerning the activities of people in Athens.

Citizens of Athens may be rendered as "people who belong to the town of Athens" or even, as in some languages, "people who were born in the town of Athens." The expression the foreigners who lived there is "those who had come to live in Athens."

The final phrase telling and hearing the latest new thing may need to be somewhat expanded: "telling others the latest new thing they had heard and hearing from others something new."

> 22 Paul stood up in front of the meeting of the Areopagus and said, "Men of Athens! I see that in every way you are very religious. 23 For as I walked through your city and looked at the places where you worship, I found also an altar on which is written, 'To an Unknown God.' That which you worship, then, even though you do not know it, is what I now proclaim to you. 24 God, who made the world and everything in it, is Lord of heaven and earth, and does not live in temples made by men. 25 Nor does he need anything that men can supply by working for him, since it is he himself who gives life and breath and everything else to all men. 26 From the one man he created all races of men, and made them live over the whole earth. He himself fixed beforehand the exact times and the limits of the places where they would live. 27 He did this so that they would look for him, and perhaps find him as they felt around for him. Yet God is actually not far from any one of us;
> 28 as someone has said,
>> 'In him we live and move and exist.'
> It is as some of your poets have said,
>> 'We too are his children.'
> 29 Since we are God's children, we should not suppose that his nature is anything like an image of gold or silver or stone, shaped by the art and skill of man. 30 God has overlooked the times when men did not know, but now he commands all men everywhere to turn away from their evil ways. 31 For he has fixed a day in which he will judge the whole world with justice, by means of a man he has chosen. He has given proof of this to everyone by raising that man from death!"
>
> (17. 22-31)

Paul begins his speech before the council of the Areopagus by a reference to the altar which they have dedicated "To an Unknown God." From this he goes on to speak, in familiar Jewish terms, of the foolishness of idolatry, and then to remind them of the ways in which God has given evidence of himself in nature. Finally, Paul brings to their attention the fact that God will judge the world, and this by means of the man (Jesus Christ) whom he has chosen.

17. 22

In some languages a transitional particle such as "so" or "hence" may be necessary at this point in the text so as to indicate that Paul, in response to those in the meeting of the Areopagus, was now addressing the group. Such a particle would be equivalent to the structure of the Greek sentence itself.

In front of the meeting of the Areopagus (see JB "before the whole Council of the Areopagus," NEB "before the Court of Areopagus") is a much more natural expression in English than a literal rendering such as "standing in the middle of the Areopagus." Luke intends to say that Paul stood before the group to speak to them, rather than that Paul stood up in the middle of the hill of Ares.

In a number of languages one cannot employ an expression of direct address such as Men of Athens! without implying that Paul is in some way ordering, or calling to, such persons. However, this expression may be incorporated as the goal of the verb said—for example, "and said to the men of Athens," after which the direct discourse begins. In some languages there may be a contradiction in the use of the expression "men" when in verse 34 it is indicated that a woman by the name of Damaris responded positively to what Paul had said. It may be necessary, therefore, to employ a term such as "people of Athens"; but in many languages an expression for "men" may, by implication, also include women.

Commentators are divided in their opinion as to whether Luke intended to say very religious (in a good sense) or "superstitious" (in a bad sense). However, the TEV, NEB, RSV, JB, Goodspeed, Moffatt, Phillips, and Barclay all accept the former alternative. In some languages it is not easy to provide an appropriate equivalent for the expression very religious. In some cases one may simply translate "worship various gods very much," "are very much interested in the gods," or "have great respect for many gods."

If one adopts the interpretation of "superstitious," a rendering might be "you are very fearful of many gods."

17. 23

The places where you worship technically means "the object of your worship" (so RSV), and is rendered by JB as "sacred monuments." Although the word may technically mean "object or thing worshiped," in reality it was an object set up at a certain place where worship was offered to the god in whose name the object had been erected. It was customary for Greeks and others to dedicate altars to "unknown gods," for fear that in their worship they had omitted some god who might otherwise be offended. Inscriptions have been found indicating that certain altars were dedicated "to unknown gods," but thus far no inscription has been found dedicating an altar "to an unknown god," though no doubt such an altar existed in Athens in Paul's day. Since in many societies there are almost the exact equivalent of such places where you worship, it is usually not difficult to find a general term for such "shrines." In any event, one can always translate "the places where you worship various gods."

In some languages a clear distinction is made between something which is "written" and something which is "cut into stone." It is quite likely that in this instance the inscription "To an Unknown God" would be cut into stone.

Though you do not know it translates a participle which in Greek modifies the subject "you" rather than the verb "worship." The KJV ("whom therefore ye ignorantly worship") is incorrect in translating the participle by "ignorantly" as though it modifies the verb "worship." Paul is either telling the Athenians (1) that the unknown god whom they worship is indeed the true God, though they do not know it (TEV that which you worship then, even though you do not know it; Zürich "what therefore you worship without knowing it"; JB "whom you already worship without knowing it"), or (2) that the unknown god whom they worship is the true God, but he is unknown to them (NEB "what you worship but do not know"). The essence of Paul's message to the Athenians may be summed up in the following way: (1) this unknown god whom you worship is the true God though you do not know it; (2) you can learn much about this unknown God by observing what he has done in the creative order; (3) this true God will remain unknown to you until you meet him in the person of Jesus Christ.

Two other observations should be taken into consideration in the translation of this verse: (1) Paul uses the neuter that which...what rather than the masculine "he whom...whom." He begins with his hearers' belief in an impersonal divine being and goes from there to tell them about the living God, who is Creator and Judge of all men. (2) In the clause what I now proclaim to you, the pronoun "I" is emphatic.

There are a number of difficulties involved in the translation of the last sentence of verse 23. In the first place, it is impossible in a number of languages to represent the neuter forms that which, it, and what. Having once spoken of God, it is necessary to use some personal pronoun—for example, "the one whom you worship." Furthermore, there are difficulties with the embedded clause even though you do not know it. In fact, in many languages this must be placed at the end of the sentence as a kind of contrastive clause —for example, "the one whom you worship is the one I am proclaiming to you, but you do not realize this." On the other hand, if one adopts another exegesis of this final sentence, it is possible to translate: "you do not know the one whom you worship, but this is the one that I am now telling you about."

17. 24

The affirmation that God is both Creator and Lord of heaven and earth leads naturally to the conclusion that he does not live in temples made by men. Made by men (literally "handmade") designates that which is material, in contrast with what is spiritual.

In some languages it is difficult to find a general expression for everything in it. Obviously this does not refer to buildings or tools (which are man-made) but primarily to plants and animals. Therefore it may be necessary in some languages to say "God, who made the world and created all the plants and animals in it."

The expression Lord of heaven and earth may be rendered as "the Lord who rules heaven and earth." In this instance, of course, heaven is "the sky." Temples are relatively common in most parts of the world, but where they are not known one can always employ "houses made especially for God" or "houses made especially for worshiping God."

Moreover, since God has created everything, he is not in need of anything that men can do for him. In most languages it is impossible to continue the negative expression merely by a conjunction such as nor. The equivalent would be "in addition to this he does not need."

The phrase gives life and breath may be equivalent in some languages to "causes all creatures to live." In many languages one simply cannot distinguish between life and breath; they are simply synonymous expressions. Where both may be employed, it is possible to say "causes all creatures to live and causes them to breathe." But it is obvious that this type of terminology is quite redundant.

To all men, that is, "to all mankind," may also be taken in the sense of "to all living things." The context suggests that the first is to be preferred. The phrase everything else to all men may be rendered as "everything that all people need" or "whatever any person may need."

17.26

The phrase rendered from the one man (so also Zürich) is literally "from one." It seems most probable that Paul is referring to the widespread belief that God created all men from Adam (see Goodspeed, Phillips "from one forefather"), rather than a more general notion that all people were "from a common origin" (Moffatt; see NAB "from one stock," NEB "of one stock," Barclay "of one common stock"). The KJV rendering, "of one blood," is based upon a textual variant which has very little support. This first clause, from the one man he created all races of men, must often be rather extensively restructured—for example, "God created first one man and from that one man came all the races of people." If one adopts the alternative interpretation of this clause, it may be rendered as "God created all the different kinds of people from one single family" or "God created one single clan from which all the different races of people have come."

Made them live over the whole earth may be rendered as "caused them to live in different places all over the earth" or even "caused them to go to different places over the whole earth and to live there."

He himself fixed beforehand correctly translates the force of the Greek participle which describes action that took place before he created and made them live. In some languages it is impossible to translate beforehand without indicating specifically what event is being referred to; therefore "before he created them he decided when and where they would live."

Made them live (v. 26) and so that they would look for him (v. 27) (these two verses form one sentence in the Greek) are actually infinitives dependent upon the main verb in the sentence, created. It is possible to understand these infinitive clauses either in the sense of purpose or of result. The TEV has translated the second clause as one of purpose, while the first has been made into a construction parallel with the main verb created.

17. 27

The introductory expression <u>he did this</u> refers back to God's creation of all the races of men. It may be necessary to specify this—for example, "he created them so that...."

In the clause <u>perhaps find him as they felt around for him</u>, both verbs are understood to express either an obtainable possibility (TEV, Goodspeed, Moffatt, NEB) or an obtainable wish (RSV, Phillips, Barclay). An expression for <u>felt around for him</u> may come from the activity of blind persons feeling around in order to identify some object or so as to determine where they are.

<u>Yet God is actually not far from any one of us</u> translates a participial clause which in Greek denotes concession: "although (or, even though) God is not far." The particle <u>yet</u> is extremely important at this point, and it may be necessary to employ some such expression as "on the other hand" or "but in contrast with this."

The first person plural expressions in verses 27, 28, and 29 are, of course, inclusive.

17. 28

The words alluded to by Paul in this verse are thought to have originated with Epimenides, a poet living in Crete in the sixth century B.C. <u>In him</u> is rendered literally by most translators (though Goodspeed "through union with him") and suggests either a mystical union with God or a spatial nearness to him. It is quite possible, however, that <u>in him</u> is to be taken in the sense of "by (the power of) him," and this is supported by the observation that Paul's next quotation, <u>"We too are his children,"</u> refers not to a spatial nearness to God but rather to God as Creator, the one "by whom" all people were created.

In most languages it is relatively meaningless to use an expression such as <u>in him</u>. One can readily speak of God being "in a person," because it is understandable that a spirit can dwell inside of a person. However, it is almost impossible to conceive of a person dwelling inside of a spirit, which would be implied in an expression such as <u>in him</u>, referring to God. Accordingly, most translators find it necessary to employ some such expression as "in close union with him" or even "because of him." In fact, in some languages it is necessary to make <u>him</u> the subject—for example, "he is the one who causes us to live and move and to be what we are" or "...to exist."

<u>It is as some of your poets have said</u> may be taken as referring either to the quotation which precedes or to the one which follows, though it is more natural to take it with the one that follows, <u>"We too are his children."</u> The clause <u>it is as some of your poets have said</u> may be rendered as "some of your poets have also said something like this" (in which "this" must refer to what follows). <u>We too are his children</u> is equivalent to "even we are his children" or "all of us are his children."

17.29

   On the basis of what Paul has just said about the nature of God, he now has grounds for an attack against idolatry. Both by the particle with which Luke has chosen to begin this verse (see 1.6) and by the content of the verse itself, Luke indicates the beginning of a new phase in Paul's argument. This significant shift in the argument may be introduced by a particle such as "then" or "therefore."

   In a number of languages it is difficult to speak of "God's nature." The closest equivalent is simply "we should not think that God is anything like an image of gold." In such a context the term "God" is itself equivalent to "God's nature."

   An image of gold or silver or stone is "an image made out of gold or silver or stone." However, a term such as "made" may need to be more specific—for example, "an image smelted from gold or silver or an image cut from stone."

   In many languages one cannot speak of something being shaped by... art or skill. An image can, of course, be shaped "by a skillful and artistic person." Therefore, it is the man who must be made the agent of the shaping, and terms such as art and skill must be made attributive to the person—for example, "shaped by a skillful artisan."

17.30

   God has overlooked means that God did not punish men as they deserved; and the times when men did not know refers to the time before men came to know God's will in Jesus Christ. A verb such as overlooked should not be rendered in such a way as to imply that God was heedless or unconcerned; rather, one should employ some such expression as "God chose not to consider." In some languages this may be equivalent to "God has decided not to count up..." or "God determined not to count against people the time when they did not know."

   Though all men everywhere are commanded to turn away from their evil ways, Paul is speaking specifically to the people of Athens who now have come to hear of God in Jesus Christ. To turn away from their evil ways represents the word which most translators render "repent." A verb such as commands may require in some languages direct discourse—for example, "but now he commands all men in every place, Turn away from your evil ways."

17.31

   The Greek expressions "in justice" and "in a man" mean, as the TEV has indicated, with justice (see Goodspeed and NEB "justly") and by means of a man. The expression fixed a day may be rendered as "has decided that on a day" or "has determined a particular day."

   Will judge the whole world must be rendered in many languages as "will judge everyone in the world." Obviously it is not the earth itself which is to be judged, but "people on the earth." Judge ... with justice is equivalent to "judge justly," "judge rightly," or "judge with fairness." Sometimes this expression is rendered in a somewhat negative fashion—for example, "judge without making a mistake" or "judge so that no one can complain."

By means of a man indicates a secondary agency. This may be expressed as "he will cause a man to do the judging for him" or "a man whom he has chosen will do the judging."

Given proof of this is literally "having given faith," but most commentators understand "faith" in the present context to mean "assurance" or "proof." It is possible, as a few have done, to understand this entire phrase to mean that God has given all men the opportunity to have faith. Has given proof of this may be equivalent to "has shown clearly that he would do this" or "has shown so well that no one can doubt."

> 32 When they heard Paul speak about a raising from death, some of them made fun of him, but others said, "We want to hear you speak about this again." 33 And so Paul left the meeting. 34 Some men joined him and believed; among them was Dionysius, a member of the Areopagus, a woman named Damaris, and some others. (17.32-34)

It may be useful in introducing this final paragraph to employ some kind of transitional particle—for example, "but." This is in keeping with the Greek text, and at the same time it helps to prepare the reader for the response of Paul's audience.

17.32

In the same way that the Jews rejected the idea that the Messiah should suffer, so the Greeks refused to believe that someone could be raised from the dead. In some languages it is quite difficult to speak about a raising from death. One can, of course, always speak about "a person being raised from death" or "causing a person to live again." Therefore it may be necessary to introduce a person as the subject of such a raising from death.

It is impossible to know whether the statement We want to hear you speak about this again is to be taken as an attempt on the part of the people to make fun of Paul, or whether they were serious in their desire to hear further information. The Greek construction would imply that there were two sets of people, those who made fun of Paul and those who wanted to hear more of what he had to say. Again refers to another occasion.

17.33

The Greek adverb translated and so may refer to the circumstances under which Paul left (see Phillips "so with this mixed reception"), or it may have the weakened meaning of result or consequence, as in most translations.

Joined him may be rendered as "took sides with him" or "identified themselves with." The term believed must probably be understood in this context as "became believers." Certainly more is implied than merely "believed what Paul had said."

It is significant that Dionysius, a member of the Areopagus, became a believer, since the Areopagus was a closed body and to belong to it was a great honor. Neither Dionysius nor Damaris are mentioned elsewhere in the New Testament.

The final phrase and some others may be expressed as "and there were also some other people who believed."

CHAPTER 18

This chapter continues and brings to a conclusion Paul's second missionary journey. It deals primarily with Paul's missionary efforts in Corinth (vv. 1-17), and tells of his return to Syria (Palestine), and perhaps to Jerusalem (see comments on v. 22). Luke interrupts the Pauline narrative in order to tell something of the work of Apollos in Ephesus and Corinth (vv. 24-28), which indicates the importance which Luke assigned to Apollos in the early Christian movement.

From the standpoint of the discourse structure, Chapter 18 is divided essentially into three parts. The first (vv. 1-17) deals with various aspects of Paul's ministry in Corinth; the second (vv. 18-23) summarizes various stages in Paul's journey from Corinth to Asia Minor, on to Jerusalem, and then back to Asia Minor; and the last (vv. 24-28) describes the effectiveness of Apollos, with special emphasis upon his learning more correctly "the way of God."

In the first section (vv. 1-17) each important episode or phase of Paul's ministry in Corinth is introduced by a temporal connective: after this (v. 1), when Silas and Timothy arrived from Macedonia (v. 5), one night (v. 9), and when Gallio was made the Roman governor (v. 12). It is important that these features of temporal setting be clearly marked.

In Corinth

1 After this, Paul left Athens and went on to Corinth. 2 There he met a Jew named Aquila, born in Pontus, who had just come from Italy with his wife Priscilla, because Emperor Claudius had ordered all the Jews to leave Rome. Paul went to see them, 3 and stayed and worked with them, because he earned his living by making tents, just as they did. 4 He argued in the synagogue every Sabbath, trying to convince both Jews and Greeks.

5 When Silas and Timothy arrived from Macedonia, Paul gave his whole time to preaching the message, testifying to the Jews that Jesus is the Messiah. 6 When they opposed him and said evil things about him, he protested by shaking the dust from his clothes and saying to them, "If you are lost, you yourselves must take the blame for it! I am not responsible. From now on I will go to the Gentiles." 7 So he left them and went to live in the house of a Gentile named Titius Justus, who worshiped God; his house was next to the synagogue. 8 Crispus, the leader of the synagogue, believed in the Lord, he and all his family; and many other people in Corinth heard the message, believed, and were baptized. (18.1-8)

The section heading In Corinth may be amplified as "Paul Visits Corinth" or "Paul Announces the Good News in Corinth."

346

18.1

    Corinth was destroyed in 146 B.C., but it was rebuilt exactly a century later by Julius Caesar, and in 27 B.C. it became the capital of the province of Achaia. It was a commercial center and noted for its sexual immorality.

    In some languages one cannot employ a temporal marker such as after this. Rather, it is necessary to stipulate precisely what event is referred to—for example, "after Paul had spoken at the court of the Areopagus."

18. 2

    Aquila is further mentioned in verses 18, 19, and 26, as well as in Romans 16. 3; 1 Corinthians 16.19; 2 Timothy 4.19.

    Pontus was a Roman province which, along with Bithynia, formed a single administrative unit under the Roman government.

    Just translates an adverb which originally meant "freshly killed," but then had the derived meaning of "recently" (see NEB, Phillips).

    His wife Priscilla is again mentioned in connection with Aquila in verses 18, 19, and 26. The "Prisca" of the Greek in Romans 16. 3; 1 Corinthians 16.19; and 2 Timothy 4.19, each time mentioned in connection with "Aquila," is undoubtedly the same person, since the form Priscilla is simply a diminutive of Prisca. Aquila is never mentioned alone. It is almost certain that the same pair is referred to in each case.

    The order from Emperor Claudius for all the Jews to leave Rome was given about A.D. 49, but very little is known about the circumstances which provoked it. From indications outside the New Testament, it would seem as if there had been a squabble between Christian Jews and non-Christian Jews in Rome, and the trouble caused by their disagreements led to their banishment.

    A verb such as ordered may require direct discourse in some languages—for example, "had ordered, All you Jews must leave Rome."

18. 3

    Most translations assume that Paul earned his living by making tents, though some commentators (Moffatt, Barclay) understand the word to mean that Paul was a leatherworker. Earned his living is translated in some languages as "earned money to buy food" or "by working making tents he received food and shelter."

    The expression just as they did may be rendered as "they also did the same kind of work" or "they also made tents." In some languages it is necessary to specify that the making of these tents was not for their own use but in order to sell as a part of their trade. Therefore the translation may be rendered as "they made tents and sold them."

18. 4

    Though "held discussions" is a possible rendering of the Greek word translated <u>argued</u>, in the present context something stronger seems necessary---for example, "argue" or "debate." In some languages the equivalent of <u>argued</u> in this type of context would be "to speak strongly" or "to talk urgingly."

The verb <u>convince</u> may be equivalent to "to cause to believe," "to receive what he said as true," or even "to cause them to say yes to what he said."

<u>18.5</u>

For the possible relationship of the movements of Timothy and Silas in Acts and in Paul's writings (1 Thessalonians 2.17—3.5), see various commentaries. It must be remembered that both Luke and Paul have included in their records only what was of concern and importance to them; neither has tried to give an exhaustive account of all that took place. This is the last time that Silas is mentioned in Acts. The introductory clause <u>when Silas and Timothy arrived from Macedonia</u> is a very important transitional device, since it marks the time when Paul gave up working with Aquila and Priscilla and devoted himself full time to preaching the message.

<u>Gave his whole time to</u> translates a verb which literally means "to hold together" (see 7.57; 28.8); here it is used in the sense of "give (one's) whole time to" or "to be completely occupied with." <u>Gave his whole time to</u> may also be rendered as "did nothing else but" or "worked only at."

In a number of languages one cannot speak of <u>preaching the message</u>. There must be some kind of goal or content of the message---for example, "the message about Jesus."

In this context the verb <u>testifying</u> may be equivalent to "showing clearly" or "explaining carefully."

When in Greek two nouns occur together as subject and as predicate complement, it is normal for the subject to occur with the article and for the predicate to be without the article. Therefore, <u>Jesus is the Messiah</u> may be translated as "the Messiah is Jesus," since the definite article appears with Messiah. As some commentators have suggested, the Christian missionaries had to begin their preaching in the Jewish synagogues with the known, <u>the Messiah</u>, and go from there to the unknown, <u>Jesus</u>, which would account for this construction in Greek. As in so many languages, the subject expression normally marks given information, while the predicate identifies new information. It is on this basis that one may argue that this final clause may be rendered as "the Messiah, whom they know about, was indeed Jesus," since Jesus would have been the unknown element as far as Paul's hearers were concerned. However, this type of order would seem quite strange to the average reader of the New Testament who would be much more familiar with the person of Jesus than he would with the designation of Jesus as the Messiah. Therefore, to the reader, it is the Messiahship of Jesus which is presumably the new information, while Jesus, as a historical person, is well accepted as given information. It is for this reason that so many translations (for example, Phillips, Luther Revised, Segond, Goodspeed, Zürich), employ the arrangement "Jesus was the Messiah." Others retain the Greek structure "the Messiah is Jesus" (RSV, NEB, Moffatt).

18.6

The verb protested is rendered in some languages as "answered back strongly," "said in response," or "declared with strong words."

By shaking the dust from his clothes is literally in Greek "shaking his clothes." Although the same verb is used here as appears in 13.51, no "dust" is specifically mentioned in this Greek text, and here "clothes" are specified, not "feet." However, it is natural to relate these two expressions and to assume that the words of Paul which immediately follow reflect the correct interpretation of this gesture. Also, the meaning of the idiom "shaking his clothes" is indicated by the verb protested. Therefore, there should be little difficulty for the reader in understanding the meaning of this action. It is always possible to introduce at this point a marginal note to explain such a gesture and to refer to other parallel expressions in the Scriptures. Some translators may prefer to employ a receptor language idiom at this point—for example, "waved his arms" or "turned his back," while in some cases indicating the idiom of the Greek text in the margin.

If you are lost, you yourselves must take the blame for it translates the Jewish formula "your blood (be) on your own head" (see 2 Samuel 1.16; Matthew 27.25). This expression means that the person upon whose head the blood comes must assume responsibility for the decision and/or action. Although most translators render this literally, it would seem best to express the meaning of the passage rather than to reproduce a verbal correspondence, since it is doubtful whether many people would understand the true significance of the phrase unless they had been conditioned by a good background in biblical terminology. In fact, the literal rendering of this Semitic idiom is often quite meaningless; and if people do try to assign meaning to it, they frequently misunderstand its implications. It should certainly never be translated literally without some kind of marginal note. At the same time, the expression if you are lost may likewise be somewhat misleading, unless one understands a good deal of biblical teaching about being lost. In some translations this expression can be rendered as "if you are lost from God," "if you cut yourselves off from God," "if you cause yourselves to perish," or "if you cause yourselves to be condemned by God." All of these expressions relate in one way or another to a person's final condemnation and separation from God.

I will go to the Gentiles should not mean merely that Paul was leaving his present residence and going to live in the house of a Gentile. It may be necessary, therefore, to render this final sentence of verse 6 as "From now on I will go and preach to the Gentiles" or "From now on I will leave you and go preach to the Gentiles."

18. 7

Them is literally "these" in Greek, but them is a more natural rendering in English. In the Greek text "these" refers back to the Jews to whom
Paul had just spoken.

If Titius Justus is the correct reading (there is considerable disagreement in the Greek manuscripts), this is the only time he is mentioned in the
New Testament. Who worshiped God is the same phrase which appears in
16.14.

18. 8

Crispus is mentioned here and in 1 Corinthians 1.14.

The word represented by family may be expanded to mean "people of
his household."

The verb tenses translated heard and believed suggest that the persons
who did so heard and believed over a period of time rather than at a single
moment. The Greek has no expressed object of the verb heard, though most
translators supply either the "message" (Phillips) or "Paul" (RSV, Goodspeed). Some translators, however, supply no object but simply have "listened and believed" (NEB; see also Moffatt).

The passive expression were baptized may be rendered active as "Paul
baptized them." Note there is a specific reference to the baptism of Crispus
in 1 Corinthians 1.14, and though the family of Crispus is not specifically
mentioned, there is a parallel reference in 1 Corinthians 1.16 to Stephanas
and his family. Rather than making Paul the agent of the baptizing, it may
be possible to use what might be called a substitute passive by saying "they
received baptism," "they underwent baptism," or "they experienced the rite
of baptism."

9 One night Paul had a vision, in which the Lord said to him,
"Do not be afraid, but keep on speaking and do not give up, 10 because
I am with you. No one will be able to harm you, because many in this
city are my people." 11 So Paul stayed there for a year and a half,
teaching the people the word of God.

12 When Gallio was made the Roman governor of Greece, the
Jews got together, seized Paul and took him into court. 13 "This man,"
they said, "is trying to persuade people to worship God in a way that is
against the law!"

14 Paul was about to speak, when Gallio said to the Jews, "If this
were a matter of some wrong or evil crime that has been committed,
it would be reasonable for me to be patient with you Jews. 15 But since
it is an argument about words and names and your own law, you yourselves must settle it. I will not be the judge of such things!" 16 And he
drove them out of the court. 17 They all grabbed Sosthenes, the leader
of the synagogue, and beat him in front of the court. But that did not
bother Gallio a bit. (18. 9-17)

18. 9

In languages which do not have a technical term for vision, one may say "the Lord appeared to Paul in his sleep" or "the Lord appeared to Paul as in a dream."

Do not be afraid and keep on speaking translate present imperatives in Greek, which have the force of "stop doing" or "continue doing what you are in the process of doing." Do not give up (literally "do not become silent") translates a Greek tense which means "do not begin (to do action of verb)." In many languages, however, one cannot speak of "being afraid" without stipulating the goal of the fear. Similarly, a verb such as "speaking" may require the identification of those to whom one is speaking, and an admonition "not to give up" may likewise require some more specific mention of what is involved. Therefore this particular statement of the Lord to Paul may be translated as "do not be afraid of these men, but keep on speaking to them and do not stop doing what you are doing."

18.10

No one will be able to harm you translates "no one will come against you to do you harm." Normally a construction of this type would express purpose; however, in light of verse 12, where an attack was made against Paul, it may be that the meaning is result rather than purpose. JB suggests purpose, "no one will even attempt to hurt you," as does Barclay, "no one will try to harm you"; see also NEB text and note. On the other hand, Moffatt, "no one shall attack and injure you," and C. B. Williams, "no one is going to attack you so as to injure you," suggest result as the meaning of the infinitive construction.

My people recalls the Old Testament terminology, "God's people"— here not the Jewish people, but the believers. My people may be translated as "people who belong to me."

18.11

This verse and the next are important for establishing a Pauline chronology, and the translator should consult the commentaries. The Greek pronoun "he" obviously refers to Paul: so Paul stayed there for a year and a half. Most commentators understand the reference to a year and a half to mean the total amount of time that Paul stayed in Corinth, rather than a year and a half after this event. If one understands the reference to a year and a half as being the total time that Paul stayed in Corinth, it may be necessary to translate this verse as "so altogether Paul stayed in Corinth for a year and a half" or "the total time that Paul stayed in Corinth was a year and a half." The expression a year and a half may be more conveniently rendered in some languages as "eighteen months," especially if a span of time such as this is more frequently described in terms of months (or moons) rather than years.

The final phrase the word of God should probably be taken in the sense of "the message that comes from God," since the content of the message was primarily Jesus Christ. It is essential to avoid an expression which will imply merely the Bible.

18.12

Gallio assumed the governorship of Greece around A.D. 51 and Luke has used the correct technical term to describe the office of Gallio, Roman governor. Greece is literally "Achaia" (18.27; 19.21), the Roman province that included the most important part of Greece. In the Roman system a governor was an "appointed ruler"; in some languages the equivalent is "an appointed big chief." But the passive expression was made is difficult to render in many languages; therefore, one may say "the Roman authorities caused Gallio to be the ruler of Greece."

Got together is actually an adverb (see 1.14) which must be taken closely with the verb seized. The verb which the TEV has translated seized appears only here in the New Testament. It appears in some other translations as "made an attack" (RSV, see Phillips) and "set upon" (NEB); and so the entire phrase got together, seized is translated "made a united attack upon" (RSV), "banded together to attack" (Phillips), and "set upon in a body" (NEB).

Took him into court may be translated in some languages as "caused him to go before the governor (or ruler) to be judged."

18.13

The phrase they said, which introduces direct discourse, may require some type of goal—for example, "they said to Gallio."

The Greek term, literally rendered "persuading," is taken by the TEV as trying to persuade. Commentators disagree in their understanding of what "law" is referred to in the expression against the law, whether Jewish law or Roman law. In 16.20 and 17.7 Paul is accused of breaking the Roman law, and some scholars assume that the accusation in 18.13 is parallel. On the other hand, the reference to law in verse 15 might be taken to support the theory that the Jewish law is the one in question. Probably what happened is that the Jews accused Paul of proclaiming a religion which did not have legal status with the Roman government, while Gallio sees in their accusations nothing more than squabbles about their own Jewish religion, so he refuses to concern himself with their charges.

Against the law is rendered in some languages as "does not agree with the law," "does not say the same thing as the law," or "causes a person to violate the law." In many languages the law cannot be used in the singular as a collective. Rather, one must employ a plural—for example, "against the rules" or "contrary to the laws."

18.14

In such contexts as the present, the literal expression "to open the

mouth" means simply to speak. In Greek the conditional sentence beginning
with if makes clear that Gallio is saying the matter is not one of some wrong
or evil crime, and therefore he will not be patient with the Jews. Evil crime,
a word which occurs only here in the New Testament (see the related word
evil tricks in 13.10), originally meant "prank" or "mean trick," but its connection with the word wrong seems to imply that for Luke and his readers it
must have had a more serious connotation. "Crime" appears in NAB, RSV,
Twentieth Century, Moffatt; JB translates both these terms together as
"crime," comparable to what the Luther Revised has done. On the other
hand, some translators attempt to keep the etymological connection and so
render "fraud" (Barclay) and "underhanded rascality" (C. B. Williams).

The passive expression that has been committed can be made active,
with Paul as the subject—for example, "that this man Paul has committed."

It would be reasonable for me may be rendered as "it would be only
right for me" or "I would rightly be patient."

The term patient, in this type of context, may be rendered as "listen
to you attentively to the end," "listening with understanding," or even as in
some languages "listen to you in a friendly way."

18.15

The pronominal reference of it may be difficult to represent readily in
some receptor languages. One may use an expression such as "this accusation involved an argument about...." When, however, one cannot employ a
noun such as argument, the appropriate equivalent may be "but since you are
only arguing about words."

The phrase your own law may be rendered as "the rules that apply only
to you" or "the laws that only you people follow."

You yourselves must settle it actually translates a future tense, but in
Greek the future is sometimes used as the equivalent of an imperative. I will
not be the judge of such things is said in such a way that "judge" is the emphatic element, literally "a judge of these things I am not willing to be." The
use of a term such as judge, referring to such issues as were presented by
the Jews before Gallio, is rendered in some languages as "decide such matters" or "say what is right and what is wrong."

18.16

Drove them out of the court must usually be interpreted as a causative
"caused them to be driven out of the court" or "caused soldiers to force them
out of the court."

18.17

In the statement they all grabbed, the pronoun they may refer either to
the Jews or to the Gentiles; the text is not clear and commentators differ.

The name Sosthenes appears only here and in 1 Corinthians 1.1. Although the identity is not certain, there are many who believe that these men are one and the same; the appearance of the name in the papyri is rare enough to make a good case for the identity of the two. If Sosthenes mentioned here is identical with the Sosthenes mentioned in the first verse of the first letter to the Corinthians, it would presumably be the Jews who beat him in front of the court. On the other hand, if Sosthenes, the leader of the synagogue was the ringleader of those who were opposing Paul, it is understandable that the Gentiles might have beaten Sosthenes. This seems to be slightly more probable in view of Gallio's complete lack of concern. Having driven the Jews from the court, it would be unlikely that he would be completely unconcerned about their attacking a Christian who was identified with Paul. The same person Sosthenes, however, could at this time have been a leader of the synagogue and later be identified with the Christian community.

The Return to Antioch

18 Paul stayed on in Corinth with the brothers for many days, then left them and sailed off with Priscilla and Aquila for Syria. Before sailing he made a vow in Cenchreae and had his head shaved. 19 They arrived in Ephesus, where Paul left Priscilla and Aquila. He went into the synagogue and argued with the Jews. 20 They asked him to stay with them a long time, but he would not consent. 21 Instead, he told them as he left, "If it is the will of God, I will come back to you." And so he sailed from Ephesus.

22 When he arrived at Caesarea he went to Jerusalem and greeted the church, and then went to Antioch. 23 After spending some time there he left. He went through the region of Galatia and Phrygia, strengthening all the believers. (18.18-23)

The section heading The Return to Antioch is not too satisfactory, since verses 18 through 23 deal with far more than the return to Antioch. In fact, going to Antioch seems to be a relatively minor aspect of Paul's continuing journey. Nevertheless, there does not seem to be any more satisfactory way of identifying these two paragraphs which are essentially transitional---that is to say, they are designed to prepare the way for a statement concerning Apollos and then to reintroduce Paul in Ephesus at the beginning of Chapter 19. It may be necessary to amplify the section heading somewhat by saying "Paul Returns to Antioch." Though in English it is common to employ the present tense of a verb in this kind of context, in many other languages it is essential to use past tense forms for all such headings: "Paul Returned to Antioch." One may, however, specify more than Antioch---for example, "Paul Journeys from Corinth to Antioch."

18.18

Left is translated by some as "said good-bye to" (Moffatt, Goodspeed,

Barclay). The choice between left and "said good-bye to" is insignificant as far as translation is concerned, and the choice is largely stylistic.

In rendering sailed off with Priscilla and Aquila one should not imply that there were only three persons in the boat. This may be avoided by translating "boarded a ship sailing for Syria; Priscilla and Aquila also went along."

The word translated shaved appears only here and in 1 Corinthians 11. 6. The basic meaning of this verb is "to cut (hair)." In the papyri it is used of shearing sheep, and later in a figurative sense of "plunder" or "ravage." In 1 Corinthians 11. 6 it appears in conjunction with another verb, and if there is any distinction to be made between the two, the word used here indicates that scissors are required, while the other verb would specify a razor. At least this distinction is apparently made in 1 Corinthians 11. 6. However, some translators (NAB, Twentieth Century, Moffatt) understand the meaning in this present context to be "shaved," which would imply the use of a razor. When used in the middle form of the verb, as here, it would mean "have (one's head) shaved." Although grammatically possible, it is not likely that Luke intends to say that it was Aquila, rather than Paul, who had his head shaved.

The word translated vow is used in the sense of "prayer" in James 5.15, though in 21. 23 (the only other place where it appears in the New Testament) it has the meaning of "vow." It is evident that the vow referred to was a Nazirite vow (see Numbers 6.1-21). Originally this was a permanent vow, but in later times one could take the vow for a stated period of time. The vow was concluded by the offering of a sacrifice and by the cutting of one's hair, since one aspect of the vow was not to cut one's hair during the length of the vow. The translation of vow may involve a phrase "make a promise to God" or, as in some languages, "make a strong promise and call upon God to witness it." The same concept may be expressed as "make a strong promise in the presence of God."

Cenchreae (used only here and in Romans 16.1) was the seaport of Corinth on the eastern side of the isthmus.

18.19-20

Ephesus was located near the mouth of the Cayster River. It was the capital of the Roman province of Asia and one of the most important commercial centers.

Paul left Priscilla and Aquila is literally "he left them," but for the English reader it helps to make the pronominal references explicit. This reference to Paul leaving Priscilla and Aquila goes most naturally with the last clause of verse 21, and so he sailed from Ephesus. In fact, this is no doubt the intent. One must certainly not give the impression that Paul left Priscilla and Aquila on the boat going on to Syria while he stopped off in Ephesus. It is Priscilla and Aquila who remained in Ephesus and were able to instruct Apollos (see v. 24). The second clause of verse 19 may, however, be made more satisfactory by translating "where Paul later left Priscilla and Aquila." This, then, makes it possible to combine this clause with the last clause of verse 21.

It is not clear who the subject of asked him is. Grammatically it would be the Jews, but it is difficult to imagine that they asked Paul to return to their synagogue if he had argued with them. Possibly Luke intends for the reader to understand that some of the persons in the synagogue were receptive, or at least not opposed, to the message of Paul, and these were the Jews who invited him back. Because of the obvious difficulties of relating they to the immediately preceding term Jews, it may be necessary to translate "some of them asked him to stay." On the other hand, one may employ "the believers asked him to stay."

18.21

If it is the will of God is a formula apparently adopted from non-Jewish sources. For similar expressions see 1 Corinthians 4.19; 16.7; James 4.15. This clause is rendered in some languages as "if this is what God wants," "if God causes it to happen," or "if God desires that I come back."

As in verse 18, it is important to select a term for sailed which implies that Paul himself did not sail his own boat—for example, "he got into a ship and was sailed off from Ephesus."

18.22

He went to Jerusalem and greeted the church is literally "he went up and greeted the church." Although Jerusalem is not mentioned in the Greek, the verb "go up" is regularly used of going (up) to Jerusalem, and for that reason a number of translators and commentators believe that Jerusalem is the object of Paul's journey here. This theory is strengthened by the observation that in the next clause Luke merely says that Paul went to Antioch. There is no mention, in this latter instance, of any greeting to the church.

Among the translations that include Jerusalem are Phillips, Twentieth Century, Luther Revised, C. B. Williams, Goodspeed; also see JB and Zürich, which give an explanatory note indicating that Jerusalem is intended. The Antioch referred to is Antioch in Syria.

18.23

In 16.6 it is said that Paul traveled through the region of Phrygia and Galatia. Here Luke states that Paul went through the region of Galatia and Phrygia. Scholars are sharply divided on the interpretation of these two phrases and the relationship between them. However, it is quite likely that the variation is a matter of style and not a change in meaning. Luke probably means that Paul went to the same regions as he visited before; and it is likely that the expression the interior of the province (19.1) is intended as a summary statement of the same geographical regions as are mentioned in these two earlier passages.

Believers is literally "disciples," but these terms are to be equated in this type of context.

Apollos in Ephesus and Corinth

24 A certain Jew named Apollos, born in Alexandria, came to Ephesus. He was an eloquent speaker and had a thorough knowledge of the Scriptures. 25 He had been instructed in the Way of the Lord, and with great enthusiasm spoke and taught correctly the facts about Jesus. However, he knew only the baptism of John. 26 He began to speak boldly in the synagogue. When Priscilla and Aquila heard him, they took him home with them and explained to him more correctly the Way of God. 27 Apollos decided to go to Greece, so the believers in Ephesus helped him by writing to their brothers in Greece, urging them to welcome him there. When he arrived, he was a great help to those who through God's grace had become believers. 28 For with his strong arguments he defeated the Jews in public debates, proving from the Scriptures that Jesus is the Messiah. (18. 24-28)

The section heading Apollos in Ephesus and Corinth may not be too meaningful in some languages, and therefore one may employ a title such as "Apollos Preaches in Ephesus and Corinth" or "Apollos Explains the Way of the Lord in Ephesus and Corinth."

18. 24

Born in Alexandria may be translated as "Alexandria was his home town" or "he came originally from Alexandria." In many languages one does not translate literally born. It may be useful to have a marginal note at this point explaining that Alexandria was in Egypt and was one of the leading cities of the ancient world. It was particularly important as a center of learning.

The word translated eloquent occurs only here in the New Testament, and though most translators prefer this rendering (NAB, NEB, RSV, JB, Twentieth Century, Goodspeed; see also Zürich and Luther Revised, as well as Segond), Moffatt and Barclay choose "a man of culture," and others have either "learned" or a "man of learning." If the term translated eloquent is a reference to Apollos' capacity as a speaker, one may translate "he could speak very well," "he was a great orator," or "he spoke so that everyone wanted to listen." If, on the other hand, one interprets this term as applying to the extent of Apollos' knowledge, one may translate "he knew very much" or "he was a man who had studied very much."

Had a thorough knowledge of the Scriptures is literally "powerful in the Scriptures," but the meaning is that Apollos knew the Jewish Scriptures thoroughly. In some languages one does not speak of a thorough knowledge of

18. 25

the Scriptures but "knowing what is in the writings," since the focus is upon the content, not upon the form.

18. 25

The passive expression had been instructed in may be rendered as "he had learned thoroughly about."

The idiom "boiling over in spirit" appears in the TEV as with great enthusiasm. Most translators take "spirit" to mean Apollos' own spirit, with the meaning with great enthusiasm or "filled with enthusiasm." However, some see here a reference to the Holy Spirit. In this type of context, enthusiasm may be rendered as "great earnestness," "he meant strongly what he was saying," or even "he spoke as one who knew that what he was talking about was very important."

On the baptism of John see 1. 22.

18. 26

As in several contexts, boldly may be translated by expressions which refer either to the content of what is said or to the speaker's attitude or reaction to the receptors. In the first instance, one may render this as "he spoke fully everything" or "he said everything strongly." If, however, a term for boldly depends primarily upon the presumed attitude toward the receptors, one may translate as "he spoke to the people without being afraid" or "he spoke to the people without fear for who would be listening."

Took him home (so many translations: NAB, Twentieth Century, Goodspeed, Moffatt) is a meaning well supported by the use of this verb elsewhere in the New Testament (see 28. 2; Romans 14.1; 15. 7a). However, it may mean simply "take aside" (Phillips). The rendering "took an interest in" (JB) does not seem strong enough. The most satisfactory equivalent in some languages is "they invited him to their home."

The phrase the Way of God is, of course, parallel to the preceding phrase the Way of the Lord (v. 25). The equivalent in a number of languages is "the way that God has shown" or "the road that God has shown that people should take." This depends upon the use of a word such as "road" with figurative meaning to designate "way of life" or "manner of conduct."

18. 27

The TEV takes him as the object of the verb helped, a verb which may also mean "encourage" or "urge." The problem is that this verb has no stated object. To whom did the believers in Ephesus give help or encouragement, to Apollos or to the Corinthians? Goodspeed and Moffatt indicate that it was given to the church in Corinth, while NAB, NEB, RSV, TEV, Phillips, Barclay, Luther Revised, Segond, and Zürich specify that the help was given to Apollos.

Urging them to welcome him there may require direct discourse in some languages: "they urged them, Please welcome Apollos when he comes there."

Those who...had become believers translates a Greek perfect tense which has the force of "those who had believed and kept on believing." Those who through God's grace had become believers translates "those who through grace had believed," but in the context grace is "God's grace." It is difficult in many languages to speak of becoming a believer through God's grace. Grace in itself indicates an activity by God, and thus in many languages one cannot employ a preposition such as through to identify an instrument, particularly if this instrument is an event such as "grace" implies. Therefore the closest equivalent is "who had become believers in Jesus because God was so good to them."

18. 28

With his strong arguments he defeated the Jews is literally "powerfully he defeated (by argument) the Jews." With his strong arguments is rendered in a number of languages as a clause with a principal verb "because he argued so strongly with them."

He defeated the Jews in public debates may be translated as "before the people he showed that the Jews were wrong."

Proving from the Scriptures may be translated as "by citing the Scriptures he proved," "he quoted the Scriptures in order to prove," or "he quoted the Scriptures and in this way showed clearly."

CHAPTER 19

In this chapter regarding Paul's work at Ephesus, Luke gives many details of local color (see exegesis below), even as he does in the account about Paul's work in Athens. Commentators raise questions on two points: (1) Why did Luke omit so many important details which are found in Paul's own letters? (2) Why did Luke select these particular events to narrate (for example, the story about the disciples of John, the narrative about the sons of Sceva, and the uproar about the goddess Artemis)? Fortunately, these are not questions which translators have to concern themselves with in detail, though a proper perspective on them will enable one to understand this section of Acts more accurately, and so to translate more effectively.

The first question itself is not very difficult and has been considered in certain other passages. We simply need to remind ourselves that it was not Luke's concern to give a detailed account of everything that happened in the early history of Christianity. Rather, he was concerned to select those events which would carry out the emphasis that he himself intended. The second question is related to the first. Luke obviously chose to give the accounts recorded in Chapter 19 because in some way or another they fitted in with his overall and/or immediate purpose. Whatever else Luke intends to accomplish by the story of the twelve believers in Ephesus, he certainly makes it clear that the gift of the Holy Spirit comes only upon those who acknowledge the Lordship of Jesus Christ (v. 5). The remainder of this chapter serves to contrast Christianity with the various magical practices, and so underlines the supernatural power of Christianity and its obvious truth, as recognized by the Gentile authorities in the city.

Though the section headings in the TEV suggest three major parts to this 19th chapter, from the standpoint of the discourse structure there are really four sections. The first section (vv. 1-7) deals with the issue of the baptism of John and how this contrasts with being baptized in the name of the Lord Jesus. The second section (vv. 8-10) describes in general terms Paul's ministry in Ephesus, the key city of that part of Asia.

The third section (vv. 11-20) is actually divided into two major parts: (1) the activity of the sons of Sceva, introduced by a mention of the unusual miracles performed through Paul, and (2) the public burning of books concerning magic. In a sense, mention of this last episode prepares the way for the introduction of the riot in Ephesus, since this was a normal reaction of persons to the growing strength of the Christian movement.

The fourth section (vv. 21-41) describes in detail the riot in Ephesus, but seems to focus primarily upon the attitude of the provincial authorities mentioned in verse 31, and of the city clerk, who provides an admirable defense of the Christian movement as far as its presumed legality is concerned.

Paul in Ephesus

1 While Apollos was in Corinth, Paul traveled through the interior of the province and arrived in Ephesus. There he found some disciples, 2 and asked them, "Did you receive the Holy Spirit when you believed?"

"We have not even heard that there is a Holy Spirit," they answered.

3 "Well, then, what kind of baptism did you receive?" Paul asked. "The baptism of John," they answered.

4 Paul said, "The baptism of John was for those who turned from their sins; and he told the people of Israel to believe in the one who was coming after him—that is, in Jesus."

5 When they heard this, they were baptized in the name of the Lord Jesus. 6 Paul placed his hands on them, and the Holy Spirit came upon them; they spoke in strange tongues and also proclaimed God's message. 7 They were about twelve men in all. (19.1-7)

The section heading Paul in Ephesus may need to be altered into a complete sentence—for example, "Paul Preaches in Ephesus" or "Paul Speaks of Jesus in Ephesus."

The first clause of this paragraph while Apollos was in Corinth is an important transitional device, since it ties this paragraph with what precedes. For the most part, this paragraph is simply an exchange of statements between some believers and Paul. It is essential that the speakers in each instance be clearly indicated, either by specific mention of who is involved, or by contrast in the words for speaking—for example, "asked" or "replied."

19.1

The interior of the province is an abbreviated statement covering the same geographical areas mentioned in 18.23. Both from the immediate context and from Luke's use of "disciples" elsewhere in Acts, one must conclude that the disciples referred to here are considered Christian believers and not merely "disciples of John the Baptist."

In some languages it is necessary to specify the means by which Paul traveled. Presumably this would have been on foot, though it is possible that he traveled on horseback or by some wagon-like conveyance.

The term there which introduces the second sentence in verse 1 is an important transitional device referring back to Ephesus.

A translation of found must not imply that Paul was necessarily looking for such disciples. It simply means that he "met up with some disciples." In this context disciples may very well be translated as "believers."

19.2

As in many other instances, receive the Holy Spirit must be translated as "have the Holy Spirit come on you" or "have the Holy Spirit control you."

19.3

The participle translated when you believed means, as the NEB and JB
have it, "when you became believers," that is, when you became Christians.

For stylistic reasons one may, in English, employ expressions such
as asked them, they answered, Paul asked, and Paul said, either preceding
or following the direct discourse. In some languages, however, all such expressions which signal direct discourse must occur preceding what is said.
In other languages they normally follow, and in still other languages there
may be an expression which precedes and another which follows every direct
discourse. Obviously, in every receptor language one must adjust to the
norms of such usage.

19.3

The question which Paul puts to these disciples is not a question regarding the manner of their baptism, as might be suggested by some translations,
"How then were you baptized?" (Goodspeed; see also JB, Phillips). When Paul
asked them what kind of baptism did you receive? (so also Barclay), he is
asking them what was the meaning or significance of their baptism. And the
answer that they give to this question is the baptism of John, by which they
indicate that the meaning of their baptism was the same as that which John
the Baptist had proclaimed.

In some languages it is extremely difficult to speak of what kind of
baptism did you receive? since one cannot "receive baptism." One can, of
course, be "baptized" or "someone can baptize someone." In some languages
the closest equivalent of Paul's question to the believers is "What did it mean
when you were baptized?" The answer would then be "It meant what John said
was involved when people were baptized." In this way one may refer to the
preaching of John concerning turning away from sins and being forgiven. A
literal translation of the baptism of John might very well apply only to John
himself being baptized, or to John doing the baptizing. But this is obviously
not what is meant in this passage. In some translations, the baptism of John
is simply indicated as "the baptism which John spoke about." (See 1.22.)

19.4

Paul now explains the relationship between the baptism of John and the
baptism of which he is speaking. A literal translation of the Greek phrase
"baptism of repentance" is of little or no meaning to the English reader, because the relationship between baptism and repentance is not qualified. According to the accounts in the Gospels, John baptized only those persons who
had repented (that is, turned from their sins), and for this reason the TEV
has made the phrase explicit: the baptism of John was for those who turned
from their sins. The word people used by Luke in this verse is a term which
is used throughout the Septuagint and also in the New Testament to refer to
the people of Israel as opposed to the Gentiles, and for that reason the TEV
has made this meaning explicit.

The verb of speaking in he told the people of Israel may need to be followed by direct discourse—for example, "he told the people of Israel, You must believe in the one who is coming after me. That is, you must believe in Jesus." This will result in one direct discourse within another, but two such levels of discourse are usually not too heavy.

19.5

The believers are willing, and so they permit themselves to be baptized. It is doubtful if this is to be referred to as rebaptism, since from the point of view of Luke these people were never really baptized in the Christian sense up to this time.

The pronoun they may be potentially ambiguous since literally reproduced it might in some receptor languages refer to the people of Israel mentioned just previously. Therefore, one may wish to say "when these believers whom Paul had found in Ephesus heard this." This will then refer the reader back to the believers mentioned in verse 1. For baptism in the name of the Lord Jesus, see 2.38.

19.6

As in the instance of the Samaritans (8.15 ff.), the Holy Spirit comes after baptism and in conjunction with the laying on of hands. If one must specify where the hands were laid, this would be presumably "on the head."

As in the case of Cornelius (10.44-46), the presence of the Holy Spirit is attested by the ecstatic speech of the believers: they spoke in strange tongues. This "speaking in strange tongues" is not to be understood essentially as "speaking foreign languages." Rather, it means "speaking in a strange manner" by using unknown or unrecognized sounds. Since, however, such forms of ecstatic speech are well known in so many religions in various parts of the world, it is usually not difficult to find some acceptable expression in a receptor language.

(They) proclaimed God's message is literally (they) "prophesied," but "to prophesy" in the biblical sense of the word primarily means "to speak God's message." It is perhaps better to avoid the word "prophesy" in the present context, inasmuch as the English word specifically means "to foretell," and that meaning seems not to be present here. To speak God's word should not be translated so as to mean "to speak God's words"; rather, it is "to speak the message which has come from God."

19.7

Luke has a fondness for using about as a qualifier of numbers (see 1.15; 2.41; 10.3). It is quite possible that in each case Luke intends for the reader to understand the exact number and that he uses about merely as a stylistic device.

8 Paul went into the synagogue, and for three months spoke boldly with the people, arguing with them and trying to convince them about the Kingdom of God. 9 But some of them were stubborn and would not believe, and said evil things about the Way of the Lord before the whole group. So Paul left them and took the disciples with him; and every day he held discussions in the lecture hall of Tyrannus. 10 This went on for two years, so that all the people who lived in the province of Asia, both Jews and Gentiles, heard the word of the Lord. (19. 8-10)

19. 8

There are certain serious complications in a more or less literal rendering of the first part of verse 8, since it could mean that Paul went into the synagogue and stayed there for a period of three months speaking boldly with the people. This is, of course, not what is intended. In a number of languages it is far better to place the temporal expression "for a period of three months" at the beginning of verse 8 so as to provide a kind of temporal setting for Paul's activity—for example, "for a period of three months Paul regularly went to the synagogue and spoke boldly with the people." This would mean that Paul's activity was regularly repeated during this period of three months, not that he was continually in the synagogue arguing with the people for this entire period of time.

The verb went has no explicit subject connected with it in Greek, though it is obvious that Paul is intended, and for this reason a number of translators have made the subject explicit (Phillips, Moffatt, Barclay).

Spoke boldly is the same verb which occurs in 9. 27; with the people has been supplied with the verb spoke boldly. Similarly, with them has been introduced with arguing. Most translations take "arguing" with the same force as the TEV has done, though some weaken the verb to mean "hold discussions" (see Goodspeed). Others understand this verb to mean "to preach," and the Zürich has rendered the whole clause as "he spoke of the Kingdom of God and tried to convince the people concerning it."

Although trying is not explicitly expressed in the Greek, many translations understand this to be implicit in the meaning of the Greek tense (Zürich, Goodspeed). Some few have combined these two verbs so that the second qualifies the first: "argued persuasively about the Kingdom of God."

The final expression convince them about the Kingdom of God may be difficult to render literally into some languages. One may, however, employ an expression such as "to persuade them that what he was saying about the Kingdom of God was true." In many languages one can convince people that something is true, but it is difficult to simply "convince people about something."

19. 9

Stubbornness is such a universal phenomenon that it is not difficult to find some appropriate term in a receptor language. This may, however, turn out to be highly idiomatic—for example, "they would not listen with their minds," "they closed their ears," "they covered over their hearts," or "they refused to answer back."

Most translations spell Way with a capital in order to indicate that this is a technical term for the Christian movement. The TEV has expanded this to read the Way of the Lord, so that the person who is listening to the Scripture being read, but not looking on the text himself, will understand the term in this way also.

As has been noted before, a literal translation of the Way of the Lord may not be adequate in some languages. It may be necessary to render this phrase as "the Way which the Lord showed," "the Way which the Lord prescribed," or "the Way of life shown by the Lord."

As the TEV points out in its list of variant readings, some manuscripts add after every day the phrase "from 11:00 a.m. until 4:00 p.m." This may well be an accurate description of what did take place. It was the custom in those days for people to carry on their public life until around 11:00 o'clock in the morning, after which they would have their noon meal and then their afternoon siesta. Thus Paul would have worked at his regular job until 11:00 a.m., when the working day was over, and would then have gone to the lecture hall of Tyrannus, where he could talk to people about the Christian Way. Held discussions is the same verb which is rendered "arguing" in the preceding verse. The word rendered lecture hall was a place used for lectures and for other gatherings; "school" gives the English reader a wrong impression.

The lecture hall of Tyrannus may be translated as "the large room where Tyrannus gave lectures" or "the large room where Tyrannus spoke to many people." This phrase could also mean "the lecture hall owned by Tyrannus."

19.10

This went on for two years must be rendered in a number of languages as "Paul did this for a period of two years." A continuous series of events cannot be expressed in some languages by a pronoun such as this, nor can one speak of such events as "going on." For these reasons one must restructure the form of this clause.

In 20.31 Paul says that he spent three years in Ephesus: he argued for three months in the synagogue (19.8), taught for two years in the lecture hall (19.9), and spent more time in the province of Asia (19.22, where Asia is perhaps equivalent to Ephesus). It was probably during this time that the churches at Colossae, Hierapolis, and Laodicea were founded, though not directly by Paul in all cases, since Luke states that during this period all the people who lived in the province of Asia, both Jews and Gentiles, heard the word of the Lord.

In a number of receptor languages, a clear distinction is made between "heard the word of the Lord" and "heard the message concerning the Lord."

365

19.12

The first would mean that the individuals had directly heard what the Lord had said, or had heard persons quoting the words from the Lord. Luke's intention, however, in this last phrase of verse 10, is to indicate that in some way or other people throughout Asia had heard about this message concerning the Lord.

The Sons of Sceva

11 God was performing unusual miracles through Paul. 12 Even handkerchiefs and aprons he had used were taken to the sick, and their diseases were driven away and the evil spirits would go out of them. 13 Some Jews who traveled around and drove out evil spirits also tried to use the name of the Lord Jesus to do this. They said to the evil spirits, "I command you in the name of Jesus, whom Paul preaches." 14 There were seven sons of a Jewish High Priest named Sceva who were doing this.

15 But the evil spirit said to them, "I know Jesus and I know about Paul; but you—who are you?"

16 The man who had the evil spirit in him attacked them with such violence that he defeated them. They all ran away from his house, wounded and with their clothes torn off. 17 All the Jews and Gentiles who lived in Ephesus heard about this; they were all filled with fear, and the name of the Lord Jesus was given greater honor. 18 Many of the believers came, publicly admitting and revealing what they had done. 19 Many of those who had practiced magic brought their books together and burned them in the presence of everyone. They added up the price of the books and the total came to fifty thousand dollars. 20 In this powerful way the word of the Lord kept spreading and growing stronger. (19.11-20)

The section heading The Sons of Sceva may, in some receptor languages, be much more meaningfully rendered as "The Sons of Sceva Try to Cast out Evil Spirits."

The discourse structure of these paragraphs is interestingly and complexly organized. In the first place, there is a reference to unusual miracles performed by Paul, including the driving out of evil spirits (v. 12b). This provides the basis for introducing the fact that some Jews, including the seven sons of Sceva, were themselves attempting to drive out evil spirits, presumably by using the names of Jesus and Paul. However, their complete failure resulted in even greater honor being given to Jesus and the decision by many people to give up magical practices.

19.11-12

These two verses are similar to 5.15 in that they serve as a summary and are also a transition to the following account concerning the sons of Sceva.

366

Through Paul is literally "through the hands of Paul." Although in most contexts the expression "through the hands of Paul" would be considered a Semitism to identify the agent of an action, many commentators understand the phrase here as one which must be taken literally. That is, the unusual miracles were performed by actual contact between Paul and the persons on whom he performed these miracles. The introduction of Paul as a secondary agent, as indicated in the phrase through Paul, may be expressed in different ways in different languages— for example, "God was causing Paul to perform unusual miracles," "God was performing unusual miracles; he was causing Paul to do them," or "God was performing unusual miracles; Paul was doing these for God."

Handkerchiefs and aprons translate words which are of Latin origin, and probably should be taken as things that were worn by Paul in his work. The handkerchief would have been the "sweat-rag" which was worn on the head, and the apron would have been the workman's apron. He had used translates the literal expression "from his skin" (NEB "which had been in contact with his skin").

Their diseases were driven away may be rendered as "these handkerchiefs and aprons caused their diseases to disappear."

19.13

Evidently Paul had used the name of Jesus in performing these miracles of healing and of ridding people of evil spirits. Luke now tells of certain Jews who seem to have looked upon the name of Jesus as another magic formula by which they could chase out evil spirits for profit (very similar to the understanding of Simon in 8.19). In the ancient world the Jews were notorious for their magical practices, and a papyrus fragment has been found on which is the statement "I command you in the name of Jesus the God of the Jews." Since the context makes it clear that the command given by the Jews is to the evil spirits, the TEV has added this phrase for clarity.

Drove out evil spirits may be rendered as "caused evil spirits to come out of people" or "caused evil spirits to leave people."

To use the name of the Lord Jesus to do this may be equivalent in many languages to "they tried to do this by pronouncing the name of the Lord Jesus." This would emphasize the usage of the name of the Lord Jesus merely as a magical device.

I command you in the name of Jesus may not be adequate in itself to express what is implied in the statement of those who are driving out evil spirits. In some receptor languages one must, therefore, specify what is involved in such a command— for example, "I command you in the name of the Lord Jesus whom Paul preaches that you come out of this person"; or, if the expression must be placed in the form of direct discourse, "I command you, pronouncing the name of Jesus whom Paul preaches, Come out of this person."

19.14

Nothing further is known of the Sceva mentioned in this verse. It may be that he actually was a Jewish High Priest, or it may be that he had simply called himself a Jewish High Priest so as to suggest that he knew the sacred name that was mentioned in the holy place of the Jews.

Who were doing this may need to be rendered as "who were commanding evil spirits to come out."

19.15

The Greek uses two different verbs which the TEV has rendered know and know about, though it is possible that they had essentially the same meaning and were not intended to be differentiated. However, most translations make a distinction. If one wishes to distinguish between the two verbs for know, it is possible in some languages to employ a translation such as "I know who Jesus is and I have heard about Paul" or "I am acquainted with Jesus and I know who Paul is."

The TEV rendering but you—who are you? is designed to represent the strong emphasis in the Greek text. In other languages this may be expressed as "but who do you think you are?" or "but who in all the world are you?"

19.16

With such violence that he defeated them actually translates a verb and a participle which are almost equal in meaning. The TEV understands the participle as intensifying the force of the verb, and so has translated it in this way. (Note JB "overpowered...and handled them so violently.")

In some languages it is preferable to invert the order of events in the last sentence of verse 16—for example, "He wounded them and tore their clothes off and then they ran away from his house."

19.17

Heard about this may be rendered as "heard about what had happened" or "heard about how the sons of Sceva were defeated."

This verse is transitional, and in style is similar to 1.19 and 9.42 (see also 2.14; 4.10; 4.16; 13.28; 28.28).

Was given greater honor translates the same verb as was rendered "praising (God's) greatness" in 10.46. The passive expression was given greater honor may frequently need to be altered into an active phrase such as "the people honored the name of the Lord Jesus even more." To honor may also be expressed as "give praise to," "speak highly about," or "consider very great."

19.18

Publicly admitting is taken by some commentators to mean "openly confessing (one's sins)." Some translators combine the two verbs which the TEV has translated separately, <u>publicly admitting</u> and <u>revealing,</u> and understand them to mean "openly confess" (NEB; see Phillips).

<u>What (they) had done</u> (so most translations) translates a noun which frequently refers to evil deeds; however, the noun is also used in the specialized sense of "magic spells," and some translations reflect this interpretation (NEB, Moffatt, JB).

19.19

Since in one way or another magic is a universal phenomenon, it is not difficult to find some expression which is adequate to translate <u>practiced magic.</u> In some instances it is necessary to describe certain kinds of magic since there are so many varieties and no general term to cover them all. One may, for example, use a phrase such as "hurt (or healed) people by using dark words" or "caused harm by using secret objects."

It is essential to indicate that <u>their books</u> are those which refer to magical practice—for example, "the books which told them how to do this."

<u>In the presence of everyone</u> may be rendered as "while all the people were watching" or "while everyone was looking on."

<u>Fifty thousand dollars</u> is literally "fifty thousand (pieces) of silver." The reference is to some silver coin, though the commentators are not in agreement as to which one Luke had in mind. The point is that the amount of money was very large, and so the TEV has rendered this as <u>fifty thousand dollars,</u> probably the closest dynamic equivalent.

In translating <u>fifty thousand dollars</u> into some other language there are a number of possibilities. One may, for example, use a somewhat general term: "fifty thousand valuable silver coins." This would carefully represent the Greek text, and since the particular size of coin is not stipulated, devaluations would not render the text meaningless, as has so often happened in various parts of the world where strictly local currencies were stipulated. It is perfectly legitimate to introduce the term "valuable" since any silver coin in ancient times had considerable more buying power than the equivalent sized coin would have today. One can also translate the <u>fifty thousand dollars</u> into some local currency (provided it is relatively stable); but in making all such adjustments in quantities, it is important to use rounded-off figures rather than attempt some precise or detailed calculations.

19. 20

In many languages one cannot speak of <u>the word of the Lord kept spreading.</u> Rather, one must change this to read "more and more people kept hearing about the message concerning the Lord."

<u>Kept spreading</u> and <u>growing stronger</u> correctly emphasize the continuous aspects of the Greek verbs in this verse. The final phrase <u>growing stronger</u> is equivalent to "more and more people were believing." In a number

of languages one cannot speak of a word becoming strong. Only some animate creature can be spoken of as "growing stronger."

The introductory phrase in this powerful way is quite difficult to translate adequately in a number of languages. Way actually specifies the manner in which the preceding events took place, including the miracles of Paul, the defeat of the sons of Sceva, and finally the public burning of the books on magic. In some languages the equivalent expression is "all this that had happened was very strong," but in many instances what happened must be directly related to the reactions of people: "all that had happened convinced people strongly." In still other instances the equivalent may be "because of these unusual events" or "because of these powerful events."

The Riot in Ephesus

21 After these things had happened, Paul made up his mind to travel through Macedonia and Greece and go on to Jerusalem. "After I go there," he said, "I must also see Rome." 22 So he sent Timothy and Erastus, two of his helpers, to Macedonia, while he spent more time in the province of Asia. (19.21-22)

The section heading The Riot in Ephesus may need to be expressed as a complete sentence—for example, "The People in Ephesus Riot," "Demetrius and His Fellow Workers Cause a Riot in Ephesus," or "The Makers of Silver Temples Cause a Riot in Ephesus."

This paragraph (vv. 21-22) is essentially transitional and anticipatory. As is so characteristic of Luke, he wishes to indicate in advance what will happen later, beginning with the first part of Chapter 20. He therefore places Paul's decision at this point in Chapter 19, so that one will not think that Paul's decision to go into Macedonia was merely the result of the riot caused by Demetrius and his fellow workers. It is also important for Luke to be able to explain the activity of Timothy and Erastus during this period.

19.21

These things may refer back either to the events described in verses 13-19, or it may refer back to the two years of verse 10. The former possibility is more probable, since two years is apparently too far removed to be the antecedent.

Paul made up his mind may also be understood in the sense of "Paul led by the (Holy) Spirit, decided" (see Goodspeed "under the Spirit's guidance"). The problem is that the literal Greek clause "Paul decided in the spirit" may refer either to the Holy Spirit or to Paul's own human spirit. Commentators and translators are divided in their judgment regarding the translation of this clause. If it is the Holy Spirit which is being referred to in Paul's decision, then one may translate "the Holy Spirit caused Paul to decide."

Must (see had to of 1.16) indicates that Paul feels that it is God's will for him to visit Rome.

See Rome implies much more than simply being "a sightseer." Paul's purpose is "to visit Rome" or "to go to Rome for a while."

19. 22

The name Erastus occurs in Romans 16. 23 (there called the city treasurer of Corinth) and in 2 Timothy 4. 20. It is not certain whether or not these three passages refer to the same person. The phrase two of his helpers may be rendered as "two of the men who helped Paul" or "two of the men who worked together with Paul."

In the province of Asia is literally "in Asia," a phrase which many commentators understand in the sense of Ephesus.

23 It was at this time that there was serious trouble in Ephesus because of the Way of the Lord. 24 A certain silversmith named Demetrius made silver models of the temple of the goddess Artemis, and his business brought a great deal of profit to the workers. 25 So he called them all together, with others whose work was like theirs, and said to them, "Men, you know that our prosperity comes from this work. 26 You can see and hear for yourselves what this fellow Paul is doing. He says that gods made by men are not gods at all, and has succeeded in convincing many people, both here in Ephesus and in nearly the whole province of Asia. 27 There is the danger, then, that this business of ours will get a bad name. Not only that, there is also the danger that the temple of the great goddess Artemis will come to mean nothing, and that her greatness will be destroyed—the goddess worshiped by everyone in Asia and in all the world!" (19. 23-27)

This paragraph (vv. 23-27) begins with a temporal setting, it was at this time, and then introduces the account concerning the riot by a general expression, there was serious trouble in Ephesus. Beginning with verse 24 the silversmith Demetrius is introduced, and the rest of this paragraph consists essentially of a summary of his statement to his fellow workers.

19. 23

The expression translated as serious trouble is literally, in Greek, "not a little trouble." Luke is particularly fond of these negative statements as a means of providing strong emphasis. By translating literally "not a little" one is, however, very likely to miss the emphasis implied in Luke's usage. Moreover, from the standpoint of the structure of the meaning, it is more difficult for people to understand "not a little" than a positive expression such as "very much" or "serious."

On the Way of the Lord see verse 9.

19. 24

In many receptor languages a typical way of introducing a person such as Demetrius would be to say "there was a silversmith named Demetrius." A term for silversmith is simply "one who makes objects out of silver," "a maker of silver things," or "a worker with silver."

Artemis (some translators identify her with the Roman goddess Diana: JB, NEB, Phillips) was a goddess of fertility. Her temple, four times larger than the Parthenon in Athens, was one of the seven wonders of the ancient world. The rendering "silver shrines of Artemis" (so most translations) is misleading, for it suggests that Demetrius made silver figurines of the goddess Artemis herself. What the Greek actually says is that "he made silver temples of Artemis," that is, miniature temples. For this reason the TEV is much closer to the meaning of the Greek: Demetrius made silver models of the temple of the goddess Artemis. It should also be noted that the TEV has added the qualifier of the goddess in order to indicate to the reader exactly who Artemis was. Archeologists have found a number of silver figurines of the goddess Artemis, and they have found a number of clay models of her temple, though no silver models of her temple have been found.

A translation of silver models of the temple may be "very small temples made of silver which look just like the large temple."

Though the TEV introduces a classifier such as goddess to identify who Artemis was, it may very well be useful to have at this point a marginal note saying that Artemis was the Greek goddess of fertility. This may help to explain to the reader something of the emotional uproar which Demetrius was able to cause in the crowd which assembled. The TEV expression a great deal is literally "no little" in Greek (see RSV), but both the NEB and the TEV have rendered this expression by a great deal of.

The last clause in verse 24 may be rendered as "his business caused the workers to receive much money" or "the workers made much money because of this business."

Profit (Moffatt, Goodspeed) may be the meaning of the Greek word as used by Paul, though some scholars take the word in its original meaning of "business."

19. 25

Demetrius apparently called together not only those who worked directly under his supervision, but all other men in the business of making model temples. One may translate this first part of verse 25 as "so he called together all of his workers, and all others who made small silver temples of Artemis."

The word rendered prosperity appears only here in the New Testament; it is rendered "prosperity" (Goodspeed, JB), "financial prosperity" (Barclay), "wealth" (RSV), and "high standard of living" (NEB). The closest equivalent to prosperity in some languages is "we have much money because of this work we do" or "our riches depend (hang) on this work we do."

The Greek imperatives "see" and "hear" have been transformed by the TEV into a statement <u>you can see and hear for yourselves</u> (see also NEB), though most translators prefer to retain the imperative. If one were to preserve the imperative forms of <u>see</u> and <u>hear</u>, it might imply that Demetrius himself was encouraging the men to listen to what Paul was saying, which, of course, is not the case.

The pronoun in Greek which is rendered <u>this fellow</u> definitely implies a slur against Paul. In colloquial English this might be rendered as "this guy Paul."

<u>Gods made by men are not gods at all</u> appears in the NEB as "gods made by human hands are not gods at all" and in the NAB as "man-made gods are no gods at all." There are certain difficulties involved in the translation of the second sentence of verse 26, since <u>gods</u> is used in two different senses. In the first instance <u>gods</u> refers to images, and in the second instance <u>gods</u> refers to "supernatural beings" or "supernatural powers." In some languages one simply cannot say <u>gods made by men are not gods at all</u>. It is necessary to employ two different types of expressions—for example, "images which men make are not gods," "the statues of gods have no power as gods," or "the images which men make are really not gods."

<u>Has succeeded in convincing many people</u> may require some type of supplementation—for example, "has succeeded in convincing many people that what he says is true" or "has succeeded in causing many people to believe that these images are not gods."

The final phrases <u>both here in Ephesus</u> and <u>in nearly the whole province of Asia</u> may need to be rendered as a complete sentence: "Paul has done this not only here in Ephesus, but in almost the whole province of Asia."

19. 27

Although the word translated <u>business</u> and the phrase translated <u>will get a bad name</u> are both unusual when rendered in this fashion, most translators have rendered both of these terms similar to what the TEV has done. <u>Will get a bad name</u> may be equivalent to "will be spoken against" or "people will speak against this business of ours."

<u>Will come to mean nothing</u> may be equivalent to "people will no longer honor" or "people will no longer think that the temple of the great goddess Artemis is important."

In many languages one can speak of destroying a person, or even a god, but one cannot "destroy greatness." One can, however, say "she will no longer be great" or "people will no longer regard her as great."

Archeologists have found evidence that the goddess Artemis was worshiped in at least thirty other places in the Eastern Mediterranean region so the statement that she was <u>worshiped by everyone in Asia and in all the world</u> (meaning, of course, the Roman Empire) is not an exaggeration.

28 As the crowd heard these words they became furious, and started shouting, "Great is Artemis of Ephesus!" 29 The uproar spread throughout the whole city. The mob grabbed Gaius and Aristarchus, two Macedonians who were traveling with Paul, and rushed with them to the theater. 30 Paul himself wanted to go before the crowd, but the believers would not let him. 31 Some of the provincial authorities, who were his friends, also sent him a message begging him not to show himself in the theater. 32 Meanwhile, the whole meeting was in an uproar: some people were shouting one thing, others were shouting something else, because most of them did not even know why they had come together. 33 Some of the people concluded that Alexander was responsible, since the Jews made him go up to the front. Then Alexander motioned with his hand and tried to make a speech of defense before the people. 34 But when they recognized that he was a Jew, they all shouted together the same thing for two hours, "Great is Artemis of Ephesus!" (19. 28-34)

This second paragraph in the episode concerning the riot in Ephesus deals with the action of the crowd before the city clerk is finally able to calm them (v. 35). The first clause is transitional, as the crowd heard these words, and this provides the basis for the uproar which followed.

19. 28

The indefinite pronoun subject of the verb heard has been made definite, the crowd. Heard these words may be rendered in some languages as "heard what Demetrius had said."

The term translated furious combines in this context components of anger as well as excitement. In some languages this is actually translated "became excited and very angry."

The form of the shout raised by the Ephesians was the usual way of cheering: Great is Artemis of Ephesus! The grammatical form of this shout by the Ephesians is in some languages rendered as "Artemis of Ephesus is very great indeed." In other instances there are idiomatic expressions equivalent to great which may literally mean "long live" or "high above all else" but which are in reality only idiomatic ways of shouting praise to an important personage or a god.

19. 29

Although "confusion" (Moffatt, RSV, NEB) correctly represents the original meaning of the word used by Luke, the present context seems to demand something stronger, and so the TEV and others have translated it uproar (Phillips, JB). In many languages, however, one cannot speak of "an uproar spreading." Rather, one must say "more and more people throughout the whole city began to shout."

In Greek the subject of grabbed is left undefined, and most translators have simply stated "they grabbed." It is clear from the context that the people of the city are referred to (see Goodspeed "the people"), though in the present setting they are acting as a mob (so also JB).

Gaius and Aristarchus are here defined as two Macedonians, while in 20.4 Aristarchus is said to have come from Thessalonica and Gaius from Derbe. But Gaius was a quite common name (see Romans 16.23; 1 Corinthians 1.14; 3 John 1), and it is very possible that two different persons are referred to in this chapter and in the following.

With them translates the same adverbial expression as was rendered gathered in 1.14 (see the discussion there).

In translating the expression rushed with them, it is important to avoid the impression that Gaius and Aristarchus rushed along with them. Rather, "they were caused to rush to the theater" or "they dragged them quickly to the theater."

The theater in Ephesus was quite large; its seating capacity has been estimated at almost 26,000. In translating theater it is important to avoid any term which would suggest simply a cinema. Although in ancient times theaters were constructed primarily for the presentation of public events, including drama, they were also used for town meetings. Unless one is prepared to have an adequate marginal note to explain the significance of a theater, it may be useful in this passage to use a descriptive equivalent of theater by translating "to the place where the people in the city gathered."

19.30

Although Phillips gives a rather literal rendering of the Greek "to go in among the crowd," this leaves a wrong impression of Paul's intention. What Paul actually wanted to do was to go before the crowd (NEB "to appear before the assembly"), and he probably had hopes of reasoning with them (see JB "Paul wanted to make an appeal to the people"). However, as is later pointed out by the city clerk, this was not a legal meeting (v. 39), and it is very possible that Paul's life would have been in danger had he appeared before the crowd at this time. Believers is literally "disciples."

In order to indicate clearly Paul's intent in going before the crowd, it may be necessary to say "to go before the crowd in order to speak to them."

19.31

The term which the TEV has rendered provincial authorities translates an expression which refers to persons who were among the most outstanding individuals in the Roman province of Asia. The cities of Asia had formed a league, the main purpose of which was to foster the religion of the Roman Emperor and of the goddess Roma, and it was the duty of these men to encourage these functions. These provincial authorities were usually elected from the wealthiest and most influential families of the province, and there would certainly have been several of them in Ephesus at the time of Paul's stay there. In Greek the verb <u>sent</u> has no object, but one must be supplied for the English reader.

<u>To show himself in the theater</u> may be equivalent to "to stand in front of the people in the theater" or "to try to speak to the people in the theater." It is this public appearance of Paul which is specifically advised against by the <u>provincial authorities</u>.

19. 32

<u>Meanwhile</u> translates a particle frequently used by Luke (see 1. 6). In the present context it is used merely to indicate a temporal relationship between what has preceded and what will now follow.

The word translated <u>meeting</u> is in reality the term which is generally used for the official gathering of the public assembly of Ephesus. The question is whether it has this meaning in the present context or not. In light of all that had transpired and of what would happen, one must assume that this was merely an impromptu gathering rather than an official gathering of the people to conduct city business.

It is difficult to say in some languages that a <u>meeting was in an uproar</u>, but one can usually say "the people attending the meeting were making a great deal of noise" or "...were shouting very much."

19. 33

The Greek of this sentence is certainly not clear. First, the verb which the TEV has translated <u>concluded...was responsible</u> may mean either "to conclude" or "to instruct, advise." Second, one would normally expect that the verb would have a double object when used with a person, that is, the person and the content of what was included or instructed. However, in the present sentence the second object is lacking, and <u>Alexander</u> is the only object of the verb. If one translates the text as it stands, one must conclude that the crowd either explained something to Alexander (see NEB) or that the crowd concluded something about Alexander (so TEV). Phillips and JB base their translation on an alternative manuscript reading. This verb appears in two other places in Acts (9. 22; 16.10). In 16.10 it definitely means "conclude" or "decide"; while its use in 9. 22 (rendered <u>his proofs...were so convincing</u>) may be taken to support either position, that is, that Paul was teaching or that he was concluding (proving) that Jesus was the Messiah. Luke gives no reason why Alexander wanted <u>to make a speech of defense</u>; there are no grounds for assuming that he wanted to defend Paul, and his entire relationship to the uproar is obscure.

It is difficult to translate <u>was responsible</u> without knowing precisely the relationship of Alexander to the issues in question; and since the Greek text does not make this clear, one can only attempt to use some meaningful equivalent which will be as general in implication as possible. However, in some languages one cannot avoid specifying the particular nature of the responsibility. In some instances the closest equivalent is "was important with respect to what had happened" or "was involved in what had happened." It may even be possible to translate this expression as "had something to say"—perhaps the most general way of talking about Alexander's role.

Motioned with his hand may be translated in such a way as to indicate that this particular gesture was designed to quiet the crowd or to induce them to listen to him. On the other hand, it may be necessary to supplement this mention of the gesture by "motioned with his hand so that people would keep quiet."

Since we do not know Alexander's role, it is difficult in some languages to translate the term defense. However, since Jews were known as opponents of idolatry, and since any riot in favor of Artemis might be interpreted by some people as an indirect attack upon the Jews, it may be that Alexander was put forward by Jews in order to explain to the crowd that the Jews themselves were not responsible for what had happened. If this was the situation, one may translate make a speech of defense as "speak to the people to show that he and his companions were not guilty of what had happened." In a number of languages it is necessary to speak of a defense in terms of "saying that one is not guilty."

19.34

The pronoun they refers, of course, to the mob or crowd—for example, "when the crowd recognized that he was a Jew." This recognition might be based upon appearance, but it could have also been derived from his accent or the manner in which he spoke in defense of himself and his fellow Jews.

This verse would indicate that the Jews were not too well received in Ephesus. "There came one voice from them all" means, as the TEV has translated, they all shouted together the same thing.

35 At last the city clerk was able to calm the crowd. "Men of Ephesus!" he said. "Everyone knows that the city of Ephesus is the keeper of the temple of the great Artemis and of the sacred stone that fell down from heaven. 36 Nobody can deny these things. So then, you must calm down and not do anything reckless. 37 You have brought these men here, even though they have not robbed temples or said evil things about our goddess. 38 If Demetrius and his workers have an accusation against someone, there are the regular days for court and there are the authorities; they can accuse each other there. 39 But if there is something more that you want, it will have to be settled in the legal meeting of citizens. 40 For there is the danger that we will be accused of a riot in what has happened today. There is no excuse for all this uproar, and we would not be able to give a good reason for it." 41 After saying this, he dismissed the meeting. (19.35-41)

This final paragraph in the episode of the riot in Ephesus begins with a temporal transition, at last, which combines this paragraph with the one immediately preceding. The content of the paragraph is essentially a summary of the statement by the city clerk, which in many parts of the world is equivalent to "the town secretary."

19.35

The city clerk was an important city official, and one of his responsibilities was to issue the decrees reached by the public assembly. He could have been, though he usually was not, one of the provincial authorities. Was able to calm the crowd is equivalent to "was able to cause the crowd to keep quiet" or "was able to cause the crowd to listen to him."

Though the Greek text literally speaks of "men of Ephesus," it is more natural in some languages to employ an expression such as "people of Ephesus."

The word translated keeper of the temple was a term originally applied to individuals and later given to cities. A city in which a particular god or goddess was honored, and in which a temple had been dedicated to that god or goddess, was called the keeper of the temple of such and such god. Is the keeper of the temple may be rendered as "has responsibility to take care of the temple," "has the work of keeping up the temple," or even "is responsible for guarding the temple."

The sacred stone that fell down from heaven is literally "that which fell (from heaven)." The reference is to a stone, perhaps a fragment of a meteorite, which fell from heaven and which the people of Ephesus looked upon as being the sacred representation of their goddess Artemis. The worship of a sacred stone, believed to have fallen from heaven, is not uncommon among religions. Sacred stone is simply equivalent to "holy stone" and may, in some languages, be rendered as "taboo stone." However, the equivalent in other languages is "a stone which is worshiped."

19.36

Anything reckless may be rendered as "something without thinking" or even "something like mobs often do."

19.37

These men refers back to Gaius and Aristarchus of verse 29. Robbing temples and saying evil things about other gods were accusations often made against Jews during the New Testament period. Robbed temples is equivalent to "carried away holy things from temples." Obviously no one would be accused of "robbing the whole building" in the sense of "carrying off a temple."

19.38

Have an accusation against someone may be rendered as "wish to accuse someone" or "have reason to accuse someone."

The regular days for court translates a rather unusual use of a word in Greek, but all commentators and translators agree that this is the meaning.

378

In referring to the regular days for court, one may say "the court is open regularly" or "on certain days one may come before the court."

The authorities is literally "the (Roman) governors," but there was only one Roman governor to a province, and so the term is best taken in a general sense, either of the governor himself or of one of his representatives who regularly held court in each of the Asian cities.

In a number of languages it may be useful to combine the two clauses there are the regular days for court and there are the authorities. One may say, for example, "on regular days the authorities sit in the court to judge cases."

It is important that they in the last clause of verse 38 refer to Demetrius and his fellow workers and to such other persons as they may accuse. This final clause may be rendered in some languages as "there people can accuse one another." This avoids a specific reference to Demetrius and the workers, but provides a general statement which is applicable to the immediately preceding clauses concerning the operation of the court.

19.39

The legal meeting of citizens is a reference to the official public gatherings of the citizens of Ephesus; it would have been presided over by the city clerk. The Roman government allowed certain cities to have freedom of government, so long as they were obedient to the Roman authority.

The legal meeting of citizens is rendered in some languages as "a meeting of the citizens which has been called by the officials" or "a meeting of the citizens which agrees with the laws."

In many languages citizens are "people who belong to the city" or "people who have a word in what happens in the city."

19.40

The city clerk expresses his fears, which are certainly not without grounds, that the right of self-government may be taken away from the city if there is a riot which they cannot explain or defend to the Roman authorities. We will be accused of a riot may be rendered as "the Romans will accuse us of causing a riot" or "the Romans will say, What has happened today is a riot."

There is no excuse for all this uproar may be rendered as "no one can defend all this uproar" or "no one can say there was a good reason for all the uproar." This latter alternative expression combines the two final clauses of verse 40 into one.

19.41

Dismissed the meeting may be equivalent to "told the people, Go home" or "told the people to go away."

CHAPTER 20

Chapter 20 records the events which lead up to Paul's journey to Jerusalem in the following chapter. The major portion of the chapter is given to Paul's farewell speech to the elders of Ephesus (vv. 17-38), and this is preceded by the mention of Paul's visits to the churches of Macedonia and Greece (vv. 1-16). It is known from Paul's own letters that he undertook a collection for the church in Jerusalem, and it is thought by many commentators that Paul is now in the process of taking this money to Jerusalem. If this is so, it would account for the large number of people accompanying Paul and also for the plot against Paul's life, which was perhaps, to some extent, an attempt on the part of the Jews to steal the money that he was taking with him.

Chapter 20 may also be regarded as a summary of Paul's activity in Asia and Greece, since it not only includes a number of places where he visited and the manner in which he was welcomed as well as how he was threatened by the Jews, but it also provides in Paul's farewell message to the elders of Ephesus a very important summary of his ministry and the extent of his commitment to the believers. In this message Paul also anticipates the theological problems faced by the church when <u>fierce wolves</u> would come in, divide, and destroy.

The first paragraph of Chapter 20 begins with a reference to what occurred in Chapter 19, <u>after the uproar died down.</u> The orientation of the rest of this paragraph is primarily geographical. The second paragraph begins with a temporal setting, <u>on Saturday evening</u>, and it constitutes only one episode in the series of places where Paul stopped.

The third paragraph (vv. 13-16) is likewise organized in terms of stages of a journey. It also is transitional to the last section of this chapter (vv. 17-38), in which Paul addresses the elders at Ephesus.

To Macedonia and Greece

1 After the uproar died down, Paul called together the believers, and with words of encouragement said good-bye to them. Then he left and went on to Macedonia. 2 He went through those regions and encouraged the people with many messages. Then he came to Greece, 3 where he stayed three months. He was getting ready to go to Syria when he discovered that the Jews were plotting against him; so he decided to go back through Macedonia. 4 Sopater, the son of Pyrrhus, from Berea, went with him; so did Aristarchus and Secundus, from Thessalonica; Gaius, from Derbe; Timothy; and Tychicus and Trophimus, from the province of Asia. 5 They went ahead and waited for us in Troas. 6 We sailed from Philippi after the Feast of Unleavened Bread, and five days later joined them in Troas, where we spent a week. (20.1-6)

The section heading <u>To Macedonia and Greece</u> may need to be expanded into a complete sentence— for example, "Paul and His Companions Go to Macedonia and Greece" or "Paul Again Visits Macedonia and Greece."

20.1

Luke makes it clear that Paul did not leave Ephesus because of the difficulties there: after the uproar died down...then he left and went on to Macedonia. There is no indication as to how much time elapsed from the day of the riot till the time Paul left for Macedonia, but one should avoid the impression that he left the same day. It must be assumed from the context that it was at least several days later.

The believers is literally "the disciples," but as has been pointed out earlier, these are synonymous terms in Acts.

With words of encouragement said good-bye to them. Although the Greek verb itself may mean "to exhort," in the present context the meaning seems to be that of "offering encouragement" (so JB, Phillips, Goodspeed, NEB).

The translation of with words of encouragement said good-bye to them may involve the use of two quite separate verbs: "encouraged them and said farewell to them." In some languages said good-bye is merely "said, I am leaving."

20. 2

Those regions refers back to the territory of Macedonia (v. 1), and would probably have included the communities of Philippi, Thessalonica, and Berea.

The people must be understood as a reference to the believers in "those regions" just referred to (see NEB "to the Christians there").

Most translators take the expression "much word" to suggest that Paul spoke many words to them on one occasion: "he said many words of encouragement to them" (JB). However, "word" is perhaps to be taken in the sense of "message," and with the meaning that Paul spoke several messages of encouragement to the Christians there: encouraged the people with many messages (see NEB "often speaking words of encouragement").

It is thought by most commentators that Greece refers specifically to Corinth.

As in a number of passages, one must be constantly aware of the problems of translating "go" and "come." In most languages one must preserve the same point of view constantly: either that of the principal character of the story (in this case Paul), or of the writer who is narrating the series of events. It would, therefore, be quite strange to say went through those regions and came to Greece unless one wishes specifically to imply that Luke himself is all the time in Greece. In that case, however, one would assume that the first verb would be "came through those regions," since this would be presumably Paul's journey from Ephesus to Greece. In most languages one must

381

adopt the viewpoint of the principal character, and therefore it would be "went through those regions" and "went on to Greece."

20.3

The three months period was probably the winter season. Paul tried to avoid sea travel during wintertime (see 27.12; 28.11; Titus 3.12). It was customary for many Jews to travel back to Jerusalem each year to celebrate the Passover, and for this purpose there were many pilgrim ships which carried them from the cities of this region to Jerusalem. It was probably Paul's intention to go by one of these ships, but since it would have been easy for the Jews aboard ship to stir up others against Paul and to have had him killed, he decided it would be better to travel by land.

In some languages the relationship between the two clauses involving preparations to go to Syria and the discovery that the Jews were plotting against him must be somewhat altered in their temporal relationships—for example, "while he was getting ready to go to Syria, he discovered that the Jews..." or "he was getting ready to go to Syria, but then he discovered that the Jews...."

In this type of context discovered may be rendered in some languages as "heard" or "learned from some people." In most receptor languages one cannot translate this term discovered by the same word which may be used to describe the finding of some unusual object.

Plotting against him may simply be translated as "planning to kill him."

20.4

Sopater may be Sosipater, who is mentioned in Romans 16.21, though this is rather questionable. Aristarchus is mentioned also in 19.29 and 27.2. Secundus is mentioned only here in the New Testament. Regarding Gaius from Derbe, see the comments on 19.29. Timothy (who came from Lystra, 16.1) is so well known to the readers that he receives no further qualification. Tychicus is mentioned also in Ephesians 6.21; Colossians 4.7; 2 Timothy 4.12; Titus 3.12. Trophimus appears again in 21.29 (see also 2 Timothy 4.20).

The grammatical structure of this fourth verse is typically Greek, but it must be rather significantly altered if it is to be translated readily into some languages. Note that according to the grammatical structure it is only Sopater who went with Paul. Then we have the addition of other persons: Aristarchus, Secundus, Gaius, Timothy, Tychicus, and Trophimus. In many languages one simply cannot use this type of structure. Rather, one must say "Several persons went with him. These included Sopater, the son of Pyrrhus, from Berea; Aristarchus and Secundus from Thessalonica...."

In a number of languages there are very convenient devices for identifying a person's relationship to his home town. Sometimes this is even done by a kind of adjectival ending to the name of the town. However, in other languages one must simply say "who came from Berea" or "who came from Thessalonica."

The so-called "we" sections resume at this point, but whom does Luke indicate by us in this passage? There are three principal possibilities: (1) us may include only Luke and Paul; or (2) us may refer to an indefinite number of Christians from Philippi, among whom was included the author himself; or (3) it may be that only Tychicus and Trophimus went on ahead, since they were from Asia and were known by the churches there, and hence us would refer to the other persons listed as well as Luke. In any event, the pronoun us is exclusive in languages which have the inclusive-exclusive contrast for the first person plural.

The same problem exists with we as with us in the preceding verse; but whatever conclusion one reaches, in both cases an exclusive form should be used, since this entire book of Acts is addressed to Theophilus, who obviously was not included in the group.

After the Feast of Unleavened Bread is taken by most commentators to indicate that Paul celebrated this festival with his friends at Philippi (on the Feast of Unleavened Bread see 12.3). But it is possible to understand this expression purely as a means of designating time (see 27.9).

Five days later (see also JB) is an unusual expression (literally "until five days"), but the meaning is obvious, that is, "within a period of five days," even though this implies relatively slow sailing.

Many translations have done as the TEV has done, translating the expression "for seven days" by a week (JB, NEB, Phillips).

Paul's Last Visit in Troas

7 On Saturday evening we gathered together for the fellowship meal. Paul spoke to the people, and kept on speaking until midnight, since he was going to leave the next day. 8 There were many lamps in the upstairs room where we were meeting. 9 A young man named Eutychus was sitting in the window; and as Paul kept on talking, Eutychus got sleepier and sleepier, until he finally went sound asleep and fell from the third story to the ground. They picked him up, and he was dead. 10 But Paul went down and threw himself on him and hugged him. "Don't worry," he said, "he is still alive!" 11 Then he went back upstairs, broke bread, and ate. After talking with them for a long time until sunrise, Paul left. 12 They took the young man home alive, and were greatly comforted. (20.7-12)

The noun form of this section heading Paul's Last Visit in Troas may be

readily modified into a verb form by rendering it as "Paul Visits Troas for
the Last Time." On the other hand, what is important is Paul's visit to the
believers in Troas, not merely his having visited the town. Therefore it may
be preferable to say "Paul Visits the Believers in Troas for the Last Time."

20. 7

On Saturday evening (see Barclay, NEB, and JB note) is literally "on the
first day of the week." This meeting would have taken place in the evening;
and according to Jewish calculation the first day of the week would have begun
on Saturday evening and continued until Sunday at sunset. Some infer, on the
basis of the phrase until sunrise (v. 11), that Luke was not counting the day
in the Jewish fashion but in the Greek way, by which the day began at sunrise.
If this is the case, then the translation should be "Sunday evening" rather than
"Saturday evening"; however, the weight of evidence is in favor of "Saturday
evening."

For the fellowship meal (see comments on 2.42) is literally "to break
bread," and some commentators take this as a reference to the celebration
of the Lord's Supper rather than to the fellowship meal which seems to have
preceded the participation in the Lord's Supper. Kept on speaking is perhaps
to be taken in the sense of "kept on preaching," since Paul is the only one
speaking. Since he was going to leave the next day explains the reason that
Paul kept on speaking until midnight.

20. 8

Commentators disagree as to why Luke mentioned that there were many
lamps in the upstairs room where we were meeting. It seems quite probable,
however, that Luke did this in order to explain one of the reasons that Eutychus fell off to sleep: the many lamps burning must have made the room hot
and stuffy and contributed to Eutychus' sleepy condition.

20. 9

Young man is a different word from the one used in verse 12 below.
According to the classification of one ancient Greek writer, the word used in
this verse would normally describe a man who was from 23 to 28 years of
age, whereas the word used in verse 12 (translated "boy" by many translators) is taken to describe a person of 8 to 14 years of age. It is quite possible that Luke is simply describing a person who is somewhere between 20
and 30 years of age. The second Greek term which would normally suggest a
person of younger age than the first term may, of course, imply some greater
degree of endearment, but more probably it is simply used in the more general sense of a young person.

The TEV has brought out the contrast that Luke has made between the
Greek progressive tense got sleepier and sleepier and the Greek verb tense
denoting instantaneous action finally went sound asleep.

The third story includes in its calculation the ground floor; therefore in some translations this would be equivalent to "the second story." In Greek "he was taken up" is an impersonal passive construction equivalent in English to they picked him up. Luke actually says that he was dead (see JB "he was picked up dead"). Had Luke intended to say that he only appeared to be dead, he could easily have done this. Therefore, such a translation as "was picked up as dead" (Phillips) or "was picked up for dead" (NEB) is misleading.

20.10

Commentators have long since seen a parallel between this account and that of Elijah in 1 Kings 17.17 ff. and of Elisha in 2 Kings 4.34 ff. Threw himself on him must not, of course, be translated literally in most languages. Rather, one may employ an expression such as "stretched himself out over him."

In the use of terms to describe this action and the subsequent action of "hugging him," it is most important to avoid any expressions which would suggest sexual behavior or interest.

Don't worry translates a present imperative, which normally means for one to stop doing the action that he is already in the process of doing (see NEB "stop this commotion"). The reference that Paul is making is either to the mental anxiety of worry (see JB "there is no need to worry" and Phillips "don't be alarmed") or to the Oriental custom of showing grief by loud noises. He is still alive does not contradict what was said in the preceding verse; Luke intends the readers to understand that the boy regained his life when Paul threw himself on him and hugged him.

20.11

He of verse 11 is, of course, a reference to Paul. Naturally Paul did not eat by himself, but he is the central figure in the narrative and therefore is the one mentioned. Some commentators take broke bread as a reference to Paul's participation in the Lord's Supper, while they understand ate to refer to a meal beyond this. Others take the two verbs together to refer either to Paul's participation in the Lord's Supper or in the fellowship meal, or simply to the fact that Paul ate for the sake of nourishment before leaving. In light of the way that Luke uses the phrase "broke bread," it seems likely that the reference is either to the Lord's Supper or to the fellowship meal which was eaten in conjunction with it.

In order to avoid the implication that Paul ate by himself, it may be necessary to introduce some reference to those who evidently participated with him in this meal, "broke bread and ate with the believers."

Until sunrise is taken by a number of commentators to mean the sunlight that comes a little before sunrise, that is, daybreak.

20.12

As mentioned above, young man is not the same word as appears in verse 9; however, for the sake of translation, it is best to render these by the same term. There are certain aspects of this verse which are not altogether clear. They may refer either to some of the Christians who were at the gathering, or more specifically to the relatives of the young man. And the verb rendered took...home is literally "took away" (see NEB, RSV), but the reference is obviously to the fact that these people took the young man either to his own or to their home. In light of the context, it seems most likely that the young man was taken to his own home. Took the young man home should not imply that "they carried him." The Greek text simply states "they led him home." This could also be rendered as "accompanied him."

The final expression, were greatly comforted, may be rendered as a causative: "this caused them to be very much comforted." One may, however, encounter a number of idiomatic expressions in various receptor languages: "their hearts became still again," "again they were happy in their hearts," or "and again their hearts sat down to rest."

From Troas to Miletus

13 We went on ahead to the ship and sailed off to Assos, where we were going to take Paul aboard. He had told us to do this, because he was going there by land. 14 When he met us in Assos, we took him aboard and went on to Mitylene. 15 We sailed from there and arrived off Chios the next day. A day later we came to Samos, and the following day we reached Miletus. 16 Paul had decided to sail on by Ephesus, so as not to lose any time in the province of Asia. He was in a hurry to arrive in Jerusalem, if at all possible, by the day of Pentecost.

(20.13- 16)

The section heading From Troas to Miletus may need to be made into a complete sentence—for example, "Paul Traveled from Troas to Miletus." Paul's means of travel might be either by walking, by horseback, or even by some type of carriage.

Before translating a paragraph such as this one, or any others in the book of Acts which are so heavily geographical in orientation, it is most important for a translator to study closely a good map of Bible lands and to read a Bible dictionary giving information about the various places. This will help considerably in employing terms for "coming," "going," "arriving at," "reaching," and "leaving."

20.13

We includes all of the companions of Paul, along with the author of the book, but for languages possessing the inclusive-exclusive distinction it is still exclusive.

No reason is given why Paul preferred to go from Troas to Assos <u>by land</u> rather than by sea, though some have suggested that he simply wanted to be alone with his thoughts. However, it seems most likely that Paul desired to avoid the rather difficult sea journey around the cape from Troas to Assos. <u>He was going there by land</u> translates a verb which originally meant "to travel by foot," but in New Testament times the meaning of the verb had been expanded to include any land travel as opposed to sea travel.

20.14

<u>We took him aboard</u> may be rendered in some languages as "he joined us on the ship" or "he came onto the ship where we were."
<u>Mitylene</u> was the main town of the island of Lesbos.

20.15

Although the root meaning of the verb rendered <u>arrived</u> means "to pass by," it may also have the meaning of "to cross over to," and therefore "to arrive." In any case, most translators understand the meaning of the verb in the present context to be "arrived."
<u>Chios</u> is one of the larger Aegean islands off the coast of Asia; it was a free state under the Roman administration.
The route taken by the ship was the most natural to follow; to have gone by Ephesus would have required extra sailing time and distance. <u>Samos</u> was also one of the larger Aegean islands, and, like <u>Chios</u>, it was a free state. It lay slightly south of Ephesus. Evidently it was felt that to sail directly from <u>Chios</u> to <u>Miletus</u> was too long a journey, and therefore the trip was broken by a stop at <u>Samos</u>. <u>Miletus</u> was a town located about 30 miles south of Ephesus.
In place of the reading <u>and the following day</u> some manuscripts read "and after stopping at Trogyllium, the following day" (see JB; RSV note, NEB alternative reading). The committee preparing the UBS text did not include this in its apparatus. The apparent reason for its inclusion in some ancient manuscripts is that the trip from Samos to Miletus would have been regarded as being too long for a single day.

20.16

Luke would have no doubt considered Miletus within <u>the province of Asia</u>, but Asia used in the present context probably refers to the city of Ephesus and to the regions around it. Not only would Paul have lost travel time in going to Ephesus, but he probably understood how difficult it would be for him to get away from Ephesus if he actually went to the city where he had ministered for such a long time.
On <u>the day of Pentecost</u> see the comments at 2.1.

Paul's Farewell Speech to the Elders of Ephesus

17 Paul sent a message from Miletus to Ephesus, asking the elders of the church to meet him. 18 When they arrived, he said to them, "You know how I spent the whole time I was with you, from the first day I arrived in the province of Asia. 19 With all humility and many tears I did my work as the Lord's servant, through the hard times that came to me because of the plots of the Jews. 20 You know that I did not hold back anything that would be of help to you as I preached and taught you in public and in your homes. 21 To Jews and Gentiles alike I gave solemn warning that they should turn from their sins to God, and believe in our Lord Jesus. 22 And now, in obedience to the Holy Spirit, I am going to Jerusalem, not knowing what will happen to me there. 23 I only know that in every city the Holy Spirit has warned me that prison and troubles wait for me. 24 But I reckon my own life to be worth nothing to me, in order that I may complete my mission and finish the work that the Lord Jesus gave me to do, which is to declare the Good News of the grace of God. (20.17-24)

Both the style and the content of this speech are different from any of the other speeches in Acts, but these differences may easily be accounted for by the observation that this is the only place in Acts where Paul is recorded as having given a speech to Christians. The speech itself may be divided into four parts: (1) verses 18-21 deal with the past, that is, with Paul's work in Ephesus; (2) verses 22-24 are concerned with Paul's present situation; (3) verses 25-31 depict the future (both the future of Paul and of the Ephesian church); and (4) verses 32-35 serve as Paul's concluding remarks.

20.17

Sent a message may be translated as "sent someone with a message." One must avoid the implications of telegraphic communication in biblical times.

The verb asking may introduce direct discourse—for example, "ask the elders of the church, Please come to meet me."

Elders is one of the terms used in the New Testament to describe church leaders; it is a term taken over from Judaism, in which the elders were the recognized leaders of the Jewish religious community. In verse 28 these same men are described in other terms. It is quite doubtful that at this time elders (or any similar term) had acquired a technical sense in its use in the church, and it is impossible to formulate any theory of church organization on the basis of this term as used here.

In general, elders is translated as "older leaders." This is because the Greek term generally rendered "elders" has two important components of meaning, age and leadership.

20.18

In Greek, verses 18 and 19 form one long involved sentence, which the TEV has divided into two sentences for the sake of clarity (see also Phillips). From the first day I arrived in the province of Asia is the emphatic element in verse 18, and the entire clause how I... in the province of Asia is best understood as the object of the verb know.

The expression how I spent the whole time may be rendered in some languages as "how I lived and worked the whole time."

The temporal expression from the first day would suggest a continuation of Paul's activity until the time he left. Therefore, in some languages this last clause is rendered as "from the very first day I arrived in the province of Asia, I lived and worked in the same manner until the day that I left."

20.19

I did my work as the Lord's servant is in the stressed position of the Greek clause.

In Greek a single preposition appears before all humility, many tears, and hard times. The meaning of this preposition when used with all humility is clear: either "with all humility" or "in all humility" (so NEB, JB). The question is whether tears should be taken along with all humility as an expression of Paul's inner attitude, or whether it should be taken with hard times as an expression of the difficulties that were brought upon Paul because of the plots of the Jews. The TEV takes with all humility and many tears as an expression of Paul's inner attitude (see also Phillips), while others take tears and hard times together as an indication of the difficulties brought upon Paul because of the plot of the Jews: "in all humility amid the sorrows and trials that came upon me" (NEB; see also JB).

The expression with all humility and many tears is extremely difficult to translate satisfactorily in some receptor languages. In the first place, one cannot conveniently combine such features as humility and tears. Humility must frequently be translated as "I was always very humble" or, in a negative fashion, "I was never proud." On the other hand, tears must refer to the sorrow or grief which Paul suffered. This cannot imply that all the time he was working he was also crying. One may, however, combine tears with the following expression I did my work, as "while I was doing my work as a servant for the Lord I was often caused to cry."

There are additional problems in the translation of hard times, for in many languages one cannot speak of "hard occasions." Rather, the term hard is equivalent to the suffering which Paul endured on various occasions. Therefore the last clause of verse 19 may, in some languages, be rendered as "by their plots the Jews caused me to suffer much."

20. 20

As with the two preceding verses, so verses 20 and 21 are one long sentence in Greek. The TEV, along with others (see NEB, JB), takes the main verb in verse 20 to mean hold back, and so understands as its object anything that would be of help to you. If this is done, the rest of verse 20 may be taken either (1) as an explanation of what Paul did in order to be of help to them (so NEB, JB), or (2) as a reference to time, as in the TEV: as I preached and taught you in public and in your homes. Others understand the verb hold back in the sense of "be silent about (out of fear)," and take the remainder of the verse as an explanation of what resulted from Paul's unwillingness to shrink back in fear: "I never shrank from telling you anything that was for your good, nor from teaching you in public or at your houses" (Goodspeed; see also RSV).

Did not hold back anything is equivalent in some languages to "did not keep from telling you" or "did not just keep for myself."

In some languages the verbs preached and taught may require a specific indication of the content of the preaching and teaching — for example, "I preached and taught you the message about the Lord Jesus."

20. 21

The verb rendered I gave solemn warning means much more than merely "testify" (so KJV), as can be seen by its use in such passages as Luke 16. 28; 2 Timothy 2.14; 4.1. It appears in other translations as "urging" (JB), "most emphatically urged" (Phillips), and "insisted on" (NEB). I gave solemn warning may be rendered as "I warned them strongly," "I said to them with strong words," or "I spoke to them harshly." The verb warning may introduce direct discourse—for example, "warned them, You must turn from your sins to God...."

That they should turn from their sins to God, and believe in our Lord Jesus is a summary of Paul's message. The first part, turn from their sins to God, is literally "repentance with respect to God." But in biblical thought "repentance" always means "to turn from one's sins," and it always presupposes that in so doing one would turn to God. Therefore, within the phrase "repentance with respect to God" there are two clearly implied elements: (1) to turn from one's sins, and (2) to turn to God. In the Christian sense one "turns from his sins to God" by believing in the Lord Jesus, though the Greek here has these two elements connected as though they were separate and distinct. Believe in our Lord Jesus is literally "belief with respect to our Lord Jesus," but "belief" is one of those nouns which is basically verbal, that is, "to believe."

20. 22

Both by the change in content and by the particles by which Luke introduces this verse, and now, he indicates the beginning of a new section in Paul's address to the elders of Ephesus.

Most scholars take the phrase "bound by the spirit" to mean either in obedience to the Holy Spirit or else "compelled by the Holy Spirit." However, it is possible, purely on the basis of the words themselves, to understand Paul as speaking of his own inner spirit. One may also translate this as in the JB: "you see me a prisoner already in spirit" (see also NEB footnote "under an inner compulsion"). But in light of the immediate context (see v. 23) and in view of the way that Luke elsewhere speaks of the Holy Spirit's leadership (see 16.6 and the alternative rendering of 19.21), it seems evident that Luke understood "spirit" in this passage to mean the Holy Spirit.

The noun phrase in obedience to the Holy Spirit is often rendered as a verbal expression: "in order that I may obey the Holy Spirit" or "because I obey the Holy Spirit."

Not knowing what will happen to me may be translated as "I do not know what people will do to me." In many languages it is much more normal to speak of people doing something to someone else rather than of something happening to a person.

20.23

Warned translates the same verb as was rendered solemn warning in verse 21. Although the TEV has rendered this verb by a past tense, in the Greek it is actually a present tense. It is customary in Greek to use a present tense in a narrative when referring to past events, if these are to be particularly stressed.

In a number of receptor languages one cannot speak of prison and troubles wait for me. A person may wait for another person or he may wait for an event, but to have an object such as prison and troubles (as a series of events) wait for an individual is simply not possible in the meaningful structure of many receptor languages. However, the structure can be readily readjusted—for example, "the Holy Spirit has warned me that people will put me in prison and cause me great trouble" or, in the passive form, "...I will be put into prison and caused to suffer much trouble."

20.24

The first part of this verse is rather awkward in Greek, so that two possibilities of translation result. One may understand the Greek to mean "but I reckon my life of no value, as though it were precious to me," and so translate as the TEV has done: but I reckon my own life to be worth nothing to me. On the other hand, it is possible to understand "reckon to be of no value" as meaning "not worth speaking of," and so translate as the JB has done: "but life to me is not a thing to waste words on" (see also Zürich and Luther). These two different renderings, however, amount essentially to the same thing. In many languages it is impossible to speak of one's "life" being "worth anything." One may, however, say "it is not important to me whether I live or die." This may then be followed by a clause stating "it is, however, important that I complete my mission...."

391

The first word of the next part of this verse has also caused difficulty for translators. Normally it is used as a particle of comparison, indicating the manner in which something is done, and is generally translated "as" or "like." It is also used, though admittedly rather infrequently, to denote purpose, and that is what seems best in the present context. It is interesting to observe the different ways by which this particle appears in the various translations: "provided that" (JB), "so long as" (Phillips), "if only" (RSV). The NEB combines this particle with the verb that follows and so translates: "I only want to finish...."

The word translated mission is literally "race" (that is, athletic contest; see 2 Timothy 4. 7), but in the present context it is evidently used in a figurative sense of the mission to which God has called Paul. Work is the same word that appears in 1.17. If mission and work have essentially the same meaning in this passage, the last clause, which is to declare the Good News of the grace of God, refers back to both of these activities; otherwise this clause may be taken to refer only to work.

In a number of languages it is not possible to make a distinction between complete my mission and finish the work. These are therefore coalesced into a single expression: "in order that I may complete the task that the Lord Jesus gave me to do."

The final clause may be difficult to render in some languages, since which must refer to the work as a whole. Therefore, it may be useful to break the sentence at this point and say "the work which I was given to do is to declare the Good News about the grace of God."

As in so many contexts, the grace of God may be rendered as "the goodness of God" in the sense of "the kindness or goodness of God toward people."

25 "I have gone about among all of you, preaching the Kingdom of God. And now I know that none of you will ever see me again. 26 So I solemnly declare to you this very day: if any of you should be lost, I am not responsible. 27 For I have not held back from announcing to you the whole purpose of God. 28 Keep watch over yourselves and over all the flock which the Holy Spirit has placed in your care. Be shepherds of the church of God, which he made his own through the death of his own Son. 29 I know that after I leave, fierce wolves will come among you, and they will not spare the flock. 30 The time will come when some men from your own group will tell lies to lead the believers away after them. 31 Watch, then, and remember that with many tears, day and night, I taught every one of you for three years. (20. 25-31)

20. 25

In the Greek text verse 25 begins with a transitional phrase, literally "and now behold." This clearly marks a shift in viewpoint and content. However, the expression which is placed first in the TEV text, namely, I have gone about among all of you, preaching the Kingdom of God, serves as a type of summary for the contents of the preceding paragraph.

Although Paul literally says preaching the Kingdom, it is agreed by the commentators that the reference is to the Kingdom of God, and so a number of translators have made this reference explicit (Phillips, Goodspeed).

The TEV has rendered the Hebraic idiom "see my face again" into meaningful contemporary English: see me again.

20. 26

So draws a conclusion from what precedes: since Paul has preached to them the Kingdom of God, he is not responsible if any of (them) should be lost. Note that the particle so should relate the first part of verse 26 to the first part of verse 25 rather than to the second sentence, which speaks of the people never seeing Paul again.

The verb translated solemnly declare is literally "testify," but in the present passage it obviously has a very strong meaning, and the TEV has attempted to bring this out (see JB "I swear"). The closest equivalent in some languages is "I tell you strongly" or "I tell you with important words."

The biblical idiom "I am pure from your blood" has been rendered by the TEV as if any of you should be lost, I am not responsible. See the similar statement in 18. 6. When used in this way, "blood" is equivalent to "death," and so the phrase could be taken to mean "I am not responsible for your death." However, since Paul is speaking of eternal death, the phrase is perhaps best rendered as in the TEV: if any of you should be lost, I am not responsible.

20. 27

Verse 27 is actually the continuation in Greek of the sentence begun in verse 26. In the same way that verse 26 draws a conclusion on the basis of what has been said in verse 25, so verse 27 draws a conclusion on the basis of what has been said in verse 26. In fact, the content of verses 25 and 27 is essentially the same: the Kingdom of God of verse 25 is equivalent to the whole purpose of God in verse 27. Held back translates the same verb as was rendered hold back in verse 20.

The phrase the whole purpose of God is often translated as "all that God plans to do" or "all that God arranges to do."

20. 28

The phrase keep watch over yourselves must not be translated in such a way as to imply "look out for yourselves," in the sense of trying to gain whatever benefit one can from circumstances. The implication here is that the church leader should be concerned about his own spiritual welfare as well as the welfare of all those whom the Holy Spirit has placed in his charge.

It is frequently impossible to carry over the idiom implied in the use of the flock, particularly since in so many parts of the world sheep are not cared for. Rather, they are the scavengers of the village or are permitted to run loose on the surrounding hillsides. Therefore, the flock must be translated as "the people" or "the congregation." If the figure of flock must be abandoned, obviously some adjustment must be made in the related figure of shepherd. The concept of shepherd may be expressed as "those who take care of" or "those who protect."

In this verse Paul is describing the function of the church leader rather than his office. For this reason the TEV has translated the literal phrase "(the Holy Spirit) has made you overseers" by has placed in your care. This word rendered "overseer" or "guardian" by a number of translators has been rendered elsewhere as church leaders by the TEV (Philippians 1.1; 1 Timothy 3. 2; Titus 1. 7; and in 1 Peter 2. 25 it appears as Keeper, in reference to Christ). Has placed in your care may be rendered as "has given to you as your responsibility to take care of."

Be shepherds is actually an infinitive, but it may be used in the sense of an imperative, parallel with keep watch. On the other hand, it is possible to take it as an infinitive of purpose after the verb keep watch: "keep watch ... so that you may be shepherds." In instances in which the metaphor be shepherds of the church cannot be employed, it is sometimes possible to approximate the meaning of this figure of speech by a simile—for example, "take care of the church of God in the same way that shepherds take care of their sheep." If the metaphor must be abandoned entirely, one can say "take care of the church of God" or "provide for the church of God."

There is a textual problem as to whether the reading should be the church of God or "the church of the Lord." The choice of the reading at this place depends in large measure upon the choice one makes regarding the phrase rendered by the TEV through the death of his own Son. The text followed by the TEV at this point literally reads "through the blood of his own." "Blood" in the present context is, of course, a reference to death and should generally be translated in that fashion. Moreover, those who accept this reading understand "his own" to mean his own Son, and so the TEV has made this explicit. The alternative reading at this point is literally "through his own blood," which also must be understood in the sense of "through his own death." However, if this second reading is followed, then it would go much easier with "the church of the Lord" than it would with the church of God. Since the textual evidence more strongly favors the reading which the TEV has in the text, through the death of his own Son, it would seem better to follow the text which reads the church of God rather than "the church of the Lord." On the other hand, if one feels bound to follow the text "through his own death," this would refer to "the church of the Lord" (that is, the Lord Jesus).

Through the death of his own Son specifies the means by which God made the church his own, but in many languages it is not easy to introduce an event such as death as an instrument. The closest equivalent may be "the fact that his own Son died made this possible," "by dying his own Son caused this to be," or "his own Son died, and this made the church belong to God."

The verb translated made his own by the TEV has been understood in the sense of "purchased" or "bought" by some translators (see KJV, JB). This gives a wrong impression, as though the Lord paid somebody something in order to acquire the church. The verb itself can mean simply "to acquire for one's self," without any thought of purchase involved. In fact, there are some passages in the New Testament where commentators understand the verb to mean "rescue from destruction" (see Luke 17.33; Hebrews 10.39), and so believe that it should be translated with that meaning in the present context. The meaning of "make one's own" or "get for one's self" seems to be the best meaning in the present context.

20.29

In this sentence, which in Greek goes through verse 30, the emphatic element is I. Even though the phrase rendered after I leave originally meant something like "after my arrival," scholars understand the meaning here as after I leave.

Fierce wolves is a reference to the false teachers who will come in and not spare the flock (that is, the church). The reference in this verse is to outsiders who will come and try to indoctrinate the church with their false teaching. The translation of fierce wolves and flock involves serious problems in a number of languages. In the first place, wolves may not even be known in the region, and therefore the closest equivalent may be "fierce wild dogs" or "fierce wild hyenas." In still other languages a more general expression must be employed, namely, "fierce animals" or "animals that kill and destroy." However, even if an appropriate term for fierce wolves may be found, it is questionable whether one can always employ this type of metaphor. It is too easy in some languages for such an expression to be understood literally. Therefore, in some languages one may employ "men will come among you and act like fierce animals."

Will not spare the flock may be equivalent to "will not leave the flock uninjured." However, as in verse 28, it may be necessary to specify that the flock here applies to "the believers" or "the congregation."

20.30

The church will be faced not only with persons from outside their ranks who will try to lead them astray, but Paul warns them that some men from their own group will tell lies to lead the believers away after them. Believers is literally "disciples," but as elsewhere in the book of Acts these two terms are equivalent expressions used to describe persons who have given themselves to the Lord.

To lead may be taken in the sense of result, though purpose is much more natural for the expression. To lead the believers away after them may be rendered as "to cause the believers to follow them" or even "to cause the believers to separate from other believers and follow only them." In some instances it may even be necessary to translate "to cause some believers to join their group."

<u>20.31</u>

The term <u>watch</u> is rendered in many languages as "be on your guard" or "watch out for people like that," in the sense of "protecting yourselves against." One may also use a figurative expression such as "keep awake" or "be alert."

The verb <u>remember</u> should not be translated in such a way as to imply that people had forgotten. The implication here is "keep constantly in mind" or "think about continuously." <u>Remember</u> is actually a participle and may be taken either in a temporal sense, "as you remember," or in a circumstantial sense, "remembering." It is also possible to understand this participle as an imperative used in conjunction with <u>watch</u>, as in the TEV (see also NEB).

The phrase <u>with many tears</u> is probably a reference to the amount of suffering which Paul had as the result of persecution and difficulties. The closest equivalent in some languages may be "I suffered very much."

The word translated <u>taught</u> is not the usual word for "teach," but it carries the overtones of "warn" or "admonish."

32 "And now I place you in the care of God and the message of his grace. He is able to build you up and give you the blessings he keeps for all his people. 33 I have not coveted anyone's silver or gold or clothing. 34 You yourselves know that with these hands of mine I have worked and provided everything that my companions and I have needed. 35 I have shown you in all things that by working hard in this way we must help the weak, remembering the words that the Lord Jesus himself said, 'There is more happiness in giving than in receiving.'"

36 When Paul finished, he knelt down with them all and prayed. 37 They were all crying as they hugged him and kissed him good-bye. 38 They were especially sad at the words he had said that they would never see him again. And so they went with him to the ship. (20.32-38)

<u>20.32</u>

<u>And now</u> introduces the final part of Paul's speech; since he can no longer be with these people in Ephesus, he places them in the care of God. In some languages the most useful transition at this point is "and finally," since this would be the normal way of introducing the last section of any discourse. In certain languages, however, the equivalent would be "at this point in what I am saying." Obviously, the Greek term <u>now</u> is not a reference to time but a transitional device.

Many translations render literally the Greek phrase "the word of his grace." The TEV has taken "word" in the sense of message: <u>the message of</u>

his grace (cf. v. 24). The NEB has employed a rather meaningless expression "his gracious word." It is difficult to decide exactly what this phrase means; it could refer to the Old Testament or to the teachings of Jesus. However, in the present context it seems to refer rather to Paul's own message which he preached about the grace of God.

It is difficult, in a number of languages, to speak about placing someone in the care of another. One can say "I ask God to take care of you" or "I put you in God's hands so he can take care of you." However, it is even more difficult to speak of placing someone in the care of the message of his grace, but one can translate "the message about God's goodness to you will take care of you."

To build you up must be taken in a spiritual sense of God's blessings to the believers in the present, while the remainder of the verse refers to the blessings which God will give to his people at the end of time. The word rendered the blessings he keeps is a word which can mean "inheritance," in the sense of what one leaves to one's heirs at death. However, in a context which speaks of God's relationship to his people, it is best understood in the sense of "that which God either promises or gives to his people." Since in the present context the reference is not to God's gift in the present but to his gift in the future, the TEV has made it explicit by translating the blessings he keeps. For all his people is literally "in all those who have been set apart (or dedicated) to him." (On this phrase see the discussion at 9.13.)

The translation of the second sentence in verse 32 is not easy. Frequently one cannot speak of "building up a person." The act of "building up" can only be applied to a house or some kind of structure. Therefore, it may be necessary to say "cause you to become strong" or "cause you to be well in your spirits," since obviously the reference here is to spiritual strength and blessing.

The second half of this sentence provides even greater difficulties for the translator, since in so many languages one cannot speak of "giving blessings." One can, however, "bless a person" or "cause a person to have a blessing." This is literally, in a number of languages, "causing good to come to a person." Since these blessings refer evidently to some future event, it may be necessary to render this final clause as "he will finally cause good to come to you, the kind of good which he has for all his people."

20. 33

In the ancient Orient, treasures consisted not only of silver and of gold but of (fine) clothing (see James 5. 2), and for this reason not only rust but also moths could be looked upon as the enemy of the rich man's treasures.

Coveted may be rendered in some languages as "wanting to take away someone's possession" or "wanting for myself what belongs to someone else."

20. 34

The Greek text of this verse is rather awkward, though the TEV has translated it in such a way as to agree with most of the commentaries. In order to understand a problem in the next verse, it is necessary to point out something which the TEV has done here. Provided everything...needed is literally "provided for (our) needs." The first word in the Greek text of verse 35 is "all things," and it has been taken by the TEV and most other translations as related to the verb shown, that is, I have shown you in all things. According to this interpretation, Paul means that in every way possible, both by example and by teaching, he has shown them that by working hard in this way (they) must help the weak (v. 35). The translators of the NEB have evidently taken "all things" as the object of the verb "provided" or "earned" (v. 34), and so have translated: "these hands of mine earned enough for the needs of me and my companions."

In most languages it is quite possible to say "I have worked with my hands," but in other languages this seems to be a very strange and even meaningless combination, since as one works more than just the hands are involved. Therefore, it may be necessary to translate merely as "I have worked." This combination of working and providing everything needed may be best expressed in some languages as "I have worked and earned enough money to buy what my companions and I have needed." Otherwise, it might appear that Paul himself had personally made and grown all that was needed for this rather primitive community of people.

20. 35

For the exegetical problem related to the translation of in all things, see 20. 34. This expression may be idiomatically rendered in a number of languages as "I have shown you in every way" or "I have shown you how under all kinds of circumstances."

By working hard in this way may be rendered as "by working hard as I have worked" or "by doing hard work as I have done."

Weak should be taken as a reference to the sick.

Paul quotes a saying from the Lord Jesus, and though this appears nowhere else in the New Testament, there is no reason to doubt its authenticity. Not everything that our Lord said and did was recorded in the Gospels (see John 20. 30-31). For the translation there is more happiness in giving than in receiving, see also the JB. Happiness is a very difficult term to translate; it refers to the kind of joy one experiences when God rules in one's life and when one's values are based upon the values of the Kingdom of God rather than on the values of this world.

Again, the verb remembering must be understood in terms of "bearing constantly in mind" or "reminding oneself constantly." This is not the remembering after a time of forgetting.

The rendering of there is more happiness in giving than in receiving may require considerable readjustment, since in so many languages it is only people who can be happy, give, and receive. Therefore one may translate as "when a person gives he is happier than when he receives" or "if a person gives to someone else, this makes him happier than if he just receives from someone."

20.36

The verb finished may require some complementary verb such as "finished speaking" or "stopped speaking to the people."

As was the custom of that time, Paul knelt down when praying. It may also be necessary to add a goal to the verb prayed, for example, "prayed to God."

20.37

The crying in this verse is the weeping which often accompanies departure from dear friends. This should not be translated as the weeping or crying at death.

The expressions hugged him and kissed him are simply typical of affectionate greetings in the Middle East. Hugged may be translated as "embraced," and the kissing was normally done on the cheek even as it is today in the Middle East. In languages in which hugging and kissing would be grossly misinterpreted as having sexual connotations, one may employ a more general expression of farewell such as "bid him good-bye affectionately" or "showed great love for him when they said good-bye affectionately."

20.38

In Greek this sentence is a continuation of the sentence begun in verse 37; once again the TEV has broken the sentence for ease of communication. They would never see him again must be taken as an explanation for the cause of their sadness. The relationship of the sadness to what Paul said may be expressed as "they were very sad indeed when he said to them, You will never see me again" or "they were very sad because he said...."

CHAPTER 21

There are three principal sections in Chapter 21. The first (vv. 1-16) describes various events in Paul's journey from Ephesus to Jerusalem. The second (vv. 17-26) describes Paul's visit to James and the plans made for Paul to undergo a ceremony of purification in company with four men who had taken a vow. The last (vv. 27-40) describes Paul's arrest and his conversation with the military commander preparatory to his message to the mob, which begins in Chapter 22.1 and continues through verse 21.

The first section is introduced by a transitional sentence, We said good-bye to them and left. The second section has a transitional clause, when we arrived in Jerusalem. The third section is introduced by a temporal transition, when the seven days were about to come to an end. These transitional devices are exceedingly important if one is to follow the discourse satisfactorily.

Note that even within the first section (vv. 1-16) there are three major divisions, each marked by a transitional device. The first one, we said good-bye to them and left, is a transitional device to the preceding chapter (as noted just above). At verse 7 there is the clause we continued our voyage, and at verse 15 there is a temporal transition after spending some time there.

Paul Goes to Jerusalem

1 We said good-bye to them and left. After sailing straight across, we came to Cos; the next day we reached Rhodes, and from there we went on to Patara. 2 There we found a ship that was going to Phoenicia; so we went aboard and sailed away. 3 We came to where we could see Cyprus, and sailed south of it on to Syria. We went ashore at Tyre, where the ship was going to unload its cargo. 4 We found some believers there, and stayed with them a week. By the power of the Spirit they told Paul not to go to Jerusalem. 5 But when our time with them was over, we left and went on our way. All of them, with their wives and children, went with us out of the city. We all knelt down on the beach and prayed. 6 Then we said good-bye to one another, and we went on board the ship while they went back home. (21.1-6)

As has been noted in certain other instances, it may be necessary in section headings in some languages to employ past tenses, for example, "Paul Went to Jerusalem." This may be necessary whenever one is referring to historical events.

21.1

Luke introduces this verse with one of his favorite transitional formulas, "and it came to pass" (KJV), which merely is a Semitic way of beginning a new phase in the narrative. To render this literally, as it has often been done, makes little sense. In the present context it introduces a subordinate clause, which is handled by most translators as "when..." (JB, NEB, Phillips; "and when" RSV). Since this is the beginning of a new section, as well as a new chapter, it is possible to do as the TEV has done and not translate this as a subordinate clause: we said good-bye to them and left.

The verb rendered said good-bye may simply mean "had parted from" (RSV, NEB). By giving this verb its literal force, the JB seems to have over-translated: "tore ourselves away from them" (see Luke 22.41, where this verb appears also).

Throughout this chapter (and especially in Chapter 27) Luke uses a number of technical nautical terms, the first of which is translated by the TEV as left; this same word has been rendered "set sail" (RSV, Phillips, NEB) and "put to sea" (JB). Sailing straight across (see 16.11) is also a technical term used in sailing; as the word indicates, it describes a ship making a straight course. Commentators believe that this implies that the wind was coming from the northeast, and this would explain once again why it was much easier for Paul to send for the Ephesian elders than for him to go to them in Ephesus. Luke apparently outlines the journey day by day in this verse: the first day was from Miletus to the small isle of Cos, the second was from Cos to Rhodes, and the third was from Rhodes to Patara, the port city of Lycia. Since Cos and Patara are the names of the main cities on the islands, as well as the names of the islands themselves, it is quite likely that Luke intended the reader to understand that these were the cities where the ship stopped.

Some manuscripts add "and Myra" after Patara. While it is possible that these words were accidentally dropped from the Greek text, it seems more likely that they were added under the influence of 27.5. This phrase does not appear in the text of most modern translations, but it is given in the margins of several—for example, RSV, NEB, JB.

21.2

It is not clear why Paul and his companions had to change ships in Patara. Perhaps the vessel on which they had been sailing was a smaller vessel used to sail close to the coast, and they needed a larger vessel to make the open sea journey from Patara to Tyre. Was going actually translates a present participle in Greek, but it has a future significance. Went aboard and sailed away are two technical terms for sailing; the second of these, sailed away, is the same word translated left in verse 1.

In attempting to deal with these relatively technical nautical terms a translator is usually either faced with a superabundance of terms, if he is translating into a language of seafaring people, or he finds that there are relatively few terms which correspond to the Greek expressions. Therefore he is required to use in almost all instances general expressions such as "went," "went by boat," or "traveled on a ship." In some languages one can simply use "left...went over the water and arrived at...." Of course, in languages where technical nautical terms are well known by all the people, these can certainly be employed; but if such terms are only known by a

21.3

relatively few persons in a society, more general expressions should be used.

<u>21.3</u>

   <u>Came to where we could see</u> apparently is a technical term for sighting land (see NEB "came in sight of"; and Phillips, JB "after sighting"). <u>Sailed south of it</u> is literally "leaving it on our left," but geographically what is meant is that the ship sailed south of Cyprus. Some translators have rendered this as a technical term used in sailing (see JB and NEB "leaving it to port" and Barclay "left it on our port beam"), but since these terms are not easily understood by most readers, it is usually more advisable to translate as the TEV has done.
   All commentators agree that the past tense used by Luke (literally "was unloading") must be understood with a future reference: <u>was going to unload</u> (see RSV and JB "was to unload"). In some languages it is not possible to say <u>the ship was going to unload its cargo</u>. Rather, one must say that "men were going to unload the ship," "men were going to carry from the ship what was on it," or "...what was being transported in it."

<u>21.4</u>

   <u>Found</u> translates a verb which means "to find by searching for" (see JB, Barclay "sought out"; Goodspeed "looked up"), which suggests that Paul and his group knew there were <u>some believers there</u>, though they may not have known who they were when they first arrived.
   <u>Some believers</u> is literally "the disciples," but once again "disciples" is used in the sense of "those who believe." Luke merely says that "we stayed there," but the implication is that Paul and his group stayed with the believers in Tyre, and so the TEV has translated this clause as <u>stayed with them</u> (see also Goodspeed and Phillips). A number of translators do as the TEV and and render "seven days" by <u>a week</u> (see 20.6).
   Luke's phrase "through the Spirit" is taken by the TEV as a reference to the power given the believers by the Spirit, thus enabling them to understand the fate that awaited Paul in Jerusalem. Accordingly, the TEV has translated this phrase <u>by the power of the Spirit</u>. This phrase may be rendered as "prompted by the Holy Spirit" or "guided by the Holy Spirit." After the verb of speaking, it may be necessary to employ direct discourse—for example, "guided by the Holy Spirit they said to Paul, You should not go to Jerusalem." In the present context <u>not to go to Jerusalem</u> means "not to go on to Jerusalem" (JB, RSV).

<u>21.5</u>

   Although this is a strange use of the Greek verb translated <u>was over</u>, scholars agree that this is its meaning in the present context. Most translators prefer to give a rather literal rendering to Luke's words "when our time was over," without indicating time spent with whom or where. The NEB refers this to time spent ashore, "but when our time ashore was ended," while the TEV relates this to time spent with the believers, but when our time with them was over. However, it is difficult in some languages to speak of our time...was over. It may be necessary to say "the time which we could spend with them was ended," "we came to the end of the time we could stay with them," or "finally we had to leave."

On the basis of the definite article used before ship (literally the ship) in verse 6, commentators conclude that the same vessel is referred to in verse 3 as in verse 6. If this is true, what caused Paul's time to be over was the fact that the ship had finished unloading its cargo and was now ready to continue on its voyage. The word used for beach (see also 27. 39) refers to a sandy beach as opposed to a rocky shore.

For knelt down...and prayed see 20. 36.

21. 6

Said good-bye is the same verb as appeared in verse 1 of this chapter. It is interesting to note that the RSV, NEB, and JB, all of which rendered this word in a different way in verse 1, agree that the meaning here is "to say good-bye."

Went on board is another technical sailing term used by Luke.

Home is the same expression rendered to his own country by the TEV in John 1.11. It is an idiomatic expression referring to one's home, but in the Gospel of John the reference is to one's home in the expanded sense of the word, that is, one's homeland.

7 We continued our voyage, sailing from Tyre to Ptolemais, where we greeted the brothers and stayed with them for a day. 8 On the following day we left and arrived in Caesarea. There we went to the house of the evangelist Philip, and stayed with him. He was one of the seven men who had been chosen in Jerusalem. 9 He had four un-married daughters who proclaimed God's message. 10 We had been there for several days when a prophet named Agabus arrived from Judea. 11 He came to us, took Paul's belt, tied up his own feet and hands with it, and said, "This is what the Holy Spirit says: The owner of this belt will be tied up in this way by the Jews in Jerusalem, and they will hand him over to the Gentiles."

12 When we heard this, we and the others there begged Paul not to go to Jerusalem. 13 But he answered, "What are you doing, crying like this and breaking my heart? I am ready not only to be tied up in Jerusalem but even to die there for the sake of the Lord Jesus."

14 We could not convince him, so we gave up and said, "May the Lord's will be done." (21. 7-14)

21. 7

We continued our voyage is taken by a number of translators to mean
"we finished our voyage" (JB, Segond, Zürich, Spanish Versión Popular).
The verb itself originally meant "to complete," but there are passages in
classical Greek where it was used with exactly the same meaning as given by
the TEV. The question is whether Luke understood Paul's voyage as being
at an end when he reached Ptolemais, or whether he looked upon this as being merely a continuation of Paul's voyage. This is related to another question, which cannot be answered definitely, whether Paul went from Ptolemais
to Caesarea by land or by sea.

Ptolemais, a city named in honor of the Egyptian ruler Ptolemy II, was
a fortress city located on the northern end of the bay directly across from
Mount Carmel, which was on the southern side of the bay.

21. 8

The distance from Ptolemais to Caesarea was 40 miles and would have
been difficult to make in a day's time. The verb translated left is a word
which simply means "to leave," without reference to whether one travels by
ship or by land. From the standpoint of translation, it is better to use a
general term, rather than a term denoting some specific kind of travel.

Evangelist (see Ephesians 4.11) simply means "a preacher of the Good
News," and it is rendered in this way by the TEV in 2 Timothy 4.5. A verb
which comes from this same stem is used to describe Philip's work in 8.12,
35,40. The New Testament itself does not clarify the distinction between
this word and the other words used of those who preached the Good News,
though it seems rather certain that evangelist did not mean in the New Testament what it means in contemporary English usage. It would seem best in
most instances to translate this phrase as "Philip who preached the Good
News."

Luke further characterizes him as "one of the seven," which means
one of the seven men who had been chosen in Jerusalem. Both the NEB and
the JB speak of Philip as "one of the Seven," but to translate even with a capital S is insufficient, for though the man who reads this for himself may immediately understand what is meant, it is quite likely that the person who
hears this read will miss its significance. On the other hand, to translate
as Phillips has ("one of the seven deacons"), may give a false meaning, since
these men are not called deacons in Chapter 6. On the whole, it seems best
to render this phrase as the TEV has done, which makes clear the meaning
that Luke had in mind, without adding an interpretation to what he said. It is
important at this point to have some type of marginal reference to 6.1-6.

21. 9

A number of commentators and translators understand Luke's phrase "virgin daughters" to mean simply unmarried daughters (see Moffatt, Goodspeed, NEB, Phillips, RSV).

21.10

We had been there for several days is a transition from the preceding statements concerning Philip to the introduction of the prophet Agabus.

For Agabus see 11.28. Nothing more is known about him other than what is mentioned there and in this verse. Although, in reference to Agabus, the term "prophet" certainly would seem to imply foretelling the future, it is important to avoid a term which simply would suggest "diviner" or "fortune-teller." One can probably most legitimately employ for "prophet" in this context the same type of expression as is used in many other places in the New Testament, namely, "one who spoke on behalf of God." (See 15.15.)

As far as the Roman administration was concerned, Caesarea was the capital of the province of Judea; however, since Caesarea was a Gentile city, it was not considered by the Jews as a part of their country in the popular sense of the word. It is quite likely, as some commentators point out, that Luke at this point equates Judea with the city of Jerusalem.

21.11

Paul's belt would have been a long piece of cloth which he wrapped around his waist. This type of belt was used not only as a part of one's clothing, but also to serve the practical purpose of being a place where one could carry money and other items. "Belt" is the nearest equivalent in contemporary English, and to translate "girdle" (JB, Phillips, RSV) is certainly misleading, since it would suggest to most people a woman's undergarment. Agabus' symbolic action reminds one of the Old Testament prophets (see Isaiah 22 and Jeremiah 13.1 ff.); and the statement this is what the Holy Spirit says is reminiscent of the Old Testament declaration "thus says the Lord." What is said of Paul (that is, he will be handed over by the Jews to the Gentiles) calls to mind the fate of Jesus. Actually Paul was not handed over to the Gentiles by the Jews, though had it not been for the Jewish hatred against Paul he would never have been arrested by the Roman authorities.

21.12

Begged translates a verb tense which places the emphasis upon the continuation of the action, that is, "they continued to beg Paul." The tense of the verb translated to go probably means "to go on" (JB) or "to continue on (to Jerusalem)." The term begged must, of course, be translated as "asked strongly" or "pled with him." Such verbs may introduce direct discourse: "pled with Paul, Please do not go to Jerusalem."

21.13

A difference in pronominal usage in Greek and English may be illustrated by the alternations in verses 12 and 13. In verse 12 Luke has in Greek the pronoun "him," while in verse 13 he has the proper name "Paul." To make this good English discourse structure, it is necessary to transform the pronoun "him" of verse 12 into "Paul," and to change the proper name "Paul" into "he" in verse 13.

The word translated breaking is a very strong term. Originally it was used of a washwoman who pounded the clothes with a rock in order to try to make them come white again. Some translators press this last aspect of this verb to mean that Paul said they were making him "turn white" (that is, "pale") from fear (see JB and NEB "weaken my resolution" and Phillips "unnerving me"). However, it seems quite unlikely that this is what Paul meant; it appears much more natural to understand Paul to be saying that they were "breaking his heart" because of their sorrow over what would happen to him. Moreover, the conclusion reached by the TEV is supported by Paul's own answer: I am ready not only to be tied up in Jerusalem but even to die there for the sake of the Lord Jesus. For the sake of the Lord Jesus is literally "for the sake of the name of the Lord Jesus," but "name" is obviously only an idiomatic reference to the person.

It is usually impossible to translate literally breaking my heart. A far more usual expression would be "you are causing me to suffer so much," "you are causing me great distress in my heart," or "you are causing me very great disappointment."

We gave up (so also NEB; see JB "we gave up the attempt") is literally "we became silent." The TEV translation has at least two advantages: (1) in the present context the meaning of "to become silent" is that they no longer tried to convince Paul; and (2) the tense of the verb suggests that they gave up doing something they were in the process of doing. We gave up may be simply rendered as "we stopped trying to convince him" or "we stopped saying to him, You should not go."

May the Lord's will be done actually translates a third person imperative in Greek, something which is difficult to express in many languages, including English. Somehow the translation should indicate that this reflects a strong resolution on the part of the people, and not merely a resignation in light of some impossible circumstances, as may be suggested by "the Lord's will be done" (NEB). The closest equivalent in some languages is to say "we pray that the Lord's will may be done" or "we pray that everything will happen just as the Lord wants it."

15 After spending some time there, we got our things ready and left for Jerusalem. 16 Some of the disciples from Caesarea also went with us, and took us to the house of the man we were going to stay with —Mnason, from Cyprus, who had been a believer since the early days.
(21.15-16)

This final section begins with a transitional clause, <u>after spending some</u> <u>time there</u>, and simply serves to complete the account of Paul's journey to Jerusalem. In a sense this is transitional between the events described in Caesarea and Paul's experiences which were to come in Jerusalem.

21.15

The verb translated <u>we got our things ready</u> is perhaps a specific reference to packing up for the trip (see NEB "we packed our baggage" and JB "we packed"). Some commentators understand this verb to mean "we hired horses," but no translation seems to go in this direction. The tense of the verb translated <u>left</u> perhaps means something like "went on" (so JB), thus indicating the continuation of the journey rather than its beginning.

21.16

Although verse 16 presents some rather unique constructions in the Greek, the meaning of this verse is clear and should cause no special problems for the translator. <u>Mnason</u> (a rather common name) appears nowhere else in the New Testament; like Barnabas (see 4.36), he had also come from Cyprus. Although it is stated that Mnason <u>had been a believer</u> (literally "disciple") <u>since the early days</u> (so also NEB), no one is quite certain what this phrase means (JB "one of the earliest disciples"). Perhaps the reference is to indicate that he was one of the first to become a disciple after the resurrection of the Lord and the coming of the Spirit.

Some rearrangement of components in the latter half of verse 16 may be useful—for example, "took us to the house of Mnason, a person with whom we were going to stay. This man was from Cyprus and had been a believer for a long time." The use of the phrase "for a long time" rather than <u>since</u> <u>the early days</u> may be necessary in some languages, since an expression such as "since the early days" would require some specification as to what happened in "the early days." In other words, one would have to indicate "the early days of (what)"; therefore saying "for a long time" may be an equivalent general expression and not involve the translator in the introduction of unnecessary or possibly unwarranted information.

Paul Visits James

17 When we arrived in Jerusalem the brothers welcomed us warmly. 18 The next day Paul went with us to see James; and all the church elders were present. 19 Paul greeted them and gave a complete report of everything that God had done among the Gentiles through his work. 20 After hearing him, they all praised God. Then they said to Paul, "You can see how it is, brother. There are thousands of Jews who have become believers, and they are all very devoted to the Law. 21 They have been told about you that you have been teaching all the Jews who live in Gentile countries to abandon the Law of Moses, telling

407

them not to circumcise their children or follow the Jewish customs.
22 They are sure to hear that you have arrived. What should be done,
then? 23 Do what we tell you. There are four men here who have taken
a vow. 24 Go along with them and join them in the ceremony of purification and pay their expenses; then they will be able to shave their
heads. In this way everyone will know that there is no truth in any of
the things that they have been told about you, but that you yourself live
in accordance with the Law of Moses. 25 But as to the Gentiles who
have become believers, we have sent them a letter telling them we decided that they must not eat any food that has been offered to idols, or
any blood, or any animal that has been strangled, and that they must
keep themselves from immorality."

26 So Paul took the men and the next day performed the ceremony
of purification with them. Then he went into the temple and gave notice
of how many days it would be until the end of the period of purification,
when the sacrifice for each one of them would be offered. (21.17-26)

The section heading Paul Visits James may need to be placed in the past
tense, "Paul Visited James." As noted above, this type of change of tense in
the section heading would need to apply to all such section headings.

There are two types of transitional and connective features in this section. First, there are the temporal transitions such as when we arrived in
Jerusalem (v. 17), the next day (v. 18), after hearing him (v. 20), then
(v. 20), so (v. 26), then (v. 26), all within the discourse attributed collectively to the church elders. Second, there are the connections in thought,
shown primarily by reciting the various objections which the Jewish believers
have to Paul and how he may be able to convince persons that such objections
are not founded.

21.17

The brothers are best understood as a spontaneous and unofficial group
of Christians who came out to meet Paul. Warmly (see JB, Phillips "gave us
a very warm welcome") is rendered in other translations "gladly" (NEB,
RSV). The equivalent of the brothers may be, in some languages, "some believers," and welcomed us warmly may be rendered as "were very happy to
greet us" or "greeted us with great joy."

21.18

James, the brother of the Lord, occupied a leading position in the early
church (see 12.17; 15.13). From all indications, Peter and the other apostles
were no longer in Jerusalem at this time. The expression see James must
often be rendered as "to talk with James" or "to visit James." It is not mere
"seeing" which is involved.

The church elders are, of course, the leaders in the Jerusalem church.

Gave a complete report of everything (literally "told them one by one each of the things") is translated "gave a detailed account" by JB (see also Phillips and NEB).

Work (most translations "ministry") is the same word used in 1.17.

As in a number of instances, it is sometimes difficult to translate an expression which speaks of one person doing something through someone else; therefore the last clause of verse 19 may be rendered as "what God had done among the Gentiles because of the work which Paul did." Sometimes the relationship between the accomplishing and the working is expressed in two closely combined clauses without formal connection—for example, "everything that God had accomplished among the Gentiles; Paul had done the work."

21. 20

Doubtless they all praised God not only because of what God had done through Paul, but also because the rumors that they had heard about Paul had proved to be false. It is difficult to understand how the entire group speaks to Paul, but that is what Luke has indicated: they said to Paul. In some languages this would be interpreted to mean that all of the persons had rehearsed this speech so they could repeat it in unison. Obviously this is not what is intended. In some languages, therefore, it is necessary to say "one of them spoke to Paul on behalf of all" or "they spoke to Paul through one person."

When Paul is addressed, Luke uses a verbal expression (literally "you see") which is intended to call Paul's attention to the situation as it existed in Jerusalem; the TEV has rendered this expression: you can see how it is. It may be necessary, however, in translating you can see how it is to specify the particular location of such events or circumstances—for example, "you can see how it is here in Jerusalem." In this context brother may be rendered as "fellow believer" or "you who believe together with us."

Who have become believers translates precisely the meaning of the Greek perfect participle "those who have believed," since the perfect tense indicates persons who have become believers. These Jewish believers are described by Luke as "zealous for the law." The TEV has translated this phrase as very devoted to the Law, and it has been rendered "staunch upholders of the Law" by JB, Phillips, and NEB (see also Goodspeed "zealous upholders of the Law" and Moffatt "ardent upholders of the Law"). Most translators render Law (with a capital L), since the reference is obviously to the Jewish Law. For the persons who only hear Scripture read but do not read it for themselves, it may be better to render Law as "our Law" or "our Jewish Law." In order to make it perfectly clear that this is not "the law of the land" or general civil laws which should be obeyed, some translators have employed here "they are very devoted to keeping the Law of Moses" or ". . . the law which came through Moses."

21.21

"Who are among the Gentiles" is a fairly literal rendering of Luke's expression. Luke has reference to the Jews scattered outside of Judea, and who therefore live in Gentile countries (see NEB "in the gentile world").

All commentators agree that by "Moses" (in the expression "you are teaching...apostasy from Moses") Luke means the Law of Moses (see also Phillips). In the present context the Law of Moses refers not only to the command for the Jews to circumcise their children, but also has reference to the Jewish customs generally, some of which came later but which were also attributed by the Jews to Moses. Paul did not tell the Jews not to circumcise their children (see 16.3), and it seems unlikely that Paul was guilty of telling the Jews to give up their Jewish customs. What Paul did teach (and this we know both from Acts and from Paul's own writings) is that one is not saved by circumcision or by living according to the Jewish customs. Evidently Paul's opponents had taken some things that Paul had said, and after twisting them around, used them against Paul. The Lukan phrase "to walk in the customs" is taken by most commentators to mean follow the Jewish customs.

In languages which normally employ direct discourse in citing opinions or statements, there may be certain complications in the translation of this verse, since there are at least three levels of discourse: "The elders... [1] said to Paul..., People have spoken to them about you. They [2] say, You have been teaching all the Jews who live in Gentile countries, [3] saying, You should abandon the Law of Moses...."

The expression follow the Jewish customs may be rendered as "live as Jews traditionally have lived" or "do what Jews customarily do."

21.22

What should be done, then? (JB "What is to be done?") is a question raised by the people who are bringing this accusation to Paul's attention. What they mean is what should Paul do, or what should they do, in order to show that the suspicions about Paul are unfounded? Though this question would seem to be directed to Paul to ask him for his opinion, in reality it is only rhetorical; that is to say, the question is asked in order to be immediately answered by the same persons who asked it. In order to deal effectively with such a question as what should be done, then?, it may be immediately followed by "let us tell you what we think you should do." This would then be the first sentence of verse 23.

21.23

Beginning with this verse the church elders explain to Paul what they think is best for him to do in light of the situation. It is generally assumed that the vow referred to was a Nazirite vow (see 18.18). In ancient Israel it was customary for some men to take a lifelong vow to abstain from wine or

anything unclean, and never to cut their hair (note Samson in Judges 13).
Later the Jewish Law provided for a man to assume a temporary Nazirite
vow, which meant that he would live as a Nazirite for a certain length of time,
and at the end of that time offer a series of sacrifices. When all of this had
been completed, the man shaved his head and burned the hair along with the
sacrifice. After this he was free to drink wine and to go back to his normal
way of life. It is known from rabbinic sources that the shortest length of time
for which one could assume this temporary vow was 30 days, so this raises
problems with the mention of seven days in verse 27. A number of solutions
have been offered, but it must be admitted that none of these are without
their particular difficulties. Perhaps the least complicated conclusion is to
assume that these men who had taken the vow had in the meanwhile become
defiled. Therefore, it was necessary for them to undergo a period of seven
days purification, at the end of which they would be permitted to offer the
sacrifices required by the Jewish Law (see Numbers 6. 9-12).

The term vow may be rendered as "a promise made before God" or "a
strong promise made to God." The process of "taking a vow" in some languages may actually be rendered as "bound themselves by a promise to God."

21. 24

Join them in the ceremony of purification (see Goodspeed "undergo the
rites of purification with them" and NEB "go through the ritual of purification with them") is literally "be made holy with them" (see JB and Phillips
"be purified with them"). It is important to observe that Luke does not say
that Paul assumed the Nazirite vow along with these men, but that he went
through the ceremony of purification with them and paid their expenses.
The expenses for the sacrifices were rather costly, and as an act of piety
people of means often paid the expenses involved.

It is not easy to translate the expression join them in the ceremony of
purification. One can say "go along with them in being purified," but it is
important to indicate that this act of purification is some kind of ritual or
ceremony. One may say, in some languages, "become one with them in
undergoing the ceremony of being purified." However, in some languages a
translation of "purified" in the sense of "to be made clean" carries no special
religious significance. Therefore one may employ some such phrase as "to
be made pure before God" or "to be made pure in God's eyes." Because of a
number of aspects of this particular passage, it is important that some marginal note provide at least minimal explanation for what is involved in a vow
and accompanying purification. Such a note may be formulated on the basis
of the exegetical information included on this passage.

Pay their expenses may be translated as "pay what it costs them to be
purified" or, as in some instances, "pay for the sacrifices for their being
purified."

In the Greek, verse 24 is only one sentence, and the second clause begins with "and everybody will know." When used in this way, "and" has the

force of introducing an explanation, rather than merely tying together two coordinate clauses. For this reason the TEV has translated "and" as in this way (see RSV "thus"; Phillips "and then"; JB "this will let everyone know").

Once again it is obvious that Luke has used "the law" in the sense of the Law of Moses (most translations indicate this by spelling Law with a capital L). Live in accordance with the Law of Moses may be rendered as "live as the rules in the Law of Moses say one should live" or "obey what it says in the Law of Moses concerning how one should live."

21. 25

This verse, which introduces the apostolic decree as though it were imparting new information, fits in very loosely with the context. Even though the words are formally addressed to Paul, in reality Luke seems to have included them for the benefit of his readers (as he did with 1.18-19). On the interpretation and translation of this verse see 15.20. The introductory conjunction but is particularly important here, since it shifts the attention from the Jewish believers to the Gentile believers.

21. 26

The transitional particle so is particularly important to mark the break between the statement attributed to the church elders and what Paul did as the result of their advice.

Took the men may be rendered in some languages as "went along with the men" or even "accompanied the men."

Once again there is the problem of defining exactly what ceremony of purification is referred to. Some commentators conclude that it would have been necessary for Paul to have undergone a type of purification ceremony before entering the temple, since he had recently returned from an extended visit in Gentile countries, and it seems quite possible that this is the ceremony of purification referred to in the present verse. Inasmuch as Paul was considered ceremonially impure, he would have undergone this ceremony of purification before entering the temple to take part in the act of purification with the four Nazirites. That this is the correct interpretation is supported by the observation that Paul did not go into the temple until after he had performed the ceremony of purification, and that this took place several days before the sacrifice for these four men was to be offered.

The word used for temple in this verse is a word that normally refers to the entire temple area, but in the present context the meaning seems to be limited to the temple proper; and this would be true also for the use of temple in verses 27 ff. The period of purification refers to the seven-day period that the four men who had taken the Nazirite vow had to undergo before they would be considered ceremonially pure to carry out the sacrifice. Each one of them refers to the four Nazirites; a sacrifice would not have been offered for Paul himself at the end of this period.

Paul Arrested in the Temple

27 When the seven days were about to come to an end, some Jews from the province of Asia saw Paul in the temple. They stirred up the whole crowd and grabbed Paul. 28 "Men of Israel!" they shouted. "Help! This is the man who goes everywhere teaching everyone against the people of Israel, the Law of Moses, and this temple. And now he has even brought some Gentiles into the temple and defiled this holy place!" 29 (They said this because they had seen Trophimus from Ephesus with Paul in the city, and they thought that Paul had taken him into the temple.)

30 Confusion spread through the whole city, and the people all ran together, grabbed Paul, and dragged him out of the temple. At once the temple doors were closed. 31 The mob was trying to kill Paul when a report was sent up to the commander of the Roman troops that all of Jerusalem was rioting. 32 At once the commander took some officers and soldiers and rushed down to the crowd. When the people saw him with the soldiers, they stopped beating Paul. 33 The commander went over to Paul, arrested him, and ordered him to be tied up with two chains. Then he asked, "Who is this man, and what has he done?" 34 Some in the crowd shouted one thing, others something else. There was such confusion that the commander could not find out exactly what had happened; so he ordered his men to take Paul up into the fort. 35 They got with him to the steps, and then the soldiers had to carry him because the mob was so wild. 36 They were all coming after him and screaming, "Kill him!" (21. 27-36)

There is a difficulty involved in the section heading Paul Arrested in the Temple. He was actually dragged out of the temple (v. 30) and there the mob tried to kill him. It was only outside of the temple that Paul was actually arrested. One may wish, therefore, to have as a section heading "The Romans Arrest Paul," "Paul Is Attacked in the Temple," or "The Jews Attack Paul."

In this section there are a number of items which mark sequence of events—for example, when (v. 27), and now (v. 28), at once (vv. 30 and 32), when (v. 32), then (v. 33), and so (v. 34). These markers of temporal sequence are extremely important in tying together the structure of these events.

21. 27

On the seven days see verses 23 and 26 above. A Nazirite who was in a state of defilement would shave his head on the seventh day and offer the required sacrifices on the eighth day (see again Numbers 6. 9-12).

The church elders had believed that the Jewish Christians might be the source of trouble for Paul (see v. 20), but as it turned out, some Jews from the province of Asia were the ones who caused Paul his difficulty.

Stirred up the whole crowd may be readily translated as "caused the whole crowd to become excited," "caused the whole crowd to become angry," or "caused the whole crowd to riot."

21. 28

On the phrase men of Israel (literally "men, Jerusalemites") see 1.16. The exclamation Help! may be rendered as "come and help us" or even, as in some instances, "come and join us against this man." "The people" is a term used in the Septuagint to refer to the people of Israel, and so the TEV has brought this out (Spanish Versión Popular "against our nation"; Barclay "God's people"; and JB, NEB "our people").

As in verse 24, "the law" is used with a reference to the Law of Moses. The significance of the word "Greeks" (so most translations) is that these people are non-Jews, that is, Gentiles (of the major translations, only the TEV appears to translate this word by Gentiles). For a Gentile to enter into the temple proper was an offense punishable by death. Inscriptions were placed over the entranceway warning the Gentiles that they took their lives in their own hands if they went beyond that point.

It is not always easy to speak of teaching everyone against the people of Israel. In fact, the concept of "teaching against" may need to be expressed as "teaching everyone by condemning" or "teaching everyone, The people of Israel, the Law of Moses, and this temple have no value."

Though in many languages it is easy enough to express the concept of defiled this holy place, in some languages the only equivalent is a relatively roundabout expression—for example, "caused harm to this holy place," "caused this holy place not to be holy," or "caused the holiness of this place to be damaged."

21. 29

This verse is a parenthetical statement given by Luke by way of explanation (see 1.18-19). On Trophimus, see 20.4 and 2 Timothy 4.20.

In some languages it is not possible to combine a series of terms merely with prepositional links—for example, Trophimus from Ephesus with Paul in the city. Rather, one must say "they had seen Trophimus going around with Paul in the city; Trophimus was from the city of Ephesus."

21. 30

Confusion spread through the whole city is literally "the whole city was stirred up" (see NEB "the whole city was in a turmoil" and Goodspeed "the whole city was thrown into confusion"). In some languages, however, one cannot speak of "confusion spreading." One must say that "throughout the whole city people were being stirred up" or "people were beginning to riot throughout the whole city."

Luke is very picturesque in his description of the events. Dragged translates a verb tense which describes progressive action in past time, whereas all the other verb tenses in this verse describe punctiliar action in past time. It is interesting to note how this lynch mob was particular in the way in which it went about trying to kill Paul: the people would not kill him within the temple precincts for this would have defiled the temple; rather, they dragged him outside and closed the door so he could not run back in for refuge. The passive expression, <u>the temple doors were closed</u>, may be rendered as "they closed the doors of the temple."

<u>21.31</u>

There is no expressed noun subject to the verb <u>was trying</u> (most translations simply have "they were trying"), but the obvious reference is to the people who had gathered together and had become a mob. <u>Commander</u> (originally a word referring to a leader of 1,000 men) was a technical term used to describe the Roman military officer in charge of a regiment (see 10.1); in other translations it occurs as "tribune" (RSV, JB), "colonel" (Phillips), and "officer commanding" (NEB, Barclay).

The expression <u>a report was sent up to the commander</u> may be rendered as "someone went and told the commander" or "some people sent a messenger to the commander."

<u>Roman troops</u> is rendered elsewhere in the TEV as regiment (10.1; 27.1). In the present context it has specific reference to the Roman garrison stationed in the tower of Antonia overlooking the temple area from the northwest corner (see Barclay "the company of soldiers on garrison duty"; Moffatt "the garrison").

Although the verb rendered <u>was rioting</u> (see JB) may mean that the people in the city were merely gathering together, almost all translations do as the TEV has done (see KJV, Phillips, NEB, Barclay "was in an uproar"). Luke has chosen to use a present tense of the verb <u>rioting</u> rather than the past tense, in order to make his description of the events more vivid.

<u>21.32</u>

This verse is a continuation of the sentence begun in the preceding verse; the pronoun with which it begins, "who," is an obvious reference to <u>the commander</u>, and the TEV has made this explicit. Luke's phrase "soldiers and centurions" (so most translations) is understood by the commentators to mean <u>officers and soldiers</u> (see Goodspeed "officers and men" and Moffatt "soldiers and officers"). "On them" of the Greek text is explained by the TEV as meaning <u>to the crowd</u> (see JB "down on the crowd") and by the NEB as "down on the rioters."

<u>21.33</u>

That the commander ordered Paul <u>to be tied up with two chains</u> perhaps means that Paul was ordered to be chained to a Roman soldier on either side of him (see 12.6). The commander's question, <u>Who is this man, and what has</u>

he done? is addressed to the crowd, not to Paul as one might conclude from a literal rendering ("he inquired who he was and what he had done"). With the exception of the TEV and Barclay, all translations apparently use indirect discourse rather than direct discourse for the commander's question. In such a setting direct discourse seems much more forceful for the English reader than does indirect discourse. In fact, in many languages direct discourse would be obligatory in this type of context.

21.34

There is no question regarding the meaning of the words which the TEV has rendered could not find out exactly what had happened, but this is rendered variously by the different translations: "impossible for him to get any positive information" (JB), "could not be certain of the facts" (Phillips), and "could not get at the truth" (NEB). The fort (see JB and Segond "the fortress"; RSV, Phillips, and NEB "the barracks") is most probably a reference to the place where the Roman soldiers were garrisoned, that is, the Antonia. The Antonia, which overlooked the temple area, was connected with it by two flights of stairs.

The expression there was such confusion may be rendered as "because people were saying so many different things, the commander could not find out."

The final phrase, he ordered his men to take Paul up into the fort, may be rendered as direct discourse in a number of languages—for example, "he ordered his men, Take Paul up into the fortress." The term fort may be rendered as "strong building," "protected building," or even "building which could be defended."

21.35

They got with him to the steps may be rendered as "they led him as far as the steps" or "they led him only as far as the steps." It may be necessary to stipulate "only" in order to indicate clearly the shift to the act of carrying Paul because of the violence of the mob.

"So it was" (KJV) translates a verb which is similar in usage to Luke's frequently used formula "and it came to pass." This verb is to be taken along with the verb "to be carried," and together they are to be translated either "he was actually carried" (RSV, Phillips) or had to carry him (TEV, NEB, JB).

The final expression the mob was so wild is rendered in some languages as "the mob was so angry."

21.36

The pronoun they which begins verse 36 must, of course, refer to the Jews, not to the soldiers.

It is agreed among the commentators that the words "away with him" (so KJV, RSV) mean kill him (TEV, Phillips, NEB, JB). The imperative expression kill him is not directed to the soldiers. The Jews were not simply asking the Romans to kill him. Rather, it was a declaration of their own intent, and therefore in many languages must be rendered as "let us kill him" or "come, we must kill him."

Paul Defends Himself

37 As they were about to take Paul into the fort, he spoke to the commander, "May I say something to you?"

"Do you speak Greek?" the commander asked. 38 "Then you are not that Egyptian fellow who some time ago started a revolution and led four thousand armed terrorists out into the desert?"

39 Paul answered, "I am a Jew, born in Tarsus of Cilicia, a citizen of an important city. Please, let me speak to the people."

40 The commander gave him permission, so Paul stood on the steps and motioned with his hand to the people. When they were quiet, Paul spoke to them in Hebrew, (21.37-40)

The section heading Paul Defends Himself may require some adjustment in certain languages, since his defense was obviously not successful. Therefore, in some languages, one must translate "Paul Tries to Defend Himself."

This section begins with a clause which provides the setting, not only in terms of time but also of place, as they were about to take Paul into the fort.

The remainder of this chapter goes closely with Chapter 22; it demonstrates one of the difficulties involved in verse and chapter division. Paul's defense follows three lines of thought: (1) He himself was a Jew, and throughout his life he was as fully dedicated to God and to the Jewish tradition as were those people who wanted to kill him. (2) God himself had intervened in Paul's life and had been responsible for Paul's decision to follow Jesus Christ. (3) God had sent Paul to tell the Good News to the Gentiles, since the Jews in Jerusalem had initially rejected his message.

21.37

It may be necessary to make clear that the pronoun they at the beginning of this verse refers to the soldiers—for example, "as the soldiers were about to take Paul into the fort."

Paul's question to the commander of the soldiers, May I say something to you?, is rendered as direct discourse in most translations, though it appears as indirect discourse in the JB.

Do you speak Greek? is not really a question asking for information, for the commander obviously understood from Paul's statement to him that he did speak Greek. Therefore, this question must be rendered in some languages as "then you obviously speak Greek" or "then you must speak Greek."

21.38

If the question is changed into a statement, the verb relating to the commander's comment must be changed from asked to "said."

21.38

That Egyptian fellow may be rendered as "that man from Egypt." Started a revolution may be rendered as "caused an uprising against the government" or "caused fighting against the government."

The term which the TEV has rendered armed terrorists (NEB "terrorists") has been translated in a variety of fashions: "assassins" (Phillips, Moffatt, Spanish Versión Popular), "cut-throats" (JB, NAB, Goodspeed); it has been transliterated by Segond with a footnote explaining the meaning of the term. These men were extreme nationalists and considered themselves the enemies of all Romans and of all Jews who were pro-Roman; they got their name from the small dagger which they carried with them and by which they would execute their enemies as they mingled with the crowds at the various festivals. By spelling the word with a capital A ("the Assassins"), the RSV and Barclay have tried to indicate that they were a special group among the Jews and not just a spontaneous group of cutthroats. The verb rendered started a revolution (see NEB "started a revolt") is the same verb translated caused trouble in 17.6. It is quite unlikely that the Egyptian fellow referred to considered himself to be the Messiah; it seems more probable that he was merely a rebel who believed that God would help his revolution.

21.39

Paul's reply to the commander (literally "but I am a man, a Jew"; see KJV "I am a man which am a Jew") is an unusual, but emphatic, way of saying merely I am a Jew (so most translations). Paul makes two emphases: (1) he is a Jew, and (2) he comes from a city outside of Palestine, which would help explain his relationship with the Greeks. Tarsus, the city of Paul's birth, was an important city noted for its cultural, intellectual, and political significance. Luke literally says that this was a "not insignificant city" (see Phillips), which is translated "no mean city" by KJV, RSV, and NEB; what Luke means is that it was an important or a "well-known city" (JB).

Let me speak to the people may be rendered as "grant me permission so that I may speak to the people." It may, however, be necessary to use a term such as "mob" or "rioting people" so that it will be perfectly clear that Paul wishes to speak to those who have just tried to kill him.

21.40

Although almost all translations say that Paul spoke to them in Hebrew, actually Paul would have been speaking in Aramaic, the language which the Jews of that day used (see NEB "in the Jewish language"). Spoke to them in Hebrew may be rendered as "spoke to them; the words he used were Hebrew words," "spoke to them, using the Hebrew language," "spoke to them in their own Jewish language," or "... in the language used by the Jews."

CHAPTER 22

Chapter 22 is a rather artificial division. It begins with Paul's address to
the Jewish people, delivered from the steps leading up to the Praetorium and
ends at verse 30 with an introduction to Paul's defense before the chief priests
and the Council. Paul's defense (vv. 1,3-21) is essentially the history of his
early contacts with the Christian movement, including his persecution of the
Christians, his conversion, and then his call to go to the Gentiles.

The second principal section of this chapter (vv. 22-29) consists of the
reaction of the Jews, the order of the Roman commander to have Paul whipped,
and finally the disclosure that Paul is a Roman citizen.

> 1 "Men, brothers and fathers, listen to me as I make my defense
> before you!" 2 When they heard him speaking to them in Hebrew, they
> were even quieter; and Paul went on,
> 3 "I am a Jew, born in Tarsus of Cilicia, but brought up here in
> Jerusalem as a student of Gamaliel. I received strict instruction in the
> Law of our ancestors, and was just as dedicated to God as all of you
> here today are. 4 I persecuted to the death the people who followed
> this Way. I arrested men and women and threw them into prison.
> 5 The High Priest and the whole Council can prove that I am telling the
> truth. I received from them letters written to the Jewish brothers in
> Damascus, so I went there to arrest these people and bring them back
> in chains to Jerusalem to be punished." (22.1-5)

22.1

In a very formal fashion Paul addressed himself both to the men of his
own age, brothers, and to his elders, fathers. In a number of languages the
equivalent of men, brothers and fathers is simply "men of my own age and
men who are older than I am" or "my elders and my companions." In many
societies there is a technical term for "age-mates" and this would be an appropriate equivalent at this point.

Listen to me as I make my defense before you is a somewhat ambiguous
construction in Greek, though the ambiguity is not too important as far as
translation is concerned, since most translations come out with essentially
the same meaning. The problem is that the verb listen may have either a
single object, my defense, or a dual object, me...my defense. However,
the meaning is clear (see JB "listen to what I have to say to you in my defense"). It is interesting, as well as valuable, to note that both me and defense are in the genitive case and are the objects of the verb listen (the same
verb that is translated heard in 9.7). This is further evidence that Luke made
no distinction between the use of this verb with the accusative or the genitive;
in either case it means that people hear something clearly and distinctly. See
the discussion at 9.7.

As I make my defense before you may be rendered as "as I explain to

419

you that I am not guilty" or "as I point out to you that I should not be condemned."

22. 2

For the phrase in Hebrew see 21. 40.

22. 3

By the use of three verbs, Paul gives the essential points in his biography: born...brought up...received (strict) instruction in the Law of our ancestors. Once again Paul emphasizes his Jewish origin: I am a Jew...brought up here in Jerusalem (literally "in this city," that is, in Jerusalem). In some languages born in Tarsus is more naturally rendered as "Tarsus, in the province of Cilicia, is my hometown" or "Tarsus...is the town from which I come."

There is some question regarding the relationship of the phrase as a student of Gamaliel to the context. It may be taken either with the verb that precedes it, brought up, or with the verb that follows, received...instruction. The TEV follows the first alternative; the JB follows the second: "I was brought up here in this city. I studied under Gamaliel and was taught the exact observance of the Law of our ancestors." (See also NEB, which parallels JB.) As a student of Gamaliel is literally "at the feet of Gamaliel," a reference to the way that the Jewish teachers taught their students; the teacher himself would sit on a stool with his students sitting on the ground in front of him. As a student of Gamaliel may be rendered either as "I learned from Gamaliel," "Gamaliel was my teacher," or "Gamaliel taught me."

I received strict instruction in the Law is equivalent to "I learned carefully just how to obey the Law" or "I was taught just how I must obey the Law."

The Law of our ancestors is merely another way of speaking of the Law of Moses and the traditions which had developed around it. The Law of our ancestors may be rendered as "the Laws which our ancestors followed," "the Law which was given to our ancestors," or "the Law which was passed on to us by our ancestors."

Luke's phrase (literally "being zealous for God as all of you are today") refers to Paul's dedication to God: I...was just as dedicated to God as all of you here today are (see Barclay "I am as whole-heartedly devoted to God as any of you here today" and JB "I was as full of my duty towards God as you are today"). By making this statement, Paul was trying to point out to his listeners that he recognized their sincere dedication to God, but that he was no less dedicated to God than they.

An expression such as dedicated to God may be rendered as "I gave myself just as much to God" or "I gave myself just as much to work for God."

22. 4

Some commentators understand Paul's statement that he persecuted to the death the people who followed this Way (see also 26.10) as a generalization of the incident mentioned in 7.54 ff. However, it is more natural to assume that Paul had other cases in mind than the single instance of Stephen's martyrdom. The people who followed this Way (see 9.2) is literally "this Way"; but, of course, Luke means that Paul persecuted the people who followed this Way. Although Barclay correctly interprets the meaning of "the Way," he misses the impact of the phrase persecuted to the death, when he translates "I was such a persecutor of the Way that I wished to put its followers to death."

The expression I persecuted to the death may be rendered as "I persecuted the people and caused their death" or "I caused great trouble to the people, even to the point of causing their death."

Threw them into prison may need to be translated as a causative: "I caused them to be thrown into prison" or "I ordered officers to put them into prison." In some languages the equivalent of prison is "to be tied up."

22.5

The word rendered Council (Greek "presbyterion") is not the technical term used throughout Acts to refer to the Jewish Council, but in light of the way that Luke uses this word in Luke 22.66, the commentators agree that this is its meaning in the present passage. The parallel passages do not mention the Council, though they do refer to the High Priest (9.1) and chief priests (26.12). The High Priest and the whole Council can prove that I am telling the truth translates the Greek clause "as also the High Priest is bearing witness to me and the whole Council." In Greek it is not uncommon for a compound subject to have a verb which agrees with the first subject, to which the second subject is joined by the connective "and."

In the present context, "to bear witness" means "to give evidence in support of (what Paul is saying)." Moreover, since the High Priest and the whole Council are not there to give their testimony in behalf of Paul, it is evident that the verb means "they can give testimony." In light of these observations, the TEV has translated the verb phrase "are bearing me witness" as can prove that I am telling the truth. (See also Barclay "can provide evidence," Moffatt and JB "can testify," and Goodspeed "will bear me witness.") Can prove that I am telling the truth may be rendered in some languages as direct discourse—for example, "can tell you, This man Paul is telling the truth."

Obviously, "the brothers in Damascus" are Jewish brothers (see Barclay "brother Jews"; NEB "fellow-Jews").

I received from them letters may also be rendered as "they gave me letters," and the Jewish brothers are "fellow Jews" or "those who are also Jews."

There may be some slight ambiguity in the expression these people. Therefore, in some languages it may be necessary to say "the people of the

Way" in order to make it perfectly clear that this is likewise a reference to those who are mentioned in the first part of verse 4.

In a number of languages one does not "bring people back in chains" but "bring them back bound with chains."

The passive expression to be punished may be rendered as "so that the officers would punish them" or "so that the Council would cause them to suffer."

Paul Tells of His Conversion

6 "As I was traveling and coming near Damascus, about midday a bright light from the sky flashed suddenly around me. 7 I fell to the ground and heard a voice saying to me, 'Saul, Saul! Why do you persecute me?' 8 'Who are you, Lord?' I asked. 'I am Jesus of Nazareth, whom you persecute,' he said to me. 9 The men with me saw the light but did not hear the voice of the one who was speaking to me. 10 I asked, 'What shall I do, Lord?' and the Lord said to me, 'Get up and go into Damascus, and there you will be told everything that God has determined for you to do.' 11 I was blind because of the bright light, and so my companions took me by the hand and led me into Damascus. (22.6-11)

The section heading Paul Tells of His Conversion may be rendered as "Paul Tells about How He Became a Believer" or "Paul Tells about How He Became a Follower of the Lord."

This section has as parallels 9.1-19 and 26.12-18.

The first clause, as I was traveling and coming near Damascus, is a transitional clause which relates this paragraph to what has just been said in verse 5 about letters addressed to Jews in Damascus.

22.6

On this verse see 9.3. In the previous account, in Chapter 9, the note of time, about midday, is not mentioned, nor is it indicated there that the light was bright. The word rendered bright (see also JB) is literally "sufficient," and so some translations render it "great" (see RSV, NEB, Phillips).

22.7

On this verse see 9.4. A different word is used for ground in these two verses, but they are synonyms (the word used in 9.4 is a more frequently used word).

22.8

On this verse see 9.5. The qualifier of Nazareth appears only here; it does not appear in 9.5 or 26.15. Elsewhere in Acts this qualifier is used of Jesus in 2.22; 3.6; 4.10; 6.14; 26.9.

22.9

On this verse see 9.7. In the earlier account the companions of Paul all hear, though they did not see the light.

22.10

On this verse see 9.6. It is possible to understand the verb rendered get up (the same verb used in 5.6 and 17) as a Semitic idiom which is either redundant or has the force of "at once" (see Lake "go at once to Damascus"). However, none of the standard translations seem to understand it in either of these ways, and most of them render the verb in the same way that the TEV renders it.

22.11

On this verse see 9.8.

> 12 "There was a man named Ananias, a religious man who obeyed our Law and was highly respected by all the Jews living in Damascus. 13 He came to me, stood by me and said, 'Brother Saul, see again!' At that very moment I saw again and looked at him. 14 He said, 'The God of our ancestors has chosen you to know his will, to see his righteous Servant, and hear him speaking with his own voice. 15 For you will be a witness for him to tell all men what you have seen and heard. 16 And now, why wait any longer? Get up and be baptized and have your sins washed away by calling on his name.'" (22.12-16)

The mention of Damascus in verse 12 is one way in which this paragraph is related to the preceding paragraph, which ends with a mention of Damascus.

22.12

There was a man named Ananias is rendered rather literally by Moffatt, "a certain Ananias," and by the RSV, "and one Ananias." The Greek phrase is merely a way of introducing a person in a narrative and of pointing him out, but a literal translation of the Greek does this rather awkwardly for the English reader. Phillips, NEB, and Goodspeed have all done something similar to what the TEV has here.

In 9.10 Ananias is identified merely as "a disciple," but the fact that he is a religious man is introduced here because of the nature of Paul's speech. Paul wants to impress on his listeners that both he and the man whom God sent to him were religious people, devoted to the will of God. A religious man may be translated as "a person who genuinely worships God" or "one who truly worships God."

Obeyed our Law is literally "according to the Law"; the meaning of this phrase in the context is that Ananias obeyed the Jewish Law. Some translators take the entire Greek phrase, "religious according to the Law," as one expression (see NEB "a devout observer of the Law"; note also Phillips, Goodspeed, and Moffatt). The phrase obeyed our Law may be translated as "lived just as the Law said he should live" or "obeyed the Law given to us Jews."

Highly respected by all is rendered by several translators as "well spoken of by all." The phrase Jews living in Damascus is rendered by most translators by something like "Jews living there." There is actually a textual problem involved, since the phrase in Damascus does not appear in all manuscripts. However, this may be handled translationally, because it is obvious that the Jews referred to were those living in Damascus. This final clause in verse 12 may be rendered as "all the Jews living in Damascus thought very highly of Ananias," "all the Jews who lived in Damascus thought that Ananias was a very good person," or "...honored him very much."

22.13

The verbs came and stood in the Greek sentence structure are actually participles dependent upon the main verb said. As has been pointed out on other occasions, it is quite often necessary to render participial expressions in the Greek sentences by finite verbs in English translation.

The verb rendered see again in the statement of Ananias is also translated later in the same verse as saw again and looked. The commentators point out that it has the basic meaning of "to regain one's sight" in both of its occurrences. However, inasmuch as in the second instance it is used with the phrase at him, it is necessary to render the verb both by "see again" and "look." Both Moffatt and Goodspeed have done something similar: "I regained my sight and looked at him"; many other translators simply render "looked at." At that very moment or "instantly" (NEB) is certainly the meaning of the Greek idiom "in that very hour" (RSV).

22.14

It may be necessary to render he said as "Ananias said to me."

The God of our ancestors, rendered in a number of translations as "the God of our fathers," was a typical Jewish way of referring to the God whom the Jews worshiped. In a number of translations it is necessary to render this very phrase as "the God whom our ancestors worshiped," since one cannot use a so-called possessive expression which would be suggested by the English preposition of or the genitive case in Greek.

The phrase to know his will may be rendered as "to know what God plans to do." Some exegetes would interpret this as "to know what God wants you to do."

For the expression righteous Servant see 3.13-14; 7.52. This is a direct reference to Jesus without specifically naming him. It may be rendered in some languages as "to see that person who is God's righteous Servant" or "to see that righteous One who serves God."

424

The phrase hear him speaking with his own voice is a correct translation of the literal Greek expression "to hear a voice from his mouth." This
is, of course, a reference to Paul's hearing Jesus Christ speak to him. In
some languages it is necessary to make clear that the pronouns him and his
refer to the righteous Servant; therefore, the phrase may be rendered as "to
hear that one speaking to you directly." In some languages it is not only artificial, but misleading, to use the expression with his own voice, since there
is no other way of speaking except by one's own voice. However, the emphasis in some languages may be given as "to hear him speaking to you personally" or "to hear his voice as he speaks to you."

22.15

In biblical thought, a witness is one who testifies concerning what he
has seen. For this reason the TEV has rendered the Greek expression "you
will be a witness for him to all men" by you will be a witness for him to tell
all men. The two verbs have seen and heard are in the Greek two different
tenses. The first of these (a perfect tense) normally places the emphasis
upon the present effects of some past action, while the second of these tenses
(an aorist) normally identifies action without respect to its present impact.
However, Luke seems to have made no distinction between the two tenses in
this verse.

22.16

Why wait any longer? (JB "And now why delay?") is a colloquial Greek
idiomatic expression. Get up in Greek is actually a participle which may be
taken either as an imperative, as in the TEV, or as a Semitic idiom describing the initiation of some action. Most scholars understand it in the way the
TEV has rendered it.

In Greek the two verbs be baptized and have your sins washed away are
both in the so-called middle voice. They mean something like "have yourself
baptized and have your sins washed away," but most translations render the
first verb as "be baptized." It seems preferable to do this in English, since
in meaning there is no difference between the command "to be baptized" and
"to have oneself baptized." In the New Testament (and especially in the book
of Acts) there is a close connection between baptism and the forgiveness of
sins. However, the New Testament does not imply that baptism is the means
by which one's sins are forgiven. In a number of languages it is impossible
to have an imperative passive such as be baptized. One can, however, in
some languages say "cause someone to baptize you" or "enter into the rite of
baptism." Similarly, have your sins washed away may be rendered as "cause
your sins to be washed away" or "cause God to wash away your sins."

The participle by calling on his name is an aorist participle and must
be taken as action prior to the main verb or verbs with which it is connected.
In the present context it is difficult to know if this participle is connected with
both verbs, be baptized and have your sins washed away, or only with the

425

latter of the two. Most translations are about as ambiguous as the Greek
here, though the TEV appears to take the participle only with the verb have
your sins washed away (note JB "It is time you were baptized and had your
sins washed away while invoking his name"). The NEB connects this participle only with the first of these verbs, something which is quite difficult to
do on the basis of the Greek: "Be baptized at once, with invocation of his name,
and wash away your sins." Goodspeed is typical of what most other translators
have done: "Get up and be baptized, and wash away your sins, calling on his
name." However, in translation it may be necessary to say "calling on the
name of the Lord" or even "calling on the Lord." This latter expression would
be used to avoid the implication that the name of the Lord was merely employed as a part of some magical incantation or formula.

Paul's Call to Preach to the Gentiles

17 "I went back to Jerusalem, and while I was praying in the
temple I had a vision, 18 in which I saw the Lord as he said to me,
'Hurry and leave Jerusalem quickly, because the people here will not
accept your witness about me.' 19 'Lord,' I answered, 'they know very
well that I went to the synagogues and arrested and beat those who believe in you. 20 And when your witness Stephen was put to death, I myself was there, approving of his murder and taking care of the cloaks
of his murderers.' 21 'Go,' the Lord said to me, 'because I will send
you far away to the Gentiles.'" (22.17-21)

The section heading Paul's Call to Preach to the Gentiles causes a number of complications in translation since it is normally necessary to have the
agent of calling identified. Moreover, the verb "call," if translated literally,
can be readily misunderstood as though someone is shouting to someone else.
Therefore, the section heading is frequently rendered as "The Lord Tells
Paul that He Should Preach to the Gentiles" or "The Lord Shows Paul that He
Must Go to the Gentiles."

22.17

In Greek, verses 17 and 18 comprise one rather awkward sentence.
Luke begins with a favorite formula of his (literally "and it came to pass,"
see KJV), which most translators do not render. The purpose of this formula
is merely to begin a new phase of a narrative and this can be done by a paragraph division in English. Once again the TEV finds it necessary to translate
a Greek participial construction (see NEB "after my return to Jerusalem") by
a finite verb: I went back to Jerusalem. This introductory reference to Jerusalem serves to relate this paragraph to the preceding narrative, which begins
with a reference to Jerusalem in verse 3 and then shifts to Damascus, where
Paul went in order to arrest people of the Way.

The expression had a vision appears in 10.10 and 11.5.

22.18

    Hurry and quickly are intended to stress the immediacy with which Paul
is commanded to act in leaving Jerusalem. The people here makes explicit
the meaning of the pronominal subject "they" of the verb will not accept. Will
not accept your witness is equivalent in many languages to "will not believe
what you say about me."

22.19

    They is an emphatic form in Greek (as is "I myself" in the following
verse), and has been rendered "they themselves" by most translators. The
TEV has brought out this emphasis by they know very well. Arrested and
beat, as they appear in most translations, suggest that these were actions
which Paul himself actually did; however, it is possible to understand these
verbs in the sense of things which Paul had ordered done to the people.

22. 20

    When your witness Stephen was put to death is literally "when the blood
of Stephen your witness was poured out." But in biblical language "to pour out
someone's blood" is to have someone put to death. It seems possible that this
passage moves in the direction of using the word "witness" in the sense of
"martyr." It may be necessary to employ an active expression at this point,
"when people killed your witness Stephen." In this type of context, your witness may be rendered as "Stephen who told people about you."
    Approving of his murder may be rendered as "I agreed with them when
they killed him," "I said yes to their killing him," or "I favored their killing
him."
    The cloaks of his murderers are simply "the coats which belonged to
those who killed Stephen."

22. 21

    For English readers it is necessary to identify the subject of the verb
said as the Lord.
    Throughout this entire account of Paul's conversion and commission to
go to the Gentiles, there is a subtle usage of the word Lord, which to Christians would refer directly to Jesus of Nazareth. To the Jewish hearers of
this word, it could, of course, refer to the God of the Old Testament known
as "the Lord." This double usage of Lord has sometimes been called the
"divine ambiguity," but in this passage especially it is most important that
this double meaning be carefully preserved rather than introduce directly
some specific reference to Jesus, since the use of the name of Jesus would
undoubtedly have provoked a strong reaction among those listening to Paul.

    22 The people listened to Paul until he said this; but then they
    started shouting at the top of their voices, "Away with him! Kill him!

He's not fit to live!" 23 They were screaming, waving their clothes, and throwing dust up in the air. 24 The Roman commander ordered his men to take Paul into the fort, and told them to whip him to find out why the Jews were screaming like this against him. 25 But when they had tied him up to be whipped, Paul said to the officer standing there, "Is it lawful for you to whip a Roman citizen who hasn't even been tried for any crime?"

26 When the officer heard this, he went to the commander and asked him, "What are you doing? That man is a Roman citizen!"

27 So the commander went to Paul and asked him, "Tell me, are you a Roman citizen?"

"Yes," answered Paul.

28 The commander said, "I became one by paying a large amount of money."

"But I am one by birth," Paul answered.

29 At once the men who were going to question Paul drew back from him; and the commander was afraid when he realized that Paul was a Roman citizen, and that he had put him in chains. (22.22-29)

22.22

This verse begins a new paragraph, and the TEV has made the participants explicit: the people listened to Paul (literally "they listened to him"). The clause until he said this may need to be somewhat more specific, since in a number of languages a pronoun such as this cannot readily refer to a statement or topic—for example, "until he spoke about going to the Gentiles."

But then they started shouting at the top of their voices is literally "then they lifted up their voices and said." The NEB takes this clause to mean "but now they began shouting," while Goodspeed understands this in the sense of "but then they shouted."

Away with him! Kill him! is literally "Away from the earth with such a person!" The phrase "from the earth" merely intensifies and qualifies "away with him," and there is no other way to understand this than in the sense of "kill him" (see Phillips "Kill him, and rid the earth of such a man!"). It is, of course, not necessary to translate both phrases away with him and kill him. The two expressions in English are simply complementary ways of translating the same Greek terms. If there is in the receptor language a strong expression for kill him, this should be sufficient.

The sentence He's not fit to live! may be rendered as "He should not be allowed to live!" or "It is not right that he should live!"

22.23

There is a question as to whether the word translated waving means "to wave" or "to tear off" (see KJV "cast off" and Phillips "ripping"). Moffatt takes the word in the sense of "to throw" ("threw their clothes into the air"). In 14.14, the tearing of clothes is the response that the people make to what they consider blasphemy. Here also the waving (or tearing) of clothes and the throwing of dust into the air must be looked upon as expressions of horror at what the Jews consider to be blasphemy on the part of Paul. At this point it may be useful to have some marginal note to explain the behavior of the crowd.

22. 24

The Greek does not make explicit the persons to whom the Roman commander gave his orders, but it is obvious that they were given to his men.

"Him" of the Greek has been made explicit in the TEV by translating Paul.

Whipping a person was not to punish him, but was the legal means of examining a person who was either a slave or an alien (see v. 29). Whipping was regarded as a kind of torture in order to guarantee that the individual would tell the truth.

Screaming...against him may be rendered as "speaking against him by their screams." This shift may be required, since in some languages one can only "speak against" and not "scream against."

22. 25

The phrase rendered to be whipped may be taken in the sense "with leather straps." That is, Luke may either be telling the reason that Paul was being tied up or the means by which Paul was being tied up. The NEB accepts the same interpretation that the TEV does, though it provides a footnote giving the alternate possibility.

The term lawful may be rendered as "according to the law," "is this what the law says," or "does the law allow you." In some languages, of course, law may always be rendered as "laws" to indicate the body of laws.

The phrase a Roman citizen may, in this context, be rendered as "a person who has all the rights of people who live in Rome" or "a person who is just like those in the city of Rome."

Who hasn't even been tried for any crime translates a Greek word which is also used in 16. 37. The word may indicate one who has not been tried or one who has been tried and found innocent. In the present context, the emphasis is clearly on the former of these two possibilities. This final clause may be translated in some languages as "a person whom a judge has not passed sentence on," "a man who has not been condemned in court," or "a man to whom the judge has not yet said, You are guilty of a crime."

22. 26

In this context the term officer is more or less equivalent to "captain" in a modern army, while commander would be equivalent to "colonel." In languages in which no such distinctions are made, one can always say "soldier" and "one who commands the soldiers."

22. 28

What are you doing? is rendered by most translations as "What are you going to do?" The question itself may indicate either action in progress or contemplated action.

22. 28

In some languages it may be necessary to state to whom the amount of money was paid. This can be "to the government," "to officers of the government," or "to government authorities." A large amount of money may simply be "very much money."

But I is a very strong emphatic construction in Greek. Paul does not state how his father or his earlier ancestors obtained Roman citizenship, and speculation is of no value for the translator. The expression one by birth may be rendered simply as "my parents were Roman citizens before me" or "I am a Roman citizen because my parents were also."

22. 29

It was legal to arrest a Roman citizen but illegal to have him put in chains, and this explains the reason for the commander's fear. Had put him in chains may be translated in some languages as "had put chains on him" or "had bound him by means of chains."

22. 30

For a discussion of this verse see Chapter 23, since this last verse of Chapter 22 actually is related to Paul's defense of himself before the chief priests and the Council contained in the first part of Chapter 23.

CHAPTER 23

The structure of Chapter 23 relates to three different episodes involved in Paul's arrest and his later transfer to Caesarea. The first section (22.30—23.11) relates Paul's defense before the Council in Jerusalem. The second section (vv. 12-22) gives certain details concerning the plot against Paul's life. The third section (vv. 23-35) tells the story of Paul's transfer to Caesarea and includes the letter from Lysias to Governor Felix. Note that verse 30 of Chapter 22 is included with Chapter 23, since it essentially constitutes an introduction to Paul's defense before the Council. In so many instances the chapter divisions are relatively artificial, and it is essential that the translator follow the basic discourse divisions rather than the chapter breaks.

Note that both the second and the third major sections in Chapter 23 begin with an expression of temporal setting, the next morning (v. 12) and then (v. 23).

Paul before the Council

30 The commander wanted to find out for sure what the Jews were accusing Paul of; so the next day he had Paul's chains taken off and ordered the chief priests and the whole Council to meet. Then he took Paul, and made him stand before them.

1 Paul looked straight at the Council and said, "My brothers! My conscience is perfectly clear about my whole life before God, to this very day." 2 The High Priest Ananias ordered those who were standing close to Paul to strike him on the mouth. 3 Paul said to him, "God will certainly strike you—you whitewashed wall! You sit there to judge me according to the Law, yet you break the Law by ordering them to strike me!"

4 The men close to Paul said to him, "You are insulting God's High Priest!"

5 Paul answered, "I did not know, my brothers, that he was the High Priest. The scripture says, 'You must not speak evil of the ruler of your people.'" (22.30—23.5)

The section heading Paul before the Council may need to be somewhat more specific—for example, "Paul Defends Himself before the Council," "Paul Is Made to Speak before the Council," or "Paul Is Brought before the Council."

22.30

This verse is related to the preceding account by taking up the same theme which has been introduced in verse 24, namely, the commander's desire to find out precisely why the Jews had accused Paul so vehemently.

In Greek, verse 30 is one sentence beginning with the phrase "so the next day." For the sake of the English reader the sentence has been broken

431

in the TEV into two sentences, the order rearranged, participants in the narrative made explicit (the commander, Paul, Paul's), and certain participles made into finite verbs (wanted and took).

Had Paul's chains taken off is understood by some to mean that Paul was released from prison (see JB "he freed Paul"), since they believe that Paul's chains would have been taken off the previous day as soon as the Roman officer found out that Paul was a Roman citizen. He had Paul's chains taken off must, of course, be understood as a causative, "he caused the soldiers to take off Paul's chains" or "he ordered the soldiers, Take the chains off Paul." One normally cannot employ a so-called possessive expression with "chains." They were not the chains that belonged to Paul, but the chains which were used to bind him.

In speaking of the whole Council, it may be necessary to say "the Council of all the Jewish leaders." This is, in fact, precisely the phrase used in some languages for the Sanhedrin.

Took Paul may be rendered in some languages as "caused Paul to go" or "had him led."

23.1

In some languages it is awkward to say looked straight at the Council. On the contrary, one must address such "straight looks" at members of the Council; therefore, "he looked straight at the men who were in the Council."

On my brothers (literally "men brothers") see 1.16.

An adequate term to express the meaning of conscience is not easy to find in some languages. In fact, such expressions may be highly idiomatic— for example, "the little man who stands within me," "my internal shadow," or "the echo of my heart." What is important about a term for conscience is that it represents one's most basic concerns about behavior and values. In some languages it is simply equivalent to "heart" and in this particular context it may be translated as "in my heart I have no serious questions about my whole life before God." In other languages one may say "my heart does not cause me questions" or "within myself I do not have doubts about my whole life before God."

The phrase my whole life may be rendered as "the way I have lived during all my life" or "what I have done during my whole life."

In a number of languages, before God must be rendered as "with God looking on" or "before the eyes of God." What is important here is that Paul brings God as a witness to what he has done during all his life.

To this very day (literally "up to this day") has been rendered by the NEB as "and still live today." Both the TEV and the NEB are so in order to indicate that Paul had not stopped living with a good conscience before God, which might otherwise be implied by the phrase "up to this day."

23.2

Ananias was High Priest from A.D. 47 to 66, when he was assassinated by the Jews because of his support of the Romans during the Jewish uprising. The reason that he ordered Paul to be slapped is not clear. It may be because he thought Paul was presumptuous by addressing the group as my brothers, or it may be that he felt it improper for a prisoner to maintain his innocence. It is interesting to recall that Jesus was also struck during his trial (John 18. 22-23).

The verb ordered may require direct discourse in some languages—for example, "the High Priest Ananias ordered those who were standing close to Paul, Strike him on the mouth." In a number of languages one must distinguish carefully between striking with the hand closed or with an open hand, that is, "hit" versus "slap." The Greek text itself makes no distinction and one can choose whichever form of striking would seem to be more appropriate within a parallel receptor context.

23.3

In Paul's reply to Ananias it is important to use the same verb to strike as is employed in verse 2. If such a verb can also suggest destruction, this may be all the better.

No one is certain what the exact analogy is that Paul had in mind when he called the High Priest a whitewashed wall. The first thing that comes to mind is the comparison that our Lord used (Matthew 23.27). However, the phrase is there used to describe hypocrisy, and it is difficult to read that into the present context. Others see in this a reference to the wall mentioned in Ezekiel 13.10-15, a wall which looked strong enough but was blown over by the wind. The problem is that the Septuagint does not use the word "whitewashed" to describe that wall. Perhaps the best solution is simply to conclude that this was a formula of abuse, the precise meaning of which is no longer known. Since we do not know the precise value of whitewashed wall, it is difficult to suggest alternative expressions in other languages. Therefore, it may very well be necessary simply to reproduce this expression in a more or less literal form (for example, "painted-over wall" or "wall that has been made to look white"), and then explain in some marginal note that this was obviously an expression of abuse, of which the precise meaning is no longer known. For the most part, however, a rendering such as "wall which has been made to look white" does provide at least a meaningful basis for an expression which would be interpreted as an insult to the High Priest.

You sit there to judge me according to the Law may be rendered as "you sit there as a judge who is supposed to follow the Law" or "you sit there as one who is supposed to judge me by what the Law says."

In a number of languages one can speak about "breaking the Law," but in many other languages such an expression simply does not make sense. One can only "break sticks." However, in many languages one can "go against the Law," "destroy the Law," or "do what the Law says one should not do."

In Greek, You are insulting God's High Priest! (JB "It is God's high priest you are insulting!") is actually a question which the TEV has rendered as an explanation. Since the form of the question in Greek is strictly rhetorical (that is to say, it is not asked for information but rather as a means of making a strong statement), the TEV has used the form of statement with an exclamation point, which reproduces in effect the emphasis of the Greek question.

In a number of languages a verb for insult is simply "saying bad things about." But since insulting is a universal feature in all cultures, there is usually no difficulty in finding any one of several terms to use in this kind of context.

23.5

Questions have been raised regarding the nature of Paul's statement in this verse. Some think that Paul was speaking sarcastically, while others insist that he was speaking in earnest. In support of the latter theory is a realization that Paul is in a judicial situation and introduces his remarks with the rather formal expression my brothers. Also in support of this thesis is the fact that Paul quotes from Exodus 22.28, and it is not likely that Paul would have used Scripture in a less than solemn fashion.

The ruler of your people must usually be rendered in such a way as to indicate that the phrase your people is the goal of "the ruling"; therefore, "the one who is ruling your people." On the other hand, in this particular context ruler refers to position of prominence and it may be rendered more effectively in some languages as "the one who among all your people is the ruler."

6 When Paul saw that some of the group were Sadducees and that others were Pharisees, he called out in the Council, "My brothers! I am a Pharisee, the son of Pharisees. I am on trial here because I hope that the dead will rise to life!"
7 As soon as he said this, the Pharisees and Sadducees started to quarrel, and the group was divided. 8 (For the Sadducees say that people will not rise from death, and that there are no angels or spirits; but the Pharisees believe in all three.) 9 The shouting became louder, and some of the teachers of the Law who belonged to the party of the Pharisees stood up and protested strongly, "We cannot find a thing wrong with this man! Perhaps a spirit or an angel really did speak to him!" (23.6-9)

23.6

Called out translates a verb tense which may indicate that Paul "kept calling out," but in this type of context called out must be understood as

434

"shouted" or "spoke in a loud voice." There is no sense here of "calling to someone."

My brothers is the same formula which appears in 23.1.

It should be noticed that Paul says I am a Pharisee, not "I was a Pharisee." Once again Paul gives indication that to be a Pharisee and a Christian are not necessarily contradictory, since in Christianity is the fulfillment of Paul's Jewish hopes (see 15.5 which tells of Pharisees who became believers). In a number of languages the expression the son of Pharisees may be more idiomatically rendered as "my parents were Pharisees."

Paul is not merely trying to cause dissension among the group of Pharisees and Sadducees when he says I am on trial here because I hope that the dead will rise to life. As a Pharisee Paul believed that the dead would be raised to life, and he saw this hope realized in the resurrection of Jesus Christ from the dead.

There is perhaps no other term more difficult to translate in some languages than hope, since it combines two very important components: (1) patient waiting and (2) confidence that something positive will happen. Therefore, in this type of context one may sometimes have a phrase such as "because I wait with confidence that the dead will rise to life."

The expression will rise to life may be rendered in some languages as "God will cause the dead to come to life again."

<u>23.7</u>

The force of the Greek verb construction in this sentence is to indicate the initiation of an action, and so the TEV has translated started to quarrel (see also Moffatt "a quarrel broke out"). The phrase started to quarrel may simply be translated as "started to talk against each other"; and the group was divided may be rendered as "the group became two groups."

<u>23.8</u>

Since this verse is an explanatory comment, the TEV (see also NEB) has placed it in parenthesis. For the Sadducees say that people will not rise from death translates "for the Sadducees say there is no resurrection." But in the context the reference is certainly to their denial of a general resurrection (see NEB "The Sadducees deny that there is any resurrection") rather than to the specific denial of Jesus' resurrection, and for this reason the TEV has made this explicit.

All three (so also JB) is literally "both" (so KJV), but this word may also be used in the sense of "all in a series" (see RSV "them all").

There are complications in some languages in the final phrase in all three, since this type of counting would combine not only an event such as the resurrection but angels and spirits, which would be in quite different classes as far as counting is concerned. In fact, some languages have quite different systems of counting, depending upon the types of objects which are being counted. In some languages, therefore, one may have to translate "believe in all of these" or it may be even necessary to repeat the three: "the Pharisees believe in people being raised from the dead, and in angels, and in spirits." On the other hand, one may express the contrast by saying "but the Pharisees believe in these things that the Sadducees do not believe in."

<u>23. 9</u>

The TEV connects the shouting mentioned in this verse with the quarrel mentioned in verse 7: the shouting became louder (so JB). It is also possible to do as the NEB has done: "so a great uproar broke out." One can, of course, translate in such a way as to specify the participants who were doing the shouting—for example, "the Sadducees and Pharisees started shouting louder and louder."

Teachers of the Law is a term which is rendered "scribes" by most translators (NEB "doctors of the law"). These people were, in fact, much more than the English word "scribe" would indicate; they were recognized teachers of the Jewish Law, and usually, though not always, they belonged to the Pharisaic party.

Protested strongly (see Phillips "protested violently") is a much stronger word than "contended" (RSV) or "insisted" (Goodspeed) might suggest.

We cannot find a thing wrong with this man may be rendered as "we have not discovered anything which will cause this man to be condemned" or "we have not found anything wrong that he has done."

Perhaps a spirit or an angel really did speak to him implies that the Pharisees believed that Paul was spoken to by an angel or a spirit.

10 The argument became so violent that the commander was afraid that Paul would be torn to pieces by them. So he ordered his soldiers to go down into the group and get Paul away from them, and take him into the fort.
11 The following night the Lord stood by Paul and said, "Courage! You have given your witness to me here in Jerusalem, and you must do the same in Rome also." (23.10-11)

Verses 10 and 11 are set off as separate paragraphs, first, because of the significant break from the violent discussion which took place in the Council, and second, because of the quite different content of verse 11 in which the Lord appears to Paul and encourages him.

<u>23.10</u>

In the clause the argument became so violent, the term argument translates the same word that was rendered quarrel in verse 7. Moffatt translates the clause, "The quarrel then became so violent." This reference to the argument serves as a link between the preceding paragraph and the decision of the commander to return Paul to the fort.

As in a number of instances, a verb such as ordered may require direct discourse—for example, "he ordered his soldiers, Go down into the group and get Paul away from them."

The expression the following night means "the night following the day on which Paul had been before the Council." In some languages this is rendered as "that night."

Though this appearance of the Lord is interpreted by some as being a vision, there is no specific indication in the Greek text that this was the case. Only by implication of the appearance being at night may one argue that this was the appearance of the Lord to Paul in a dream. It is best simply to render the text as it appears, without specifying dream or vision.

Courage has been rendered both as "take courage" (RSV) and "keep up your courage" (NEB). The former of these two possibilities seems to fit the Greek better.

Given your witness...do the same actually translates two different verbs (note RSV "have testified...must bear witness"), but it is best to regard these essentially as synonyms (note Moffatt "testified...must testify" and NEB "affirmed the truth about me...do the same").

The Plot against Paul's Life

12 The next morning some Jews met together and made a plan. They took a vow that they would not eat or drink anything until they had killed Paul. 13 There were more than forty of them who planned this together. 14 Then they went to the chief priests and elders and said, "We have taken a solemn vow together not to eat a thing until we kill Paul. 15 Now then, you and the Council send word to the Roman commander to bring Paul down to you, pretending that you want to get more accurate information about him. But we will be ready to kill him before he ever gets here." (23.12-15)

The section heading The Plot against Paul's Life may also be rendered as "The Jews Plot to Kill Paul" or "The Jews Make Plans against Paul's Life."

This section consists of two principal parts: the first (vv. 12-15) describes the plot which the Jews made against Paul, and the second (vv. 16-22) describes the manner in which Paul's nephew informs the commander Lysias of what the Jews intend to do. Note that the first paragraph begins with the temporal phrase the next morning. This immediately links this paragraph with the preceding account. On the other hand, verse 16 begins with the conjunction but, which serves as an appropriate transition to show the manner in which the plot, as described in the first paragraph, is now thwarted by what Paul's nephew does.

The word translated plan in this verse and the word translated planned

437

in the following verse are from two different stems, though there are indications that they are used as synonyms. In each case the meaning may be that of "a plot" or "a conspiracy."

The verb rendered took a vow is a very strong term, signifying that one has placed himself under God's curse if he does not achieve what he vows he will do. Immediately following the word "vow" in Greek is the participle "saying." However, in the context this is merely a marker of indirect discourse, and so most translators have tried to follow the most natural way of introducing indirect discourse into the context. The intensity of the vow is indicated by the fact that the men had sworn neither to eat nor drink until they had killed Paul. The rabbis made it possible for persons to release themselves from such vows, and so it is quite improbable that these persons either starved to death or died of thirst. In a number of languages vow is rendered as "made a promise to God," "made a strong promise to God," or "made a promise to God with a threat to themselves."

In a number of languages the content of the vow may be most appropriately expressed as direct discourse—for example, "made a promise calling God to witness, and they said, We will not eat or drink anything until we have killed Paul."

In order to express the concept of until some languages require a change in order—for example, "first we will kill Paul and only then will we eat and drink anything."

23.13

Note the number forty which reinforces the requirement in some languages to employ the expression "some Jews" in verse 12.

23.14

Although this verse begins with a participle, most translations employ a finite verb—for example, they went.

The difference between vow in verse 12 and solemn vow in verse 14 is simply an expression of the intensity with which the vow is affirmed. One might reflect this difference in some translations by using in verse 12 "have made a promise," and in verse 14 "have made a very strong promise."

23.15

You and the Council is more accurately rendered in some languages as "you on behalf of the Council," since it was not the chief priests, elders, and Council who collectively or individually sent the word to the Roman commander, but the leaders who did this on behalf of the Council as a whole.

Send word is a term which means "to impart official information," and in the present context it seems to be used at least in a semitechnical sense. The same verb occurs in 23.22; 24.1; 25.2,15.

Since this message to the Roman commander was primarily a request, it may be necessary to indicate this fact so as not to imply that it was an order—for example, "request the Roman commander, Please bring Paul down to us."

Pretending... may be translated as "say to him...."

To get more accurate information about him renders a verb phrase in which the verb combines both the ideas of inquiry and of decision. More accurate information may be rendered as "to learn better just what he has done."

> 16 But the son of Paul's sister heard of the plot; so he went and entered the fort and told it to Paul. 17 Then Paul called one of the officers and said to him, "Take this young man to the commander; he has something to tell him." 18 The officer took him, led him to the commander and said, "The prisoner Paul called me and asked me to bring this young man to you, because he has something to say to you."
>
> 19 The commander took him by the hand, led him off by himself, and asked him, "What do you have to tell me?"
>
> 20 He said, "The Jewish authorities have agreed to ask you tomorrow to take Paul down to the Council, pretending that the Council wants to get more accurate information about him. 21 But don't listen to them, because there are more than forty men who will be hiding and waiting for him. They have taken a vow not to eat or drink until they kill him. They are now ready to do it, and are waiting for your decision."
>
> 22 The commander said, "Don't tell anyone that you have reported this to me." And he sent the young man away. (23. 16-22)

23.16

The expression the son of Paul's sister may be rendered in this specific form, or it may be adapted to the more natural expression in a particular receptor language—for example, "Paul's nephew." The Greek of this verse seems rather awkward, but the sense is clear. The word rendered plot is a different word from the word plan (v. 12) and planned (v. 13), though it is quite likely that all three of these terms are used synonymously.

23.17

The terms rendered officers and commander (NEB "centurions" and "commandant") in this verse are literally "men in charge of one hundred men" and "a man in charge of a thousand men."

23.18

The prisoner Paul is not contradictory to what was said in 22.30. Whatever was indicated there, whether Paul was released from his chains or released from prison, he was not given absolute freedom in any case.

23. 21

In the Greek, <u>will be hiding and waiting</u> are actually in the present tense, though it is quite common for a Greek writer to use the present tense as a future when he wants to make something vivid.

<u>They are now ready to do it</u> is no doubt a reference specifically to killing Paul, though it could be understood that they are ready to make the request.

<u>Waiting for your decision</u> may be rendered as "waiting to hear what you say" or "waiting to hear what you reply."

23. 22

A comparison of the TEV with a translation such as the RSV will show how the TEV has rearranged this verse in chronological order. As a matter of fact, the participial phrase "charging him" (RSV) is misleading, since in the Greek this is a participle which indicates action prior to that of the main verb <u>sent ... away</u>. Considered from this point of view, the Greek itself is actually in chronological order.

Paul Sent to Governor Felix

23 Then the commander called two of his officers and said, "Get two hundred soldiers ready to go to Caesarea, together with seventy horsemen and two hundred spearmen, and be ready to leave by nine o'clock tonight. 24 Provide some horses for Paul to ride, and get him safely through to Governor Felix." 25 Then the commander wrote a letter that went like this:
26 "Claudius Lysias to his Excellency, the Governor Felix: Greetings. 27 The Jews seized this man and were about to kill him. I learned that he is a Roman citizen, so I went with my soldiers and rescued him. 28 I wanted to know what they were accusing him of, so I took him down to their Council. 29 I found out that he had not done a thing for which he deserved to die or be put in prison; the accusation against him had to do with questions about their own law. 30 And when I was informed that some Jews were making a plot against him, I decided to send him to you. I told his accusers to make their charges against him before you." (23. 23-30)

23. 23

In Greek, verses 23-25 comprise one sentence. Most translators, however, divide this sentence into several parts for the sake of clarity.

The first reference to <u>two hundred soldiers</u> identifies the most common kind of soldier, namely, those which in ancient times employed a shield and sword. In addition, there were seventy soldiers who rode horseback.

The word rendered <u>spearmen</u> is of uncertain meaning, though many translators render it in this way. The term spearmen may be translated as "soldiers who fought with spears."

Get ... ready ... and be ready to leave translates the verb rendered by many other translators as "get ready." Nine o'clock tonight is literally "the third hour of the night." Since the night would have begun around six o'clock, the TEV is in agreement with most other translations. However, the RSV has rendered the translation literally, and the NEB has "three hours after sunset." In most languages it is increasingly more useful to employ generally accepted expressions for time, whether "nine o'clock at night" or "at twenty-one o'clock" (if in the language the twenty-four hour system of reckoning is more general). However, in a number of languages a local system of determining time is widely employed, and since it often seems far more natural, particularly for this kind of context, its use is certainly to be encouraged.

23. 24

The word rendered horses may either mean horses or mules; the reason that Paul was provided with more than one is not indicated. It may be that one was to carry Paul's belongings, or it may be that an exchange horse was to be available when the first became tired.

Get him safely through to Governor Felix may be translated as "be sure that he arrives safely where Governor Felix is."

Felix was governor of Palestine beginning in A.D. 52. Tacitus, the ancient Roman historian, characterized him as one who exercised the power of a king with the mind of a slave.

23. 25

That went like this may be translated as "that had these words in it" or "that said this."

23. 26

The form of the letter in verses 26-30 reflects the letter form as used in the first century A.D.

In a number of receptor languages it is necessary to speak of one's self in the first person singular. Therefore, the introduction to this letter would need to be modified as follows: "I, who am Claudius Lysias, write to you, Most Excellent Governor Felix."

Excellency is a title of honor used to address important persons; it is used of Roman officials in 24.2 and 26.25. The closest equivalent in a number of languages to the term Excellency is an expression of honor due to one's importance. For example, in some languages one may use "to the very important Governor Felix," "to Governor Felix who deserves great honor," or, in some instances, "to the big chief, Governor Felix."

Terms of greetings differ vastly from one language to another. In some instances one greets another simply by saying "I am talking to you." In

441

another language one may say "may you live well" or "may all kinds of happiness be yours." What is important is that a natural and normal form of greeting be employed at this point, something which would be fully in keeping with this type of context.

23. 27

The Jews seized this man and were about to kill him translates a passive construction in Greek: "this man was seized by the Jews and was about to be killed by them." The reference to his having discovered that Paul was a Roman citizen and therefore went to rescue him is, of course, a misrepresentation of the facts. But this is so typical of bureaucratic correspondence that there is every reason to believe it to be an accurate report of what Lysias wrote.

23. 28

The phrase rendered what they were accusing him of may possibly be taken with another meaning, but most translators apparently understand it as a reference to the charges made against Paul.

23. 29-30

The TEV has inverted the Greek sentence order of verse 29 to make it easier for the English reader. The Greek sentence construction of verse 30 is quite difficult, though the meaning is clear.

For which he deserved to die or be put in prison may be translated as "which would cause him to be killed or be put in prison" or "which would justify us in killing him or putting him in prison."

The accusation against him may be rendered as "they accused him."

Here the TEV has made the pronominal reference "them" explicit by rendering some Jews, and has translated "the man" by him. The last sentence of verse 30 may be rendered as "I told those who accused Paul, You can go to see Governor Felix and there make your accusations against Paul."

At the end of verse 30 some manuscripts add, as a closing salutation to the letter, an expression which may be rendered as "best wishes" or "farewell." If this closing greeting had been a part of the original text, it is difficult to see why it was dropped. It may, however, have been added through the influence of 15. 29.

31 The soldiers carried out their orders. They got Paul and took him that night as far as Antipatris. 32 The next day the foot soldiers returned to the fort and left the horsemen to go on with him. 33 They took him to Caesarea, delivered the letter to the Governor, and turned Paul over to him. 34 The Governor read the letter and asked Paul what province he was from. When he found out that he was from Cilicia, 35 he said, "I will hear you when your accusers arrive." Then he gave orders that Paul be kept under guard in Herod's palace. (23.31-35)

Verse 31 relates this paragraph to what has already been mentioned as an order in verses 23-24.

23.31

In Greek, verse 31 is one sentence with carried out their orders and got as two participles dependent upon the main verb took. However, most translators tend to make at least one of these participles (usually "took") into a finite verb; the TEV has made both of them into finite verbs for ease of comprehension.

From Jerusalem to Antipatris would have been a journey of about 40 miles, a difficult distance for foot soldiers to cover during a night's march. The usual march for a group of soldiers was set at 24 miles, but during the cool of the night they could possibly have covered more distance than they could during the heat of the day on a normal march.

It is important in terms such as got and took to preserve the appropriate geographical point of view. Since in verse 32 the soldiers returned to the fort (that is, to Jerusalem), it would seem that the point of view of the narration was certainly Jerusalem.

23.32

The next day the foot soldiers returned, since the road from Antipatris to Caesarea was in predominantly Gentile territory, and Paul would no longer have needed such a large guard to protect him.

23.33

They took him to Caesarea actually translates a participial phrase meaning "when they had entered Caesarea." Although a number of modern translators render this participial phrase by a finite verb, most of them evidently prefer to retain the idea of "they entered Caesarea."

Turned Paul over to him may simply be rendered as "put Paul under the charge of Governor Felix" or, as in some languages, "they said to Governor Felix, Paul is now your responsibility."

23.34

The Governor read the letter translates a participle which has neither an explicit subject nor a given object (literally "having read"). Phillips has translated in a way very similar to the TEV: "when the Governor had read the letter."

In a number of languages a verb of "asking" must introduce direct discourse: "he asked Paul, What country do you come from?" or "...What province are you from?"

<u>23.35</u>

   <u>I will hear you</u> translates a legal technical term (appearing only here in the New Testament), and means something like "to hold a hearing." The equivalent in some languages is "I will listen to your case," "I will listen to what you are accused of," or "I will listen and judge what you have done." The addition of the term "judge" is sometimes necessary to indicate the official character of such a hearing.

   In order to avoid the possibility of ambiguity for English readers, the TEV has rendered the Greek pronoun "him" by <u>Paul</u>.

   The phrase <u>kept under guard</u> may be translated as "had soldiers watching him" or even "commanded soldiers to watch him."

   <u>Herod's palace</u> (rendered literally as "Herod's praetorium" by the RSV) is a reference to the palace which Herod the Great built and which was used as the headquarters by the Roman governors in Palestine.

   The translation of <u>Herod's palace</u> should not imply that Herod was still alive and therefore using the palace. This phrase may be rendered in some languages as "the palace that Herod had built."

CHAPTER 24

Chapter 24 deals primarily with Paul's defense before Governor Felix. This is divided into two sections: (1) the accusation against Paul (vv. 1-9) and (2) Paul's defense (vv. 10-21). Verses 22-23 constitute a kind of postscript to Paul's defense.

Verses 24-26 describe Paul's continuing relationship to Governor Felix and give the reasons why Paul was kept a prisoner for some two years. The final verse (v. 27) provides the transition to Chapter 25 and introduces Porcius Festus.

Paul Accused by the Jews

1 Five days later the High Priest Ananias went to Caesarea with some elders and a lawyer named Tertullus. They appeared before Governor Felix and made their charges against Paul. 2 Tertullus was called and began to accuse Paul as follows:

"Your Excellency! Your wise leadership has brought us a long period of peace, and many necessary reforms are being made for the good of our country. 3 We welcome this everywhere at all times, and we are deeply grateful to you. 4 I do not want to take up too much of your time, however, so I beg you to be kind and listen to our brief account. 5 We found this man to be a dangerous nuisance; he starts riots among the Jews all over the world, and is a leader of the party of the Nazarenes. 6 He also tried to defile the temple, and we arrested him. [We planned to judge him according to our own Law, 7 but the commander Lysias came in and with great violence took him from us. 8 Then Lysias gave orders that his accusers should come before you.] If you question this man, you yourself will be able to learn from him all the things that we are accusing him of." 9 The Jews joined in the accusation and said that all this was true. (24.1-9)

The section heading Paul Accused by the Jews may be rendered as "The Jews Accused Paul" or "The Jews Accused Paul before Governor Felix."

24.1

Five days later presumably is the time from the first interview that Paul had with Felix (23.34). Very little is known about Tertullus except that he was a lawyer acting in behalf of the Jews. He could possibly have been Roman, Greek, or Jewish. In verses 3,4, and 6, by the use of we and our, he seems to identify himself with his clients, the Jewish people. On the other hand, in verse 2 he refers to "this country" (TEV our country), and in verse 5 to the Jews, as if to imply that he was not one of the Jews himself. In the last part of verse 6 he does refer to our own Law, but this part of the verse is not secure in the Greek text. All of this is to say that the identity of Tertullus is not definite, though the TEV suggests that he was one of the Jews.

The term <u>lawyer</u> is not to be understood in the sense of a "specialist in the Jewish law." He was rather a "specialist in the Roman law" or "an interpreter of the laws of the country." In some languages, however, the term for lawyer is rendered as "an accuser of people" or, in other contexts, as "a defender of people." In some instances some reference to the law may be attached to such words as "accuser" or "defender"—for example, "one who accuses according to the law" or "one who defends another using the law."

<u>Went to Caesarea</u> in the Greek text is literally "went down," but this is a normal term used when referring to travel from Jerusalem to some other city, and Caesarea is the city of destination.

<u>Appeared before Governor Felix</u> must be understood in the sense of "appeared before Governor Felix in court" or "stood before Governor Felix as he was judging the case."

<u>Made their charges against Paul</u> may be rendered as "accused Paul" or "listed their accusations against Paul."

24. 2

<u>Tertullus was called</u> is in the Greek a very ambiguous participle "when he was called" (see RSV). Verse 2 suggests that Tertullus was the one called upon to speak; but it is also possible to understand this participle as Paul being called to the hearing (see 25. 6, 17, 23). Goodspeed, Moffatt, NEB, and Phillips all explicitly identify Paul as the subject of this verb. Neither does the Greek give any object of the verb <u>began to accuse</u>, though all agree that Paul is its object.

In a number of languages one cannot say <u>Tertullus was called</u>. This would imply that he had not been there and someone "called to him." The equivalent expression in some languages is simply "Governor Felix motioned to Tertullus to speak" or, in some instances, one may use a very general subject "they indicated to Tertullus that he should speak."

<u>As follows</u> is literally "saying." However, the force of this expression in Greek is merely to introduce an address (see Phillips "in these words"; NEB merely says "Tertullus opened the case"). In some languages the equivalent is "and these are his words" or "and this is what he said."

In the Greek sentence structure Tertullus' address begins with the words "much peace" (TEV <u>a long period of peace</u>). Apparently in the first century A.D. it was quite common and proper to begin an address with the word "much," and then later introduce the person addressed. However, in English it is more natural to begin a speech by addressing the person or persons to whom one is speaking, and so this has been followed in the TEV.

In some languages it is not possible to speak of <u>your wise leadership has brought us a long period of peace</u>; only persons can be spoken of as causing peace. Therefore, one may translate as "because you are such a wise leader, we have had peace for a long time."

Of course, this introductory statement by Tertullus is pure flattery, but it was typical of all such statements made to government officials who in ancient times served not only as executives but also as judges.

Many necessary reforms is literally "reforms," and has been rendered as "needed reforms" (Goodspeed), "improvements" (NEB; see Moffatt), and "improved conditions of living" (Phillips).

For the good of our country is literally "for this country," but these reforms must be understood in terms of something good for the country. It is proper to understand the Greek expression "for this country" as an equivalent of "for our country," since this is a natural way in Greek for one to refer to his own country. On the other hand, if one understands Tertullus not to have been a Jew, then perhaps he is referring to "their country" rather than our country. In this type of context, however, one must employ the exclusive first person plural in Tertullus' remarks to Governor Felix since he certainly would not imply to the governor that the governor himself was to be identified with the country.

24. 2

It may be that Tertullus, like any good lawyer, tries to identify himself with the position of his client. This would not mean, therefore, that Tertullus would necessarily be a Jew even though he might use we.

In some few languages there is a highly specialized distinction in the first person plural of pronouns. One is the nonrestrictive "we" which involves everyone in a group. Another form of "we" is the restrictive "we" and identifies within any particular group a subgroup which is aware of its own identity. For this type of language an expression such as our country would certainly employ the restrictive our.

24. 3

The object of the verb we welcome is not explicitly stated in Greek, though the reference is to the long period of peace and the many necessary reforms that Felix is said to have brought about. The verb is stronger than a translation such as "we accept this" (RSV) might suggest; actually the verb may also mean something like "we thank you very much for this." We are deeply grateful to you translates a noun phrase ("with all gratitude"), qualifying the verb "we welcome this."

24. 4

I do not want to take up too much of your time is understood in this same fashion by most other translations, though it is faintly possible that the meaning may be "I do not want to tire you out." Ancient orators, as well as modern, felt it advisable to promise their hearers only a short speech. To be kind and listen (literally "to listen with kindness") is an expression which appears frequently in the papyri and is often used in complimentary addresses to officials. Our brief account may be rendered as "but we shall say briefly," "what I shall say briefly," or "what I shall say briefly on behalf of us here."

24.5

In the use of a term such as found one must not suggest that the Jews were out looking for this man. Rather, the meaning is "we experienced the fact that this man" or "we realized the fact that this man."

The term rendered dangerous nuisance is a word which in other contexts may mean "plague" or "pestilence." The accusations made against Paul in this verse are three: (1) he is a dangerous nuisance, (2) he starts riots among the Jews all over the world, and (3) he is a leader of the party of the Nazarenes. Even though all three of these charges are actually made on the basis of religious grounds, they are calculated to make the Roman governor suspect Paul as a political nuisance and danger. The designation of the Christian movement as the party of the Nazarenes came from the fact that its founder was Jesus of Nazareth (see 2.22). It is quite likely that the term rendered party in the present context is used in a rather derogatory sense (see JB).

The rendering of dangerous nuisance may be "he causes trouble and he is a danger to the country" or "...a danger to the government." Tertullus obviously has in mind an accusation which would not only indicate that Paul was a troublemaker but that he was potentially dangerous to the Roman power.

The reference to the party of the Nazarenes is no doubt also an attempt by Tertullus to implicate Paul as being politically active and therefore, by implication, a threat to Roman power.

24.6

In Greek, this verse is a relative clause continuing the sentence begun in the previous verse. It is interesting to note that the verb rendered to defile is not the usual term that Jews used to describe someone who had defiled their temple, but it is a more general term which would more likely appeal to someone who was not a Jew. To defile the temple may be rendered as "make the temple unholy" or "take away the holiness from the temple."

The verb rendered arrested may possibly mean "caught" (Goodspeed) or "seized" (RSV). It should be noticed that everything from the last half of verse 6 through the first half of verse 8 has been placed in brackets. The reason for this is that there is a considerable degree of doubt regarding the text at this point. In fact, the UBS Textual Committee has rated this passage as a "D" reading, indicating that there is the highest degree of doubt regarding the original text at this place. Most modern translations either omit these verses entirely (see Moffatt, Goodspeed, and Phillips) or place them in a footnote (see RSV and NEB). Even if one does include these verses as a genuine part of the text, they appear in somewhat different forms in the various ancient manuscripts. The longer reading which the TEV has included is the one which is generally accepted as the most probable of the various alternative renderings.

Judge him according to our own Law may be rendered as "judge him as our own Law says we should," "judge him by what it says in our Law," or "judge him by quoting our own Law."

24.7

The verb rendered came in almost has the force "interfered," and the Jews would have looked upon the action of Lysias in exactly this manner. With great violence would characterize the violence of the soldiers against the Jews—for example, "by attacking us, took him from us" or "by using strong force against us, took him from us."

24.8

In Greek, this verse is a continuation of the sentence begun in verse 7 and is actually a dependent clause. The TEV has changed the participle "having given orders" to a finite verb with the subject stated explicitly: Lysias gave orders. The expression gave orders or "ordered" may require direct discourse—for example, "Lysias ordered us, You must accuse Paul before Governor Felix."

The expression learn from him implies that what Lysias would learn would be that the accusations made by Tertullus against Paul were true. Therefore one may translate as "you will learn from him that all these things we are accusing him of are true."

24.9

Joined in has been rendered by Phillips as "kept joining in," an attempt to bring out the continuous force of the Greek imperfect tense. The verb rendered said that indicates the making of an assertion to challenge the truth of what someone else has said; in Phillips and the JB it appears as "asserting," and in the NEB as "alleging." Jews joined in the accusation may be rendered as "Jews also made the same accusations against Paul" or "the Jews also accused Paul of the same things."

Paul's Defense before Felix

10 The Governor then motioned to Paul to speak, and Paul said, "I know that you have been a judge over this nation for many years, and so I am happy to defend myself before you. 11 As you can find out for yourself, it was no more than twelve days ago that I went up to Jerusalem to worship. 12 The Jews did not find me arguing with anyone in the temple, nor did they find me stirring up the people, either in the synagogues or anywhere else in the city. 13 Nor can they give you proof of the accusations they now bring against me. 14 I do admit this to you: I worship the God of our ancestors by following that Way which they say is false. But I also believe in all the things written in the Law of Moses and the books of the prophets. 15 I have the same

hope in God that these themselves hold, that all men, both the good and the bad, will rise from death. 16 And so I do my best always to have a clear conscience before God and men. (24.10-16)

The section heading Paul's Defense before Felix may be rendered as "Paul Defends Himself before Felix" or even "Paul Defends Himself against the Jews before Felix."

Paul's defense is divided essentially into two parts. The first (vv. 10b-16) is a general statement of Paul's attitude with regard to his ministry and his relationship to the Law of Moses. The second (vv. 17-21) relates specifically to the accusation that he had defiled the temple or had in some other way done something wrong when he was in Jerusalem.

24.10

In Greek, verses 10-13 are one sentence, and this requires a good deal of restructuring in order to make sense for the English reader. The order in Greek is: and Paul said, which is followed by a participial phrase indicating that the governor had motioned him to speak; and then the content of Paul's speech is given. In English it is more natural to follow the chronological order, indicating that the governor motioned to Paul and then Paul spoke. Paul begins his speech with the words for many years, which is also a complimentary way of beginning an address (see v. 2).

Have been a judge over this nation may be rendered as "you have judged the people of this nation."

24.11

As you can find out for yourself refers back to the words of Tertullus in verse 8: if you question this man, you yourself will be able to learn.... The references to time in this section are rather vague, and exactly what Paul meant by twelve days is not clear. It is possible to understand this to mean that he had not been in Jerusalem for more than twelve days when they arrested him. However, most translations take it to mean a total of twelve days from the time Paul entered Jerusalem up to the hearing. This is arrived at by adding the seven days of 21.27 to the five days mentioned in 24.1.

To worship translates a verb which commentators point out as often having the meaning of "to go on a pilgrimage" (see JB). It may be necessary in translating to worship to specify who was being worshiped—for example, "to worship God" or (since in some languages one may need to specify the place) "to worship in the temple."

24.12

In some languages an expression such as did not find me arguing may be rendered as "when they saw me, I was not arguing." The same would, of course, apply to the next phrase.

There is some question regarding the exact meaning of the phrase stirring up the people (see Goodspeed "creating a disturbance among the people" and Moffatt "causing a riot"), though in the present context it seems to have a much stronger force than what is given to it in the NEB, "collecting a crowd," or in Phillips, "gathering a crowd."

The last two phrases, either in the synagogues or anywhere else in the city, may require some additional neutral verb—for example, "I was not doing this in their synagogues, and I was not doing it any place else in the city." In the city is not the normal way of expressing the idea of "in"—for example, "throughout the city" (see NEB "up and down the city" and Goodspeed "about the city").

24.13

Give you proof translates a verb which literally means "to place evidence alongside of (the accusation)." Nor can they give you proof of the accusations may be rendered as "they are not able to show that what they are accusing me of is true."

24.14

The introductory expression I do admit this to you must refer to what follows, not to what has just preceded. In some languages one must translate: "but I do say the following to you," "I do confess that the following is true," or "I do agree to the following words."

The God of our ancestors may very well be rendered as "the God whom our ancestors worshiped."

By following that Way may need to be somewhat restructured in some languages: "by living according to that Way" or "by believing in that Way." That Way in the present context is, of course, a reference to the Christian way.

The word rendered false is the same word rendered party (of the Pharisees) in 15.5. Later this word came to be used in the sense of "a heresy" (see Phillips), and in the present context the meaning seems to be in this direction. That is, Paul is stating that the Jews are accusing him of worshiping in a way that is not in keeping with what they consider to be the truth. However, Paul reminds them that he also believes in all the things written in the Law of Moses and the books of the prophets, indicating that he is still faithful to what he understands to be the truth of his Jewish heritage.

The clause which they say is false must, in some languages, be translated as a clause introduced by a conjunction such as "but"—for example, "but they say that way is false" or "but they say that way is not right." The reason for this shift is the fact that in many languages a relative clause tends to specify the characteristics of the word which it modifies rather than state the attitudes of people concerning it, especially those who might oppose it. The complexity of this relationship is implied in the embedded expression they say, and therefore a shift to a clause introduced by "but" may be far more accurate.

451

24.15

As in many other contexts, the Law of Moses may be translated as "the laws which came through Moses," and the books of the prophets may be "the books that contain the words of the prophets" or "the books which the prophets wrote."

24.15

Have the same hope in God is rendered in some languages as "I wait expectantly for God in the same way as they." In some instances hope, as in this context, implies trust—for example, "wait trustingly."
These themselves is probably a reference to the Pharisees, who are representatives of the basic outlook of Judaism, since the reference is made to Paul's belief in the resurrection.

24.16

I do my best translates a word which was originally used of athletic training, that is, "I exercise" (see NEB "train myself"). Most translators try to carry through the idea of "doing one's best." Always is placed emphatically at the end of the sentence. Clear is the same word that is translated cause no trouble in 1 Corinthians 10.32. With reference to conscience, the meaning of clear is the nearest equivalent for the English reader, and most translators have so rendered this word. For a discussion of the translation of clear conscience see 23.1.

17 "After being away from Jerusalem for several years, I went there to take some money to my own people and to offer sacrifices. 18 It was while I was doing this that they found me in the temple, after I had completed the ceremony of purification. There was no crowd with me, and no disorder. 19 But some Jews from the province of Asia were there; they themselves ought to come before you and make their accusations, if they have anything against me. 20 Or let these men here tell what crime they found me guilty of when I stood before the Council—21 except for the one thing I called out when I stood before them: 'I am being judged by you today for believing that the dead will rise to life.'" (24.17-21)

24.17

The introductory clause, after being away from Jerusalem for several years, relates the paragraph back to what has already been mentioned, namely, Paul's visit to Jerusalem to worship (v. 11). This makes this first clause an important linking device.
Once again there is a long involved Greek sentence, as verses 17-21 are one sentence in Greek. For the English reader the literal Greek expression "after several years...I came" is unclear; what Paul means is after being away from Jerusalem for several years, I went there.

To take some money is doubtless a reference to the collection that Paul gathered from the churches of Macedonia, Achaia, Galatia, and Asia for the Christians in Jerusalem. On this collection see Romans 15. 25 ff.; 1 Corinthians 16. 1-4; 2 Corinthians 8. 1 ff. Most translators render this either as "alms" (see RSV) or as "charitable gifts" (NEB, Phillips; see Goodspeed "charitable donations"). Take some money should probably be rendered as "take some money as a gift" and to my own people should not be a reference simply to Paul's own family or kinsmen; rather, it is a reference to "some Jewish people." It would not be a reference to the Jewish people as a whole.

To offer sacrifices may also be understood in the sense of "to give offerings," but in light of what Paul in fact did do, to offer sacrifices seems more in keeping with the context. To offer sacrifices is, in many languages, simply "to cause animals to be killed as gifts to God" or "to give slain animals to God."

24.18

Paul points out that when the Jews found him, it was after he had completed the ceremony of purification (see 21. 24-26), which refutes the charge that they found him defiling the temple (v. 6). Again, the verb found must be understood in the sense of "saw me."

After I had completed the ceremony of purification is equivalent to "after I had gone through the rite of being purified" or "after I had gone through the rite which caused me to be pure."

No disorder may be rendered as "no people were causing a noise" or "the people were not causing any disturbance."

24.19

Now Paul indicates that the real troublemakers were some Jews from the province of Asia. If they have anything against me is stated in such a fashion as to indicate that in fact they did not have anything against Paul.

24. 20

These men here is literally "these men themselves," but the reference is to the men who are standing there accusing Paul (see NEB "these persons here," JB "those who are present," and Moffatt "these men yonder").

What crime they found me guilty of may be equivalent to "what bad they proved that I had done" or "what evil thing they showed that I had done."

When I stood before the Council must be rendered in some languages as "when I defended myself before the Council," since in a number of languages the mere fact of standing before the Council would not imply making one's defense.

24. 21

Except for the one thing I called out correctly translates the Greek idiomatic expression "or concerning this one voice which I called out." Most translations have rendered this in a way similar to what the TEV has done. In a number of languages, however, it is difficult to introduce a clause with except for. One can therefore say "but I did do one thing, I called out...."

The passive expression I am being judged by you can be changed into the active "you are judging me," but in this particular instance "judging" does not imply neutral determination of a case but primarily condemnation. Therefore one may translate in some languages "you are condemning me today because I believe that the dead will rise to life."

On the remainder of this verse see the comments on 23. 6.

22 Then Felix, who was well informed about the Way, brought the hearing to a close. "I will decide your case," he told them, "when the commander Lysias arrives." 23 He ordered the officer in charge of Paul to keep him under guard, but to give him some freedom and allow his friends to provide for his needs. (24. 22-23)

24. 22

Well informed (so also NEB) should possibly be taken in the sense of "somewhat well informed" (Goodspeed), "had a rather accurate knowledge" (Moffatt), or "a rather accurate knowledge" (RSV). Some translators render well informed as "knew a good deal about" or "had learned much about." As in a number of other contexts, it may be necessary to translate the Way as "the Way of the Lord."

Brought the hearing to a close translates a technical judicial term (Goodspeed "adjourned the trial," JB "adjourned the case"). Evidently the RSV rendering, "put them off," comes from an understanding of the word as meaning "to withhold judgment for the time being."

I will decide your case is rendered as "I will make a judgment on these matters" or "I will say whether you are guilty or innocent."

24. 23

The TEV, the JB, and the NEB have translated the pronoun "him" as Paul to clear up a possible ambiguity from the point of the English reader (note the RSV "then he gave orders to the centurion that he should be kept in custody").

It is difficult to determine precisely what is involved in to give him some freedom. This could involve "freedom to go in and out of the prison" or "freedom from being guarded so closely." Some translators may want to render this as "to be considered like a person who was not a prisoner, even though he was still being guarded."

Allow his friends to provide for his needs is actually given in the Greek in a negative statement, "and to prevent none of his friends from providing for his needs," but in English this is stated much more naturally in the positive. This last clause may be rendered as "to permit his friends to help Paul in any way they wanted to."

Paul before Felix and Drusilla

24 After some days Felix came with his wife Drusilla, who was Jewish. He sent for Paul and listened to him as he talked about faith in Christ Jesus. 25 But as Paul went on discussing about goodness, self-control, and the coming Day of Judgment, Felix was afraid and said, "You may leave now. I will call you again when I get the chance." 26 At the same time he was hoping that Paul would give him some money; and for this reason he would call for him often and talk with him.

27 After two years had passed, Porcius Festus took the place of Felix as Governor. Felix wanted to gain favor with the Jews, so he left Paul in prison. (24. 24-27)

The section heading Paul before Felix and Drusilla might imply that this is a further defense which Paul makes before Felix and Drusilla. In reality it is simply "Paul Speaks to Felix and Drusilla" or "Felix and Drusilla Listen to Paul."

24. 24

In Greek, this verse is actually one sentence; came in the Greek sentence structure is a participle dependent upon the main verb. However, most translators prefer something similar to what the TEV has, rather than to maintain the Greek sentence form. Drusilla was the youngest daughter of Herod Agrippa I, and also the sister of Herod Agrippa II and Bernice (see 25.13). When she was only sixteen years old, Felix lured her away from her first husband, Azizus, king of Emesa.

Listened to him as he talked about faith in Christ Jesus may be rendered as "listened to Paul talking about faith in Christ Jesus" or "listened to what Paul said when he spoke about faith in Christ Jesus." However, the phrase faith in Christ Jesus may itself be best translated as a verbal expression "about believing in Christ Jesus" or "talked about what it meant to believe in Christ Jesus."

24. 25

Goodness translates the word generally rendered "righteousness" (see Goodspeed "uprightness" and RSV "justice"). Some understand it to be limited to the more specific idea of "morality" (Moffatt) or "morals" (NEB), while the TEV has understood it in the more general sense of goodness. In some languages there is no noun "goodness," but one can employ an expression such as "discussed what it meant to be good."

The other two topics which Paul discussed, self-control and the coming Day of Judgment, are understood in most translations in precisely the same manner that the TEV has taken them. Self-control is rendered in some

455

languages as "the ability to command one's self," "being able to say no to one's own desires," or "holding one's self down." The coming Day of Judgment may be rendered as "the day when God would judge everyone" or "the day when God would judge all the good and bad things people have done."

You may leave now is in Greek an imperative, which a number of translators have also taken in this softened sense (note Goodspeed, Moffatt, and JB "you may go for the present"). Now must be taken to mean "for the present time."

Felix's reply to Paul should be understood either in the sense of when I get the chance (RSV "when I have an opportunity") or with the meaning of "when I have time" (see Moffatt "when I can find a moment"). Felix was not putting Paul off, as might be implied by such a translation as "when I find it convenient I will send for you again" (NEB; see also JB), and Goodspeed is probably correct in making this into an unqualified statement: "I will find time later to send for you." Despite all the other characteristics that the Herodian family may have possessed, Luke always gives the impression that they were interested in persons connected with the Christian faith. See, for example, Luke 9. 9 and 23. 8.

24. 26

He was hoping may be translated in this context as "he was wishing" or "he wanted." Although Felix is pictured as hoping that Paul would give him some money, the very fact that he would call for him often and talk with him suggests that his interest was not solely in what he might get from Paul. It was not uncommon for government officials to take money either for the imprisonment or the release of prisoners, though there was a law against such activities.

24. 27

It is difficult to determine precisely what time is referred to in the clause after two years had passed. It is most naturally taken to refer to the amount of time that Paul was in prison before Festus succeeded Felix, though others take it to mean that Felix was removed after two years in office. After two years had passed is rendered in some languages as "two years later" or "this took place for a period of two years, then Porcius Festus took the place of Felix."

Porcius Festus took the place of Felix as Governor may be rendered as "Porcius Festus became governor; Felix was no longer governor," "Porcius Festus occupied Felix's place as governor," or "Felix no longer sat in the seat of the governor, but Porcius Festus sat there." In some languages there are, of course, idiomatic expressions referring to the transfer of "the ruler's fan," "the ruler's stool," or even "the ruler's boar's teeth."

The Greek of this sentence apparently means to gain favor with the Jews (so most modern translations) rather than "to do the Jews a favor." The same expression appears in 25. 9. In this type of context, to gain favor may be translated as "to make them his friends," "to cause them to like him," or "to cause them to say, Festus is a good governor."

CHAPTER 25

Chapter 25 is divided into two principal sections. The first (vv. 1-12) relates Paul's defense before Festus and his appeal to be judged by the Emperor, which was his privilege as a Roman citizen. The second (vv. 13-27) is really an introduction to Paul's defense of himself before Agrippa, contained in Chapter 26. However, this second section of Chapter 25 contains two important statements concerning Paul: one by Festus privately to King Agrippa, in which he relates something of the background of Paul's imprisonment; and a second (vv. 23-27) in which he makes a public statement (though primarily to King Agrippa) concerning Paul's case. Most of the paragraphs of this chapter begin with some type of temporal and spatial reference—for example, three days after Festus arrived in the province (v. 1); Festus spent another eight or ten days with them, and then went to Caesarea (v. 6); some time later King Agrippa and Bernice came to Caesarea (v. 13); the next day Agrippa and Bernice came with great pomp and ceremony (v. 23).

By introducing a number of statements concerning Paul by Felix, Festus, and Agrippa, Luke has very successfully shown the reader that Paul was essentially innocent of any serious charges which would justify the death penalty.

Paul Appeals to the Emperor

1 Three days after Festus arrived in the province, he went from Caesarea to Jerusalem. 2 There the chief priests and the Jewish leaders brought their charges against Paul. They begged Festus 3 to do them the favor of having Paul come to Jerusalem, because they had made a plot to kill him on the way. 4 Festus answered, "Paul is being kept a prisoner in Caesarea, and I myself will be going back there soon. 5 Let your leaders go to Caesarea with me and accuse the man, if he has done anything wrong." (25.1-5)

The section heading Paul Appeals to the Emperor is probably the most effective, since it highlights this section and helps to prepare the reader for what follows, namely, Paul's continued imprisonment and final journey to Rome. However, it may be necessary to alter slightly the form of the section heading—for example, "Paul Appeals to be Tried by the Emperor," "Paul Insists that Only the Emperor Can Try Him," or "Paul Asks to be Sent to the Emperor."

This first paragraph of Chapter 25 is closely linked to the last part of Chapter 24 by the mention of Festus arriving in the province (see 24.27). The mention of Caesarea and Jerusalem also link this section with the preceding narrative (see 24.1, 11, 17).

25.1

It should be pointed out that the first three verses are actually one sentence in Greek. By specifying three days, Luke intends for his readers to

understand that the new governor attended to Paul's case as soon as possible
after he had assumed his authority. Arrived in the province may be taken
geographically as in the TEV and most other translations, or administra-
tively as in the NEB ("taking up his appointment") and Phillips ("taken over
his province").

25.2

Brought their charges against translates the same verb which appeared
in 23.15. This expression brought their charges against is rendered in some
languages as "accused Paul of having violated various laws" or "told Festus,
This man Paul has committed various crimes." A term such as "various" or
"some" must be introduced in some languages in order to indicate the indefinite nature of these particular charges.

The sense of the verb used in verse 2 seems to be that of begged (so
also Phillips, Goodspeed, Moffatt; JB "urgently asking") rather than merely
"asked" (NEB). The tense of the verb indicates action in progress, that is,
"they were begging Festus." Both in this verse and in the following verse the
TEV has made pronominal subjects explicit; here "him" has been rendered
as Festus, and in the following verse "him" has been rendered as Paul. In
trying to relate the verb begged to the favor which was asked of Festus, it is
often useful to place the content of what was requested in the form of direct
discourse—for example, "they begged Festus, Please cause Paul to come
here to Jerusalem." The use of a term such as "please" not only suggests
the concept of favor but also reinforces the meaning of begged. In some languages a term such as favor is translated as "to do good for them," "to do
them a kindness," or "to be helpful to them."

25.3

The word rendered plot is the same word that is used in 23.16.

25.4

In the Greek sentence structure verse 4 is in indirect discourse; direct
discourse begins in verse 5 of the Greek text. The TEV has made both verses
into direct discourse (so also the NEB).

The passive expression is being kept a prisoner may be rendered in
the active form by "soldiers are guarding Paul in Caesarea" or even as "Paul
remains a prisoner in Caesarea."

25.5

Let your leaders go to Caesarea is, of course, not an expression of
permission, but of implied command—for example, "cause your leaders to
go to Caesarea with me."

If he has done anything wrong (see Moffatt "and charge the man with whatever crime he has committed") is a direct interpretation of the Greek expression (literally "if there is anything out of place in the man").

> 6 Festus spent another eight or ten days with them, and then went to Caesarea. On the next day he sat down in the judgment court, and ordered Paul to be brought in. 7 When Paul arrived, the Jews who had come from Jerusalem stood around him and started making many serious charges against him, which they were not able to prove. 8 But Paul defended himself, "I have done nothing wrong against the Law of the Jews, or the temple, or the Roman Emperor."
>
> 9 Festus wanted to gain favor with the Jews, so he asked Paul, "Would you be willing to go to Jerusalem and be tried on these charges before me there?"
>
> 10 Paul said, "I am standing before the Emperor's own judgment court, where I should be tried. I have done no wrong to the Jews, as you yourself well know. 11 If I have broken the law and done something for which I deserve the death penalty, I do not ask to escape it. But if there is no truth in the charges they bring against me, no one can hand me over to them. I appeal to the Emperor."
>
> 12 Then Festus, after conferring with his advisers, answered, "You have appealed to the Emperor, so to the Emperor you will go."
>
> (25. 6-12)

One should not presume that all that Paul said in defending himself is contained in verse 8. This is naturally only a summary, even as so many of the speeches or paragraphs of direct discourse are in Luke's writings.

25. 6

In Greek, this sentence begins with a participle "having spent," which is rendered by the TEV as Festus spent. Inasmuch as this is the beginning of a new paragraph, it is felt important for the needs of the English reader to qualify the participant (Festus) and to make this into a coordinate, rather than a subordinate, clause.

Another eight or ten days is a negative expression in the Greek (literally "not more than eight or ten days"). There is a potential ambiguity in the expression Festus spent another eight or ten days with them. Translated literally in some languages, this might imply that Festus was the guest of the chief priests and Jewish leaders and therefore would be prejudiced against Paul as a result of this hospitality. In reality, it only means that Festus spent another eight or ten days in Jerusalem.

In some languages, he sat down in the judgment court must be rendered as "he took his place as judge" or "he sat down as judge." The final clause, ordered Paul to be brought in, is rendered in some languages as direct discourse: "ordered the soldiers, Cause Paul to come in" or "...Bring Paul in."

The two verses 7 and 8 are one sentence in Greek, beginning with the participle "when he arrived." Since the subject of verse 7 is different from the subject of the previous verse, it is helpful to identify "he" as Paul. The TEV understands the force of the verb to be started making; most translators render merely "making." The phrase making many serious charges against him may be rendered as "accused him of many serious crimes" or "said, This man has done many bad things."

Since the last clause of this verse states something which was not true of the charges, it may be important to introduce this with some kind of adversative conjunction—for example, "but they were not able to prove these charges" or "but they were not able to show that what they said about Paul was true."

25.8

Paul is quick to point out that he has done nothing wrong (literally "not sinned") against the Law of the Jews (see 21.21), or against the temple (see 21.28), or against the Roman Emperor. The less known term, "Caesar," appears as the Roman Emperor (see NEB "the Emperor").

I have done nothing wrong against the Law of the Jews may be rendered as "I have done nothing which violates the Law of the Jews" or "...which is contrary to the Law of the Jews." It may be much more difficult to speak of "nothing wrong against the temple." In some languages this is "have not harmed the temple in any way" or "have not caused trouble as far as the temple is concerned."

Frequently one cannot use the same expression, "doing anything wrong against," with three such entirely different objects as the Law of the Jews, the temple, and the Roman Emperor. Therefore, especially in the final case, it may be necessary to say, "I have said nothing bad against the Roman Emperor" or "I have said nothing harmful against the Roman Emperor."

25.9

To gain favor with is the same verb which appears in 24.27.

Inasmuch as the crime which Paul was accused of committing took place in Jerusalem, it was quite natural for Fèstus to ask Paul if he were willing to go there and be put on trial. Before me is emphatic in the Greek sentence structure. Be tried on these charges before me may be rendered as "have me judge these charges against you" or "have me judge if what they say against you is true."

25.10

Paul is convinced that Festus must certainly know of his innocence, and you yourself is an emphatic expression in Greek. Thus Paul seemingly suspects that Festus' question is only a device for gaining favor with the Jews.

25.11

It is not at all easy to introduce meaningfully an expression such as I am standing before the Emperor's own judgment court. In fact, this first clause may very well be combined with the second clause, and the entire sentence translated as "I insist that my case should be judged in the Emperor's own court" or "I insist that the Emperor should judge my case."

I have done no wrong to the Jews may be rendered as "I have not caused the Jews any harm" or "I have not hurt the Jews."

25.11

Broken the law may be translated variously, as "violated the law," "done contrary to the law," "done what the law says I should not do," or, idiomatically as in some languages, "twisted the law," "bent the law," or "went around the law."

Done something for which I deserve the death penalty may be rendered as "done something which should cause me to be killed" or "...for which I should be punished by being killed." The following clause, do not ask to escape it, may accordingly be rendered as "do not ask not to be killed" or "do not ask to escape death."

A number of languages have no noun such as truth, but it is possible to employ an adjective in an expression such as "if the crimes they accuse me of are not true" or "if what they say that I have done is not true."

No one can hand me over to them may possibly mean something like "no one can make a gift of me to them," but the idea of "making a gift of someone" is difficult to carry over into translation (note NEB "it is not open to anyone to hand me over as a sop to them"; in verse 16 NEB has "hand over" for the same verb).

In many languages one must indicate clearly that an auxiliary verb such as can implies here "the right to," not simply "the strength or power" to do something—for example, "no one has the right to turn me over to them" or "...to cause me to come before them."

Very little is known about the details of an appeal to the Emperor, though apparently in Paul's day it was something that only a Roman citizen could do, and perhaps only then in the case of the threat of capital punishment. In translating I appeal to the Emperor, it may be necessary to say "I ask that the Emperor judge my case" or "I ask that I be sent to the Emperor."

25.12

The appeal to Caesar was of such moment that Festus thought it best to confer with his advisers before making the decision regarding Paul's fate. The first part of this verse may be translated as "then Festus first conferred with his advisers and then answered Paul."

Paul before Agrippa and Bernice

13 Some time later King Agrippa and Bernice came to Caesarea

462

to pay a visit of welcome to Festus. 14 After they had been there several days, Festus explained Paul's situation to the king, "There is a man here who was left a prisoner by Felix; 15 and when I went to Jerusalem, the Jewish chief priests and elders brought charges against him and asked me to condemn him. 16 But I told them that the Romans are not in the habit of handing over any man accused of a crime before he has met his accusers face to face, and has the chance of defending himself against the accusation. 17 When they came here, then, I lost no time, but on the very next day I sat in the judgment court and ordered the man to be brought in. 18 His opponents stood up, but they did not accuse him of any of the evil crimes that I thought they would. 19 All they had were some arguments with him about their own religion and about a man named Jesus, who has died; but Paul claims that he is alive. 20 I was undecided about how I could get information on these matters, so I asked Paul if he would be willing to go to Jerusalem and be tried there on these charges. 21 But Paul appealed; he asked to be kept under guard and let the Emperor decide his case. So I gave orders for him to be kept under guard until I could send him to the Emperor."

22 Agrippa said to Festus, "I would like to hear this man myself." "You will hear him tomorrow," Festus answered. (25.13-22)

There is some awkwardness in the section heading Paul before Agrippa and Bernice, since actually Paul does not make his defense before them until Chapter 26 and does not even come before them until 25.23. Therefore it is perfectly possible, in this instance, to use as a heading for this section (vv. 13-22), "Festus Explains Paul's Case to King Agrippa" or "Festus Talks to King Agrippa about Paul." It would then be necessary to introduce another section heading before the last paragraph of this chapter (vv. 23-27), which might read, "Paul Is Brought before Agrippa and Bernice."

25.13

The King Agrippa mentioned here is Agrippa II, son of Herod Agrippa I. He actually ruled over only a few small territories north of Palestine, though he did have the authority, given him by the Roman Emperor, to appoint the Jewish High Priest. Bernice, the oldest daughter of Herod Agrippa I, was not without her faults. She had been given by her father to his brother as a wife, and when he died she lived for a while in the home of her own brother, Agrippa II. After this she married the king of Cilicia, but then left him and came back to live with her brother. Later she became the mistress of the Roman general Titus, who felt it necessary to leave her when he was made Emperor.

The temporal expression some time later can probably be best interpreted as "some months`later" or perhaps "several weeks later," but it is certainly neither a matter of years nor of days.

To pay a visit of welcome translates a term which is used of general greetings, though it is also used in a specialized sense of "to pay an official visit of welcome to someone" (see NEB "on a courtesy visit to Festus").

25.14

A visit of welcome to Festus may be rendered as "to visit Festus and to say to him, Welcome" or "... We are glad you have come."

25.14

Explained Paul's situation to the king is translated by most as "lay Paul's case before the king." The particular emphasis (whether of Paul's "situation" or his "case") is determined by what Festus tells the king in the following verses. In rendering Paul's situation, one may say "how it was with Paul" or "how Paul had made his appeal to the Emperor," since this is really the crucial issue in Paul's case.

25.15

Brought charges against is the same verb which appears in 23.15. Asked me to condemn him is literally "asking against him a condemnation." In this construction, however, it is understood that Festus is the person whom they are asking to pass this decree of condemnation on Paul. Asked me to condemn him may be rendered as "asked me, Condemn this man" or "begged me, Declare this man guilty."

25.16

In a number of languages it is difficult to translate the relationship of the various events mentioned in this verse, if they are kept in their present order and employ a conjunction such as before. However, with some shift of order it is possible to translate quite accurately and idiomatically—for example, "but I told them that it was the practice of the Romans first to have an accused man meet face to face those who accuse him and so have a chance of defending himself against what he has been accused of. I told him it was not the practice of Romans to hand over a man accused of a crime unless this had been done." By breaking up this verse into two different sentences, one can often reproduce the meaning far more satisfactorily.

25.17

I lost no time (see JB "I wasted no time") must be understood in the sense of "I acted as quickly as I could." In the Greek sentence the only finite verb is ordered, with all of the other verbal forms either participles or infinitives depending upon this main verb.

As in other contexts, an expression such as I sat in the judgment court may be rendered as "I took my place as judge." Similarly, the final clause following the verb ordered may be put into the form of direct discourse: "ordered the soldiers, Bring the man in."

25.18

That I thought they would must be taken to indicate that Festus thought

Paul's opponents would have charges of serious crimes to bring against him. Some translators render this phrase rather ambiguously, so that it suggests that the men did not bring serious crimes against Paul, and Festus knew all along that they would not (see RSV "they brought no charge in his case of such evils as I supposed").

In some languages it may be useful to shift somewhat the order of clauses in this verse—for example, "his opponents stood up to accuse him, and I thought they would accuse him of evil crimes, but they did not accuse him of any such evil crimes." This type of restructuring may be necessary in some languages, because the qualifying relative clause, that I thought they would, introduces something which is different from what is a normal characterization of evil crimes.

25.19

The word rendered arguments basically means "questions," but in the present context it refers either to arguments or "differences of opinion."

The word rendered religion here is the same term which was discussed in 17. 22; in both occurrences of this word in Acts it means religion and not "superstition." It is difficult to imagine that Festus would refer to the Jewish religion as "a superstition" when speaking with persons of Jewish background.

Their own religion may be rendered in some languages as "the way in which they worship God."

A man named Jesus, who has died is literally "a certain dead Jesus," but the construction is similar to that discussed in 22.12.

Claims that is the same verb rendered "said that" in 24. 9. Since, however, this final clause is in contrast with the preceding, it may be necessary to introduce it with some kind of adversative conjunction—for example, "but Paul says that this man Jesus is alive."

25. 20

I was undecided renders a verb that indicates Festus felt thoroughly confused about what to do. Both Phillips ("I did not feel qualified") and the NEB ("finding myself out of my depth") express this idea on a rather high level of language.

Get information on these matters may be rendered as "learn more about these matters" or "find out exactly what was involved in these matters."

25. 21

The clause but Paul appealed must be amplified in some languages to read "but Paul appealed to the Emperor" or "but Paul insisted that he be tried by the Emperor."

In reality, of course, Paul did not directly ask to be kept under guard. However, by appealing to the Emperor, he indirectly placed himself under guard until his case could be tried in Rome.

25.22

The clause I gave orders for him to be kept under guard may be rendered as direct discourse: "I ordered the soldiers, Guard him."

The TEV has transformed the noun phrase "for the decision of the Emperor" into a verbal expression: let the Emperor decide his case.

25.22

For the clause Agrippa said to Festus, the verb said does not appear in the Greek sentence. However, it is not uncommon for Greek to leave out a verb such as "is" or "said" when this can be understood from the context. I...myself may be understood as "I...also," though the former of these two meanings seems preferred in the present context. Once again the TEV has made explicit the pronominal subject of the verb answered, that is, Festus rather than "he."

The Greek structure of the expression I would like to hear this man myself leaves open the possibility that it may be understood in the sense of "I have been waiting to hear this man" (Phillips). The TEV renders this verb as have most translators, namely, as an expression of a present wish rather than as a wish experienced over a period of time. On the other hand, it may be that Luke is intending to stress the parallel between Agrippa's desire to hear Paul and Herod's desire to hear Jesus, as is indicated in Luke's Gospel (Luke 23.8).

> 23 The next day Agrippa and Bernice came with great pomp and ceremony, and entered the audience hall with the military chiefs and the leading men of the city. Festus gave the order and Paul was brought in. 24 Festus said, "King Agrippa, and all who are here with us: You see this man against whom all the Jewish people, both here and in Jerusalem, have brought complaints to me. They scream that he should not live any longer. 25 But I could not find that he had done anything for which he deserved the death sentence. And since he himself made an appeal to the Emperor, I have decided to send him. 26 But I do not have anything definite about him to write to the Emperor. So I have brought him here before you—and especially before you, King Agrippa! —so that, after investigating his case, I may have something to write. 27 For it seems unreasonable to me to send a prisoner without clearly indicating the charges against him." (25.23-27)

25.23

In Greek this verse is one sentence, but it has been broken into two by the TEV. With great pomp and ceremony depicts the great fanfare with which oriental kings would have entered a public gathering. The phrase with great pomp and ceremony may be translated in some languages as "and were honored very much with ceremonies" or "and people honored them very much by what they did."

The audience hall was used not only for times such as this, but could also be used as a place for public trial. In some languages, the audience hall would be "a large hall" or "a large building for people to assemble in."

Military chiefs translates a word which may be rendered as "men in charge of a thousand soldiers," while leading men may be taken in the sense of "the most prominent men."

Festus gave the order is literally a participial clause: "Festus having given the order." It may, however, be necessary to stipulate "and soldiers brought Paul in."

25. 24

Note that here Festus indicates that it is all the Jewish people, not merely the Jewish leaders (see vv. 2, 7, 15), who have brought accusations against Paul.

25. 25

But I is very emphatic in the Greek sentence.

Anything for which he deserved the death sentence may be rendered as "any crime which would cause him to be killed" or "any crime for which it would be right for us to execute him."

25. 26

To the Emperor is literally "to the Lord," a term which was very often applied to the Roman Emperor. One of the early conflicts between Christianity and the Roman government grew out of the fact that the Christians said "Jesus Christ is Lord," whereas the Roman people said "the Emperor is Lord."

It may be necessary to imply with the verb brought him that Paul has been brought "in order to speak before you."

25. 27

Seems unreasonable to me may be rendered as "does not seem right to me," "does not seem good to me," or "does not seem proper to me."

Without clearly indicating the charges against him translates the Greek expression "not to indicate the charges against him."

CHAPTER 26

Chapter 26 consists essentially of Paul's defense of himself before King Agrippa. Note that it is to King Agrippa that he addresses his defense, which includes not only a denial of the accusations brought against him, but also an explanation of his conversion and his work.

Paul's defense is interrupted briefly at verse 24 by the statement of Festus concerning Paul's "being mad," but Paul continues his defense to King Agrippa and appeals directly to him.

The final paragraph (vv. 30-32) concludes the account with a statement from Agrippa declaring Paul's innocence.

The structure of Paul's defense is very well developed. Notice how, for example, in verse 3 Paul introduces the question of Jewish customs and questions, and then immediately in verse 4 refers to what all the Jews know about him. In verses 7-8 he introduces the theme of the resurrection, and immediately in verse 9 shifts to a specific reference to Jesus of Nazareth. At the end of verse 11 he mentions his desire to persecute the Christians, and this introduces the following paragraph, where in verse 12 he cites his experience on the way to Damascus. Toward the end of this paragraph, Paul cites what the Lord said to him, and in verse 19 he takes up the same theme of this vision from heaven. It is essential, in translating this chapter, that the same carefully constructed links between succeeding events and episodes be reproduced.

Paul Defends Himself before Agrippa

1 Agrippa said to Paul, "You have permission to speak on your own behalf." Paul stretched out his hand and defended himself as follows:

2 "King Agrippa! I consider myself fortunate that today I am to defend myself before you from all the things the Jews accuse me of. 3 This is especially true because you know so well all the Jewish customs and questions. I ask you, then, to listen to me with patience.

(26.1-3)

26.1

As in 25.22, the verb said is missing from the Greek sentence and must be supplied in translation.

You have permission to speak may simply be translated as "you may now speak" or "you are allowed to speak."

Paul stretched out his hand and defended himself must be translated in such a way as to indicate that the stretching out of his hand was a gesture, and not a means by which he was defending himself from physical injury.

Verses 2-3 must be understood as the introduction to Paul's defense. In Greek, these verses are the continuation of the sentence begun in verse 1. Although from all the things the Jews accuse me of is the first element in the Greek sentence order, it is difficult to reconstruct English naturally in this fashion; but see Phillips, who has tried to do so.

In the setting in which Paul was speaking, the word King would have been understood in a much lesser sense than the English word is understood today; however, there seems to be no better way to render the term for the English reader. The equivalent of this use of King is in a number of languages simply "an important chief." He was certainly by no means "the head chief."

I consider myself fortunate reminds one of 24.2,3,10, where the speaker indicates his good pleasure at being able to address a particular person or audience.

26.3

Especially may be taken either as a modifier of true or as a modifier of the verb know (see RSV "because you are especially familiar"; Lake "especially since you are expert"). Know so well translates a noun meaning "expert."

Questions (JB "[matters of]...controversy"; NEB "disputes") is the same word translated arguments in 25.19; here it refers to the questions regarding theological issues that were often discussed within Judaism. Jewish customs and questions may be translated as "the way the Jews live and their differences" or "the ways in which they differ from one another."

I ask you, then, to listen to me with patience serves the same purpose in this present address as I beg you to be kind and listen to our brief account did in the speech of Tertullus (24.4). Patience may be rendered as "with your heart open" or, in some languages, with an expression which is more or less equivalent to "sympathetically." The focus here is upon the patience which is required because of the presumed length of the account which is to follow.

4 "All the Jews know how I have lived ever since I was young. They know from the beginning how I have spent my whole life in my own country and in Jerusalem. 5 They have always known, if they are willing to testify, that from the very first I have lived as a member of the strictest party of our religion, the Pharisees. 6 And now I stand here to be tried because I hope in the promise that God made to our ancestors—7 the very promise that all twelve tribes of our people hope to receive, as they worship God day and night. And it is because of this hope, your Majesty, that I am being accused by the Jews! 8 Why do you Jews find it impossible to believe that God raises the dead? (26.4-8)

26. 4

26. 4

As is indicated by the particle with which Luke introduces this section (see 1. 6), he indicates that this is the real beginning of Paul's defense. This paragraph points out that Paul is, in fact, on trial for what is one of the very basic beliefs in Judaism, that is, the belief in the resurrection from the dead.

Although the phrase rendered from the beginning in this verse and from the very first in the following verse are different, it is not likely that any difference in meaning is to be sought in them. The same two expressions appear in Luke 1. 2,3 and there have been rendered by the TEV from the beginning and from their beginning. The use of different terms in the present context is merely for stylistic effect.

In my own country (that is, Cilicia) is the meaning that most see in this phrase, though some few understand it to mean "in my own province" (that is, in Judea).

26.5

Always translates the adverb rendered "long enough" in NEB and "for a long time" in JB. In Luke 1. 2 the same adverb is used with the meaning "from the beginning" (see TEV; NEB "in detail").

The clause if they are willing to testify may seem to be strange in this kind of context. Obviously, what the Jews know about Paul is in no sense dependent upon their being willing to testify. Therefore, in some languages this clause must be rendered as "and they can testify that this is true if they want to."

Party is the same word rendered false in 24.14. That the present meaning is intended in this context is clear, and illustrates that in different contexts the same word may have a variety of meanings. In this type of context, party obviously refers to a "group"—for example, "a member of the group that was most strict" or "a member of the group that followed regulations more than any other."

The word which Paul uses for religion is especially suited in a Gentile context. Basically, the word refers to the entire mode of worship of a particular people; it is not the same word used in 25.19. As in so many other contexts, our religion may be rendered as "the way in which we worship God."

The expression the Pharisees may need to be identified as the name of the particular group—for example, "a member of a group which worshiped our God in a way which was more strict than any other group. This group is called the Pharisees."

26. 6

In Greek, this and the following verse are one sentence. In this verse Paul moves from the discussion of his past as a Pharisee to his present position. The hope which Paul has in mind is not explicitly stated in this verse, though it is clear from such passages as 23. 6 and 24.15 that it is the hope in the resurrection from the dead. I hope in the promise may be somewhat re-structured in some languages to read "I wait trusting that God will accomplish the promise he made to our ancestors." As has been noted in other contexts, hope normally involves two components, one of waiting and the other of positive expectancy, suggesting trust or confidence. Hope may thus be described in some contexts as "confidence projected into the future."

26. 7

The very promise that is in Greek a pronoun phrase referring back to the word promise in the preceding verse. Since it appears to be emphatic in the present setting, the TEV has rendered it by the very promise. The very promise may be rendered as "the same promise." However, promise may need to be expressed as a verb—for example, "all twelve tribes of our people hope to receive that which God has promised." In view of this type of re-structuring, it may be important to place the clause as they worship God day and night at the beginning of verse 7.

In the Greek sentence worship has no specified object, though it is clear that God is intended.

The expression day and night (literally "night and day") is used also in 20. 31; in Luke 2. 37 it is said of Anna that day and night she worshiped God. In some languages a literal translation of day and night would imply that the Jews worshiped day and night continuously and did nothing else. The implication, of course, is "as they habitually worshiped God" or "...continually worshiped God."

It may be necessary to transform the noun hope in the phrase this hope into a verb—for example, "because they hope in this way."

Your Majesty (so also NEB and Goodspeed) is rendered "O king" by most translators. American English in particular is deficient in terms used to address royalty, though your Majesty appears much more natural for the reader of American English than does "O king." In some languages the equivalent of "O king" would simply be "you who have power," "you who sit on the stool," or "you who carry the spear."

By the Jews is in an emphatic position in the Greek sentence structure. In Greek "the" does not appear before "Jews," and some have taken this to mean something like "and by Jews themselves," so as to indicate a very surprising turn on the part of the Jews who denied this hope (so NEB).

26. 8

You Jews is literally "you" (plural), but Jews has been added by the TEV in order to bring out the fact that Paul now addresses himself to the entire group of Jews present, rather than merely to the king. The RSV has "by any of you," NEB "among you," and Phillips "to you all." Goodspeed, Moffatt, and the JB (along with KJV) keep the ambiguous form "you."

Although God raises the dead is a general statement, Paul's argument is that the denial that God has raised Christ from the dead is a denial of a general belief in a resurrection. The sequence find it impossible to believe that is, from a semantic standpoint, relatively complex. In some languages this type of combination of concepts is somewhat simplified by introducing direct discourse—for example, "Why do you Jews say, It is not possible for us to believe that God raises the dead?" or "...We cannot believe that God raises the dead?"

> 9 "I myself thought that I should do everything I could against the name of Jesus of Nazareth. 10 That is what I did in Jerusalem. I received authority from the chief priests and put many of God's people in prison; and when they were sentenced to death, I also voted for it. 11 Many times I had them punished in all the synagogues, and tried to make them deny their faith. I was so furious with them that I even went to foreign cities to persecute them." (26. 9-11)

Although the UBS Greek text does not make a paragraph division here, it is obvious that a new section of Paul's thought begins at this point. This is indicated not only by the transitional particle which is used (the same as in v. 4 and 1.16), but by the difference in content. In this section Paul describes in detail his zeal to uphold what he thought to be the tradition given by his ancestors. Specifically this was shown by his persecution of the Christian community.

It might appear that there was no basic connection between Paul's statement in verse 8 concerning the resurrection of the dead and his continuing statement in verse 9 concerning Jesus Christ. However, for all those present, certainly the key issue was the resurrection of Jesus Christ as proclaimed by Paul.

26. 9

Since "I" is emphatic in the Greek sentence, it has here been rendered as I myself. Everything I could is literally "many things," but the meaning in the present context is clear.

On the name of Jesus see 4. 7.

Do everything I could against the name of Jesus of Nazareth may be rendered as "do everything I could to harm the name of Jesus of Nazareth." In some languages, however, one simply cannot use the name in this type of context. One must refer to the person himself, for the use of the name would imply some type of magic incantation or verbal sorcery.

26.10

In Greek, this and the following verse are one sentence. I received authority from the chief priests may be rendered as "the chief priests gave me the power," "the chief priests appointed me with power," or "the chief priests gave me the power to put many of God's people in prison."

When they were sentenced to death is literally "when they were put to death," but most translations understand it in the sense followed by the TEV (see NEB "were condemned to death"). The phrase I also voted for it would suggest that Paul himself had been a member of the Council in Jerusalem, which alone would have passed judgments of this kind. In order to render I also voted for it, some languages employ "I also said, I agree" or "I showed that I also was in favor."

26.11

I had them punished is literally "I punished them," but the meaning is not that Paul did this on his own but that he had others punish them.

Most translators understand the Greek phrase "made them deny their faith" in the sense of tried to make them deny their faith, though the KJV and Moffatt indicate that he did in fact make them deny their faith. The question cannot be settled absolutely and depends on whether or not one assumes that Paul was successful in making the Christians deny their faith. No doubt he found himself successful in some cases, while in others he was unsuccessful, otherwise he would not have had them put in prison and sentenced to death.

Tried to make them deny their faith is rendered in some languages as "tried to make them say, We no longer believe in Jesus."

To persecute them may simply be rendered as "to cause them harm" or, in a more technical sense, "to bring accusations against them," but such actions were designed primarily to cause serious difficulty and harm.

Paul Tells of His Conversion

12 "It was for this purpose that I went to Damascus with the authority and orders from the chief priests. 13 It was on the road at midday, your Majesty, that I saw a light much brighter than the sun shining from the sky around me and the men traveling with me. 14 All of us fell to the ground, and I heard a voice say to me in the Hebrew language, 'Saul, Saul! Why are you persecuting me? You hurt yourself by hitting back, like an ox kicking against its owner's stick.' 15 'Who are you, Lord?' I asked. And the Lord said: 'I am Jesus, whom you persecute. 16 But get up and stand on your feet. I have appeared to you to appoint you as my servant; you are to tell others what you have seen of me today, and what I will show you in the future. 17 I will save you from the people of Israel and from the Gentiles, to whom I will send you. 18 You are to open their eyes and turn them from the darkness to the light, and from the power of Satan to God, so that through their faith in me they will have their sins forgiven and receive their place among God's chosen people.'" (26.12-18)

The section heading Paul Tells of His Conversion is rendered in some languages as "Paul Tells How He Became a Believer." In some instances conversion may be translated as "turn to God"; but in this context it is important

473

to use some expression referring to Paul's faith in Jesus Christ rather than a more general belief in God.

On these verses see 9.1-19 and 22.6-16.

26.12

On this verse compare 9.2 and 22.5. It was for this purpose may be understood in the sense the TEV has taken the word (see Moffatt "on this business"), or in a temporal sense (see Goodspeed "once" and NEB "on one such occasion"), or in the sense of "under these circumstances." Note, however, that the phrase for this purpose is important in relating the following paragraph to what has just preceded, namely, Paul's intent to persecute the churches.

In Greek the word orders is singular and is rendered "commission" by many translators. The reference would be to a document indicating the authority given him by the High Priest. In some languages it is not possible to say I went to Damascus with the authority and orders. Since such authority and orders would be given in written form, one can only go with this type of document—for example, "I went to Damascus with a document which stated I had authority and orders from the chief priests."

26.13

On the road differs from near Damascus of 22.6, while at midday differs slightly in wording from about midday of the same verse. Much brighter than the sun intensifies what is said in 22.6 and 9.3. Shining also differs from what was said in the earlier accounts; there the verb flashed was used. It is not strange, however, that Luke in recounting the conversion of Paul uses slightly different details of wording. For him to have reproduced the exact wording in every instance would have certainly produced a rather monotonous account. These stylistic modifications are precisely what one would expect from a writer as skillful as Luke.

26.14

According to 9.4 only Paul fell down, while here it is stated all of us fell to the ground. It is explicitly stated here that Saul (Paul) was spoken to in the Hebrew language, while in 9.4 and 22.7 only the use of the word Saul implies this fact.

"It is hard for you to kick against the stick" must be understood in the sense of "you hurt yourself by kicking against the stick." The kind of stick referred to was a sharp-pointed stick used by a person goading an ox or a donkey while working. What appears as a metaphor in Greek is rendered here as a kind of simile, since it would be difficult for the average person to understand what is really involved in an ox kicking against its owner's stick and how this might apply to an individual.

26.15

Compare 9.5 and 22.8.

26.16

It should be pointed out that verses 16-18 comprise one sentence in the Greek. Also of importance for these three verses is the number of Old Testament allusions that Paul makes.

Get up and stand on your feet is stated somewhat differently in 22.10 and 9.6. Here the command reflects Ezekiel 2.1,3. In a number of languages there is a single expression which means get up and stand on your feet. Under such circumstances a single verb may very well be sufficient to translate all of the components implied in this phrase of seven words in English.

My servant may be rendered as "one who is to help me" or "one who is to work for me" (see 13.5).

You are to tell others translates "(you are to be) a witness." What you have seen of me ... and what I will show you represents a difficult construction in Greek, but the meaning is understood in this sense by all commentators and translators. Although the weight of manuscript evidence favors the omission of the phrase of me, the strongest argument for its inclusion is the fact that it makes the kind of awkward Greek that is best assumed to be original.

The TEV has made the temporal relationship explicit by today and in the future.

26.17

Although the word rendered save may also mean "appoint," all translators understand it in this sense in the present passage. It is also used in the sense of "save" or "rescue" in 7.10,34; 12.10; 23.27. The words addressed to Paul reflect those spoken to Jeremiah (Jeremiah 1.7-8). In some languages the concept of "being saved from" is expressed as "I will save you from the people of Israel, and the Gentiles will not harm you" or "I will cause you not to be harmed by the people of Israel and by the Gentiles." In this circumstance a term such as "harm" must be a relatively strong expression.

People of Israel is literally "people," but here as elsewhere the term is used with the specific meaning of the people of Israel.

26.18

As pointed out above, verses 16-18 are actually one sentence in the Greek, and you are to open is, in the Greek sentence structure, an infinitive. The idea of "opening their eyes" in many languages is simply "cause them to see" or even "to remove their blindness."

To open their eyes reflects Isaiah 42.7, while to turn them from the darkness to the light is an allusion to Isaiah 42.16. In some languages it is relatively meaningless to speak of "turning people from darkness to the light."

One can, of course, say "turn them around from looking into the darkness so they will look into the light," but in a number of languages the equivalent expression is "cause them to come out of the darkness and into the light."

The remainder of the verse has parallels in Colossians 1.12-13. The expression from the power of Satan to God is translated in some languages as "to cause them to come away from being under Satan's power and to enter into being under God's power" or "to cause them to leave the place where Satan rules and to come to the place where God rules."

Through their faith in me may be equivalent to "because they believe in me." They will have their sins forgiven may be rendered as "God will forgive their sins."

Their place among God's chosen people, though expressed differently in various translations, is without doubt the meaning of the Greek expression here. This final expression in verse 18 may be rendered as "they will occupy the place which they should have among the people whom God has selected."

Paul Tells of His Work

19 "And so, King Agrippa, I did not disobey the vision I had from heaven. 20 First in Damascus and in Jerusalem, and then in the whole country of the Jews and among the Gentiles, I preached that they must repent of their sins and turn to God, and do the things that would show they had repented. 21 It was for this reason that the Jews seized me while I was in the temple, and tried to kill me. 22 But to this very day I have been helped by God, and so I stand here giving my witness to all, to the small and great alike. What I say is the very same thing the prophets and Moses said was going to happen: 23 that the Messiah must suffer and be the first one to rise from death, to announce the light of salvation to the Jews and to the Gentiles." (26.19-23)

The section heading Paul Tells of His Work may be misleading in some languages if work could only refer to his making tents. Therefore, in some languages one may translate: "Paul Tells about How He has Preached" or "Paul Describes How He has Served Jesus."

26.19

I did not disobey the vision is an emphatic way of saying "I obeyed the vision." In many languages, however, it is quite misleading to talk about did not disobey. The double negative will be misunderstood in many instances as merely an emphatic expression for "disobey." Therefore it may be much better to employ a strong positive "I certainly obeyed the vision."

The vision I had from heaven (literally "the heavenly vision") is a reference to the heavenly being who appeared to Paul. For Paul this was a decisive fact; it was impossible for him to disobey the command from heaven. In some languages it is difficult to speak of a vision coming from heaven. Rather, one must employ some such wording as "the vision of a person who came from heaven" or "the vision of one who came from heaven."

26. 20

Paul preached <u>first in Damascus</u> (9.19-25) and then <u>in Jerusalem</u> (9. 28-29). There is a great deal of difficulty regarding the grammatical form of the phrase <u>in the whole country of the Jews</u>, though from the standpoint of translation it should be construed in the way in which the TEV has rendered it. Though the geographical locations of Paul's preaching are emphasized in this verse, in many languages it is necessary to place the verb of "preaching" first—for example, "I preached first in Damascus and then in Jerusalem and then in the whole country of the Jews and also to the Gentiles."

As with the earlier part of the book of Acts, the content of Paul's preaching is to tell people <u>they must repent of their sins and turn to God</u>; to this has been added the affirmation that they must <u>do the things that would show they had repented</u> (see Luke 3. 8). The purpose of Paul's remarks is to show that his preaching was exactly the same that any Jewish missionary would have used in trying to convert the heathen.

26. 21

<u>It was for this reason</u> may be rendered as "because I had done this" or "because I had preached in this way."

<u>Seized</u> is the same verb rendered <u>seized</u> in 23. 27 and <u>arrested</u> in 1.16 and 12. 3, and <u>kill</u> is the same verb which appears in 5. 30.

26. 22

The exact relationship of <u>to this very day</u> to the rest of the sentence is ambiguous in Greek; it may be taken with <u>I have been helped by God</u> (as in the TEV), or it may be taken with the verb <u>I stand</u> (as in the NEB "and so to this very day I stand and testify"). <u>Have been helped by God</u> may, of course, be placed in the active form as "God has helped me."

The expression <u>I stand here giving my witness to all</u> may very well be translated in this kind of context as "I stand here to speak the truth to all."

The <u>small and great alike</u> is a Semitic way of including all people. The idiomatic equivalent of <u>to the small and great alike</u> may be simply "to all men everywhere in the same way." One may always reproduce something of the significance of this idiom by saying: "I tell the same truth to those of no importance and to those who are of great importance."

<u>What I say is the very same thing the prophets and Moses said was going to happen</u> is the means by which Paul verifies the truth of his message. In a number of languages to <u>say...the very same thing</u> is represented by the use of a verb meaning "to agree"—for example, "what I say is going to happen agrees with what the prophets and Moses said was going to happen" or "what I say is going to happen is the very same thing the prophets and Moses said was going to happen."

26. 23

The content of this verse specifies what Paul understood was the message of the prophets and Moses. The belief that the Messiah must suffer is not found explicitly in any known Jewish source. However, Paul must have felt that this was in keeping with Jewish tradition and thought. In this type of context must suffer may be rendered as "must die," "had to die," or "was put to death."

The light of salvation is the manner in which the TEV has made explicit Paul's phrase "a light." This passage reflects the thought of Isaiah 9. 2. In a number of languages it is difficult to speak of the light of salvation. In some instances the closest equivalent is "to announce to Jews and to Gentiles that they can be saved, and this is like light to them."

To the Jews is literally "to the people," a phrase used consistently in this sense.

> 24 As Paul defended himself in this way, Festus shouted at him, "You are mad, Paul! Your great learning is driving you mad!"
>
> 25 Paul answered, "I am not mad, your Excellency! The words I speak are true and sober. 26 King Agrippa! I can speak to you with all boldness, because you know about these things. I am sure that you have taken notice of every one of them, for this thing has not happened hidden away in a corner. 27 King Agrippa, do you believe the prophets? I know that you do!"
>
> 28 Agrippa said to Paul, "In this short time do you think you will make me a Christian?"
>
> 29 "Whether a short time or a long time," Paul answered, "my prayer to God is that you and all the rest of you who are listening to me today might become what I am—except, of course, for these chains!"
>
> (26. 24-29)

It is possible to introduce a section heading at this point, for example, "Paul Appeals to Agrippa to Believe."

This final section is introduced by a transitional clause, as Paul defended himself in this way. This is an important device to relate Festus' words to what Paul had just said.

26. 24

In the Greek, defended himself is a participle having a pronoun subject "he," which the TEV has made explicit as Paul. Shouted is literally "said with a loud voice." The use of the present tense along with the emphatic expression "with a loud voice" means either shouted or "shouted at the top of his voice" (NEB).

The term mad in this context means "insane" and may be translated in various ways—for example, "out of your mind," "you are no longer yourself," "you cannot think straight," or "your thoughts are twisted."

Great learning is a phrase which describes not merely elementary knowledge but also higher learning. In this type of context, great learning may be rendered as "because you have studied so much" or even, as in some languages, "because you have read so much."

26.25

In keeping with acceptable Greek style, there is no verb answered in the text, but it must be supplied from the context (see 25.22; 26.1).

The word rendered sober is a term used in other contexts as the exact opposite of mad (that is, "out of one's mind"). The final sentence of verse 25 may be translated as "what I am saying to you is true, and I am speaking like a person completely sane." This type of restructuring may be required, since one can speak of words as true, but only of persons as being sane.

26.26

This verse has been completely restructured in the TEV. For a rather literal rendering of the Greek see the RSV.

With all boldness, in this type of context, is sometimes rendered as "without holding back anything" or "with complete openness."

In a corner is a good Greek expression, and not a Semitism. In many languages one cannot refer to an event by an expression such as this thing. Therefore, one may say "what has happened did not take place in a corner." However, the phrase in a corner may be relatively meaningless in some languages. The closest equivalent would therefore be "in some dark place" or "in some unknown place"—for example, "what happened did not take place in an unknown location."

26.27

King Agrippa, as a pious Jew, would have to affirm that he believed the prophetic writings of Judaism. Paul's question to King Agrippa was obviously a rhetorical one, since he was not specifically asking for information but rather suggesting that King Agrippa obviously believed what the prophets had written. In some languages the equivalent would be "King Agrippa, I know that you believe what the prophets have written."

26.28-29

The Greek text here translated In this short time do you think you will make me a Christian? has been rendered in a number of ways by other translators, as can be easily seen by consulting various translations. The sentence itself may be understood either as a statement of fact, indicating Agrippa's interpretation of Paul's intention, "you are trying to make me a Christian," or as a sarcastic statement on the part of Agrippa, "so you think you can make a Christian of me!" The TEV interprets this as a sarcastic statement and expresses it by means of a question.

In this short time may be understood as in the TEV, though there are several other possibilities: (1) "with such little effort"; (2) "with a few words"; (3) with the sense of "to sum it all up," that is, "briefly what you intend...." The same possibilities exist for the interpretation of the phrase in verse 29, a short time. Another question that is raised is whether or not Luke used this phrase in the same sense in both places. The TEV implies that the phrase has the same sense in both occurrences, and for that reason the translation is the same in each instance. No firm conclusion can be reached, but the TEV has the advantage of suiting the context quite well. Agrippa realizes that in the short time Paul has to speak to him, he is trying to make him a Christian. To this Paul replies, Whether a short time or a long time ... my prayer to God is that you and all the rest of you who are listening to me today might become what I am (that is, a Christian).

My prayer to God is may be rendered as "I pray to God that...."

The final expression except, of course, for these chains may be rendered as "of course, I do not pray that you should be in chains," "of course, I do not want you to be chained," or "but of course, I do not want you to be a prisoner."

> 30 Then the King, the Governor, Bernice, and all the others got up, 31 and after leaving they said to each other, "This man has not done anything for which he should die or be put in prison." 32 And Agrippa said to Festus, "This man could have been released if he had not appealed to the Emperor." (26.30-32)

26.30

Then the King, the Governor, Bernice, and all the others got up translates a clause which has a singular verb connected with four subjects joined in pairs of two each. Literally, the clause reads: "then the king got up and the governor, also Bernice and those with them." However, in most languages a series of coordinate subjects is much more likely to be acceptable than any device to reproduce the rhetorical balance of the Greek expression.

26.31

The Greek of this verse reflects a Semitic formula (though not expressed in translation) which may be rendered literally "they said to each other saying." In such a context, "saying" is redundant and is merely an indication of direct discourse (see Matthew 5.2, literally "he taught them saying").

In some languages it may be necessary to change the order of should die or be put in prison since death would automatically rule out being put in prison. Therefore, the lesser penalty would normally occur first. On the other hand, it may be useful to preserve the present order but to translate it as "for which he should be put to death, or if not put to death, then at least be kept in prison."

26.32

This man could have been released if he had not appealed to the Emperor is a statement by which Luke intends to verify not only the innocence of Paul but the truthfulness of the Christian message. Could have been released is emphatic in the Greek sentence structure. The treatment of this kind of condition, which is contrary to fact (that is to say, Paul had appealed to the Emperor and therefore could not be released), poses certain problems in translation into some receptor languages. In some languages one must say, for example, "if he had not appealed to the Emperor, but he has, then he could have been released, but now he cannot be released." In certain other languages, however, this type of condition contrary to fact is represented as causal—for example, "but because he has appealed to the Emperor, this man cannot be released."

CHAPTER 27

Chapter 27 describes the journey of Paul toward Rome, but only as far as Malta. Basically, the account is divided into three principal sections: (1) the journey from the coast of Palestine to the coast of Crete (vv. 1-12); (2) the storm at sea which describes the serious plight of the ship and those on board (vv. 13-38); and (3) the final destruction of the ship but the survival of all the persons on board (vv. 39-44).

The transitional features which link the various sections of this chapter are primarily temporal—for example, when it was decided that we should sail to Italy (v. 1); we sailed slowly for several days (v. 7); after the men had gone a long time without food (v. 21); it was the fourteenth night (v. 27); day was about to come (v. 33); and when day came (v. 39). Within certain of these principal divisions, marked usually by temporal expressions, there are a number of links which describe geographical features. This would not be so evident to a person who is not fully familiar with the geographical relationship of the various cities and islands mentioned. However, the whole account is very skillfully organized, with Paul presented as the hero of the event.

Paul Sails for Rome

1 When it was decided that we should sail to Italy, they handed Paul and some other prisoners over to Julius, an officer in the Roman army regiment called "The Emperor's Regiment." 2 We went aboard a ship from Adramyttium, which was ready to leave for the seaports of the province of Asia, and sailed away. Aristarchus, a Macedonian from Thessalonica, was with us. 3 The next day we arrived at Sidon. Julius was kind to Paul and allowed him to go and see his friends, to be given what he needed. 4 We went on from there, and because the winds were blowing against us we sailed on the sheltered side of the island of Cyprus. 5 We crossed over the sea off Cilicia and Pamphylia, and came to Myra, in Lycia. 6 There the officer found a ship from Alexandria that was going to sail for Italy, so he put us aboard. (27.1-6)

The section heading Paul Sails for Rome may in some languages be misleading, since one might presume that Paul took the initiative in taking this trip to Rome. Therefore, it may be necessary to say "Paul Is Put Aboard a Ship for Rome" or "Soldiers Take Paul to Rome."

27.1

By his use of we, the author of Acts evidently includes himself among those who went with Paul from Caesarea to Rome. But, as in other instances of the so-called "we" passages in Acts, the form should be exclusive for those languages which make a distinction between inclusive and exclusive

482

first person plural. This use of the exclusive form is necessary, since Luke is addressing this entire account to Theophilus.

Neither the subject of the passive verb <u>it was decided</u> nor the subject of the impersonal third person plural <u>they handed ... over</u> is made explicit by Luke. Perhaps Governor Festus is intended to be the subject of the verb <u>it was decided</u>, while the Roman authorities were the ones who <u>handed Paul ... over to Julius</u>. Accordingly, if it is necessary to stipulate who does the deciding and who hands Paul over, one can employ Festus in the first instance and "Roman officers" in the second instance. To translate <u>handed ... over</u> one may say: "put Paul and some other prisoners in the charge of Julius," "gave Julius authority over Paul and some other prisoners," or even "said to Julius, You are responsible to see that Paul and some other prisoners get to Rome."

The Emperor's was an honorary title frequently given to auxiliary troops. An <u>army regiment</u> is in some languages simply "a large number of soldiers," though in most parts of the world a group of soldiers such as a <u>regiment</u> is relatively well known. However, it is important to indicate that this army regiment did not necessarily consist of Romans. It was simply an army regiment under the command of Rome or which "fought for Rome." The expression <u>The Emperor's Regiment</u> may be translated as "the regiment which belonged to the Emperor."

27.2

The <u>province of Asia</u> is literally "Asia." The reference may be either to the province of Asia, or more precisely to the seaports along the western coast of Asia, of which Ephesus was the center. The NEB is also explicit in speaking of "the province of Asia." The ship which they boarded had its home harbor in <u>Adramyttium</u>, which was southeast of Troas.

<u>Aristarchus</u> is mentioned in 19.29; 20.4; Philemon 24; and also in Colossians 4.10, where he is called "a fellow prisoner."

27.3

The noun <u>what he needed</u> appears only here in the New Testament; its verb form appears in Luke 10.34 and 35 in the sense of "take care of." <u>To be given what he needed</u> may be translated as "so that his friends could give him what he needed."

27.4

As has been noted in previous passages dealing with voyages by sea, languages differ very widely in the type of terminology and the explicitness with which they describe various types of sea journeys. For languages in the South Pacific, there are a great many technical terms which are known by practically all of the local population. But in societies in which there is a great deal of specialization of activity, such technical vocabulary is simply not known by the majority of people and cannot be readily introduced into a translation meant for the populace as a whole. In languages where there is practically no specialized vocabulary for sailing (for example, some of the languages on the edge of the Sahara in Africa), one can only imply very general terms such as "to go in a ship." In all instances, the translator himself must decide what type of vocabulary is appropriate for an audience for which he is translating.

We sailed on the sheltered side of the island of Cyprus must be taken to mean that the ship sailed around the eastern end of Cyprus. As a rule, in the late summer the wind comes from the west or northwest, and there is also a westward current moving along the southern coast of Asia Minor with practically no tide. In some languages the sheltered side of the island must be represented by "the side from which the wind was not blowing," "the side from which there was not much wind," or "the side where we were protected from the wind."

27.5

The verb rendered crossed over is a verb meaning "to sail on the open sea," as opposed to sailing along the shore. The sea off Cilicia and Pamphylia may be translated in some languages as "that part of the sea which was by the provinces of Cilicia and Pamphylia" or "that part of the ocean which touched the provinces of Cilicia and Pamphylia."

It may be necessary to stipulate that Myra is a city and Lycia a province—for example, "we came to the city of Myra in the province of Lycia."

27.6

Ships from Alexandria on their way to Rome generally went by way of Myra, because of the winds in the late summer. It was not too difficult to sail from Alexandria to Myra, and from there to Sicily, and then on up to Puteoli, though it was very difficult to make the voyage straight from Alexandria to Sicily at this time of year.

Since at this point Paul and others had to change ships, it may be necessary to indicate that "they got off one ship and were put aboard another," or it may be better to stipulate in verse 5 that "we came to the city of Myra in the province of Lycia where we disembarked." Otherwise the last clause of verse 6 may seem strange.

7 We sailed slowly for several days, and with great difficulty finally arrived off the town of Cnidus. The wind would not let us go any farther in that direction, so we sailed down the sheltered side of the island of Crete, passing by Cape Salmone. 8 We kept close to the coast, and with great difficulty came to a place called Safe Harbors, not far from the town of Lasea. (27.7-8)

484

It may be necessary to indicate why the sailing was so slow. This is implied later on in verse 7, but one can state "because the wind was against us, we sailed slowly for several days."

<u>Arrived off the town of Cnidus</u> means that they came near to the town of Cnidus, though they did not land there.

<u>The wind would not let us go any farther in that direction</u> may be rendered as "because the wind was blowing against us, we could not go any farther in that direction."

<u>The sheltered side of the island of Crete</u> was the southern side. No one would have dared to sail on the northern side of the island.

Though many languages have a term for <u>Cape</u>, it may be necessary in some languages to use some kind of descriptive equivalent: "a point of land sticking out into the water," "a hill that extends out into the water," or "a part of land which goes out into the water."

27. 8

<u>The coast</u> is literally "it" in Greek; the reference, of course, is to the southern coast of Crete. There is some question as to whether the phrase <u>with great difficulty</u> should be taken with the verb <u>we kept close to</u> or with the verb <u>came</u>, as the TEV has done. Most translators take it with the first of these two verbs (for example, Goodspeed "with difficulty coasted along it and reached a place").

In all of these "we" passages there is the possibility of the reader assuming that those identified by <u>we</u> were the sailors. One must, therefore, in some languages translate as "the ship in which we were going kept close to the coast" or "the ship in which we were, traveled along very close to the land."

<u>Safe Harbors</u> appears in most translations as "Fair Havens." Both <u>Safe Harbors</u> and <u>Lasea</u> were towns located on the southern side of Crete about midway. The name <u>Safe Harbors</u> may be translated as "harbors for protecting ships" or "harbors where ships could remain safe."

9 We spent a long time there, until it became dangerous to continue the voyage, because by now the day of Atonement was already past. So Paul gave them this advice, 10 "Men, I see that our voyage from here on will be dangerous; there will be great damage to the cargo and to the ship, and loss of life as well." 11 But the army officer was convinced by what the captain and the owner of the ship said, and not by what Paul said. 12 The harbor was not a good one to spend the winter in; so most of the men were in favor of putting out to sea and trying to reach Phoenix, if possible. It is a harbor in Crete that faces southwest and northwest, and they could spend the winter there.

(27. 9-12)

27.9

A long time is a vague expression of time, as is several days in verse
7. In both instances Luke uses one of his favorite expressions (literally "sufficient days" and "sufficient time"). This reference to time is better rendered as "many days" rather than being a reference to weeks. "Many weeks"
would certainly have involved a couple of months or so, and by that time no
one would have set out on a journey to Rome by ship.

It became dangerous to continue the voyage because the end of the sailing season was approaching. According to one ancient source, not much
sailing was done after the middle of September, and it stopped entirely after
November 11.

The exact date on which the day of Atonement (literally "the fast") was
celebrated differed from year to year, though it would have been either in
September or October. Some commentators believe that this was the year
A.D. 59, and that the fast came in this year on October 5. In any case, all
the men considered that it was dangerous to continue the voyage to Sicily at
this time. It is important in translating the final clause of this verse not to
suggest that there was some religious factor involved in the danger of continuing the voyage. It was purely a matter of the season of the year. Therefore, in some languages one must translate: "because it was so late in the
year, the day of Atonement was already passed."

It may be very useful at this point to have some brief marginal note explaining the significance of the day of Atonement. However, even in translation some meaningful equivalent should be employed—for example, "the day
on which atonement was made for sins," "the day when there was a special
ceremony for the atoning for sins," or "the day which celebrated the forgiveness of sins."

So Paul gave them this advice may be rendered as "so Paul advised
them with the following words" or "so Paul warned them," since the advice
given is essentially in the form of a warning.

27.10

In many languages the equivalent of dangerous is simply "bad," "will
cause great trouble," or even "will almost destroy us."

Damage to the cargo may simply be rendered as "the cargo will be
wrecked" or "what is in the ship will be lost."

Loss of life is literally "loss of souls"; but the Greek word for "soul"
is often used in the sense of life (see Matthew 6.25-27; Luke 12.22-24).
Loss of life may be rendered as "people will die because of this." Note that
in reality all persons did get safely ashore (v. 44), but no doubt the loss of
life was a part of Paul's warning at this point in the account.

27.11

Most translators understand captain in the sense employed in the TEV,

though there are some who render this term as "pilot" or "helmsman." It
was quite customary either for the owner himself or for his representative
to travel aboard a ship. The captain may be rendered as "the one who gave
orders to the sailors" or "the one who bossed the men who had charge of
making the ship go."

27.12

Putting out to sea may be rendered as "leaving the harbor and going out
on the sea" or "leaving the protected water and going out where the water is
not protected by the land."

It may also be important to stipulate Phoenix as a harbor, though this
is specified later in verse 12.

That faces southwest and northwest (so most translations) is rendered
"looking northeast and southeast" by the RSV; however, the RSV does have a
note indicating the possibility of "southwest and northwest." In Greek, the
terms "southwest" and "northwest" are names referring to winds that come
from those respective directions. The different translations are based upon
different interpretations of the prepositions which precede these nouns in the
Greek sentence. The RSV takes this preposition to mean "facing the direction toward which the winds blow," while the TEV takes it to mean "facing
the direction from which the winds blow." The latter interpretation has
two factors in its support: (1) the use of this preposition in similar constructions in the Septuagint supports it (see 2 Chronicles 4.4; Ezekiel 8.3; 9.2;
11.1; 40.6; 43.1; 44.1), and (2) the modern Phineka, a harbor open to winds
from the west, is evidently Phoenix. If the RSV rendering is correct, the
reference must be to the harbor of Lutro, which is separated from Phineka
by an extension of land into the sea called Muros. Phineka is open to winds
from the west, while Lutro is open to winds from the east.

In dealing with directions there are often a number of complications.
In a number of languages, references to directions are based entirely upon
local geographical objects—for example, names of particular rivers, head-
lands, or mountains. However, in a high percentage of languages, east and
west are designated primarily by reference to the rising and setting of the
sun, and terms for north and south are frequently described in terms of the
right hand or the left hand of the rising or setting sun. For example, in this
instance a harbor...that faces southwest and northwest may be translated
as "a harbor that is open to the sea to the left of the setting sun and to the
right of the setting sun." In some languages an expression such as "to the
right of the setting sun" would designate due north, but in other languages it
may designate northwest. Some languages make a distinction between "a little
to the right of the setting sun" and "very much to the right of the setting sun"
as a way of talking about northwest and north respectively.

The Storm at Sea

13 A soft wind from the south began to blow, and the men thought

that they could carry out their plan; so they pulled up the anchor and sailed as close as possible along the coast of Crete. 14 But soon a very strong wind—the one called "Northeaster"—blew down from the island. 15 It hit the ship, and since it was impossible to keep the ship headed into the wind, we gave up trying and let it be carried along by the wind. 16 We got some shelter when we passed to the south of the little island of Cauda. There, with some difficulty, we managed to make the ship's boat secure. 17 They pulled it aboard, and then fastened some ropes tight around the ship. They were afraid that they might run into the sandbanks off the coast of Libya; so they lowered the sail and let the ship be carried by the wind. 18 The violent storm continued, so on the next day they began to throw the ship's cargo overboard, 19 and on the following day they threw the ship's equipment overboard with their own hands. 20 For many days we could not see the sun or the stars, and the wind kept on blowing very hard. We finally gave up all hope of being saved. (27.13-20)

The section heading The Storm at Sea may in some languages be translated as "A Storm" since there may be a specific type of term which applies only to a storm at sea. Another term may be employed when speaking of a similar type of violent wind on land. Where there is, however, no such term for storm, one can always employ a descriptive equivalent—for example, "The Wind Blows Very Hard over the Sea" or "The Wind Causes Great Waves on the Sea."

27.13

Perhaps it is worthwhile to point out that while the Greek text of this verse has twelve words, the TEV rendering has thirty-seven words. One reason for this is that the TEV uses six words, so they pulled up the anchor, for what in Greek is a single word, a technical term meaning "to pull up the anchor." The Greek sentence itself is structured with only one finite verb, sailed, while the remaining verbs are either participles or infinitives. In order to restructure the sentence most naturally for the English reader, the TEV has transformed these participles and infinitives into a series of finite verbs. However, what is important in translation is not the number of words which are employed, but the extent to which the words reflect accurately the meaningful components of the original text. Accuracy of translation cannot be determined by the number of words, but by the extent to which the structure of the meaning is accurately reproduced.

A soft wind from the south began to blow (Goodspeed "a moderate south wind sprang up") is literally "when the south wind began to blow softly." In many languages one cannot speak of a soft wind; on the other hand, it is possible to speak about "a wind which is weak," "a wind which is not strong," or "a wind which does not make waves."

For languages which are spoken by people far removed from a coast, an expression for anchor may be extremely difficult to find or even to develop.

In some languages an anchor is represented as "a heavy object which keeps the boat from moving" or even "a heavy object which holds the boat in one place." However, if the people in question have no experience with anchors, it may be important to have a marginal note to indicate specifically what an anchor is, and then to employ some abbreviated form of that description as an identification for such an object.

They tried to sail <u>as close as possible along the coast of Crete</u>, in order not to be blown out into the open sea.

27.14

<u>A very strong wind</u> is in some languages "a very fast wind" or "a wind which makes large waves."

This wind that <u>blew down from the island</u> was so well known that the sailors had given it a proper name, and this has been rendered by <u>Northeaster</u>. The equivalent of <u>Northeaster</u> is, in some languages, "a wind from the northeast" or "a wind that blows from the left of the rising sun."

<u>From the island</u> is literally "from it," a reference to the island of Crete. In some instances it is necessary to make some adaptation in the expression <u>blew down from the island</u>, since seagoing persons would soon recognize that a wind which only came from an island would not be strong enough to cause a great storm. Therefore, an expression such as "blew down across the island" would be necessary.

27.15

<u>It hit the ship</u> may need to be somewhat altered in some languages since winds cannot be spoken of as "hitting anything"; therefore, "the wind blew against the ship" or "the wind caused the ship to shake" (as a means of describing the suddenness with which the wind came upon the ship).

In an effort to bring the ship back into the harbor, the place called Safe Harbors, the sailors apparently tried to head the ship into the wind. Since they found this to be impossible, they had to let the ship be carried along by the wind.

In the Greek sentence there is a phrase which may be understood either in the sense of "into the wind" or "by the wind." At first glance it may seem as if the TEV has translated this phrase twice, but that is not the case. This phrase is rendered in the TEV by <u>into the wind</u>, while <u>by the wind</u> is the means whereby the TEV has made explicit what it was that <u>carried</u> (the ship) <u>along</u>.

27.16

<u>We passed to the south of</u> is a synonym of the verb <u>sailed down the sheltered side of</u> used in verse 7. Both words are technical nautical terms referring to sailing that is done on the side of the island that protects the ship from the winds. In this instance, it was the south side of the island that offered

shelter, and so the TEV has rendered we passed to the south. There is some difference of opinion as to whether this island should be called "Cauda" or "Clauda." NEB, JB, and Goodspeed, along with TEV, accept Cauda.

The ship's boat was a small boat sometimes towed and sometimes tied down on deck; it was used for a variety of purposes, especially for landing. We managed to make the ship's boat secure refers primarily to what was done immediately following in verse 17, namely, pulling the boat aboard and tying it down with ropes. This entire clause may be translated in some languages as "then we were able to make safe the little boat that was towed behind the ship, but it was difficult to do this." In some languages "to make safe" would be equivalent to "to keep from being broken."

27.17

In order to make the ship's boat safe from the waves, they pulled it aboard. In some languages one must specify pulled it aboard in terms of two different events: "raise it up and put it on top of the ship" or "put it on the deck of the ship."

The word rendered ropes is of uncertain meaning in Greek, and there are at least two possible meanings. (1) The word may refer to the ship's tackle which was used to pull the ship's boat aboard (see Lake "they lifted it up by using their tackle"). (2) On the other hand, most scholars understand this in the sense of ropes (perhaps made from the ship's tackle, see NEB) that were fastened tight around the ship in order to keep it from coming apart in the storm. It may be necessary in some languages to be quite specific about the placement of these ropes around the ship—for example, "they placed ropes underneath the ship and tied them tight."

Sandbanks off the coast of Libya is literally "Syrtis" in the Greek text. As the TEV has made clear, the reference is to the dangerous quicksands along the coast of Libya towards which they feared the ship might drift (see JB "on the Syrtis banks"; NEB "the shallows of Syrtis"). Sandbanks may be rendered as "sand just beneath the water" or "dangerous sand just beneath the water."

The meaning of the phrase lowered the sail is ambiguous in Greek. Other than the interpretation rendered in the TEV (also followed basically by NEB, Goodspeed, Moffatt, Phillips), there is the possibility that the word rendered sail should be taken in the larger sense as a reference to the ship's "gear." This would mean that not only were the sails brought down, but the spars and the rigging as well were lowered to the deck of the ship. A third possibility, and one which does not have much acceptance, is to understand the word in the sense of "sea-anchor" (so JB). A sea anchor would probably have been a large piece of canvas designed somewhat in funnel shape which would have been tied to the stern of the ship and which would have slowed down the ship's movement considerably, thus presumably preventing it going ashore off the coast of Libya. However, lowering the sail would have accomplished somewhat the same results, and this alternative is far more likely.

By translating and let the ship be carried by the wind, the TEV has made explicit the meaning of the Greek clause, "in this way they were being carried along," though others take this to mean "and so let themselves drift" (JB). This final clause may be rendered in some languages as "let the wind blow the ship along" or "let the wind blow the ship wherever it wanted."

27.18

The violent storm continued translates the Greek participle "as we were being tossed about violently in the storm." An equivalent expression in some languages is simply "the strong wind kept blowing" or "the wind kept blowing very hard."

They began to throw the ship's cargo overboard translates a technical nautical term which means "to jettison the ship's cargo" (see JB). This jettisoning of the ship's cargo may be rendered in some languages as "they took what was in the ship and threw it into the water."

27.19

As in the TEV, so in Greek, verses 18 and 19 are one sentence. On the following day (NEB "next day") is literally "on the third day."

The ship's equipment is the same word rendered sail in verse 17; in both cases the word perhaps renders a technical term, the meaning of which is lost. Other translations render this either as "the ship's tackle" or "the ship's gear." In some languages the ship's equipment would simply be rendered as "the ropes, sails, and poles." However, one must note that it would be wrong to say that all of the equipment was thrown overboard, since in verse 29 there is a reference to four anchors, and in verse 40 a reference to a sail that was placed at the front of the ship. It may therefore be necessary to say: "part of the ship's equipment" or "some of the ship's sails, ropes, and poles."

27. 20

For sailors of ancient times, the fact that they could not see the sun or the stars was perhaps of more importance than a storm itself, because the sun and the stars were the points by which they navigated.

The wind kept on blowing very hard (see NEB "a great storm was raging") is literally "no little storm was upon us."

We finally gave up all hope of being saved (JB "at last we gave up all hope of surviving") appears in the NEB as "our last hopes of coming through alive began to fade," of which "began to fade" is an attempt on the part of the NEB to bring out the force of the Greek imperfect tense. This final clause may be rendered in some languages as "at last we thought we would not possibly be saved," "finally we thought, We cannot possibly remain alive," or even "at last we said to ourselves, We will certainly drown."

21 After the men had gone a long time without food, Paul stood before them and said, "Men, you should have listened to me and not have sailed from Crete; then we would have avoided all this damage and loss. 22 But now I beg you, take courage! Not one of you will lose his life; only the ship will be lost. 23 For last night an angel of the God to whom I belong and whom I worship came to me 24 and said, 'Don't be afraid, Paul! You must stand before the Emperor; and God, in his goodness, has given you the lives of all those who are sailing with you.' 25 And so, men, take courage! For I trust in God that it will be just as I was told. 26 But we will be driven ashore on some island." (27. 21-26)

27. 21

After the men had gone a long time without food must not be taken to imply either that there was no food or that the men were deliberately fasting for religious or other reasons. It seems, rather, that the men had been so busy trying to protect themselves and the ship from the storm that they had not taken time to eat, or that the violence of the storm had taken away their desire for food.

Paul stood before them is literally "Paul stood in their midst" (see the quite similar scene in 17. 22). Should have translates the same verb rendered had to in 1.16 (see the comments there). It is difficult to know whether or not Luke intended the verb to be taken here with the same force of divine necessity as it apparently had in 1.16. You should have listened to me is rendered in some languages as "it would have been better if you had listened to me."

And not have sailed from Crete may also be rendered as "it would have been better if you had not sailed from Crete" or "you did what you should not have done—you sailed from Crete."

The final clause, then we would have avoided all this damage and loss, is difficult to render in some languages, since it implies a condition contrary to fact—for example, "if we had not sailed, we would have avoided...." The equivalent in many languages, however, is a statement of actual events: "but now that we have sailed, we have incurred this damage" or "but since we have sailed, we have suffered this damage."

27. 22

Take courage! may in some languages be expressed negatively—for example, "do not lose your hearts" or "do not become weak in your thinking."

Not one of you will lose his life is literally "there will be no loss of souls from among you," with "soul" used once again in the sense of "life" (see comments on v. 10). The closest equivalent in some languages is "not one of you will die." In speaking of the destruction of the ship, however, one often cannot say "will be lost." This would appear as though the ship "had lost its way." A more precise equivalent would be "only the ship will be destroyed" or "but the ship will be completely destroyed."

492

27. 23

The introductory conjunction for must be rendered with care since a literal translation might imply that the ship would be destroyed because an angel of the Lord spoke to Paul. In some languages it may be necessary to specify at the beginning of verse 23 exactly the basis for the following clause beginning with for. One can, therefore, say: "I know this because last night an angel of God...."

Last night is literally "in this night," but the reference is clearly to the night immediately preceding. In its rendering of this phrase, the TEV is in agreement with many other modern translations.

The phrase angel of (the) God is a favorite Lukan expression. In most languages the equivalent of angel of (the) God is "an angel who comes from God."

To whom I belong (literally "whose I am") is typically biblical (see Genesis 50.19 in the Septuagint). To whom I belong may be rendered "who possesses me."

27. 24

Don't be afraid, Paul! is a present imperative in Greek and may have the force of "stop being afraid, Paul." Most translations render it with this same force.

On the necessity to stand before the Emperor see 23.11. Must translates the same verb rendered should have in verse 21 (see 1.16).

God, in his goodness, has given (Phillips "and God, as a mark of his favor toward you") is an attempt to render the force of the Greek verb which most translations give merely as "God has granted." On the use of this verb see 3.14; 25.11, 16. The conjunction and which introduces this final clause in verse 24 seems perfectly natural in English, but in some languages it would be misleading since it would imply that (1) Paul's stand before the Emperor and (2) God having given to Paul the lives of those sailing with him, were two coordinate events. In some languages, therefore, one must simply drop the conjunction and.

The equivalent in some languages of in his goodness is "because he is so good" or "because of his kindness."

In some languages one simply cannot speak of a person being "given the lives of others." In fact, a literal rendering of this phrase might even imply the death of such individuals. The equivalent expression in some instances, therefore, is "because God is so good, he has done you a kindness: he will cause that all those who are sailing with you will remain alive" or "...none of those sailing with you will die."

27. 25

The clause for I trust in God that it will be just as I was told involves complications in some languages, and a certain amount of readjustment of order may be required—for example, "for I trust in God that what he has told me will happen just as he said it would" or "I trust in God, and I am sure that everything will turn out to be just as he told me it would."

27.26

Will be once again renders "must" (see vv. 21 and 24 above).
Will be driven ashore may be rendered actively as "the wind will blow us onto the shore."

> 27 It was the fourteenth night, and we were being driven by the storm on the Mediterranean. About midnight the sailors suspected that we were getting close to land. 28 So they dropped a line with a weight tied to it and found that the water was one hundred and twenty feet deep; a little later they did the same and found that it was ninety feet deep. 29 They were afraid that our ship would go on the rocks, so they lowered four anchors from the back of the ship and prayed for daylight. 30 The sailors tried to escape from the ship; they lowered the boat into the water and pretended that they were going to put out some anchors from the front of the ship. 31 But Paul said to the army officer and soldiers, "If these sailors don't stay on board, you cannot be saved." 32 So the soldiers cut the ropes that held the boat and let it go. (27.27-32)

27.27

It was the fourteenth night may be more appropriately rendered in some languages as "it was at night, two weeks after the storm began."

By the storm is the manner in which the TEV has made explicit the rendering of the Greek verb "being driven." However, a number of translators understand the meaning of this verb to be "we were drifting." The closest equivalent in some languages is "the wind kept blowing us along" or "the wind kept blowing from behind us and making the boat move."

The exact boundaries that Luke had in mind for the Mediterranean (literally "Adria") are not known, but they would have at least included the sea between Crete and Sicily.

The sailors suspected may be rendered as "the sailors thought." If a specific term for sailors is lacking, one can employ "those responsible for taking care of the ship" or "those who were in charge of the ship."

We were getting close to land is literally "land was approaching them," but for the English reader the TEV is much more natural. In other languages, however, it may be more natural to say "the ship was getting closer to the land" or "the ship and the land were coming closer together."

27.28

Dropped a line with a weight tied to it is actually one word in Greek, a technical nautical term used of measuring the depth of water under a ship.

One hundred and twenty feet is literally "twenty fathoms"; while ninety feet is literally "fifteen fathoms." A fathom (equivalent to six feet) was a standard measurement of ocean depth. This measurement was calculated on the basis of the distance between one's hands when the arms are stretched out full length. In a number of languages there is a local equivalent of this type of measurement; however, increasingly all such measurements are given in terms of meters (a meter is approximately one-half of a fathom). The depth would therefore be given in terms of first "forty meters" and later "thirty meters."

27.29

Our ship is literally "we," but in most languages our ship would have to be translated as "the ship in which we were traveling." In a number of languages the appropriate equivalent would simply be "the ship."

Would go on the rocks must be translated in some languages as "would be blown onto the rocks" or "the wind would blow the ship to where rocks were."

The four anchors may be translated as "they lowered from the back of the ship four heavy weights to keep it from moving."

The phrase back of the ship translates a technical Greek term referring to the "stern."

They...prayed for daylight is appropriately rendered in some languages as "they...prayed that daylight would soon come." One should not suggest that they were praying for daylight to occur in the middle of the night.

27.30

This verse and the following comprise one sentence in Greek. Verse 30 is actually a subordinate clause dependent upon the main verb said in verse 31.

The first clause in this verse states the purpose of the sailors, and the remainder of the verse describes the manner in which they were trying to escape. This relationship needs to be made quite clear—for example, "the sailors tried to escape from the ship by lowering the boat into the water" or "in order to try to escape from the ship, the sailors lowered the boat into the water."

It may be necessary in some instances to indicate specifically what the boat is, that is, "the small boat that was tied on deck."

The verb pretended is rendered in some languages as "they said, We are going to put out...."

From the front of the ship translates a technical Greek term denoting the "bow" of a ship. Already the back of the ship was being held firmly by anchors, and the sailors' statement that they wished to put out anchors in the front of the ship was obviously an attempt to get away from the ship and thus to escape with their own lives.

27.31

Sailors (NEB "these men") is a rendering of the pronoun "they." In the present context it is obvious that the verb saved is used of the deliverance from physical danger. You cannot be saved may be rendered in this type of context as "you cannot save your lives" or "you cannot get ashore alive."

27.32

The TEV has made explicit the meaning of the ambiguous Greek phrase (literally "ropes of the boat") by rendering ropes that held the boat. Let it go may be equivalent to "let it fall into the water" or "let it drift away."

> 33 Day was about to come, and Paul begged them all to eat some food, "You have been waiting for fourteen days now, and all this time you have not eaten a thing. 34 I beg you, then, eat some food; you need it in order to survive. Not even a hair of your heads will be lost." 35 After saying this, Paul took some bread, gave thanks to God before them all, broke it, and began to eat. 36 They took courage, and every one of them also ate some food. 37 There was a total of two hundred and seventy-six of us on board. 38 After everyone had eaten enough, they lightened the ship by throwing the wheat into the sea. (27.33-38)

27.33

This verse begins with an unusual construction (literally "until when"), rendered in most translations by "when." The TEV has made this subordinate temporal clause into a coordinate clause: day was about to come. The equivalent of this clause in some languages is "it was just beginning to be light" or "the day was not far away."

On the phrase eat some food see verse 21.

27.34

I beg you, then, eat some food may be rendered as "I ask you very strongly, therefore, please eat some food" or "therefore I am asking you with strong words, Do eat some food."

You need it in order to survive translates a noun phrase (literally "this is necessary for your salvation") in which the word "salvation" is used in the sense of physical survival, as is the verb saved in verse 31. The NEB renders this as "your lives depend on it." In order to survive is equivalent in some languages to "in order not to die."

Not even a hair of your heads will be lost is a proverbial expression occurring frequently in the Old Testament; it means, of course, "no harm will come to you." The equivalent of this expression in some languages is "you will in no way be harmed" or "you will not suffer at all."

27.35

Paul took is literally "he having taken."

Gave thanks to God before them all may be rendered as "prayed to God in front of them all, thanking him for the food."

Broke it is equivalent to "broke off a piece of it" or, as in some languages, "tore off a piece."

27.36

Most translators connect every with the subject of the first verb in the sentence, rather than with the second verb as the TEV has done. (See RSV "then they all were encouraged.") The meaning is essentially the same either way.

27.37

As the TEV alternative rendering points out, there is the possibility that in place of two hundred and seventy-six one should have two hundred and seventy-five, or seventy-six, or seventy-five. The difference in Greek is not nearly so much as might be intimated from the English, but the UBS Text Committee is rather firm in its agreement that the text should read "two hundred and seventy-six."

In some so-called "primitive languages" there is no regular way of calculating a number such as two hundred and seventy-six. One can use a general term for "many, many people," and then in a marginal note employ the specific number from a major language of the area. On the other hand, most translators under such circumstances simply borrow expressions for numbers such as two hundred and seventy-six and introduce these directly into the text. If this is done, a footnote may be employed to suggest to the reader how this can be calculated (though in rather paraphrastic ways), using the indigenous system of counting, limited though it may be.

Once again the Greek word "souls" (in the phrase "a total of ... souls") is used in the sense of "persons."

27.38

Wheat is best understood as a reference to what remained of the ship's cargo, rather than to the ship's provisions. Evidently they had not previously thrown overboard all of the ship's cargo (see v. 18). The reason for throwing the ship's cargo overboard initially was to keep the ship from being swamped in the storm; the present reason for throwing the remainder of the cargo overboard seems to be so that the ship would "float high" and would go up on the beach as far as possible.

The Shipwreck

39 When day came, the sailors did not recognize the coast, but

they noticed a bay with a beach and decided that, if possible, they would run the ship aground there. 40 So they cut off the anchors and let them sink in the sea, and at the same time they untied the ropes that held the steering oars. Then they raised the sail at the front of the ship so that the wind would blow the ship forward, and headed for shore. 41 But the ship hit a sandbank and went aground; the front part of the ship got stuck and could not move, while the back part was being broken to pieces by the violence of the waves. (27.39-41)

The section heading The Shipwreck may be more appropriately rendered in some languages as "The Waves Break the Ship" or "The Waves Cause the Ship to Break into Pieces."

27.39

In some languages one does not speak of "a day coming." One can, however, say "it became light" or "the sun was almost up."

The sailors makes explicit the Greek pronominal subject "they." It is not surprising that the sailors did not recognize the coast, for the storm had carried them away from their usual sailing route.

Most translators understand the Greek word to mean bay, though some understand it in the sense of "a creek" (KJV, Moffatt). The only way the sailors felt it would be possible to save the ship would be to run the ship aground there, and so that is what they tried.

If possible may be related to the process of running the ship aground by translating "decided that they would try to run the ship aground."

Run the ship aground is rendered in some languages as "cause the ship to reach the land," "cause the ship to touch the land underneath the water," or "cause the ship to go against the ground under the water."

27.40

Cut off (see Moffatt, Phillips) is rendered "cast off" by the RSV and Goodspeed. The JB and the NEB have used the technical sailing term, "they slipped the anchors." In some languages it will be necessary to say "cut the ropes that held the anchors" or "cut the ropes that were tied to the anchors."

Ancient ships had steering oars, one on each side sticking out toward the back. In some languages the steering oars would be translated as "rudders" or "oars which served like rudders." In other languages one must use a descriptive phrase such as "large oars at the back of the boat used for steering." For languages in which there is no regular term for oar one may even use an expression such as "large pieces of wood at the back of the boat used to steer it."

Each ship was also equipped with a mast toward the front on which a small sail could be raised. All of these actions were designed so that the wind would blow the ship forward as far as possible up on the shore. In languages in which there is no technical term for sail, one can employ "a large piece of cloth."

498

The last expression, and headed for shore, may need to have as the subject "we" rather than merely "they," since obviously all in the ship went together, not merely the sailors. On the other hand, one may also translate as "the ship moved toward the shore" or "the ship was blown toward the shore."

27.41

The meaning of the word rendered sandbank ("shoal" or "reef" in many translations) is disputed. It literally means "a place between two seas," and for this reason the NEB has rendered it as "between cross currents" (see JB "But the cross currents carried them into a shoal"). It is not, of course, strange to encounter this type of difficulty of translation in the rendering of sandbank, since such a bank normally does develop when there are two currents running either parallel or even against each other.

The term sandbank may be translated in some languages as "a mound of sand underneath the water" or "a hill of sand underneath the water."

The phrase went aground may be translated as "stuck in the ground," "hit the ground and stopped," or "was stopped by the hill of sand."

The second clause of verse 41 explains more precisely what is involved in "going aground"—for example, "the front part of the ship hit the sandbank, and no one could move it" or "the front part of the ship struck a hill of sand and stopped firm."

The last clause of this verse is rendered in some languages by "the strong waves broke to pieces the back part of the ship." This is a perfectly possible rendering in most languages, since one often cannot say that something is broken...by the violence of the waves. The term violence must in some way be related to the waves since they are the objects which do the breaking.

> 42 The soldiers made a plan to kill all the prisoners, so that none of them would swim ashore and escape. 43 But the army officer wanted to save Paul, so he stopped them from doing this. Instead, he ordered all the men who could swim to jump overboard first and swim ashore; 44 the rest were to follow, holding on to the planks or to some broken pieces of the ship. And this was how we all got safely ashore.
>
> (27.42-44)

27.42

The final verb escape may be rendered in some languages as "run away."

27.43

This and the following verse are one sentence in Greek. It may be of some interest to note that the word rendered to save in this verse is the same verb rendered <u>when we were safely ashore</u> in 28.1 and <u>he escaped</u> in 28.4. <u>Wanted to save Paul</u> is rendered in some languages as "wanted to prevent Paul from being killed" or "wanted to save Paul's life."

<u>He stopped them from doing this</u> may need to be more explicit in some languages—for example, "he stopped the soldiers from killing the prisoners." However, in some languages this could be ambiguous, suggesting that they had started to kill some of the prisoners. Therefore one may translate as "he prevented the soldiers from carrying out their plan to kill the prisoners."

After the verb <u>ordered</u> it may be preferable to have direct discourse— for example, "he ordered all the men who could swim, Jump into the water first and swim ashore" or "he ordered, All of you men who can swim must jump overboard and swim ashore." The fact that those who could swim were the <u>first</u> to go may actually be rendered by placing a conjunctive adverb such as "then" or "later" at the beginning of verse 44.

27.44

The phrase rendered <u>to some broken pieces of the ship</u> could possibly be taken in the sense of "on (the backs of) some of the crew." This possibility arises from the ambiguity of the Greek, which literally reads "on some of those (either masculine or neuter in form) from the ship." Nevertheless, most translators, both ancient and modern, take this phrase as a reference to the wreckage which came from the ship, rather than as a reference to the ship's crew.

<u>Got safely ashore</u> is the same verb mentioned in verse 43, and it may be rendered as "reached the shore and were safe" or "reached the shore without suffering harm."

CHAPTER 28

Chapter 28 consists essentially of three major sections. The first (vv. 1-10) describes what happened on the island of Malta. The second (vv. 11-15) is somewhat transitional and outlines the journey from Malta to Rome. The third (vv. 16-31) deals with Paul's experiences in Rome, and consists primarily of two parts: (1) a description of the introductory meeting of Paul with the Jews in Rome (vv. 17-22), and (2) his final discussion with the Jewish leaders in Rome (vv. 23-28), with special emphasis upon the quotation from the prophet Isaiah.

The various sections of this final chapter are very carefully linked, and except for the second paragraph, which begins with a spatial link, not far from that place (v. 7), all the other transitionals are temporal ones: when we were safely ashore (v. 1), after three months (v. 11), when we arrived in Rome (v. 16), after three days (v. 17), so they set a date with Paul (v. 23), and for two years (v. 30). The most difficult structure in this chapter is found in verses 25-28, for at the beginning of verse 25 the Jews leave disagreeing among themselves, but the latter part of verse 25 through 28 introduces what Paul had to say to the Jews just before they left. This particular problem causes a number of complications in translation, and they will be discussed.

In Malta

1 When we were safely ashore, we learned that the island was called Malta. 2 The natives there were very friendly to us. It had started to rain and was cold, so they built a fire and made us all welcome. 3 Paul gathered up a bundle of sticks and was putting them on the fire when a snake came out, on account of the heat, and fastened itself to his hand. 4 The natives saw the snake hanging on Paul's hand and said to one another, "This man must be a murderer, but Fate will not let him live, even though he escaped from the sea." 5 But Paul shook the snake off into the fire without being harmed at all. 6 They were waiting for him to swell up or suddenly fall down dead. But after waiting for a long time and not seeing anything unusual happening to him, they changed their minds and said, "He is a god!" (28.1-6)

In some languages a title such as In Malta would not be adequate; therefore, it may be necessary to have something such as "What Paul Experienced on the Island of Malta" or "What Happened to Paul on the Island of Malta."

28.1

Malta is a Mediterranean island, in a straight line about 150 miles southwest from the "toe" of Italy.

When we were safely ashore appears in most translations as something like "after we had escaped" (see 27.43 and 28.4 for the same verb). The

28.2

clause when we were safely ashore may be rendered as "when we had reached the shore and were safe" or "when we had escaped by reaching the shore."

No doubt those who had escaped safely to shore learned the name of the island from the local people. Certainly there would have been no signs to identify the place. Since in some languages there are very distinct terms for learning, depending upon whether one reads something or hears it from someone else, it may be necessary to say "we learned from the people who lived there."

28.2

The natives (JB "the inhabitants") renders a term which refers primarily to people who speak a language other than Greek; to render as "barbarous people" (KJV) or "rough islanders" (NEB) is to press the meaning of the word too far. The equivalent in some languages is "the tribe of people who lived there."

Friendly comes from the same root as the word rendered kind in 27.3. In some languages friendly may be rendered as "they welcomed us," while in other languages the closest equivalent is "they helped us."

In order to present what is a more logical and chronological order for the English reader, the remainder of this verse has been inverted from the Greek order. The kind of fire referred to here is a wood fire built out in the open. The two references to us in this verse are very vague. Did Luke have in mind all of the persons from the ship or, more specifically, merely the Christian group? It seems almost impossible to imagine that two hundred and seventy-six people could have gathered around a fire, and it is quite likely that Luke is now limiting his interests to the attitude of the islanders toward Paul and his companions.

28.3

A snake came out must sometimes be specified as "a snake came out of the bundle of sticks."

Fastened itself to must be understood in the sense of "bit and kept hanging onto."

28.4

The natives is the same expression which occurs in verse 2 and may be rendered in some languages as "the local people," "the people who lived on the island," or "the people whose homes were there." The choice of a term or phrase depends upon the normal manner in which a receptor language designates local inhabitants of a region.

This man must be a murderer is often rendered as "this man is surely a murderer" or "this man most certainly has killed someone."

The word rendered Fate is the name of a god whom people worshiped, and must be translated so that the readers get this meaning. The TEV has

502

tried to accomplish this by spelling the word with a capital F (see also Moffatt "Justice"; NEB "divine justice"). To render merely as "justice" (RSV, Goodspeed, Phillips) seems inadequate. It may be necessary to qualify this as "the god Justice," "a god called Justice," or "a god called Retribution."

28. 5

The TEV has made it explicit that Paul (Greek "he") is the subject of the verb shook. In Greek there is a very evident contrast between the subject of this sentence and the subject of the following sentence, "he shook...they were waiting."

The final phrase, without being harmed at all, may be translated as "and he did not suffer anything" or "and the snake did not cause him harm."

28. 6

Waiting for him to swell up or suddenly fall down dead may need to be somewhat recast in some languages—for example, "they were expecting him to soon swell up or suddenly fall down dead." In some languages this may even be expressed as direct discourse "they kept thinking, He will certainly soon swell up or suddenly fall down dead."

Not seeing anything unusual happening to him may be translated as "they did not see that Paul was suffering anything" or "they saw that Paul was not in any way suffering anything."

Just as to be bitten by a snake was considered to be an indication of divine punishment, so to be protected from the bite of the snake was considered to be an indication of divine protection; and so they changed their minds and said, "He is a god!" It is known from other Greek sources that persons who underwent divine protection were called "friends of the god," but it is not known where people were themselves called gods because of some act of divine protection.

7 Not far from that place were some fields that belonged to Publius, the chief of the island. He welcomed us kindly and for three days we were his guests. 8 Publius' father was in bed, sick with fever and dysentery. Paul went into his room, prayed, placed his hands on him, and healed him. 9 When this happened, all the other sick people on the island came and were healed. 10 They gave us many gifts, and when we sailed they put on board what we needed for the voyage. (28. 7-10)

28. 7

The first phrase of this verse, not far from that place, serves as a transition to the account of Paul's relationship to Publius, the chief of the island. Paul's healing of the sick also serves to explain why Paul and his colleagues were so well treated by the people on the island.

503

28. 8

Not far from that place appears in the RSV and NEB as "in the neighborhood of that place." The meaning is simply "near that place" and therefore may be translated as "not far from where this happened to Paul." This may be the only way of identifying that place satisfactorily.

Chief seems to have been an official title, perhaps either of the leading government official on the island or of a native official. In some languages the closest equivalent of chief would be "headman," but in other languages the most appropriate term would be "the leading official."

The same problem of ambiguity exists here as in verse 2 with us. Does Luke refer to all the persons who arrived on the ship, or does he limit his thoughts to the Christians? If a choice has to be made in translation, the latter seems preferable.

The adverb kindly is taken by most translators to modify the manner in which Paul and his companions were received as guests, rather than to modify the manner in which they were welcomed (note Moffatt "he welcomed us and entertained us hospitably"). We were his guests translates the Greek statement, "he entertained us (as guests)."

28. 8

Inasmuch as the word rendered fever is in the plural, some understand this to refer to recurring attacks of fever (see NEB "recurrent bouts of fever"; JB "feverish attacks"). Most translations merely indicate that he was sick with fever and dysentery, without indicating the possibility that there were intermittent attacks of fever. Since fever and dysentery are of universal occurrence, there is no difficulty in finding appropriate terms. However, in many languages one cannot say that a person was sick with fever. The corresponding receptor-language equivalent may be "fever had grabbed him," "he was sick because of fever," or even "fever had made him sick."

Paul went into his room is literally "to whom Paul went in," which is rendered in most translations as "Paul visited him." If it is necessary to specify the place where Paul placed his hands, it may be appropriate to say "he placed his hands on his head." Healed him may be rendered as "caused him to be well," "caused the disease to disappear," or "caused the fever and dysentery to leave him." It is almost incredible how many different expressions there are for becoming sick and for being healed.

28. 9

The word used for healed in this verse and in the preceding verse are different words. Some have suggested, though without wide acceptance, that whereas the former refers to miraculous healing, the latter indicates healing that Luke did as a physician. It is much more natural to assume that these were both acts of miraculous healing and that the verbs are not to be differentiated in meaning. The tenses of the verbs rendered came and were healed are such as to suggest that this is something that took place over a period of

504

time, rather than at one time only. <u>Were healed</u> may be recast as an active expression, "and Paul healed them."

28.10

In the Greek, verse 10 is a continuation of the sentence begun in verse 9. Although it is possible that the word rendered <u>gifts</u> may refer to the money given to a physician for his fee, in the present context it means either "presents" or "honors." The NEB accepts the latter possibility: "they honored us with many marks of respect" (so JB). However, it is quite unlikely that the islanders would have shown their respect in any other way than by presenting gifts.

In rendering the last clause of this verse, it may be necessary to introduce some such expression as "later" or "some time after that." Otherwise, it might appear, at the end of verse 10, that Paul and his comrades had sailed from Malta, whereas the sailing is actually not specifically mentioned until verse 11, where it is clearly stated that this took place three months later.

From Malta to Rome

11 After three months we sailed away on a ship from Alexandria, called "The Twin Gods," which had spent the winter in the island. 12 We arrived in the city of Syracuse and stayed there for three days. 13 From there we sailed on and arrived in the city of Rhegium. The next day a wind began to blow from the south, and in two days we came to the town of Puteoli. 14 We found some believers there who asked us to stay with them a week. And so we came to Rome. 15 The brothers in Rome heard about us and came as far as Market of Appius and Three Inns to meet us. When Paul saw them, he thanked God and took courage.
(28.11-15)

The section heading <u>From Malta to Rome</u> may need to be amplified somewhat: "Paul Goes from Malta to Rome," "Paul and His Companions Go from Malta to Rome," or "The Journey from Malta to Rome."

A careful examination of this paragraph will indicate clearly the so-called spatial structure of this discourse, depending as it does upon verbs of leaving and arriving—for example, <u>sailed away</u> (v. 11), <u>arrived</u> (v. 12), <u>from there ... sailed on</u> (v. 13), <u>arrived</u> (v. 13), <u>a wind began to blow from the south</u> (v. 13), <u>came to</u> (v. 13), <u>stay with</u> (v. 14), and <u>came to</u> (v. 14).

28.11

If the ancient historian Pliny is correct, sailing began on February 7, the beginning of spring. Assuming that the ship left as early as possible, <u>after three months</u> would indicate that they had been shipwrecked since the early part of November. It may, however, be necessary to relate <u>after three</u> <u>months</u> to some intermediary verbal expression—for example, "after we had stayed there three months, we sailed away," "after being there three months, we sailed away," or even "we stayed there three months, and then we sailed away."

A ship from Alexandria may either be "a ship whose home port was Alexandria" or simply "a ship which was coming from Alexandria."

The word translated called may have the meaning of "having as a figure-head." The precise meaning of this word is disputed, though it is known that the ancients often named their ships by the figurehead on the bow of the ship. For this reason it is safe to assume, along with the TEV (so also Goodspeed and NEB), that the meaning here is "called" or "named." It is important, however, that the name The Twin Gods be applied to the ship and not to Alexandria. It may be very useful at this point to have some marginal note to explain that the principal beam at the prow of the ship may have been carved into the shape of The Twin Gods. The Twin Gods (JB "the Twins") translates one word in Greek, which refers to the twin gods Castor and Pollux (see NEB), who were often worshiped by sailors.

The equivalent of winter in some languages is "the cold months"; in other languages it is "the time of storms." Either reference would be perfectly appropriate in this context.

28.12

Syracuse was a port on the southeastern coast of Sicily. The TEV has identified it as a city and has also employed the term city in speaking of Rhegium in verse 13. The classifier town has been employed for Puteoli.

28.13

We sailed on means literally "sailed around (something)." This same verb appears in 27.40 and is used there with anchors as its object. Puteoli, near Naples, was the regular seaport for ships coming to Rome from the east. However, since Puteoli was essentially a harbor, it may be useful to employ at this point "came to the harbor of Puteoli" or "came to the town of Puteoli which was a harbor."

28.14

The verb found should probably not be interpreted as meaning "looked for and then discovered." It is more appropriate to render this as "there we met some believers" or even "there were some believers there who asked us...."

Believers is literally "brothers" (NEB "fellow-Christians"); and a week (so NEB, JB) is literally "seven days."

And so we came to Rome may be rendered as "and this is the way we arrived at Rome," "and this was the kind of journey we had in coming to Rome," or "...in going to Rome" (depending, of course, upon the point of view of the narration). Since Luke himself is accompanying those who went to Rome, one would assume that the point of view would be "going." If one assumes that this account was written in Rome, it might very well be rendered as "coming." In Greek the same verb is used for either "coming" or "going."

<u>28.15</u>

The <u>brothers</u> are Christian believers (see NEB "the Christians").

<u>Heard about us</u> may be rendered as "had heard about us" or "had heard that we were coming."

<u>In Rome</u> translates the Greek adverb "there," but the reference is to the city of Rome. The <u>Market of Appius</u> was a famous market place on the Appian Way, 43 miles from Rome. <u>Three Inns</u>, a place with inns for travelers to stop, was about 33 miles from Rome on the same Appian Way. In view of the fact that these two places mentioned are at different distances from Rome, one must presume that there were at least two groups of believers who went out to meet Paul and his companions, one group going as far as the Market of Appius and the other group going only as far as the <u>Three Inns</u>.

The final phrase <u>took courage</u> may be equivalent to "was encouraged" or "this encouraged him."

In Rome

16 When we arrived in Rome, Paul was allowed to live by himself with a soldier guarding him.

17 After three days Paul called the local Jewish leaders to a meeting. When they gathered, he said to them, "My brothers! Even though I did nothing against our people or the customs that we received from our ancestors, I was made a prisoner in Jerusalem and handed over to the Romans. 18 They questioned me and wanted to release me, because they found that I had done nothing for which I deserved to die. 19 But when the Jews opposed this, I was forced to appeal to the Emperor, even though I had no accusation to make against my own people. 20 That is why I asked to see you and talk with you; because I have this chain on me for the sake of him for whom the people of Israel hope."

21 They said to him, "We have not received any letters from Judea about you, nor have any of our brothers come from there with any news, or to say anything bad about you. 22 But we would like to hear your ideas, because we know that everywhere people speak against this party that you belong to." (28.16-22)

The section heading <u>In Rome</u> may not be sufficient in some languages. An extension of this may involve some such expression as "What Paul Experienced in Rome," "Paul Meets with the Jews in Rome," or "Paul Preaches in Rome." This last type of section heading would shift the attention from the immediate encounter with Jewish leaders to Paul's ministry in Rome over a period of some two years.

28.16

Verse 16 is set off as a separate paragraph since it indicates Paul's
general living conditions and is not related to the immediately following discussion which Paul had with Jewish leaders. The following two paragraphs
(vv. 17-22) are, however, very important in understanding what Paul later
said to the Jewish leaders, mentioned in verses 23 ff.

28.16

This is the conclusion of the so-called "we" sections in the book of
Acts, in which the author identifies himself as participating in the narrative.

Paul was not placed in prison, but he was allowed to live by himself
with a soldier guarding him. From the context it is obvious that this permission was granted him by the Roman government. The passive expression was
allowed may be rendered as "the Roman authorities permitted Paul to live by
himself" or "... in a separate house." The final phrase with a soldier guarding him may be translated as "only there was a soldier who guarded him" or,
as in some languages, "only there was a soldier that kept watching in order
that he would not escape." It is important, in this particular context, to indicate that the soldier was to prevent Paul's escape rather than to guard Paul
from the attacks of other persons.

28.17

Luke begins this verse with one of his favorite transitional formulas
(literally "and it happened"), which may be indicated in translation merely by
the introduction of a new paragraph, and since a new paragraph is begun at
this point, the TEV has made the mention of the subject explicit: Paul.

After three days may be rendered in some languages as "three days
later" or "after Paul had been in Rome for three days."

The verb called must be translated in some languages as "invited to a
meeting" or "asked them to come see him."

In order to specify that the Jewish leaders in this instance were those
in Rome and not the Jewish leaders of Jerusalem, the term local has been employed.

On my brothers see 2.29. It is obvious that in the present context reference is not made to fellow believers, but to fellow Jews.

In Greek, the first word in Paul's address is I, placed in an emphatic
position. It was important for Paul to point out several matters: (1) that the
accusations made against him by the Jews were false; (2) that he was not
found guilty by the Roman government and would have been released, had he
not appealed to the Emperor; and (3) that he himself had no accusation to make
against his own people.

I did nothing against our people may be translated as "I did not in any
way harm our people." In this quoted context the pronoun our is to be rendered
as inclusive first person plural for those languages which make a distinction
between inclusive and exclusive first person. In speaking about doing nothing
against ... the customs, it may be necessary to say "I did not violate the

508

customs" or "I did not speak against the customs," with customs often being
translated as "the way in which our people live."

The customs that we received from our ancestors may be expressed
more naturally in some languages as "the customs which our ancestors
handed down to us."

I was made a prisoner in Jerusalem may be translated in the active
form as "the Jews caused me to be a prisoner in Jerusalem."

The word rendered handed over always carries overtones of wrongdoing
on the part of those who did the handing over; it is the same word used
by Jesus in Luke 9. 44 and 18. 32.

28.18

In Greek this continues a sentence begun in the preceding verse.

The pronoun they, which begins verse 18, must refer to "the Roman
authorities." Questioned is the same verb used in 24. 8. Questioned me may
be translated as "asked me exactly what I had done" or "by asking me found
out exactly what I had done."

In this context found is equivalent to "learned" or "found out by inves-
tigating."

In some languages it is hardly sufficient to say I had done nothing for
which I deserved to die. A receptor-language equivalent may be "I had done
nothing bad and therefore did not deserve to be put to death" or "I did nothing
so bad that it would cause me to be put to death."

28.19

What the Jews opposed was, of course, Paul's release, and therefore
this may be made specific in the first clause: "the Jews did not want me to be
released" or "the Jews opposed the Romans releasing me."

I was forced to appeal to the Emperor may be rendered as "it was necessary for me to appeal to the Emperor," "it was necessary for me to say,
I wish to go to the Emperor," or "...I wish the Emperor to try my case."

Even though I had no accusation to make against my own people is stated
in a very strong fashion in the Greek sentence (literally "not as against my
own nation having anything to accuse"). From the point of view of the Roman
readers, it would have been important for Luke to emphasize that Paul was
in Rome to defend himself and not to bring an accusation against the Jews.
The Romans had very strict laws regarding what should be done with persons
who had accused others of being guilty and were unable to prove their charges.

28. 20

The pronoun that beginning verse 20 refers back to all of the preceding
events. In some languages this may be more appropriately rendered as "because of all that had happened, I asked to see you" or "these are the reasons
why I have asked to see you."

There is a problem in translating the conjunction because which introduces the expression I have this chain on me. If translated literally, in some
languages it would mean "I wish to talk with you because I have this chain on
me." This is, of course, not the meaning. The Greek conjunction which is
rendered because in this context often points out merely some type of logical
sequence, without indicating that it is specifically causal. A more appropriate transition might be "in fact, I have this chain on me for the sake of him
for whom the people of Israel hope." This would act as a kind of link between
the recounting of the previous events and Paul's claim that the real issue is
his preaching of the resurrection or of the Messianic fulfillment in Jesus
Christ.

I have this chain on me is equivalent to "I am here a prisoner" or "I am
chained as a prisoner."

For the sake of him for whom the people of Israel hope is taken by the
TEV and certain commentaries as a reference to the Jewish Messianic hope.
Other commentaries take this as a reference to the Jewish belief in the resurrection (see 23.6). The Greek expression is literally "for the sake of the
hope of Israel" and may support either of these interpretations. Most translators prefer to leave this phrase ambiguous (see NEB "for the sake of the
hope of Israel"). One may render this final expression, for the sake of him
for whom the people of Israel hope, as "for the sake of the one in whom the
people of Israel have placed their hope" or "for the sake of the one the people
of Israel look forward to with confidence."

28. 21

They said to him may be made more specific in some languages as "the
local Jewish leaders said to Paul" or "the local Jewish leaders responded."

In this context our brothers is, of course, "fellow Jews."

Of the two expressions come...with any news and or to say anything,
the first refers to an official and the second to a private communication. The
RSV translates these as "reported or spoken," and the JB "with any report or
story."

Say anything bad about you may be equivalent to "say that you have done
anything bad," "say bad words about your reputation," or "put bad words upon
your name."

28. 22

Your ideas may be rendered "what you think."

The word rendered party appears in 24.5 and is the normal word used
to refer to a recognized group within Judaism. The TEV has made Paul's relationship to this party explicit by the words that you belong to. In some languages one cannot speak of "belonging to a party." One may, however, say
"to be one with the party," "to be a member of this group," or "to be counted
together with those who form this party."

23 So they set a date with Paul, and a larger number of them came that day to where Paul was staying. From morning till night he explained and gave them his message about the Kingdom of God. He tried to convince them about Jesus by quoting from the Law of Moses and the writings of the prophets. 24 Some of them were convinced by his words, but others would not believe. 25 So they left, disagreeing among themselves, after Paul had said this one thing, "How well the Holy Spirit spoke through the prophet Isaiah to your ancestors! 26 For he said,

'Go and say to this people:
You will listen and listen, but not understand;
    you will look and look, but not see.
27 Because this people's minds are dull,
    they have stopped up their ears,
    and have closed their eyes.
Otherwise, their eyes would see,
    their ears would hear,
    their minds would understand,
and they would turn to me, says God,
    and I would heal them.' "

28 And Paul concluded, "You are to know, then, that God's message of salvation has been sent to the Gentiles. They will listen!" [29 After Paul said this, the Jews left, arguing violently among themselves.] (28.23-29)

Note that the main substance of what Paul had to say to the Jewish leaders is contained in indirect discourse (v. 23). Here Luke emphasizes the typical response to Paul's preaching, namely, that some believed and others would not; and, as a result of this, there was strong disagreement among the Jewish people.

The quotation from Isaiah is particularly appropriate as a prophetic justification for Paul's turning to the Gentiles. Note that the last words of Paul as quoted in Acts emphasize his ministry to the Gentiles since they will listen. This is a fitting climax to a book evidently designed to help people understand the relationship of Christianity to Judaism and just how and why it had such a strong appeal to the Gentile world.

28.23

With Paul is literally "with him" in the Greek. The phrase which the TEV has rendered to where Paul was staying (see also RSV, Moffatt, Goodspeed, JB) may also be understood in the sense of "as his guests" (NEB). Even though this phrase when used with the verb "to call" may mean "to invite someone as a guest," it is doubtful that it has this meaning in the present context.

From morning till night appears in the last part of the Greek sentence

28. 24

and is in an emphatic position; in English it is more normal to place it at the beginning of the sentence.

In the Greek sentence structure gave ... his message about is a participle dependent upon the main verb explained, and it may be understood in the sense of amplifying what is meant by the verb explained. The relationship of these two verbs in Greek may be rendered as "he explained to them what he meant by giving to them his message about the Kingdom of God." On the other hand, in some languages it is more accurate to say: "he talked to them about the Kingdom of God and explained this message to them." It would be quite wrong to translate his in such a way as to imply that Paul's message concerning the Kingdom of God was distinctly his own and not shared by the Christian community.

He tried to convince is also in the Greek a participial construction dependent on the main verb explained. The force of the verb here is that he "tried to convince," not that he "did convince" (see KJV "persuading"). Tried to convince may be rendered in some languages as "tried to show that what he was saying was true" or "tried to cause them to believe that what he was saying was true."

By quoting from is literally "from," a phrase which the NEB takes in the sense of "by appealing to" and the JB in the sense of "arguing from." On the basis of verses 26-27, it is quite possible that "from" should be taken in the sense of "by quoting from," though the other possibilities are not to be excluded. In some languages an equivalent of quoting from may be "he used the law given to Moses and the writings of the prophets to show that what he was saying was true."

28. 24

Some of them were convinced may be rendered as "some of them believed that what he said was true."

28. 25

It is quite likely that Luke intended for his readers to see a contrast between the Jews who disagreed among themselves (see 23.10) and Paul who said one thing. It is interesting that Luke always pictures Paul as getting in the last word.

How well is the same adverb rendered "how right" in Mark 7.6.

This verse poses a serious problem of linguistics versus historical order in the relating of events. The first clause indicates that the Jews left. The next clause, however, introduces what Paul said (vv. 25b-27), which obviously occurred before the men left. This lack of agreement between the linguistic and the historical order must be very carefully indicated or a serious misunderstanding is likely to arise. One may, for example, translate this passage as "so they left disagreeing among themselves, but only after Paul had already said to them, How well the Holy Spirit spoke ...." In other

512

languages it is necessary to say "but before they left, disagreeing among themselves, Paul said this to them, How well the Holy Spirit spoke...."

The Holy Spirit spoke through the prophet Isaiah is rendered as a causative in a number of languages: "the Holy Spirit caused the prophet Isaiah to say." In other languages this secondary agency is expressed as "the Holy Spirit spoke; the prophet did it."

28. 26-27

In Greek, verse 26 begins with a participle (literally "saying"), which the TEV has rendered for he said. The Old Testament passage cited in these verses is Isaiah 6. 9-10, and, as quoted here, it is in almost word-for-word agreement with the Septuagint. Both in Isaiah and in its use in Acts the phrase to this people is a specific reference to the Jewish people.

Listen and listen...look and look (JB "hear and hear...see and see") translate Hebraic idioms which indicate intensive action. The contrast between listening and understanding, and between looking and perceiving, may be rendered in some languages as "though you listen and listen you will not understand, and though you look and look you will not perceive." However, in certain languages emphasis cannot be indicated by a mere repetition of a verb in phrases such as listen and listen or look and look. It is necessary to indicate that this is an intensive action—for example, "You will listen very intently but not understand; you will look very hard but not really see."

The word rendered minds is literally "hearts," but in Hebrew thought the heart was the center of the intellectual activity. One should not translate the term dull in this type of context to mean that the people's minds are simply below normal in intelligence. It is not their lack of intellectual capacity, but their stubborn refusal to understand what their senses tell them. In some languages one must translate "because the minds of this people are hard," while in other languages precisely the opposite idiom would be employed "because the minds of this people are soft." Basically what is required here is an idiom which indicates refusal to comprehend. In some languages this is rendered as "because these people do not wish to understand."

The Hebraic idiom "they hear with ears of heaviness" has been transformed into an English idiom: they have stopped up their ears. This expression stopped up their ears may be rendered as "covered over their ears," "have put something in their ears," or even "have closed their ears."

Two other Semitic idioms, "lest they should see with their eyes...hear with their ears," have also been transformed into more natural English expressions: otherwise, their eyes would see, their ears would hear. In a number of languages one cannot say "their eyes see," but one can say "they see with their eyes and they hear with their ears."

In some languages it is necessary to specify the relationship of the last two lines of verse 27 to what has preceded. This can be indicated as "and as a result they might turn to me."

The verb heal should be understood in the broadest possible sense, since

28. 28

it should include not just physical healing but spiritual transformation as well ---for example, "cause them to be well again."

<u>28. 28</u>

<u>And Paul concluded</u> must be rendered in some languages as "and Paul also said before they left." Otherwise it might appear that this was Paul's final judgment on the Jews after they had departed.

In this verse, as in 13. 48 and 18. 6, a proclamation of God's message to the Gentiles is initiated by the refusal on the part of the Jews to hear it. <u>You are to know</u> is a very strong and solemn expression (see 2.14; 4.10; 13.38). The equivalent rendering of <u>you are to know</u> may be "you must know." In some languages this can only be adequately reproduced as "I must tell you so that you will know."

The phrase "the salvation of God" has been taken by the TEV with the meaning <u>God's message of salvation</u> (see also Goodspeed). From the context it is quite evident that Paul's emphasis is on the message of salvation rather than on salvation itself, though in the final analysis these two ideas cannot be separated from one another. <u>God's message of salvation</u> may be rendered as "the message about salvation that comes from God." However, in such a phrase it must be perfectly clear that it is the message that comes from God, though theologically speaking, it is also the salvation which proceeds from God. To make this perfectly clear, one may translate "the message that God has proclaimed about his saving people." In some languages, however, one cannot speak about "sending a message." One can only "send a messenger" or "send a person to speak a message." Therefore, in this clause one may translate: "those who announce what God has said about salvation have been sent to the Gentiles."

In the statement <u>they will listen</u>, the <u>they</u> is emphatic.

<u>28. 29</u>

This verse is omitted from many modern translations because its place in the text is quite doubtful, and for this reason the TEV has placed the verse in brackets. Note that the contents of this verse simply duplicate what is said in verse 25. Because of the difficulty of historical and linguistic order, some early scribe may have thought it was necessary to try to resolve the problem by the addition of verse 29.

The TEV has made the subject <u>Paul</u> explicit, whereas the Greek has simply "he."

30 For two years Paul lived there in a place he rented for himself, and welcomed all who came to see him. 31 He preached about the Kingdom of God and taught about the Lord Jesus Christ, speaking with all boldness and freedom. (28. 30-31)

514

The reference to two years would indicate that Luke knew that a change took place after this period, and that he also knew what happened, though he did not care to indicate this to his readers.

As in the preceding verse, so in this verse the subject has been made explicit: Paul. The phrase in a place he rented for himself (JB "in his own rented lodging") may also be taken in the sense of "at his own expense" (see RSV, NEB). The problem is that the word rendered place he rented basically means "money paid" and may refer either to money that Paul earned or to the money that he paid out. The TEV, along with a number of other translations, understands this in a specific sense of "money paid out for a place to live in."

28.31

In Greek, this verse is a continuation of the sentence begun in the preceding verse and forms a dependent clause referring back to the verb welcomed. Preached and taught are actually participles defining the manner in which he welcomed all who came to see him.

By closing his book with the words all boldness and freedom, Luke indicates that though Paul's message was rejected by the Jews, he was not hindered in his preaching by the Roman government. The first of these words, boldness, refers to Paul's own inner attitude, while the second, freedom, refers to the attitude of the Roman government toward Paul's activities. Boldness may be rendered as "he spoke to everyone," "he did not hesitate to speak to everyone," "he had no fear whatsoever," or "he was not at all intimidated." In contrast with this, freedom may be translated as "he was not stopped in any way from preaching," "he was allowed to speak to everyone," or "there was no one to whom he could not speak."

BIBLIOGRAPHY

BIBLE TEXTS AND VERSIONS CITED

Bibel. 1956 (NT), 1964 (OT). Stuttgart: Würrtenbergische Bibelanstalt.

Bible: A New Translation. 1922. James Moffatt. New York: Harper and
Brothers.

Good News for Modern Man: The New Testament in Today's English Version.
1966. New York: American Bible Society.

Holy Bible: A Translation from the Latin Vulgate in Light of the Hebrew and
Greek Originals. 1950. John Knox. New York: Sheed and Ward, Inc.

Jerusalem Bible. 1966. Garden City: Doubleday and Company.

King James Version. 1611.

New American Bible. 1970. Washington: Confraternity of Christian Doctrine.

New English Bible. 1970. London: Oxford University Press and Cambridge
University Press.

New Testament: A New Translation. 1968. William Barclay. New York:
Collins.

New Testament: A Translation in the Language of the People. 1950. Charles
B. Williams. Chicago: Moody Press.

New Testament: An American Translation. 1923. Edgar J. Goodspeed.
Chicago: University of Chicago Press.

New Testament in Modern English. 1962. J. B. Phillips. New York:
The Macmillan Company.

Revised Standard Version. 1952. New York: Nelson and Sons.

Segond Revisé, Nouveau Testament. 1964. Paris: French Bible Society.

Synodale Version, La Sainte Bible. 1956. Paris: Alliance Biblique Française.

Twentieth Century New Testament. 1904. Chicago: Moody Press.

Versión Popular, Dios llega al hombre: El Nuevo Testamento de nuestro
Señor Jesucristo. 1970. New York: United Bible Societies.

Zürcher Bibel. 1931. Zürich: Zwingli-Bibel.

GENERAL BIBLIOGRAPHY

A New Testament Wordbook for Translators. 1966. New York: American Bible Society.

Bible Translator, The. London: United Bible Societies.

Bratcher, Robert G. (ed). 1961a. Old Testament Quotations in the New Testament. London: United Bible Societies.

------. 1961b. Section Headings for the Old Testament. London: United Bible Societies.

------. 1961c. Section Headings for the New Testament. London: United Bible Societies.

------. 1961d. Short Bible Reference System. London: United Bible Societies.

------ and Eugene A. Nida. 1961. A Translator's Handbook on the Gospel of Mark. Leiden: E. J. Brill.

Bruce, F. F. 1955. Commentary on the Book of Acts. The New International Commentary on the New Testament. Grand Rapids: William B. Eerdmans.

------. 1960. The Acts of the Apostles. Grand Rapids: William B. Eerdmans.

Conzelmann, Hans. 1963. Die Apostelgeschichte: Handbuch zum Neuen Testament. Tübingen: J. C. B. Mohr (Paul Siebeck).

Foakes-Jackson, F. J. The Acts of the Apostles. The Moffatt New Testament Commentary. New York: Harper and Brothers.

------ and Kirsopp Lake (eds). 1920-33. The Beginnings of Christianity. 5 vols. London: Macmillan and Company. (Especially volume 4 A Commentary on Acts and volume 5 A Series of Essays on Studies Related to the Study of Acts.)

Haenchen, Ernst. 1961. Die Apostelgeschichte: Kritisch-Exegetischer Kommentar über das Neue Testament. Göttingen: Vandenhoeck und Ruprecht.

Jordt-Jørgensen, K. E. 1972. Fauna and Flora of the Bible. New York: United Bible Societies.

Metzger, Bruce M. 1971. A Textual Commentary on the Greek New Testament. London: United Bible Societies.

Munck, Johannes. 1967. The Acts of the Apostles. The Anchor Bible. Garden City: Doubleday and Company.

Nida, Eugene A. 1964. Toward a Science of Translating. Leiden: E. J. Brill.

------ and Charles R. Taber. 1969. The Theory and Practice of Translation. Leiden: E. J. Brill.

Reiling, J. and J. L. Swellengrebel. 1971. A Translator's Handbook on the Gospel of Luke. Leiden: E. J. Brill.

Stagg, Frank. 1955. The Book of Acts. Nashville: Broadman Press.

Williams, C. S. C. 1957. The Acts of the Apostles. Harper's New Testament Commentaries. New York: Harper and Row.

GLOSSARY OF TECHNICAL TERMS

The terms included in this glossary are those which are either inherently technical or are used in this book in a sense other than their everyday meanings. The order of entries is strictly alphabetical and ignores all space and word boundaries. The definitions and examples are necessarily brief and limited. For further information as to the meaning of some of the terms, the reader is urged to consult Toward a Science of Translating and The Theory and Practice of Translation (see Bibliography, page 519).

abstract is a designation of qualities and quantities, which are properties of objects, events, or even of other abstracts. Terms such as red (in a red dress), fast (in run fast), and three (in three bottles) may be called abstracts, since they are never entities in themselves, but only specify features of other entities.

active voice is the grammatical form of a verb and/or clause which indicates that the subject of the clause is the one who performs the action—for example, John returned; that is, John, who performs the action, is the subject of the verb returned. (See passive voice.)

adjectives are typically a grammatical class of words which modify nouns —for example, tall, big, funny, good.

adverbs are typically a grammatical class of words which modify verbs, adjectives, or other adverbs—for example, quickly, soon, greedily, very.

affix is a part of a word which cannot stand alone and which is added to a root or stem—for example, im- (in impossible), -ly (in friendly), -est (in largest).

agent is the object which accomplishes the action, regardless of whether the grammatical construction is active or passive. For example, in John hit Bill (active) and Bill was hit by John (passive), the agent in each case is John.

ambiguous describes a word or phrase which in a specific context may have two or more different meanings. For example, Bill did not leave because John came could mean either (1) "The coming of John prevented Bill from leaving" or (2) "The coming of John was not the cause of Bill's leaving."

anacolouthon (plural anacoloutha) is a sentence which begins with one type of grammatical structure and ends with another.

analysis is the process of determining what are the various units which enter into any complex structure and describing how these units are related to one another.

animate identifies objects which are regarded as alive and normally able to move voluntarily. For example, man, dog, and fish are animate objects, but tree is not.

521

apposition is the placement of two expressions together which identify the same object or event—for example, my friend, Mr. Smith.

article is a grammatical class of words, usually obligatory, which indicate whether the accompanying word is definite or indefinite. In English the articles are the and a (an).

aspect is a grammatical category which specifies the nature of an action— for example, whether the action is completed, uncompleted, repeated, begun, increasing in intensity, or decreasing in intensity.

benefactive goals are those for whom (or which) something is done. For example, the pronoun him is the benefactive goal in each of the following constructions: he showed him kindness, he did the work for him, and they found him an apartment.

causative is a semantic category relating to events and which indicates that someone caused something to happen rather than that he did it himself. For example, in John ran the horse, the verb ran is a causative, since it is not John who ran but rather John who caused the horse to run.

central meaning is that meaning of a word which is generally understood when the word is given without a context. This is also called the "unmarked meaning." For example, the central meaning of tree is a large perennial plant. However, tree may have a wide variety of other meanings, depending on the context. (See figurative meaning, referential meaning.)

classifier is a term used with another term (often a proper noun) to make clear what category the latter belongs to. For example, city may serve as a classifier in the phrase city of Jerusalem, and river as a classifier in the phrase river Jordan.

clause is a grammatical construction, typically consisting of a subject and a predicate. (See predicate.)

communication load is the degree of difficulty in a message. It may be regarded as indirectly related to the problems encountered by receptors in understanding a text.

componential analysis is a process of determining the meaningful features of a word or phrase and describing the relations of those features to one another.

connotation is that aspect of meaning which concerns the emotional attitude of the author and the emotional response of the receptors. Connotations may be good or bad, strong or weak, and they are often described in such terms as colloquial, taboo, vulgar, old-fashioned, and intimate.

context is the relevant part of a message in which a particular form occurs. For example, in the clause Poor John was sick yesterday, the context of John is Poor...was sick yesterday.

countable refers to classes of objects which can be counted—for example, table, boy, house, tree. Countables differ from terms of "mass" (for example, gas, water, oil, grain), which are not normally regarded as countable and hence do not have plurals in their usual meanings.

decoding is the operation or process which the receptor employs to understand a message. (See encoding.)

dependent clause is a grammatical construction, consisting normally of a subject and predicate, which is dependent upon or embedded within some other construction. For example, if he comes is a dependent clause in the sentence, If he comes, we'll have to leave.

direct discourse is the reproduction of the actual words of one person which are embedded in the discourse of another person. For example, He declared, "I will have nothing to do with this man." (See indirect discourse.)

direct object is typically the goal of an event or action specified by a verb. For example, in the clause the ball hit John, John is the direct object of hit.

dynamic equivalence is a type of translation in which the message of the original text is so conveyed in the receptor language that the response of the receptors is (or, can be) essentially like that of the original receptors or that the receptors can in large measure comprehend the response of the original receptors, if, as in certain instances, the differences between the two cultures are extremely great.

ellipsis is the omission of some expression which is readily constructible from the context. For example, John is taller than Bill is readily understood to mean John is taller than Bill is tall. The phrase is tall is an ellipsis in the first statement. Again, I will go if possible contains the ellipsis it is between if and possible.

encoding is the operation by which a sender plans and composes a message. (See decoding.)

euphemistic term is one which substitutes for another which is connotatively more objectionable. For example, to pass away is a euphemistic term for to die.

event is a category of semantic elements in all languages which refer to actions, processes, etc., in which objects can participate—for example, run, fall, grow, think. In English and some other languages, many nouns may refer to events—for example, baptism, fall, game, song.

exclusive first person plural excludes the audience. For example, a speaker may use we to refer to himself and his companions, while specifically excluding the person(s) to whom he is speaking. (See inclusive first person plural.)

exegesis is the process of determining the meaning of a text, normally in terms of "who said what to whom under what circumstances and with what intent."

explicit refers to information which is formally represented in a discourse. That is, it is expressed in the words of the discourse. This is in contrast to implicit information.

expository discourse is a type of text which primarily explains some object, event, or principle.

false passive is a grammatical structure which is active in form but passive in meaning. For example, John received the gift is active in form, but semantically John is the goal of the giving; therefore the meaning is passive.

figurative meaning is an extended meaning of a term, depending generally upon some supplementary, rather than basic, feature of the meaning. For example, calling Herod a fox involves a figurative meaning of fox, and speaking of the Jews as the circumcision involves a figurative extension of the meaning of circumcision. (See central meaning.)

first person plural includes the speaker and at least one other person: we. (See exclusive first person plural and inclusive first person plural.)

first person singular is the speaker: I.

flashback is a reference in a narrative to events prior to the time of the portion of the narrative under consideration.

focus is the center of attention in a discourse or portion of a discourse.

formal correspondence is a type of translation in which the features of form in the source text have been more or less mechanically reproduced in the receptor language.

generic refers to a broad, inclusive domain or experience. For example, the term animal is generic, while dog is more specific. However, dog is generic in comparison to poodle.

genitive case (or construction) is a grammatical set of forms occurring in many languages and usually indicating among other meanings the possessive relationship.

goal is the object which undergoes the action of a verb. The goal may be the subject of a passive construction (John was hit), or of certain intransitives (the door shut), or the direct object of a transitive verb (...hit the man).

hierarchical arrangement is one in which the meanings of certain terms include the meanings of others. For example, the terms animal, canine, dog, and poodle constitute a hierarchy of four terms, with animal as the most inclusive and poodle the least inclusive.

homonyms are words which are written or pronounced alike, but which are different in meaning.

honorific is a form used to express respect or deference. In many languages such forms are obligatory in talking about royalty and persons of social distinction.

idiom is a combination of terms, the meaning of which cannot be derived by adding up the meanings of the parts—for example, have a green thumb, behind the eight ball.

imperative is a grammatical category of commands.

inclusive first person plural includes both the speaker and the one(s) to whom he is speaking. (See exclusive first person plural.)

indirect discourse is the reporting of the words of one person embedded grammatically in an altered form in the discourse of another person. For example, the direct discourse expression John said, "I will go" may be transformed into indirect discourse in the expression John said that he would go. (See direct discourse.)

intransitive is a predicate construction in which there is no direct or indirect object—for example, John ran. (See transitive.)

kernel is a sentence pattern which is basic to the structure of a language. Kernels may also be called "basic sentence patterns," to which transformations may be applied to derive surface structures. (See surface structure and transformation.)

linguistic refers to language, especially the formal structure of language.

marginal helps in Bible Society usage are notes, normally occurring on the same page as the text and providing purely objective, factual information of the following types: alternative readings (different forms of the source-language text), alternative renderings (different ways of rendering the source-language text), historical data, and cultural details, all of which may be necessary for a satisfactory understanding of the text. Notes which are doctrinal or homiletical interpretations of the text are excluded from Scriptures published by the Bible Societies.

Masoretic text is the form of the text of the Hebrew Old Testament which was established by Hebrew scholars around the eighth and ninth centuries A.D.

narrative discourse is a text consisting of a series of successive and related events.

nominal refers to nouns or noun-like words.

nominalized verbs are verbs which have been made into nouns—for example, involvement (from involve), developer (from develop), and love (in such expressions as the love of God).

noun is a class of words, which in most languages may function as subject, direct object, and indirect object of a verb.

papyri are, in the context of this Handbook, those texts of the Scriptures which were written originally on papyrus (an early form of paper) and which are often representative of the earliest forms of the Greek text.

paraphrase is a restatement of a meaning in a different form. Paraphrases are of two principal types: (1) grammatical (for example, John hit the man and the man was hit by John) and (2) lexical (for example, the man refuses to work and he declines all employment).

participant is an object in relation to an event. A participant may be an agent, a goal, or an instrument. For example, in John worked, the agent is John; in ... struck the boy, the goal is boy; and in ... cut with a knife, the instrument is knife.

particle is a small word which does not change its grammatical form. In English the most common particles are prepositions and conjunctions.

partitive construction is one in which one constituent identifies a part of the other. For example, in the phrase the hand of the man, the noun hand identifies a part of the man.

passive voice is a grammatical construction in which the subject is the goal of the action. For example, in the man was hit, the grammatical subject man is the goal of the action hit. (See active voice, agent, goal.)

phonological refers to the sounds of language, especially their formal similarities and differences.

phrase is a grammatical construction in which the entire expression typically functions in the same way as the principal word or words. For example, a noun phrase such as the old man has the same general range of usage as the noun man.

predicate is the division of a clause which contrasts with, or supplements, the subject. The subject is the topic of a clause and the predicate is what is said about the subject.

progressive is an aspect of an event referring to its continuation. Progressive is often used more or less synonymously with continuative and durative. (See aspect.)

proper noun is the name of a unique object—for example, Jerusalem, Joshua, Jordan. However, the same proper name may be applied to more than one object—for example, John (the Baptist and the Apostle) and Antioch (of Syria and of Pisidia).

punctiliar is an aspect of an event regarded as a "point of time," in contrast with continuative or durative aspect, which describes events as continuing over a period of time. (See aspect.)

receptor is the person receiving a message.

receptor language is the language into which a translation is made.

redundancy is the expression of the same information more than once. Anything which is completely redundant is entirely predictable from the context.

referential meaning is that aspect of the meaning of a term which most closely relates to the portion of the nonlinguistic world which the term symbolizes. For example, the referential meaning of the central meaning of father consists of such components as human, male, immediately preceding generation, and direct line of descent. This referential meaning is in contrast with certain connotative or emotive meanings of father, which suggest care, love, protection, and discipline. (See central meaning.)

restructure is a process of changing the form of a discourse without changing any essential elements of the meaning.

rhetorical question is an expression cast in the form of a question but which is not intended to elicit information. Rhetorical questions are usually employed for the sake of emphasis.

root is the minimal base of a derived or inflected word. For example, friend is the root of friendliness.

second person is the person (or persons) spoken to: you.

semantic refers to meaning.

semantic components are the distinctive features of the meaning of a term. For example, the central meaning of man has the components of human, adult, and male.

semantic domain is a definable area of experience which is referred to by a set of words whose meanings are in some way related. For example, kinship terms constitute a semantic domain. Similarly, the color terms of a language may be said to form a semantic domain.

Semitic languages are those which belong to a large family of languages spoken primarily in western Asia and North Africa. Hebrew and Arabic are Semitic languages.

sentence is a grammatical construction composed of one or more clauses and capable of standing alone.

Septuagint is a translation of the Old Testament into Greek, made some two hundred years before Christ.

sequence of tenses is the manner in which the tenses of successive verbs may be related to one another. For example, He has said, "I will come" may be transformed into indirect discourse as He had said he would come. The tenses are different, but the relative sequence of tenses is the same.

527

simile is a metaphorical expression which is specifically marked as a comparison. For example, he is a fox is a metaphor, but he is like a fox is a simile.

source language is the language in which the original message was produced.

stem is the base for a specific derivation or inflection. For example, demonstr- is the stem of demonstrable.

substantive is a noun or anything that functions as a noun.

substitute is any of a class of words which may be used in the place of other words. The most common substitutes are pronouns—for example, he, she, they, some, this. However, in a particular context my friend might be a substitute for Mr. Wallace Smith, and even later in the discourse reference to the same person might be made by such a lexical substitute as the man I referred to.

surface structure is the grammatical form of a discourse as it is actually spoken or written. (See kernel.)

symbol is a form, either linguistic or nonlinguistic, which is arbitrarily and conventionally associated with a particular meaning. For example, the word cross is a linguistic symbol, referring to a particular object. Similarly, within the Christian tradition, the cross as an object is a symbol for the death of Jesus.

synonyms are words which are different in form but similar in meaning—for example, boy and lad.

syntactic components are the basic units of a grammatical construction, considered in their relations to one another.

temporal relations are the relations of time between events.

tense is a grammatically marked identifier of time, generally relative.

third person is the person(s) or thing(s) spoken about: he, she, it, they.

transformation is a process of grammatical modification, usually beginning with the so-called deep structures and proceeding to the more elaborate surface structure. For example, a basic expression such as John hit Bill could be transformed into Wasn't Bill hit by John? This would involve three primary transformations: (1) active to passive, (2) positive to negative, and (3) statement to question. A back-transformation is the reverse of this process.

transitional expressions are words or phrases which mark the connections between related events. Some typical transitionals are next, then, later, after this, when he arrived.

transitive is a predicate construction in which the verb has a direct object—for example, ...hit the man. (See intransitive.)

528

translation is the reproduction in a receptor language of the closest natural equivalent of the source-language message, first, in terms of meaning and, second, in terms of style.

verb is in most languages a word of a grammatical class which functions most typically as the principal word of the predicate.

verbal has two meanings. (1) It may refer to expressions consisting of words, sometimes in distinction from other forms of expression which do not employ words. (2) It may refer to other word forms which are derived from verbs. For example, coming and engaged may be called verbals.

Aaron. The brother of Moses, who was chosen by God to be the chief priest in Israel (7.40).

Abraham. The earliest ancestor to whom the Jews traced their origin. He is noted not only because he was the first ancestor of the Jewish race, but because he is the one with whom God made the covenant.

Akeldama. A burial ground outside the Jerusalem wall (1.19).

apostle. One of the group of twelve men whom Jesus chose to be his followers and helpers. Apostle means "messenger," and is also used in Acts to refer to Paul and some other Christian workers.

Areopagus. A hill in Athens where the city council met. For this reason the city council itself was called Areopagus, even after it no longer met on that hill (17.19, 22).

Babylon. A country in ancient Mesopotamia (which see) which took its name from its capital city (7.43).

Beautiful Gate. Generally thought to have been one of the gates on the eastern side of the temple (3.2,10).

Cenchreae. The eastern seaport of Corinth (18.18).

census. The registration of citizens and their property, to determine how much tax they had to pay.

Chaldea. A later name for the country of Babylon in southern Mesopotamia (7.4).

circumcise. To cut off the foreskin of a Jewish baby boy as a sign of God's covenant with the people of Israel.

Council. The supreme religious court of the Jews, composed of seventy leaders of the Jewish people, and presided over by the High Priest.

covenant. The agreement that God made with Abraham, and later with the people of Israel.

David. The most famous of the Jewish kings. The later Jews idealized the time of his rule, and often thought of the coming Savior as a descendant of David who would rule as David once ruled.

Day of the Lord. The name given by the Jews and Christians to the last day of history when God will reveal his power and come to judge the world.

disciple. A person who follows and learns from someone else. The word is used of the followers of Jesus, particularly of the twelve apostles; in 9.25 it is used of the followers of Paul.

Elam (2.9). See Mesopotamia.

531

elders. Christian church leaders who had general responsibility for the work of the church.

Epicureans. Those who followed the teaching of Epicurus (died 270 B.C.). They taught that happiness is the highest good in life.

eunuch. A man who has been made physically incapable of having normal sexual relations.

fast. To go without food for a while as a religious duty.

Gentile. A person who is not a Jew.

Haran. A city of northern Mesopotamia where Abraham lived (7. 2, 4).

hell. The place of eternal destruction of the wicked.

High Priest. The priest who occupied the highest office in the Jewish priestly system and who was president of the supreme Council of the Jews. Sometimes used in the plural (chief priests) to designate members of the Jewish Council who belonged to the high priestly family.

Isaac. One of the three famous ancestors of the Jewish race. He was the son of Abraham and the father of Jacob.

Isaiah. One of the most famous of the Old Testament prophets.

Jacob. One of the three famous ancestors of the Jewish nation. He was the son of Isaac and the grandson of Abraham.

Jesse. The father of King David, one of the ancestors of Jesus.

Joel. One of the prophets of ancient Israel. His words are quoted by the apostle Peter (2.16).

Joseph (of the Old Testament). The son of Jacob who was sold into slavery by his own brothers, but later became the highest official of the king of Egypt. His brothers encountered him when they went to Egypt to buy food because there was a famine in their own land (7. 9,13-14,18).

Joshua. Successor to Moses who led the Israelite people into the land that God had promised them (7. 45).

judge. A title used of those men who from time to time gave leadership to the people of Israel in the period immediately preceding the time of the kings (13. 20).

Kingdom of God. A title used to refer to God's ruling over the world. It refers primarily to his possession and exercise of power, and not to a place or time in history.

Law (Law of Moses). The name the Jews applied to the first five books of the Old Testament. Sometimes the word Law is used in a more general sense of the entire Old Testament.

Levite. A member of the priestly tribe of Levi, who had the duty of helping in the services in the temple.

Media (2. 9). See Mesopotamia.

Mesopotamia. The original homeland of the patriarchs (7. 2). The name means "the land between the rivers" (that is, between the Tigris and Euphrates rivers). It was northeast of Palestine and east of Cappadocia. To the east of Mesopotamia were the territories of Elam, Media, and Parthia, representing Eastern peoples outside the Roman Empire (2. 9).

Messiah. The title (meaning "the anointed one," that is, "the chosen one") given to the promised Savior whose coming was predicted by the Hebrew prophets; the same as "Christ."

Moses. The first great leader of the Israelite people. At first he was rejected by his own people in Egypt, but later God sent him back to lead them out of slavery in Egypt. After he had led them out, God gave him the Law that became the basis of the life and religion of the Jewish people.

Nazarenes, party of. Evidently a term of abuse used by the Jews for the Christians (24. 5).

Parthia (2. 9). See Mesopotamia.

patriarchs. The famous ancestors of the Jewish race, such as Abraham, Isaac, and Jacob, with whom God made his covenant.

Pentecost, Day of. The Jewish feast of the wheat harvest, on the 6th day of the month Sivan (around May 20). The name Pentecost (meaning "fiftieth") comes from the fact that the feast was held 50 days after Passover.

Pharaoh. The title of the kings of ancient Egypt.

Pharisees. A Jewish religious party. They were strict in obeying the Law of Moses and other regulations which had been added through the centuries.

priest. One who led in the performance of religious services in the temple.

prophet. A man who proclaims God's message to men. (1) The term usually refers to the Old Testament prophets, such as Isaiah and Joel. (2) It also may be used to refer to prophets in the church (2.16). (3) In 3. 22-23 it is used of "the Prophet" who was expected to appear and announce the coming of the Messiah.

Sabbath day. The seventh day of the Jewish week, the holy day on which they worshiped God and on which no work was permitted.

Sadducees. A small Jewish religious party, composed largely of priests. They based their beliefs exclusively on the first five books of the Old Testament, and so differed in several matters of belief and practice from the larger party of the Pharisees.

Saul. (1) The Hebrew name of the apostle Paul. (2) The first king of Israel (13.21).

Servant (and Holy Servant). A title taken from the book of Isaiah and used to refer to the coming Savior.

Solomon's Porch. Generally thought to have been the roofed colonnade that ran the length of the eastern side of the outer court of the temple (3.11).

Son of Man. The title used by Jesus to refer to himself as the one chosen by God to be the Savior. Outside of the Gospels it is used only in 7.56.

Stoics. Those who followed the teachings of the philosopher Zeno (died 265 B.C.). He taught that happiness is to be found in being set free from pleasure and pain.

synagogue. The place where Jews met every Sabbath day for their public worship. It was also used as a social center and as a school for Jewish children during week days.

teachers of the Law. Men who taught and interpreted the teachings of the Old Testament, especially the first five books, known as the Law of Moses.

temple. The central place of Jewish worship and a symbol of their national unity. There were many synagogues but only one temple, and it was the only place where sacrifices could be offered.

Unleavened Bread, Feast of. The Jewish feast, lasting seven days after Passover, which also celebrated the deliverance of the ancient Hebrews from Egypt. The name came from the practice of not using leaven (or yeast) in making bread during that week. It was held from the 15th to the 22nd day of the month Nisan (around the first week of April).

vow. A strong declaration or promise, usually made while calling upon God to punish the speaker if the statement is not true or the promise is not kept.

Way or Way of the Lord. A term used to designate the Christian religion.

world of the dead. In Jewish thought, the place where the dead went. It was believed to be under the earth, and that when one went there, it was the end of all meaningful existence.

285, 286, 295, 297, 299, 303, 304,
305, 308, 311, 317, 319, 325, 328,
330, 335, 336, 339, 341, 342, 343,
349, 350, 354, 356, 357, 358, 362,
364, 370, 372, 375, 381, 390, 393,
402, 405, 409, 411, 414, 415, 418,
421, 423, 424, 428, 436, 446, 447,
448, 451, 453, 454, 455, 456, 459,
471, 474, 485, 488, 490, 498, 503,
506, 511
governor 244, 247, 352
grace 267, 275, 285, 286, 359, 397
Great Power 175
ground their teeth 167
group 62, 66, 110, 120

hand 108, 177, 249
happened 236, 273
heal (healed) 67, 103, 278, 504
heard 189
heart 111, 116, 165, 178, 228
heathen 165
heaven 167, 223, 281
Hebraic (Hebrew) 43, 45, 54, 87, 96,
105, 159, 160, 163, 178, 205, 256,
265, 279, 280, 295, 418, 513
hesitate 224
holy 78; — ground 155
Holy Spirit (Spirit) 13, 33, 35, 43, 95,
105, 118, 135, 136, 167, 176, 181,
192, 198, 210, 216, 218, 219, 220,
248, 249, 311, 391
homes (house) 65, 66, 150, 151, 163,
164, 211, 296, 315
honor 241
hope 51, 470, 471
hurry 201

idiom 46, 54, 55, 70, 74, 77, 82, 83, 87,
91, 99, 106, 111, 112, 115, 123, 127,
132, 139, 147, 155, 157, 174, 185,
187, 190, 197, 200, 206; 215, 220,
232, 256, 282, 285, 292, 305, 323,
331, 335, 349, 358, 365, 374, 393,
398, 403, 406, 423, 424, 425, 432,
435, 453, 462, 464, 477, 513

ignorance 81
ignorant show-off 336
immorality 298
in the name of Jesus Christ 60
inclusive and exclusive plural pronouns 253, 259, 261, 269, 307, 312,
342, 383, 386, 445, 447, 482, 508
indirect discourse 210, 284, 324, 416,
417, 438, 459, 511
insulted 267, 268
Israel 47, 76, 257, 261

jail (prison) 123, 125, 233, 234
Jerusalem Bible 13, 23, 41, 48, 65, 66,
84, 91, 93, 98, 99, 111, 112, 120,
121, 124, 125, 126, 130, 136, 137,
139, 146, 148, 149, 150, 151, 153,
154, 155, 156, 157, 158, 159, 162,
163, 170, 171, 174, 175, 178, 179,
180, 182, 184, 185, 186, 187, 189,
190, 191, 193, 194, 195, 198, 201,
204, 210, 211, 213, 217, 219, 222,
228, 231, 232, 233, 237, 238, 239,
242, 248, 249, 250, 253, 257, 259,
262, 266, 268, 270, 279, 281, 282,
289, 291, 292, 293, 299, 300, 301,
302, 303, 304, 305, 306, 309, 311,
314, 317, 318, 319, 323, 324, 325,
330, 331, 336, 337, 338, 339, 340,
351, 353, 356, 357, 358, 362, 368,
369, 372, 374, 375, 376, 381, 383,
384, 385, 387, 389, 390, 391, 392,
393, 395, 398, 401, 402, 403, 404,
405, 406, 407, 408, 409, 410, 411,
412, 414, 415, 416, 417, 418, 419,
420, 421, 422, 425, 426, 432, 434,
435, 436, 448, 449, 450, 453, 454,
456, 459, 464, 469, 470, 471, 490,
491, 498, 502, 504, 505, 506, 510,
511, 512, 513, 515
Jew (Jewish) 36, 39, 41, 55, 60, 88, 98,
111, 125, 130, 134, 137, 160, 167,
187, 194, 200, 204, 205, 207, 208,
211, 212, 217, 219, 222, 225, 227,
232, 237, 246, 247, 261, 273, 276,
280, 291, 314, 410, 467, 510

United Bible Societies Greek text 198, 215, 242, 254, 257, 297, 472

upset 335

visions 43, 44, 207, 476
voice 189, 425
vow 355, 410, 411, 438

walking 73
warn (warning) 102, 390, 391
way 187, 269, 281, 282, 286, 365, 370, 421, 451
"we" sections 307, 312, 342, 383, 386, 445, 447, 482, 485, 508
went up 221; — down 246
whitewashed wall 433
wicked 61, 62, 88
will 48

Williams, C. B. 351, 353, 356
witness (witnesses) 18, 30, 425, 427
wolves 395
wonder (wonders) 109, 119, 120, 157, 275
wood 320
words 61, 137, 295
work 26
world 51, 97
worms 241
worship 339
worthy 268

Zürich 91, 162, 179, 180, 195, 198, 199, 213, 224, 226, 229, 231, 232, 233, 242, 268, 286, 316, 328, 340, 341, 349, 356, 357, 358, 364, 391, 404